D1502771

For struggling for a better world all of
us are fenced in, threatened with death.
The fence is reproduced globally.
In every continent,
every city,
every countryside,
every house.

Power's fence of war
closes in on the rebels,
for whom humanity
is always grateful.

But fences are broken.

The rebels, whom history repeatedly has given
the length of its long trajectory,

struggle and the fence is broken.

The rebels search each
other out. They walk
toward one another.

They find each other and
together break other fences.

First published by Verso 2003

10 9 8 7 6 5 4 3 2 1

Verso
UK: 6 Meard Street, London W1F 0EG
USA: 180 Varick Street, New York, NY 10014-4606
www.versobooks.com

Verso is the imprint of New Left Books

ISBN 1-85984-447-2

British Library Cataloguing in Publication Data
A catalogue record for this book is available from the British Library

Library of Congress Cataloging-in-Publication Data
A catalog record for this book is available from the Library of Congress

Designed and typeset by Notes from Nowhere
Printed in the UK by Bath Press

The labour of the authors and the editors of this book was given freely. All royalties received by Notes from Nowhere from sales of this book are being donated to the social movements featured in *We Are Everywhere*.

Contact us directly at: info@weareeverywhere.org
www.WeAreEverywhere.org or via Verso

we are everywhere

edited by
Notes from Nowhere

the irresistible rise of global anticapitalism

VERSO

London • New York

Foreword

We are Everywhere is the first book to truly capture and embody the exuberant creativity and radical intellect of the protest movements opposing neoliberalism around the world.

This book is not just about these movements; it is genuinely of these movements, in the best possible way. It is the only project I have seen to emerge so authentically from the movement's own culture, mirroring its core values of decentralization and radical democracy in its own structure and tone. By allowing activists to tell their own personal stories, focusing on glimpses instead of top-down official history, the stories somehow become instantly iconic. If a book could be a carnival instead of a linear narrative, it would read like this.

Because of the unique process behind the book, I have no doubt that *We are Everywhere* will be claimed by thousands of activists around the world as a cultural creation that is truly their own. But this is not just an activist book. There is an insatiable appetite outside activist circles for information about what this movement really stands for. Many claim to be answering this question but this book will do something much more valuable: allow a general readership to catch an unmediated glimpse of what it looks like from the inside, and what it feels like to be there.

Naomi Klein, author of *No Logo*

Contents

Opening Salvo

"Never again will a single story be told as if it is the only one."
– John Berger

We are Everywhere falls somewhere between an activist anthology and a grassroots history, agitational collage and direct action manual. It traces the anticapitalist movements from their emergence in 1994 to the present, documenting the rise of an unprecedented global rebellion – a rebellion which is in constant flux, which swaps ideas and tactics across oceans, shares strategies between cultures and continents, gathers in swarms and dissolves, only to swarm again elsewhere.

But this is a movement of untold stories, for those from below are not those who get to write history, even though we are the ones making it.

The powerful look at our diversity and see only miscellany. The media report that we don't know what we're talking about, we have no solutions, we represent nobody, we should be ignored. If they would stay quiet for a while, they might begin to hear the many different accents, timbres, voices, and languages in which we are telling our myriad stories.

We wanted a way to document, broadcast, and amplify these unheard stories coming from the grassroots movements that have woven a global fabric of struggle during the last decade. And so we came together as an editorial collective, Notes from Nowhere, to produce this book.

But how does one begin to tell the history of a movement with no name, no manifesto, and no leaders?

The answer is that you tell it the way you live it. Just as there is no single banner we march behind, no little red book, and no doctrine to adhere to, there is no single narrative here. Rather than one dominant political voice, one dogma, one party line, we present you with a collision of subjectivities. These are moments both intimate and public, charged with inspiration, fear, humour, the everyday, and the historic.

Like this movement, we relish intimacy, subjectivity, and diversity, and we think that personal stories have as much (if not more) to teach us as any manifesto. In this, we differ from many past traditions of struggle. We are part of a new, radical, transformative politics based on direct democracy; one that values our individual voices, our hopes, our joys, our doubts, our disasters, and requires no sacrifice from us except that we sacrifice our fear. And so this book subverts the conventional reporting of such movements, taking as its starting point the experiences of those actually involved.

The book is divided into seven sections, each introduced with essays on key characteristics of the movement, written by the editors. After each essay comes a series of stories, in roughly chronological order, which show the progression of the movement as it emerges, comes together, and matures. Interspersed among these texts are do-it-yourself guides to direct action.

Running throughout the book is a historical timeline. We

chose to begin with the Zapatistas as we see their uprising on 1 January 1994 as heralding a new era of resistance movements, and we come full circle, ending with their retaking of San Cristóbal de las Casas on 1 January 2003. It reveals the sheer scale and number of undocumented struggles that go on, almost daily, all around the world.

We are Everywhere does not, and could not, seek to present a packaged whole or complete overview, and its limitations, its editorial choices, are our own. In following a few threads of this complex, dispersed, and centreless web, the threads that we began to pull were the ones closest to us, which wove through our own memories and experiences. As we followed them, we realized that there were many places we couldn't reach, where barriers of language, culture, and distance prevented us from hearing the voices of those directly involved. Inevitably, this was particularly true of the global South, and, in some cases, we have only been able to translate these movements through the voices of Northern visitors working with those movements. Whenever possible, these pieces have been read and commented on by the social movements themselves before making their way into the book.

The Zapatistas have taught us through their struggle founded on radical notions of dialogue and participation to embark on a rebellion which listens. In this spirit, we produced in the summer of 2001 a 100-page preview booklet, *Notes from Everywhere*, which we gave for free to activists at gatherings and actions in 11 countries on three continents, soliciting critiques, feedback, and further contributions. We continue that dialogue through our website.

When we started to bring these stories together, we were excited to confirm what we'd always suspected – that separate movements converge, recognize each other as allies, and struggle together.

So where do you fit into all of this? Well, the Zapatistas, from behind their masks, are saying not "Do as we do", but rather, "We are you".

But don't forget that what you hold in your hand is only a book. As Gerrard Winstanley, one of the English Diggers – who through exemplary direct action demanded the abolishment of private property and encouraged the poor to reclaim the commons – wrote in 1649: "Thoughts and words ran in me that words and writing were all nothing, and must die, for action is the life of all, and if thou dost not act, thou dost nothing."

Notes from Nowhere Spring 2003

"If you listen carefully to the celebrating voices, those of the rich and the powerful in their corporate offices and government buildings, you can pick up a nervous undertone. If you watch the policy-makers closely, you may notice that the smiles are often thin and the hands that hold champagne glasses sometimes twitch, involuntarily.

If you listen even more carefully, you can discover why. In the background you can hear another set of voices – those from below – far, far more numerous. These are voices the powerful do not want to hear, but they are having a harder and harder time ignoring them.

Some of these voices are quiet and determined, talking together in bare tenements. Some are singing and reciting poetry in the plazas, or stirring young hearts with old tales deep in the forests.

Some are discussing, planning their future, inventing lines or chanting in the streets. All are talking about revolution, whether they use that term or not."

– Harry Cleaver

This book wouldn't exist if it wasn't for the tireless, unsung efforts of people everywhere working for no reward except the sweet knowledge that they are in the right place, at the right time in history, doing the right thing. This book is for them.

Emergence an irresistible global uprising

"It is not only by shooting bullets in the battlefields that tyranny is overthrown, but also by hurling ideas of redemption, words of freedom and terrible anathemas against the hangmen that people bring down dictators and empires ..."
– Emiliano Zapata, Mexican revolutionary, 1914

The new century is three days old when the Mexican army encampment of Amadór Hernandez, nestled deep in the Lacandón jungle of Chiapas in the country's southeast, comes under attack from the air. The air force of the indigenous Zapatista Army of National Liberation (EZLN) swoops down in its hundreds on the unprepared troops.

This is an army of paper aeroplanes, which soar, curve, and dive in the dappled forest sunlight. Some are caught in the teeth of the barbed-wire fence. Some fall to the forest floor, and are silenced. But many are well-thrown – they rise, dip, bank, and swerve past the bracken and black plastic sheeting straight into the army dormitories.

They are heavily armed with words of resistance and launched over the fence around the base by the local people, indigenous Tzeltals. For weeks, months now, they have been chanting, singing, crying to the troops – that they want peace. They want the low-flying military aircraft to stop terrorizing their village. They don't want the army to build a road through their forest. They want their rights, their dignity as indigenous people. But their voices are lost in the damp canopy of forest as the camp commanders drown them out by blasting military marches, Musak, and the William Tell Overture over the PA system. And the soldiers are just children, far from home, frightened of the Zapatistas, who the state Governor has warned are about to launch a violent attack on the base.

Yuriria Pantoja Millán

But now, finally, the Tzeltal voices have penetrated the fence of power with their message of resistance to the federal troops, and lampooned the hyped threat of Zapatista violence. On each plane is written the words: "Wake up! Open your eyes so you can see ... Soldiers, we know that poverty has made you sell your lives and your souls. I also am poor, as are millions. But you are worse off, for defending our exploiters."

A year and a half later on a shimmering hot day in July 2001, Air Force One carries George W Bush into Christopher Columbus airport in the Italian city of Genoa for the G8 summit, where the eight most powerful men in the world are gathering to decide the fate of six billion human beings. They meet behind a vast, reinforced fence which marks the heavily militarized 'red zone', where democratic law has been suspended, expressing opinions on the fate of the global economy rendered illegal, and protest forbidden. It exists to keep 300,000 protesters away from the eyes and ears of the G8.

And so the Zapatista air force launches its second attack. These paper aeroplanes, covered with messages of resistance and colourful images of Zapatista rebels, have been carefully constructed by the small hands of school children in Oventic, an autonomous Zapatista community in the highlands of Chiapas, and posted to activists in Genoa. Arms curve, planes rise and fall, littering the ground inside and outside the red zone.

Once again, rebel voices breach the fence of the powerful.

But what is it that connects the Genoa protesters and the Zapatistas? To uncover the character of the world's largest social movement, you must follow the flight of a paper aeroplane, from the Lacandón jungle in southeastern Mexico to the streets of the Italian port city of Genoa. It's a paper aeroplane carrying a message of hope, and of resistance.

Breaking fences

"Borders crumble; they won't hold together on their own; we have to shore them up constantly. They are fortified and patrolled by armed guards, these fences that divide a party of elegant diners on one side from the children on the other whose thin legs curve like wishbones, whose large eyes peer through the barbed wire at so much food – there is no wall high enough to make good in such a neighbourhood. For this, of course, is what the fences divide."

– Barbara Kingsolver, *Small Wonder*, Harper Collins, 2002

The fence surrounding the military base in Chiapas is the same fence that surrounds the G8 meeting in Genoa. It's the fence that divides the powerful from the powerless, those whose voices decree, from those whose voices are silenced. And it is replicated everywhere.

For the fence surrounds gated communities of rich neighbourhoods from Washington to Johannesburg, islands of prosperity that float in seas of poverty. It surrounds vast estates of land in Brazil, keeping millions who live in poverty from growing food. It's patrolled by armed guards who keep the downtrodden and the disaffected out of shopping malls. It's hung with signs warning you to 'Keep out' of places where your mother and grandmother played freely. This fence stretches across borders between rich and poor worlds. For the unlucky poor who are caught trying to cross into the rich world, the fence encloses the detention centres where refugees live behind razor wire.

Built to keep all the ordinary people of the world out of the way, out of sight, far from the decision-makers and at the mercy of their policies, this fence also separates us from those things which are our birthright as human beings – land, shelter, culture, good health, nourishment, clean air, water. For in a world entranced by profit, public space is privatized, land fenced off, seeds, medicines and genes patented, water metered, and democracy turned into purchasing power. The fences are also inside us. Interior borders run through our atomized minds and hearts, telling us we should look out only for ourselves, that we are alone.

"THIS IS AN UPRISING AS BIG AS THE REVOLUTION THAT SHOOK THE WORLD BETWEEN 1890 AND 1920. BEWARE."

– Asian Vice-President of Goldman Sachs

But borders, enclosures, fences, walls, silences are being torn down, punctured, invaded by human hands, warm bodies, strong voices which call out the most revolutionary of messages: "You are not alone!"

For we are everywhere.

We are in Seattle, Prague, Genoa, and Washington. We are in Buenos Aires, Bangalore, Manila, Durban, and Quito. Many of these place names have been made iconic by protest, symbols of resistance and hope in a world which increasingly offers little room for either.

The Zapatistas have joined with thousands around the world who believe that fences are made to be broken. Refugees detained in the Australian desert tear down prison fences, and are secreted to safety by supporters outside. The poor, rural landless of Brazil cut the wire that keeps them out of vast uncultivated plantations and swarm onto the properties of rich, absentee landlords, claim the land, create settlements, and begin to farm. Protesters in Québec City tear down the fence known as the 'wall of shame' surrounding the summit meeting of the Free Trade Area of the Americas, and raise their voices in a joyful yell as it buckles under the weight of those dancing on its bent back, engulfed in euphoria even while the toxic blooms of tear gas hit. The radical guerrilla electricians in South Africa break the fence of privatization that keeps the poor from having electricity by installing illegal connections themselves. Peasant women across Asia gather to freely swap seed, defying the fences of market logic that would have them go into debt to buy commercial seed. "Keep the seeds in your hands, sister!" they declare.

Those who tear down fences are part of the largest globally interconnected social movement of our time. Over the last ten years, our protests have erupted on continent after continent, fuelled by extremes of wealth and poverty, by military repression, by environmental breakdown, by ever-diminishing power to control our own lives and resources. We are furious at the increasingly thin sham of democracy, sick of the lies of consumer capitalism, ruled by ever more powerful corporations. We are the globalization of resistance. But where we came from, what we have done, who we are, and what we want have remained untold. These are our stories.

An army of dreamers

"And you, are you so forgetful of your past, is there no echo in your soul of your poets' songs, your dreamers' dreams, your rebels' calls?" **– Emma Goldman**

Depending on who you ask, the resistance began 510 years ago when the indigenous of the Américas fought Columbus, or 700 years ago when Robin Hood rode through the forests of England to protect the rights of commoners, or a little over 100 years ago when slavery was abolished throughout the Américas, or 150 years ago when working people became an international revolutionary movement, or 50 years ago when colonized countries gained their independence, or 30 years ago when populations across Africa, Asia, and Latin America started rioting over the price of bread as the International Monetary Fund (IMF) began restructuring their economies.

Or perhaps it was in 1988 when the IMF and World Bank were almost run out of Berlin by 75,000 protesters, or 1999 when the same number disrupted the World Trade Organization (WTO) meeting in Seattle in 1999? For those who like their history neat, 1994 emerges as a landmark year as resistance to capitalism snowballed. Resistance to IMF policies in the global South increased dramatically that year; around the world there were more general strikes than at any previous time in the 20th century according to the labour journalist Kim Moody; radical ecological movements were re-introducing creative direct action tactics to popular protest during in the US and the UK – and as the Mexican economy crashed and burned, the Zapatista uprising took the world by storm. For simplicity's sake, let us start the story there.

As the clock chimed midnight on 1 January 1994, indigenous Zapatista rebels emerged for the first time from the mists of the Lacandón rainforest. The new year ushered in corporate rule in the guise of the North American Free Trade Agreement (NAFTA), a treaty that threatened the Zapatistas' land rights. Article 27 had been eliminated from the Mexican constitution, land reform fought for by Emiliano Zapata, folk hero and revolutionary, which created a nationwide system of collectively owned and cultivated land, and which was absolutely incompatible with NAFTA. And so a courageous band of women and men launched a unique resistance movement that was to reinvent the radical political imagination for the world.

Under the cover of night the Zapatistas took control of seven cities, set prisoners free, set fire to police headquarters and expropriated weapons found there, occupied City Halls, secured major highways, and declared war against the Mexican Government and the policies they called *neoliberalismo*. Many were armed only with rifle-shaped sticks and toy guns. Their most powerful weapons were their words. They said they were "leading by obeying"; that they were invisible people who had "masked themselves in order to be seen"; that they didn't want to seize power for themselves, but to break it into small pieces that everyone could hold. The war lasted for twelve days, until Mexican civil society demanded a cease-fire and peace negotiations, but the inspiration, the poetry, and the hope that run deep in the hearts of the Zapatistas was contagious, and the tale of the unlikely army found its way into the hearts and minds of activists around the world for whom hope had become a rare commodity.

At the time, the Zapatista uprising seemed to come from out of nowhere. The 1990s was a time of triumphant optimism for capitalism. The old enemy of the Soviet Empire had collapsed, and with it the remaining opposition to the capitalist system. Economic globalization – the imposition of the 'free' market into every corner of the globe – was worshipped by economists as a kind of fundamentalist religion. Every piece of earth, every natural resource, and billions of pairs of human hands, feet, and backs became raw material to create products to sell on the global market, and that created growth, and growth, we were told, was good for everyone. Capitalism was so ubiquitous people forgot they were living under an 'ism' – the time for all isms, in fact, seemed over.

During this period, the disappointed fragments of the left had either turned towards the ascendant neoliberal sun, or withdrawn into disillusion. They didn't know what to do with the Zapatistas. As indigenous people, they didn't fit into a Marxist model of proletarian revolution of the sort that had flourished in Latin America in previous decades. But as the embers of the old left faded, and capitalism declared itself immutable, inevitable, there were pockets of resistance abroad ready to hear a new story.

Or rather, stories. For the time of single ideologies and grand narratives was over. People were sick of sacrificing themselves for the sake of gigantic game plans which didn't account for their individual needs, their humanity, their culture, their creativity. They were unwilling to be soldiers or martyrs in movements whose big-picture and top-down solutions were to be imposed on the 'masses', which too often existed only in the imaginations of vanguard revolutionaries. People had grown weary of being ordered about, whether by their oppressors or their self-appointed liberators.

Into this chapter of history entered the Zapatistas, masked people the colour of the earth, women wearing multi-coloured clothes and carrying make-shift weapons, and speaking a quite different language of resistance – of land, poetry, indigenous culture, diversity, ecology, dignity. The Zapatistas understood the power of subjectivity, spoke the language of dreams, not just economies.

Though their army had a hierarchical command structure, the communities they represented had no leaders, only those who led by following the will of the people, who demanded an end to the war, and who have led the army into pursuing an unusual path towards peace – a true peace, which includes dignity and justice, which has no room for hunger, for death by military and paramilitaries, or loss of their land. They did not march on the capital to seize the state, nor did they want to secede from it. What they wanted was autonomy, democracy, "nothing for ourselves alone, but everything for everyone".

Activists from around the world declared their solidarity with the Zapatista autonomous zones, and asked: "What do you want us to do?" The Zapatistas, taken aback by so much attention, replied that for them, solidarity would be for people to make their own revolutions in ways which would be relevant to their own lives. As one activist put it: "The Zapatistas translated struggle into a language that the world can feel, and invited us all to read ourselves into the story, not as supporters but as participants." And in doing so, the Zapatistas unleashed an international insurrection of hope against the forces of global capital.

In 1998, a year before protesters shut down the meeting of the WTO in Seattle, Subcomandante Marcos, military strategist and spokesperson of the Zapatistas, said: "Don't give too much weight to the EZLN; it's nothing but a symptom of something more. Years from now, whether or not the EZLN is still around, there is going to be protest and social ferment in many places. I know this because when we rose up against the government, we began to receive displays of solidarity and sympathy not only from Mexicans, but from people in Chile, Argentina, Canada, the United States, and Central America. They told us that the uprising represents something that they wanted to say, and now they have found the words to say it, each in his or her respective country. I believe the fallacious notion of the end of history has finally been destroyed."

"The naming of the intolerable is itself hope," wrote John Berger. With their uprising the Zapatistas named an old enemy in new clothing – neoliberal globalization. Their rebel yell: "Ya Basta!" (Enough!) announced the end of the end of history. This cry, and their communiqués posted on the internet, echoed around the world. They were heard by urban street reclaimers in London; by land squatters in Brazil; by Indian farmers burning genetically modified crops; by hackers, cyberpunks, media guerrillas; by Seattle anarchists; by Africans rioting against the IMF; by white-overalled Italian dissidents. Not a homogenized band of revolutionary proletariat, but a diverse band of marginal people – vagabonds, sweatshop workers, indigenous peoples, illegal immigrants, squatters, intellectuals, factory workers, tree-sitters, and peasants.

History, like resistance, began to accelerate. In 1996 the Zapatistas called this diverse band to an 'International *Encuentro* Against Neoliberalism and For Humanity' in the rainforests of Chiapas; this was the historic moment when these rebels recognized each other and their common enemy. Also in 1996, arguably the first tear gas-wreathed summit of the globalization era was held in Manila in the Philippines, when 10,000 protesters against the Asia Pacific Economic Community (APEC) meeting faced 30,000 police and soldiers, the slums were bulldozed to sanitize the city, and dissenters filled the jails. In 1997 another Zapatista-inspired Encounter led to the creation in 1998 of Peoples' Global Action, a network of grassroots social movements who swore to resist capitalism with direct action, whilst throughout 1998 unrest and wave upon wave of strikes and 'people power' uprisings in the wake of financial crisis broke across South East Asia. The networks strengthened further as internationally co-ordinated days of action targeted the WTO in May 1998 and the G8 in 1999 with a global Carnival against Capital.

But the anticapitalist movement only became visible to the Northern media during spectacular moments of confrontation at global economic summits in the rich world. The first to make it onto their radar screen was on

30 November 1999 when the WTO meeting was rudely interrupted in Seattle.

The city ground to a halt when a new generation of activists, using radically decentralized, creative tactics, outwitted the police and successfully prevented the WTO from launching a fresh round of free trade negotiations. Locked-down, tear gassed, and beaten with truncheons, they blocked the WTO delegates' way to the conference centre, argued with them about patents on life, the global forest logging agreement, and enforced privatization. They insisted that their world was not for sale. Business leaders looked on, stunned. None of them could tell if Seattle was a carnival or a riot, where it had come from, or who these people were. It was an epic confrontation to decide who would go forth into the new century ascendant – people or corporations.

US Trade Representative Charlene Barshefsky, due to greet 5,000 international trade delegates at the summit's opening ceremonies, was trapped in her hotel room by the street blockades, as was US Secretary of State Madeleine Albright. By 10.00 am, Albright was screaming down the telephone to the Governor to call in the National Guard. At 10.05 am the tear gas started. Mass arrests, concussion grenades, curfews, plastic bullets, beatings, and prison followed for many of the protesters, hundreds of whom refused to give their names when arrested. The police entered them on the arrest records as "John/Jane WTO". A few days later, the summit ended in failure – collapsing from within while attacked from without. "The twenty-first century started in Seattle," ran the headline of French newspaper *Le Monde* the following morning.

Together, through the process of international gatherings, global networking and joint mass actions, the movement has created a rich fabric, both strong in its global solidarity and supremely flexible in its celebration of local autonomy. This global fabric of struggle breaks with single-issue politics, transcends divisions of class, race, language, religion, and nationality, is strengthened by diversity, stretches around the globe, and yet is the natural outgrowth of resistance cultures as different as Korean auto-parts manufacturers, indigenous Andean farmers, and European squatters.

Rule of the market, by the market

"To attract companies like yours… we have felled mountains, razed jungles, filled swamps, moved rivers, relocated towns… all to make it easier for you and your business to do business here." – **Philippines Government advert in *Fortune*, placed in 1975**

Neoliberalism, an economic theory which is the latest incarnation of capitalism, means rule by the market. In other words, the market should be the predominant arbiter of all the decisions in a society.

The central fact of our time is the upwards transfer of power and wealth – never have so many been governed by so few. The economy has globalized but in this new world order there is no room for people. We are ruled over by transnational corporations and the World Trade

Organization, the World Bank, and the International Monetary Fund; our lives can be ruined at the whim of the financial markets. In their view, a deregulated, privatized, corporate-led global 'free' trade regime is the answer to humanity's problems.

But 'free' trade is on an inevitable collision-course with democracy. For history shows that the exercise of genuine democracy will always act as a brake on the free market. The dawning of the twentieth century saw along with deepening democracy and universal suffrage, an increase in social safety nets for the working poor. All this has been rolled back since the 1980s by the advent of neoliberalism. As economies are liberalized and public assets sold off, political freedoms are increasingly curtailed and the state is employed in keeping down the objections of its own protesting populations. The key decisions of our lives do not belong to us. We are the uninvited, standing on the peripheries as others shape the world in their own image. We are disconnected from what we produce and what we consume, from the earth and from one another. We live in an arid, homogenized culture.

Neoliberalism achieves this by use of its two most potent weapons. Firstly, messages of prosperity – we can all have what the rich have, as long as we keep our heads down and keep working. Secondly, when this doesn't work, economic muscle. Between 1990 and 1997, 'developing' countries paid out more in servicing their debt than they received in loans – a transfer of $77 billion from South to North, through the machinery of the IMF and the World Bank, organizations which ensure the continued dominance of the rich nations. Meanwhile, ironically, those rich nations are being 'structurally adjusted' too, as the World Trade Organization rolls back democracy in the name of trade, unravelling decades of social progress.

Ours is the complex task of resisting this power exercised through a web of political, economic and military systems, representing entrenched and often invisible interests. In a global economy, there is no seat of power for the new guerrillas to storm. This is why protesters have been targeting international summit meetings. Unaccountable institutions that determine the fate of the global economy – the World Trade Organization, the World Bank, the International Monetary Fund, the G8, the World Economic Forum – have not been able to meet in recent years without being accompanied by protest.

The spectacle of carnivalesque theatres of popular democracy outside these summits contrasts sharply with the undemocratic and secret negotiations of trade ministers and corporate lobbyists going on behind the police lines. These tactics are potent weapons, unmasking the true nature of neoliberalism's economic mythologies and institutions, and simultaneously blowing apart the cultural malaise of late capitalism with authentic cries of rebellion, of culture re-engaged with the real.

For together we are the inversion, the mirror opposite, of a strata of concentrated power from above, in which decisions that affect billions of human lives are made at a transnational level where the market is king. We embody the real world below, the sphere of all those factors not reducible to a commodity to be bought and sold on a global marketplace; human beings, nature, culture – an international multitude that in its diversity challenges the idea that the global surfaces of the world market are interchangeable.

Dollars in the soil

"We are not a market – first and foremost, we are a people."

– Declaration of South American Chemical and Paper Workers

In April 2001, a few weeks before thirty-four heads of state met in Québec City to hammer out details of trade liberalization throughout the western hemisphere, a mob of merry men and women dressed as Robin Hood and Maid Marian occupied the Pacific Stock Exchange in San Francisco, demanding that the secret negotiating text of the Free Trade Area of the Americas (FTAA) be released to the public. As he was carried away by police officers, one Robin Hood yelled: "I do not recognize the authority of the Sheriff of Nottingham!" The bemused police bundled him into the back of their van as he shouted to the cheering crowds, "Robin Hood will be back!"

In thirteenth-century England, Robin Hood and his band of merry men defied the authority of the Sheriff of Nottingham, but not just by robbing the rich to feed the poor. One theory suggests that Robin Hood is a fable of resistance against the ruling classes' policy of transforming common land available for the use of all, into fenced-off grazing areas for sheep to encourage the native wool industry for their own private gain. This process, known as 'enclosure', remains one of the most powerful concepts in understanding contemporary capitalism, just as tearing down fences is one of the most powerful symbols of resistance to enclosure.

These unprecedented enclosures were precursors to mass clearing of the lands of peasants, and the eventual ushering of these people into the cities to become the factory workers of the industrial revolution where their labour, too, became an 'enclosed' commodity. The dramatic upheaval of industrialization in Britain between 1785 and 1830 was the first of its kind in the world. Sweeping Enclosure Acts led to millions of acres of commonly held land being fenced off, pushing people off land, taking away their common rights of usage: collecting fire wood, growing crops, grazing animals, gathering food, hunting, and fishing. Over half of all cultivated land in England was put into private hands, until no county had more than three per cent of its area held in common. An entire class of people experienced a loss of independence and freedom, traditions of local exchange and mutual assistance were shattered, and formerly self-sufficient people became wholly dependent on what they could earn and buy in a cash economy.

Compare this to the contemporary process by which communal lands from Africa to the Pacific are torn apart under the World Bank and IMF's Structural Adjustment Programmes. The Economist magazine invoked the fence of capital when it declared that Africa's land, "must be enclosed and traditional rights of use, access and grazing extinguished," as it is "private ownership of land that has made capitalism work".

And so the peasant, indigenous, and social movements of the South are facing something similar to the first wave of enclosure in rural England; they are being thrown off their lands, and having their rights to water, to pasture, to forests, to seeds taken away from them. Via Campesina, the international peasant farmers union uniting farmers, rural women, indigenous groups and the landless is one of the most extraordinary examples of the movements' capacity for international networking, a veritable international peasants' revolt in the making. With a combined membership of millions, from Brazilian landless to Indonesian farmers it represents probably the largest single mass of people opposed to the WTO. The first points of resistance to global capitalism have been those who still depend upon natural resources directly for their livelihoods.

Meanwhile, in post-industrial societies which went through this process hundreds of years ago, today neoliberalism is penetrating the everyday, having to 'enclose' new areas of our lives, areas previously unimaginable: From the invasion of the material fabric of life through the patenting of gene types, from the opening of markets in health, social care and education through to the assertion of intellectual property rights over medicines – all are tainted by the logic of capital and the elevation of the commodity above all else.

As a result the Northern post-industrial rebels against enclosure began as culture jammers, software hackers, GM crop-pullers, road protesters. Making the connections Native American poet John Trudell calls them "blue indians", because, he says: "The world is now an industrial reservation and everybody is the Indian, and our common colour is the blues."

These two groups; the natural resource-based movements – the indigenous, the farmers – of the South, and the post-industrial marginalized of the North, have somehow recognized in one another a shared enemy – global capital. Suddenly, the "blue indians" and the real Indians are speaking the same language. Subcomandante Marcos rejects the "plastic playlands" of corporate development that will dispossess the people of Chiapas of their land, while Northern anticapitalists reject the spectacles of consumer capitalism, those same plastic playlands that have covered every inch of their towns, and their souls. Together they are creating a movement of movements that defies easy classification, a rebellion whose character is one of anarchic hybridity, a potent mixture of the symbolic and the instrumental.

All over the world similar struggles, struggles against the commodification of every aspect of life, are being waged every day. A poster attached to the fence in Québec City read, "Capital is enclosure: First it fenced off the land. Then it metered the water. It measured our time. It plundered our bodies and now it polices our dreams. We cannot be contained. We are not for sale." Unbeknown to each other a Thai rural coalition, the Assembly of the Poor, had used almost the same terms one year earlier. When thousands of rural Thais – farmers, fisherfolk, the landless – converged to protest against the Asian Development Bank meetings in Chiang Mai in May 2000, they carried a tombstone on their backs inscribed with the words, "There is a price on the water, a meter in the rice paddies, dollars in the soil; resorts in the forests."

Spaces of hope

"The longing for a better world will need to arise at the imagined meeting place of many movements of resistance, as many as there are sites of enclosure and exclusion. The resistance will be as transnational as capital. Because enclosure takes myriad forms, so shall resistance to it."

– Iain A Boal, *First World, Ha Ha Ha!*, City Lights, 1995

One of the great strengths of this movement of movements has been its capacity to rekindle the idea of a global political project defined by notions of diversity, autonomy, ecology, democracy, self-organization and direct action. This activism is an attempt to intervene directly in the process of corporate globalization. These spaces of hope are reclaimed urban streets, the de-privatized wells and irrigation canals of Cochabamba, in Bolivia, the community gardens of New York City, the appropriated farmland of the Landless Movement of Brazil, the open publishing wire of the Indymedia websites.

Against the single economic blueprint where the market rules, we represent diverse, people-centred alternatives. Against the monoculture of global capital, we demand a world where many worlds fit.

Today, the different movements around the world are busy strengthening their networks, developing their autonomy, taking to the streets in huge carnivals against capital, resisting brutal repression and growing stronger as a result, and exploring new notions of sharing power rather than wielding it. Our voices are mingling in the fields and on the streets across the planet, where seemingly separate movements converge and the wave of global resistance becomes a tsunami causing turbulence thousands of miles away, and simultaneously creating ripples which lap at our doorstep. Resisting together, our hope is reignited: hope because we have the power to reclaim memory from those who would impose oblivion, hope because we are more powerful than they can possibly imagine, hope because history is ours when we make it with our own hands.

Notes from Nowhere

Over the Wall: so *this* is direct action!

by Noam Leven

Everyone was pushing hard; *school children and their parents, eco-activists, elderly local residents. First it creaked, then cracked and then crash – the huge wooden fence fell. Erected by the Department of Transport (DOT) on Wanstead Common in east London in the winter of 1993, the fence surrounded an old chestnut tree, condemned to sawdust because it was growing in the way of a new road. It took no time for people to push it down, to reclaim their commons. But weeks later the DOT came back. Despite the resistance, they cut down the 250-year-old tree, but it took them ten hours.*

Demolishing that fence was a spontaneous act of popular rebellion and it became a defining moment for the British direct action movement in the early 1990s. It catalyzed a campaign of direct action against the M11 link road, which helped inspire road protest camps to multiply across the country. Tactics imported from environmental activists in the United States and Australia (such as building tree houses and using bodies to block bulldozers) were highly effective and proved very expensive for the road builders. Public opinion was behind the movement and the government's road programme was soon in tatters. Budgets were cut and over 500 road plans scrapped. In response the government introduced a draconian piece of legislation, the 1994 Criminal Justice Bill, which included criminalizing direct action, removing the right to silence, and banning rave parties.

Instead of stopping the movement, the Bill did quite the opposite. A broad, and uniquely diverse coalition emerged to fight it as all the disparate factions whose interests were threatened banded together: hunt saboteurs, peace protesters, football supporters, squatters, radical lawyers, gypsies, ravers, disabled-rights activists. The idea of single-issue politics dissolved as new relationships formed, and new networks were born.

We were late, as always. Lost in a part of London neither of us had ever been to before. A place far across the river and way to the east, with a postcode, E11, that indicates a zone on the endless periphery of our sprawling city. Eventually we found where we were meant to be, a nondescript semi-detached house, pebble-dashed in grey, steeped in normalcy and surrounded by a sea of suburbia.

Someone opened the door and quickly whisked us inside. A strong smell hit us – the smell of wet clothes and bonfire smoke, and a group of about 30 people sat on the floor of the living room. Young dreadlocked hippies, elderly women sipping mugs of tea, a few people looking like bike messengers, all listening attentively to a woman in her late twenties who was enthusiastically explaining the ins and outs of Operation Road Block. For a suburban house, it was uncannily bare, empty of trinkets and the amassed stuff that so often suffocates suburban interiors. We were in one of the many squatted houses on the route of the M11 link road, which was being built through this area, destroying 350 homes and several patches of ancient woodland in its wake. Operation Road Block was a month of daily direct action intended to delay the construction of the much-contested road scheme and cost the developers large amounts of money.

Half an hour later we were walking in a single file through one of the threatened pieces of woodland, crouched one behind the other, a bunch of clumsy urbanites desperately trying to make as little noise as possible while creeping through the undergrowth. I wasn't really sure where we were going, or exactly what we were meant to do. I knew why I was there – to disrupt the road builders; to place my body in the way of the machinery which was destroying this neighbourhood and to try and prevent another triumph of crazy car culture. The training told us our legal rights and some basic tactical tips, but what exactly I was going to do once I got there, I had no idea. And frankly I was scared – terrified. I'd never taken direct action, never jumped on a bulldozer, never even been arrested, and in seven months time I would be a father. Was this a responsible thing to be doing?

A high wall topped with sharp shards of broken glass embedded in concrete marked the edge of the woodland. We stopped beside it. I looked up and wondered – were we really going to go over that? Someone threw a roll of carpet over the protruding bits of glass. "Quick – over the wall," they whispered breathlessly. I froze, hit by one of those moments where the normal flow of life is suddenly interrupted. A tiny fraction of time expanded, encompassing everything, filling itself with many thoughts, questions, dilemmas. Am I really going to go over that wall? It's too tall, I'm not going to make it. I'll hurt myself. What's on the other side of it, anyway? Aren't we just going to fall into the waiting arms of the police?

Although a thousand thoughts flowed through my mind in that moment, it was actually my body that took over and made my decision for me. My muscles, by now bathed in adrenaline, knew exactly what to do. My knees bent, my arms reached up, and I jumped. Someone held out their

"All I was trying to do was defend our local bit of land. I've never thought of myself as political before but this has shown me that all life is politics – if you step out of line."

– East London resident and protester against the M11 link road, 1994

The Restless Margins

moments of resistance and rebellion: 1994 - 2003

\\ 1994 //

>> January 1 >> The EZLN (Zapatista Army of National Liberation) declares war against Mexico, bringing its inspirational struggle for life and humanity to the forefront of political imaginations across the planet. Within 24 hours, the Mexican army responds, bombing communities and killing at least 145 indigenous people. An outraged Mexican civil society retaliates with massive demonstrations calling for an end to military repression. The date of the uprising marks the implementation of the North American Free Trade Agreement (NAFTA), which condemns millions of

hand and pulled me over the top of the wall. As if weightless, my body complied and seemed to fly over what had seconds ago seemed like an unassailable obstacle. I landed on my feet, leaves crunching on impact, and began to run. At first I did not know where to go; I couldn't see any machinery to jump on. We seemed to be on some cleared land, bounded on one side by the wall and on the others by newly erected steel fencing. The only thing that made sense was to head towards one of the two large oak trees that I could see a few yards away. I propelled my body towards the base of one of the trunks as a flash of fluorescent clothing lurched at me. Security guards, everywhere.

A group of us huddled around the base of the tree trunk. Half an hour ago I had never met any of these people; now we were intimately entangled, arms locked together, limbs thrashing, a mass of squirming bodies resisting the guards' attempts to remove us. I remembered the trainer's words: "Keep your thumbs tucked in so they can't prise open your hands." That strange suburban house now felt several worlds away.

I'm not sure what happened next. The clarity of the peak moment – jumping over the wall – turned into a blur populated by frantic security guards and police. But after much pulling on limbs, something extraordinary happened. They gave up and just walked off the site. "We've done it!" someone shouted from one of the piles of bodies. "We've squatted the land, taken it back!" A cheer went up, whoops of joy. Our pragmatic embraces turned into warm hugs of victory. We stood up and immediately began dismantling the steel fences enclosing this piece of land, which was destined to become a four lane motorway one day.

So this was it, this was direct action. Not asking someone else to do something for us, but doing it ourselves. We had crossed walls, broken down fences, and claimed this land as ours. Our bodies had trespassed. Our feet had walked across the line that separates the private from the public. Our minds had evicted the fear that tells us not to disobey and had ignited the hope that anything is possible.

That day was the first step of a journey which would transform my entire life – a journey to places, struggles, and rebellions I never imagined on that spring morning as I crouched beside the wall, wondering if I should jump or not.

Noam Leven is a pseudonym

Resources:

» Extensive site with links and infomation on radical ecological direct action movements: www.eco-action.org

"At times hidden by the clouds that floated in and out of the trees stretching beyond, mile after mile after mile, they sensed that they were part of a 'historical event' with no clear precedents; with the density; depth, and shape associated with turning points – with palpable far-reaching changes in movements that, starting small, can yet sweep over vast spaces of the world. Who knows how this day will unfold into the unforeseeable future? Will it be analogous to the day the Luddites first smashed the machines of the Industrial Revolution? Or will this day mark one of the several small steps taken towards the demise of global neoliberalism?"

– Gustav Esteva, describing the first day of the First Intercontinental Encuentro for Humanity and Against Neoliberalism, 27 July 1997, *Grassroots Postmodernism*, Zed Books

---

indigenous people, peasants, farmers, and workers across North America to poverty, and accelerates environmental destruction and corporate ascendance.

>> **January 27** >> New labour laws set off a 24 hour general strike across Spain. Major cities are occupied by police, and rioting erupts sporadically as hundreds of thousands take to the streets. Shops, airports, and railway stations close, and tourists must fend for themselves in hotels.

>> **February 3** >> Thousands of Indian villagers gather on the banks of the Narmada River to celebrate victory in their year-long campaign to halt the Maheshwar hydropower dam – the first to be built in India using private finance.

>> **March** >> Campaign against the M11 link road begins in earnest in London, UK, as anti-road activists team up with local people to try and defend their public space.

>> **April** >> Peasants form 850 self-defence committees across Bolivia to block roads and resist militarization, the result of the US demand that the Bolivian government eradicate 1,750 hectares of coca production, under threat of an international economic embargo from the International Monetary Fund (IMF)

In January 1996, two years after the uprising, the Zapatistas sent an invitation to social movements on every continent to hold regional gatherings in preparation for what they called the "First Intercontinental Meeting for Humanity and Against Neoliberalism" planned to take place deep in the heart of the Lacandón jungle at the end of July.

They didn't expect many people would want to make the arduous journey to the jungle of Chiapas, endure the military checkpoints with their strip searches and interrogations, and brave the mud and the mosquitoes just to attend a meeting. But the response was overwhelming. On 27 July 1996 over 3,000 grassroots activists from more than 40 countries spanning five continents gathered in five hand-built conference centres, beautifully carved out of the jungle, each hosted by a different autonomous indigenous community.

Berlin squatters sporting green mohawks exchanged tactics with Mayan rebels in ski masks; the mothers of the disappeared of Argentina swapped stories with French strikers; and Iranian exiles listened to Rage Against the Machine. It was a hallucinating mixture of cultures. "Next time we will have to invite the Martians," Subcomandante Marcos quipped. This was the beginning of the movement as a global entity, a movement that was about to radically redefine the political landscape. Despite the multitude of differences, everyone agreed on a common enemy: neoliberal globalization and the desire, as the initial invite stated: "not to conquer the world but simply to make it anew".

Many dared to hope that the scattered pockets of resistance that had gathered here in the Mexican jungle would link up and grow, but no-one quite knew what was going to follow this extraordinary gathering. This is an extract from Subcomandante Marcos' closing remarks on the last night of the Encuentro, held in the Zapatista outpost community named "La Realidad," which means reality.

Tomorrow Begins Today: invitation to an insurrection

by Subcomandante Insurgente Marcos

Welcome to the Zapatista reality. Welcome to this territory in struggle for humanity. Welcome to this territory in rebellion against neoliberalism.

When this dream that awakens today in La Realidad began to be dreamed by us, we thought it would be a failure. We thought that, maybe, we could gather here a few dozen people from a handful of continents. We were wrong. As always, we were wrong. It wasn't a few dozen, but thousands of human beings, those who came from the five continents to find themselves in the reality at the close of the twentieth century.

The word born within these mountains, these Zapatista mountains, found the ears of those who could listen, care for and launch it anew, so that it might travel far away and circle the world. The sheer lunacy of calling to the five continents to reflect clearly on our past, our present, and our future, found that it wasn't alone in its delirium. Soon lunacies from the whole planet began to work on bringing the dream to rest in La Realidad.

Who are they who dare to let their dreams meet with all the dreams of the world? What is happening in the mountains of the Mexican southeast that finds an echo and a mirror in the streets of Europe, the suburbs of Asia, the countryside of America, the townships of Africa, and the houses of Oceania? What is it that is happening with the peoples of these five continents who, so we are all told, only encounter each other to compete or make war? Wasn't this turn of the century synonymous with despair, bitterness, and cynicism? From where and how did all these dreams come to La Realidad?

May Europe speak and recount the long bridge of its gaze, crossing the Atlantic and history in order to rediscover itself in La Realidad. May Asia speak and explain the gigantic leap of its heart to arrive and beat in La Realidad. May Africa speak and describe the long sailing of its restless image to come to reflect upon itself in La Realidad. May Oceania speak and tell of the multiple flight of its thought to come to rest in La Realidad. May America speak and remember its swelling hope to come to renew itself in La Realidad.

May the five continents speak and everyone listen. May humanity suspend for a moment its silence of shame and anguish.

May humanity speak.
May humanity listen....
Each country,
each city,
each countryside,
each house,
each person,
each is a large or small battleground.

On the one side is neoliberalism with all its repressive power and all its machinery of death; on the other side is the human being.

In any place in the world, anytime, any man or woman rebels to the point of tearing off the clothes that resignation has woven for them and cynicism has dyed grey. Any man or woman, of whatever colour, in whatever tongue, speaks and says to himself, to herself: "Enough is enough! – *¡Ya Basta!*"

For struggling for a better world all of us are fenced in, threatened with death. The fence is reproduced globally. In every continent, every city, every countryside, every house. Power's fence of war closes in on the rebels, for whom humanity is always grateful.

But fences are broken.
In every house,
in every countryside,

---

and World Bank. Filemán Escobar of the Bolivian miner's federation points out: "The Andean world was born with the coca leaf thousands of years ago and the coca leaf and coca chewing are part of our culture.... The transformation of coca leaf into cocaine is a problem of the industrialized countries who discovered that cocaine could be extracted. Yet we Bolivians are the victims."

>> April 5-6 >> More than 150,000 Indians protest in New Delhi against the soon-to-be-signed General Agreement on Tariffs and Trade (GATT) treaty which will create the World Trade Organization. The police react to the demonstrators shooting arrows, and throwing stones and sandals by attacking with water cannons and tear gas. 80 people are injured, including several police officers with arrow wounds.

>> April 15 >> The treaty establishing the World Trade Organization (WTO) is signed in Marrakesh, Morocco. Trade representatives from 120 countries sign on, presumably having read its 22,000 pages which weighed in at 11,395 pounds.

>> May >> An entire street in London, Claremont Road, is squatted by activists in an attempt to halt the construction of the M11 motorway. Barricading the street transforms it into a car-free community in

in every city,
in every state,
in every country,
on every continent,
the rebels, whom history repeatedly has given the length of its long trajectory, struggle and the fence is broken.

The rebels search each other out. They walk toward one another.

They find each other and together break other fences.

In the countrysides and cities, in the states, in the nations, on the continents, the rebels begin to recognize each other, to know themselves as equals and different. They continue on their fatiguing walk, walking as it is now necessary to walk, that is to say, struggling....

A reality spoke to them then. Rebels from the five continents heard it and set off walking.

Some of the best rebels from the five continents arrived in the mountains of the Mexican Southeast. All of them brought their ideas, their hearts, their worlds. They came to La Realidad to find themselves in others' ideas, in others' reasons, in others' worlds.

A world made of many worlds found itself these days in the mountains of the Mexican Southeast.

A world made of many worlds opened a space and established its right to exist, raised the banner of being necessary, stuck itself in the middle of earth's reality to announce a better future.

But what next?

A new number in the useless enumeration of the numerous international orders?

A new scheme that calms and alleviates the anguish of having no solution?

A global program for world revolution?

A utopian theory so that it can maintain a prudent distance from the reality that anguishes us?

A scheme that assures each of us a position, a task, a title, and no work?

The echo goes, a reflected image of the possible and forgotten: the possibility and necessity of speaking and listening; not an echo that fades away, or a force that decreases after reaching its apogee.

Let it be an echo that breaks barriers and re-echoes.

Let it be an echo of our own smallness, of the local and particular, which reverberates in an echo of our own greatness, the intercontinental and galactic.

An echo that recognizes the existence of the other and does not overpower or attempt to silence it.

An echo of this rebel voice transforming itself and renewing itself in other voices.

An echo that turns itself into many voices, into a network of voices that, before Power's deafness, opts to speak to itself, knowing itself to be one and many.

Let it be a network of voices that resist the war that the Power wages on them.

A network of voices that not only speak, but also struggle and resist for humanity and against neoliberalism.

The world, with the many worlds that the world needs, continues.

Humanity, recognizing itself to be plural, different, inclusive, tolerant of itself, full of hope, continues.

The human and rebel voice, consulted on the five continents in order to become a network of voices and of resistances continues.

We declare:

That we will make a collective network of all our particular struggles and resistances. An intercontinental network of resistance against neoliberalism, an intercontinental network of resistance for humanity.

This intercontinental network of resistance, recognizing differences and acknowledging similarities, will search to find itself with other resistances around the world.

This intercontinental network of resistance is not an organizing structure; it doesn't have a central head or decision maker; it has no central command or hierarchies. We are the network, all of us who resist.

Subcomandante Insurgente Marcos is the Zapatista's masked spokesperson

---

Resources:

» *Our Word is Our Weapon: Selected Writings of Subcomandante Insurgente Marcos*, Serpent's Tail, UK/ Seven Stories, US, 2001

» Everything you ever wanted to know about Zapatismo: www.flag.blackened.net/revolt/zapatista.html

---

resistance which lasts for six months. One hundred foot towers rise from the rooftops, a network of tunnels are built beneath, nets are hung across the street, junked cars are filled with plants and used as blooming barricades. When the $3.3 million eviction takes place, 1,300 police and security guards work nonstop for four days to remove 500 residents and locked-down activists. Activists from this campaign go on to form Reclaim the Streets.

>> June >> A World Bank delegation appraising the Kaeng Sua Ten dam in northeast Thailand is surrounded by 5,000 angry villagers, who demand that the World Bank leave. "There is no need for any more studies, because we oppose the project," they say. When several consultants return two days later, they are dragged from their car and beaten. No further delegations are sent.

>> July 8-10 >> The G7 meet in Naples, Italy. The local communist mayor insists on having grand receptions for the heads of state and for participants in "The Other Economic Summit," part of the protests which have stalked the G7 summits since 1984. Seven activists from the poorest countries of five continents send the G7 a message: "Keep your wealth. Enjoy your consumer civilization. Withdraw completely your interest,

__Goods and money__ cross borders freely, but when people try to do the same they face repression. In the global economy, the migrant is the ultimate subversive. On 23 August 1996 the French police broke down the doors of the Church of St Bernard in Paris with axes, throwing tear gas canisters inside. They evicted the building occupied by 300 immigrants who were conducting a 50 day hunger strike for recognition of their rights. This was the second church from which the group had been evicted. On 18 March 1996, three hundred foreigners 'sans papiers' (without papers) had occupied the Church of St Ambroise, also in Paris. Women, children, and men together, refusing the label of 'illegals', had decided to live in dignity and in the open in France. "Whenever we go out to work, we are hunted down like animals and denied our dignity; we are stopped by police, often simply for the colour of our face, although we have committed no crime," explains Ababacar Diop, spokesperson for the Sans-Papiers of St Bernard.

At first, their demands were not political. They wanted 'papers for all', that is, general regularization in France. But the French state responded with the forcible eviction from St Ambroise. The Sans-Papiers then moved from place to place, housed here by a Parisian gymnasium, there by a theatre in Vincennes.

As the State dug its heels in and popular support for the Sans-Papiers grew, with up to 2,000 visitors a day coming to St Bernard church, it became a political movement, highlighting the inhumane situations that undocumented immigrants experience in France, and demanding the repeal of laws which restricted further the right of foreigners to reside in or even visit the country.

The origins of current movements for the rights of asylum seekers and immigrants that form a key part of the anticapitalist movement – the No Borders network, the border camps, and most directly the German 'Kein mensch ist illegal' (no one is Illegal) initiative – all grew from the seeds of inspiration sown by the Sans-Papiers.

The *Sans-Papiers*: a woman draws the first lessons

by Madjiguène Cissé

Where do we come from, we *Sans-Papiers* of St Bernard? It is a question we are often asked, and a pertinent one. We didn't immediately realize ourselves how relevant this question was. But, as soon as we tried to carry out a 'site inspection' [of all of the migrants seeking refuge in the church], the answer was very illuminating: we are all from former French colonies, most of us from West-African countries, Mali, Senegal, Guinea, and Mauritania. But there are also among us several Mahgreb people (Tunisians, Moroccans and Algerians); there is one man from Zaire and a couple who are Haitians.

So it's not an accident that we all find ourselves in France: our countries have had a relationship with France for centuries. There are among us many Soninké [who live in the east of Senegal, Mauritania, Mali, Guinea, the Ivory Coast, and Burkina Faso] and it is often said that the Soninké 'are a travelling people' who come together in the Empire of Mali and who were scattered across five or six different countries: that might also explain why they always feel the need to go beyond national borders. And of course, as soon as there is any question of leaving our country, most of the time in order to find work, it's natural that we turn to France. It's the country we know, the one whose language we have learned, whose culture we have integrated a little.

The time of neocolonialism

We hear, including from French government sources, that the solution would be to eradicate the causes of immigration; to help developing countries, in such a way that the people of these countries can find the jobs they need where they are. It's a good idea. But it is not at all what France is doing in Africa. French governments have never really aimed at their former colonies becoming truly independent. On the contrary, France has put in place more subtle forms of domination and exploitation. In Senegal, French investments are not made in the sectors which could help us but only in those which are already profitable.

Structural adjustment policies, which are little by little strangling our countries provide the background: we are lent money on condition that we fit into the Western, neoliberal model of 'development'. Of course this doesn't work; little by little our countries find themselves in considerable debt. And the governments cannot repay the interest of the debt and at the same time finance a policy of development, even if they wanted to.

I say even if they wanted to. Clearly there are corrupt African leaders who divert the aid money and fill their own pockets. Quite simply, we must add that they do this before the eyes and with the full knowledge of their French advisers, even with their collusion. In a way, it's a small tip for 'good and loyal services'.

For France has never stopped being there, advising African leaders and suggesting to them which policies they should implement. For decades now we have been living in a neocolonial situation while passing for independent countries.

It is not for nothing that there is still a French military base in Dakar (and another one in Gabon). It was the French army which quelled the Bangui riot a few months ago. It must be said that even after the colonial period, they have had a solid tradition in these matters. It is they who took charge of repressing the movement of the youth and of the trade unions in May 1968. That's an episode little known in France: but our May movement in Senegal lasted five months, from February to June. And if the French army hadn't intervened, it is probable that power would have been overturned under the combined pressure of the

---

companies, investment, tourist resorts, and good humanitarian intentions from our countries. Leave us to confront ourselves and face our own cultural values. Leave us to pursue our own indigenous road of self-development. It shall be hard and long. But it will be our own choices to determine it. And we will never find ourselves worse off than we are today."

>> July 9 >> Sixty-seven workers at a local McDonald's in a suburb of Paris, France pull a surprise strike, closing the store down during its busiest period. Their demands: "Respect of our right to engage in union activity, paid vacations, the right to choose our own delegates and recognition of our personal needs." Less than 24 hours after the strike begins, a contract is signed between management and the General Confederation of Workers (CGT) union. A few days later, McDonald's workers in the town of Ulis walk out. In Nantes, McDonald's workers prepare a week of action with CGT trade unionists.

>> July 12 >> Four thousand United Rubber Workers in five states of the US walk out, beginning a bitter strike against Bridgestone/Firestone, the world's largest tyre manufacturer, which leads to a lock-out lasting 27 months. The workers respond to slashes in wages and

National Union of Senegalese Workers and the youth movement. The French army doesn't care in the least about 'eradicating the causes of immigration'. They are there to protect the very real economic interests which are at the same time the interests of French neocolonialism and of the African bourgeoisies.

Democracy and autonomy

The struggle has taught us many, many things. It has taught us first of all to be autonomous. That has not always been easy. There were organizations which came to support us and which were used to helping immigrants in struggle. They were also used to acting as the relay between immigrants in struggle and the authorities, and therefore more or less to manage the struggle. They would tell us, "Right, we the organizations have made an appointment to explain this or that;" and we had to say, "But we can explain it very well ourselves." Their automatic response is not to get people to be autonomous, but to speak for them.

If we had not taken our autonomy, we would not be here today. Because there really have been many organizations telling us that we could never win, that we could not win over public opinion because people were not ready to hear what we had to say.

We can see the results today: From ACT UP to the Festival of Cinema in Douarnenez, we've won a wide range of support, including in the most remote parts of France. Little by little masses of people have understood that our struggle was raising questions which go beyond the regularization of the *Sans-Papiers*. New questions have gradually emerged: "Do you agree to live in a France where fundamental human rights are trampled on? Do you agree to live in a France where democratic liberties are not respected?" And we have also learned that if we really wanted to be autonomous, we had to learn about democracy. We had to make our own decisions, get them acknowledged as truly representative of us, not allow them to be called into question from the outside, respect them ourselves and therefore learn to make others respect them, and to implement them ourselves. We have learned that in six months. Without the struggle we would not have learned it in ten years.

It has not been easy. It was not obvious at the beginning that we needed general meetings; it was not obvious that women had to take part in them; it was not obvious that delegates had to be chosen. Let's take, for example, the role

"We are only just starting ... The struggle of the *Sans-Papiers* has to go beyond obtaining our papers and must address the underlying questions, not only in France but also, especially, in our countries of origin.... What is the purpose of migration policies? Should frontiers be open?" – Ababacar Diop, *Sans-Papiers*

of the families, which the press has helped to highlight. At the beginning, when the 'families' got together, it was mainly the 'heads of the families' who tended to express their views. There was an *esprit de chef* (leader spirit) like the head of a region or the village headman in Africa.

Now the reference to 'families' has become more a reference to the family, the African family, very extended, flexible, boy cousin, girl cousin...

Even at this stage, problems still remained. For example, there was a proposal to elect a president. The idea was that we give ourselves a 'head of the family' (a man of course) who would be above the college of delegates, and who would eventually have all powers bestowed on him. Fortunately, this did not happen.

So we elected delegates. At first, we elected ten of them. Today we are no more than five. Each time there is a problem there is in effect a general meeting, and it happens that some *Sans-Papiers* say: we don't want such and such a delegate any more; they're not doing their job. Thus of the ten delegates elected at the beginning of the movement, only two of us are left.

The role of women

Women have played an extremely important role in this struggle. And it was not obvious that this was going to happen. At the beginning it seemed to be taken for granted that women would not participate in general meetings: it wasn't necessary, since the husbands were there! Not only did women not have the right to speak; they didn't even have the right to listen to what was being said at general meetings.

Two or three women began by imposing their presence at general meetings. Then they spoke. The third stage was to have women's meetings. Then the men were really puzzled; they saw us as scheming, plotting, up to no good; they used to hang around our meetings to try and find out what we were saying. In fact, these meetings gave great strength to the women, and enabled them to play an important role in the direction of the struggle. When we were in the 15th *arrondissement*, at Catholic Aid, and the priest of SOS-Racisme suggested that we submit our case files to the Ministry and that we go home, the men were ready to do that, because they trusted the priest. It was the women who didn't want to.

They decided that they were not going home and they

---

benefits, and a threatened implementation of around-the-clock production with seven-day weeks and 12-hour shifts. Imaginative actions take place, including demonstrations at car races, a protest camp outside the corporate HQ, international solidarity-building campaigns launched in Japan and Europe, and a successful boycott campaign. The company eventually agrees a deal and reinstates all strikers who were discharged.

>> July 20 >> One million Turkish workers stage a one-day strike to protest cutbacks ordered by the World Bank and private lending sources. The government threatens arrests, but is overwhelmed by the sheer size of the walkout.

>> August 6-9 >> The Zapatistas organize the National Democratic Convention, held in rebel territory in a newly built convention centre called Aguascalientes, in honour of the 1914 site of the constitutional convention during the Mexican revolution. Over 6,000 people representing a broad range of civil society come from across the country to join the Zapatistas in planning what the government is refusing to discuss or negotiate – a fundamental reform to the Mexican state that would ensure democracy, justice, and a peace with

gave me the job of finding premises. I managed to find an offer of shelter at the Women's Centre (which just celebrated its tenth anniversary) but it was not mixed; it was only for women. The women didn't need long to think about it. Since you want to go home, they said to the men, we'll take the belongings, we'll take the children, and we'll move into the Women's Centre. Then the men told us that meanwhile they had been thinking that we should all stay together and that they would find a place big enough for everybody. In fact, each time the movement ran out of steam, the women met and worked out initiatives which relaunched the struggle.

Thus, there was the women's march on 11 May, at the time when we were in Pajol [a disused railway site made available to the *Sans-Papiers* by the rail workers' trade union CFDT] and when the media were no longer reporting about the struggle. The march unblocked the situation in relation to the press. On 25 June there was the occupation of the town hall of the *18th arrondissement* by the women who hadn't 'warned anyone': it is no accident that the next day the Ministry gave us the first results on the cases we had submitted.

It has to be said that the fighting spirit of women has a long history in Senegal. It was mainly the Senegalese women who spearheaded the protests against the rigging of elections in 1988. For three months, again from February to June, there were demonstrations almost every day. A National Coordination of women of the opposition was set up, and it was this Coordination which took the initiative most of the time, and organized most of the demonstrations.

In fact, the Senegalese women don't only have a tradition of struggle, we also have a tradition of self-organization. It is in some way linked to our education: as women, we are used to managing on our own from a very early age. Because back home, it is the woman who is in charge of the home, who is in charge of the compound [the plot of land on which several families live together]. Little girls from the age of eight look after their younger brothers, go to market, cook. And they have a very important role in forging links with the other families in the compound.

The spokeswoman and the mobile phone

When I was arrested after the police had invaded St Bernard, two events seemed significant to me.

The first is the way I was stripped by policewomen in front of my daughter. It was obvious that their aim was to humiliate me, to break me. So I stripped amid sarcastic comments and questionable jokes. "She's not being that clever any more, the spokeswoman", or "You're not supposed to wear a bra inside out." (A man wouldn't have thought of that.) But the nature of the mocking, the sarcastic comments and the jibes also said much about the state of mind of the police: "Aha! The spokeswoman doesn't have her mobile phone any more." The mobile phone had become the symbol of the modernity to which as a foreigner, as an African, as a Black woman, as a Negro, I had no right: "They've hardly come down from the trees, and they already have mobiles in their hands."

The second one was that I was immediately taken to

court, even though I had a perfectly valid leave to stay. It was obviously another attempt to break the symbol represented by an African woman chosen to be the spokeswoman of her comrades in struggle. And for this, they were prepared to commit many illegalities: they did not themselves respect the laws which they praised so much.

During that whole period, we had many identities to re-establish. For example, our identity as workers. So after St Bernard we insisted on holding our press conference at the *Bourse du Travail* [trade union office] to make people understand that we are not only foreigners, but that we're also workers, men and women who work in France.

The purpose of the attacks against us is of course to casualize us. But we're not the only ones threatened with casualization: many French workers are in this position. Therefore we were keen to signal this 'shared social fate' by where we held our press conference. I must add that our relations with trade unions are now very good. A system of sponsorship has been set up: the *Sans-Papiers* of St Bernard have been shared out among the various trade unions which take care of them, and invite them to speak in their workplaces. For us, the involvement of the trade unions is fundamental to our struggle.

We have also become aware of the importance of our struggle through the support that we immediately found in our home countries (at least from the people; the governments were in less of a hurry). We believe that the struggle, in Senegal and elsewhere, against structural adjustment programmes, and our struggle here, is one and the same struggle. Coordination is not easy from 4,400 miles away, but we must constantly ensure that we are making the connections between our different battles.

Integration and respect

In France up until now our fate as immigrants was: either take part in the Republic's process of integration, or be deported like cattle. At the heart of this approach was the notion that we are 'underground', which has a very strong negative charge. A person who is underground is someone who hides, who conceals themselves, and if you conceal yourself it must be because after all you have something to hide. The French person who thinks that they must oppose

---

dignity and social justice. In the opening ceremony, Subcomandante Marcos expresses the wishes of the Zapatistas, saying: "We hope that the horizon will open up so that we will not be necessary anymore, we the dead since always, who have to die again in order to live. We hope...to disappear in the same way we appeared, one morning, without a face, without future. To return to the depths of history, of the dream, of the mountains..."

>> September >> Italy's infamous Tute Bianche [white overalls] movement is born, when the neofascist mayor of Milan orders the eviction of the squatted social centre, Leoncavallo, saying: "From now on, squatters will be nothing more than ghosts wandering about in the city!" Activists respond humorously, dressing in ghostly white overalls and taking to the streets; riots ensue, and the squat is saved. The white overalls, symbols of the invisibility of those excluded from capitalism, spread across the world, from Finland to Mexico.

>> September 21 >> Doctors in 25 Bangladesh government hospitals walk out over demands for higher wages, promotions and new employment, virtually paralyzing the public health sector.

people who are underground, illegal immigration, etc. always has at their side an immigrant friend they've known for a long time.

The immigrant you reject is always the one you don't know. We have made ourselves visible to say that we are here, to say that we are not in hiding but we're just human beings. We are here and we have been here a long time. We have been living and working in this country for many years and we pay our taxes. In the files of the St Bernard people you will find wage slips, income tax declarations, old documents giving leave to stay. There are also passports and visas issued by the consulates of our countries of origin.

At the beginning of our struggle, they tried to label us as people who are underground. But they couldn't: the authorities of this country have known us for a long time. Now we feel that we have taken a step forward: even the media no longer talks about people who are underground, but of *Sans-Papiers*. The fact that we've been seen on TV, that we've been interviewed in the press, I think that has helped people to understand that we've been here for years, that we haven't killed anyone, and that we are simply demanding the piece of paper which is our right, so that we can live decent lives.

In my view, our struggle also says a number of things about the difference between the model of French integration and the model which respects our founding cultures. I think that we have understood, and maybe helped others to understand, that it isn't a question of one model or the other, but of finding a balance between the two. I have understood this by also thinking about my origins, about the culture of my ethnic group. I am from the Serere ethnic group. My first name is typically Wolof, and it's a Tiado first name. In Africa, the majority of first names are either Christian or Muslim. When you are a Christian, you are called either Paul or John, and when you are a Muslim, you are called Ali or Mohammed. A Tiado first name is the first name of someone who is neither Christian nor Muslim. We have resisted all attempts to convert us, whether to Christianity or to Islam. Our resistance is legendary. We are non-conformists. But our experience has also taught us how to live in a pluralist society.

When you want to live in a country there is a basic

"We are now at a crossroads. Immigrants have been designated as scapegoats for every crisis in France and in the rest of Europe. By attacking immigrants, the French government is drawing closer to the policy of the National Front [extreme right-wing party] against a background of racism and xenophobia."

– Ababacar Diop, *Sans-Papiers*

minimum, not only of rules to abide by but also of the effort you have to make: to learn the language, to fit into the social and institutional fabric of the society, and not to be satisfied with community education structures for the children but for them to go to the state schools of the country in which their parents live and work. On the other hand, there must be in this country a minimum of respect for our cultures of origin.

Nobody forces French people who have lived in Senegal for a long time to dress like the Senegalese. And it is not because we live in a country where women are keen to wear trousers that we must decree that women who put on their African cloth and who wear the scarf cannot integrate. A bottom line must be firmly established on both sides: a minimum of will to integrate, a minimum of respect for our cultures of origin. As soon as these two pillars are firmly established, everyone can find their own balance: it will not necessarily be the same for each person. But balance will be found along this middle way which can be reached largely by consensus.

Madjiguène Cissé is the spokeswoman of *Sans-Papiers*. In 1998 *Sans-Papiers* and Madjiguène Cissé received the prestigious Carl-von-Ossietzky Medal from the International Federation of Human Rights League (German section), in recognition of their "public-spirited courage" in campaigning for the rights of immigrants and refugees. Her book, *Parole de Sans-Papiers*, was first published in France in 1999. She now lives in Dakar, Senegal.

Original French version published in *Politique*, la revue, n°2 October, 1996
Published in English with a chronology of the *Sans-Papiers* movement,

English translation by Selma James, Nina Lopez-Jones, Helen West

Resources:

» **Sans-Papiers : www.bok.net/pajol**

>> September 29 >> A nationwide strike is held in India called by the National Platform of Mass Organizations in protest against the structural adjustment programmes (SAP) of the World Bank and the signing of GATT (WTO). The strike affects functioning of banks, financial institutions, and public sector units across the county, and is the eighth in a series of protests against SAPs during the previous two years.

>> October 2 >> Bolivian workers fight back against World Bank-ordered 'reforms,' which require that the country cuts wages of public workers and privatize the national phone system. The resulting general strike, hunger strikes, and road and rail blockades result in the government declaring a state of siege. After 23 days, the government agrees to wage demands, and backs down from privatization.

>> October 2-4 >> Eleven people scale overhead beams of a conference centre in Madrid, Spain, and shower thousands of dark-suited delegates below with fake dollar bills that say "50 Years of Destruction" during the opening ceremonies of the IMF/World Bank's 50th anniversary meetings. The financial institutions face their biggest demonstrations since they were run out of town a day early in Berlin in 1988. Outside the

In August, 1995, the Los Angeles Times reported on 63 Thai immigrant women, found locked in a complex surrounded by barbed wire, working 84 hours a week. This slave labour didn't occur in China, Indonesia, or Honduras, where we've sadly come to expect such working conditions; it took place in El Monte, California, USA.

At the same time, other stories of horrific abuse and exploitation were emerging from factories producing clothes for the global market. In what became known as the 'race to the bottom', multinational corporations could move to where the labour force was the cheapest and the labour laws the weakest. From Manhattan to Tangier, workers were beginning to reveal the oppressive, dangerous, and often illegal conditions under which they were working to produce the clothes bearing popular labels like Nike, Levi's, and the Gap. Thus the word sweatshop – which dates back to the nineteenth century – was reintroduced into popular use.

Although university apparel makes up only two per cent of the US garment market, students have been at the forefront of anti-sweatshop organizing. Early on, students around the US realized that their universities were directly profiting from the exploitation of women who make the clothes bearing the university logo. A campaign for a 'Sweat-Free Campus' was launched in the summer of 1997, and the idea spread like wildfire. Demanding that universities hold clothing producers accountable, students expressed their outrage that their fashion was dependent on exploitation and violence. For many students, it was their first – and perhaps their only – political action, but for others, it was their entrance into the movement, their introduction to the (il)logic of economic globalization. They learned that women make up 90 per cent of the sweatshop work force, and work gruelling hours, unprotected by wage or safety laws, subjected to mandatory pregnancy testing (sometimes even injection with contraceptives without consent). Armed with this information, students began connecting the stories of these women's lives with the broader economic system which thrives on such exploitation.

The Sweatshop and the Ivory Tower

by Kristian Williams

The first thing we did was set up a prayer meeting. An odd start, it's true, but Georgetown was an unusual setting for an anti-sweatshop campaign. It's a conservative university catering to the upper-upper-middle class, jealous of the Ivy League, a Catholic school where both a gay rights organization and a pro-choice group had been suppressed by the administration, and a financial leviathan with ties to Nike and Disney. Georgetown was not where one would go in search of anarchists and revolutionaries.

Still, the school's financial dealings did draw the attention of the Georgetown Solidarity Committee (the GSC) – a student group formed a few years earlier to support a union drive among the cafeteria workers. When that campaign failed, the group languished briefly, then found new direction with the help of the Union of Needletrades, Industrial and Textile Employees (UNITE) – the garment workers' union. UNITE brought some much-needed scrutiny to the conditions under which apparel featuring Georgetown's name and logo was being produced. These sweatshirts and ballcaps sold widely and provided a key source of income for the school's sports program; they were also made in sweatshops in Central America. So, armed with facts about the wages of the workers and the profits of the college, the GSC set out to expose – and eliminate – the

Georgetown sweatshop connection.

Our plan was to get the university to adopt a code of conduct governing the licensing of its name and logo, with independent monitoring and enforcement through the Workers' Rights Consortium (WRC). Student groups around the country were pursuing similar strategies at their own schools; the sweatshop profiteers countered by forming the Fair Labor Association (FLA), with an intentionally meaningless code of conduct of their own. The trick, then, was to get the university to go with the WRC and not with the FLA.

I must confess I was skeptical about the prayer meeting. I did not expect God to put things right, and felt very strongly that the only way to persuade the administration was to apply pressure of a sort they could not ignore. In the end, that pressure came to bear: on Friday, 5 February 1999, 27 students took over the University President's office and refused to move until the school committed to the WRC code of conduct.

This move led to a decisive (if modest) victory at Georgetown, as the same tactic had a few days earlier at Duke University, and as it did later at a number of other schools. Though the school did not wholly accept the WRC position, they did accept key points of it. Companies producing Georgetown apparel would be required to publicly disclose the locations of their factories, opening the possibility of third-party monitoring by human rights and labor organizations. Any company which failed to comply with this requirement would have its contract cancelled.

The sit-in itself lasted 85 hours and was extremely well organized. Press releases were issued twice daily, support rallies were held, fliers printed and placed under every door in every dormitory and office building, and the school's stately stone walls were covered with posters and chalk-scrawled graffiti. I had a hand in all that, but that's not what I want to talk about here.

This is what I want to say: I was right about the need to pressure the administration; but I was wrong about that prayer meeting. And that's not the only thing I was wrong about. During the months between the September prayer meeting and the February sit-in the GSC engaged in tame tactics that the university could (and usually, did) ignore. We had rallies, vigils, petitions, leaflets, and a public forum. I expected

---

building, a carnivalesque march of 5,000 people declare their opposition to IMF policies. Press conferences and banquets are further disrupted by infiltrating activists. The 50 Years Is Enough network is founded at a counter-conference. Simultaneous protests take place in several countries.

>> October 6 >> One thousand French workers invade the Paris stock exchange, halting the billion-dollar trade in financial futures and options for the entire day, in protest against the partial sale of car maker Renault, and all privatizations in France. One huge poster reading "Sacrifices, Unemployment, Privatizations" obscures the computer screens which normally provide prices for stock options. "If we called the police there would be a complete riot," one security guard complains.

>> October 9 >> Over 100,000 people march in London, UK, against the Criminal Justice Bill, which criminalizes direct action, rave music, and squatting, as well as terminating the right to remain silent under interrogation. A diverse group takes to the streets opposing the law – festival and party goers, squatters, travelers, hunt saboteurs, anti-road protesters, and gay rights groups. The day ends with rioting in Hyde Park.

>> October 26 >> All schools in Sierra Leone are shut

nothing to come from these, but I was in for a surprise.

It was at the public forum that I was first impressed by the course of the campaign. We supplied three speakers – GSC's vice president and two sympathetic professors. The administration sent a representative from the sports program and Dean of Students (with whom we would later negotiate). Following the speakers was a time for public comment, creating the sort of 'open discussion' so often called for in universities. We had, of course, planted half a dozen reliable people in the audience, scattered throughout the auditorium to make sure the conversation went the way it ought.

None of our people spoke. None of them needed to. The students who did speak – most of whom I had never seen in either a meeting or at a rally – spoke eloquently and with passion. They shamed the administration. They called the Dean a hypocrite and a liar. One woman broke into tears as she quoted scripture: "Inasmuch as ye have done it unto one of the least of these..." Another, a member of the rowing crew, explained in no uncertain terms that her recreation was not worth the exploitation of teenaged girls half a world away. No student spoke in favour of the FLA or defended the administration. As I left that night it occurred to me – I think, for the first time – that the students might actually be on our side.

It should be understood that the students at Georgetown are, as a group, notoriously conservative. They are – almost uniformly – rich, young, white, and Catholic. Privileged and ambitious, they represented to my mind about the least likely source of sympathy to the plight of the toiling masses.

"In 1996 a Nike advertising man said innocently: 'Why write this kind of copy if not to incite people to riot?' – thinking that he was boosting the rebellious image of the brand, rather than predicting the Nike brand backlash." – *Stay Free* magazine

But during the sit-in, support came from some unexpected places: business students, a College Republican (a pro-lifer who literally winced at the word 'leftist'), a military cadet, and the Skull-and-Bones-type secret fraternity devoted to upholding Georgetown's Catholic traditions. The student government half-willingly donated their office for the GSC to manage its support operations. (We jokingly called this "the other occupation"). The security guards joked that they'd call us when their contracts expired (and I believe they might); they did nothing to interfere with the sit-in, or to discourage donations from coming into the office. Professors forgave students their late papers. And a Jesuit priest performed a mass in the occupied President's office.

The truth is that I never expected to win, in large part because I never expected such support. In retrospect, it seems that I must not have understood what we were doing when we held those rallies, printed leaflets, issued statements to the school paper. I was thinking tactically, you see, focusing on what we could do to force concessions from the administration. And so I overlooked the strategy that was being employed right in front of my face.

If I had been in charge – also, I suspect, if the GSC had been comprised of more radical types – things would have gone a great deal differently. We would not have bothered with leaflets at the basketball games. We would not have sung the fight song at our rallies, or put Jack the Georgetown Bulldog on our posters and picket signs. We would not have organized prayer meetings. And we would not have won.

The GSC tailored its campaign to the conservative culture of the school. This was not the type of organizing I was used to, and it often made me uncomfortable. My mistake – a terrible mistake for a radical – was in thinking too small. I was focused on discrediting the administration in the eyes of the GSC members, while they were busy discrediting the administration in the eyes of the entire school.

I spent a year at Georgetown, and this is the biggest thing I learned: you win by organizing, and you organize by approaching people on terms they can accept. You do not win because of your radical rhetoric. You do not win by writing off potential allies, or insisting on ideological purity. You do not win by denigrating popular culture or ignoring the decent impulses of your peers. You do not win because you have the 'right line' or are able to quote Gramsci. You do not win through heroics or martyrdom. You win by organizing, and you organize by approaching people on terms they can accept.

It is often tempting to think that 'moral feeling' has no political worth. And indeed, a pious moralism is worse than useless unless it can be directed into meaningful collective action. But if it can be so directed, the results are sometimes astonishing. It was not Marx's critique of capitalism or any ideological rejection of authority which led those twenty-seven privileged college kids to risk arrest and expulsion on behalf of sweatshop workers thousands of miles away. Nor was it an urge toward internationalism or student-worker solidarity that moved scores of others to support this shocking act. These ideological developments came later. Instead, it was a sense of basic human decency, the idea that it is simply wrong to abuse workers in the global South so

---

down as 35,000 teachers go on strike. Demanding prompt payments of salaries and allowances and a 30 per cent pay increase, teachers also demand of the military government that they repeal a decree banning the right to strike.

>> October 27 >> More than 15,000 workers in Siberia and the far east of Russia take to the streets in the first stage of a nationwide protest against falling living standards and huge salary arrears. Similar protests take place across the country, with the participation of well over two million people.

>> November 8 >> At least 40 people in masks ransack a McDonald's in Mexico City's fashionable Zona Rosa, protesting an anti-immigrant ballot initiative passed in California. Windows are broken, bins tipped over, cash registers hurled to the ground, and graffiti with messages of solidarity and anti-imperialism painted. The new law denies all social services to illegal immigrants in California, clearly showing that voters have by and large forgotten that California was stolen from Mexico (and from Native Americans before that) by force and that the definition of "illegal immigrant" is an insult to those originally inhabiting that land.

>> November 24 >> In Beirut, Lebanon, striking

that Georgetown can sell its hats and sweatshirts at a higher profit. These motivations may be reformist and bourgeois. They are certainly not as tough-sounding as 'class interest', for example. But I doubt if such distinctions matter very much to the 16-year-old girl, chained to her sewing machine, stitching hats for a few dollars a day.

Kristian Williams is the author of *Our Enemies in Blue: Police and Power in America*, Soft Skull Press, 2003

Resources:

» US-based information, including how to get involved: www.sweatshopwatch.org

» Detailed info on starting and maintaining campaign: www.maquilasolidarity.org

» *Sweatshop Warriors*, by Miriam Ching Yoon Louie, South End Press, 2001

Traffic moves sluggishly *through the grey London haze. Suddenly people dart into the road with scaffolding poles. They quickly erect a tripod, and someone climbs to the top, balancing gracefully 20 feet above the tarmac. The road is now blocked to traffic but open to pedestrians. Louis Armstrong's "What a Wonderful World" drifts from a sound system as thousands of people pour out of the nearby underground station and fill the street. People shinny up lampposts and hang huge banners, some supporting the striking public transport workers, others saying "Breathe", or "Street Now Open". A band plays from the roof of a bus stop, people dance, a choir sings, and a tonne of sand is dumped onto the tarmac, turning it into an instant beach for children. Welcome to a Reclaim the Streets party.*

Reclaim the Streets (RTS) emerged in London from the campaign against the construction of the M11 link road, the environmental direct action movements of the early 1990s, and the unusual network of ravers, travellers, and protesters brought together by the Criminal Justice Act of 1994. By using creative tactics which fused carnival and rebellion they reintroduced notions of pleasure and play into radical politics. RTS also merged social and ecological principles into a wider cultural critique; their agit-prop questioned: "Won't the streets be better without cars? Not if all that replaces them are aisles of pedestrianized consumption or shopping 'villages' safely protected from the elements.... The struggle for car-free space must not be separated from the struggle against global capitalism."

The creative audacity of RTS proved to be contagious and spread across the emerging activist networks. In the late 1990s, street parties began to pop up across the global North, and a new generation of activists was inspired to rethink political action. In July 1996, RTS ambitiously reclaimed a motorway, the M41. While 10,000 people partied, huge carnival figures were wheeled through the crowd. Hidden underneath and drowned out by the sound system, people were tearing into the tarmac with jack hammers and planting saplings. This story tells how RTS pulled it off ...

Reclaim the Streets: an arrow of hope

by Charlie Fourier

I have a pain in my stomach. As the fog of sleep gives way to daylight, dawn and the strangeness of someone else's house are the first things of which I'm aware. I don't want to remember why. But my memory, usually unfailingly bad, lets me down again. It's strange, this morning has been the object of so much nervous pondering over the last six months. Will it be raining? How will the police intervene? Will I panic? Will we panic? And now, as future and present collide, it's as if there never was a past, there had always only been this day.

I'll explain. There's a group organizing what we hope will be a massive illegal street party. We want to fire an arrow of hope and life into the heart of our dying city. We're going to take back the M41, reclaim it, steal it back from the machine. But occupying a motorway is no easy business. You can't just walk up saying "Excuse me, could you go away, we're going to have a street party here." We've been planning this for about five months. Everything has been looked at in detail. Every possibility scrutinized and coordinated. Even the likelihood (certainty?) that we'll miss something. Backups for mistakes, contingencies for backups. It's our own Frankenstein's monster. Our own Catch 22. Once we've realized it's essential to stop, to back out, it's become impossible to do so.

This is the basic plan. The crowd meet up at Liverpool Street station, the meeting place we've advertised in advance. Then when there's around two thousand people, they're directed onto the tube by people in the crowd. Then, they're taken right across London to Shepherd's Bush where they're directed out of the station in groups of eight hundred, and onto the motorway. The basic plan is quite simple but it's the smaller details that really hold it together. The crowd block the northbound traffic, but for technical reasons they can't stop the southbound traffic. That's our job. At exactly the same time as the crowd arrives at Shepherd's Bush, we have to drive onto the south lane, block it (by crashing two cars together and

---

dockers completely shut down the port for six days.

>> December 1 >> United States Congress approves joining the WTO without having read the treaty. Prior to the vote, an offer of a $10,000 donation to the charity of choice had been made to any congressperson who had read the entire thing and could answer ten simple questions about its contents. Not one member of congress accepted, until after the vote was postponed, and then one Republican, a "free" trade supporter, stepped forward to the challenge. He answered all ten questions correctly and then held a press conference, stating that he had planned to vote in favour, but after reading the text of the agreement, he had changed his position.

>> December 2 >> Hundreds of indigenous people from Chile, Mexico, Peru, and Bolivia march in Temuco, Chile to protest against Chile joining in the North American Free Trade Agreement, decrying the ease with which multinational corporations would be able to take their land.

>> December 3 >> Police arrest thousands of people heading for a demonstration in Bhopal, India, on the tenth anniversary of the chemical leak from the Union Carbide plant that caused 7,000 deaths. As one Bhopal

putting up tripods), and drive trucks carrying the sound systems, bouncy castles, etc. onto the road to meet the crowd. I'm in the group driving the trucks from their secret location to two points. One about two miles away, and then on signal, to another one about quarter of a mile from the motorway. A short wait, one more phone call, and we drive onto the road, block it and unload all the gear. That's the plan anyway.

I make Andy some tea. I'm staying at his address because it's one the police don't know. We guess they might bust the main organizers the night or morning before the event. It sounds paranoid, but it turns out to be sound thinking. I leave the house on my bike around 9.00 am. I don't exactly feel calm but I'm on automatic, I'm pre-programmed. It's a beautiful day. The bleached blue of sky cuts strange shapes against the jumbled horizon of a city full of question marks. I hope we can answer, I hope we can pull this off. After half an hour I arrive at the factory, our secret rendezvous. A group of Spaniards are squatting it and holding parties every now and again. Ian, a man with siesta in his blood, has sniffed them out and for the last few weeks we've been storing equipment and practicing the erection of our forty-foot tripod which is to be used for blocking the road. The Spaniards hung out, sitting cat-like in the sun, looking sexy and listening to weird mixes of Mozart and techno. I think they liked us, the way you might like a furry alien. We must have seemed strange. Coming in at all hours, dropping things off, being very secretive. Then we'd rush around the courtyard, putting up creaking tripods in minutes with military precision. Well almost. Sometimes the contrast was ridiculous. Their endless dreamy siestas, us charging up and down shouting and sweating. One morning we caught the tail end of one of their parties. There were about 20 Spaniards lying around tired and happily stoned listening to very ambient, end of party music. We were there in the courtyard putting the upper section of our tripod on for the first time. Twenty bodies melting into the furniture haphazardly strewn around, us 12 maniacally constructing. Just as we lifted the last 20 foot section into place, the DJ started playing a dramatic remix of the Space Odyssey 2001 soundtrack. I realized that they were willing us on, hoping we'd succeed in our bizarre project.

It's quiet when I arrive. The sound crew are in the warehouse. They've been packing the trucks all night and their techno sculpture is now complete. My arrival is greeted with tired hostility which turns to laughter when they realize it's me. But it's the laughter of people bemused, worried even. The sound system people treat us with some suspicion. It's not surprising. Ask anyone from a rig what they do and their answer will be reasonably clear. Ask someone from RTS and the answer will be as clear as the Thames on a foggy night. Ours is the politics of the margins, the margins where words fear to tread. But a shaman needs an audience, a religious site, and they know that we'll try our best to provide it.

Soon the RTS road crew (yeah I know) arrive, and yet despite enjoying the feeling of comradeship, the feeling of purpose, this feels like the spinning point around which months of fantasy become a terrifying reality. The two trucks are parked behind each other in the bigger of the two warehouses. The front truck contains one sound-system and three tons of sand (a beach for the kids). The other truck has a huge sound system and four 20 foot tripods, which together make the 40 foot tower. After some last-minute running around looking for that crucial remix, petrol for the generators, and so on, everybody is on board. Two drivers, two co-drivers, and the sound crews happily hidden in the back with their systems. It's one of life's rarer moments. Everything's organized, we've taken our responsibilities seriously, and everything is going to plan. I feel like I'm going to burst but there's also a sense of calmness that preparation allows you. Dean and I are in the front tuck. Dean's driving, the others are waiting for us to move off. "Shall we...?" I venture. "Give us the keys then." "Oh yeah, the keys."

I am water. The plug has been pulled. I've forgotten the keys. I'VE FORGOTTEN THE FUCKING KEYS. The keys to the truck. The truck with the stuff. The truck in front of the other truck. The other truck with the rest of the stuff. The truck with the tripods for the blockade, the truck with the sound systems, the beach, the everyfuckingthing. Two trucks. Eight sad tons of useless metal. One small piece of brass, a shudder of electricity, compression and life. But the key, the key whose ninety degree shift gives meaning, is four miles away. I slip from a rigidity of shock to a catatonic nothingness. It takes half an hour to drive to Muswell Hill. We've got to be parked up in three quarters of an hour. Without these two trucks there will be no blockade, no sound systems, and probably no street party. People are getting out, wondering what the hold-up is. I'm sitting in the cab shaking, unable to move or speak properly. This event confirms all my most firmly held doubts about myself. That: (1) I am, and always have been stupid. (2) I am not worthy of love, friendship, or trust. (3) That I will have a miserable life. Dean is staring at me from the driving seat. His eyes say it all. I know he's thinking that I'm totally stupid, utterly untrustworthy and deserving of a miserable life. People, having discovered what's going on, are pacing the courtyard like a troop of headless chickens. I pull back into my vacated self and maniacally start scraping every

---

activist puts it, "Bhopal is not something unfortunate that is only happening to the people of a central Indian city. It is happening everywhere around the world. The routine poisoning of living systems that accompanies the storage, transport, production, consumption and waste treatment of hazardous chemicals are part of our industrial society. The silent and slow Bhopals that are happening in everyday life often go unnoticed and are seldom resisted."

\\ 1995 //

>> January >> Wildfire wins a victory as a result of one of the most successful actions of Earth First! at Warner Creek, Oregon, US. Activists maintain an 11 month blockade of logging roads, through harsh winter snowfall, and frequent visits by curious tourists! The camp, christened Cascadia Free State, features a watchtower, a moat and drawbridge, a wide variety of barricades, and frequent trainings and planning meetings for establishing other "Free States." As part of the fallout of new "salvage logging" legislation, the forest service had plans to log over 1,200 acres after the second largest wildfire in the region. In addition to the blockades, activists hold a thorough educational campaign explaining the ecology of fire, and the natural

pore of my bag in the forlorn hope that.... A woman arrives in the courtyard in her car. It's an old Fiesta, which to us shines with the perverted curves of a sports car. Like zealots we explain our plight to this goddess of fortune. She hands us the keys and a ghost of sadness shadows her face as we leave in the car, that in a strange, human way she kind of loves. Turnpike Lane passes in a blur as we speed towards the Hill.

Somehow we get to the flat in 15 minutes. I charge up to the top floor. There are the keys. I run back to the car, clenching the key in fearful grip, a tiny sliver of brass thawing the ice that has entered my body. Dean's smile mirrors my relief, and we race back towards the factory, our fragile hopes of success alive again. We arrive at the factory ten minutes over the 30 minutes we had in hand. A phone call to Liverpool Street establishes that the crowd has started to gather. I ask them to give us an extra ten minutes to get in place. Now we have to drive the trucks across London, park up in a quiet industrial estate and wait for a phone call which tells us to move to a final pitch less than half a mile from the motorway.

We drive across London, every now and then spotting a group of people obviously heading for the meeting place at Liverpool Street station. I'm too vain not to feel a sense of pride, and too scared for it to make me feel anything but more nervous. We join the Westway, which rises majestically out of the chaos like a giant silver-backed reptile winding over the city. I feel young, like a child on a great adventure, the blue skies echoing our new found mood. London seems to be waiting, almost conspiring with us, as if somehow it's a living participant in the day's events. We pull off the motorway and drive to our first pitch.

"We are basically about taking back public space from the enclosed private arena. At its simplest, it is an attack on cars as a principle agent of enclosure. It's about reclaiming the streets as public inclusive space from the private exclusive use of the car. But we believe in this as a broader principle, taking back those things which have been enclosed within capitalist circulation and returning them to collective use as a commons."

– London Reclaim the Streets agitprop, 1996

The industrial estate is virtually deserted. A jumble of silent, blank warehouses. Our cars, which are to crash and block the road, are parked at the back of the estate. With the cars are the four people responsible for the block: Louise, John, Anna, and Beth. You can tell they're nervous. You would be if you had to stage-crash a car on one of London's crowded motorways. A tailback of a thousand overheated motorists and you caused it. On purpose.

We've bought the two cars for 100 pounds each. Scrap on wheels and it shows. One has died on us. NO amount of mouth-to-exhaust can bring it back. Blocking the road with one car is going to be difficult. Luckily we have a backup car. I call Des, the driver, who starts heading over. Now it's just a case of waiting and hoping. Waiting for the call to say "move," hoping that Des arrives before the call. So, of flesh and beating hearts we wait among the silent and formless warehouses. People are out of the trucks and lolling about in the sun.

The phone rings. "Pete, it's Des. I've run out of fucking petrol." Maybe it's right and proper that a group who claim to be against car culture should be jinxed when it comes to using them. Anyway, we're going to have to manage the road block with just one. These problems aside, I feel surprisingly confident. It feels like some kind of miracle to be in this nowhere place waiting to pounce. If we can get this far, anything is possible. Every now and then the mobile rings. Things are OK at Liverpool Street. The crowds have started moving off and are heading towards us on the tube. And we wait. I feel like we're on some strange island, isolated from a world we can only dream of. And then this guy wanders over, wearing a big coat and black clothes to match his long black hair. He seems vaguely pissed or stoned or both. "So, what's happening?" "Errh... nothing much." I sound nervous as hell. "So, what's in the trucks?" It may have been a casual inquiry, but it's like someone has thrown a bucket of icy water over us. I'm staring at the others and trying to look relaxed at the same time. Lee tries to shake him off, "What's up, what you doing down here?" "Oh, my truck's broken down. I'm parked up round the corner. Is that a sound system in the back?" Fuck. Fuck. Fuck. This is getting stranger. I'm feeling panicky again. My next words sound hollow, "Yea we're doing a party in Hampshire tonight, should be good." He ignores my synthetic voice and carries on, "Oh right, did you hear about the Reclaim the Streets party?" The words hang in the air like branding irons. He mutters something indiscernable and wanders off, leaving us to our paranoia.

Then, as if to balance things, Des arrives. He'd managed to hitch to the petrol station and back to the car in under 20 minutes. Recent strangeness is soon forgotten as we explain the practicalities of the road-block to our new arrival. The crowd is on the way. We wait some more. The mobile rings

---

regeneration that will occur if allowed. The blockade ends when a presidential decree withdraws the salvage sale and the forest is allowed to continue its cycle.

>> January 1 >> The General Agreement on Tariffs and Trade (GATT) becomes the World Trade Organization (WTO).

>> January 25 >> Protesting tuition hikes and education cuts, the Canadian Federation of Students take action on the Pan-Canadian Day of Action, as 16,000 students take to the streets in Montreal, and at least 100,000 participate nationwide. As a result, tuition fees are frozen in the provinces of British Columbia and Québec.

>> February 12 >> Over 100,000 people demonstrate in Mexico City, demanding that the military withdraw from Chiapas, in response to the issuance of arrest warrants for 11 Zapatistas, the "unmasking" of Subcomandante Marcos as a former philosophy professor, increased military aggression in Chiapas, and the government's breaking of the ceasefire with the EZLN. The aggression backfires, as not only do the Zapatistas fight off the Federal Army troops and retain control of most of the southern regions of the state, they turn the offensive to their advantage by organizing

again. It's John. "The first tube's gone past Marble Arch!" Now we have to move to the final pitch. It's only just down the road, but we want to be as close as possible when the final call comes, so we can time our arrival just right. The next parkup is next to a riding school squeezed in behind a block of flats. We pull up and park in a line next to some bushes. This time there's no lolling about, no jokes, just the weight of our nervous anticipation. If the plan goes well we shouldn't be here for more than five minutes. The mobiles are going mad. There's a call from D, her gentle nervous voice sounding strange amongst the aggressive chaos. She says there are police vans crawling all over the location, but that her group is in place. She's part of a group of ten hiding behind a wall next to the motorway. When our cars crash, we pull the trucks up next to the wall and they all jump over, get the tripods out and put them up. We thought the police might work out where we were going by looking at the map and the direction we were heading. Our hunch was that by the time they'd worked it out we'd be too close for it to make any difference. Still, their arrival is like salt water to our already flayed nerves.

Gideon Mendel/RTS archives

'Above the tarmac the beach', reclaiming the M41 for play. London, UK

In the distance we can hear police sirens above the low grumble of traffic. What is usually the slightly annoying sound of somebody else's problem, today strikes fear into our hearts. There are probably only two or three of them, but to us it sounds like thousands. Then Clive calls. Clive is the spotter at Shepherd's Bush, who will give us the final go ahead. He tells me that there's a thick line of police blocking the crowd in at Shepherd's Bush and they can't get through onto the motorway. His words crash through me like a vandal in a greenhouse. In the background I can hear the noises of the crowd. It almost sounds like the party's started. I tell the others, a desperate gloom envelops us, and our collective mood shifts with the speed of a retreating tide. I have spent months telling myself that even if we failed it will have been worth it. I could never have carried on if I'd thought everything hung on success. Now I see I've been conning myself. I feel sick. Everyone looks crushed. Jim calls. "Pete is that you?" "Yeah, fuck's sake what's going on." "We can't get through. We're going to have to have it at

Shepherd's Bush. You'll have to go round the back." Even through the electronic echo I can hear the tension in his voice. He knows as well as I do that Shepherd's Bush is a dire location. A strip of dog-shit covered lawn squeezed between two hideous shopping parades. It seems pretty unlikely that we could drive through the police cordons, and even if we could, would it be worth it? How could all those coppers get there so quickly? Why can't the crowd break through the cordon? The hopeless, pointless, questions of loss drown out my thoughts. A mood of desolation fills me like the first cold rains of winter. It's over. We fought the law and the law won.

Sitting there in that truck in the London sunshine with those people feels like the end of hope. We start looking at the A-Z trying to work out a back route to Shepherd's Bush. There's no enthusiasm, this is a job now. Jen calls. She was to call if things were going badly. This call signifies a last ditch attempt to rectify things. When Clive sees there's no way through he calls Jen. She's waiting at the nearest station. She runs down the tube and tells people coming from Liverpool Street that there's no way through. They then get out and approach the motorway through some back streets. "There's a hundred or so people heading down through the back route." By this time a small group of us are gathered round the front truck, analyzing all the information as it arrives. Everyone looks at everyone else. Hope releases tiny vascular muscles and blood lights our pale faces. A straw is floating out there on the stormy waters.

This is the moment the plan comes alive. It's like the question of artificial intelligence. I viewed the plan a bit like that. It was so complicated (too complicated) and intricate that I felt it might develop a life of its own. For months we'd worked on it in meetings without end, a tangled mess which often threatened to pull us under. Now, on the day, the plan is boss. Dean takes the initiative. "Come on, let's fucking go for it." The change of mood is instantaneous. A recklessness born of desperation, grabbing at straws that can give us our dreams back. This is it. The beginning. It's like being interviewed for a job you don't want – you can take it easy. An action that can't succeed. I feel almost relaxed. As the convoy pulls off I'm hit by a

---

a popular consultation of the people, or *consulta*.
>> April 13 >> Huge solidarity demonstrations erupt in Tierra del Fuego, Argentina, following the brutal eviction of 200 workers who had occupied their electronics plant and shut it down, demanding their back pay. The police attack, killing Víctor Choque, a 37-year-old construction worker, and wounding sixty others workers. The Metalworkers Union and the Union Front, which includes government employees, teachers, taxi drivers, and sanitation workers, organize a general strike.
>> April 15 >> International protests take place to mark the fortieth anniversary of the opening of the world's first McDonald's restaurant, and to celebrate ten years of coordinated international resistance to the corporation. There are actions in at least 20 countries including Aotearoa/New Zealand, Spain, Sweden, Ireland, Poland, Denmark, Australia, Czech Republic, Croatia, Netherlands, Germany, Finland, US, and the UK.
>> April 19 >> Following a six week strike against privatization by Bolivian teachers, a general strike is called in solidarity with them, and against the neoliberal policies of the government. Roads are blocked throughout the country and one southern province declares independence from the government. The

wave of guilt. We may well be consigning thousands of pounds worth of other people's equipment to the scrap heap. Appallingly, I ignore these moral qualms, my sense of relief is too great.

It will take us a couple of minutes to reach the location. I swing between elation "Thank fuck we're doing something," and profound doubt, "We're doing this because we can't face not doing it, we should be going to Shepherd's Bush." The cab is silent. Too much emotion, too much tension, words, forget it, they come from another dimension. I realize I haven't called Dee. With fingers of lead I fumble desperately with the mobile. "Dee, we're on the way." "Oh, OK. I think we're ready." She doesn't sound confident. We circle the final roundabout which leads onto the M41. There's a riot van waiting on the roundabout. My sense of fatalism sets like concrete. We drive past, followed by the two cars. We take the second exit and follow the gentle curve of the slip road onto the motorway, a black unflowing river, the motorway of dreams. The slip road is held aloft by giant concrete pillars. A thin concrete wall bounds each side; on the left behind the wall there's a skateboard park and our twelve hidden activists.

Behind us the cars are slowing down to block the traffic, they hit each other, stop, and the road is sealed. We pull up next to the skateboard park and jump out. The tripod team are scrambling over the wall to join us. Now things just become a frantic chaotic blur. As we heave the tripods out of the truck I can see coppers coming through the blocked traffic towards us. Three tripods are up within 45 seconds and we're trying to join them together. It's like trying to communicate in a gale, we can't hear each other above the adrenaline. The others look at me for direction, but my map has blown off in the wind. Only Dee knows what's going on but she can't raise her voice above the din of maleness. People climb the tripods. Incredibly the road is blocked.

I look round and see the M41 stretching away from us like a desert. Utterly empty. No thousands of people, no hundreds, no-one. In the distance I can see the two trucks parked up on the hard shoulder. They're already surrounded by coppers and still no party goers have arrived. I don't think any of us know why, but we just start running towards the trucks. We arrive and find that Carl from Express Sounds has managed to dodge the police and get to our side of the wall. He looks dazed and wanders about aimlessly. He's probably just lost his sound system. Just over the wall the police are arresting people and rifling through the lorry cabs. On the one hand I recognize that the street party is probably over, deep down I'm bracing myself for the humiliation of failure. On the other hand we're all clutching at every straw, filled with a belief that even now it might still be possible. We realize that we've got to get onto the truck roofs. The police will want to move them, but the longer we can keep them there the more the chance of the mythical crowd appearing.

The police are concentrating on their conquest. Flushed with the joy of victory they fail to see us skulking just feet away on the other side of the wall. They're already arresting the drivers and searching the trucks. We see a space, a lucky moment when their attention is distracted. We haul ourselves over the wall and launch ourselves at the trucks. As we begin climbing I'm struck by a trembling fear that some unseen hand will grab my leg. But the police are too slow and two of us find ourselves standing on the thin aluminum tops laughing with relief. The coppers have handcuffed the drivers and sound crews, more of them are arriving all the time. Three hundred and thirty yards to the south, a wall of police vans and cop infantry has formed what looks like an impenetrable barrier blocking access from the roundabout. Anyone who managed to get through the cordon outside the tube station would be faced by this.

And then we see it, our mythical crowd, shimmering mirage-like at the roundabout. They've managed to get through at Shepherd's Bush. Ian and I start jumping and screaming at the crowd, our hopes alive again. Then, like a giant beast stumbling, the police line falters, and somehow the smallest breach seems suddenly to threaten the stability of the whole. The faltering becomes panic, police vans drive madly all over the place, and then the crowd bursts through. At first a trickle, the odd person sprinting onto the silent tarmac beyond the police line. Then, with sheer determination and weight, the dam bursts and 3,000 people charge onto the waiting road. At this point I look down and see a senior police officer walk over to the people under arrest and pinned to the wall. "De-arrest them." If he hadn't, we would have. I almost feel sorry for him. Within moments what was empty motorway, hot strips of tarmac, utterly dead, is living and moving, an instant joyous celebration. It is our moment; everyone and everything seems incredibly and wonderfully alive. Seconds later a sound-system fires up and our fragile dashed hopes become resurrected in the certainty of the dancing crowd.

Charlie Fourier is a pseudonym

Resources:

» **For photos and more accounts of the day: www.reclaimthestreets.net**

---

government imposes a 90-day state of siege, and over 1,000 trade union, student, peasant, and political leaders are arrested.

>> April 24 >> The government's firing of 12,000 bus drivers and its closure of bus routes in Mexico City generates a demonstration of 50,000 people. The bus drivers, members of SUTAUR, the independent and militant Mexico City Bus Driver's union, continue their daily protests. Two days later, students seize several buses in support of the drivers and hold them for several days. The following year, after a dogged struggle, which includes countless marches, constant clashes with the police, the year-long imprisonment of 12 union leaders, several 40-day hunger strikes, and an offer from a union leader to crucify himself on Good Friday, the union becomes a worker-owned cooperative, taking control of two of the ten newly privatized lines, and struggling to increase their control and regain jobs for the thousands who remain unemployed.

>> May 1 >> One and a half million demonstrate in Mexico City calling for an end to NAFTA, an increase in salaries, and declaring their support for the EZLN. The government declares a ceasefire, for the time being.

>> Continues page 75 >>

Tripods block the road to traffic and open it for pedestrians. Streatham, UK

Street Reclaiming

"CARS CANNOT DANCE: When they move they are violent and brutish, they lack sensitivity and rhythm. CARS CANNOT PLAY: When they diverge from the straight and narrow, they kill. CARS CANNOT SOCIALIZE: They privatise, separate, isolate, and alienate."

– London Reclaim the Streets agitprop

Imagine a packed city street in London, shoppers mingling on the thin strip of pavement that separates the store-fronts from the busy road. Two cars careen into each other and block the road. The drivers get out and start to argue. One of them brandishes a hammer and starts to smash up the other's car. Passersby are astonished. Suddenly people begin to surge out of the anonymous shopping crowd and jump on top of the cars, others fling multicoloured paint everywhere. Before anyone has time to catch their breath, 500 people emerge from the underground station and take over the street, reclaiming it from commerce and cars, for people and pleasure. An enormous banner is unfurled over the two destroyed vehicles. "Reclaim the streets – free the city – kill the car," it proclaims.

Thus began the first Reclaim the Streets party, in Camden High Street, May 1995. All afternoon people danced to the sound of the mobile bicycle-powered Rinky Dink sound system. Free food was served at long tables stretching down the middle of the road while children played on a climbing frame placed in the middle of the now-liberated crossroad junction.

This was the birth of the street party as a tactic, and it spread rapidly across the world – sometimes involving tens of thousands of participants, other

Andrew Testa/RTS archives

times a few hundred. The magical collision of carnival and rebellion, play and politics is such a potent recipe and relatively easy to pull off, that anyone can do it. Even you…

How to sort a street party:

Step 1: Get together with some like-minded people. Possibly your friends. Work on a plan of action. Sort out different roles, jobs and time frames. Imagine. What's possible?

Step 2: Decide on a date. Give yourselves enough time. Not too much – a deadline is a great motivator – but enough to sort the practicals: materials, construction etc. You may need money.

Step 3: Choose the location. Your street, the town centre, an underground train, a shopping mall, a corporate lobby, a busy road or roundabout, a motorway! A separate meeting place is good: people like a mystery, bureaucrats don't.

Step 4: Publicize! Word of mouth, leaflets, posters, email, carrier pigeon. Make sure everyone knows where and when to meet. Posters and paste go well on walls, billboards, and phone boxes. Leaflet shops, clubs, pubs – everyone, even your mum.

Step 5: Sort out your sound system. A party needs music – live, some DJs, acoustic, samba drums, yodelling – go for diversity. Invite jugglers and clowns, poets, prophets, and performers of all kinds. Ask campaign groups to come along and set up a stall in the middle of the road.

Step 6: How will you transform the space? Huge banners with a message of your choice, colourful murals, a bouncy castle, a ton of sand and a paddling pool for the kids, carpets, armchairs. The materials and money from earlier may come in useful here. Print up an explanation for this collective daydream to give to participants and passersby on the day.

Step 7: For opening the street – or rather stopping it being re-closed by the traffic – ribbons and scissors are not enough. A large scaffold tripod structure with a person suspended from the top is useful. Practice in your local park. Blocking the road with a car that can then be dismantled is nice. Even the traditional barricade will do.

Step 8: Rescue some young trees from the road of your local "development" and have them ready for planting. You may need a pneumatic drill and safety goggles for the last bit.

Step 9: Have a street party! Enjoy the clean air and colourful surroundings, the conversation and the community. Bring out the free food, dance, laugh, and set off the fire hydrants.

Some boys in blue may get irate. Calm them down with clear instructions.

Step 10: At least a couple of the boys in blue will fail to get the point and nick people – six is generally the minimum to convince their paymasters it was worth all that overtime. Of course you found a solicitor who understands about street protests and distributed a bust card with their number, a phone number to collect details of arrestees, and basic advice. Make sure someone stays awake, alert and near that phone to take messages, gather names, and organize a defendants' meeting a week or two later.

Get together with even more like-minded friends and plan the next one. Organize in your community, workplace, school and street.

from www.reclaimthestreets.net

311min SP 0:17:19:14
311min SP 0:18:16:0
311min SP 0:18:33:22
wanted to colonise the
Square, all the way
Just heard that there
some stuff kicking off up the top
It's nice to be here today and I feel safe despite the
potential violence coming from the media. I just regret that
for something with such mainstream relevance and appeal it
hard to get positive media coverage on what the whole
bout.
311min SP 0:19:34:1
Access Point
Independent Media Centre
www.indymedia.org.uk

Networks the ecology of the movements

"In the age of global flows and networks ... the small scale and the local are the places of greatest intensity." – **Jean Franco, *What's Left of the Intelligensia?*, North American Congress on Latin America's Report on the Americas, vol. 28, no.2, 1994**

A black balloon drifts across the dusty cement floor, pushed by an invisible draught. Printed on it in small, neat, white letters are the words, "Everything is connected to everything else." It's late September of 2000, and I'm in an enormous factory hangar on the outskirts of Prague. The machines have all gone, and in their place are thousands of bustling human beings. Some of them rush around, occasionally bumping into one another, exchanging a few words and then continuing on their way; a few stand alone, cell phone in hand, engaged in distant dialogues, while still others sit in intimate circles on the floor, talking, plotting. I'm inside the convergence centre, a space where activists are preparing the actions against the World Bank and International Monetary Fund (IMF) meetings due to begin in a couple of days.

Indymedia uk

There are Catalonians building large yellow skeleton puppets, friendly-looking Polish punks with scary dogs, haggard protest veterans huddled over detailed maps of the city, and fresh-faced newcomers trying to work out how to put on gas masks. There is a German squatter building a police radio scrambler, a Maori activist being interviewed by an Indymedia camerawoman, and an Italian from a squatted social centre trying on his makeshift armour of inner-tube-and-cardboard. In one corner, British Earth First!ers are planning a street communications team, in another Colombian peasants hold a workshop about the US funding of Plan Colombia and Czech anarchists learn street first aid. Outside, the sound of a marching band from Seattle practicing its driving rhythms bounces off the building, while a few desultory Marxists attempt to sell their books and newspapers. Amidst the chaos, Dutch cooks prepare a massive meal to feed the rabble. And then there's me and my companion – an Indian activist from Narmada Bachao Andolan, the struggle against the Narmada dam project. He is wrapped in a brown wool cardigan and shivering slightly.

"What do you make of this?" I ask. "These people!" he says fiercely, throwing out his hand to encompass the entire chaotic scene, in which hundreds of people are taking part in a mass meeting to collectively agree on the plan to disrupt the summit, arguing over endless points of principle, in five different languages, "These people have NO LEADERS!" He pauses, waggling his head sternly. "It's very, very, very good."

The strength of stories

"Act in assembly when together, act in network when apart."

– Mexican National Indigenous Congress

How does this seemingly chaotic movement of movements – without leaders, with overflowing diversity and contradictions, without clear organizational structures, without a shared programme or manifesto, without a command and control centre – manage to bring thousands of activists from around the world to cities, such as Prague, Genoa or Seattle to protest a summit? How did swirling affinity groups besieging the IMF/World Bank meetings in Prague manage to force them to close a day earlier than scheduled? How was the agenda, according to one World Bank delegate, "effectively seized" by the protesters? And how did this movement coordinate a simultaneous global day of action in over 110 cities across the world in solidarity with the Prague mobilization? Surely this high level of organization is only possible with some form of leadership?

"Take me to your leader," is the first demand of aliens to earthlings, police to protesters, journalists to revolutionaries. But it's a demand that falls on deaf ears whenever directed to participants in this global uprising. Ask the neighbourhood assemblies of Argentina, the indigenous Zapatistas of Mexico, the autonomous island-dwellers of Kunayala off the coast of Panama or participants in the spokescouncils of the US Direct Action Network who shut down the WTO in Seattle. All will speak of horizontal, as opposed to pyramidal structures of power, dispersed networks rather than united fronts.

Movements of the past are laden with charismatic leaders – Che Guevara, Rosa Luxemburg, Huey Newton, Karl Marx, Emma Goldman, Lenin, Mao Tse-Tung. But whose face can be found in the foreground of today's movement? Ironically, the first face that comes to mind is masked and bears the pseudonym "Subcomandante Marcos". This is the spokesperson for the Zapatistas, whose words have profoundly influenced the spirit of the movement. But he, like so much of this movement, thrives on the power and creativity of paradox, for he speaks of leading by obeying, carrying out the policies of a committee of indigenous campesinos. Note the 'sub' commander, and the anonymity of the mask. He warns that the name Marcos is interchangeable – anyone can put on a ski mask and say "I am Marcos." In fact he says that Marcos does not exist, but is simply a window, a bridge, a mediator between worlds. He says that we are all Marcos. Not what one expects from a traditional leader.

It follows that a movement with no leaders organizes horizontally, through networks. And it was the poetic communiqués and powerful stories that trickled from the Zapatista autonomous zones in the Chiapas jungle onto the relatively new medium of the internet which told of their suffering, their struggles, their mythologies, that began to weave an electronic fabric of struggle in the mid-nineties. This web of connections between diverse groups gave birth to a series of face-to-face international gatherings – the Zapatista Encuentros – which soon grew to become the roaring, unstoppable torrent of movements for life and dignity and against capital that are emerging across the world. "We are the network," declared the Zapatistas, "all of us who resist."

Like a virus, uncontrollable and untameable, this inspiration flowed from city to city, country to country, spreading at the same speed as the trillions of dollars involved in the reckless unsustainable money game of transnational capital. Like the financial markets, the inspiration fed on rumour and myth. Unlike the markets, it thrived on the rejection of ownership and enclosure.

Capital's dream of super fast networks that will spread consumerism across the planet was turned on its head. For while the networked money markets were tearing the planet apart, our grassroots networks were bringing us together. People were using the global communications infrastructure for something completely different – to become more autonomous, to get the state and corporations off their backs, to live in a more healthy way. To talk to one another.

As the links grew, more stories were added to the flow, accounts of audacity and courage, moments of magic and hope. The tale of the Indian farmers demolishing the first Kentucky Fried Chicken in the country, or the news of five million French workers bringing the country to a standstill and reversing their government's neoliberal policies – layer upon layer of stories travelled along the thin copper threads of the internet, strengthening the global network and developing relationships between diverse groups and individuals. People found strength in the stories, which expressed a sense of identity and belonging, communicated a shared sense of purpose and mission. The movement was learning that it was as important to capture imaginations as to command actions.

Perhaps the first victim to be defeated by this nascent network of subversive information-sharing was the Multilateral Agreement on Investment (MAI), a treaty whose text was cooked up in the sweaty boiler rooms of the most powerful corporate lobby group on earth, the International Chamber of Commerce. If it had been implemented, the MAI would have enabled corporations to sue governments – it was a veritable charter for corporate rule. The network was galvanized when US campaigners Public Citizen circulated the secret text on the internet in 1997. "If a negotiator says something to someone over a glass of wine, we'll have it on the internet within an hour," the campaigners claimed.

Against a total media blackout, the email inboxes of activists began bristling with life, with information, with strategy, with education. List-serves bulged as the nascent global network took shape with messages from Canadian truckers, Maori groups, Harvard trade lawyers, French cultural activists. Their defeat of the MAI in 1998 was the first real success story of the movement, sending a shiver down the spine of its next target: the World Trade Organization, which would meet the following year in Seattle. A rich blend of past political forms (especially from feminist, ecological, and peace movements) of the global North and various indigenous forms of organizing from the global South, these new hybrid networks didn't quite fit any previous models of political practice. Police forces, journalists, academics, politicians, and traditional leftist parties were at a loss to understand them "Who ARE these guys?" wondered the *Financial Times* after the defeat of the MAI. Something important was stirring as the way of doing and thinking about politics was changing radically – yet still it remained below the radar screen.

The logic of the swarm

"Those who dance are considered insane by those that cannot hear the music." – **George Carlin**

"We don't consider them terrorists.... We're not yet sure how to even label them," says a spokesman for Europol, Europe's transnational police agency, struggling to describe the new breed of protesters. British political commentator Hugo Young attacked the "herbivores" behind anticapitalist protests for making "a virtue out of being disorganized", while the head of the World Wildlife Fund referred to us in Genoa, as a "formless howling mob". It was the RAND Corporation, a US military think tank, who actually came up with most accurate description. In their 2002 book, *Networks and Netwars*, they describe the Zapatista uprising, the web of interconnected activists' groups and NGOs, the affinity groups of Seattle, and the tactics of the Black Bloc as *swarms*, and predicted that swarming would be the main form of conflict in the future. While for most commentators, a bottom-up system that functioned so effectively was totally outside their conceptual framework, the RAND Institute, steeped in the latest developments of systems theory and complexity, turned to the natural world for the best metaphor. They realized what others failed to see – that there is enormous power and intelligence in the swarm.

Since the seventeenth century scientists have made enormous technical discoveries through taking the world apart, piece by piece, to try and understand how it works. Their mechanical model of reality saw life as a giant machine made up of separate parts. Linear processes of cause and effect, command and control dominated their thinking.

These mechanistic perceptions have been central to our patriarchal, Western 'scientific' worldview. But this formulation of reality involves an enormous blind spot, one which science has only relatively recently started to uncover. As a result they have failed to recognize, complex, interdependent systems. This is one of the root causes of our current ecological crises. Problems as different as global warming, homelessness, and mental illness are all seen in the context of single cause and effect processes. But these cannot be cured like a clock's workings can be mended. They require a different way of looking at the world – in other words, they require whole-systems thinking.

Witness how recent tests studying the effects of

genetically modified organisms (GMOs) on the environment have taken place in so-called controlled field settings, ignoring the fact that such control does not exist in nature. GMO flowers produce pollen, as does any ordinary flower, and bees will take the pollen to other fields, thus contaminating other plants. There is nothing isolated in nature. Mechanistic thinking develops a world view which is unable to see the interconnection and interdependence of life, unable to see the world for what it is – a huge, complex, dynamic system where everything is connected to everything else, as the balloon in Prague so eloquently suggested.

But over the last few decades there has been a paradigm shift in scientific understandings of living systems. Scientists are now discovering what indigenous knowledge has long taught – everything is connected. Ecologists, biologists, physicists, and mathematicians have begun to be able to describe vastly complex connected webs of life, which are made up of networks within networks. They have gradually realized that life has the ability to self-organize and mutually adapt, without anyone in control. Their descriptions of living systems are perhaps the best model yet for how the movement functions.

Imagine watching thousands of birds take off one by one. As they begin to rise into the air, a pattern emerges. They group together and then, if a predator approaches, the flock rapidly turns direction, swooping up, down, left, right; all the birds stay together, and none of them bump into each other. The whole flock moves as one, as if it's one organism. Yet no one is in charge; it seems to happen as if magically. High-speed film reveals that the movement spreads across a flock in less than one-seventieth of a second. Yet this should be impossible, as it is much faster than a single bird's reaction time. The flock is clearly more than the sum of its parts. But how is this possible?

Observing the movement of affinity groups from police helicopters during many of the mass mobilizations of the past few years, or trying to map the daily flow of information between the forever-transforming activist groups on the internet must create a similar sense of bafflement for the authorities. Even participants in the movements are often confused as to how everything seems to somehow fit together so well. The logic of the swarm is an eerie thing, especially when you don't understand its simple rules. Those who are unable to learn from these observations will remain frozen in mechanistic logic, which thinks the whole is never greater than the sum of its parts.

The swarm phenomena can be observed everywhere. Think of the billions of neurons in your brain. A neuron on its own cannot have thought, cannot write poetry, move a muscle, or dream, but working with other neurons it can produce extraordinary things. Now think of a dense mass of bees swarming across a landscape in search of the perfect location for a new hive; all this happens without anyone in charge, without any single command centre.

It wasn't until the advent of high speed computers that scientists were able to begin to unravel this mystery. Prior to that, they had observed the phenomena, but because they were attached to their clockwork view of the world, they literally couldn't believe their eyes. For years after the idea had first been posited in the 1950s by Alan Turing, inventor of the computer, scientists couldn't believe it, and kept looking for a head bird, a leading cell. Only computers could model these hugely complex self-organized, and interconnected systems. What scientists saw was astounding – each element, seemed to be following simple rules, and yet when the multitude was working together they were forming a highly intelligent sophisticated self-organized system. Nowadays software designers, urban planners and ecologists all use these concepts in their day-to-day work; the realm of politics has yet catch up.

For this is truly organizing from below. The process of simple local units generating complicated global or group behaviour, a process not directed by a conscious entity, but rather emerging through the interrelationships of the system's parts is known in scientific circles as *emergence*.

If numbers, neurons, crowds, computer programmes, cells, city dwellers, birds behave like this, why not a networked movement of movements?

Learning to self-organize

"Chaos is a name for any order that produces confusion in our minds." – **George Santayana**

Emergence may seem to 'just happen', but it's actually the result of clear sets of mathematical principles and processes that govern a highly connected network. Through these, we can learn how to organize creative actions and build sustainable movements in our local communities. There is a tendency within some aspects of anticapitalist movements to think that actions happen spontaneously, without planning or structure. An email from Australia inaccurately suggested that the Reclaim the Streets street parties in London resulted from pure spontaneity. The email's author bemoaned the fact that Australians somehow did not possess this magical ability to just turn up and create a street party from nothing. As any organizer can confirm, creating situations in which spontaneity can occur is a lot of hard, and mostly not magical work.

Spontaneity is a vital tool of resistance, but it occurs only under certain conditions. The most successful movements are those that are able to adapt to situations rapidly and spontaneously, much like the flock of birds avoiding the predator, precisely because of a stunning amount of preparation, interconnection, and flow of communication that is already in place.

What are the ingredients of successful mass actions? Incredible structures are developed beforehand: we find large buildings and transform them into convergence centres; we organize workshops, trainings, and coordinating meetings; we form affinity groups which meet each other and form clusters; we work out communication channels via mobile phones, pagers and so forth; we set up independent media centres and pirate radio stations, ready to compile information from multiple street reporters and feed it back to the streets; we develop beautiful and enticing printed propaganda; the list is endless. It takes months of planning to set up the networks from which can emerge the intelligence of a magically moving, thinking swarm, a shape-shifting organism that can survive the chaos of the streets or the disruption and repression of the state.

The Pentagon think-tank RAND, in its highly informative analysis of the successful swarming strategies of the Zapatistas' civil society networks and the Direct Action Network's WTO shut down in Seattle, suggests that this movement is ahead of state authorities in its mastery of swarming. But it also suggests that the police learned a lot from their failures, and that activist groups have learned little from our victories. Although mass mobilizations have grown steadily since then, there has been a tendency in the latest mobilizations to repeat ourselves, to attempt to reproduce Seattle, or even worse, to return to familiar forms of struggle, the mass marches instead of decentralized actions, rallies and speeches instead of assemblies and spokescouncils – forms which squander our new-found advantages, and do not reflect the new worlds we want to build. The new is always more daunting than the familiar, but if we don't want to repeat the failures of great rebellions of the past, we need to continue to develop ways of working that learn from our victories, which build on the past and yet are always reaching into the unmapped and unknown future.

Sustainability comes to those who can adapt and change the quickest, a concept that is alien to many older forms of political organizing. Many of the groups in these new networks call themselves '(dis)organizations', implying that they are loose networks rather than formal organizations.

Yet in order to give up control and allow the system to govern itself, we need to develop structures that will enable us to lose control with dignity and thus be able to overwhelm the dry and brittle forces of state repression with our invincible fluidity. Authoritarian systems are good at changing laws but not habits, and it seems that in the race for true network mastery in the political arena, we are already in the lead. By learning some of the principles of swarm logic and emergence, we can develop creative tactics and strategies that will put us even further ahead, not just for mass street actions, but for all forms of organization and mobilization in our networks, whether through the global reach of the internet, or within the local spaces of our communities. The future of the planet and society may well depend on who builds the most successful network of networks.

Watching the ants

"We need to work like the Zapatistas do, like ants who go everywhere no matter which political party the other belongs to. Zapatistas proved people can work together in spite of differences." – **Anna Esther Cecena of the FZLN (Mexican support committee of the Zapatistas)**

Systems theorists know there is no better way to learn about emergence than by looking at the extraordinary behaviour of ant colonies – one of nature's most successful examples of bottom-up intelligence. Ants are found virtually everywhere, from the tropics to the desert to the tundra, and account for over 18 per cent of the earth's biomass (the combined weight of every living thing on the planet). They grow fungi in farms, raise aphids as livestock, and have extraordinary engineering skills and city planning, building recycling dumps, lavatories, and graveyards situated away from the main body of the colony.

Ant colonies are perfectly self-managed without any single ant in charge. They can switch rapidly between roles of foraging, nest-building, and raising pupae; they can work out the shortest route to food, and prioritize food sources based on quality, ease of access, and distance from the nest; and the entire colony seems to know exactly how many ants are needed where and for what jobs at any given time. The best way to think of a colony is as a self-regulating organism, with its millions of cells and all its bio-chemical feedback loops constantly adjusting itself to reach homeostasis – regular heart beat, body temperature and so on.

Our cultural images of ants evoke military columns, with proud soldier ants marching in a straight line, one column going towards the food and the other back to the colony (just like a motorway), with isolated individuals tirelessly working for the queen. But if you really observe what is happening, you will see something quite different – the ants are actually all weaving in and out of line, and touching each other! Every single ant greets each ant coming from the other direction, heads and antennae stroke one another, communicating with pheromones, then going on its way and meeting the next ant. In any line of ants, virtually every ant will meet and briefly exchange information with every other ant. Somehow, these simple interactions multiplied enable the colony as a whole to adjust the tasks allotted to each ant, allowing the colony to run efficiently. In this cooperative conversation between separate local parts can be found the extraordinary phenomenon of emergence, where the sum of all the parts becomes greater than the whole.

Clearly, ants are very different from people. But the way the ant colony as a whole works, its process, is comparable to that of the movement of movements – the numerous email lists, the autonomous local groups networking globally, the face-to-face gatherings, the convergence centres, the ebb and flow of crowds in the occupied streets. This not only how our local actions produce global behaviour; but shows us how important the quality and amount of communication is in the maintenance of effective networks.

Most of the anticapitalist global days of action happened not because of central commands, but simply because a small group sent out a proposal. If the proposal captured other groups' imaginations, they disseminated it on email lists, discussed it at meetings, mentioned it in publications, web pages and so on. It multiplied exponentially in every direction, a kind of ricochet rebellion, and in the end, no one takes responsibility and yet everyone takes the credit. In emergent systems, you influence your neighbours and your neighbours influence you. All relationships are mutual feedback loops.

Paying attention to the lessons of the ants, and their emergent systems can help teach us how to build efficient trickle-up systems, networks where the local becomes global, where the top-down chains of command are broken and replaced by a multitude of individual, communicative links acting simultaneously.

Four ways to act like an ant and dream like a giant

"Our enemies did not cross our borders, they crept through our weaknesses like ants." – **Nizar Qabbani**

If we want to build networks that behave like a swarm, these four rules from the ant world can guide us:

More is different: A few ants roaming across your kitchen floor might find the bread crumb hiding under the table, a lone affinity group might find the breach in the fence around the summit, a few independent researchers might manage to find the link between the Enron scandal and their local council.

But increase their numbers and interconnect them and you'll have something which behaves quite differently – you'll get systematic change – a movement that can cause an entire summit to be cancelled, or the entire corporate accounting system to come crumbling down. Many interacting smaller pieces create the exponential magic of emergence: swarm logic.

Our movements are multiplying at an incredible rate. Every day new connections are developing both face to face and virtually as the internet grows to connect more sentient beings than any other technology before it. New webpages, email lists and Indymedia centres are springing up like grass after a downpour, leading to more networking, more co-ordination, and more actions. The crowd has always terrified those in authority, but a crowd where each individual is able to think and act autonomously, a crowd where everyone is connected to everyone else, will cause more than a shiver down their spine, because it behaves in ways that no one will ever be able to predict.

Stay small: The greatest feature of the ant colony is the simplicity of each ant; if one ant began to somehow assess the overall state of the whole colony, the sophisticated behaviour would stop trickling up from below, and swarm logic would collapse. Emergence teaches us that not to know everything is a strength and that local knowledge is sovereign. The magic is in densely interconnected systems made up of small simple elements.

As soon as our groups become too big, communication tends to break down and hierarchies develop. We must learn to divide like cells before this happens; big is unwieldy, small and connected is what we should aim for.

A network of a million small interconnected groups cannot be stopped by any of the world's police agencies, no leaders can be singled out for assassination or corruption, no single headquarters raided, no central party committee infiltrated. But that doesn't mean our movement is small – for we are all networked into a whole that is larger than anyone can possibly imagine.

Encourage randomness: Haphazard encounters are key to network-building – they are where creativity lies. Without the lone ant exploring new territory, no one would find new sources of food or develop ways to adapt to environmental conditions.

Decentralized systems thrive on the creativity of random encounters. How often have you been in a huge swirling crowd on the streets during a festival or an action and bumped into exactly the right person, or found out a key piece of information you were seeking? How often have you received a seemingly randomly forwarded e-mail from someone that happens to point you to someone else who will enable your new project to get off the ground?

Some may think that with perfect unity the revolution begins, but without randomness, evolution ends. While some toe the party line, others are drifting and dancing into new ways of changing the world. What may look like chaos to some is actually brimming with creativity.

Listen to your neighbours: 'Local' turns out to be the key term in understanding swarm logic. Emergent behaviour happens because the ants are paying attention to their neighbours, rather than waiting for orders from a distant authority. The more ants do so, the more quickly their colony will solve problems. Local information leads to global wisdom; this is the secret of the intelligent swarm.

The ants teach us that by working locally and continually sharing our local stories globally, by connecting everything and creating a plethora of feedback loops, we don't need to – indeed cannot - 'organize' the global network, it will regulate itself, swarm-like, life-like, if we develop the right structures and conditions.

The (r)Evolution will be improvised

"I saw everyone and saw no one, for every individual was subsumed into the same, countless, meandering crowd: I spoke to everybody but could remember neither my own words nor others, for my attention was at every step held by new events and objects, by unforeseen developments." – **Mikhail Bakunin**

When Bakunin wrote of his experience on the streets of Paris during the 1848 revolution, he was unknowingly describing emergence. Thinking and technology has evolved exponentially since he wrote, yet our thinking around political change has not evolved to the same degree. Although a revolution has occurred in our perception of the world, many of our perceptions of political change remain stuck and fixed in centuries old models – centralized parties, uniformity, manifestoes, taking control of power, hierarchical leadership.

Now that we better understand the workings of decentralized, diverse interconnected networks within networks, where everything is in flux – there is no excuse for our political forms to remain stuck in ways of seeing and thinking from the past, it's time to evolve.

One thing that has not changed since 1848 is the fact that revolutionary moments always open up the social space for people to begin to connect in new and manifold ways, spontaneous convergences occur, and a multitude of unaccustomed conversations arise. If we look at any revolutionary situation we see human interactions multiplying as the streets and squares are filled, groups and networks coalescing, as the human desire for conviviality swamps the alienation of capital. The town hall meetings of the American Revolution of 1776, for example, or the sections of the 1789 French revolution; the clubhouses of the 1871 Paris Commune or the numerous syndicates during the Spanish Civil War of 1936; the *Räte* in Hungary during the uprising of 1956 or the workers' councils of May 1968; the popular assemblies that appeared spontaneously across Argentina after the uprising of 19 December 2001.

What is emerging now is a dialogue of a million voices, which is building the first truly interconnected global uprising, an unprecedented transnational social revolution, a revolution made up of thousands of revolutions, not just one. A revolution that is not predetermined, or predictable: not going around in circles but moving in every direction simultaneously. What we are witnessing now is actually a lot more like evolution, a work in progress that makes itself up as it goes along, constantly adapting to each others' needs. An unprecedented global (r)Evolution, is taking place and many of us don't even recognize it.

Activist Hazel Wolf lived through a Russian Revolution, a Chinese Revolution, and the fall of the Berlin Wall. "The thing about all of them is, nobody knew they were going to happen," she says. A revolution, by its nature, hardly seems possible before it takes place; but it may seem obvious, even inevitable, in hindsight.

As the networks grow more connected, by webs and actions, wires and stories, many things will emerge that we, as mere neurons in the network, don't expect, don't understand, can't control, and may not even perceive. The only way to understand an emergent system is to let it run, because no individual agent will ever be able to reveal the whole. The global movement of movements for life against money, for autonomy and dignity, for the dream of distributed direct democracy, are following an irresistible logic. It is a logic as old as the hills and the forests, an eco-logic, a bio-logic, the profound logic of life.

Notes from Nowhere

Inspired by the Zapatistas' invitation to weave a global network of resistance, and following the success of the 1996 Encuentro for Humanity and Against Neoliberalism in Chiapas, a second encuentro took place exactly a year later in Spain.

Organized horizontally without a central committee through co-operation between numerous European social movements, involving planning meetings in Prague, Zurich, and Barcelona, the second encuentro brought 3,000 activists from 50 countries together under the banner "For a World Which Contains All Worlds."

For nine days in locations spread across Spain, Tuareg nomads from the Western Saharan desert mingled with German anti-fascists, Indian Ghandians with landless Brazilians, British anti-road protesters with Zapatista delegates. The nebulous network began to take shape as disparate groups met face to face to continue the growing global conversation about fighting capitalism and building alternatives.

Despite the intense heat, difficulty of coordinating workshops separated by hundreds of miles, and complaints of too many fiestas (six in nine days) the main themes of the gathering began to take shape as people explored questions like: How do we learn from each others' struggles? What kind of network do we want? What are the new forms of struggles and politics?

Many new initiatives and groups were born during those long dusty days, including the idea of a more concrete global campaign against the World Trade Organization and the development of a global alternative media network. There was no doubting that the global network of resistance was becoming a powerful reality.

Dreaming of a Reality Where the Past and Future Meet the Present

by Andrew Flood

> *"Everywhere there are people who are fed up with the dominant values, who seek to change their own lives, to open new spaces and construct a more dignified present. Everywhere there are willing accomplices desiring to live an adventure."*
>
> **– Manifesto for the convocation of the Second Intercontinental *Encuentro* for Humanity and Against Neoliberalism**

Imagine for a moment marching up a hill, lit only by starlight and a distant bonfire on a hot August night, in Andalucia, near the very tip of southern Spain. Looking at the stars you point out the red twinkle of Mars to the comrade whose arm you entwine. She comes from the opposite end of Europe. Behind you lies an agriculture estate, left derelict by its owner but now seized by agricultural workers. Behind you hundreds of comrades try and ford the shallow river in the dark. On either side, olive groves stretch up the hills in neat rows, the red soil now dark and cool.

Someone on the road ahead starts singing 'A Las Barricadas' (To the Barricades) in Spanish. Slowly this is taken up by others behind and ahead, in Italian, Turkish, and other languages, sometimes just hummed or whistled by those who don't know the words. The Spanish version is familiar to me from a scratchy recording an Italian comrade passed on to me on tape. The original recording is of 500,000 people singing this working class anthem at a rally of the anarchist National Confederation of Workers (CNT) in Barcelona, July 1936, days after the revolution there.

Those on this road have gathered from all over the world, over 50 countries in all. They have temporarily left the struggles in their own countries to come here to dream of a new reality together. Here the weather-beaten features of a male campesino from Brazil are found beside the sunburned face of an 18-year-old female squatter from Berlin. Do you feel you are imagining something impossible, something from a Hollywood blockbuster, or the past? Then add one more detail: a gasp goes up from those on the road, for overhead a shooting star briefly appears. Were it not for the collective gasp each of us might have imagined this was a vision we alone were seeing. But no, we look around and realize we are marching, seeing, and dreaming together.

In our modern world The Power tells us such dreams are no longer possible. History has ended, there is no dream, just the reality of alienation, work, and obedience. Yet the scene above is not from a film or from a history book, rather it took place on the evening of 2 August 1997. This was the Second Encounter for Humanity and against Neoliberalism. I could describe it in cold, political terms alone but this would miss the 'for humanity' part and in truth for every day we discussed organizing 'against neoliberalism' we spent another 'for humanity.'

The encounter was organized without a central committee through co-operation on a continental level. News of it flowed along many paths in many languages. It made huge leaps via the internet and fax, and smaller ones via leaflets, pamphlets, on radio shows, in photo exhibitions, and during a million conversations. In various ways the news of the encounter-to-be was put into the hands of those marching in Derry in February 1997 against the massacre of civilians by the British army there 25 years earlier; landless campesinos occupying land in Brazil; refugees from the Western Sahara in camps in Southern Algeria; anti-road protesters in Britain; First Nation activists in Canada, those running a 'pirate university' for workers in Turkey; environmental campaigners in Columbia; academics in South Africa; anarchists in Poland –

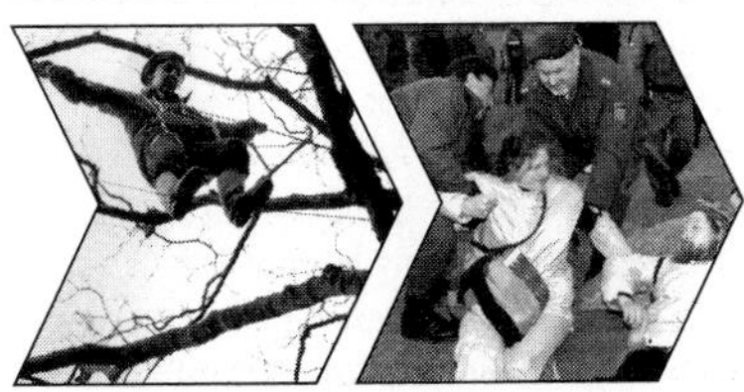

>> **May 3** >> Declaring "The oil is ours," 50,000 workers at Brazil's government-run oil company, Petroleo Brasileiro, walk off the job over pay cuts and a plan to privatize the company. The strike is reinforced by a strike of thousands of rail workers and truckers, as well as tens of thousands of other government workers demanding higher wages and an end to privatization.

>> **May 14** >> Two cars collide and block Camden High Street, a busy shopping district in London, UK. The drivers argue, and then begin smashing up the cars. Suddenly, 500 people pour out of the underground station and occupy the street. The first Reclaim the Streets street party begins, challenging the privatization of public space by the car, while bringing together the spirit of carnival and rebellion, rejuvenating creative forms of direct action.

the list goes on and on. It echoed right down to the Zapatista villages in the mountains and jungle of the Mexican south east where the idea of the first encounter had come from.

Flowing to Spain

And so in July people from everywhere came on boats, by plane, by car, bus, and train, even a few by bicycle. Alongside them came messages bearing titles like *Resistance to Neoliberalism: A View from South Africa* as dozens of papers began to arrive to be translated and circulated. As we got closer, the streams started to merge until a river of people arrived from the Metro station to fill the public buses to San Sebastian de los Reyes, a small and dusty town outside Madrid.

The opening ceremonies were held in a nearby bull-ring, Plaza de Toros, where two delegates from the Zapatista communities read out greetings in which they prophetically warned us that: "As companions in the struggle for harmony in our world, we say that it is necessary to put up with heat, thirst, and tiredness, like a farmer who puts up with everything because he has faith in his work in the fields." These were indeed prophetic words for the week ahead of us.

We split up for discussions on a variety of issues which were held in five different locations in the Spanish state. I set out for the train station alongside others heading north to Barcelona for the economics and culture group. We travelled overnight on a specially chartered train to Barcelona. Many of us felt Barcelona was a fitting location, the centre of the anarchist revolution that had swept much of Spain some 61 years earlier, a revolution that in the last few years had become a point of redefinition for sections of the left.

Arriving at 8.00 am in the morning we first formed a cordon through the train station for the security of the Zapatista delegates who had travelled with us. Then we marched in a long column through the streets, at one point passing under a squat from the roof of which large exploding fireworks were being fired in welcome. This brought the neighbours out on their balconies along the route to wonder what this motley, tired, and unwashed sample of the world's population were up to.

One of the strange features of our group was how many of the delegates sleeping on mats in school halls were equipped with portable computers, digital cameras, and other play-things. But with these we succeeded in putting up on-the-spot accounts and pictures of the encounter in process.

The sub-group I worked with dealt with the issue of how to form the network of information between struggles. The call for this network had emerged from the previous encounter in Chiapas and was contained in the closing statement: "That we will make a network of communication among all our struggles and resistance's... this intercontinental network of alternative communication will search to weave the channels so that words may travel all the roads that resist."

Most of us had experience in communication, from pirate

radio and small circulation magazines to regional TV stations. We decided to work in English and Spanish, as everyone there had a working knowledge of one of these languages.

We began by rejecting the traditional pyramid structure of news media where local sources feed up to region level, which feed to national and perhaps the global level before news trickled down again to other regions. In discussing what a network without a centre could look like (but in recognizing that some people have more time and resources to dedicate to the flow of information than others), we came to use the human brain as an analogy. Here the many nodes have major paths that carry information between them but it is possible for any two nodes to form a connection and for any connection to improve in speed and the amount of information it can carry if this is needed. Therefore many minor paths also exist. There is also a two way flow of information and feedback on the information that is sent.

This image flowed out of what the network already is, in practice. The network we described is an organic one already in existence and already growing. Our role was more to begin a description of it and come up with ways to develop this existence and improve the flow of information.

We considered, for instance, the path a communiqué from Subcomandante Marcos might take after he has written it in the heights of some *ceiba* tree in the mountains of the Mexican south east. Perhaps it goes on horseback to the nearest settlement, from there by car to San Cristóbal where it is typed onto a computer, translated and suddenly takes more paths, perhaps by fax to newspapers and solidarity groups on the one hand, on the other it jumps onto the internet and runs down the telephone lines to listserves like Chiapas 95. Here it replicates hundreds of times and make its way onto a desktop in Ireland where it jumps onto webpages and more lists but also gets printed out and stuck up as a poster in a bookshop or reproduced and distributed in the Mexico Bulletin. Simultaneously it has arrived in Istanbul, where it is also printed out and travels by bus to some distant town and a union meeting. Multiply this path by thousands and consider all the alternatives and we see the network already exists without a centre; indeed the different nodes have not only never met but can be unaware of each others existence.

>> June >> Health care workers occupy hospitals throughout Cordoba, Argentina. Nurse Ana María Martoglio says, "We've taken over this hospital because they haven't paid us in two months and because the government has sent the health-care system to hell."

>> June 1 >> About 5,000 Argentinian students surround the Congress, preventing deputies from entering, and forcing the government to postpone discussion and voting on President Menem's proposal to introduce tuition fees for the first time. Days later, the vote is in favour of fees, and riots erupt throughout the night.

>> June 5 >> Over 3,000 people occupy the Mexico City stock exchange, protesting against election fraud in the state of Tabasco. Three hundred people arrive on foot, having walked 500 miles from Tabasco to draw attention nationwide to what has become known as "Tabascogate."

>> June 8 >> South Korean President Kim Young Sam warns unions that a planned strike at the state-owned telephone company would be akin to "an attempt to overthrow the state".

>> June 15-17 >> The Halifax People's Summit in Canada, brings together international non-governmental organizations (NGO) and local networks of activists, and linking global issues with local concerns. Workshops,

In the course of the week in Barcelona we also mobilized in support of one of the squats where the encounter was being held. In a piece of blinding stupidity the council had announced its intention to evict this in the middle of the week. They backed down on the day of the demonstration, which became a victory march through the Hospitalet district complete with samba bands, stilt walkers, and fire jugglers. An enduring image from the demonstration is one of a Brazilian carrying the flag of the MST, the movement co-coordinating the occupation of farmland by landless campesinos, in support of the occupation of a building in one of the big industrial cities of Europe.

Another highlight of the week was a video-showing of the Milan train occupations. These occurred in June of this year when 4,000 Italians occupied two trains in Milan and succeeded in travelling right across Europe to the demonstration against the EU summit in Amsterdam, focal point of the European march against unemployment. The video was produced by Italian autonomists from a social centre in Rome which, we were thrilled to learn, was in an old military fort with a castle and a drawbridge.

Jordi Blanchar

Second Encuentro for Humanity and Against Neoliberalism. Spain

The encounter was bringing people from different traditions of struggle into contact with each other so that we could draw inspiration and learn from each other. The value of this sort of exchange cannot be over-estimated. By seeing the struggles of others, we come to understand our struggles better.

After several days, we boarded the train for the closing gathering and settled down for the long night-journey across the Spanish state to El Indiano. Throughout the night, and into the next day, vast amounts of liquid refreshment were consumed to the sound of revolutionary songs from every corner of the globe, which emanated from the dining car. By the early hours of the morning the songs were becoming shorter as words were forgotten, but the spirit was there. On that long train journey south many kindred spirits living in this temporary and mobile 'free world' reached out to each other in the dark of one hundred compartments. All through that night and into the next day the train rolled south and as the sun rose, so did the heat, and it kept rising and rising as further south we went into a land of red soil – sunflowers and olive trees stretching into the distance.

The journey took 20 hours by train and another 30

minutes by coach to the small town of Puerto Serrano. Here we ran into two gates, each guarded by a large bearded man shouting at us to go to the other one. Eventually something was sorted out and thousands of activists flooded into the schools and their grounds to stake out spaces for sleeping.

That evening there was the inevitable fiesta. We formed into a long column outside the schools and marched there – definitely more of a manifestation than a demonstration. The locals turned out in force to watch. At one point an old man stood outside the house, both arms above his head, cheering those marching by. From his age and obvious joy we speculated that here was a participant whose eyes had seen the struggle that Spain represented to so many of us, the Spanish revolution of 1936. We were, after all, in the olive groves of Andalucia where a previous generation had fought and died for their vision of a new world.

On the final day of the encounter we walked to El Indiano, an agricultural estate squatted by the *Sindicato de Obreros del Campo* (Union of Rural Workers). We were passed at one point by a digger, its front bucket crammed with several punks who had hitched a lift from a local. Revolutionary Spain briefly met Mad Max on that road.

The end was an anti-climax; throughout the long, hot day each group from the numerous discussions reported back in three languages, Italian, Spanish, and English and in the evening we returned to hear the closing words of the Zapatista delegates before making our way back along the road; this is where the shooting star appeared and this account begin. From here there is little to tell or there is everything to tell. The Second Encounter ended but the encounter for humanity and against neoliberalism goes on.

Andrew Flood is an Irish anarchist who has followed the Zapatista rising online since 1994, travelled to Chiapas for the first encuentro in 1996, and spent time in a community there in 1997

Resources:

» Documents from the second Encuentro can be found at www.geocities.com/CapitolHill/3849/encounter2dx.html

---

protests, carnivalesque street theatre, and outdoor picnics prevail, while the G7 meet under extremely low security, with delegates freely walking about the city, and meeting in a Maritime Museum which features, ironically, a deck chair from the Titanic.

>> June 19 >> Workers at Hyundai Heavy Industries in South Korea approved a provisional wage agreement providing for a 5.6 per cent wage increase and bonuses of three months pay.

>> July 13 >> Energy workers in Ecuador begin a long strike that threatens to halt electricity and petroleum production. The unions demand the repeal of laws restricting the right of public workers to strike. Administration buildings of the state-run companies are occupied by workers.

>> July 17 >> Some 50,000 teachers in Costa Rica strike, closing about 4,000 public schools, as well as four state universities. The teachers demand a presidential veto of a recently approved pension law. Another 10,000 state workers join the teachers' strike two days later, protesting government plans to reduce the work force. Meanwhile, the central labour union in Costa Rica prepares for a general strike.

>> July 21 >> One thousand mothers and children march

__By 1998__, the sense of hope and possibility emerging from the spirit of Zapatismo was spreading. With the proliferation of new websites, list-serves, and international activist gatherings, it seemed like a whole new cycle of struggle was taking place. Yet daily in the autonomous Zapatista communities, deep in the humid Lacandón jungle, the low-level war continued.

Chiapas is one of the areas richest in natural resources in Mexico; it has oil, natural gas and hydroelectric power, is the largest producer of coffee and second largest producer of beef, corn, bananas, honey, melons, avocados, and cocoa, all sold for export. Yet 80 per cent of the indigenous communities suffer from malnutrition, and more than half have no access to drinking water or electricity. Over a third cannot read and have never been to school, and in 1994, poverty-related disease accounted for an estimated 15,000 indigenous deaths.

Roberto Barrios, a community of 2,000 people, was one of the five places that hosted the first International Encuentro in 1996. Not everyone that lives there supports the uprising – supporters of the government live side by side with Zapatistas, and less than half a mile away (until 2001) sat one of the largest military bases in the area. The tension was always high, with low flying army planes and helicopters buzzing overhead. Fear of a repeat of the army's invasion of February 1996 was punctuated by the constant threats and attacks by paramilitary gangs.

The situation in Chiapas has drawn numerous international activists to visit and work as peace observers and to help build clinics, schools and sanitation projects with the autonomous municipalities. Despite the daily grind of poverty and fear, the Zapatista communities maintain a tenacious spirit of dignity and hope, a spirit which every visitor can't help but bring back home.

Death of a Zapatista

by Jeff Conant

Robert Barrios, Chiapas, Mexico, 1998

"Welcome to Zapatista Rebel Territory," a hand-painted sign reads as we enter the village, yellow letters on a black background, over what used to be a Coca-Cola advertisement. "Corn and peace, yes. Drugs and soldiers, no." Below the welcome is the five-pointed red star of the Zapatistas, the star representing the five continents united in struggle, representing the human figure standing up in dignity.

This past month has been especially tense, with military occupations of many villages and constant helicopter surveillance following the recent massacre in Acteal, where government supporters with AK-47s gunned down 45 unarmed men, women, and children. Everywhere there are threats that the massacre will be repeated in other villages. After Acteal, with federal police and military officials implicated in planning the massacre, both the secretary of the interior and the governor of Chiapas were forced to resign. But the murderers remained free, and the threat of open war put the Zapatistas on red alert. In response to international pressure, the government claimed to be applying the Federal Law of Firearms and Explosives to disarm paramilitaries. But they were really applying the law only as a form of harassment against Zapatista communities.

When I came into Roberto Barrios in December, a week after the Acteal murders, loaded down with seeds for the community garden, my friend Trinidad greeted me at the entrance. He stood near the hand-painted sign, a tall, stocky campesino, muscular, with kind eyes and a long hunting knife at his belt.

"*Como estás?*" I greeted him warmly, relieved to have successfully passed through the army base and crossed the river. Trinidad smiled, shaking my hand. "*Pués, aquí, jodido pero acustumbrado*". Just here, screwed but used to it.

This time, coming into the village in March, Trinidad's not here to welcome me, because he's dead. He was killed two days ago by machete blows to the head, along the road just above the army base. The killers were leaders of a local paramilitary group, *Los Chinchulines*, similar to those who killed with impunity in Acteal, in Sabanilla, in Nueva Esperanza, in Tila, in Agua Blanca, in San Geronimo Tulija, and who will continue killing as long as the government and the press continue to portray the Zapatistas as the source of violence in Chiapas. They are *Priistas*, supporters of the PRI, the [then] ruling party. In exchange for their support, the government, by way of the soldiers who surround these villages, gives them guns, trains them to kill, allows them to take what they can and what they want. They are the local enforcement team of the global massacre known as neoliberalism.

Trinidad's nickname was Trino, which in Spanish means the warble or trill of birdsong. The name fit him – he was gentle like that. After working on the village water system or in the gardens I sometimes looked for Trino in the community's library. He could often be found there studying by lamplight, reading books on history or newspapers brought in by the international observers, or recent communiqués from Subcomandante Marcos.

The first time I met Trino he led me for a walk around the village. We walked down to the river, to the waterfalls where the jungle's limestone shelf falls away in steps below towering *ceiba* trees and swallows make their nests in holes at the water's edge. He told me a story:

"In 1992, after the government changed our constitution so that they could buy and sell our lands, some men came to the village. They were dressed like men from the city, we'd never seen them before. They said they came to help us, that

---

in Toronto, Canada against proposed cuts in social services, including changes in child care benefits which would no longer grant teenage single mothers free day-care.

>> August >> Coal miners in Ukraine go on strike for back pay, higher wages and pensions, and better medical benefits. "I haven't been paid in two months," says Aleksi Tsybin, a miner from the eastern town of Makayevke. "This is a gross violation of workers' rights." The miners, who have launched sporadic strikes at some of the country's 246 mines in the past few weeks, are also demanding more control over the industry, such as setting coal prices and their own wage scale. The miners' union has warned the government that a broader strike is likely in the winter if negotiations collapse.

>> August 5 >> In a campaign to get multinational corporations out of India, the Karnataka Rajya Raitha Sangha (KRRS, Karnataka State Farmers Association), a ten million strong direct action movement of Indian farmers, manages to close down India's first Kentucky Fried Chicken outlet, on health grounds. At the same time billboards belong to KFC owner PepsiCo are destroyed by activists throughout the state, while the KRRS sets up training centres in organic agriculture and seed banks. The KFC eventually reopens under full-time guard.

they wanted to bring money and work to Roberto Barrios. They said they knew about our beautiful waterfalls and that they wanted to build a hotel for tourists right here, looking over the falls. They said the hotel would bring jobs and money, that it would be good for the village, that it would be development in a positive way.

"We had a community meeting that night to talk about it. And we agreed what we thought would happen. They would come with their men to plan the hotel and we would go to work building it. We would work for them like slaves levelling the ground and putting up the building, and they would try to trick us and pay us in liquor. And we would build the hotel, and then we would build a big fence around it, and then a big fence around the waterfalls, and once it was built they would make us pay to come in. And if we want to bathe in the river and wash our clothes in the river they would try to make us pay for the water in the river and they would not let us over their fence.

"So we made a decision. We told them to leave and never come back. And we told them to tell all of their other friends in the hotel business to not bother coming here, because our waterfalls are not for sale, and neither are we."

Arriving two days after his death, on 17 March 1998, a sea of familiar faces was gathered together in the *Aguascalientes*, the community meeting centre at the entrance to the village, not in anticipation of our arrival, but in expectation of police, soldiers, or paramilitaries to continue the wave of violence. Getting down from the jeep, I greeted everyone sadly, with hugs and handshakes, in the mute way of greeting the families of the dead. I walked off up the road to find my friend Moises, campesino poet and songwriter, and spiritual brother to Trino.

Moises' house, like the rest of them, is a quickly built shack of hand-cut boards with a thatch roof and a mud floor. In the yard, marked off by a low stone wall, he had planted beans and amaranth among the weeds, epazote, and chrysanthemum that grew randomly around the muddy lot.

> **"Considered from a Western political perspective, the autonomous municipalities make no sense. They have no resources or real power or legal legitimacy, and they are dying, encircled by hunger, diseases, the paramilitary threat, and the security forces. However, for the indigenous peoples, they constitute an eloquent symbol of a culture which is resisting and defying the dominant culture, making a reality of a different way of understanding politics and of organizing the economy, society, and even human relations."** – Servicio Internacional para la Paz

"*Buenos tardes!*" I called out from the yard, to make Moises and his family aware of my presence. He came out of the house barefoot and shirtless, followed by three of his sons, all calling out my name. The children were young, brown, mostly naked, their bellies swollen and round. In his hands Moises carried a few loose papers and a pen, and his eyes were wet from crying. He greeted me solemnly.

"I'm sorry I have nothing to offer you," he said, "but I'm poor."

"I just came to talk, to see how you're doing." I paused. "How are you doing?"

He held out the papers, and repeated, "I have nothing to offer you, but I can offer you my words."

I looked at the papers, at his crooked handwriting and the misspelled Spanish text he'd been working on. "You've already written a song for Trino?" I asked.

"It's not a song," he said, "just something I wrote."

He flattened out his papers and began reading.

"People accuse the Zapatistas of violence," he read, "They say that we bring war and death to the communities. But in one year we have seen two murders in our community, in one year we have seen two acts of war. Two brothers have been killed at the hands of paramilitaries, and not a single paramilitary has suffered in return. Who is violent here? Who is on the side of peace? Maybe after this everyone will see who is on the side of justice and who is on the side of war. Maybe Trinidad's death at the hands of the *Priistas* will help them see."

He put down the paper but continued talking. His initial shyness gave way to a flood of words.

"The *Priistas* have something wrong," he said. "The *Priistas* think that when you throw a bit of grain to the ground, it dies there. In this they are wrong. When you throw a bit of grain to the ground, it takes root and grows there, and it comes back stronger than before. They will find out how wrong they are."

He paused for a moment. In the jungle heat, the sweat dripping from my brow ran into my eyes, humid like his. A few yards away the river cut quietly through the afternoon, washing over the rocks towards the military post beyond. One of his children, his brown arms streaked with white patches of scabies, handed me a muddy wheel broken off a

---

>> **August 7** >> Oil workers in South Trinidad begin a six-week strike over wages, resulting in a seven per cent pay increase.

>> **August 7** >> One hundred thousand striking teachers, state workers, oil workers, and others march in San José, Costa Rica, in one of the largest demonstrations in 25 years. Some of the strikers occupy the Inter-American Court of Human Rights after the march, saying they will remain until the government listens to their demands.

>> **August 8** >> Nearly 600,000 public workers in Turkey go on strike against the government's austerity programme. Three days earlier, 100,000 workers marched through the capital city, Ankara, calling for an increase in the minimum wage, higher pay, and broader trade union rights.

>> **August 12** >> Nearly 1,500 landless peasants try to occupy the National Bank for Housing in Guatemala. Many are beaten by police. The peasants demand the land promised to 2,800 landless and homeless families. Lorenzo Pérez, a representative of the Guatemala Council for the Displaced, says 500,000 of the two million inhabitants of Guatemala City are displaced peasants who live in extreme poverty and are homeless.

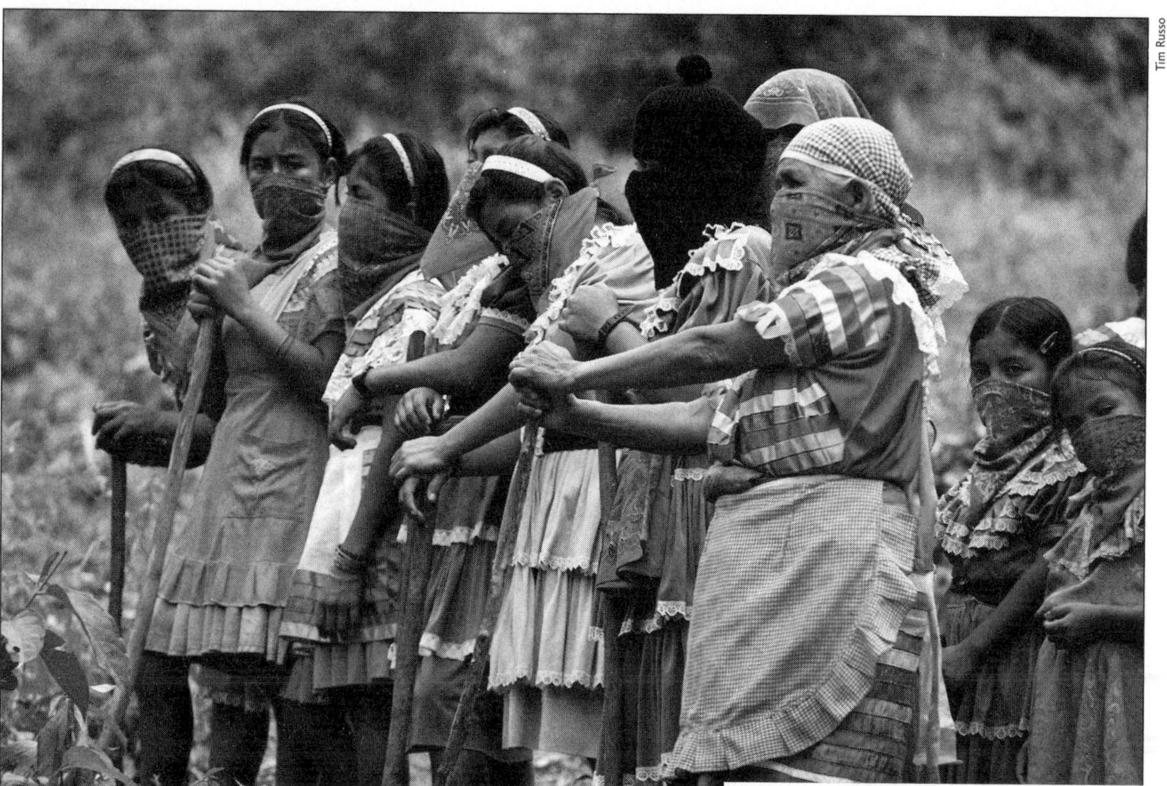
Tim Russo

Zapatista women defending their community. Chiapas, Mexico

wagon. I began to speak, but Moises cut me off.

"There is something that needs to be cleared up, a lie that has been told. The *Priistas* say that they have killed a Zapatista leader, that they have killed the Zapatista leader of this community. But they lie. They lie because the Zapatistas have no leaders. They think that by killing our leaders they can destroy the movement, but this is not so. It is true that there are people who command and people who obey, but those who command do it for those who obey, and those who obey do it out of pure will, out of service to the people. There are no Zapatista leaders, only Zapatistas, and so the *Priistas* have made a great mistake."

"I would have come for the funeral," I told him, "but we only heard yesterday. They say you gave a beautiful speech."

The three children, with bloated bellies and scabs all over their little bodies, ran around the yard with plastic bowls on their heads like helmets, laughing.

"Do you want to hear what happened at the funeral?" he asked, and before I had time to respond, he began the story.

"I was sitting there looking for something, anything, to help me understand what had happened, why they took Trino and not me, and I couldn't find anything in Heaven or Earth that would make me understand. I was tired of looking at the body of my friend in its coffin and I looked up into the branches of a *guanacastle* tree. Sitting up there, on one side of the grave, was a toucan, and the toucan looked at the grave, and looked at me, and started bobbing its head back and forth the way they do when they're about to sing. And he started singing, and it made me angry and I thought, "Goddamned toucan, why can't you shut up! My brother is lying there dead and all you can do is sing." But he kept singing. And then, across from him, on the other side of the grave in an *higuero* tree, a *kashcan* started singing. It looked at the grave and it looked at me and it started singing. And then I thought, well maybe they have a message. So I listened, and I was relieved because I was tired of looking at the grave and at my friend's body in his coffin, and after a little while I thought they were telling me to pay attention to the trees. So I started paying attention to the trees, and I noticed that all the trees suddenly swayed in one direction, that a wind had come up out of the North. And then the wind died back, and the

---

>> August 27 >> The Zapatistas hold the first international *consulta*, with the participation of over 1.2 million Mexicans, and more than 100,000 people from outside of Mexico. Voters overwhelmingly agree with the principal demands of the EZLN, call for a broad united opposition to struggle for those demands, and agree that women should be guaranteed equal representation and participation at all levels of civil and governmental responsibility. In a country where the ruling PRI's own plebiscite on its economic plan only managed to achieve a voter participation of 600,000 voters in the spring of 1995, the Zapatista's success at dialogue with national and global civil society is illustrative of the will to change.

>> September 27 >> Hundreds of Honduran students clash with police during protests against a rise in urban bus fares.

>> September 28 >> More than half a million teachers in Russia go on a nationwide strike to protest against unpaid wages, low pay, and severe government underfunding of social services.

>> September 28 >> "Reclaim the Future," an alliance of Reclaim the Streets, rave activists, and the Liverpool dockers commemorate the anniversary of the dockers lock out. Activists break through fences, occupy cranes,

trees all swayed in another direction, with a wind from the West, where the sun sets. And then the trees all moved in a third direction with a wind that came up out of the South. And that wind died back, and then a fourth wind came up, out of the East, where the sun rises, and moved the trees in that direction. And I was watching the trees move in the wind when suddenly I heard thunder – and it hasn't rained here in two months – and then I saw rays of lightning shoot out of the clouds. And suddenly it started to rain, and just as it rained, they were lowering Trino's body into the grave, and I thought of his blood being washed off the earth by the rain, and I thought of the seeds planted that need the rain. Rain is a blessing.

"And a few minutes later the rain stopped and I heard the call of a howler monkey nearby. And all of this happened just like this, I can't share it with anybody but I can share it with you. And if they think our struggle is over because they killed Trino they're wrong, because the rain came and washed his blood off the earth and blessed the seed, and everything that I do, in my work and in my struggle, Trino is right here with me and we're going to struggle more than ever for justice. We don't want vengeance, but we want justice."

Saying farewell to Moises, I made my way back to the *Aguascalientes* walking along the river, a wide foaming swath of blue that cuts through the jungle and marks the tentative border between the villagers and the war made on them by the government. The journalists I'd travelled with had gotten their interviews, and I joined them for a visit to the village up the road, beyond the river and the army base, where the murder had happened.

Stopping by a tiny collection of shacks and a cement church straddling the road, we were invited to sit and share a cup of coffee. As in the village we'd just left, the air was thick with sorrow and fear. And here, like in the other village, mine was a familiar face, so the normally reticent villagers felt comfortable, maybe even relieved, to share their story with me.

We talked to Miguel, one of the eyewitnesses of the murder, a gentle, firm man who runs the co-operative store right along the road there. He told us the story of the *Priistas* harassing Trinidad in the truck on the way home from Palenque, how they pressured him to drink *aguardiente* with them. He told us how they threatened Trinidad, how they accused him of being a leader of the Zapatistas, saying: "You are going to witness another Acteal here in the North. We have orders."

Miguel described how once drunk, Trinidad became docile, and how at a crossroads, the five *Priistas* pulled him out of the truck and threw him to the ground and whipped him across the face with a belt, putting his eye out. The driver and another *compañero* managed to get Trino back in the truck, and they took off with the *Priistas* running behind. When they caught up to the truck, at the stop in this village, Trinidad, drunk and half-blind, blood still rushing from his head, confronted the attackers. He named them, roaring that they were leaders of the *Chinchulines* paramilitary, and accused them of having killed his brother-in-law a year previous.

"You'll pay for what you've done!" he shouted, but he was surrounded by the five of them, wielding stones and machetes, and before he could fight back they had him on the ground and one of the men had taken a piece out of his skull with a machete. The five ran off up the road, towards the river and the army base that lay before it.

Miguel told the story in great detail, how he tried to stop the killers by insisting that violence only brings more violence, how his brother-in-law came running with a machete to join the fray but he begged him off, how Trino, splayed on the ground by the low concrete church, called out for water and repeated "They've killed me, they've killed me, they've killed me," until his one eye closed and his voice died into silence. He told us that he was scared, that the killers will come again.

Trinidad died that night in the hospital in Villahermosa, Tabasco, several hours away by truck. It was only the second time in his life that he'd left his home state of Chiapas. The first was a year earlier, to participate in the National Indigenous Congress in Mexico City.

Miguel continued: "They said they want another Acteal, and they mean it. They have the soldiers on their side and they want to kill us all. We don't want war, we want peace, but they won't leave us alone. Trinidad wasn't from our village but he died here. His blood is on the ground here. The war is spreading. We're afraid of more blood spilling here, we don't want to fight. We will fight if they make us, but we only want peace. We only want peace."

Jeff Conant is an activist and writer of non-fiction, fiction, and poetry living in Berkeley, California. He has translated a book about Mayan traditional medicine, *Wind in the Blood*. Currently, he's developing a popular education guide to environmental health with the Hesperian Foundation.

Resources:

» Excellent information on working as a peace observer in Chiapas: *The Zapatistas: A Rough Guide*, available from AK Press: www.akpress.org
Available online: www.chiapaslink.ukgateway.net/cho.html

---

and fly the RTS flag from the roof of the corporate headquarters. The actions trigger a 24 hour strike by tug boat captains. No vessels enter or leave Liverpool, and Mersey Docks shares fall a further 14p, despite the company's claims of continued normal operations.

>> October 10 >> During their annual meetings in Washington D.C., US, the IMF/WB are stunned by four days of demonstrations when activists from the Native Forest Network and Earth First! hang banners from a crane at the construction site of the lavish new World Bank headquarters. A crowd of demonstrators gathers on the sidewalk, heckling World Bank and IMF employees on their way to work. Five people are arrested; the two white people are released while the three people of colour are charged.

>> October 20 >> Security services disperse 20,000 Romanian students after three days of protest against Bucharest government control over education in the post-communist era. The students win a victory when the government withdraws controversial taxes on students who fail exams.

>> October 31 >> Some 5,000 people participate in a "Death of Education March" in Honolulu, US, to protest against budget cuts totaling $50 million over two years.

Affinity Groups

An affinity group is the fundamental unit of direct action. It is a self-sufficient support system which may develop actions on its own, or may work with other affinity groups toward a common goal in a large action. The most effective groups consist of 5-15 people, and they usually strengthen over time. They differ from other groups of friends in that participants tend to have more in common, there is an absence of hierarchy, and over time, a deep trust in the group's intelligence can develop, allowing us to let go of some of our own prejudices and consider what is best for the group.

Every affinity group must decide for itself how it will make decisions and what it wants to do. This process starts when an affinity group forms. If a new person wants to join an affinity group, she should find out what the group believes in and what they plan to do, and decide if they are compatible. Ideally, you will have a shared idea of your individual and collective goals for the action or campaign, what support you will need from others, and what you can offer each other. It helps if you have agreement on certain basic things: how active, spiritual, nonviolent, touchy-feely, militant, or willing to risk arrest you'll be – however, it may be that you just work together at a job, play music or hike together, and that's okay too. The point is that doing things together is safer, and much more fun, than doing them alone.

The concept has a long history. It developed in Catalonia and was used in the 1930s during the Spanish Civil War, when anarchists, communists, and other libertarians fought desperately against Franco and the fascists. In 1969, affinity groups organized a massive nonviolent blockade during the 30,000 strong occupation of the Ruhr nuclear power station in Germany. In 1971 in the US occupations of the Seabrook nuclear power station, when 10,000 were arrested, affinity groups were key, as they were throughout the highly successful anti-nuclear movement. More recently, they were used with outstanding success in the mass actions in Seattle, Prague, and Québec City, where the open manner of organizing created a framework within which affinity groups could plan autonomous actions.

Affinity groups form the basic decision-making bodies of many mass actions; they also frequently work together as study groups, or provide services to their community. Within the group, there is a whole range of roles that its members can perform, which could include: a media liaison, a facilitator for meetings, a note taker, someone trained in first aid, a legal observer.

As well as fulfilling these roles, the affinity group can take on a specialized role in the way it interacts with other groups, or operates within the action or community. There can be affinity groups specializing in copwatching, communications, health care, street theatre, or blockading. With a focus, each affinity group can do its job and support the work of others. In this way, many affinity groups form a network that achieves exponentially more than equal numbers of unaffiliated activists ever could.

The thing to remember is that an affinity group belongs to you – you can decide what actions and what degree of risk you wish to take. Bringing creative people together to work and play collectively is one of our most powerful acts of resistance.

Resource:

» Temporary Anti Capitalist Teams: www.temporary.org.uk

Bette Lee

Radical cheerleading unleashes silliness for the crowd. Portland, Oregon, US

*"**He who sows poverty shall reap anger!**" declared a banner of the unemployed movement which swept through France during the winter of 1997-98. The Paris Stock Exchange had announced record growth that year, yet national statistics revealed four million under-employed people, with 12 million living in extreme insecurity and poverty. Coming three years after the widespread strikes of 1995, which brought to light the effects of neoliberalism on French society, the unemployed movement signalled a break in the traditional party and union-dominated forms of political action in France.*

Beginning as a series of small local actions demanding emergency benefits in Marseille, the movement spread with extraordinary speed to cover 26 towns. They occupied unemployment offices and electricity companies, they expropriated supermarket food, blocked roads and railway lines. The wide range of protests across France had a huge political impact. For the first time a movement of the unemployed caused a government to take national measures, (an emergency fund for the unemployed, among others).

Although parts of the movement were tightly stage-managed by official unemployment groups, much of it relied on small, self-organized collectives, taking local actions and initiatives without central coordination. Refusing a life that demanded dependence on the crumbs of state welfare, people imagined a world with a radically different concept of work. "We have the time, you have the money," they shouted as they took over motorway toll booths, opened the barriers, handed out flyers, and collected 'toll' money from passing motorists to fund their campaign, sometimes at the rate of $1,800 per hour.

In Paris they organized their actions with a daily assembly in the occupied hall of a university, and in order to eat they helped themselves to lunch at corporate cafeterias, distributing their leaflets and increasing their network of support. Many of the networks developed during these intense months became strands of the anticapitalist movement.

We Have the Time, You Have the Money: the French unemployed get busy

by Chômeurs Heureux

Monday in the sun: the story of a stroll through Paris, Friday 6 February 1998

Isn't it great to meet a few dozen smiling faces again this Friday? Armed with a serious desire for a good laugh, we're going to make a bit of history today, tell it, build it, write about it too. And we're determined to make it mean something.

It's noontime, so we invite ourselves to lunch with the elite, at the School of Higher Studies in the Social Sciences, right in the middle of a ritzy neighbourhood... The cafeteria workers give us a warm welcome: "Don't forget to take some dessert! And have some of the pork, it's really good!" The Appeal of the Jobless is passed round, it's our ticket for a first-class meal. It gets read or skimmed by the intellectuals we sit down to eat with, scattered here and there. Of course some of them feel threatened by the arrival of this crowd of strangers. But others pay friendly attention, like the two women research directors who unmask us right away: "With smiles like that you can't be from here!" You're right. And next comes a free-wheeling conversation about jobs becoming a myth for three million people, about the utopia of a world without money, without work, about dreams halfway between reality and fantasy, about the colossal time that's at our fingertips thanks to the lack of work, time enough to give those dreams materiality. Those women's eyes fairly flamed with enthusiasm as they heard the call of activities that set them dreaming.

They said, "Did you know that we're the ones keeping this cafeteria out of the red, which means we're the ones paying for your lunch today? But it's our pleasure. It's an awful lot better than greasing the wallet of the last manager we had here, the one who took off with the till. And now we can put faces to the jobless people and casual workers. The media tells us you're a bunch of retards looking for affection. Well, we're not going to believe that anymore!" And before you know it, they're thanking us for the visit.

At the cafeteria some clever guy requests 45 coffees for the participants of a conference on labour and reification. We sip our stimulant with pleasure, and our good mood becomes insolent when one girl suggests we take it out on the repossession men. Who has never cursed those vultures? This would be the high point of the day. The action is set for 3.00 pm, at the ground floor of a building where one of those legal killjoys is due to stop in. On the way we nab some over-ripe remains from a street market at closing time, yesterday's tripe and last week's tomatoes, some dodgy sardines and a few pounds of flour for good measure.

So we're there waiting for Mr. Bourge with the attaché case, who shows up right on time and freshly shaven, the kind of face you can't mistake among ten thousand. And one, two, three, it's open season on the repossession man, with rotten food flying in all directions: a sardine on the shoulder is all the rage, a few rotten bananas land like huge spitwads, and his glasses dangle as he tries to protect his precious bag, looking for an exit. Despite the vain flight of the guy who's always there when you don't need him, still every one of us makes good on our aim each time, and splatters him with insults too, but not the slightest blow. A few passers by watch, laughing, while the human rodent lets his eyes overflow with question marks and whimpers now and then, "But what did I do? What did I do?"

Free transport on the subway is not a demand, but a reality. Few of us pay anyway. The difference here is taking it together: the first holds the door for the others and all

---

Governor Benjamin Cayetano is shouted down by protesters while telling University of Hawaii faculty members and students that the state administration had no choice but to slash the school's budget.
>> October 31 >> Riots break out in Bryansk, Russia, as car workers demand payment for over five months' back wages. Coal miners and other workers have organized strikes and demonstrations also demanding back pay. The Russian government has accumulated massive debts to hundreds of enterprises in attempting to adhere to a budget arranged with the IMF last spring.
>> November-December >> In protest against the French government's liberalization of labour laws in an unpopular effort to reform the welfare system, five million union members and students go on strike, demanding that telecommunications and all other services not be privatized, and that more funding be allocated to overcrowded state universities. Hundreds of thousands take to the streets. The transport strike results in a 350 mile traffic jam in Paris. Strikes spread to Belgium and Luxembourg. The French government eventually backs down.
>> November 10 >> Protests against Shell erupt around the world, as the Nigerian government executes nine

the better if strangers take advantage. It's enough to drive the ticket-men crazy! At Météo-France [the national weather bureau] the door-keeper didn't take much notice of these nondescripts, nonetheless quite out of place, as we went through one by one. Only later did he start to get surprised. In any case he was wiser to stay at his post, because numbers were on our side. But so are laughter, dreams, and intervention in public life. We met an insider and asked him where to find a photocopier and a fax. He hesitated, then asked us how we got in. It's an almost ritual question: "Through the door, how else?" We let him go along his way. Office doors open up, the employees smiling. Our tracts give them a laugh and make things easier. A director or some official forbids the employees from letting us use the fax, but civil disobedience has always been an effective weapon. And so the weather bureaus of the Paris region would receive our appeal to the natural elements. In another office, nobody goes against orders, but they let us use the equipment with a few indispensable tips. And Agence France Presse (AFP) receives our weather report too.

Here again, we created a momentary break in the routine, brought an unexpected breath of fresh air, in a place where such things are ceaselessly predicted and detected in advance. The AFP didn't transmit our rainbow, too bad! It would have warmed up the atmosphere and cut right through the Parisian smog.

In this late afternoon we start feeling the pangs. It's time for a sportsman's drink. Let's go do the shopping at the local supermarket! No more paranoia about the security in the store. You don't have to be aggressive, it's just a matter of numbers and willpower. Half of it gets eaten without any discussion. We split the rest out in the street together, with whoever might want to stop and cut a steak around an improvised stand.

On this Friday 6 February, our 'Monday in the Sun' stroll was rich in meetings, amazed looks, knowing smiles, and shared laughter.

The city is not just a barracks where bureaucrats tap on their computers, cops settle violations of the law, and judges cut to the quick by doling out years in prison, while the prolos groan. We live in this city, what the fuck! Let's not leave it in the hands of imposters and vultures.

PARIS IS AN IMMENSE PLAYGROUND!!!

Jussieu, an Extraordinary Assembly

For three weeks now there has been an assembly every day at Jussieu. Born of the jobless people's movement, it's the home base and meeting place of this struggle, addressed to all those who see themselves in its mirror... How did it come to be, what has it begun to build, with what resources, and in what spirit?

On Saturday 17 January 1998 several hundred people gathered round the banner, "We Want A Shitty Job For Peanuts." The irony of a few joyous masochists struck a chord. People came together around a shared dissatisfaction, as much with the boredom and routine of the demos as with the often miserable demands (because we minimize ourselves when we ask for 'social minimums'). There were the young and the not-so-young, workers and people without a job. Many of the individuals and small groups had participated in the occupations of the preceding weeks, notably of the *Ecole Normale Supérieure on rue d'Ulm*. The idea arose of keeping in touch, of taking what we had in common a little further. For that we'd need a place. Since the police blocked off any occupation that night, a *rendez-vous* was set for Monday evening in an amphitheatre of Jussieu university. It wasn't our first pick, and far from the nicest place we could imagine, but the police occupation of Paris didn't leave us much choice.

For a very long time, 'general assembly' has suggested an impossible encounter, deafening and suffocating all at once. Our assembly has been able to go beyond certain shortfalls. It's often a pleasure, because people actually listen to each other. It's only general because everyone is invited to participate; it's not a meeting of delegates. For the moment we're responsible to no-one but ourselves, that is, to the people who participate in creating this collective intelligence.

In the early days we saw improvised session leaders emerge. Their role turned out to be worse than freewheeling debate, where everyone addresses everybody else and everyone can answer. The debate doesn't follow a speaking order, but the order of the subjects.

The question of voting came up. We rejected it as an artifice of democratic traditions, inadequate to our needs

---

environmental activists, including writer Ken Saro-Wiwa, who were imprisoned on fabricated murder charges. The activists were resisting Shell's environmental destruction of Ogoniland, Nigeria, which has resulted in the loss of agricultural land to oil wells, spillage, pipelines and blowouts. In Ken Saro-Wiwa's closing statement at his trial, he predicts that "...the ecological war that [Shell] has waged in the delta will be called to question, and the crimes of that war duly punished."

>> **December 4** >> To the accompaniment of bagpipes, 500 Earth First! activists storm the largest stone quarry in England, in Whatley, Somerset, swarming over gates, scaling fences, and erecting a tripod blocking the rail line leading out from the quarry. Sixty-five feet of railway track "disappear;" the surveillance system falls apart; a two-story crane pulls itself to bits; three control rooms dismantle themselves; and several digging and conveyer belts "break down." At the end of the day, the media reports that $163,000 of damage occurred, with an additional loss of production of $325,000.

>> **December 13** >> Students, professors, and university staff in Managua, Nicaragua, rejecting proposed tuition hikes and administrative fees, demand that the government abide by the constitution and

right now: it's a form of decision that often annuls the debates, reducing them to the caricature of 'for' and 'against'. But our position isn't our principle, and some circumstances might lead us to vote. Our number varies from 80 to 400. The proposals for action submitted to the assembly are not necessarily ratified by it: we discuss the spirit, rather than imposing anything, or blocking anyone from acting at their own will. Tracts are written by hand, from repugnance for computers. We gradually shake off the tic of applause, which is the accounting machine of demagoguery.

A style emerges from original actions and the self-critiques that follow: inviting ourselves into cafeterias, transforming the streets of Paris into playgrounds, distributing tracts and rants in public places (schools, businesses, bistros, social services, post offices, metros, markets, restaurants, unemployment offices, etc.), with splash appearances in unexpected spots (Le Monde, Météo-France, the Fine Arts school), pie-throwing at social menaces, free generosity lessons for store owners, parties and banquets, passionate debates....

In addition to the possible police consequences, the presence of journalists and other outside eyes seemed contradictory to the assembly's will to maintain control over its means of expression and the meaning of its acts. The defenders of the media-hounds argued our dependency on information. The response was that if we had something essential to say, then no-one but ourselves could say it.

After a tumultuous debate we therefore kicked out photographers, cameramen, and those doing studies of the jobless people's movement. But we welcome individuals who break with their social functions, including journalists who stop being voyeurs to become sensible again, artists who give up their exhibitionist performances, unionists who cease kow-towing to their bureaucracy. The unionist from one of France's most mainstream unions who came on 27 January to say that we warmed his heart by our presence and our humour means more to us than any professional revolutionary.

We refused to go along with the combined maneuvers of the parties, unions, and associations seeking to confuse the jobless people's movement with the illusion of the 35 hour work-week. About 800 of us got a real kick out of a banner and a tract with the socialist party logo saying "Let's Sacrifice our Lives to the Economy," while we handed out hot wine and drank it too.

On the way back to Jussieu, the provocation of a policewoman and the mistakes of one of us didn't keep 400 people from making it to the assembly. That night, people looking for a fight saw the importance of collective issues, the promise of a greater pleasure than the immediacy of direct conflict. That night we obeyed neither the union lullaby (dignified and peaceful demonstrations) nor the activist outcry (let's hit back!). It's a kind of collective lucidity that knows there's no fixed recipe. Our idea was that it's as important to act as it is to take our time. An intelligent understanding; a kind of suave mixture of old and new friends, between groups that existed previously and individuals discovering the possibility to act. The punks are not just hoodlums, the debaters are not just big talkers; we began to be something better than all those categories, which were still separate in yesterday's movements. We don't have any choice, we have to organize our agreement.

It's kind of tough for us to introduce ourselves. We're not a group of mercenaries, or a support committee. We're not the leaders of some stinking splinter faction that only sees the other as a potential member, and addresses them as an object. It's not a question for us of casting a larger net, of mobilizing (like troops are mobilized), but of creating favourable conditions for mutual recognition and encounter. Collective intelligence also arises from the fact that the assembly doesn't only define itself by its enemies, not by a political line, an idea raised above it, but by what it is, that is, the people who compose it, and the steps it takes. So far we've been able to talk about everything, including what for some people is obvious. That's one of the qualities of this assembly: being able to go backwards in order to get further ahead. We dream of multiplying assemblies like ours, to put an end to the feeling of an inevitability at the heart of things.

We're an assembly of *déclassés* who want to transform social structures, to do away with the parasitic side of individual and collective relations, to return to simpler and more direct ties. We're conscious that the strength of a movement depends on its ability to eradicate fears and reinforce individuals. Our actions, games, debates and parties build the confidence needed to put our ideas into practice.

We think it's important to clarify and understand the questions posed by the unemployed people's movement. That means the problem of salaried labour, of the economy that produces it and the money that's associated with it. How to transform this society which eliminates work while maintaining it as the supreme value, into a society founded on human activity, a society that doesn't produce commodities? To answer this central question, to quell the confusion that reigns on this subject – even among us – we want to refine the style and spirit invented by this assembly: the mix of seriousness and play that we have been experimenting with in the demonstration that made us known and visible.

---

allocate six per cent of the national budget for university education. Riot police break up demonstrations at the National Assembly with tear gas followed by gunfire. Two students are killed, one loses a leg, and more than 60 are injured.

>> December 13 >> Members of the Machinists' Union in Seattle, US, celebrate victory with a new contract with Boeing, Inc, which finally capitulated after a strike of 34,500 workers. They picketed 69 days in almost non-stop rainstorms and sacrificed $6,000 per worker in wages.

\\ 1996 //

>> January 1 >> During the first hours of 1996, the EZLN announce the formation of the Zapatista Front of National Liberation (FZLN), "a civil and nonviolent organization, independent and democratic, Mexican and national...A political force which does not struggle to take political power but for a democracy where those who govern, govern by obeying...Our word, our song and our cry, is so that the dead will no longer die. So that they may live we struggle, so that they live we sing."

>> January 30 >> Continuing their campaign to rid India of mutinational corporations, the KRRS chooses the anniversary of Ghandi's death to dismantle a Kentucky Fried Chicken outlet in Bangalore. Its windows

We'll claim what we've won, but we aren't just going to make demands: that would let those we're addressing believe they can just make up for all that they've taken away. To satisfy our needs we prefer to go looking rather than just ask. It's something we're proud of. We have already found allies, and by coordinating our shared disgust we begin to get beyond it. Three weeks have gone by, banishing boredom and bringing hope back alive. We don't want to stop!
WE INVITE EVERYONE TO JOIN OUR STROLLING COMMITTEES, OUR GAMES, OUR DEBATES.

Extract from *Le Lundi au Soleil: Recueil de textes et de récits du mouvement des chômeurs*, novembre 1997 – avril 1998, Paris: L'insomniaque éditeur, 1998

English translation by Brian Holmes

When French unemployed activists *got together with Indonesian fisherfolk, Columbian U'wa tribal elders, and South Korean strikers, they were participating in the birth of a unique radical network which was to provide the impetus for many of the summit-disrupting actions which were to hit the headlines over the next few years.*

The idea of Peoples' Global Action (PGA) was born at the Second Encuentro (encounter) in Spain. It arose out of the need to create something more tangible than the encuentros, which were ostensibly international talk shops. Aiming to be "a global instrument for communication and coordination" of grassroots groups who believe in taking confrontational direct action, "while building up local alternatives and people power," the PGA was one of the first networks to target the World Trade Organization (WTO) specifically, and capitalism in general.

The WTO, reckless promoter of 'free' trade and corporate rule which, according to its director-general, "is writing the constitution of a single global economy," was to have its second ministerial meeting in Geneva, in May 1998. The founding PGA conference was held a stone's throw away, that February. Over ten chaotic days, activists from a mind-boggling array of cultures and backgrounds drafted a manifesto and hatched plans for the first global day of action against the WTO and G8 summits the following May.

While the PGA does not define itself as an organization, it holds a distinctive organizational philosophy based on decentralization and autonomy. It has no head office, no central funds, no membership, and no representatives – a difficult way of working on a local level, let alone a global one. But despite the disparity, chaos, and confusion that pepper the process, thousands of grassroots organizations from every continent have participated in the global days of action called by the PGA, and it continues to be a catalyzing focus for global action.

Peoples' Global Action: the grassroots go global

by Olivier de Marcellus

"It is difficult to describe the warmth and the depth of the encounters we had here. The global enemy is relatively well known, but the global resistance that it meets rarely passes through the filter of the media. And here we met the people who had shut down whole cities in Canada with general strikes, risked their lives to seize lands in Latin America, destroyed the seat of Cargill in India or Novartis' transgenic maize in France.

The discussions, the concrete planning for action, the stories of struggle, the personalities, the enthusiastic hospitality of the Genevan squatters, the impassioned accents of the women and men facing the police outside the WTO building, all sealed an alliance between us. Scattered around the world again, we will not forget. We remain together. This is our common struggle."

– Letter from the Geneva PGA Welcoming Committee

For Geneva, the job of hosting the PGA conference was an interesting challenge. As in many places, the Genevan activist scene, allergic to traditional organization and hierarchy, has never been capable of organizing itself in numbers that go beyond 15-20 which can function in spontaneous small group dynamics. In practice, other potentially interested people were excluded simply because it isn't possible to give more people a hearing, or a clear task to do with that sort of organization. And of course people who didn't correspond to the usual profile of the 'alternative' scene rarely felt like they could fit in.

The huge practical necessities and the amazingly wide response to the PGA perspective got us past that way of functioning. Already the Zapatista calls "against neoliberalism and for humanity" had attracted very diverse kinds of people to meetings. Preparing the conference allowed us to organize half a dozen different practical groups for accommodation, food, visas, translations, fund raising, etc. At least a hundred people worked on it in one way or another, none of them receiving a wage, of course.

---

are smashed, furniture broken, ledgers burnt, and utensils flung into the streets. Over 100 people are arrested, and the KRRS spokesperson, Professor Nanjundaswamy, is accused of attempted murder. He uses Ghandi's words to defend his actions against property: "If you had a goods train carrying arms, blowing it up does not amount to a violent act. It would however be violent to blow up a passenger train."

>> February >> In Britain around 5,000 march against the construction of a road to bypass the town of Newbury.

>> February 7 >> Over 20,000 students in 30 cities across Canada go on strike in a national day of action against cuts in education and social programmes by the federal government.

>> March 10 >> The largest gold mine in the world, located in West Papua, a colony of Indonesia, and owned by US company Freeport McMoRan, is closed down for six days by riots. The company has dug out top of a sacred mountain, an act Papuans describe as "beheading our mother". More than 90 per cent of the mined mountain end up as tailings, poisoning rivers for miles downstream. The company has also been responsible for the murder and torture of independence

Katharine Ainger

Grassroots rebels from every continent are brought together by the Peoples' Global Action network. S26, Prague, Czech Republic

On a political level, we managed to combine the decisive participation of the Genevan squatters/alternative scene (who offered most of the lodging and work, cooked the meals in the Usine – the local alternative culture centre) with the political and financial support of some progressive trade unions, "Third World" support groups, and NGOs. Finally, even the left-wing parties were obliged to declare their support. Geneva makes a business of hosting all kinds of international gatherings, but it had never hosted a conference of radical popular movements. With people coming to represent a ten million-strong Indian farmers' movement, it was easy to ask for support; the legitimacy of the request was difficult to deny.

At the same time the PGA's proposal for direct but nonviolent action provoked an excited political discussion, particularly when the Indian Karnataka farmers' union leader Swamy, on a preliminary speaking tour of the country, threw a bottle of Nestlé iced tea (which had very incorrectly found its way onto the speakers' podium) against a wall, proclaiming: "This is not violence! Violence is only actions directed against living things!" This he

"There is no centre anywhere that could hope to organize and oversee all this mutual thickening of ties. It would be like trying to instruct a forest how to grow."

– PGA bulletin five, February 2000, UK edition

followed with his favorite story about Gandhi's judgement that blowing up a British munitions train was not really violent. Radical anti-WTO groups started springing up behind his stops across Switzerland.

Typically for PGA, it all seemed megalomaniac and doomed until the last moment, when more than 300 delegates finally made it, almost half of them from the global South – 71 countries in all. It was preceded by four days of workshops and six large public meetings which drew an unprecedented number of Genevans to hear and discover the most diverse people and struggles: from Medha Patkar from India – with her goddess-like style and

---

fighters who have fought a long struggle against the company, and the colonizing Indonesian military who get rich defending the mine.

>> March 28 >> Thousands of people take to the streets in La Paz, Cochabamba, and Santa Cruz, Bolivia, demanding a raise in salaries and denouncing the privatization of Bolivia's oil fields. In Cochabamba, 250 people, most of them elderly, are detained while on hunger strike, protesting for the same reasons. On the same day, workers in Paraguay initiate a general strike demanding salary increases of 31 per cent and calling for a referendum on the rapid privatization of their nation's wealth and resources. Meanwhile, in São Paolo, Brazil, more than 5,000 students are attacked and detained by the police while protesting against tuition fee hikes and other neoliberal policies on education.

>> March 29 >> Adding their voices to the continent-wide uprisings, thousands of farmers in southern Chile block national highways in protest against Chile's imminent inclusion in the 'free' trade agreement, Mercosur, which will result in the unemployment of at least 80,000 Chilean farmers. At the same time, street vendors in Lima, Peru, confront

gestures – denouncing the Narmada Dam project, to towering Maori – expert activists on neoliberal policy. A particularly significant discovery for the Genevans and other Europeans was from less far away – the attractive example of that strange post-Thatcherite phenomenon called Reclaim The Streets, whose practice of 'street parties' would be imitated the world over during future global days of action. The press was very good, particularly the local progressive daily that worked with us on an excellent 12 page supplement, entitled 'WTO: A world government in the shadows', and even designed a snappy PGA logo, which we promptly adopted.

The conference itself brought together far too many fascinating people and experiences for anyone to appreciate them all (and we Genevans were generally too busy carrying around mattresses etc, anyway). I am often still surprised when looking through the list of participants to see how many organizations we work with now were present back then!

The most important part of the conference was devoted to a collective elaboration of the manifesto by the delegates meeting in different working groups: indigenous peoples, peasant, trade unions, gender, education, migrations, and racism. The conference was finally prolonged a day to finish the job. Just by totally random chance, and unknown to us at the time, this was occurring during the week of the one hundred-fiftieth anniversary of the writing of the Communist Manifesto! Our manifesto, evolving slightly from one conference to another, has

"We have to start aiming at the head; we have been militants fighting against nuclear power, against homelessness, sexism – different tentacles of the monster. You are never really going to do it that way, you really have to aim at the head." – **Olivier de Marcellus at the founding conference of Peoples' Global Action, 1998**

proved to be one of PGA's most important tools. With the four (later five) 'hallmarks', it gives a pretty clear picture of what the organizations and movements involved in the PGA network are like and stand for. It spares us a lot of tedious discussion with organizations and people that we don't really have enough in common with. The manifesto, as it took form in Geneva, already reflected a significant evolution. PGA was conceived as a tool to radically oppose the WTO and 'free' trade, but it became increasingly clear that the movements committed to direct action against this latest form of capitalism, were in fact also for the most part against capitalism as such, and were looking for ways to reaffirm a revolutionary perspective internationally.

The last day of the conference, a demonstration marched from our meeting hall to the WTO headquarters.

It was the moment when a unifying characteristic of all those disparate delegates appeared: we like to talk, but we love to get into the streets! It was not a large demonstration, just a few hundred people, but no one there will ever forget it, for the sheer energy and passion that expressed itself. The Genevan police, used to dealing with unruly young people, were thunderstruck. Medha Patkar and other very 'respectable looking' women in magnificent saris suddenly were swinging themselves gracefully over the police barriers; a huge Maori woman, six feet tall and very broad, leaning over a helmeted young policeman, sticking her tongue out about six inches in the traditional grimace of provocation; an irrepressibly jolly young Spaniard, diving into the police lines, consistently being thrown back over the barriers and then diving over again; a nimble elf from Reclaim The Streets climbing like a monkey to the top of the WTO gates; the incredible, from-the-gut speeches of a Canadian postal worker, of our local *passionaria*.

Finally, a woman from the Bangladesh garment workers' organization burst into a diatribe of such fury that I (who was holding the mike) was actually a little afraid that she might have some sort of a fit. Absolutely rigid, her eyes fixed on the top stories of the WTO building, she was asking for nothing. She was telling them, positively screeching, "We are warning you! You have caused enough suffering! Enough deaths! That time is going to end, because we are going to stop you!" The external relations officer of the WTO abandoned his attempts at dialogue and retreated into the building, no doubt thinking, "So that was what they mean by being opposed to lobbying." And we marched back to dinner, I think each of us saying to ourselves: "These are people after my own heart!"

Olivier de Marcellus fled the US (and Vietnam) in 1966, and has been happily hyper-active in many movements: anti-imperialist, anti-nuclear, squats, etc. They all pale, however, in comparison with the impetuous piece of history unleashed by the Zapatista uprising.

Resources:

» PGA online and in seven languages: www.agp.org

---

the police and defend their right to work as the police attempt to expel them from the historic (read, touristic) centre. And in Santa Ana, Costa Rica, thousands protest against the installation of a waste dump in their town which would add more than one thousand tons of rubbish a day to the heap already dumped on them by neoliberalism.

>> April >> Hundreds demonstrate against the military government as a UN team tours the Ogoniland region to investigate the execution of writer and activist Ken Saro-Wiwa.

>> April 17 >> About 1,500 families of landless peasants from the Movimento Sem Terra blockade the highway near the town of El Dorado dos Carajas in the state of Paraná, Brazil, demanding land reform and defying the authorities insistence that the occupation of a wealthy landowners' farm nearby end. Military police, their ID tags removed, open fire on the demonstrators. Nineteen dead men are left beside the highway, though survivors talk of an open grave containing women and children hidden nearby. 69 are wounded. The MST are still seeking justice. In memory of this day April 17 is henceforth declared International Peasants' Day.

>> Continues page 123 >>

STR/Reuters

Unionists, unemployed workers, and landless peasants march on the capital from four corners of the country. Brasilia, Brazil

Global Day of Action

Party and Protest against 'Free Trade' and the WTO

May 1998

"Riots are not just taking place on the streets of Jakarta but also here in Geneva. Alienation has reached the streets of the North too."
– Martin Khor of Third World Network, May 1998

The first global day of action is called by groups involved in Peoples' Global Action's inaugural meeting and takes place in May 1998 to coincide with both the G8 meeting of the world's eight most powerful leaders in Birmingham, Britain, and the WTO's Second Ministerial meeting in Geneva, where global, corporate-friendly trade rules are being determined. More than 70 cities take part in the first globally co-ordinated action against these multilateral institutions by grassroots groups demanding their abolition rather than reform.

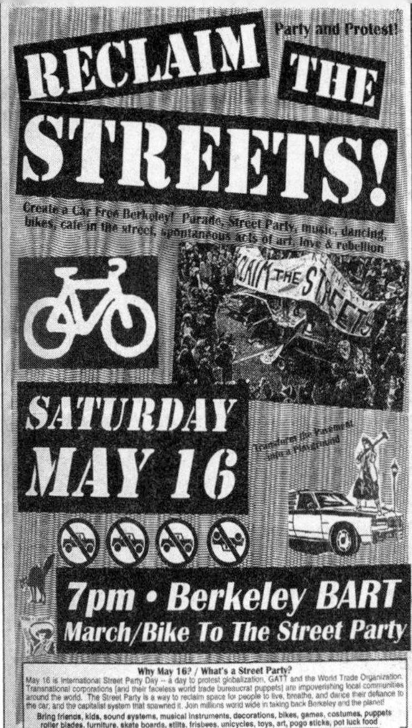

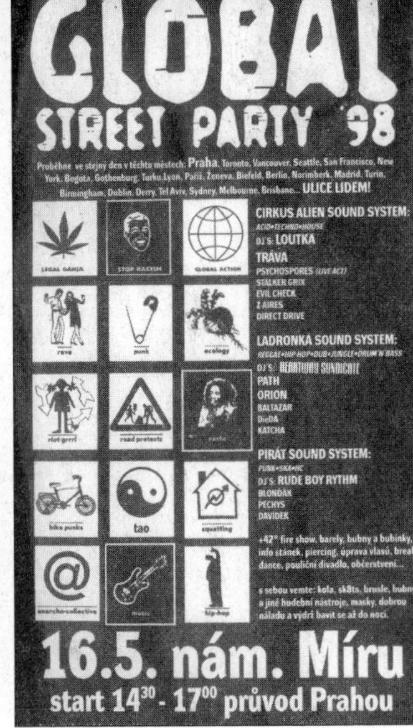

On 2 May, hundreds of thousands of peasants, farmers, tribal people, and workers from all regions of India take to the streets of Hyderabad against a backdrop of a wave of peasant suicides, calling for a rejection of neoliberal policies and demanding the immediate withdrawal of India from the WTO. Two weeks later in the Philippines, 10,000 fisherfolk march in Manila, calling for the cancellation of treaties signed with the WTO and APEC, "in order to reorient our food production and market to feed the Filipino people and not aristocrats abroad". In Nepal, a forum and publication against globalization is born out of workshops attended by farmers, teachers, and tea plantation workers.

On 16 May, the first global street party takes place, called by London Reclaim the Streets, under the slogan "our resistance will be as transnational as capital." Over 30 street parties happen around the world, spreading carnival and rebellion from Helsinki to Sydney, Berkeley to Toronto, Ljubljana to Ghent, Lyon to Berlin. In Prague, the biggest single mobilization since the Velvet Revolution in 1989 brings over 3,000 mostly young people out for a mobile street party, which is attacked by police, and

Nick Cobbing

Clowning around against the G8, Global Street Party. Birmingham, UK

Thomas Schlijper

Cars give way to people, Global Street Party. Utrecht, Netherlands

JOINT ACTION FORUM OF INDIAN PEOPLE
AGAINST WTO AND ANTI-PEOPLE POLICIES
29,30 APRIL AND MAY DAY 1998
HYDERABAD.
Fight against
Imperialist Exploitation

KRRS archive

India's peoples' movements converge against the WTO. Hyderabad, India

ends with an assault on several McDonald's and other transnational stores. The following days' media saturation brings issues of globalization to the forefront of public discussion for the first time since the Czech Republic accepted capitalism in 1989. Meanwhile, people in a tiny midwestern town in the US decide to block the highway with a picnic table. No-one comes past to disturb their picnic the entire day, except a single truck, which they turn back.

In Birmingham, UK where the G8 is meeting, 75,000 Jubilee 2000 anti-debt campaigners make a human chain around the summit, and a Reclaim the Streets party blocks the town centre with 6,000 people, many dressed as clowns. The eight world leaders choose to flee the city to a local manor in order to continue their meeting in a more tranquil location.

In Geneva, which is preparing for the following week's WTO ministerial and celebration of the fiftieth anniversary of the General Agreement on Tariffs and Trade (GATT – the forerunner of the WTO), the media publish scare stories of anticipated riots, and protesters are turned back from the borders. However, over 10,000 march to the WTO headquarters, a few banks have their windows smashed, the WTO

Interfoto

Protesters respond to the presence of the WTO Director-General's Mercedes in their midst. Geneva, Switzerland

Director-General's Mercedes is turned over, and three days of the heaviest rioting ever seen in the city follows. The security surrounding the summit on the final day is so robust that many delegates miss their flights home. It was not the last time that a city hosting the WTO ministerial was to be filled with billowing clouds of tear gas …

Four days later, Brazil's 50,000 landless peasants, unemployed workers, and trade unionists who had been marching from the four cardinal points of the country, converge on the capital, Brasilia. During the week as they approach the city they redistribute food from supermarkets to feed the poor.

The global scale and co-ordination of the protests goes unnoticed to most observers but China's English-language paper, *The China Daily*, says of the protest in Geneva: "It was planned as a grand birthday celebration to mark the fiftieth year of the free trade system. But the second ministerial conference of the WTO will instead be remembered as a turning point in the rush towards globalization."

Autonomy creating spaces for freedom

"How many peoples in the worlds that make up the world can say as we do, that they are doing what they want to? We think there are many, that the worlds of the world are filled with crazy and foolish people each planting their trees for each of their tomorrows, and that the day will come when this mountainside of the universe that some people call Planet Earth will be filled with trees of all colours, and there will be so many birds and comforts.... Yes, it is likely no one will remember the first ones, because all the yesterdays which vex us today will be no more than an old page in the old book of the old history." **– Subcomandante Insurgente Marcos, *Our Word is Our Weapon*, Seven Stories Press, 2001**

Autonomy is our means and our end. It is both the act of planting our 'tree of tomorrow', and that tomorrow of many different hues: rich, diverse, complex and colourful. Autonomy is freedom and connectedness, necessarily collective and powerfully intuitive, an irrepressible desire that stalls every attempt to crush the will to freedom. As the politics of escape attempts from capitalism in the North and the experience of liberated realities in the South, it is a global theme. The movements against capitalism have once again brought it to the fore, vibrant, alive and urgently needed.

Sebastião Salgado / Amazonas Images

In the middle of the nineteenth century, a simple question was asked of a utopian community in England, and it is just as relevant today as it was then: "How do you get to a place where people live in harmony, and manage without money – by railway or rainbow?" By dreaming or doing? There are many answers and plenty of examples, some of which arise in this chapter, some of which are woven through the book, and some of which you have seen, thought of, imagined or fantasized about.

We call these experiments in autonomy, though others might prefer freedom, liberation, or self-organization. The appeal of autonomy spans the entire political spectrum. Originally coming from the Greek and meaning 'self' plus 'law', it is at the core of the liberal democratic theory of justice and values such as freedom of speech and movement. Understood radically, however, it has been the terrain upon which revolutionary social movements have encountered each other throughout Europe; 'autonomy at the base', from the grassroots, is the core organizational principle of the influential social movement known as *Autonomia* in Italy. Globally it has been a refrain of countless uprisings, struggles, rebellions, and resistance movements from the Zapatistas in Chiapas to the *Organisasi Papua Merdeka* (the Free Papua Movement) in West Papua, a colony of Indonesia. From the Cauca people of Colombia to the communities of Kerala in southwestern India and on to the *asamblistas* and *piqueteros* of the Argentinean uprisings, people worldwide are developing political and social forms rooted in differing concepts of autonomy.

What is the appeal of autonomy today? We seem to have reached the point where trust in representative democracy has run out. The consistent betrayal by those who promise everything and deliver nothing has led many of us into apathy and cynicism. More profoundly some have begun to question the idea that our involvement in decision-making should be limited to a simple vote every few years. Participation, deliberation, consensus, and direct democracy are emerging from the margins and, in many instances, are being reaffirmed as the centre of gravity for communities the world over.

Autonomy appropriated

"The public be damned! I work for my stockholders."
– William H. Vanderbilt, 1879

"Break the rules. Stand apart. Keep your head. Go with your heart." **– TV commercial for Vanderbilt perfume, 1994**

Our desire to influence the decisions that affect our everyday lives, however, has a powerful enemy disguised to seduce and lull into sleep that very desire. The culture of capitalism portrays autonomy as a key mechanism of the 'free' market. For us to be free, the mythology goes, we must exercise our autonomy as consumers in the marketplace, where our bank balance determines our level of participation – in other words, we are free as consumers, where one dollar equals one vote.

By this same logic, the World Trade Organization, the International Monetary Fund, and the World Bank become advocates of 'freedom'. Freedom, that is, from 'unnecessary regulation' and 'barriers to trade' (such as environmental standards, trade union rights, corporate taxation, bans on child labour) – the freedom of money to flow around the globe at will. In such a 'free' world, food, water, shelter, education, and healthcare are all trackable commodities. Insisting on them as basic rights rather than something to be bought, however, is a barrier to trade. But those basic rights provide the security that is at the root of a positive understanding of freedom as a freedom to do or to be.

For in order to be truly free – to create, co-operate, produce, dream, and to realize one's own autonomy through the respect and recognition of the autonomy of others – requires the freedom to be in the world and to have a network of care and support. The corruption of autonomy by 'free' marketers is at the heart of the capitalist project – to capture the idea of freedom and sell it back to us. From 'self' plus 'law', they have fashioned the idea that individuals are actually a 'law unto themselves'. The market is presented as the logical development of our self-interest as well as the mechanism for its fulfilment.

We refute this notion of autonomy. It is not the tree of tomorrow that our movements are planting today. Our understanding of autonomy includes community owned and run healthcare, education, and social support; direct democracy in zones liberated by the people who live in them – not as enclaves or places to withdraw to – but as outward looking and connected communities of affinity, engaged in mutual co-operation, collective learning, and unmediated interaction. This is the reason for our impassioned defence of the mechanisms and support structures that have been fought for and won, the hard toil of movements who have struggled for hundreds of years – indigenous, revolutionary, and democratic.

Autonomy and capitalism

Autonomy is always in process. But autonomy is often mistaken for individual independence which most of us understand as growing up, leaving home, finding work, earning money, making our own decisions: where to live, what to eat, what to wear, buy, and so on. But even where these decisions can be made (and in most of the world this fiction of independence is impossible), these choices are, in reality, entirely dependent upon the actions of others. That is, dependent upon the labour, transport, distribution, and exchange involved in the production of the food, clothes, house and so forth from which we gain our experience of 'independence'. Our lives are manufactured for us, instead of being the outcome of our choices and desires. Not only are we produced by this system, we in turn reproduce it by acting within its established parameters and boundaries and as long as we remain within these boundaries, we are perfectly 'free' to go about life according to the paths offered to us by governments and corporations. In short, we are free to choose anything, as long as it doesn't defy the logic of capitalism. When we defy that logic, we soon discover the true limits of our 'freedom'.

The relationship between those with power and those under their command lies at the foundation of capitalism. Our capacity to create and to produce is separated from that which is produced – the 'product', so instead of deciding together the best ways we can meet our own needs, while respecting the needs of others and the planet, our energies are appropriated to produce for the profit of others. Consequently, we are alienated from the very fruits of our work and work itself becomes something tedious, imposed, and suffered, rather than something imagined, anticipated, and creatively experienced. The creation of value and its concentration in things, or products, is then confirmed through their exchange in a market. This value invested in things means they quickly come to own us, rather than us owning them.

Of course, most of us are not slaves. We can refuse, walk away, desert, quit, but where should we go and what should we do? This is the question and the challenge at the core of our consideration of autonomy. Refusal is only a real weapon if it is collective, with the combined creativity and strength that implies. Autonomy can never be about simple individualism, as we have been encouraged to believe. Autonomy is not about 'consumer choice', whether wearing brands or boycotting them, choosing to drive an SUV or a biodiesel bus. No amount of 'ethical consumerism', self-help, no amount of therapy, no retreat inside ourselves will allow us to make the jump. Autonomy is necessarily collective.

You are not alone

Of course, this is a simple way of describing a very complicated set of processes and the world is far too complex for easy explanations to hold up for very long. The means of producing, the nature of production, and what we might think of as products are all changing and have all changed. However, evidence that this powerful logic surrounds us and penetrates the everyday can be found in every sphere of life: from the marketization of basic needs such as water, to the patenting of gene types; from the opening of markets in healthcare, social services, and education, to the assertion of intellectual property rights; from the simulation of dissent to sell cultural experiences in everything from fashion to cinema and art, to the erosion of any distinction between the simulated and the real in popular culture – all are tainted by the logic of capital and the elevation of the commodity above all else. Under these circumstances it is no wonder that many of us respond with a sense of incredulity at the pace and complexity of life, a sense of helplessness, a feeling of being overwhelmed, and a general state of apathy in response to the wilful appropriation of creativity and energy for which we are offered in exchange the most meaningless level of participation – produce, consume, die.

"WE'VE BEEN LIVING AUTONOMY, BUT WE'VE ONLY JUST DISCOVERED THERE'S A WORD FOR IT. WE COULDN'T FIND ANYTHING OUT THERE THAT ANSWERED OUR NEED FOR CHANGE SO WE CREATE THIS AS WE GO ALONG. THERE'S LOTS OF CONTRADICTIONS IN IT. IT'S NOT A THEORY BUT A PRACTICE IN DEVELOPMENT."

- Raúl Gatica, indigenous community activist from Oaxaca, Mexico

But once we act purposefully despite these constraints, we embark on a journey – a process of becoming which leads simultaneously towards freedom and connectedness, towards autonomy. We realize it through our connections to others, through interaction, negotiation, and communication. To be autonomous is not to be alone or to act in any way one chooses – a law unto oneself – but to act with regard for others, to feel responsibility for others. This is the crux of autonomy, an ethic of responsibility and reciprocity that comes through recognition that others both desire and are capable of autonomy too

So when we talk about autonomy, we are not talking about or advocating a few journeys of independence;

much less a withdrawal from the world into a kind of retreat. Something else entirely is happening, something rooted in this concept of autonomy as freedom and connectedness. A dynamic geometry of social struggle is emerging, fractal-like, where local autonomy is repeated and magnified within networks that overflow geographical, cultural, and political borders. On the horizon is an exodus – thousands of escape attempts, a mass breakout that is taking place globally. People are passing around the keys, exchanging tunnelling techniques, tearing down the fences, climbing the walls... learning to fly.

What follows are a few of the branches of the complex tree of tomorrow that is autonomy. Through these stories, we hope to move beyond the idea that autonomy is 'just' about deciding things with others of like mind in 'ideal' communities that are often very different from those we usually experience in the everyday. Like stars on the horizon, some of these examples have burned themselves into our collective consciousness, while others are now faded distress signals echoing across other realities, re-visioned, transformed, and partially renewed in forms that may not even be recognizable to their founders and catalysts. None are perfect, and none are offered as 'blueprints'. All have in common an experimental quality, openness to possibility and contingency, and an intoxicating blend of creativity and courage which resonates across ideological barriers and national borders.

Italy – autonomy at the base

"Political autonomy is the desire to allow differences to deepen at the base without trying to synthesize them from above, to stress similar attitudes without imposing a 'general line', to allow parts to co-exist side by side in their singularity."

– Sylvere Lotringer & Christian Marazzi, "The Return of Politics" in *Italy: Autonomia, Post-Political Writings*, Semiotext(e), 1980

"Autonomy at the base" was the core principle of *Potere Operaio* (Worker's Power) the influential group and magazine that was at the heart of social unrest in Italy during the late 1960s and early 1970s, dissolving itself in 1973 to become part of a broader movement known as *Autonomia (Autonomia Operaio)*. *Autonomia* as a movement never unified; as a series of fluid organizations and shifting alliances, it refused to separate economics from politics and politics from everyday existence. This approach led ultimately to the idea of refusing waged labour and to the extension of struggle from the factory (occupations, sabotage and strikes were commonplace) to the city (20,000 buildings were squatted between 1969 and 1975) and on in to the lives of what was termed the 'socialized worker'. The state finally crushed *Autonomia* as an active political force beginning with the 7 April 1979 arrests. Over 1,500 intellectuals and militants were imprisoned within a year.

But how does this relate to us today? In many ways, Italy remains something of a political and cultural experiment in the possibilities and potentials of autonomous forms and processes, currently embodied in the *Disobbedienti* (Disobedients), the network of social centres and autonomous groupings that has grown in the wake of the G8 protests in Genoa, 2001. The *Disobbedienti* emerged from the *Tute Bianche*, a movement tool and strategy of confrontation that became renowned during the Prague protests against the World Bank and IMF for wearing white overalls (or coveralls) and deploying body armour made of foam padding and bubble wrap to ward off police batons. Their white overalls are an ironic celebration of the Mayor of Milan's comments on the eviction of a social centre in 1994, a popular community space in which cultural events, free meals, and political discussion brought workers, immigrants, students, and neighbours together. The mayor remarked, "From now on, squatters will be nothing more than ghosts wandering about in the city!"

These 'white ghosts' sought a visibility from which to celebrate the margins, experiment with both local democracy and terrains on which diverse social groups can encounter each other. Tute Bianche's use of the body as barricade and bludgeon during actions epitomizes the need for presence, the desire to be an obstacle; it also dramatizes the futility of endless debate about violence and nonviolence. Putting bodies on the front line in this manner allows for confrontation while calling for restraint, for resistance to the temptation of resorting to further violence, engaging in a battle with the state on its own terms. It clearly opposes the needless descent into civil war:

> "*...we do not have to turn this space of revolt into a war zone. We have to think of the conflict in a different way. We call it 'disobedience', conflict and consensus, an action always open to experimentation, open to transformation and rethinking the movement. We could have gone to Genoa carrying molotovs and we decided not to, because it does not work against the bullets and the Carabinieri's trucks that chase demonstrators. We also had to confront the police force. We built barricades after they shot at us. But we are always holding ourselves back in order not to be dragged into a civil war. That is what power wants: for the conflict to become a war.*"
>
> **– Luca Caserini, a spokesperson for the *Disobbedienti*, interviewed by Ezequiel Marcos Siddig in *Z Magazine***

The deepest desire of the state in such circumstances is for an escalation through violence that leads to the prison cell and grave. The Italian legacy of armed struggle, which ended with hundreds in prison in the 1970s, was instrumental in teaching the *Disobbedienti* this lesson. Refusal to engage in a confrontation whose rules are established by the state is a pre-requisite of autonomous action; the stakes are incredibly high as the experience of a generation of Italian activists indicates.

The danger of celebrating confrontation whether (as the Seattle slogan suggested) "we are winning" or not, is that our aspirations and tactics are once more reduced to a simple binary opposition. In reality, who 'we' are is never clear, what winning means is always difficult to ascertain, and those who would rather 'we' didn't win often take a far longer or broader perspective. As the *Disobbedienti* argue, strategy is crucially important, as is communication, adaptability, knowledge, and willingness to listen and change. Where confrontation is necessary – and it is always likely to be necessary – an autonomous strategy requires us to be free both from the constraints of rules established by the powerful and from our own expectations that resistance requires us to always meet force with force. True autonomy means new and variable tactics, learning patience in order to flow around and above obstacles, learning to retreat, disperse, and then re-group to swarm and surround. It requires us to educate and communicate, and to be grounded in and to nurture support within constituencies beyond narrow communities of activism. All of this is essential to the practice of radical social change and all of it is essential to the idea of autonomy as freedom and connectedness.

Wild autonomy: local inspirations and global visions

A journey off the beaten track that highlights fascinating examples of autonomous initiatives could take us anywhere in the world – for they are numerous, and often include people, organizations, or activities that we might not suspect of being subversive to the status quo. Think, for example, of those forms of mutual aid that provide the webs of support on which huge numbers of people already rely: community education and health care, food and housing co-ops, social centres and info-shops, shared transport initiatives, independent media, art, and publishing projects, and many other local and often unsung alternatives. All form a self-organized matrix dedicated to the construction of alternative social relationships. These are the support structures for our collective escape attempts.

Some of the most interesting are coordinating through networks of communication and information exchange. Some are shaped by specific issues, or are clustered around social divisions such as race, class, gender, disability, sexuality, or age. Others are unique because of particular cultural traditions or sensibilities, or because of geographical location, or perhaps their courage in the face of overwhelming opposition. And for some autonomy is a whole way of being, living in communities that are liberated, directly democratic, and self-organizing, communities of struggle where the politics of autonomy have been realized in the social practices and day-to-day existence of alternative realities.

Autonomous communities

The Kuna people live on a series of 50 tiny islands in an archipelago of 360 known as Comarca Kuna Yala, situated in the Pacific Ocean and straddling the Colombia-Panama border. They gained autonomy after a bloody struggle with colonial police in 1925. Today 70,000 Kuna manage their day-to-day affairs through an elaborate system of direct democracy that federates 500 different autonomous communities within the Kuna General Congress, which meets once every six months. Each community and each inhabited island has their own internal rules and regulations, and is completely autonomous from the others; the only obligation is to send four delegates to the congress in order to enable coordination and to facilitate decisions on issues that relate to all Kuna. As Ibe, a Kuna activist points out in an interview: "If the government (ie: the Panamanian Government) wants to carry out any kind of project within the region it has to consult the congress. It has to be subordinate to the Congress, and the Congress has to make the decision – it has the last word."

Their autonomy is not a matter of mere theory, or of the formal but tokenistic recognition of indigenous rights. When the Panamanian Government granted a Canadian mining company license to explore and exploit Kuna territory that permission was revoked by the Kuna. Equally, the Government was refused permission to install a naval base in Kuna territory. And the Kuna are neither localist or naive: they have independently negotiated rights to their territorial waters for the purposes of laying trans-Atlantic fibre optic cable for improved web links between South America and Europe. They are also active with local and regional groups within Peoples' Global Action in resistance against Plan Colombia – a joint project between the Colombian, US, and EU governments which has heavily militarized the region. As Ibe puts it: "Our organization wishes to struggle and to fight together, as fighting is necessary, without distinguishing between different ideologies, colours or nationalities.

The practical effects of globalization for PGA affect all oppressed people, and not only the Kuna or the indigenous people are oppressed: blacks, peasants, unions and syndicates are also oppressed. But we should act with respect for diversity of culture, diversity of opinions, and the diversity of all the people who live on the planet."

"IT IS NO ACCIDENT THAT MOST OF THE REMAINING NATURAL RESOURCES ARE ON INDIGENOUS LAND. FIRST THE WHITE WORLD DESTROYS THEIR OWN ENVIRONMENT, THEN THEY COME ASKING FOR THE LAST PIECES OF LAND THEY HAVE PUT US ON, THE EARTH WE HAVE PROTECTED." **– Luis Macas, spokesperson for indigenous Ecuadoran organization, CONAIE**

Now we are awake

Of course, the most globally influential of recent experiments in autonomous organization is the Zapatista communities in Chiapas, Mexico. The Zapatistas' emphasis upon direct democracy – so familiar to the indigenous peoples of Chiapas – combined with the collective project of the EZLN has allowed them to advance local affairs and settle differences for themselves, without the imposition of general rules or norms of behaviour.

Networks such as the Zapatista-inspired National

Indigenous Congress show that far from a retreat to localism, the organizational dynamic of the EZLN has always been towards regional, national, and international collaboration. Autonomy as practiced by the Zapatistas is about inclusion and connection, about projects and actions that form a whole, over and above the capacity of any group or individual to determine or impose a particular direction or outcome.

Zapatismo is therefore the emergent philosophy of a constellation of essentially autonomous projects. From the indigenous women's initiative which specified a series of women's rights contrary to the patriarchal culture that surrounded them, to the autonomous Zapatista National Liberation Front (the unarmed civil society branch of the Zapatistas), to the national and international gatherings known as *encuentros* that subsequently led to the founding of Peoples' Global Action and had a significant influence on the development of the world and regional Social Forum movement.

All these examples of autonomy challenge the basic tenets of state power and the continuance of government in anything like its present form. In a similar way to the Kuna, the Zapatista revolution in thinking and practice did not taken place in a vacuum, but is rooted in an analysis of the national and international context within which they find themselves. Consequently, while negotiating for indigenous autonomy and civil rights during peace talks in San Andrés Sakamchíén, the Zapatistas were simultaneously pushing for profound constitutional reforms that would have in effect begun the process of dismantling the existent power structure of Mexican society. This was only realized by the government after their representatives and negotiators had reached the final stage of the peace accords – and it is a major reason why the Mexican Government failed to implement those accords.

The Zapatistas also bypassed the state through the organization of a *consulta*: a programme of popular education involving 5,000 Zapatistas travelling the length and breadth of Mexico followed by a plebiscite on the San Andrés peace agreement. As a result, over three million Mexicans voted for its ratification. "You came and found us sleeping, but now we are awake," said one old man from Morelos who took part. Participation, deliberation, transparency, and democracy are at the forefront, essential to the transformative power of autonomy.

Examples such as these are found globally, and everywhere the refrain is the same. In Indonesia, a system of regional autonomy introduced in 1999 as a means of responding to global market pressures for productive flexibility has instead led to incredible innovation amongst civil society, as well as a qualitatively different way of doing politics in some areas. In the Mentawai Islands, the ideal of replacing government with a *lagai*, a consultative and deliberative body is gaining momentum as, they suggest: "the functioning of mainstream politics contradicts the ideals of dialogue in pursuit of a generally acceptable *lagai*-based consensus".

In the village of Mendha in the Gadchiroli district of Maharashtra State, in India the slogan is "*Mawa mate, mawa Raj*," (in our village we are the government). This autonomy began with their opposition to the incursions into their forests by Ballarpur Paper Mills, which they subsequently defeated. In defiance of central government, they developed a system of forest and watershed management, as well as new methods of honey production realized through their system of participatory democracy and self-organization. Up to 1,500 such villages across rural India have been recorded taking similar steps. In these villages, government officials fear to tread.

The everyday reality of autonomy then, is one which is rich, diverse, and complex and once embedded is difficult to root out, for like Mendha's honey, the taste of freedom and the inspiration of connectedness are unforgettably sweet. In many communities of struggle, autonomy is the beating heart of defiance, simultaneously echoing the rhythms of the everyday, which are also the rhythms of resistance.

Networking: new social spaces and old social realities

There are many examples of communities that have been able to make the leap, albeit precariously, towards a form of autonomy that is rooted, indeed is given meaning, through everyday existence in liberated zones where ideas and practices are one. Elsewhere, autonomy is more fragmented and incomplete. It can be the experience of working in an affinity group and making consensus decisions based upon trust and respect, or the kick of growing your own food, organizing a co-operative, or joining a group of people agitating for community control of vital services.

"BECAUSE OUR HISTORICAL VISION HAS BECOME SO USED TO ORDERLY BATTALIONS, COLOURFUL BANNERS, AND SCRIPTED PROCLAMATIONS OF SOCIAL CHANGE, WE ARE AT A LOSS WHEN CONFRONTED WITH THE SUBTLE PERVASIVENESS OF INCREMENTAL CHANGES OF SYMBOLS PROCESSED THROUGH MULTIFORM NETWORKS, AWAY FROM THE HALLS OF POWER. IT IS IN THESE BACK ALLEYS OF SOCIETY, WHETHER IN ALTERNATIVE ELECTRONIC NETWORKS OR IN GRASSROOTED NETWORKS OF COMMUNAL RESISTANCE, THAT I HAVE SENSED THE EMBRYOS OF A NEW SOCIETY, LABOURED IN THE FIELDS OF HISTORY BY THE POWER OF IDENTITY."

– Manuel Castells, "The Rise of the Network Society" *The Information Age: economy, society and culture*, Volume 1, 1996

It is educating your child, occupying a building, refusing a job, working for satisfaction rather than money, and achieving everything. These escape attempts, though small and often unseen, coalesce in cycles, and sometimes they grow and spread exponentially. Previously they were easily co-opted, their threat neutralized, because they were isolated attempts – from brief transgressions to large mobilizations, they often signified singularity rather than solidarity.

In contrast, the movement of movements against capitalism is composed of groups, (dis)organizations, networks, and constellations of networks that are linked to each other through struggle. There is nothing new in this except that most of those active within these movements are now vibrantly aware of these links – the strategies, forms of action, modes of decision-making, and of course, the common enemies. Previously, episodes of resistance such as the rise of Zapatismo would have been a footnote in the history of indigenous rebellions, a brief flare on the horizon; now they are the digital archive of a global revolutionary consciousness, a whole vista set alight. These links are fostered by communication technologies, travel, and gatherings where people can meet, interact, learn, teach, and struggle together. These spaces have been and continue to be crucial to the vitality and the continued expansion of this global cycle of resistance.

Keeping these spaces open is essential, as is retaining a balance between the need and desire of groups to operate independently – autonomously. We also need a level of coordination to increase communication flows between ourselves, and to ensure that participation at regional and global levels is participatory and democratic. Network forms of organization, such as Peoples' Global Action have been crucial to the development of global resistance and the coordination of autonomous projects within a broader framework which itself seeks to be autonomous.

Other spaces of coordination reflect the emphasis on popular processes of deliberation, discussion, and education that are such a feature of the liberated zones of the Kuna, the Zapatistas, and others. In 2000 in Spain, for example, activists facilitated a social *consulta* on the question of abolishing external debt. Over 10,000 people got involved in 500 neighbourhood assemblies, and ultimately over one million people voted by 97.5 per cent to abolish the external debt. This process was subsequently made unlawful by the state judicial authorities. Fourteen countries across Latin America have conducted social *consultas* on the Free Trade Area of the Americas – in Brazil ten million voted against it in a civil society referendum in September 2002. A European social *consulta*, is now being organized, seeking popular involvement catalyzed by autonomous promoter groups working in their own localities.

In Los Angeles, the Bus Riders' Union is a trilingual organization composed of the urban poor who are dependent upon public transport for work, education, and leisure. Militant and carnivalesque strategies of confrontation, including non-payment of fares, theatre skits, and onboard teach-ins through bus-based educators and organizers has forced the Metropolitan Transit Authority and the courts to recognize them as the voice of an incredibly diverse coalition. Race, class, gender, disability, and the environment have been highlighted in a vibrant and massively effective campaign that has helped keep fares low, led to the replacement of older diesel buses with newer compressed gas models, and ultimately increased passenger numbers as confidence grows amongst the black and ethnic minority, female, and poor communities that are so in need of decent public transport. Organized independently of political parties and operating with a high degree of autonomy and internal democracy, this organization has resonated with others across North America, and new Bus Riders' Unions have sprung up in many large cities.

In Canada, the Ontario Coalition Against Poverty (OCAP) is another example of autonomous organizing based upon alliances forged across social divisions. OCAP was founded in 1990 and intervenes using instrumental direct action aimed at obstructing the application of neoliberal policies employed by the state or national government. This involves "direct action case-work", focusing on issues and events which are directly relevant to the quality of everyday life experienced by oppressed communities. The casework involves a process that requires active resistance at the point where it can make a difference – not symbolic protest, or advocacy, but

"THE MONEY KING IS ONLY AN ILLUSION.
CAPITALISM IS BLIND AND BARBARIC. IT POISONS THE WATER AND THE AIR. IT DESTROYS EVERYTHING.
AND TO THE U'WA, IT SAYS THAT WE ARE CRAZY, BUT WE WANT TO CONTINUE BEING CRAZY IF IT MEANS WE CAN CONTINUE TO EXIST ON OUR DEAR MOTHER EARTH."

– The U'wa people in Colombia, after oil corporation Oxy was forced to withdraw from their land in 2002

building communities of struggle and respecting the autonomy of those communities to self organize.

OCAP has had success working against homelessness, poverty, police harassment, privatization, deportations, and corporate power. As an avowedly anticapitalist organization not allied to any political party, they have attracted members from different ethnic and class backgrounds, and have shown clearly that to organize in a way which can make a difference often means being prepared to fight. As OCAP organizer Jeff Shantz says, "as long as movements remain trapped in methods of limited protest, governments and profit-seeking regimes will continue to escalate their attacks on poor people, people of colour, and the Earth."

It is easy to call for a fight and easier still to lose one, but it is very difficult to sustain a serious defence against the ever-more regressive and brutal tactics of the state. However, OCAP's autonomy and vitality has enabled them to mount such opposition. For their strength lies in the roots of their organization – rather than being content to mirror the liberal call to "tolerate diversity", they practice an actual unity in diversity, and this means they draw upon a wider constituency than many similar activist organizations.

As Thomas Walkom wrote in the Toronto Star, OCAP is: "An eclectic band that includes not only poor people, but students, retirees and the odd university professor, OCAP doesn't play by the usual rules. It is direct, in your face and occasionally rude. Where other protest groups try to make their points by holding demonstrations in authorized public spaces such as Nathan Phillips Square, OCAP tends to take the fight right to where its enemies live."

In OCAP, we have an example of how 'new' strategies of direct action have reinvigorated campaigns around perennial social realities of poverty and inequality. Similarly, in the new networked spaces of PGA and the myriad processes of consultation, we have a model for how everyday social realities might come to inform each other while retaining the autonomy each prizes so highly.

The tree of tomorrow

The nature of autonomy is necessarily different in different locations; both political philosophy and grounded practice, an aim of self-organization and the outcome of participatory democracy. We have sketched out the bare bones of what this might mean: liberated zones, networked social spaces for organizations, coordinating across geographic and cultural barriers, and the tough resolve required to organize autonomously in the shadow of the state, across difference and division. Yet, it will always be difficult to do justice to autonomy. For as theory and practice it is the life-blood of the movements against capitalism: as freedom and connectedness, as unity in diversity, as recognition of the other.

The politics of autonomy encourage us to push for and take, to refuse, to be prepared to fight, and to escape, exit. For to exit is also to take, to take ourselves out of the context within which we are ensnared, to choose differently, to re-invent our circumstances, and to decide what it is we should, or need, to do. Autonomy is a key demand of a complex movement, a tree of tomorrow whose deep roots were planted in yesterday and today, and are spreading everywhere.

Notes from Nowhere

Homeless families living in squatted building. Porto Alegre, Brazil

Squatting Spaces

In the broadest sense, to squat means to occupy a space that is poorly utilized, or not used at all, and transform it. Squatting is an ancient practice, ongoing since there have been empty buildings or unused land. Wherever you find inadequate housing, a lack of meaningful public space, or landless people in rural areas, you will also find squatters.

Long perceived as dirty low-lifes who just want a free ride, squatters have developed a world-wide social movement, challenging capitalist notions of property while providing an impetus for self-determination, independence, experimentation, and creativity.

One of the earliest documented groups of squatters were the Diggers, in England. Declaring that "the earth is a common treasury for all", they took over unused land in 1649 to farm it communally. They hoped that their ideas and practice would spread, and that property owners would surrender their estates and join their communal living project. Although they were eventually evicted, their vision lingers on.

Modern examples of squatting are found in Brazil, where landless peasants have reappropriated millions of acres of unused farmland, in Manhattan, where a diverse mix of young punks, immigrants, and the local homeless occupy tenement buildings; and in Italy, where there is a vast network of squatted social centres – community hubs for activism, art, youth, and free living space.

Andrew Stern

Squatting exists everywhere, not only in the places where it has developed into a social movement. Squatters become masters at living in the in-between spaces, the cracks in the system – sometimes living furtively, blankets covering the windows so no light spills out, other times decorating with bright murals and colourful banners, proudly proclaiming a liberated space for all. Anyone, from anywhere, can squat. It just takes a few determined people who yearn for free space to play with, or live in – or both!

How to squat:

1) Form an affinity group
It's no fun to squat alone, and can be downright dangerous.

2) Name your desires
Do you want living space? A social centre or community space? Something temporary, for a publicity stunt or a party? A convergence centre for an action? A secret hideout for you and your friends? Clear goals from the beginning can help you select an appropriate site. Preparedness and planning are key, before you actually break any locks.

3) Learn local laws
Do some research on your area and, if possible, talk to local squatters. Legal issues and local tolerance are different everywhere; it's best to know what you're up against, and what will work to your advantage. For example, in the UK, once you're in and change the locks, it becomes a civil matter and the police can't remove you from the premises without taking you to court. However in most US cities, the cops are more likely to kick your head in, so different tactics are necessary.

4) Select your site
Explore a few different places. Ensure that the site is unoccupied, and carefully assess the best way of gaining entry. From this you can determine what tools you'll need. Bolt cutters for locks are great, yet unwieldy; crowbars are essential. Try to do as little damage as possible while cracking (opening) the place; if you're successful, it will be your home, and you'll have to fix whatever you break!

5) Fix 'er up
Once you've changed the locks and secured the place, the real work begins. If possible reconnect the electricity and water (if you don't know how, get help). Then, redecorate! Feel free to knock out walls, paint murals on the ceiling, and move the bathtub into the living room if you want. The space is yours.

Another crucial thing to consider is your profile in the neighbourhood. Sometimes survival depends on total secrecy, other times, on community support. If you decide to meet your neighbours, be friendly and open about your intent. People might be stand-offish initially, but may warm up once they realize that you aren't running a crack house. However, they may be opposed to your presence and make you pack up and try a different place. Squatting requires experimentation and perseverance; its lifeblood is the commitment to reclaiming space, and the rebel pioneer spirit which fuels us to take control of our lives in yet another way.

Resources:
» International internet magazine focusing on squatted houses and other free spaces: www.squat.net
» Information from the Advisory Service for Squatters (ASS) who have run a daily advice service for squatters and homeless people in the UK since 1975: www.squat.freeserve.co.uk

In Brazil one per cent of farmers own over half of the land. Almost two-thirds of these vast latifundios remain idle while millions go hungry in the favelas (city slums) and tenant farmers pay crippling rents. Enter the Movimento dos Trabalhadores Rurais Sem Terra (MST) – the Landless Rural Workers Movement of Brazil – which has been carrying out its own 'land-reform from below' for the last 20 years. It identifies these latifundios and occupies them. Under MST occupation, large houses belonging to the landowners can play host to dozens of poor families, who cultivate the land, and gradually turn the encampments into settlements replete with co-operative stores, decent housing, and MST schools. The MST is the largest and most successful social movement in Latin America with one million members and has won 81,081 square miles of land. But it has paid a high price – hundreds of its members have been assassinated.

Today it is evolving from a more centralized, traditional leftist movement as the younger generation grow up on the settlements, into one that is making the move towards green and sustainable farming, and improved internal democracy. MSTs in Bolivia and elsewhere have sprouted, as has a Movimento dos Sem Teto – movement for those without roofs – comprised of homeless people squatting buildings in Brazil's cities.

Brazilian agriculture is where feudalism meets capitalism, and the MST fight both. Globalization is land reform in reverse as big farmers take over, expanding vast corporate monocultures, and forcing small farmers to compete with the forces of giant agribusiness on international markets. On the global battlefront, the MST is a member of Via Campesina, the international peasant farmers' union which includes the Karnataka State Farmers' Association of India, the Confédération Paysanne of France, and the Assembly of the Poor of Thailand. Together, they have been fighting global agribusiness and marching on WTO meetings from 1994 onwards.

Cutting the Wire: the landless movement of Brazil

by Sue Branford and Jan Rocha

"When the pliers cut the wire and it snaps like the string in a violin and the fence tumbles down, the landless lose their innocence."
– Pedro Tierra, MST poet.

For the MST the act of occupying land – which they call 'cutting the wire' – is the cornerstone of their movement. It is the baptism of fire for the militant, an essential part of their identity. It plays a key role in the *mistica*, the moment of collective theatre and myth-making that kicks off all MST events. MST leader João Pedro Stedile recognizes that it is a huge step for a poor rural family to take part in an occupation. "The vehemence of this action means that no-one can sit on the fence," he says. "You have to have a position, either in favour or against."

Until the moment that the wire breaks, explains Roseli Salete Caldert, rural workers "have been trained always to obey, to obey the landowner, the priest, the political boss. They learnt this from their families and from the short period they spent in school." Taking their life in their own hands, they gain political awareness. They realize that they will never achieve what they want if they restrict their demands to what the establishment sees as acceptable. And they learn to impose their own agenda. "We have always been told that agrarian reform is a good idea in principle, but the *conjuntura*, or present moment, isn't right," said Monica, a woman leader from the northeast. "Well, we make the *conjuntura* right." In other words, they become subjects of their own history. And, in taking this step, they turn their world upside down. They start to realize that the established values are not immutable. As the historian, Christopher Hill, has pointed out: "Upside down is after all a relative concept. The assumption that it means the wrong way up is itself an expression from the top." The act of occupation becomes the fuse for a profound process of personal and political transformation.

"Land that we conquer through struggle is land that we win without the help of anyone," says Darci Maschio, a MST activist. "We don't have to go down on our knees to give thanks to anyone. This allows us to go on to fight for other things." He says that government authorities try hard to stop the families believing that they had rights. "In the beginning," he said, "the authorities made a point of saying to us 'you're here to beg for land, aren't you, because no one here is going to demand anything. You don't have that right.' But we do have the right, a right constructed through struggle."

The MST has never won a single acre of land without first carrying out an occupation. "I tell everyone who hasn't got land to do what we did, join the MST," said Zezilda Casamir, a settler from Rio Grande do Sul. "But the MST won't give you land. You'll have to win it for yourself." Stedile says that the act of occupation is "the organizational matrix of the movement, in that it was around this concept that the organization was built." The MST has to conquer every right it is demanding at every stage of the struggle; nothing is bequeathed.

In 1996, shortly before his death, the educationalist, Paulo Freire, who was a fervent supporter of the MST, recalled a visit he had made to an MST settlement. "I shall never forget a beautiful speech from a literacy worker, a former landless worker, who was living in an enormous settlement in Rio Grande do Sul. 'We managed through our work and our struggle to cut the barbed wire of the *latifundio*, the big estate, and we entered it,' he said. 'But when we got there we discovered that there was more barbed wire, like the barbed wire of our ignorance. I realized that the more ignorant we were, the more innocent we were of the ways of

>> April 18-21 >> Via Campesina, a network of peasants and farmers groups fighting globalization, meets for its second conference in Tlaxcala, Mexico. 69 different groups from 37 countries meet; they range from the Thai Forum for the Poor, to the Brazilian Movimento Sem Terrra, to the French Confédération Paysanne.

>> May 30-June 2 >> About 1,000 people from 26 European countries participate in a "Continental Meeting for Humanity and against Neoliberalism" under the banner of "Ya Basta - Enough!" in Berlin, Germany. The meeting is organized by the Mexican branch of the Berlin Research and Documentation Centre on Chile and Latin America.

>> May 30 >> Driven to desperation by food shortages fostered by the peso devaluation, drought, and the

the world, the better it was for the landowners, and the more knowledgeable we got, the more frightened the landowners became.' As he was speaking, I realized what real agrarian reform was about." "We have three fences to cut down," says Stedile. "They are the fence of the big estate, the fence of ignorance, and the fence of capital."

The long line of raggedly dressed rural workers, men and women and children marched around the rows of black polythene-covered tents they had put up on a hurriedly cleared patch of undergrowth. They marched behind the red flag of the MST, their left fists punching the air as they shouted slogans, hoes and spades raised in their other hand. There were 264, including the 40 children who marched at the front of the columns. Ten days ago, very few of these largely illiterate people had had any contact with the MST. Outside the camp, standing by the sugar plantation's distinctive white and green Toyota pick-ups, some 30 gunmen looked on as the marchers shouted lustily: "Agrarian reform! When do we want it? Now! When do we want it? Now!"

Zona de Mata is a region of large, semi-feudal sugar plantations in the northeast of Brazil. When we arrived in the area, we found that the MST activists had planned a daring occupation. They wanted to occupy an estate which belonged to the most powerful landowner in the region – Jorge Petribu. They had chosen as their base the small town of Igarassu, which forms part of the disorderly periphery around Recife. The MST wanted to recruit in both the large shantytown in Igarassu and the small rural hamlets scattered among the plantations.

We travelled around with the MST activists, often balanced precariously on the back of a motorbike. It was the beginning of the sugar harvest, which lasts from December to March. As we sped dangerously along the rough roads between the villages, we watched the rural labourers as they set fire to the sugar cane fields to burn the young vegetation and then, wielding sharp machetes, cut down the thick, charred stems that contain the sugar cane juice. It was a scene that had changed little over the last 400 years. At the end of the day workers are blackened from head to toe. The talk in the villages was about the growing unemployment and the loss of the *sitios* that a job in the plantations used to guarantee. There was real hunger in the hot dusty villages of wooden huts.

The story of Antonio Jose de Santos, 50 years old, was typical. He explained, his voice tinged with sadness: "I've been living here in Tres Ladeiras for 30 years. We moved here, because we were turned off the sugar plantation we used to work on. When we lived on the plantation, we had a hard life. We were paid very little and we were badly treated. But we had our *sitios*, our plots of land. We could grow all the food we needed – cassava, beans, rice, pumpkin, breadfruit, oranges, lemons and so on. Since we've been here in Tres Ladeiras, we've only had these tiny plots, which aren't any good at all. And it's getting worse. So many of the plantations have closed down. There's really just this Petribu left. And there's not much work with them.

I can't get any work there. I'm too old. And those that do are treated badly. They've turned us back into slaves. We don't earn enough to survive. We get odd jobs when we can. Those of us who get over our feeling of shame go begging in the streets. But there's a lot of hunger. There are 600 or 700 children living here. Their lives are a calamity."

"The only way out for us is through land invasions with the MST," he continued. "It's only together, through union, that we'll be able to get land, feed our children, help our friends. For some families are in a desperate situation, overwhelmed with debts. And there's plenty of land out there. There are a lot of landowners who aren't planting any more. It's our right to invade this land, so that we can plant crops and feed our children. It's going to be difficult. I don't think we can get back to the time of plenty, but we can't go on as we are. I've got 11 children. Fathers should be able to help their children, get them started in life. But I haven't been able to. We're going on the occupation. My wife and children are coming too."

The MST has drawn up guidelines for choosing the area for the first occupation in a new region: talk to local people and select an area that has water, is potentially fertile, and over which there is some controversy as to its legal ownership. In the past, the MST had always chosen areas that were unproductive, that is, were not being farmed by the landowner. This allowed them to justify the apparently illegal occupation of private property by pointing to Article 184 of the 1988 constitution that states that land not being used productively should be expropriated and distributed in an agrarian reform programme. But at the time of this occupation (1999) the MST was tentatively adopting a new strategy: in rural areas of great poverty and hunger, it was occupying land being used to produce commercial crops, such as sugar cane, not food for the local population. "We want to create a debate over the use of land," Cicero Onario Alves, an MST organizer from a poor northeastern family of peasant farmers who was rallying local people for the occupation, told us. "We think that the government's first priority in a region like the Zona da Mata should be to end starvation, and that means giving the land to poor families so that they can grow their own food."

The sugar plantation beside the church, known as

---

impact of NAFTA and GATT trade rules on peasant farmers, 400 women and children stop and loot a train near Monterrey, Mexico, carrying away 40 tonnes of yellow corn in buckets and plastic bags.

>> June 19 >> Large parts of the South Korean car industry are shut down as workers at Kia Motors Corp., the country's second largest auto corporation, go on strike over a wage dispute.

>> June 27-29 >> The G7 meet in Lyon, France. Eight counter summits take place and for the first time in the G-7's 21-year history, 25,000 trade unionists take to the streets, protesting against job cuts, labour deregulation, attacks on public services, and the "sinister impact of the global economy." The summit, as always more ceremony than content, costs $40 million to organize, and delegates promise next year's meeting will be a cheaper, scaled down affair.

>> July 23 >> London Reclaim the Streets occupies the M41 motorway with a 10,000 person street party. Lurking near the sound system are 20 foot high carnival figures in hoop skirts, which conceal jack hammers busily digging up the tarmac. Trees are then planted in the fast lane.

>> July 27-August 3 >> In Chiapas, Mexico, the

Engenho Pasmado, fitted the MST's new criteria. Until the mid-1950s there had been a thriving community around the church. All the families had worked on the plantation and during the off-season they had cultivated large *sitios*. The old labourers looked back nostalgically to life during this period. Alice, an old labourer who as a child lived nearby in another village, remembered visiting the community. "The workers had big *sitios* and we ate so well during festivities – there were wonderful harvests of cassava, beans, maize, bananas, mango, breadfruit, and coconuts. People were poor but no one ever went hungry. It's so different today."
In 1956 the plantation was sold. The new owners, Votorantim, claimed it was wasteful to allow the workers to have so much land for their own use. They caused great resentment when they transferred the families to a nearby village, and planted sugar cane on the land around the church. "People cried when their houses were knocked down and their crops destroyed," Alice said. Mauricio Henrique de Nascimento, who had been the plantation administrator and now lives in Igarassu, said it still pained his heart when he drove past the church and saw sugar cane fields where so much food had once been harvested.

More recently, all the plantations had been sold to Petribu. It was widely assumed that the land around the church had been included in the sale, for Petribu's guards patrolled the area. When we later phoned up Votorantim's office in Recife, we were told that the company no longer owned any plantations. Yet Petribu said that the area still belonged to Votorantim, information that was eventually confirmed to us by Votorantim's lawyer. This contradictory information led Jessimar Pessoa Boracho, the lawyer working with the MST, to suspect that Votorantim did not have proper land titles for the plantation, and for this reason had been unable to sell to it to Petribu. So there was a jumble of information over the legal ownership – which was all grist to MST's mill.

All the villagers were certain that the MST occupation would be on Petribu land, as it was the only big plantation owner in the region. In their chats with the villagers, the MST militants did little to hide this, or the likelihood that Petribu would illegally send its security guards – in other words, gunmen – to prevent the occupation.

Everywhere we went we heard stories of Petribu's brutality. Jesimar Pessoa Boracho, one of the few lawyers in the region to defend the rights of rural labourers, told us that most of his cases involved Petribu. "The Petribu family is part of that old established elite of plantation owners who have ruled the north east since it was colonized by the Portuguese in the sixteenth century. They have that in-built arrogance that comes from centuries of domination."

Soon it became evident that Petribu was prepared to use violent tactics to prevent the occupation that we were hoping to join. Daniel Quirino da Silva, a 32-year-old unemployed cane cutter, after showing us festering wounds on his legs, told us his story. Ten days earlier, he had been cycling home when he had stopped "for an urgent necessity", as he put it, going into the cane fields. Gunmen employed by Petribu happened to be driving past in one of their pick-ups. For no good reason, they stopped, seized him as he was squatting down, hauled him out of the cane fields, and kicked and beat him. Bleeding from the head, chest, and legs, he was dragged off to the local police station, and thrown into a cell.

The only possible reason for the attack was a desire by Petribu to show the villagers what they could expect if they dared to take part in the occupation. A week later Daniel was still unable to walk without help, because of the wounds he had suffered from the iron tips of the gunmen's boots. His attackers had left him incandescent with rage at the humiliation he had suffered. "I got beaten up for nothing," he told us. "I can't even work now. So I've joined the MST. I want to show Petribu that it doesn't own the world. My problem was that I was alone. Now we're in it all together. And I'll go to the bitter end."

The MST was organizing that first difficult step – the initial occupation. Cicero outlined their plans – where the occupation would take place, the dispute over land titles, the three buses they were organizing, the villages where they would pick up families.

Everyone was excited and optimistic, but we felt apprehensive. This was a region where the MST had not worked before. Despite the warm reception the MST activists had received in the villages, we were not convinced that many people would actually take that first step and join in what was widely known to be a dangerous undertaking. But it was too late to be having second thoughts. At 3.30 am on the Sunday morning, a bus pulled up outside the MST headquarters in Igarassu. We got in and, after Cicero had explained to a somewhat startled bus driver that he was not going to take people on a fishing trip but on a land invasion, we left.

We picked up about 25 people, carrying farm implements, clothing and a little food, in the village of Botafogo. They included a young woman, whose two year-old daughter was shivering with cold and had to be wrapped up in a blanket, and an old man, wearing a trilby hat and a raincoat, who seemed in his element, laughing and joking with the others. Then on to Alto do Ceu. We found the main road into the village blocked by four white and green Toyotas. So we drove round to the back entrance, a rough dirt track leading to the village up an exceptionally steep hill. The driver said that

---

Zapatistas organize the first Intercontinental Encuentro for Humanity and Against Neoliberalism. Thousands of people representing social movements from all five continents attend the seminars in the autonomous town of La Realidad, where they identify a common struggle and develop and strengthen networks of resistance.

>> August >> Enraged mothers organize an August march of more than 150,000 campesinos in the provinces of Guaviare, Putumayo, and Caqueta, Columbia after aerial spraying of Ultra Glyphosate pesticide on 45,000 acres causes convulsive vomiting and hair loss among children. Colombian *federales* diffuse the protest with false compromises, then assassinate march organizers. The US then insists that Colombia allow it to switch to the far more poisonous tebuthiuron.

>> August 8 >> An estimated 90 per cent of all Argentinean workers honour a general strike, decrying President Menem's neoliberal policies and the IMF-imposed structural adjustment, which has privatized virtually anything of value in the country, including highways and zoos.

>> August 16 >> Riots break out in Karak, Jordan, after IMF-imposed subsidy removal results in the price

his bus could not take the gradient, so a couple of MST activists and one of us climbed up the hill in the dark to tell the villagers to come down on foot, while the rest stayed in the bus. After about a quarter of an hour, three Toyotas appeared. Their lights flashing, they drove up and down. Eventually, one of them stopped by the bus and four men, one with his revolver clearly visible, came up. "Where are you going?" demanded the leader of the gunmen. "To do a job on a sugar cane plantation," replied Cicero, unconvincingly. "Well, this job better not be on Petribu land. If it is, we'll be waiting for you." And with that the Toyotas drove off up the hill.

Quick as a flash, Cicero pulled out his mobile phone. "Look out," he shouted down the phone to the MST activists who had reached the group of villagers at the top of the long hill. "The gunmen are on their way up." He rang off and, in a climate of growing tension, the people in the bus waited.

Dan Baron Cohen

Art installation at an MST encampment. Brazil

Up at the top of the hill, the group of villagers ran to hide at the back of a bar on the edge of the square. One was holding a rifle, while an old man clutched a rolled up MST flag. The mothers hugged their children, telling them to keep very quiet. The Toyotas drove around the square, stopped, conferred, and then drove away. After waiting a while, the group emerged from behind the church and began walking down the road. The mobile phone rang again. "Look out, the gunmen are coming back!" This time the only place to hide was in a prickly hedge. We crouched down while a Toyota drove past the end of the road. They did not see us. Then we picked our way over the stones down a steep gully, a short cut to the road below. It was a difficult scramble in the half-light. Suddenly it felt as though we had travelled back 200 years, and this was a group of runaway slaves, fleeing the plantation to set up a *quilombo*, or free community. At last, we reached the bus at the bottom of the hill.

The Toyotas, too, had returned and were parked about 100 yards away. Taking care not to be seen, the villagers clambered aboard. The bus departed hastily and, rather to everyone's astonishment, the Toyotas did not follow. It gradually dawned on us that the security guards had jumped to the wrong conclusion. They certainly knew all about the planned land invasion, and all day Saturday they had been cruising around Alto do Ceu in their Toyotas, distributing leaflets with warnings about "evil elements" and "agitators" who were deceiving the population with false promises of land. During the night they had been back in the village, speaking through loudspeakers and threatening the villagers with violent reprisals if they took part in the occupation. But – and this proved decisive – the gunmen believed that the MST was planning to launch the land invasion from Alto do Ceu itself into an area of the plantation that bordered the village. They thought that the bus was trying to take people into the village, rather than out of it, so, when the bus drove off, they believed they had won.

Almost miraculously, the occupation went ahead as planned. After a ten minute drive, the bus reached the church of Nossa Senhora de Boa Viagem. With dawn breaking, the families hurried out of the bus, carrying their farm implements, bags of food, pots and pans. Within an hour or two, they had cleared away the tangled scrub and bushes and put up their polythene tents. The camp held its first assembly. The red flag was hoisted and, in a climate of exultation, the people commemorated their first victory, singing and laughing. Many of the activities organized by the militants followed a planned routine, taught to members on training courses.

This first assembly consisted almost entirely of *mistica* – the morale boosting, quasi-religious communal ceremony at the heart of the MST culture, involving songs and chants. One slogan proclaimed: "*Che, Zumbi, Antonio Conselheiro na luta pela terra, somos todos companheiros*", invoking Che Guevara, an icon of the movement, and two northeastern revolutionaries: Zumbi, a Brazilian slave who headed a revolt in the sixteenth century, setting up a *quilombo* known as Palmares, which lasted 95 years, and Antonio Conselheiro, a mystic who led a rebellion among the rural poor in the nineteenth century and set up the quasi-communist community of Canudos. "We are all comrades in the struggle for land," affirms the slogan. Both Zumbi and Antonio Conselheiro have acquired the aura of romantic freedom fighters in the north east, and roaming minstrels still sing about them in street markets around here.

One enterprising man climbed up a big stone cross in front of the church and tied a red flag on the top of it.

---

of bread tripling. The king suspends Parliament when it refuses to support price hikes. Protesters also target the Ministry of Education because of drastic increases in school fees – also imposed by the IMF.

>> August 21-31 >> Active Resistance, a gathering in Chicago which coincides with the 'Democratic' Party's national convention, brings together nearly a thousand people who engage in intensive work on building sustainable communities of resistance. Police harass activists, particularly those involved in creating alternative media, make 14 arrests, and raid the site, pepper spraying participants and confiscating (and damaging) equipment and personal belongings. Yet the seeds of inspiration are sown for Indymedia and other new ways of resisting.

>> August 23 >> Three hundred Africans occupy a church in Paris in an effort to bring attention to the plight of immigrants, and to demand regular papers. The French government refuses to negotiate with them, and they are eventually evicted.

>> September >> In the ongoing campaign to save the ancient redwoods, 8,000 people gather across from a Pacific Lumber mill in northern California, US, to defend the Headwaters Forest. Over a thousand of them are

Another climbed even higher, to the top of a billboard on the main road that passed the camp and tied a red MST flag above an advertisement for insurance. The crowd below cheered enthusiastically and started to sing and dance. It seemed like Carnival. Yet the celebrations were at best premature. We were by then just 40 people, for the other two buses had failed to turn up. It later emerged that the telephone call from the labourer in Tres Ladeiras to say that he had arranged a bus had been an act of sabotage. He was really working for Petribu. The other bus had picked up some people in a couple of villages and then stopped in Cruz de Reboucas, only to find no-one waiting. As it made its way half-empty towards Engenho Pasmado, two green and white Toyotas had swung across the road, blocking its way. Wielding a revolver, one of the gunmen then threatened to set fire to the bus with everyone inside it, and understandably the driver, who had also not known beforehand that he was carrying people for a land invasion, had refused to go any further.

At about midday several jeeps and cars drew up near the church, and some 30 men marched in a phalanx towards the camp. About half wore the smart beige uniforms of official Petribu security guards, while the rest, wearing jeans, old t-shirts, and cowboy boots, were our acquaintances from the previous night. At the sight of them marching towards the camp, men and women seized their hoes and ran to block their path. It was clear that the guards and gunmen would have to use violence to evict the families and they hesitated. They admitted, when we questioned them, that the land

"The most dramatic and far-reaching social change of the second half of this century, and one that cuts us off forever from the world of the past, is the death of the peasantry." – Eric Hobsbawm, *Age of Extremes – The Short Twentieth Century 1914–1991*, Michael Joseph, London, 1994

around the church did not belong to Petribu. In threatening language, they warned the villagers not to move into the adjacent cane fields, turned around, and strode back to their Toyotas. More celebrations.

We were still talking to Antonio Severino da Silva when the camp received its first visitors – José Servat, a French priest who has been living in this region for 35 years, and a nun, who immediately busied herself making sure that the children had enough to eat and were not ill. They had brought several sacks of rice and beans, which the women immediately began to cook. Father José had been delighted by the news of the occupation. "Workers in these sugar plantations were organized in the 1950s and early 1960s but then they experienced dreadful repression and the movement collapsed," he said. "They were abandoned by the Catholic Church. Just one or two of us struggled on. Some members of the Church are frightened by these occupations, but I'm not. The people are simply saying that they're not animals, they're humans. They want land. They want to be part of society. I've been hoping for years that something like this would happen."

Although clearly unwell, Father José spoke to a hastily convened assembly. To much applause he said, "This land does not belong to Votorantim or Petribu. There used to be a community around this church and, with God's help, you will build it again." More cheers. "I should like to make a proposal, that you christen this new community with its old name – Nossa Senhora de Boa Viagem." At which point Cicero intervened so that the MST's democratic procedures for presenting a proposal and voting on it would be followed. The assembly voted by an overwhelming majority to accept the proposed name.

The head of the security commission immediately called on the men to volunteer for two shifts, one from 6.00 pm to midnight and the other from midnight to 6.00 am. One of the volunteers was Junior, an openly gay young man who had been on the bus with us the previous night. A makeshift bell was quickly made out of a piece of metal. The head of the security commission said that, in the case of an emergency, day or night, the watch would ring the bell and everyone was to grab a farm implement and assemble under the red flag.

It did not take long for the first emergency to happen. At about 10.00 pm, just as everyone was settling down to sleep in the tents, the bell rang out. The Toyotas – which by then had become a symbol of fear and violence – had returned and were driving up and down the road. It was pitch black outside. The only source of light was a smouldering wood fire, on which the women had been cooking. A Toyota tried to drive in, to be confronted once again by mass resistance. The villagers shouted slogans and brandished their implements. The vehicle finally backed off. After an hour or so of considerable tension, all the Toyotas drove off. It was a long night and few slept, but the gunmen did not return.

The next day was full of activity. The camp had survived the first crucial 24 hours and the news spread like wildfire in the region. People began pouring in from the neighbouring villages. A delegation arrived from Cruz de Reboucas, begging the MST to send another bus to the shanty town to pick them up, but Cicero was adamant: "The bus came for you on Sunday morning, and you weren't there. If you want to join our camp

---

arrested for trespassing before the police run out of plastic handcuffs.

>> October 1 >> The longest strike in the United States steel industry begins against WCI Steel Inc. over diminished job security and deep cuts to pensions. Eight communities in Pennsylvania, Ohio, and West Virginia buckle under the collective loss of $5 million in weekly wages. Steelworker families in the Ohio and Mon valleys are going to food banks instead of the grocery store. Strikers target banks and financial institutions linked to the corporation.

>> October 16 >> The global day of action against McDonald's coincides with the UN's World Food Day. Actions take place in over 50 cities in 21 countries, and include distribution of the now-infamous 'What's Wrong With McDonald's?' leaflet. The leaflet prompts the 'McLibel' suit, which gose on to be the longest libel suit in British history.

>> October 25 >> One million people take part in a general strike in Toronto, protesting against massive national health care cuts and the widespread homelessness exacerbated by a 50 per cent increase in evictions in the previous year.

>> November 8-17 >> The World Food Summit is held

now, you'll have to find your own transport." Somehow they managed and a dozen or so families arrived a few hours later. More commissions were set up, with the people in the camp playing a more active role in the selection of their representatives. The new commissions were given a variety of responsibilities – to build more tents; to set up communal kitchens; to organize literacy classes for adults and children; to set up a women's collective; and to organize a young people's collective for collecting litter and for organizing games. Everyone was busy.

Still, the problems seemed immense. There was very little food. One activist was sent off to ask for food from MST settlements. Another MST delegation travelled to Igarassu and other neighbouring towns to make contact with the local authorities. Surprisingly, several mayors promised to send in some basic supplies of rice and beans, even though they were not sympathetic to the MST's cause. Even so, it was clear that food would run out if the camp continued to grow rapidly. Cicero, who has organized dozens of occupations, was unperturbed. "If necessary, we'll loot lorries on the highway," he told us. "It all helps to raise people's awareness, shows them that together we can overcome all obstacles. People have been kicked around by the plantation owners since the days of slavery. It takes actions like this to make them aware that they can throw off oppression."

There was also the challenge of training the new arrivals for future confrontations with gunmen. Again Cicero was unfazed: "People can change very quickly in these camps. They gain a sense of their own power and become fearless. New leaders emerge and they soon take responsibility for running the camp and for preparing people for conflict. As you saw, we don't need to encourage them. We even have to caution them against running unnecessary risks."

By the end of the week there were 620 families living in the camp. Cicero had gone off to help organize yet another camp, set up spontaneously by families who thought that Nossa Senhora de Boa Viagem had become too crowded.

But, as the MST activists had thought likely, a major setback occurred. At 4.00 am on Saturday morning 100 police, accompanied by 200 gunmen, arrived at the camp, equipped with a legal order, issued by the courts in the name of Votorantim, to re-occupy the land and to evict the villagers. The families refused to move and a long standoff ensued. The gunmen set fire to the tents. One labourer was seriously injured. Eventually, after mediation by a lawyer, Jessimar Pessoa Boracho, and a Catholic priest from Scotland, a compromise was reached. The local Catholic bishop agreed to open the doors of the long-closed church and the families moved into the area immediately surrounding the church. As the families had technically moved off the land under dispute, the gunmen withdrew. The priest and the lawyer, still convinced that the land really belonged to the Church, promised to challenge the legality of the expulsion order in the courts. The scene seemed set for a long legal battle.

Early on Monday morning, before the eyes of a small group of gunmen, the families, reinforced by seven MST activists brought in from other regions, reoccupied the plot. They had to begin everything again. Many families had left, intimidated by the violence, so they had to send out the word that they were now back on the land. They had to build new huts, bringing in fresh supplies of black polythene. They had to construct another communal kitchen, another open-air school. Conditions were even worse than before, as the gunmen had infected the only stream bringing water close to the camp with dead animals. Undeterred, several of the workers began to clean the old well that had been used in the past by the village but was now heavily polluted with diesel oil. The long process of conquering the land – which could well involve further evictions and reoccupations – was underway.

Sue Branford and Jan Rocha have been accompanying the MST in Brazil since the first occupations in 1984. Both freelance writers, they are the authors of *Cutting the Wire: the story of the landless movement of Brazil*, from which this piece is adapted. Please acknowledge when reproducing.

Resources:

» *Cutting the Wire: the story of the landless movement of Brazil*, Sue Branford, Jan Rocha, Latin American Bureau, 2002

» Extensive multilingual information on the MST: www.mstbrazil.org

» History and documentaion of Via Campesina: www.viacampesina.org

---

in Rome. The Hunger Gathering, a counter summit, brings together diverse groups ranging from Bangladeshi farmers to the Brazilian MST. Their work lays the foundation of protest against genetically modified organisms (GMOs) in Europe.

>> November 20 >> Massive student strikes in Québec City, Canada take place, demanding an end to cuts in education funding, lifting of new restrictions on loan qualifications, a tuition freeze, bans on administrative fees, and abolition of a restrictive enrollment policy.

>> November 22 -25 >> Mass mobilizations against 'free' trade occur throughout the Philippines during the Asia Pacific Economic Cooperation (APEC) summit. The authorities ban certain foreigners (including Archbishop Desmond Tutu and former French first lady Danielle Mitterand) from entering the country as they might cause "disharmony." The government bulldozes shantytowns to create a fantasy of technological and social wealth for delegates. Protests include a march of 130,000 which is stopped by police blockades as it heads for the summit, as well as a massive blockade of the road connecting Manila to the summit site of Subic Bay.

>> November 23 >> On the US' National Day of

Few cities are as desperately in need of transformation as New York. This became even more evident during the eight-year reign of Mayor Rudolph 'zero tolerance' Giuliani, who rigorously applied neoliberal principles to the city. He slashed university funding, criminalized the homeless, gentrified neighbourhoods faster than eviction notices could be delivered, and waged a concerted campaign against the urban poor's last bastion against hunger and misery: their colourful and productive gardens, vehicles for social organizing, cultural renaissance, ecological recovery, and spiritual regeneration.

For politicians, city planners, landowners and developers alike, food growing as a land use is never going to take priority over housing developments, shopping centres, parking lots and hotels. After all, food can never hope to compete with this form of 'development' in terms of financial returns. By cultivating unused derelict land without consent of local authorities and other landowners we present a positive demonstration of community initiative and resistance to the set of priorities that sees our local environment as just another tradable commodity.

This is why illicit, or 'guerrilla' gardening is not just about planting vegetables in cities and towns, nor limited to one-off, symbolic stunts, such as planting in locations like Parliament Square, or the White House lawn. At its deepest level, gardening is a way of reconnecting people to land, teaching children that carrots come from the earth, not the supermarket; it's a way of reminding us of our incredible power to plant seeds and create sustenance autonomously, to experiment, to build connections with other gardeners which cross generations and borders. It's remembering that we also can be pollinators, fusing ideas together to make new ones, collecting and broadcasting seeds and shared visions.

Cultivating Hope: the community gardens of New York City

by Brad Will

"Here's a story that you may not understand,
but the parking lots will crack and bloom again.
There's a world beneath the pavement that will never end.
Seeds are lying dormant, they will never end."
– songwriter Dana Lyons, "Willy Says"

In New York City in the 1970s, while the white flight flew and the city coffers choked up blood, a procession of torched buildings tumbled down, block after block, at the same time that firehouses were closed, trash services cut off, police retreated. The public face of NYC hung its head and caved in. These rubble-strewn lots were magnets for trash, rats, prostitution, drug dealing, dirty needles, hepatitis. The city's only response was to spend thousands on fences. But then, something really amazing happened. Realizing the government was not interested in helping them, people took back their neighbourhoods, one lot at a time. They cultivated unique community greenscapes. They brought their homes with them: from the rural south to Harlem; from Puerto Rico to the Lower East Side; from Jamaica to East New York; from the Dominican Republic to the South Bronx. They disregarded property rights and did what was right for their neighbours. The story of the community gardens is thousands of stories. I can tell a few.

I moved to the big shitty as Giuliani-time kicked in. Hard times for the fiscally disinclined. Hardest of all for communities of colour. Land under your feet grew more expensive by the minute – they still call it real estate, even under a garden. Down at the 5th Street squat, we cleared out the adjacent lot of rubble, junk carts, piss bottles, and rot. We started a green space. The neighbourhood kids ran wild between the fragile beds. The nuns from the Cabrini old folks home came across the street to praise our goodly green emergence. The year before they were lobbying for our eviction. We turned the ghost fragments of rubble into elaborate brick walkways and stone-raised beds. I heard the tale of the cobblestones, cut in debtors' prison in England, used as ballast for the rough sea, and dumped on the docks in exchange for old growth white pines. They became streets, then were ripped up and poured black. We tried to set them right. Getting your hands in the soil is such a simple and human thing. You are moving contrary to the concrete.

A crew of us went out to the Liz Christy garden for the Green Guerrilla annual plant give-away. In the 1970s, the Green Guerrillas formed a band of night-time raiders, kick-starting the gardening movement with bolt cutters, trainings on appropriate trespass tactics, 'seed bombs', direct support. Natural allies. We cleaned house: a rickety wheelbarrow, shovels, dozens of plants, and a compost bin. It took three trips to haul it away. We planted a row of thorny bushes whose berries would attract birds and doubled as security. We planted a pear tree for sweet Sammy the plumber who passed away. Never got to see it come to fruit.

When they came for our building there weren't any eviction papers, and they came with a wrecking crane. I snuck inside, felt the rumble when the ball pierced the wall. I was alone. From the roof I watched them dump a chunk of my home on my garden. Everyone screaming from behind police lines. When it was all over: a rubble heap. And later, it returned to a junkie's trash den.

I was feeling displaced. The good people at Chico Mendez Mural garden wanted to fight. I shared some Earth First! blockade techniques. It was a brand new confrontational stance for the gardeners. It became Fort

---

Mourning, also known as Thanksgiving, Native Americans converge in Plymouth, Massachusetts and bury Plymouth Rock to protest against the celebration of genocide.

>> December >> The culmination of a year-long campaign against GMOs by German eco-anarchists results in prevention of one third of all test sites nation-wide being sown, and the sabotage of many more. Squatted protest camps sprout throughout the nations' fields; the squatters experience unprecedented support from inhabitants of the surrounding villages and small towns. People from all ages and social groups give money, bring food, and live there for days or weeks at a time. One camp produces its own electricity with donated solar panels from a local company. Prior to the occupations of many of the plots, a broad coalition of activists and local citizens collected thousands of signatures in order to prevent the experiment.

>> December 16 >> Two Sanyo Universal Electric PLC buildings are torched by Thai workers after wage negotiations break down, marking a break in Thailand's record of relatively harmonious labour negotiations. Labour disputes have more than doubled since 1991, and strikes and lockouts are becoming more confrontational.

Chico. Barricades went up. We had pre-dawn bike reconnaissance, patrolling for police mobilizations. Squatters from the Tompkins Square riot days dropped by. The city got nervous.

Chico Mendez Mural garden was a miracle. Neighbours dug in next to the most notorious crack house in the city – a tenement fortress dubbed 'The Rock'. The kids with negligible parents were almost adopted by Agi, the garden saint. They didn't understand when Don Garcia from Little Puerto Rico garden walked up to me on the stoop of a friend's squat and offered to buy us beer. The next day I was in his beautiful garden where the sound of merengue charged the cool night air. This small liberated piece of land brought us together; I never thought I could set foot there, and I was welcomed as an honoured guest.

The Angels' garden had a little *casita* with old men playing dominos with a bottle of rum. Maria's garden had an intricate *nuyorican* (Puerto Rican New Yorker) shrine. A rooster called me as I biked past at the crack of dawn. All were destroyed one day before New Year's, 1999, when most were out of town. They were turned into government subsidized condos. The developer, Donald Capoccia, showed up as the bulldozer finished off lovely Chico. About a dozen community members lunged with a volley of spit. The police turned the other way.

Rapid response. Activists chained themselves across a rush hour street in front of the Manhattan Institute, the right-wing think tank that was the Frankenstein behind the Giuliani monster and had shaped the neoliberal policy sweeping the city. NAFTA for the South Bronx, bringing all of the five boroughs under the thumb of Wall Street wizards, making nothing out nothing and the bubble was yet to burst. People were making the connections.

It was a non-profit shell game. They called them "blighted vacant lots". Public-private partnership. And the spin was that they would be low-income housing, even though only 20 percent were lower than market rate, and only for ten years. After that they were sitting pretty. Gentrify your portfolio. And it is never enough.

Giuliani went for the jugular. No more pretence of 'affordable' anything. "This is a free-market economy – welcome to the era after communism." One hundred and nineteen gardens going to the auction block. This was an act of war.

More Gardens!

"Even in this city where the shadows seem victorious,
Sunflowers stand tall and put them all to shame."
– songwriter Casey Neil, "Emma's Garden"

In a green space between the towering dark projects in the South Bronx, the More Gardens! Coalition was formed. Gardeners, squatters, and young activists changed the language of the struggle. Sharing food cooked over an open fire, we strategized a fresh mix of direct action (with puppets) and lobbying with love for the land.

The smell of garlic, greens, and tomatillos in an old squat. A gang of friends making puppets by candlelight. Standing in a circle for the solstice. We were a new

communication of dissent. Proactive element – not only protection, but extension of green space. We fought before the execution was imminent. We brought the gardeners together to decide for themselves what to do.

Talking democracy while walking to the hearings at City Hall. Whole classrooms coming downtown to tell the truth. We came dressed as flowers and bugs. My testimony was a song. Went to the gardeners on their block to gather information for the court battle. Helped get the court actions moving. Sweet escalation. I stole a kiss in the paddy wagon leaving city hall, and when they lined us up, boys versus girls, we did the hokey-pokey at the station house. The cops were impressed.

Training folks to sit down and get busted for the first time. I got hauled away with granny gardeners and a preacher. And still that day was coming. We came at them from all sides. Actions in their offices, up in a tree, down in their courthouse with a lawyer playing for real. One sister compiled all the information needed for a court challenge against the auction and, dressed like a sunflower, delivered it to the State Attorney General Eliot Spitzer in Albany.

I stumbled out of jail, bleary-eyed at dawn, and stumbled to another rally to support the legal battle at the federal courthouse. They raised the money for my fine on the spot. Just days to go. Right down to the wire with many interesting plans for the auction and a photo finish. The mayor conceded defeat. May 1999. Every garden on the auction protected. He should have known better.

El Jardín de la Esperanza

There is a myth in Puerto Rico. A monster approaches the forest intending to destroy it. The tiny thumbnail-sized *coquí* tree frog steps up, and is able to scare away the monster with the loudness of its voice. This was the perfect analogy for a community facing off against bulldozers.

Alicia Torres, a saintly grandma, came from the embattled island of Vieques, Puerto Rico and started *El Jardín de la Esperanza* (The Garden of Hope) in 1977. Across the street there was a line down the block for the dope shop for years. It took the Drug Enforcement Agency with machine guns to put an end to it. But the Torres family just kept digging,

---

>> December 23 >> Subcomandante Marcos receives a used pipe in the mail from Denmark. A group of activists occupying the Parliament building and the office of the Minister of Foreign Relations took the pipe from the Minister's desk and mailed it to the mountains of the Mexican southeast.

>> December 26 -29 >> The largest series of strikes and walkouts in South Korean history, involving hundreds of thousands of workers, takes place to protest against new labour legislation that allows companies to lay off and fire workers more easily and to avoid paying overtime in a more flexible work system.

\\ 1997 //

>> January >> South Korea is rocked by a three week wave of massive general strikes – the largest in the country's history - as workers protest new casualization laws. The strikes costs $3 billion in lost production. The government backs down and withdraws the new laws.

>> February >> A leaked copy of the draft Multilateral Agreement on Investment (MAI) text – secretly being negotiated at the "rich-man's club," the Organization for Economic Cooperation and Development (OECD) – is posted onto the internet. Up to this point negotiations are conducted in relative isolation—the revelation

clearing out their lot and building up a *casita* through it all. They grew medicinal plants for healing teas. A 22 year old rose bush, and lots of changes in the 'hood. But there was a plan to destroy hope.

Doña Alicia talked to the plants and prayed for them. She even prayed for the developer, that he would have a change of heart. With the go-ahead from Doña Alicia, we started a full time encampment. We built a giant *coquí* guardian in the front of the garden, with room inside for three to sleep, raised up ten feet with window watchtower eyes and concrete-sealed lock-boxes. In the back of the garden rose a twenty-six foot sunflower made of steel with a lock-box on top, nested between the petals, which read: "*Esperanza*/Hope, *Lindo*/Beauty, *Communidad*/Community, *Oxygeno*/Oxygen, *Comida*/Food."

We recycled Christmas trees to feed the fire and pitched tents to stay warm as winter drove in hard. They always come in winter. Our day in court had come, and Giuliani sent in his troops to steal it. We had 12 hours notice. Over 100 people gathered. We filled the lock-downs on the fence and buried in the ground. We sang to gather strength. Dawn came quick, with the special Emergency Service gestapo cutting open the front fence. Sudden surge of police. Yelling, scrambling, friends dragged away. Cold wet smother from the fire. Soon the taste of burning steel close to my lips, and a burn on my wrist. I asked the cop if he was going to tell his kids what he did today. He didn't answer. On the other side of town, the State Attorney General was arguing a case that would put a temporary restraining order (TRO) on the destruction of any garden in the city. We held on to the ground. The TRO came 40 minutes too late. But it protected all of the gardens in the city, for the time being. When asked why he took the case Spitzer said, "A sunflower asked me to."

In Washington DC, we inspired actions during the World Bank meetings. The A16 Guerilla Gardening Collective hit the streets armed with seedlings and kale seeds. These anarchists didn't come to break windows, they came to break the ground.

Mayday 2000. The kids in NYC Reclaim the Streets marched in solidarity with immigrant workers, then broke off and beelined it for a neglected spot by the East River, where they pulled the chain and cleaned and cleared and got the green rolling with hundreds of NYPD watching. The only thing we smashed was a *piñata* in the shape of a bulldozer. Inside were seeds I had saved from destroyed gardens. They scattered on the opened ground.

Under your feet

A quiet moment in Melrose neighbourhood of the South Bronx. It is Luis' fourth garden, *Cabo Rojo*. This is one of the poorest congressional districts in the US – they can't afford to leave their job for a week, let alone summer in the Hamptons. The neighbourhood has the highest rate of asthma in the country. The gardeners saved their blocks from blight but they don't get awards for all their hard work – they don't even get notice of demolition. These are the real heroes of the city.

A shock wave. An endless cloud of dust. The financial district burning for months. A new tourist attraction downtown. A new billionaire mayor. A cold winter by the wood stove in the *Cabo Rojo* encampment. I remember the smell of squash baking in the coals. The garden was destroyed, another death in the family. I watched the kids walking home from school stop in horror. The work crew clearing out the garden was doing 'community service' to pay off fines owed the courts.

At the time of this writing [2002] the TRO is about to be lifted. Either the city will sell out half of the gardens to a land trust, or city council legislation will establish a process for community boards to decide their fate one by one. A big shift is under way, and 200 plus gardens definitely will be put at risk. But one thing is certain: whatever deals they try to swing, people will fight for the land. Now we are connected.

I shared a meal with the *Movimento Sem Terra* in the countryside of Brazil. I slept with eco-warriors in the high canopy of an old growth forest. I joined in a sweat lodge at an occupation with the American Indian Movement. I sat in a circle and decided together with my friends that we would not obey. Luis began his fifth garden. We are dreaming the same dream.

The humble story of stones returning to the ground. A family growing their food, and growing with their food. This is a quiet revolution. The soil churns. And lead turns to gold in a sunflower. Simple alchemy of days. Because there is no such thing as 'nature'. It is always under your feet.

Brad Will is an anarchist and environmental activist who is now doing solidarity work in South America with Black Bridge International

---

Resources:

» Coalition of New York community garden activists: www.moregardens.org

» Network protecting biodiversity and creating local food security: http://primalseeds.nologic.org/

---

sparks off a world-wide campaign, which scuppers the agreement before it can pass.

>> February -May >> In Thailand, a coalition of 20,000 disenfranchised farmers, refugees of dam flooding, and other rural people from the Assembly of the Poor stage a 99-day protest camp in front of Government House in Bangkok.

>> February 5 >> IMF restructuring in Ecuador forces overnight price rises of electricity (500 per cent), gas (340 per cent) and telephone charges (700 per cent), among others. A general strike brings over two million people into the streets under the slogan, "No one stays home." Leaflets circulating before the event declare: "We invite all Ecuadorians to the giant going-away party for [President] Bucaram... This event will take place in the country's plaza and streets... Dress informally. The entrance fee is a street barricade, a burning tyre, and the will to save the country's dignity." President Bucaram flees and is dismissed by Congress two days later.

>> March 9 >> In Glasgow, Scotland over 50 people occupy the City Council chambers for 19 hours, in an attempt to prevent the Council from announcing nearly $131 million worth of cuts, 1,500 redundancies, the

Power Generation: the protest villages of Thailand

by Velcrow Ripper

Pak Mun Dam, Thailand, July 2000

In the soft gold of magic-hour an old man is weaving a fishing net that will catch few fish. Behind him is the metal mesh of a chain-link fence emblazoned with the Thai words, "Danger! High Voltage!" and the silhouette of a man killed by the misuse of power. Inside the fence stand the hulking transformers connected to the turbines of the dam, the dam that destroyed the old man's village. High-tension power-lines stretch off to massive pylons disappearing into the distance, taking the electricity to the city. A meagre output – the dam delivers a fraction of what it was supposed to, and then only in the rainy season.

But the actual productivity of a dam is rarely the issue. The World Bank contributes a generous loan, contractors get fat, everyone at the top of the food chain benefits – at least until it's time to pay off the debt. The government can feel a step closer to joining the exclusive club of 'developed' nations.

And the price? Incalculable. The loss of a way of life for a people, the loss of life for countless species. And for some, that existed only here in the Mun River, the greatest loss, extinction. Worse than mere death: the end of birth.

The first towering metal pylon rises above a new village, *Mae Mun Yuen One*, Mother Mun Protest Village Number One, Thailand's first protest village. Six thousand villagers are

---

***Assembly of the Poor** is the strongest peoples' organization in Thailand, with its roots in the struggle against the World Bank-funded Pak Mun dam, completed in 1994, which displaced at least 600 families from their villages, starved the river of fish, and gave the people meagre and unfertile lands in recompense. Primarily fisher-folk, fishing was a deep part of their culture and the basis for their livelihoods. As a result of displacement by the dam, many were forced to join the ranks of the destitute in Bangkok. Dam-affected villagers have never given up their fight, and have fuelled Thailand's dynamic anti-dam movement which also opposes the Rasi Salai dam further down the Pak Mun river, among others.*

They have also fuelled a wider movement against globalization made up of all those, rural and urban, left out of the Thai economic 'miracle'. On 25 January 1997, the Assembly of the Poor made a huge impression on the Thai political imagination when 20,000 dam-affected villagers, small farmers, fisher-folk erected a makeshift 'Village of the Poor' of plastic shacks which stretched back nearly a mile down the Nakhon Pathom Road outside Government House in Bangkok. A spanner in the works of the globalization project, they camped there in the stink of the smog and the traffic for 99 days, growing vegetables illegally along the banks of the city's river.

Then in 1998, international speculators betting against south east Asian currencies, caused the economy to go into free fall, revealing that Thailand's prosperity was built like a house of cards. The Government bowed to resulting austerity measures imposed by the International Monetary Fund (IMF), belts tightened and unemployment soared.

So in 1998 the village came again, this time to join the coalition of protest movements against the IMF, and protests and resistance have continued ever since against structural targets of globalization such as the WTO and the Asian Development Bank.

spread around the land surrounding the dam in thatched roofed bamboo huts built on stilts. They've been here for 15 months. The numbers keep growing, their spirit of resistance strengthening with time, not weakening as the officials hoped. Instead, the shacks are spreading out, gaining more ground in a nonviolent wave of people power. It has become an autonomous zone, attracting like-minded people from across the country, from around the world. The state does not enter here. Taxes are not collected, laws are applied by the community. There are refugees from the military dictatorship in Burma, landless peasants from the Cambodian border, activists from Canada, Australia, India, here in solidarity, to offer their bodies, to receive shelter, to learn from the strength of this movement. The wave of resistance is spreading throughout Thailand, which is now witness to more than 200 protests a year.

A diverse spectrum of factory workers, fisher-folk, students, landless farmers, urban poor, all those affected by so-called 'development', have banded together under an enormous umbrella group called the Assembly of the Poor. Throughout the camp hand-silk-screened red or yellow flags proudly proclaim "Poor!" in Thai and English. The Assembly was born in 1997 from a protest encampment of 20,000 people in the centre of Bangkok. That moment gave a focus and unity to the movement which still resonates in Thailand today, the way Seattle sends out waves of inspiration.

The struggle against the Pak Mun Dam has been going on since 1990. Initially the Electricity Generating Agency of Thailand (EGAT), ran into a snag: the dam site was located on national park land. That was easily worked around – the staff of EGAT simply had themselves declared park rangers. They were merely improving the park. They moved in and began blasting away the 50 rapids of the Mun River – the spawning beds for the fish, the fish the villagers depended on for their lives. What was once a parking lot for the dam's visitor centre is now the headquarters for the dam protest. Sentries sit next to a bamboo gate which is raised and lowered with the help of a makeshift pulley system. Standing guard on one side of the gates, a giant fish trap towers up 20 feet, woven from reeds, a long slender cone. It was used to capture a single fish, the giant dinosaur fish that lived only in the Mun

---

closure of 130 community projects, and a 22 per cent rise in council tax. George McNeilage of the North Pollock Community Council says, "We have as much right as the councillors to be in this building; they were voted in two years ago in a stand against cuts and redundancies. Now they have betrayed every citizen of Glasgow and should resist or resign."

>> April >> One of Britain's last colonies, the tiny island of St Helena, goes into open revolt against its dictatorial British Governor, setting the island's only police van on fire.

>> April >> A large white tent is erected in Buenos Aires. It will play host to 1,500 teachers on a rotating liquid diet strike, and to more than 5,000 personalities and 3 million supporters. Known as the 'White Tent of Dignity', it is erected by a teachers' union as part of a campaign for an increase in funding to guarantee the future of the Argentinean public education system. Within a few weeks, however, the tent far exceeds this original purpose, and becomes the focus for other popular demands - and eventually the symbol of a social movement opposed to the spread of official neoliberal policies. Other 'white tents' spring up around the country.

River. Now they live nowhere on earth.

In the centre of the paved lot, in a little green island, is a bronze coloured statue of three life-sized human figures, two kneeling on the ground, another standing proud with fist raised to the sky in a gesture of defiance. A sign reads "Monument to the Poor". There is a stage with speaker system and microphones hooked up to loudspeakers and a bamboo hut on stilts that is the nerve centre of the operation. Inside I am surprised to see a fax machine, a couple of computers, and a line of cell phones charging. Political posters adorn the walls – a dove impaled on a machine gun, commemorating the anniversary of the students massacred in 1992. Another photo from the student massacre of 1976. A soldier in the foreground, holding a rifle, and hundreds of students lying on the ground with their hands behind their heads. A batik painting of the Village of the Poor, electricity pylon rising in the centre, bamboo huts spread out around the hillside.

Morning, and we gather on the deck of the big house to eat sticky rice, fish paste, and a basket of greens harvested from the river, seated on a woven reed mat under the shadow of the enormous pylon. EGAT, the village dog, comes sniffing around hoping for hand-outs. People love to say, "Bad EGAT!" to him. Poor dog, stuck with the moniker of the enemy.

I meet Pon, who has been an activist for a over decade, though he is only 30. He was beaten and arrested in the early years of the struggle to save the Mun and thrown in jail along with many other activists. Ugly scars on his chest bear witness to the severity of the beatings he received. While on that action he met a young woman, a passionate, committed activist like himself. She was also arrested, and though they couldn't see each other, they began sending notes sent back and forth and a courtship began. Soon after their release they were married, and now they share their lives together as activists.

"Rivers and forests on which the survival of rural families depend have been plundered from the people ... the collapse of agricultural society forces people out of their communities to cheaply sell their labour in the city.... The people must set up the country's development direction. The people must be the real beneficiaries of development." – Assembly of the Poor, 1997

Paolo is a young boy of 14. He's a skinny little guy with crazy tousled hair, a high nasal voice, and sparkling eyes. He generally runs around shirtless and shoeless, with long baggy shorts that almost reach his ankles. Without any hesitation, he'll grab a megaphone at the daily demos and launch into a passionate speech. He first came to a protest when he was seven. Paolo is focused, determined. "This river is not for me, myself but for all people everywhere and in the future too," he says. "Everyone uses the river. No one is an owner. No one owns the forest. So I'd like to tell everybody who can see this that they should look out for nature. In our free time what do we do? We go out and have fun. We waste time. We should use this time to educate ourselves on what is the actual situation. What is the effect of these mega-projects. We're still kids. Not long from now we will grow up. Our children, our grandchildren gonna have children. They'll have children and are they gonna see that nature returns?"

I hop on back of a motorcycle with Pon and a Filipino-American media activist named Cray. We speed along the broad paved road and out onto the dam crest.

On 15 May 2000, a year after the establishment of the protest village, the villagers awoke at 2.00 am and made their way here to the fence, blocking the dam itself. There was only one guard in his little house by the gate that night, asleep. Unbeknownst to him, he was also locked inside. The villagers, young and old, carrying reed mats and pots of food, scaled the fence and began running across the crest of the dam. High above the water rushing through unseen turbines, past the surveillance cameras, to a second gate. Again they climbed, and they were in! The gate was cut and a sound system on a truck pulled in, blasting out traditional Thai music. The villagers danced ecstatically while the sun slowly rose.

Today the protest village extends along the entire top of the dam. The fishermen climb down the catwalks above the turbines and string out their nets to catch a few of the meagre remnants of fish that still swim the river. It's a startling juxtaposition of the villagers with their traditional nets against the metal and concrete monolith of the dam. At night guitars around campfires strum out protest songs: "I'm tired, but I'm still fighting..."

Rasi Salai dam

One day I climb into the back of a pick-up truck with Sikyamet, an activist with the South East Asia Rivers Network, for a two hour drive south, down to the site of *Mae Mun Yuen* Protest Villages – Numbers Two, Three, and Eight

---

>> April 12 >> In Cutral-Có and Plaza Huincol, south-west Argentina, protest flares into outright rebellion when police attack a protest of unemployed workers and fatally shoot Teresa Rodríguez, a 24-year-old domestic worker. Roads are blocked with barricades and burning tyres, preventing police reinforcements from entering the city at several strategic points. "This is Chiapas" says a frightened police chief as he orders his forces to withdraw and the government is forced to send aid packages and work subsidies to the area.

>> April 12 >> The March for Social Justice takes place on the eve of the general election in London, UK, demanding a repeal of the Criminal Justice Act, the reinstatement of jobs and union privileges for sacked workers, and more. It is organized by a unique alliance between Reclaim the Streets, the Liverpool Dockers, Women of the Waterfront, and the Hillingdon Hospital Workers. The original plan of squatting government buildings is foiled by police, but 20,000 people march through London and end up enjoying what the music media describe as "the best illegal rave or dance music party in history." The radical coalition is clearly a threat to the authorities; police confiscate all printed propaganda

– which surround the Rasi Salai Dam, another blockage downstream on the Mun River. We pass a long row of deserted concrete buildings high on stilts – the houses the government had built in hopes of enticing the villagers away from the protest site. No-one had taken the bait, and the houses, surrounded by infertile soil, sit empty.

Now the reservoir of the Rasi Salai dam stretches before us, murky water, remains of a forest rising up from its depths, dead trees, twisted forms against a threatening sky. This dam was ostensibly built to provide irrigation to the surrounding fields. Unfortunately, the land contains underground repositories of salt – a legacy of the distant past when this land was a sea bed – and the water of the reservoir became salinized, useless for agriculture. The government did an environmental impact assessment, the villagers later told me, after the completion of the dam. They were able to laugh at this incredible stupidity when they told me, though it was the ruin of their lives. They have encountered nothing but lies and manipulation by the dam builders, who would prefer them to conveniently disappear. But they will not disappear. Instead, they have made their presence well-known, constructing a protest village in the middle of the reservoir, above the flooded land that was once their homes. They have spent nine months living in this makeshift village, perched on stilts, waters slowly rising around them.

We climb into the middle of a long dug-out, sat cross-legged on a flat platform of woven reeds, and push out into the water. Our smiling boat driver starts up the outboard engine and lowers the propeller, jutting six feet out the back of the boat at the end of a long metal shaft. We glide past lily pads dotted with lotus flowers. Purple tinged white. The lotus is a Buddhist symbol of awakening. It emerges from the mud of existence, but is unstained, only strengthened, fed. For the villagers, there can be no compensation for the loss they have experienced. Yet, they have had to plumb their depths for previously unknown strength, to stand up and fight, and have learned to fight without violence. To live in unity, united in their opposition, supported around the country, and gradually learning that they are part of a much larger community, coming to understand the greater world of resistance, in the face of the greater world of repression.

After 20 minutes we pass four outhouses sheltered by tarpaulin atop a little island. Soon we enter "water world": a collection of thatch roofed huts with bamboo walls and floors, interconnected with precarious one-plank walkways high above the water. Outside many of the huts, ancient dug-out canoes bob in the murky water. We pull up to the big house and hoist ourselves up onto a catwalk. We remove our shoes as we step onto an open bamboo platform covered with a thatched roof. In the centre of the room a large brown painting depicts three men in uniforms holding aloft a huge scroll which represents the constitution of the country. Around them are the faces of peasants, in their conical woven straw hats, or wearing bandannas emblazoned with revolutionary symbols. The boots of one of the uniformed men rests firmly atop the head of a peasant man.

The villagers stand up to their waist in the water, the rising waters threatening to drown them, as it has drowned their very way of life. Their hands are raised in prayer position as they enact their morning ritual of thanks to the river, of apology to the river, of thanks to the Buddha. Each night, another ceremony is dedicated to their brothers and sisters in the struggle at the Narmada Dam in India. We slowly drift towards them in a dug out canoe as they chant in front of their sinking village, past the lines of committed faces, ending in silence, hands in prayer position, standing unmoving in the water that was their land. They don't spend all day standing in the water, just each morning, and night. The fact is, however, that the villagers are prepared to drown. They will not leave unless the dam is decommissioned. A similar protest is held at the Narmada dam site at monsoon time. Villagers chain themselves to their original homes as the waters rise, determined to drown until they are removed by force.

Early morning, we're gliding above the flooded land in a long dug out canoe that needs constant bailing. "This is where the forest was," say the villagers accompanying me. They point to dead twisted trees rising from the murky water. Eerie silence. "The sound of the birds used to accompany us on our walks. There were deer, wild chickens. We would gather herbs and mushrooms." Through the light rain, threatening clouds reflect on a glassy surface. "We believe that there is a spirit in everything, in the forest, in the river. We call the forest grandfather. The river is female." Running parallel to us is another boat filled with villagers. In the bow of our boat, an old woman with wrinkled face and betel-nut-stained teeth sits in contemplation, her gnarled hands weaving reed into basket. Hours pass. In the distance, through the skeletal trees draped in seaweed, the Rasi Salai Dam appears, disappears, re-appears. The little engine of the boat is the only sound in the dead calm of the stagnant water, stopped up by the slowly approaching monstrosity.

Colourful tents become visible atop the dam, the tents of the protest village, Mae Mun Yuen Number Eight. "A few days after the protesters at Pak Mun dam took over their dam crest, we did the same thing, marching from the first

---

and try to frame people with the "attempted murder" of a policeman.

>> April 17 >> The streets of Brasilia, capital of Brazil, are lined with 120,000 people to welcome thousands of Brazilian landless (MST) ending a two month march from São Paulo to demand land-reform and protest against the violent clampdown on their movement, arriving on International Peasant Farmers' day, the one-year anniversary of the massacre.

>> April 28 >> Two factories of workers making Nike shoes for subcontractors near Jakarta, Indonesia, go on strike separately on consecutive weeks to demand a ten per cent wage increase.

>> May >> Throughout the month protests against unemployment and privatization take place in numerous provincial towns of Argentina. In Libertador General San Martín, where unemployment is over 33 per cent, the highway is blocked for three days and police attack with rubber bullets. Defending the police, Argentina's president declares, "I am not going to allow them to block my highways. This is a legitimate and democratic government."

>> May 20 >> In La Plata, Argentina, police provoke rioting by removing street vendors. After occupying the

protest village, along the road, to the gates of the dam. We waited for the news from Pak Mun and when we saw that they hadn't been arrested, we too climbed the fence and took over this dam," a villager explains, laughing. We drift parallel to the massive impassive grey concrete of the dam with its incongruous cavalcade of fabric from the protesters sprouting from the crest. There are 700 protesters at this site, many of them the original villagers. The sound of water rushing through the partly opened gates reverberates. We pull up to an enormous concrete-covered slope, and hop out of the boat, scrambling up to the camp above.

A man in army fatigues walks through the lines of tents, shouting through a megaphone, calling people to their daily meetings. Sykamet explains that "the larger group is split into a number of smaller groups, and every day they get together in meetings to discuss problems, discuss strategy. Each group is of about ten to twenty people." Like the concept of affinity groups, smaller autonomous groups within the larger community.

From the dam, fisherfolk hang nets 100 feet down to the rushing water to try and snare the few fish that make it through. Stretching away from the dam, Pak Mun takes on the appearance of a river once again – though what I am seeing can no longer be accurately described as a river. Scientists would call it "reservoir outflow", a sadly depleted echo of its former existence. The water coming from the reservoir is severely de-oxygenated, and much of the usual life cannot survive.

Further down the road, near the gate they had scaled a month earlier, a group of villagers are busy digging a tunnel. They have decided to take matters into their own hands, and with picks, shovels, and their bare hands, are creating a channel through the road, to drain the reservoir, and return the Mun river to its old course. Fifty villagers, men and women, young and old, are toiling in the heat of the sun, on both sides of the road and have already succeeded in making an appreciable dent in the artificial earthen mound. Four men in longs, stripped to the waist, stand in the mucky water of the reservoir, chopping into the red clay with energy. A huge banner hangs along the roadside above proclaiming, "Assembly of the Poor." A man with a megaphone paces back and forth, urging the workers on. After about half an hour, the exercise is terminated for the day, and villagers return to the camp, in two orderly rows of men and women.

The whole day I find myself smiling broadly, invigorated

"Gleaming there and humming, [the dam] stands like a very talisman of change, a miraculous intrusion, as though its engineers have flown down from Mars itself and brought their anvils with them." **– James Morris, *The Road to Huddersfield*, here commenting on World Bank-funded Bhumipol dam in Thailand in a book commissioned by the World Bank, 1964**

by the feeling of resistance and solidarity in the air. These people are not content to sit quiet and be victimized. They are standing up. Chances of the dam being completely decommissioned are slim. But they will always know that they fought, they did not allow themselves to be silently, meekly transformed into yet another poverty-stricken community, tribal people dependent on the government for handouts.

UPDATE: Since 2000, the protest villages and marches have successfully pressured the government into opening the sluice gates of the Pak Mun dam to let fish through. As a result, for the first time in the ten years since the dam was built, a single giant fish, thought to be extinct, has been seen in the river, and fishing has resumed. A ground-breaking study of villagers' ecological knowledge of the river's ecosystem has done much to raise the issue of rural participation and knowledge in development, and public understanding of the ecological and social issues involved.

However, the villagers continue to face serious crackdown – in January 2003 one of the protest villages was burned down by a gang of unidentified thugs. International campaigners are pressuring the World Bank to remove funding for the dam.

Velcrow Ripper is a Canadian Academy Award (Genie) winning documentary filmmaker, writer, media activist and web artist. In progress is *ScaredSacred*, a book, documentary, and web project based on journeys to the 'Ground Zeros' of the world in search of stories of transformation, resistance, and hope.

Resources:

» The International Rivers Network supports local communities working to protect their rivers and watersheds: www.irn.org

» A multimedia website documenting a long term project documenting scared and sacred places of the world: www.scaredsacred.org

---

TV station, vendors seek refuge in the university where students protect them against mounted police charges, though many are injured. In Buenos Aires, outraged students hold rush hour actions in solidarity, blocking major avenues at five key points and organizing teach-ins and rallies. As they march, they are greeted with confetti raining down from balconies and cheers from the local residents.

>> June 8 >> The first (known) action against GMOs in Britain takes place outside of Cambridge. Activists stage a rousing game of cricket with a test crop of GM potatoes, destroying the entire crop.

>> June 14 >> The European march against unemployment, job insecurity and social exclusion converges in Amsterdam, Netherlands, arriving from all points in Europe and culminating with a demonstration of 50,000 during the EU summit. Several thousand Italian activists commandeer a train from Italy to Amsterdam. Throughout the course of the summit, 750 people are arrested, in the largest mass arrests in the Netherlands since 1966.

>> June 19 >> The McLibel case, England's longest ever trial, ends after 314 days. McDonald's was suing two activists for handing out leaflets criticizing the

Peace Message to the Public

by the Assembly of the Poor

"For us, it's a dam of tears. We don't have water to drink, nor rice to eat. And we can't eat tear drops." – Paw Lert, a villager displaced by Bhumipol dam who helped to launch the Thai anti-dam movement. Two years later he was assassinated by an unknown gunman.

Formerly, we were not poor. We had farmlands and self-reliant livelihoods based on nature, land and the rivers. We were not rich, but never had we been hungry. When the governments built dams on the land where we had lived and farmed for generation after generation, we protested. The governments used legal measures to evict us and gave us chicken feed and futile land as 'compensation' for uprooting our lives. So we became poor, or to be more exact, the governments and their rural resources-exploiting urban development approach impoverished us.

International Rivers Network archives

Sit-in outside Government House. Bangkok, Thailand

If 'development' means that thousands of households and abundant natural resources must be ruined in exchange for a few megawatts of electricity, then we're not willing to sacrifice our sustainable resources and the future of our descendants for such worthless development. The Assembly of the Poor came to camp out in front of Government House, time and again. We didn't come to ask for what's not ours. Is it wrong to demand what has been robbed from us?

Over the past several days, the Assembly has asked ourselves, "What's most important in our lives?" Houses and farmland; we've already lost them all. The most important thing for us now is our dignity. Physical assets such as houses, farmland and resources can be taken away from us. But we'll never let ourselves be looked down upon. Though deprived of wealth, we'll not let our human dignity be wrenched from us.

We've realized that to preserve our dignity is to fight for justice and righteousness; not to fight for personal gains.

We have to fight to keep our cherished local culture, our rivers, mountains, forests as well as wildlife and riverine animals for the future sake of our descendants. We carry on our hunger strike not to torture ourselves but to control our minds. We don't do it in protest of the government or the public at large. We refrain from taking food to maintain *dhamma*, to communicate the truth about the problems of poverty. Poverty is caused by the structural system of misdirected development and economic policies. There are at present a great number of hungry people. Our plight is just a mirror of structural hunger of millions of people in this country.

While we're fasting, we'll send our loving kindness and well wishes to the government and the policemen who have to be on duty. They are not our enemies. Our actual enemies are unjust economic and social structures, which we, the government, and every member of Thai society have to join hands to get rid of. For the government, if it still considers itself as the people's government, should treat the poor's problems as equally as they did with the economic ones. If the government had guts enough to amend and change legislations, regulations and structural policies to solve problems for the business sector, it must do the same for the sake of the poor.

Excerpt translated by Friends of the People, Thailand

Resources:

» Assembly of the Poor website: www.thai.to/aop/index.html

---

corporation. The verdict devastates the corporation. The judge rules that they exploit children with their advertising, produce misleading advertising, are culpably responsible for cruelty to animals, are antipathetic to unionization, and pay their workers low wages. But the judge also rules that the activists had libeled McDonald's and should pay close to $98,000 damages. They refuse and McDonald's declines to pursue it further, having already spent over $16 million on the trial, unintentionally inspired a global solidarity campaign, and generated an enormous amount of negative exposure.

>> June 20-22 >> The G8, having officially brought Russia into the group, meet in Denver, US. Several counter-summits take place, including a Women's Summit which features a "hunger banquet" to show up the feasting going on inside. A trial is held of the eight most industrialized nations and their multinational corporations in front of an international panel of judges from eight indigenous nations. Unsurprisingly, the G8 are found guilty.

>> July >> Financial crisis hits Southeast Asia and reverberates across the world's markets. The IMF steps in to rescue the region with a $100 billion restructuring

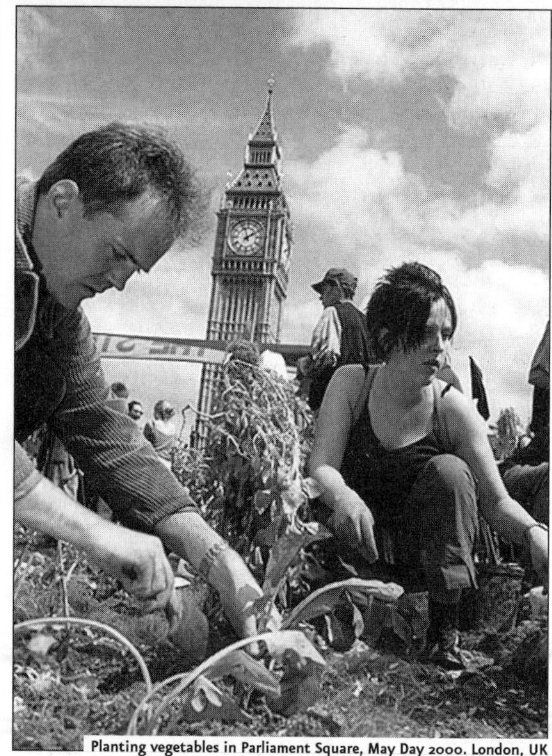
Planting vegetables in Parliament Square, May Day 2000. London, UK

Nick Cobbing

Guerrilla Gardening

"Armed with trowels, seeds, and vision, the idea is to garden everywhere. Anywhere."
– Primal Seeds

Capitalism is a system that separates everything from everything else. Take food, for example. What was the last thing you ate? Where was it grown? How far did it have to travel to get to you? How many lorries, planes, boats were required, and how much oil used? How much did you pay for it, and how much did those who grew and picked it get? How many chemicals were used to grow and package it? How much control did you have on how the food that passed your lips was produced?

There is a way out of this ignorance and dependence – growing our own food. Learning to produce our own food is a threat to capitalism as it begins to break us free of the cycle of supply and demand, liberating us from the role of passive consumer, remote from real decisions, alienated from nature.

To grow food we need land, yet most of us have none. Capitalism's first act is often the privatization of common, or public, land, whether we are talking about the enclosures of seventeenth century England or the Mexican Government's repeal of Article 27, the law which until 1992 guaranteed common ownership.

But whether you're in the countryside or the city, there are always little gaps, holes, places that can be transformed into small oases providing food for you and your neighbours. This is where guerrilla gardening comes in.

Guerrilla gardening can take many forms, and is practiced all over the world – from the hundreds of community gardens on vacant lots in New York, to the squats on decontaminated GMO test sites in Britain and Germany; from the London May Day 2000 action to the landless Thai and Filipino peasants who plant vegetables on squatted golf courses; from the neighbourhood in San Francisco who used broken parking meters as planters, to the IMF/World Bank protesters in Washington DC, who developed a tree planting project which involved going door to door with saplings and a flyer linking deforestation with Bank policies, and offering to plant trees outside people's houses if they agreed to care for it.

And if any one tells you that growing our own food is not 'realistic' for large cities, tell them about Havana, the Cuban city of 2.2 million people which has over 1,000 public gardens, employing 30,000 people producing 70 per cent of the city's fresh fruit and vegetables. It's also worth remembering that a lot of what we call weeds – nettles, dandelions, chickweed, nuts, and berries – provide wonderful food for free and require little effort, and no need for clandestinity.

How to Guerrilla Garden:

1) Do some reconnaissance

First find your ideal site. It could be a railway embankment, golf course, roof top, car park, vacant lot, quiet corner of a local park, crack in the pavement – the choice is endless. Consider ease of access, contamination, and your impact on the surrounding community.

2) Arm yourself

Growing things is not as difficult as you think. You don't need to be born with green fingers, nor do you have to buy the latest tome by celebrity TV gardeners. A wide variety of food can be grown with a minimum of tools or external energy inputs. All you need to start is a trowel, some seeds, a small bag of compost, some water, and ingenuity.

3) Break ground

Best to do it at night or without drawing too much attention to yourself. Plant your seeds, make sure they will get some light, and give them a good water. Weeds can be left alone except where they threaten to engulf your crop, as they provide initial camouflage for your activities.

4) Enjoy the harvest

After several months of tending, your garden will be ready for harvest. Why not invite friends and neighbours to share your first home grown meal? You can turn it into an event, share your stories of guerrilla gardening exploits, show them before and after photographs, and eventually turn the conversation to abolishing capitalism. You never know, the taste of locally grown fresh food might convince them to join the guerrillas!

"Putting plants where they are not expected – something common in an uncommon place, or an unusual plant in an everyday situation – lifts them out of the ordinary and allows them to be seen again for what they really are: beautiful, incredible, alive."

– Primal Seeds

"Humanity is born free
but everywhere is in
supermarket chains
buying 14.7 cm long carrots
stripped of dirt, geography, effort, labour
stripped of content, context, joy and flavour
buying 14.7 cm long carrots
stripped of carrothood".

– Steve Hancock, "all power to the allotments," *In Between Poems*, Pig and Ink books, 2000

Resources

» **Primal Seeds**: **http://primalseeds.nologic.org/**

Cremating Monsanto: genetically modified fields on fire

by Professor Nanjundaswamy

"We are aiming to consolidate the entire food chain." – **Monsanto, 1998**

In November 1998, *activists from the Karnataka State Farmers' Association (KRRS) – one of the largest and most radical farmers' movements in India – began Operation Cremate Monsanto, a programme of direct action against the infamous US biotech corporation. Unbeknownst to the farmer Basanna Hunsole the 'experimental' seeds Monsanto had given him to plant were genetically modified (GM). When Hunsole discovered this, he helped KRRS activists rip up the crop – the first trial of GM cotton in India – then they threw the plants into a pile and made a bonfire.*

Monsanto had been illegally conducting 40 field trials of genetically modified cotton across five Indian states for at least three months. As that first GM crop went up in flames, KRRS activists declared: "We send today a very clear message to all those who have invested in Monsanto in India and abroad: take your money out now, before we reduce it to ashes." The action inspired a mass movement of direct action and crop-pulling against GM crops around the world. In Karnataka State there were several more GM bonfires, and the banning of similarly undeclared field trials which Monsanto were discovered to be operating in other Indian states too.

An enormous and radical farmers' movement is building, not just in India but across the world as agribusiness moves in to monopolize the seed, pesticide, and food markets. The KRRS are the pioneers of this peasants' revolt. The prospect of having to buy patented, hybrid, and genetically modified seeds each year is motivating Indian farmers to defend the practice of saving seeds for the next crop. Currently 80 per cent of Indian seed is saved for the next harvest. Breaking that ancient relationship is crucial for the expansion of the profitable seed market in India. As KRRS leader Nanjundaswamy says, they are: "forcing seed dependency on farmers who cannot afford to buy seeds."

Open letter – November 1998

Dear friends,

Monsanto's field trials in Karnataka will be reduced to ashes, starting on Saturday. Two days ago the Minister of Agriculture of Karnataka gave a press conference where he was forced by the journalists to disclose the three sites where field trials with [Monsanto's GM] Bt cotton are being conducted. KRRS activists have already contacted the owners of these fields, to explain to them which action will be taken, and for what reasons, and to let them know that the KRRS will cover any losses they will suffer. On Saturday the 28th of November, at mid-day, thousands of farmers will occupy and burn down the three fields in front of the cameras, in an open, announced action of civil disobedience.

These actions will start a campaign of direct action by farmers against biotechnology, called Operation Cremation Monsanto, which will not stop until all the corporate killers like Monsanto, Novartis, Pioneer etc. leave the country. Farmers' leaders from the states of Maharastra, Gujarat, and Madhya Pradesh (states where Monsanto is also conducting field trials) were yesterday in Bangalore to prepare the campaign.

The campaign will run under the following slogans: "Stop genetic engineering", "No patents on Life", "Cremate Monsanto", "Bury the WTO", along with a more specific message for all those who have invested in Monsanto: "You should rather take your money out before we reduce it to ashes".

We know that stopping biotechnology in India will not be of much help to us if it continues in other countries, since the threats that it poses do not stop at the borders. We also think that the kind of actions that will be going on in India have the potential not only to kick those corporate killers out of our country: If we play our cards right at a global level and co-ordinate our work, these actions can also pose a major challenge to the survival of these corporations in the stock markets. Who wants to invest in a mountain of ashes, in offices that are constantly being squatted (and if necessary, even destroyed) by activists?

For these reasons, we are making an international call for direct action against Monsanto and the rest of the biotech gang. This call for action will hopefully inspire all the people who are already doing brilliant work against biotech, and many others who so far have not been very active on the issue, to join hands in a quick, effective worldwide effort.

This is a very good moment to target Monsanto, since it has run out of cash in its megalomaniac attempt to monopolize the life industry in record time. It is going now through a hard time of lay-offs and restructuring in a desperate effort to survive, since it cannot pay its bills. It is also a good time because several recent scandals (like the pulping of *The Ecologist* magazine's exposée of Monsanto , the whole Terminator Technology [seeds genetically modified so they cannot reproduce] affair, the illegal introduction of Bt cotton in Zimbabwe [similar to the scandal in India], etc) have contributed to its profile as a corporate killer, which, being the creators of Vietnam War's Agent Orange and [bovine growth hormone] rBHG, was already good enough, anyhow.

We are hence making a call to:

» Take direct actions against biotech transnational corporations (TNCs), particularly Monsanto (be it squatting or

---

programme, generating protests across the region. Social movements from Indonesia to Thailand link the crisis to economic globalization and predatory financial speculation.

>> July 26-August 2 >> Over 3,000 people gather in Spain for the Zapatista-initiated Second Encuentro for Humanity and Against Neoliberalism to continue the first Encuentro's work by building networks of resistance and communication to link struggles around the globe. A decision is made to target the Second Ministerial meeting of the WTO in Geneva in May 1998.

>> July 31 >> A 24 hour general strike brings Bangladesh to a standstill; ports and factories close, and all public transport grinds to a halt. Workers demand that the government agree to an eight point plan, which includes safeguarding jobs, guaranteeing a minimum wage, and reopening abandoned factories.

>> August >> Thailand's economy collapses, causing a domino effect of social and economic crisis across Southeast Asia. Unrest ripples out across the region.

>> August 14 >> A general strike called by unions and government employees wreaks havoc through much of Argentina. Bridges, ports and roads are blockaded, and teachers walk out of their schools. The government

burning their fields, squatting or destroying their offices, etc)
» Maintain the local and/or national press informed about all the actions going on around the world
» Take direct actions at stock exchanges targeting Monsanto, to draw attention to its state of bankruptcy

We are making this call for action on the line of Peoples' Global Action (PGA), a worldwide network of peoples' movements, in order to emphasize the political analysis beyond our opposition to biotechnology. This analysis does not only take environmental concerns into account, and is not limited to the defence of food security – it attacks neoliberal globalization as a whole, the World Trade Organization regime as its most important tool, and the global power structures (G8, NATO, etc.) as the root of all these problems. You will find the complete political analysis in the manifesto of the PGA.

We are calling ONLY for nonviolent direct actions. Nonviolence in this context means that we should respect all (non-genetically modified) living beings, including police and the people who work for these TNCs.

The campaign will take place in a decentralized manner, and nobody should speak on behalf of other people involved in the campaign without their consent (also not on behalf of PGA, of course); however, people are welcome to report about the actions of others without pretending to represent them.

Friendly greetings,
Professor Nanjundaswamy – President, *Karnataka Raiya Ryota Sanghe* (Karnataka State Farmers' Association)

An Introduction to the Karnataka State Farmers Association, 1998

Context: Indian agriculture and trade liberalization

The situation of Indian agriculture (and of the whole society) is deteriorating very rapidly due to the globalization process. The wave of suicides of peasants (since they cannot anymore compete on the market and are covered with debts) has stopped now (it will start again after the next harvest), but the desperation is leading to an escalation of tension and violence in rural areas. In Haryana, 23 peasants were killed by the police in October, and five were killed in Karnataka in early November. In the case of Karnataka, these peasants were protesting for the drop in the price of the peanuts that they produce, which took place due to the liberalization in the import of vegetable oils that can substitute peanut oil (like palm oil). The Agreement on Agriculture of the WTO is at the root of these problems.

The farmers' movement that was to give birth to KRRS in 1980 was initiated by five people in 1965. They see the movement as part of a very long process of construction of a new society, which must be driven by people at the local level but must reach the global level, and which cannot take place without the active and direct involvement of society as a whole.

There is no central register of KRRS members (it would be impossible to maintain, unless a huge bureaucracy was set up). However, according to the information coming from the village units, the membership of KRRS is now estimated to be around ten million people.

The dream of the Village Republic

The KRRS' work goes beyond the specific problems of farmers – it is aimed at social change on all levels. Another important element is that the autonomy and freedom of the village should be based on the autonomy and freedom of its individual members.

In terms of coherence and elaboration of its analysis and practice: KRRS is a Gandhian movement. This means that the final objective of its work is the realization of the Village Republic, a form of social, political and economic organization based on direct democracy, on economic and political autonomy, on self-reliance, on the participation of all members of the community in decision-making about the affairs that affect them, and on creating ways to ensure that affairs affecting several communities are decided upon through processes of consultation involving all affected.

This model is applied to the internal organization of the movement. The basic unit of organization is the village unit, which decides on its own forms of organization and finance, programmes and actions.

Above the village level there are several other levels of organization: the *Taluk* [sub-district] level, the district level and the state level. The decisions that affect more than a village but not more than a *Taluk* are taken at *Taluk* level. The decision-making body for the state level is the State Executive Committee, which consists of 400 delegates from all the districts. (KRRS is present in 17 of 19 Karnataka districts).

Since its beginning, the movement has also aimed towards cultural change. It has always denounced the caste system, promoting its elimination as a necessary step towards social justice in India. An example of cultural change promoted by the KRRS is the organization of what it calls "simple, self-respect weddings" as an alternative to the very expensive and extravagant regular weddings (where peasants usually spend a fortune).

The KRRS also has other programmes aimed at challenging patriarchal structures. Women have their own structures, mobilizations and programmes within KRRS,

---

continues to make empty promises and forges ahead with free market policies and social spending cuts.

>> August 21 >> "It's a good day to pie!" The Biotic Baking Brigade (BBB) emerge from their Secret Headquarters and Ovens, located somewhere in the mountains of the Californian northwest, and commit their first act of pie-rect action. Infamous corporate raider and Maxxam CEO Charles Hurwitz receives an apple pie on top of his head for his role in clear-cutting ancient redwoods in Headwaters Forest. He responds "Too bad it's peach. I like blackberry." As Special Agent Apple says, "What does one say about a man who can't tell an apple pie even when he and his stained suit are wearing one?"

>> August 22 >> Earth First! activists in Humboldt County, California, US lock down to a gate at Pacific Lumber's main entrance into the Headwaters redwood forest. Blocking the road is a 'living room', with couch, coffee table, and smashed up television. The activists are covered in mud to spotlight the local town of Stafford, which recently experienced a mud slide from a Pacific Lumber clearcut. Three arrests are made. Three weeks later, 7,000 people converge for the third annual mass rally for Headwaters, and help Stafford residents

organize women's rallies, present their own demands, etc. The KRRS (both women and men) participated in the mobilizations against the celebration of the Miss Universe ceremony in India. It also has for a long time demanded and mobilized for the creation of women's constituencies so that a minimum percentage of the parliament seats are reserved for women. As a result of this pressure (which was joined by other, smaller organizations), the *Panchayats* [village councils] in Karnataka became the first entity of India to create women's constituencies, so that now 33 per cent of seats and offices are reserved for women.

KRRS works under a clear commitment to nonviolence (understood as violence against living beings, not against inanimate objects), and promotes the use of nonviolent

KRRS Archives

Burning genetically modified crops. Karnataka, India

methods (particularly direct action) in order to solve conflicts and overcome problems. This anti-violent stand does not only apply for the protest against governments or companies; it is also generalized to broader areas of conflict, like communal conflict. For example, in the regions where KRRS is strong, the level of violence between different religious groups is much lower than the average.

The KRRS is one of the most important targets of the BJP (the Hindu fundamentalist party which is now running the central government in coalition with 31 other parties), which has unsuccessfully used all kinds of means in its attempt to weaken the movement.

Ecological approaches: alternatives and resistances

The KRRS has always integrated ecological issues in its work in a complete natural way, since the livelihoods that they are defending are a brilliant example of what 'experts' call 'sustainable development'. They have hence taken direct action against eucalyptus plantations [commercial invasive species which deplete the groundwater]. For KRRS there is no sense in dividing resistance and alternatives, since none of them can take place without the other. Rejecting chemical agriculture and biotechnology necessarily implies promoting traditional agriculture.

One district unit in the south of Karnataka is building up a Global Centre for Sustainable Development, which will include the in-situ conservation and development of traditional varieties of seeds, a centre for traditional technologies, a centre for traditional medicines, a green school, etc.

"The American Ambassador in Delhi has written to the Government of the State of Karnataka asking to provide a strong police protection to all American companies in the city. Pointing out the previous repeated attacks on American companies by 'miscreants', the Ambassador ... has stressed the need for a special security for companies related to science and technology and also for their hundreds of foreign companies in the city." - from article in local newspaper *Samykta Karnataka*, 25 November 1998

The fact that traditional technologies and knowledge plays a key role in the alternatives proposed by the KRRS does not mean that we reject new technologies. For instance, the electric fence that will surround the centre for sustainable development (needed given the presence of wild elephants in the area) will be powered by solar energy. The criteria for the acceptance or rejection of technologies in KRRS are not related to their age; they are related to factors such as whether the technology can be directly operated and managed by the people who use it, whether it is labour-intensive or capital-intensive, and other political criteria.

KRRS has been opposing so-called 'Green Revolution' technologies (ie: chemical- and capital-intensive agriculture) since day one, and now it is mobilizing different sectors of society (not just our own constituency) against biotechnology.

Very related to agricultural issues, trade liberalization has also been a basic target of KRRS mobilizations for a long time. The KRRS was the first peoples' movement in India (probably in the world) to organize massive mobilizations against the GATT (the previous incarnation of the WTO) with demonstrations of up to half a million people.

---

sandbag their homes.

>> August 23 >> One thousand Hondurans from the Lenca indigenous nation arrive in Tegucigalpa for what they called the "First civic day for the dignity of the Lenca people." After a march, a public meeting takes place in which they outline their demands to the government: land titles; the creation of a National Council of Ethnic Groups; definitive delimitation of municipalities; recognition of the National Lenca Indigenous Organization of Honduras (ONILH) as the only legal organization representing the Lenca people; and community development programmes, among other demands.

>> September >> Workers in Ecuador occupy the Paute Power Works in an attempt to prevent privatization of the company during a wave of threats to publicly-controlled health care, social security, oil, telecommunications, ports and docks, education, water, and irrigation.

>> September >> Workers protest against a World Bank/IMF meeting in Hong Kong, saying they take inspiration from workers resisting lay-offs and privatization in Sichuan, China and in South Korea.

>> September 8 >> An international day of action for

The main tools of action of KRRS are civil disobedience and direct action. They have organized a large range of really impressive actions, including an action of civil disobedience where 37,000 people were arrested in a single day. (This action was part of a period of intensive mobilizations on which such mass arrests were provoked by KRRS activists every single day).

An important component of KRRS' work is bringing global issues to the local constituencies, and fighting against global institutions and transnational corporations in Karnataka. They have also done spectacular direct actions, including the occupation by 1,000 activists of the Cargill office in Bangalore (they threw all the equipment through the windows and made a big bonfire), the physical dismantlement with iron bars of a seed unit of Cargill that was being constructed in Karnataka, and the occupation of a Kentucky Fried Chicken outlet. "Monsanto, quit India!!" is the running campaign from the KRRS against Monsanto.

They have also created awareness (in Karnataka and beyond) about the impact of global policy-making bodies, tackling issues that are really not easy to bring close to people's lives, like the multilateral trading system, the WTO, intellectual property rights on life, etc.

Besides taking global issues to the local level, KRRS is also very actively involved in national networking processes, since it is clear for them that global issues cannot be tackled unless awareness-raising and mobilization take place beyond the local level. They have played a key role in bringing about national networking processes such as the one that gave birth to the BKU (Indian Farmers Union) or the JAFIP (Joint Action Forum of Indian People against the WTO, which includes movements representing farmers and other social sectors like industrial workers, women's groups, academics, etc).

"Genetically modified seeds are polluting the local species. It will not solve the food problem – in fact it will terminate food security along with biodiversity."

– Nanjundaswamy, quoted in *The Times of India*, 20 November 1998

International networks

In terms of international networking, they were also a key initiator of the PGA process, and they were the ones to propose the Intercontinental Caravan. They are also one of the main actors within *La Via Campesina*, a worldwide network of peasant movements. KRRS hosted both the Second PGA Conference in April 1999 and the Third International Conference of *La Via Campesina* in October 1999.

There is now an effort going on to include representatives of other mass movements besides the peasant movements (tribals, anti-dam, women's, fisherfolk, etc), provided that they share the kind of analysis reflected in the PGA manifesto.

Participation in the caravan

The movements that will send representatives to participate in the Caravan are the state-level branches of the BKU (Indian Farmers' Union) in Punjab, Haryana, Rajasthan, Gujarat, Uttar Pradesh, Maharastra, Madhya Pradesh, Bihar, Andhra Pradesh, and of course Karnataka, where the idea came from and where the largest movement of India (the KRRS, part of the BKU) is based. There will be about 170 people participating from Karnataka (selected directly by the district units of the KRRS, plus a special group of people who will be helpful for all the participants, like ten doctors, one dentist, one gynecologist, etc.) and about 330 from the other states. However, the number of people who want to participate from each of these movements (especially from KRRS) is larger than the quota given, and the number keeps growing and growing. The Indian man and woman know, although the most of them don't speak English and a lot of them can't write, a lot about their problems with and in relation to the WTO. They're also very motivated to come to Europe.

Professor Nanjundaswamy is the leader of the KRRS

Resources:

» Comprehensive site with excellent articles devoted to increasing awareness of the food crisis in India: www.agbioindia.org

» KRRS – Karnataka Raiya Ryota Sanghe, c/o Professor Nanjundaswamy, 2111, 7th-A Cross,3rd Main, Vijayanagar 2nd Stage, Bangalore-560 040-India, Phone: +91-80-3300965 Fax: +91-80-3302171
E-mail: swamy.krrs@vsnl.com; krrs_123@yahoo.com

---

dockers who were sacked in Liverpool, UK, for fighting casualization results in dockers taking action in 21 countries spanning five continents. Every port on the West coast of North America, from Mexico to Alaska, is shut down.

>> **October 3** >> The peoples' movement Narmada Bachao Andolan (Save Narmada Movement) bring together 10,000 villagers in Mandleswar, Madhya Pradesh, India, who will be displaced by the proposed Maheshwar dam. The villagers call for a work stoppage and review of the project in consultation with residents. The company responds with a speed-up of work, and the police seal off roads to prevent an occupation. However, the villagers reach the dam site in the middle of the night, using pathways only known to area residents, and the occupation begins.

>> **October 6** >> Workers in a Hyundai-affiliated *maquiladora* (Mexican sweatshop) in Tijuana, Mexico, vote overwhelmingly for an independent union, despite the company's efforts to sway the vote by paying unemployed people to illegally vote. The union would be the first in the vast *maquiladora* system along the US border. All other *maquila* workers are 'represented' by a company union with close ties to the ruling Institutional

The Karnataka State Farmers' Association of India (see previous text) was one of the first social movements to target the World Trade Organization and corporate globalization. In India they dismantled a Cargill factory. They demanded India's withdrawal from the World Trade Organization – whose Agreement on Agriculture was shaped by Cargill – because opening up India's farm produce to competition from monopolistic global corporations and heavily subsidized US farm products was destroying their livelihoods. They vilified the WTO's global patent regime, written by Monsanto, which facilitated corporate patenting of traditional Indian food crops like basmati rice. But they wanted to go to the belly of the beast. And so in 1998 they conceived of an intercontinental caravan of protest across Europe. Now the Indian farmers could face the WTO and the agribusiness corporations down right on their doorsteps.

450 activists from Southern grassroots movements took part in the Intercontinental Caravan protest tour of Europe in the summer of 1999. Participants included not just 400 Indian farmers, but activists from the Movimento Sem Terra *(Landless Movement of Brazil), and from Columbia, Mexico, Bangladesh, and other places. They came together with European activists to organize the caravan which culminated at the protests at the G8 summit in Köln, Germany on 18 June 1999 as part of a global day of action.*

"We do not want Western money, technologies or 'experts' to impose their development model on us. We refuse to be used as political tools to ask the elites for reforms that we never demanded. We only want to organize our strength and combine it with the strength of other movements in the North and the South in order to regain control over our lives. We are not working for a place on the global table of negotiations, nor for a bloody revolution; we are just working on the long-term process of construction of a different world, a world which will come about from the local to the global, from a shift in the values and everyday choices of millions of persons." – KRRS, 18 June 1999.

Life Is Not Business: the intercontinental caravan

by Katharine Ainger

"Brilliant idea," I'd thought when Nanjundaswamy, leader of the Karnataka State Farmers' Association (KRRS), first explained the vision of an Intercontinental Caravan at a gathering on globalization and resistance by Lake Geneva, the World Trade Organization headquarters glittering in the sun on the far shore. "It'll never happen."

Ten months later, and I'm at the airport to meet a hundred Indian peasants from the KRRS off their chartered Russian plane. I still can't believe they'll ever reach Europe, a feeling which persists until I round a corner, and there they are.

They walk in the white sterility of the airport with a banner proclaiming their arrival, past adverts for corporate bank accounts, global financial services and consumer items for business travellers. Their contingent fills an entire baggage-reclaiming belt. Then, with Indian flags flying on their airport trolleys, they pour into Fortress Europe under the startled gaze of immigration officials.

They seem to me a small but significant rent in the silent curtain that separates the planet into rich and poor.

The following morning, I wake beside dozens of sleeping bodies, my hair filled with straw. We have spent the night in the hayloft of an enormous, dilapidated thirteenth-century monastery on the far eastern German border. As I descend the wobbly ladder, the mist lifts off the surrounding fields, and I try to take in the improbable view below me.

A rural Indian hamlet has been dropped wholesale into the German countryside. Hundreds of Indian farmers are wandering around in the chill of the early morning, many wrapped in the trademark green shawls (the "colour of growing things") of the Karnataka farmers. A serene old man wearing kurta pajamas and plastic shoes seated in the centre of the courtyard takes a long, slow draw from a hookah pipe as large as himself, and still with its Aeroflot baggage-tag attached. He nods towards me graciously. In the far corner, steam rises from the vast vats of chai (tea) being brewed by local and international volunteers. In another corner a group of shivering Indians with fur hats are watching a kid with a shaved head and three dreadlocks sticking out the back of his head trace a route across a map of Europe. Women expertly wash themselves without removing their saris by the taps.

Grabbing a chewy piece of bread and some tea, I catch a glimpse of my friend Kolya and run over to him. "You did it!" is all I can say, as we clutch each other somewhat hysterically. He, and several hundred other European activists have been working for ten months to do the impossible. Defying staggering odds, logic – and possibly common sense – they have brought hundreds of members of Southern social movements to Europe for a one-month protest tour that will traverse nine countries. This includes 400 peasant farmers from India and 50 movement representatives from other regions, including *Movimento Sem Terra* (Landless Movement) from Brazil, the Indigenous Mapuche movement from Chile, the Process of Black Communities from Colombia, environmentalists from Pakistan, a women's farmers movement from Bangladesh, human rights activists from Nepal, a member of the Mexican civil society support group for the Zapatistas, and many more.

This is the Intercontinental Caravan of Solidarity and Resistance, or ICC. It's an unprecedented initiative to bring members of Southern social movements at the forefront of resisting globalization and capitalist exploitation, en masse, to protest for themselves at Northern centres of power. They will swarm at the headquarters of the World Trade

---

Revolutionary Party (PRI) dynasty. Days later, the company fires the pro-union workers, and one month later the election is declared invalid by the National Conciliation and Arbitration Board.

>> October 15 >> Zimbabwe's impoverished farm workers, the largest single group of workers in the country, win a hefty wage increase as a result of their first organized national strike against the country's wealthy, predominantly white, commercial farmers. Farm workers, who walked out at the end of September, were demanding wage increases and additional leave days. During the strike, thousands of singing, chanting workers blocked highways, invaded farms, and chased union officials from a tea plantation after suggestions that the strikers return to work.

>> October 15 >> Thousands of members of two Zambian public workers unions, the Civil Servants Union of Zambia (CSUZ) and the National Union of Public Service Workers (NUPSW) start a three day strike, demanding implementation of a 1997 contract. Hospitals, courts, and all government offices come to a virtual standstill nationwide. On the second day, with thousands more joining the strike, the government declares the strike illegal, threatening unions with

Organization. They will scream "Biotechnology down, down!" at the headquarters of Cargill, the biggest seed corporation in the world. They will destroy GM rice with French farmers. They will surround the NATO buildings in Brussels. The tour will end on June 18 at the meeting of the G8 leaders in Köln, Germany with an enormous 'laugh parade', the spirit of which recalls the cry of the Zapatistas: "First world? Ha! Ha! Ha!" Together, they want to resist the globalization process that they call corporate colonialism.

For 30 days, 11 buses will altogether travel 56,000 miles, take part in 63 direct actions, 85 public meetings, visit 38 farms, and go to 30 parties. The ICC. It's at least as full of genius and insanity as it sounds.

Comfortably ensconced on a bench nestling in the ruins of a giant tree stump beside the monastery, Vijay Jawandhia of the All India Farmers' Union explains to me why they have come. "The farmers were told we'd benefit from joining the WTO, that we'd get better prices for our produce. But due to globalization, the prices paid for our food are going down and down while the cost of production for the same farmer is going up."

He's also sceptical about the costs of the 'Green Revolution', which brought intensive and corporate agriculture to India in the 1960s under the auspices of the World Bank, and American foundations and corporations. "Pests have become immune to the pesticides, and the fertilizer has depleted the soil so we have to add more to get the same level of production." This becomes a desperate cycle of debt and dependency as farmers borrow money to buy chemical inputs. Jawandhia tells me about the 1,200 farmers who have committed suicide in the state of Andhra Pradesh over the previous two years. They'd got seeds and pesticides on credit at crippling rates of interest from a toxic alliance of ruthless moneylenders who were also seed and pesticide agents of transnational corporations. Monsanto used its local seed agents in a massive push towards planting cotton in Andhra Pradesh. When the harvest failed, many indebted farmers committed suicide by swallowing their own pesticides.

The mist of the morning is burning off under midday heat, and a German peasant woman with headscarf grins toothlessly at us as she passes. I ask Jawandhia what his message to the G8 will be when they join the protests in Köln at the end of the tour.

"We want to say to the G8 leaders: 'We do not want your charity, we do not want your loans.' Those in the North have to understand our struggle and realize it is also part of their own. Everywhere the richer are getting richer, the poor are getting poorer, and the environment is being plundered. Whether in North or South, we face the same future. We see the European farmers also being affected by 'free trade' policies. Just as Europe exported its development model to the rest of the world, now it is our turn to bring an alternative development model to you."

Later that day I am wandering through the welcoming ceremony, and wondering why most political speeches are identically boring no matter what country the speaker comes from, when I meet a man with a kind face, patiently seated on the outskirts of the audience. Mr. Somalingiah looks like he is in his late sixties, with a sparse beard, sandals, pajamas, and a green shawl. At first he is diffident. "My English is not good. I am not an educated man," he says quietly. We sit together in silence for a while, contemplating our chai. I ask about his farm. He grows coconut and silk on five acres of land in the southern state of Karnataka. Then, all of a sudden he leans forward and asks me intensely: "Tell me. Have you read Bertrand Russell?"

"Er ... no," I say.

Quoting Russell, Gandhi, Einstein, and the Indian plant geneticist Jadadesh Chandra Bose, and drawing on an extensive knowledge of ecology and traditional farming methods, Mr. Somalingiah then startles me with a trenchant critique of Western materialism. He believes, he says, clutching his tea, in Gandhi's vision of self-government and self-sufficiency. "Only then", he explained, "can persons have self-respect. The self-sufficient personality is not dependent. I came here because I want to tell European people about this idea of self-sustaining village life, to tell them of the importance of an economy that includes the ecology of living systems."

I am rather lost for words.

"America and Europe," he continues, "they are part of a materialistic mega-system. This system does not allow people to live an independent lifestyle. People have no liberty. Every youth thinks only of profit. But this is something inhuman. This mentality had developed based around a profit-oriented megasystem. It is impossible to reach mutual understandings under such a system."

Then this man, who never graduated from primary school, gave the most cogent summary I've heard of what this movement is for, and what it is against. "Globalization means we want to globalize human society, not business. Life," he said earnestly, settling the full force of his gaze onto me, "life is not business."

It takes the best part of the day to load the 11 buses headed for different destinations. The bus I am coordinating is the last to be loaded. I watch with mounting horror as the all of the enormous tins of rice are put onto other buses – and

---

degregistration and individuals with jail sentences. The unions comply, and call on their workers to return to work the next day.

>> November 10 >> A US coalition of labour, environmental, farm, and other groups block the passage of 'fast track' legislation which would have allowed the president to negotiate new trade agreements without Congressional approval. This defeat is seen as the first major check to the growing power of global trade organizations.

>> November 11 >> A two day general strike in the Dominican Republic is declared 80-90 per cent effective in the capital and 100 per cent effective in much of the interior. Striker's demands include a 40 per cent wage increase, lowered prices on basic goods and fuel, improved transport and electricity services, and reincorporation of workers fired from the state-run electricity corporation. The president declares the strike illegal, as his government's efforts to neutralize the strike, which included preemptive arrests of hundreds of organizers and journalists, and the distribution of about $4 million had so clearly failed.

>> November 16 >> Over 250 unionists and activists from 20 countries participate in the

there is none left for us. We are in the middle of nowhere, going on a 12 hour journey heading to Amsterdam with no food. No one can help. I can't speak a word of German. The other buses pull away. "We'll fill you up with some jars of food from the Ukraine that the monastery has donated," some helpful soul offers. We set off with 14 crates filled with dusty jars of pickled rutabagas from the Chernobyl region that the monastery has thus far found no use for, and eight litres of rapidly turning milk in the belly of the bus.

My fellow bus coordinator is a lovely woman, an authentic free spirit, but even less practical a soul than I. When I confer with her about how to feed our 40 caravaners, she puts her head on one side, thinks for a moment, then smiles and pulls from the depths of her enormous yellow satchel a cabbage covered in mud, which she passes around the bus.

Meanwhile I am filled with the aching awareness that forcing as much food as physically possible on the guest is at the profound and unchangeable heart of the Indian psyche. And here I am with 40 Indians on a bus in the middle of nowhere, with a tonne of radioactive rutabagas in the boot. We stop at a Shell service station.

This is many of the caravaners' first taste of Western consumerism. Several finger plastic ornaments, socks, and key chains in admiration until I translate some of the prices into rupees. We buy some supplies and the Indians unhappily munch on damp sandwiches. Fortunately my fellow bus-coordinator pulls vast quantities of sweets she has expertly shoplifted from the petrol station out of her voluminous coat pockets. We munch on them all the way into Amsterdam. She, however, is the only one who tries the Chernobyl rutabagas.

The caravan is a mixture of inspired genius and terrible folly, and over the coming weeks it becomes increasingly impossible to disentangle the two. It stretches European activists to the breaking point or beyond, yet leaves a network of groups within and between countries who have never worked together before. In India, too, the farmers movements post-caravan are far more focused on working together on national issues.

Many Europeans have embarked on this project understanding little or nothing about the context of struggle in India. Some show little imagination in understanding the reality of the caravaners, condemning as 'bourgeois' their wishes to spend time out sight-seeing.

And some of the Indian men have difficulty adjusting their assumptions too: few women from the South are on the caravan – it is difficult for Indian women to travel alone or leave their families to travel. Many European women bus coordinators report disrespect from some of the male participants, and in a few cases even harassment. And, as one caravan email list posting notes, "It was probably stunning at first for many middle-aged, male leaders from a highly patriarchal society to be organized and treated on an equal footing by very young people – often female, and dressing and acting in apparently outlandish and shocking ways to boot!"

While in Amsterdam, a several-hour-long battle with a tight-lipped civil servant lends me renewed respect for the mindboggling achievement of those who won the battle to get the caravaners visas for Europe. We are still trying to get British visas for almost all of the 100 caravaners en route for London in two days time.

Fifteen farmers from the Punjabi farmer's union the BKU (Bharatiya Kisan Union) and 20 from the Gujurati union (Khedut Samaj) and two Nepalese human rights workers have got UK visas, but every single member of the KRRS has been turned down. They made their applications back in Madras, India. But the high commission there treated them 'like dirt', throwing their forms away because they had written in blue ink, despite the fact that the letters of invitation gave financial guarantees and support by several British MPs. "They are still in the colonial mindset at the Madras High Commission," one green-scarved KRRS farmer tells me, sadly, when I tell him we have failed to get the visas. Clearly, the KRRS's reputation has gone before them.

It is the summer of 1999 and Britain is in the middle of a popular revolt against genetically modified (GM) food, to the irritation of the government which has made great investment in a GM future. Fields of farm-scale GM trials are being felled, by day and by night, by armies of activists in white decontamination suits.

In response, the Life Science industries' PR machine is on the war-path. They're trying to convince the public that anti-GM activism is preventing the hungry in the global South from feeding themselves. In this context the entrance of 100 Indian peasant veterans of a Cremate Monsanto campaign into Britain this summer would be political dynamite – something to be avoided at all cost.

The day the 30 farmers from the Gujurat and the Punjab arrive in the UK, an article appears in the *Telegraph* about a new Nuffield Foundation report which concludes that Britain has a "moral imperative" to develop GM crops to feed the global South, accompanied by a picture of an appropriately emaciated Biafran.

As it happens, the Nuffield Foundation offices are round the corner from the shambolic London forum where the caravaners are speaking. Learning of the Nuffield report's conclusions, they are infuriated by the fact that no actual farmers from the global South have been consulted.

Several of the UK's most talented genetics activists,

Western Hemispheric Conference Against Privatizations and NAFTA in San Francisco, US, to hear testimony from across the Américas of the effects of Mercosur, NAFTA, and rampant privatization. Strategizing occurs about how to fend off the MAI and the FTAA. A call for a common day of action at next April's FTAA meeting in Chile is developed from the conference.

>> **November 25** >> Canadian students protest against the annual APEC summit in Vancouver, BC, and are met with preemptive arrests and an unprecedented attack with pepper spray, leading to a national inquiry known as "Peppergate." Intelligence files later released show that police requested the arrests of, and specified criminal charges for, certain activists "with a view of eliminating some of the more high profile members" of anti-APEC groups.

>> **November 28** >> MST members establish a protest camp in front of the state Rural Development Secretariat in Fortaleza, Brazil. Military police attack as the protest begins, injuring five peasants. The camp survives the attack, remaining in place for over two weeks until 1,000 military police agents surround the group of landless protesters, sealing off the area, and harassing

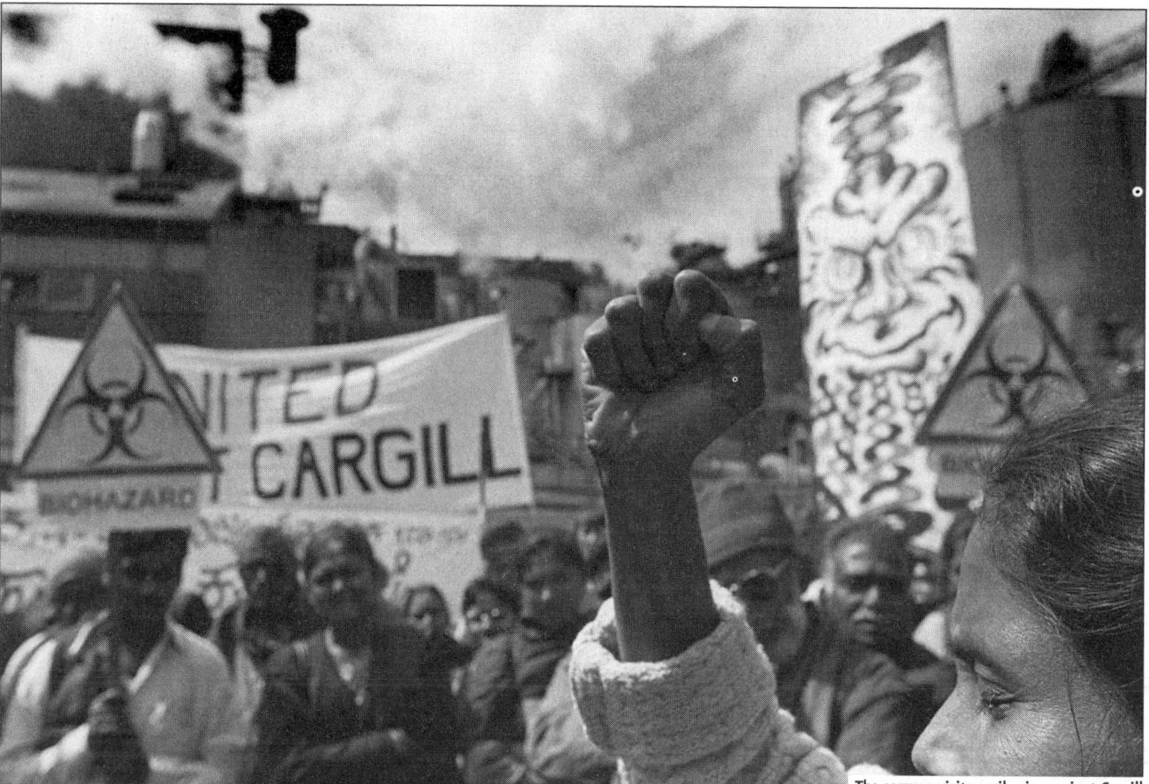

Thomas Schlijper

The caravan visits agribusiness giant Cargill

without whom this leg of the trip would have been a disaster, get on the case. By the afternoon the farmers have spread out over the road, blocking London traffic. They carry home made banners: "No to the WTO;" "Food Control Eats You," and a big one split in two which reads "Say no to GMO" and sometimes, when the banner carriers get mixed up, "To GMO say no."

Reaching the Nuffield offices, the crowd blocks the entrance and the farmers at the front demand an audience with the director. Eventually he arrives, looking very unhappy. He's not sure whether to call the police or be excessively polite to his uninvited foreign guests – so he does both. Several of us accompany the farmers into the building to record what is said.

Around the table sit the leaders of some of India's largest farmers unions. Manjit Kadran, the Secretary General of the BKU, an imposing man with an enormous turban; Ajmeri Lakshowal, the President of the BKU union; Lal Shankar Upadhyaya of the Gujurati State Farmers' Association; G. Singh Haribe, Mukhtian Rana, and Hasmukh Patel, all give eloquent testimony to Antony Dumay, the director, who looks nervous, sweaty, and extremely uncomfortable, and Peter Murray, the assistant director, who looks like he hasn't had this entertaining a day at work in years.

"We understand," says Manjit Kadran imperiously, looking as frightening as a Sikh can, "that you have issued a report insisting that there is a moral imperative to develop genetically modified foods to feed the world.

"Perhaps you believe that India needs genetically engineered seeds, or there will be famine? I am from north west India. India has a surplus of food, and we have a problem of storage, not of shortage. What we need is facilities and political will for the distribution of this food. This surplus is largely due to the production of small-scale peasant farmers. Even without genetically engineered seeds, we have surplus. So you can imagine our astonishment to hear from your report that we need genetically engineered food to feed ourselves."

The director made demurring noises that he hadn't actually written the report himself, and that full details of the report's authors were available on their website, and

---

and attacking journalists.

>> December >> Support groups around the world protest at the news that 45 unarmed peasants have been massacred by paramilitaries in Acteal, Chiapas, in one of the worst incidents of repression during the Zapatista conflict.

>> December 2 >> About 120 people from the Committee of Unemployed of Central Montreal carry out a 'Commando Bouffe' food grab at a posh hotel in Montreal. They storm the exclusive buffet restaurant and reappropriate the food, taking it into the street to feed fellow homeless and unemployed people. Riot police are called and 108 of the commandos are arrested.

>> December 3 >> In Brasilia, Brazil, a group of people from the MST seize the Ministry of Land Policy and the national headquarters of the National Institute of Colonization and Agrarian Reform for four hours. The protestors issue a list of ten demands, including the immediate settlement of the landless families in encampments set up on expropriated lands, the expropriation of 20 more rural properties, and the provision of grants and seeds to those already living in the encampments. This action

that they couldn't engage in debate then and there...

"This very bio-engineering," interrupts a white-haired man in a *dhoti*. "What about our ecological and cultural biodiversity? When you limit seed varieties to one or two? Now we have 100 varieties. If one fails, we have many others we can use if we have only one and it fails, all fails."

Luke Andersen, a British activist who has written a book on genetic engineering, adds: "And in any case, not a single GE seed has so far produced higher yields."

Hashmukh Patel says, "Seventy per cent of Indians rely on agriculture, and most of us are small farmers. We are really concerned with these developments. Our past experiences, for example with hybrid seeds, show they are useless after one or two or three crops, and require huge amounts of pesticides and fertilizers.

"Your report gets heard. But we don't have a voice that gets heard. This is why we came in a crowd. It is the only way to show our agony. No one hears us. We are frustrated. Kindly tell our agonies to your scientists, the decision makers, tell them our miseries. And we have been collecting the tribal knowledge of our indigenous farmers. Kindly convey that to the decision makers too."

Another explains, gently, "You see, this is not a question of intellectual debate to us, but a question of survival. This is life and death for us."

And then he adds, with a smile, "You paid a lot of expensive researchers and consultants for that report. But we have given you our good opinion for free."

And then we leave.

Outside, a police officer asks for our names. When we refuse to give them, he says, "Suit yourselves. We'll just take your pictures and get them on file."

The next day we are on a bus heading for Bishop's Stortford, where a field trial of Monsanto's genetically modified oil seed rape was pulled up by activists two weeks previously.

Anarchist Teapot, a group who serve food at actions, have set up a bender (wooden tent-like structure) and are cooking lunch. A tripod rises out of the field, fortifying us from eviction, and as an imposing line of Indian farmers comes over the horizon, their union banners fluttering in the wind, three activists get up a folk song on flute and fiddle to welcome them.

A few neighbours from nearby houses turn up to read the information signs about GM crops, and are fascinated by the sight of Indian farmers and British eco-warriors planting organic vegetables in the soil together. Everywhere you look something bizarre and wonderful is happening. A protest veteran shows an Indian housewife how you 'lock on'. The Indian farmers are shocked to learn that it is illegal to save or swap seeds that are not on the official seed list in the UK. One listens to the anti-GM feeling sweeping Britain and says, amazed, "We're overjoyed to see that European people are also opposing biotechnology!" Someone shins up the tripod, until the activist banner of red, green and black is joined by the green and white Punjabi farmers' union flag fluttering in the breeze.

This, for me, is the best afternoon of the entire caravan. One man plays an Irish song and says, "These lyrics are about resistance against British colonialism." Then a Punjabi named Jagdish Singh sings one in return, explaining it has exactly the same theme. Dave thumbs an obscure traditional English folk string instrument called a sitan and Jagdish improvises lyrics. It stops me in my tracks. It's the oddest and one of the most beautiful musical combinations I've ever heard – delicate English folk sounds to haunting Indian vocals – and suddenly my eyes are filled with tears. Finally, Jagdish ends with a song he describes as "a promise to our guru that we will not run away from our fields of struggle." The activists who've been living in this field for days, and been organizing tirelessly to raise British public awareness of GM crops for months and even years, look like they understand.

Accompanying us is the agricultural correspondent from *The Economist* magazine. As we leave for home, I ask her what she thinks of her first crop squat. "I've had more intelligent conversations here than I've had in six months of café-squatting in Kensington," she says, looking surprised.

In France, the ICC's passing launched a mini-revolution. In Montpellier they destroyed a greenhouse of GM rice with the radical French farmers, in particular Renée Reisel and José Bové of *Confédération Paysannes* (the radical French farmers' union). They left a populace that was dry tinder for a popular rebellion against the WTO, GM foods, corporate power, and *malbouffe* (junk /industrial food). Two months later, Bové dismantled a McDonalds in protest and became an international media star.

This was the caravan, perhaps the most ambitious attempt yet to connect up different traditions of struggle, North and South. Sometimes they combined in the most beautiful and unexpected of ways, emblematic of this new kind of politics. Sometimes they collided in ways that were more like farce than solidarity, as 400 Indian farmers discovered when they joined up with a peace march outside the NATO headquarters in Brussels. When a contingent of naked hippies arrived, the distressed Indian farmers spent much of the next half an hour entreating them urgently, "Please! Please sirs! Put on your clothes!"

They stayed in Berlin squats, stood on anti-genetics platforms in Pamplona. They were turned back at the Polish border, where the local farmers were rioting and sent a note

---

is one of a series of similar, and mostly successful, MST protests in five states.

>> December 9 >> The Bolivian Workers Central (COB) labour federation stages a national 24-hour strike and a march in La Paz to protest the *gasolinazo*, or governmental fuel price hikes. The march in the capital brings together nearly 8,000 teachers, campesinos, factory workers, miners, retirees, university students, oil workers and even small-scale business people and artisans in a broad-based rejection of the government's economic policies. The strike is widely honored in Cochabamba, site of a second mass demonstration, which also pays homage to Pablo Rocha, a miner who recently died of silicosis.

>> December 10 >> Julia "Butterfly" Hill climbs 'Luna', an ancient redwood in the Headwaters Forest, California, US She lives in the tree for over two years, protecting the trees surrounding her and helping to draw international attention to the destruction of the redwoods.

>> December 11 >> More than 30,000 people, mainly auto workers, march in São Paulo, Brazil, to defend their jobs and to protest against the central government's economic policies, including a rise in interest rates to 40

of solidarity instead. In Geneva, they marched to the WTO building. "*ICC zindabad! WTO murdabad!*" they yelled. (Long live ICC, kill the WTO). Italian caravaner Maurizio Cucci describes, "The green scarves of the Karnataka farmers, together with the red flags of Brazilian *sem terra*, the turbans of the Punjabi farmers, the coloured hair of the European squatters, a tractor of Swiss farmers...thousands of voices rise in a multilingual speech of testimony against the threat the WTO poses to their lives."

Once, back in Karnataka's capital, Bangalore, the KRRS laughed all day outside the state government's buildings. The next week the government collapsed. There is a mass arrest of caravaners at the culmination of the ICC when they converge on Köln, Germany for the G8 meeting on June 18. But all is not lost: in downtown Köln – a group of laugh-paraders spot the G8 leaders' wives visiting an art gallery, and a spooky "Ha! Ha! Ha!" erupts from their lips. Despite the chaos and the contradiction, the caravan has the last laugh.

UPDATE: In 2002, Reisel and Bové served six months in jail for destroying the GM rice during the caravan. The judge made no mention of the 150 letters he had received from Indian farmers in 1999, proclaiming their own guilt for this piece of direct action, and insisting they be arrested and charged too.

Katharine Ainger is one of the co-editors of this book

Together We Start A Struggle

excerpt from a speech given by Intercontinental Caravan participant Jorge, of Brazil's Movimento Sem Terra (landless movement), during the protests in Köln, 18 June 1999

Compañeras y compañeros:

We, of the Brazilian and Latin American delegation of the caravan, saw, heard and learned many things on European soil. Two big lessons in particular:

We saw beautiful cities, large buildings, luxurious cars. An architecture that reflected history and radiated wealth. We did not always understand what we heard. For it seemed that amidst all this beauty, people spoke of bad things. We heard little laughter, and saw little happiness.

We saw with astonishment that many seemed half-dead, imprisoned in their own bodies without a spark of life, addicted to television and radio – doped by the sound of the religious ritual of consumption, of cheap and expensive drugs. Doped with indifference and illusion.

Thus we saw humans, empty, in the midst of beautiful things, but – without humanity. That is how this continent, which we call 'the cradle of Western civilization', appears to us. Now it is a grave, a cave, a cemetery, a consequence of the human race.

But here we also learned another lesson.

We understood that there is resistance, which attacks this order between all these bad things – when houses are squatted, when war is denounced, when the persecution of migrants is condemned. When international collectives carry messages against 'Third World' debt, when the environment is defended against economic globalization, whose soul is called capitalism.

We learned that we are many minorities. In us, who fight together, hope catches fire for the coming millennium. The governments of the wealthy G8 countries meet to discuss the fate of peoples under all possible forms of force, forced to suffer the world, the destruction of our rivers and plants and the lives of millions of human beings.

Thus the force of the neoliberal model is imposed on poor countries. For example, in Brazil we have the murder of the example that the *Movimento Sem Terra* embodies, and without condemnation, the murder of more than fifty-six of our *compañer@s* – this is the cruel face of capitalism. But we know that what remains for us, the peoples of the world, is to mobilize those who still resist imperialism, to carry out our resistance, and not to bend.

We, peoples from different continents, who have joined together in this caravan, started a struggle. We have understood that capital has no boundaries.

Therefore we must create an enormous uprising of peoples on all continents, to continue to call for respect for life and human rights, and also for the environment and nature.

Down with the IMF! Down with the WTO! Down with Monsanto and many other multinational companies, who think only of accumulating capital! The fight of the people lives! The Intercontinental Caravan lives! ICC *zindabad!*

Note: The use of the "@" in the word compañer@ is used by some radicals in Spanish and Portuguese to render words gender-inclusive, as the symbol includes an "a" and an "o".

---

per cent. The protest takes place in the industrial zone, San Bernardo, where most of the automotive factories are located. Workers' Party leader Luiz Inacio 'Lula' da Silva speaks at the protest, blaming the central government for the economic crisis and demanding that authorities lower interest rates.

\\ 1998 //

>> January 17 >> The Global March against Child Labour kicks off in Manila, Philippines with over 10,000 participants, largely children. One march continues for 14 weeks, passing through several Asian countries and hosting educational forums. Many of the marchers regroup in Geneva in June for the annual conference of the International Labour Organization.

>> January 18-19 >> In Stockholm, Sweden, activists from Action for Social Ecology severely damage four road building machines, temporarily stopping the construction of the southern link road. The link is a part of a large road building project that has extreme environmental impacts. After much hard work in the courts and on the streets, the road project is canceled.

>> Continued on page 189 >>

ABOLISH
CAPITALISM
NOW!

Carnival resistance is the secret of joy

"The goal of the revolutionary artist is to make revolution irresistible." – **Toni Cade Bambara**

"We will make revolution irresistible," assured a bit of Direct Action Network propaganda, in the final days of November 1999. Writing those words late at night, I was hunched on the floor of the near-empty warehouse in downtown Seattle with a friend and a laptop, with only 30 minutes before going to print, and eight hours before we opened the convergence centre – a networking hub and training facility for activists – to the world. After having gone for months with too much to do and too little sleep, I grumbled about how utterly resistible this particular aspect of 'revolution' seemed, before getting on my bike and weaving my way home – to yet another meeting. Organizing a Festival of Resistance didn't feel particularly festive that night.

But the nights flew past and the day, 30 November 1999, a date fixed in our heads for months and now engraved into the history books, dawned. Bleary-eyed, my affinity group gathered at 7.00 am. Running late, we hurried to catch up with the main march as it headed down the hill into downtown Seattle. The perspective from above was incredible – all we could see was people – our people – spilling out of the streets and onto the sidewalks, a cacophony of colour and exhilaration. Sleeplessness didn't matter anymore. We passed a tripod blockade, a man dangling from its apex, a line of cars immobilized impatiently, not yet understanding how futile they were that day. Those were the last cars I saw for 12 hours.

Andrew Wiard

As we entered downtown something shifted. It was partially the fresh air blowing off the Puget Sound, unpolluted by the choking exhaust that was the normal scent of the city. We controlled the streets, all of them, and in every direction we looked were more and more of us, and thousands still arriving. There were stilt walkers dressed as butterflies, a giant inflatable whale blockading an intersection, a hip hop crew rhyming through a mobile sound system, a stage being built to double as a road blockade where performances would take place all day long, giant puppets, butoh dancers, acrobats. The sounds were incredible – the sound of drums resounding off skyscrapers, the sound of chanting and singing, the sound of laughter – no honking, no engines roaring.

I looked up at the high-rise hotels where the world's trade representatives were just waking up, preparing to go to work, turning on the TV or looking out the window and perhaps beginning to realize that they weren't going to make it to work that day, that they were trapped in their hotels. Perhaps they had already figured out that the city streets, normally the domain of cars and capital, of commerce, trade, and profit, were ours now; perhaps the delegates recognized that for once, they were the excluded ones, the ones with no place in our ideal society. The dominant colour of the city was no longer a shade of dark suit, and making history was triumphing over making money. Just then the rain let up. I think it was in that moment that we all realized that we really were going to do it, that history belonged to us that day, that we really were going to shut down the WTO. Later, left-wing journalist Geov Parrish would write, "'Seattle' became a one-word rallying cry, used to invoke horror by free trade advocates, used to evoke inspiration by those new generations around the world."

Almost all of us that were in Seattle on November 30 felt like we were personally responsible, like our participation in the day's events was crucial to things unfolding as they had. Goethe wrote that carnival "is not really a festival given for the people but one the people give themselves," and we gave ourselves the best we could. We came away in triumph, not only having succeeded at bringing to a halt the trade negotiations of the WTO's millennium round, but also at withstanding the brutal repression unleashed upon us. For many of us, it was the first time we had directly experienced the state's power, and it changed us for life. But a deeper imprint was left by the experience of the carnival – halfway between party and protest, resisting at the same time as proposing, destroying at the same time as creating. Our 'carnival against capital' brought together the volatile mixture of carnival and revolution, creativity and conflict, using rhythm and music to reclaim space, transform the streets, and inject pleasure into politics.

Turning the world upside down

Revel *(rev'l) vi. from MFr. reveler, to revel, lit., to rebel; L. rebellare, see* **REBEL.** **1.** *to dance, drink, sing, etc. at a party or in public; to be noisily festive;* **2.** *to take intense pleasure; to delight (in) [to revel in one's freedom]*

Reinventing tactics of resistance has become a central preoccupation for the movement of movements. How do we make rebellion enjoyable, effective and irresistible? Who wants the tedium of traditional demonstrations and protests – the ritual marches from point A to B, the permits and police escorts, the staged acts of civil disobedience, the verbose rallies and dull speeches by leaders? Instead, why not use a form of rebellion that embody the movements' principles of diversity, creativity, decentralization, horizontality, and direct action? These principles can be found at the heart of a ancient form of cultural expression, the carnival.

Throughout history carnival has been a time for inverting the social order, where the village fool dresses as the king and the king waits on the pauper, where men and women wear each others' clothing and perform each others' roles. This inversion exposes the power structures

"EROTICISM IS EXCITING, LIFE WOULD BE A DRAB ROUTINE WITHOUT AT LEAST THAT SPARK. THAT'S THE POINT. WHY HAS ALL THE JOY AND EXCITEMENT BEEN CONCENTRATED, DRIVEN INTO THAT ONE NARROW, DIFFICULT-TO-FIND ALLEY OF HUMAN EXPERIENCE, AND ALL THE REST LAID TO WASTE? THERE'S PLENTY TO GO AROUND WITHIN THE SPECTRUM OF OUR LIVES." – **Shulamith Firestone, *The Dialectic of Sex: The Case For Feminist Revolution*, Harpercollins, 1970**

and illuminates the processes of maintaining hierarchies – seen from a new angle, the foundations of authority are shaken up and flipped around. The unpredictability of carnival with its total subservience to spontaneity, where any individual can shape her environment and transform herself into another being for an hour or a day, ruptures what we perceive to be reality. It creates a new world by subverting all stereotypes, daring imaginations to expand their limits, turning the present world upside down, if only for a moment.

It is in the capricious moments of history when we can best see that carnival and revolution have identical goals: to turn the world upside down with joyous abandon and to celebrate our indestructible lust for life, a lust that capitalism tries so hard to destroy with its monotonous merry go round of work and consumerism. In its immediacy, carnival refuses the constant mediation and representations of capitalism. It opens up an alternative social space of freedom where people can begin to really live again.

This also means turning what we consider to be political on its head. Mention the word *politics* and many people will imagine a world filled with words, and debate, a sterile, pleasureless world of talking heads. The pleasures of the body have been banished from the public sphere of politics and the excitement of the erotic pushed into the narrow private confines of the sexual realm. But carnival brings the body back to public space, not the perfect smooth bodies that promote consumption on billboards and magazines, not the manipulated plastic bodies of MTV and party political broadcasts, but the body of warm flesh, of blood and guts, organs and orifices.

During carnival the body sticks its tongue out as far as it can, it laughs uncontrollably, sweats and farts as it dances in the heat of other bodies. It's a body that refuses the static images of itself developed by capital, frozen in immortal youthfulness, aloof from natural cycles of eating and shitting, being born and decomposing. In carnival the body is always changing, constantly becoming, eternally unfinished. Inseparable from nature and fused to other bodies around it, the body remembers that it is not a detached, atomized being, as it allows its erotic impulse to jump from body to body, sound to sound, mask to mask, to swirl across the streets, filling every nook and cranny, every fold of flesh. During carnival the body, with its pleasures and desires, can be found everywhere, luxuriating in its freedom and inverting the everyday.

We live in a world already turned on its head, writes Eduardo Galeano, a "desolate, de-souled world that practices the superstitious worship of machines and the idolatry of arms, an upside-down world with its left on its right, its belly button on its backside, and its head where its feet should be." In this upside-down world, children work, 'development' impoverishes, the poor pay the rich, and people are bombed in order to be 'liberated'. In this grotesque looking-glass wonderland, 'free' speech is paid for, cars are in streets where people should be, public servants don't serve, free trade is a monopoly, the more you have, the more you get, and a handful of the global population consumes the majority of the resources. And, Galeano asks: "If the world is upside-down the way it is now, wouldn't we have to turn it over to get it to stand up straight?"

Everything was topsy-turvy in London on 18 June 1999. The world's largest financial centre, a square mile district known as the City of London, is normally a place resounding with the sounds of profit. The ringing of mobile phones, the click of high heels on the sidewalks, the clink of wine glasses over power lunches, the hiss of espresso machines on every corner, the hum of CCTV cameras turning to follow movements. A modern-day fortress, with police checkpoints at every entrance, the City is one of the most heavily surveilled square miles in the world. It is a tribute to the acquisition of wealth, with a foreign exchange turnover equal to that of Tokyo, New York, and Paris.

> "THE REVOLUTION, IN GENERAL, IS NO LONGER IMAGINED ACCORDING TO SOCIALIST PATTERNS OF REALISM, THAT IS, AS MEN AND WOMEN STOICALLY MARCHING BEHIND A RED, WAVING FLAG TOWARDS A LUMINOUS FUTURE. RATHER IT HAS BECOME A SORT OF CARNIVAL."
>
> **– Subcomandante Marcos**

Yet this Friday was different. Mobile phones were still ringing, but for a very different purpose. The clicking high heels were replaced by the sounds of boots pounding pavement, the clinking wine glasses by the cascade of shattered windows, the hiss of steaming milk by the whoosh of water let loose from a fire hydrant, and all to the beat of the overarching samba rhythm, resounding off the fortress' walls. The City was occupied by 10,000 people wearing carnival masks, who evaded the police by splitting into four different groups, all headed for a secret location – one of the most important financial hubs, the London International Financial Futures Exchange (LIFFE).

One of London's 75 buried rivers was freed and water spurted 30 feet into the air, cooling off the dancing crowd, flooding the street, and flowing into the basement of LIFFE. Around the corner, another entrance to the Exchange was being bricked up as if it were an abandoned building, obsolete in the post-capitalist world the carnival hoped to help bring about.

Carnival's mockery, chaos and transgression have always threatened the sobriety and seriousness of the state, which is why it was often banned or heavily controlled. What carnivals remain in most parts of the world have themselves become spectacles – specialist performances watched by spectators – with police lines and barriers placed between the parade and audience. Thus the vortexed, whirling, uncontrollable state of creative chaos is shoe-horned into neat straight lines and rectangles. A visit to many contemporary carnivals sanctioned by the state (such as Carnaval in Rio de Janeiro, or the Notting Hill Carnival in London) where consumption and corporate sponsorship has taken over from the creativity and spontaneity is enough to illustrate how carnival under capitalism has lost its vitality. But carnival has been with us since time immemorial and it has always refused to die. Reappearing in different guises across the ages it returns again and again. Freed from the clutches of entertainment, the anticapitalist movements have thrown it back into the streets, where it is liberated from commerce for everyone to enjoy once again.

Participate, don't spectate

"Carnival does not know footlights, in the sense that it does not acknowledge any distinction between actors and spectators. Footlights would destroy a carnival, as the absence of footlights would destroy a theatrical performance. Carnival is not a spectacle seen by the people; they live in it, and everyone participates because its very idea embraces all the people."

– Mikhail Bakhtin, *Rabelais and his World*, Indiana University Press, 1984

Passivity disappears when carnival comes to town, with its unyielding demand for participation. It is the time for celebrating the joy of collectivity, the exhilaration of creating something that snowballs into something much bigger, and more amazing than previously imagined possible. It is a moment when we can break free from the alienation that capitalism enforces in so many ways. We find ourselves separated from each other and from our environment as we move from place to place in the isolation of private car or the silence and averted eyes of public transport.

We face it at work, forced into competition with our colleagues, under constant threat of being 'downsized', 'laid off', 'made redundant'. We suffer from it even when we try and relax, watching television or movies, which promote lifestyles we can't afford, and which require that we sit silently, passive recipients of someone else's visions. Consequently, we leave important questions about politics, economics and foreign policy up to experts, having been told that these matters are too complicated for us to understand.

But carnival denies the existence of experts, or rather, insists that everyone is one – that each person possesses something unique and essential, and success depends on freeing that in us all. It demands interaction and flexibility, face-to-face contact and collective decision-making, so that a dynamic and direct democracy develops – a democracy which takes place on the stage of spontaneously unfolding life, not raised above the audience but at ground level, where everyone can be involved. There are no leaders, no spectators, no sidelines, only an entanglement of many players who do their own thing while feeling part of a greater whole.

That sense of belonging to – that the carnival belongs to me, and I to the carnival – generates a feeling of collective ownership, of responsibility, of being part of a community and caring deeply about the fate of the whole. Participants may be dancing or blockading, reading poetry or writing graffiti, breaking windows or playing drums; they may be long-term activists or curious neighbours, students or trade union organizers, yet they all come together, albeit briefly, in the space opened up by carnival.

It is the spontaneous eruption of joy that draws people into carnivals, the limitless play – which as it freewheels and spins outside the drudgery of everyday life, gives us the possibility of changing our goals and, therefore restructuring what our culture states to be reality. This playfulness works as a charm, protecting resistance against hierarchy and mediation; it's the opposite of a barricade in that it prevents separation rather than enforcing it, it doesn't allow for abstraction, for distancing yourself from your beliefs, your dreams, and your struggles. It demands that you take yourself less seriously and have a good time.

In fact, recent research by psychologists at the University of Sussex found that people who participate in political demonstrations experience psychological benefits which may help reduce stress, pain, and depression, the most common ailments of late capitalism. According to Dr John Drury, "Participants [in collective action] experienced a deep sense of happiness and even euphoria in being involved in protest events. Simply recounting the events in the interview brought a smile to the face of the interviewees."

Terrorists in tutus

"Carnival laughter is the laughter of all the people. Second, it is universal in scope; it is directed at all and everyone, including the carnival's participants. The entire world is seen in its droll aspect, in its gay relativity. Third, this laughter is ambivalent: it is gay, triumphant, and at the same time mocking, deriding. It asserts and denies, it buries and revives. Such is the laughter of carnival." – **Mikhail Bakhtin**

Québec City's Carnival Against Capital, during the Free Trade Area of the Americas summit in April 2001, is in full swing. Suddenly undercover police officers break through

"CAPITALISM IS BORING!"

– Graffiti on a bank, Carnival Against Capital, Québec, April 2001

the crowd. Brandishing telescopic batons, they pounce on their target, bundle him into an unmarked van and drive away at speed. The man they have arrested is an organizer with the Anti-Capitalist Convergence, one of the key groups organizing the carnival. When he appears in court, he is charged with possession of a dangerous weapon, and denied bail.

The weapon in question is a 25 by 10 foot catapult. It was smuggled into the most heavily fortified city in Canadian history by a group calling themselves the Medieval Bloc, who wear pots on their heads and carry the lids as shields. During the action they wheeled the wooden catapult up to the fence that surrounded the summit and fired dozens of teddy bears over it. A dangerous act indeed and yet, one the kidnapped organizer had nothing to do with. But the police just don't get it. Not understanding the tactics or the means of this movement, they assume that as an organizer, he must have had something to do with the catapult. They are confounded when teddy bears turn up in droves at the jail, many of them locked up in birdcages, with notes demanding the release of the innocent organizer.

Such actions defy interpretation, and are intensely problematic for police to control because of their inherent ambiguity. When people dressed as ballerinas, clowns, nurses, or Santa Clauses confront police who are dressed like the villains of your worst nightmares, the result is inevitably hesitation and confusion – no police department wants a reputation for beating a battalion of ballerinas or arresting a sleigh full of Santas.

When politics leaves the space of boredom and bureaucracy, when resistance becomes joyful and not a sacrifice, then the process of changing the world becomes dangerously infectious, so it should have been no surprise that a year after Seattle, the FBI added Carnival Against Capital to its list of 'most wanted' terrorist groups. This may seem absurd now, in the midst of the seemingly endless 'war on terror' that carnival could be considered such a dire threat. Even more absurd – not only is 'Carnival Against Capital' nothing to do with terrorism, it's not an organization at all. It has no cells, no leaders, no ten-point programs. It is a tactic, nothing more. It is the embodiment of the spirit of contemporary resistance to global capitalism. It is: a pink fairy; a pie in the face; a man in a devil suit holding hands with a nun; a fire breather; a driving samba rhythm.

It's impossible not to laugh out loud as you look at the Carnivals against Capital that have taken place across North America and Europe, and try to root out the 'terrorists' in their midst. Does the FBI honestly believe that the Tactical Frivolity women posed a terrorist threat during the International Monetary Fund meetings in Prague? They were dressed in outrageous pink dresses, wild bouffant wigs, and nine-foot-high fan tails, and danced towards lines of confused Czech police waving magic wands and dusting off the riot shields with feather dusters. Was there a chance that capitalism would be brought to its knees by the Revolutionary Anarchist Clown Bloc in Philadelphia, with their unicycles, squeaky mallets, and big shoes, who confused the cops by attacking each other? Has the comedy army of the Italian *Tute Bianche* movement, who wrap door mats and cardboard round themselves for protection and attempt to push through police lines with inner tubes for shields and armed with water pistols, threatened the hegemony of the market economy?

Perhaps, as global institutions of capital continue suffering from a crisis of legitimacy, they are realizing that our irresistible resistance is indeed eroding their monopoly on power. Perhaps they realize that their hold on power, their legitimacy, is maintained by keeping us, their protesting populations, in fear of repression, of being labelled 'terrorists'. And perhaps they know that fear is dispelled most effectively, not by anger or determination, but by laughter.

Meanwhile, subversion, ridicule, and joy erupt all over the global South, in addition to their widespread appearances across the North, benefiting long term struggles for subsistence and survival. In India, 50,000 farmers from all over the state spent an entire day outside the Karnataka state government, laughing. The government, unable to handle the ridicule, was replaced the following week. In Mexico City, shortly after the Zapatistas emerged from the jungle and declared war

"PUPPETS AND SONGS DON'T KILL CHILDREN, BULLETS AND POVERTY DO."

– Nigerian activist, Oronto Douglas, commenting on media reports labeling activists as 'violent', A16 IMF meeting, Washington, 2000

against neoliberalism and for humanity, 100,000 people marched in solidarity with the rebels, shouting "First world, Ha! Ha! Ha!" Not only were they expressing open solidarity with the Zapatistas, they were also identifying the roots of poverty, rejecting the opening of the Mexican market to foreign investment, and thumbing their noses at the possibility of repression.

Carnival works all over the world, as political action, as festive celebration, as cathartic release, as wild abandonment of the status quo, as networking tool, as a way to create a new world. One of the key reasons for its wild success was overheard during the WTO shut down in Seattle, "Even if we are getting our asses kicked, we're having more fun than they are."

Festive Precedents

"Every one of these [historical] revolutions has been marked by extraordinary individuation, by joyousness and solidarity that turned everyday life into a festival. This surreal dimension of the revolutionary process, with its explosion of deep seated libidinal forces, grins irascibly through the pages of history like the face of a satyr on shimmering water." **– Murray Bookchin, *Post-Scarcity Anarchism*, Black Rose Books, Montreal, 1986**

Carnivals of resistance didn't begin with this movement. Many of the great moments of revolutionary history were carnivalesque – revelatory and sensuous explosions outside of the accepted pattern of politics. From the clubhouses of the Paris Commune of 1871, to *capoeira* –martial arts disguised as dancing to keep it secret from Brazilian slave owners, from the seven mile long Suffragette parades that brought early twentieth century London to a standstill, to the colourful be-ins of 1960s Berkeley – if you look hard enough, you can find carnival between the cracks of many of history's unpredictable moments of rebellion.

In nineteenth century south Wales, farmers facing extraordinary hardship banded together to protest against proliferating and expensive tollgates. Men and women dressed in bonnets and petticoats, called themselves Rebecca, after a Biblical prophecy that the seed of Rebekah would "possess the gate of those which hate them," (Genesis 24,60), and performed street theatre in front of the despised gates before destroying them. The Rebecca Rioters, as they became known, operated for five years, inspiring others to refuse to pay the tolls.

Parisian students lit the spark of rebellion with a spontaneous uprising in May, 1968. They decorated Paris with graffiti deeply influenced by the Situationists – an international network of radical intellectuals and artists, whose poetic slogans included: "I take my desires for reality because I believe in the reality of my desires," "Be realistic: Demand the impossible." The Situationists called for the immediate and constant transformation of everyday life, through celebrating creativity, and constructing 'situations' which disrupted the status quo, jolting people out of customary habits and thoughts. The students' rebellious carnival quickly spread to the factories, where it became one of the greatest general strikes in history. While workers nationwide were occupying the factories, students occupied the Sorbonne University and held enormous council meetings, taking decisions collectively, and calling for the dissolution of power.

The fall of communism across central Europe in 1989, often described as something that occurred out of the blue, was in fact preceded by years of planning and playfulness. Much of it was influenced by groups using carnivalesque tactics. One such group from Wroclaw, Poland, was called the Orange Alternative. On Carnival day in 1988, a crowd of about 5,000 was enticed by a flyer, reading, "Dress for a party. This time the police won't touch us. We'll say a magic word and either they'll disappear or they'll join the carnival." A makeshift orchestra with a giant drum kept time while a Red Riding Hood danced with a wolf, a group of Smurfs cavorted madly, and people chanted, "Police party with us!" and "Hocus pocus!" in an effort to disappear the police. According to the newspaper of the main opposition group, *Solidarity*, "This was a scene to make any surrealist's head spin." Other fusions of culture and politics proliferated across central Europe, setting the stage for transition, and acclimating a fearful population to taking to the streets and expressing its hopes and desires in public.

You can't predict the outcome of a carnival and neither can you predict history. The history of the twentieth century was one of utter unpredictability – few could have predicted the Russian Revolution, the fall of the Berlin wall, the end of apartheid, the internet? Who could have predicted that anticapitalism would be back on the agenda at the end of the twentieth century which has seen capitalism touch, subsume, and subjugate everywhere and everything on the planet?

Judging from the early years of this century it seems that we are living in times that are just as unpredictable. But allow us to make one prediction. The time of waiting for the right historical moment for revolution is over, and movements will not repeat this mistake. This is one of the great lessons that we have learnt from history, and it will influence the way political action is taken in the future. Carnival teaches us not to wait, but to live out the future we desire now, it implores to those who follow the path of previous repressive and ascetic struggles which postpone pleasure, along with racial and gender equality, until 'after the revolution'. In its celebration of all that is moving and changing, in its hostility to everything immortal and complete, carnival reminds us to refuse the idea that revolution is a ready-made permanent blueprint that we wait for, but a process that begins right here, right now.

In fact, the urgency of the current ecological crisis makes it impossible to wait for the future, unless we want to celebrate victory in an uninhabitable desert. Instead of simply saying, "NO – we are against this", Carnival yells, "LOOK – this is what we are for and we are not going to ask for it. We are doing it right now." It gives us a glimpse of what is possible, igniting our imagination, our belief in utopia – a utopia defined not as no-place but as this-place.

"TO WORK FOR DELIGHT AND AUTHENTIC FESTIVITY IS BARELY DISTINGUISHABLE FROM PREPARING FOR A GENERAL INSURRECTION." – **Raoul Vaneigem, *The Revolution of Everyday Life*, Rebel Press/Left Bank Books, 1983**

The revolutionary carnival may only last a few hours or days, but its taste lingers on. It is not simply a letting-off of steam, a safety valve for society, enabling life to return to normal the next day. It is a moment of intensity unlike any other, which shapes and gives new meanings to every aspect of life. The everyday is never the same after one has tasted a moment that is ruled only by freedom. Tasting such fruit is dangerous, because it leaves a craving to repeat the exhilarating experience again and again.

The Indian movement against the Narmada Dam says that resistance is a process for creating something new, and carnival prepares us for this process, by changing our perceptions and behaviours, giving us confidence, and inspiring our passionate collective imagination. In a world dictated by the rationalism of economics, a world where we are mere cogs in a market mechanism, radical imagination becomes one of the rare human faculties that can rupture capital's curse of 'realism'. 'Realism' can never be the foundation for envisioning a new society, because it determines limits before these limits are themselves known. Hindering free creative action and the possibility of searching for what is new, in the name of 'realism' denies the fact that change is cumulative, not sequential; that the present is always conditioned on the future. They may well call those of us who have the courage to be 'unrealistic' – romantics, dreamers, extremists. But as Herbert Read wrote: "What has been worthwhile in human history – the great achievements of physics and astronomy, of geographical discovery and of human healing, of philosophy and of art – has been the work of extremists – of those who believed in the absurd, dared the impossible."

So if the FBI wants to infiltrate this movement – a movement of pink fairies in solidarity with Indian farmers, of taxi drivers and graffiti artists issuing the same demands, of indigenous Ogoni identifying the same targets as pie-throwing utopians – it may have to do so wearing tutus. And when it identifies 'Carnival Against Capital' as a terrorist group, it exposes its greatest fear, and perhaps its greatest weakness. Unable to think fluidly, boxed in by hierarchical structures, frozen by the straight-jacket of 'realism', it is incapable of comprehending the decentralized dynamism of carnival, where anyone can have leadership momentarily before dissolving into the sea of the crowd again. And as it attempts to isolate, influence, and infiltrate groups in a great effort to break these movements, our spontaneity, unpredictability, and irresistibility are blossoming, scattering seeds of inspiration across cultures and continents. We learn to work together, we become better at being human, and we are able to live prefiguratively, in the most radical of all carnivals – a world which will not wait for the future, a world which embraces diversity, a world which contains many worlds.

Notes from Nowhere

Sonja Kellenberger

The beautiful words of the Diggers return to the City of London after 350 years, Carnival Against Capital. UK

Global Day of Action

June 18th 1999

J18 – Carnival Ambushes Capital

Desiring to strengthen the global resistance networks following the success of the first global day of action in May 1998, various UK groups including Reclaim the Streets, people from the McLibel campaign and Earth First! circulate a proposal for an "International day of protest, action and carnival aimed at the heart of the global economy: the financial centres and banking districts" to take place on Friday 18 June , the opening day of the 1999 G8 summit in Köln, Germany. The proposal identifies capitalism, not just 'free' trade and multilateral institutions, as "the root of our social and ecological problems", and is taken up by the Peoples' Global Action network, translated into seven languages, and distributed by email and post to thousands of groups worldwide. Unable to find a catchy name for the day, the simple tag J18 is used, a practice that continues with each global action, N30, S26, A20, and so on.

SPECIAL EDITION

Evading Standards

LONDON, FRIDAY 18 JUNE, 1999 — INCORPORATING THE UNCENSORED NEWS — FREE

FREE trip to Cologne for G8 Summit celebrations. see page 19

WAR STARS Clinton and Albright's dark secret

NEW TODAY: INTERFERENCE FM - TUNE IN TO THE SOUND OF THE STREETS ON 107.4 FM

GLOBAL MARKET MELTDOWN

Panic stalks Square Mile following dramatic collapse of world financial markets.

By Watt Tyler and Emma Goldman

SHARES plummeted around the world today following last night's meltdown of Asian financial markets. Triggered by the collapse of Japan's national bank.

Mass produced J18 propaganda spoofs London's *Evening Standard* newspaper. UK

Nick Cobbing

Party replaces profit in London's financial centre

Nick Cobbing

Police evict protesters from the London International Financial Futures Exchange

From Brazil to Malta, Nepal to Zimbabwe, actions take place in 40 different countries. In the City of London a Carnival Against Capital attended by 10,000 turns Europe's largest financial centre upside-down. Attempts to physically occupy and electronically hack into the Financial Futures Exchange are met with police charges. Simultaneously, a Carnival of the Oppressed in Nigeria brings nearly 10,000 Ogoni, Ijaw, and other tribes together in closing down the country's oil capital, Port Harcourt. In downtown Seoul, Korean activists dressed as Subcomandante Marcos and financial speculator George Soros engage in a street theatre debate about 'free' trade.

Stock exchanges are invaded in Madrid and blockaded in Amsterdam, Vancouver, and New York. In Melbourne, anti-logging activists deposit roadkill wombats on the steps of the Australian Exchange. A spoof trade fair in Montevideo invites Uruguayan garbage haulers to deposit their refuse in local bank branches before a festive invasion of the stock exchange takes place. In Israel, a 'goodbye to the mall' street party is held in Tel Aviv's financial district, while in Barcelona, a piece of squatted land

Nick Cobbing

The rebel caravan makes its way towards Köln, Germany for the G8 summit

Gopal

The Carnival of the Oppressed shuts down oil capital Port Harcourt, Nigeria

Nick Cobbing

Love meets rebellion under the freed River Walbrook. City of London, UK

is turned overnight into an urban oasis complete with vegetables, medicinal herbs and a lake, and a street party hands out free food to drivers stuck in traffic. A multi-faith assembly marches through the Buenos Aires financial district demanding an end to Argentina's debt, while Bangladeshi domestic and garment workers demonstrate against the IMF in Dhaka. A simulated bank demolition takes place in Lisbon, Portugal; real banks are attacked in Eugene, US, painted pink in Geneva, occupied in Bordeaux, France, and picketed in several Spanish cities. In Minsk, Belarus, two groups organize a picket at McDonald's, handing out pamphlets and toilet paper to people entering the restaurant and an illegal No Corporations open-air festival is staged. Los Angeles holds its first street party complete with sound system, trashed car, and a skate park, during which 17 people are arrested and the bomb squad is called to investigate the trashed car! In Bologna, Italy, overnight autonomous zones block traffic and stage interactive street performances. Similar actions happen in Milan, Rome, Siena, Florence, and Ancona. In Senegal, 600 people assemble for performances and speeches in protest against child exploitation.

Colin Beere/FT

The traces of carnival prove difficult to erase the day after J18. City of London, UK

On a more virtual level, the Electronic Disturbance Theatre launches an international internet blockade of the Mexican embassy in solidarity with the Zapatista communities; 18,000 people from 49 countries participate, clogging the embassy website all day.

Meanwhile, in Köln, the Intercontinental Caravan, made up of 400 Indian farmers and other activists from the global South, plans to conclude its tour with a Laugh Parade but police detain 250 of them before they get the chance to guffaw at the G8. For the first time reports of the global events are transmitted over the internet by alternative media activists, with news, video, and photos uploaded by street reporters using innovative software that later becomes the backbone of the Indymedia network.

"The enemies of capitalism will be back," proclaims the editorial of the *London Times* the following day, perhaps predicting the shut down of the World Trade Organization in Seattle five months later.

Dancing at the Edge of Chaos: a spanner in the works of global capitalism

by Wat Tyler

Part of the second *PGA global day of action, J18 took months of preparation. Educational materials were produced in order to demystify the arcane games of financial capital, and included a map of potential protest targets (banks, exchanges, corporate HQ's, investment houses, etc.) in the square mile known as the City of London. 30,000 copies of a spoof newspaper with a front-page headline declaring "Global Market Meltdown", were distributed across London the night before.*

The City was chosen as a target due to its looming importance on the world financial stage. With a daily turnover of $504 billion in foreign exchange, its infrastructure completely ennervates the body of global capitalism. If it were a country, it would be ranked the twentieth richest in the world. The City contains more foreign banks than anywhere else in the world, is the primary market for international insurance, and is also the world's leader in currency exchange, most of which is speculative, and has led to global economic crises like the devaluation of the Mexican peso in 1994, the collapse of the Asian 'tiger' economies of 1998, and the 2001 financial meltdown in Argentina.

Despite media hype about the "organized anarchists… plotting on the internet", and complex security precautions (City workers were instructed to "dress down" for the day), the event took everybody by surprise. 10,000 revellers wearing carnival masks split into dozens of autonomous groups and invaded the heart of London's financial district, disrupting trading while dancing to the wild sound of samba music, and causing over a million pounds worth of damage. The police reported that they had never witnessed a demonstration with such a "level and sophistication of planning".

"City of London Besieged by Anticapitalists", proclaimed the Financial Times *the next day. The sheer audacity of J18 gave confidence to US activists, already organizing for the seemingly impossible task of shutting down the WTO in Seattle five months later.*

Glistening. Silver and white. The river escaped over the shadows of the narrow city street. Released from centuries of subterranean captivity, the Walbrook rose and fell in billowing arcs, sending clouds of spray onto the growing crowd below. Laughing, people danced under the cool fountain. Shrieks of delight mixing with the sound of falling water. Between their toes, the water slipped down the dark tarmac retracing an ancient course to the Thames below. Looking upwards. Breathing the moist air. I grinned to myself. We'd done it. The roar of profit and plunder in the world's largest financial centre had been replaced with the sounds of party and protest.

Ten months earlier, a number of predominantly anarchist grassroots direct action groups had come together to plan and co-ordinate UK actions against the G8 summit on June 18th in 1999. The lack of a handy name for this coalition, and the day of action, led to the adoption of the simple tag 'J18' (as in 'J-eighteen' or 'J-one-eight'). A habit which has continued for every global action since (simple and meaningful acronyms to counter the wilfully obscure abbreviated titles of the ruling institutions of capitalism). Our action would be directed against financial centres. The thinking behind this was straightforward. These small urban areas, dotted with glass and concrete towers, wield inconceivable power. Decisions made in an instant on the trading floor, behind a desk, or in a wine bar, affect the fate of people and their environment in distant lands. Who dies, who lives. What grows, who goes hungry, who is well fed. What is destroyed, what is preserved. All for private profit. Consequently, financial centres are vital nerve centres in the anatomy of global capitalism. For J18 in the UK, our coalition decided to take action in the financial centre of London, 'The City' or 'Square Mile'. For all its ancient history, grand architecture, and glittering monuments, the City has no soul. IRA bombings in the early nineties prompted the authorities to erect a 'ring of steel' around the Square Mile. Police checkpoints, roadblocks, and blanket CCTV surveillance cameras, transformed the City into a modern fortress. A sanitized surveillance zone delimiting a territory ruled by profit fundamentalism, where the foreign exchange turnover equals that of Tokyo, New York, and Paris combined.

I became involved in the J18 coalition through Reclaim the Streets (RTS). I'd been part of RTS for a couple of years. An involvement that grew from a frosty January walk along the route of a proposed road in the English countryside on the edge of a town called Newbury. Ancient woodland and floodplain had been earmarked for destruction. Nine miles of dual carriageway wrecking a beautiful lowland landscape, sacrificed to satisfy an unsustainable and pointless car culture. Instead of conceding quietly when the farce of liberal petitioning and lobbying inevitably expired, opponents of the road took direct action. Treehouses, tunnels, digger-diving, sabotage. Till Newbury registered on my consciousness, I'd relied on annual subscriptions to environmental NGOs, recycling once a week, buying 'green' in the supermarket, and taking public transport, as the sum expression and solutions of my ecological concerns. What I experienced at Newbury went beyond any of that. My view of the world underwent a radical metamorphosis. Here was something that finally made sense, the antithesis of the passive abdication of representative politics and what we're told is democracy. Later that year, I danced on the M41 motorway with 10,000 other people. RTS had organized the

>> January 30 >> In a dramatic midnight announcement the Indian government orders work on the Maheshwar dam to stop. The site of the enormous hydropower project has been occupied for three weeks by up to 8,000 demonstrators from 2,200 families In 61 villages whose homes would have been submerged by the reservoir. Resistance to the Narmada Project had been ongoing. The people demanded a complete halt to construction warning that they intended to launch a major campaign against the project if it was not halted by 31 October that year. People from all over India hail the importance of this victory, seen as not only the first milestone in the fight against the destructive development symbolized by dams, but as an important symbol in the on-going struggle against economic globalization.

illegal party and protest, and the experience filled me with an irresistible urge and impetus to join them. A few months later I made it to the weekly RTS meeting, and was hooked. For me RTS offered a rare union of the cerebral and the visceral, acting as a catalyst but never a vanguard, with no leadership or static membership, and motivated by eclectic but coherent inspiration ranging from the sixteenth-century Diggers movement to the Situationists of 1960s Paris. It didn't take long for me to progress from going to meetings to taking action.

A dozen pubs, community centres, lecture halls, kitchens, bedrooms, and parks provided shifting venues for J18 meetings. The monthly coalition meetings, and weekly open RTS meetings, provided punctuation that marked the rhythm of our planning, and when people weren't meeting in the same room, an email discussion list with over a thousand participants added to the mix. Lists of books were swapped. Everything from impenetrable tracts on the inner workings of the global economy to exhilarating histories of carnival. There's always a certain looming inevitability once you get deeply involved with action on the scale of J18 that it will gradually take over your life. Other commitments are waylaid as missionary fervour takes hold. Piece by piece we began to put together a plan for the RTS action on J18. In my vision the City would get a green makeover. Dismantled block-by-block. Tarmac dug up. Exchanges and banks levelled. Steel girders ripped down. Trees planted in place of towers. Rivers flowing in place of roads. Allotments in place of wine bar and chain coffee stores. A lush garden to replace an urban desert, somewhere vegetables, not fortunes, could be grown. Countless meetings passed before we had managed to distil a common theme from our individual dreams. Our action would be a carnival. A carnival of resistance, a carnival against capitalism. The carnival would meet in the City, and then tour notable institutions of global capitalism. As pragmatism slowly set in we decided to focus the carnival on one financial institution, the London International Financial Futures Exchange (LIFFE).

In the mid-nineties, LIFFE had an average daily turnover of 160 billion pounds. Three thousand traders working a two storey trading floor. Big business doesn't get much bigger than this. Roughly two thirds of all global economic activity is speculative gambling on short term price fluctuations, and it's places like LIFFE which act as the venue for this insane casino. Our plan continued to grow, and eventually took on a life of its own, mutating, evolving. By the time J18 came 'round, not one of us knew the plan in its entirety. Just a handful of many interlocking pieces. Our plan to take the carnival to LIFFE had to remain secret; only a handful of us knew what the end location would be.

J18 started not long after midnight passed. Paintbombers redecorated the London Metal Exchange pink. A young couple visited each of the City's guardian dragons, whose occult significance is as carefully guarded as the treasure they protect, and left offering of flowers to nullify the dark magic. As morning came, a banner reading 'Life Before Profit' hung on Tower Bridge. Upstream, London Bridge was blockaded, disrupting commuters trying to reach their jobs in the City. Hundreds of cyclists joined together in a slow moving Critical Mass, stopping traffic around the City. Animal rights protestors marched, and McDonald's junk food outlets were picketed. Anti-arms trade activists staged a fake-blood covered die-in, chaining themselves to Lloyds Bank in Cheapside. Early editions of the Evening Standard, London's daily right-wing newspaper, mistook prologue for climax and wrote the day off prematurely: "...the forces of Mammon proved once again that it takes more than a mere protest to bring to a halt the money-making machine that is the Square Mile". They hadn't counted on the 'mere protest' of the carnival yet to come.

While the morning actions unfolded, I met my affinity group to go over our part of the plan one last time. After convincing ourselves we were all accounted for and holding it together, we went our separate ways. I took a circuitous and nervous tube journey to Liverpool Street Station, a large rail terminus in the City that we'd advertised as the meeting place for the carnival.

Arriving at the station, not knowing what to expect, I realized the transformation had already begun. The usual miscellany of lost-looking tourists and harried grey-faced City workers yelling into mobile phones had been supplanted. Waves of thumping samba rhythms merged with scents of expectation. Journalists worked the gathered masses. The environment correspondent of *The Guardian* asked a well-dressed City worker, company ID hanging on a slim chain around her neck, what she thought of it all. "I think it's f*@kin excellent John, don't you?" came the reply in a gruff voice, as the cross-dressing anticapitalist disappeared into the crowd. Thousands filled the concourse and the galleries above. Optimism and excitement surged through my body. We began to hand out masks. Whispering the message written on their reverse: On the signal follow your colour! We'd made 8,000 masks in four colours, red, green, black, and gold. The idea was simple; we'd split the carnival into four groups, each group wearing the same colour mask, and each taking a different route to LIFFE, some overground, some underground. That way the cops could never stop us all. Coloured streamers, waved above our heads, would guide each group through the City. What's more the masks would work at several

---

>> February 4 >> In Brussels, Belgium, Bill Gates, the Microsoft CEO, receives a cream pie in the face while on his way to give a talk on education. The action, carried out by the International Pastry Brigade, gives light to the fact that the richest man in the world has standards higher than can be met by Belgium's renowned patisseries. In what is sure to become an international scandal, Gates is overheard complaining that the pie "didn't even taste that good."

>> February 23-26 >> A network called People's' Global Action Against Free Trade and the WTO is born at a meeting of about 400 people from all continents in Geneva, Switzerland. Inspired by work done at the Zapatista encuentros, PGA's intent is to coordinate global days of action, and to link activists worldwide through face-to-face meetings and improved communication channels.

>> March >> Three thousand Nepali protesters demand an end to child labour in the country as part of a global drive to highlight the situation of the world's 250 million child workers.

>> March 23 >> A battle against a new uranium mine in Australia's tropical Kakadu National Park in Jabiluka kicks off when 9,000 people protest in three major

levels. Not only would they give us the means to move the carnival, but they would protect individuals from the Big Brother-like impositions of CCTV, while giving us a collective identity as a carnival.

Preoccupied with handing out masks, I missed the shut down around us. Every entrance to the underground was closed up by the cops. There wasn't a plan B for this. People started moving, but the signal hadn't been given. It wasn't time. Hundreds of people wearing red and green masks lurched their way out of the lower concourse, heading west. This wasn't meant to be happening. All those months of painstaking planning. A few seconds and they had become meaningless. Making eye contact with my worried affinity group, I held up my streamer and started waving. Desperate gesturing in the hope something would happen. A handful of people followed suit, then a few more. Everyone taking their prearranged cue from someone else. I led our red with a hint of green group east, up the stairs and escalators, out onto Bishopsgate Street. Red streamers writhing overhead we wove a serpentine trail through the straight lines of the City, looking for the path of least resistance to LIFFE.

A likely route beckoned, and we left the sun and onlookers of Bishopsgate, for the shadows of the side streets. Ahead, a deserted street curved gently towards Bank Square, the centre of the City. Buildings rose up on either side of us like stony walls in a dead-end gorge, forcing the sky far away. An eerie calm descended around us. We kept the pace up. Not knowing what we'd find. Take it a step at a time. Then the ominous and unmistakable drumbeat of hooves clattering on tarmac echoed around the bend. The line of mounted riot police , long batons swinging at their sides, trotted into view. We stopped in our tracks. I swallowed. Someone else swallowed. Run. I sprinted ahead into a beckoning alley and could hear everyone frantically following behind. Blindly careening down twist after turn, we emerged just two streets away from LIFFE. We'd shook off our mounted pursuers. Lost them in a medieval maze of back alleys. Now there was only one direction to go. Downriver. We were at the top of Walbrook Street, its sign the only visible clue to the presence of the buried river beneath our feet. Red streamers fluttering in the summer sun, we followed the flow. Move like water, adapt to the situation, stay fluid, and ride on the submerged river's energy.

I could see the non-descript ugly functionality of Cannon Bridge House, the rented home of LIFFE, looming ahead. Four-tonne grey and brown cladding interspersed with metal ventilation grilles, and sharp triangular doorways. A stale presence choking the life out of the narrow road running alongside. No visible sign on the outside to mark the significance of the activity that took place within. The bulk of the building sits over Cannon Street rail station, whose concealed platforms span the B132 dual carriageway carrying traffic east and west along the north bank of the Thames. Suspended, unconnected to the earth, LIFFE feeds off the energy of travelling commuters.

It was difficult to convince the flowing carnivalistas not to pond up on Cannon Street. The lure of stopping traffic was too seductive. Here was a situation that made sense. A road. Traffic. Let's stop it. I started to yell at people. We're not there yet. We have to keep going. My affinity group took up the call. Our frantic gesticulating managed to convince enough of the crowd to cover the last few yards of our journey. It was time to check in with the rest of the carnival. "We're there", I whispered into my mobile phone. "What, at the station?" "No, LIFFE !"

Things started to happen. CCTV cameras were put out of action. A fire hydrant was opened and the buried Walbrook was freed. A couple of guys with a ladder started to prise open the cladding that covered the side of the LIFFE building. One of them climbed in. I didn't see him come out. Maybe he managed to penetrate the inner sanctum of LIFFE or maybe he just ended up confused on platform seven.

It didn't take long for Upper Thames Street, – normally an exhaust-choked and gloomy four lane arterial conduit in the capital's private 'autogeddon' – to undergo a radical metamorphosis. Instead of cars and lorries racing between traffic lights, colourful banners hung across the street. Each sending out a clear message about what we thought of global capitalism: "Global Ecology Not Global Economy", and "The Earth is a Common Treasury for All". A soundsystem boomed out electronic techno and the dub-ska-punk supergroup PAIN played further down the street. People danced, dozed in the sun, bumped into old friends, and made new ones. But this was only a small part of what was happening.

The City had been declared off limits. Bridges closed to traffic, trains not stopping. A group of a few hundred had gathered outside the Stock Exchange, using steel crowd control barriers to ram reinforced glass doors. It was like this everywhere. Sounds of breaking glass harmonized with the sounds of celebration. Passion for change mixed with frustration and anger against the present system. Some are content to dance. Some take it further. Everyone expresses themselves differently. Unplanned and unexpected, carnival finds its own voice.

By mid-afternoon attention turned to LIFFE. Word had got round about what the building in the backdrop symbolized. The lower entrance got bricked up. Grey breeze blocks, joints oozing cement, walled up the lower entrance. Messy but solid, a sealed doorway, representing the future we desire, when such institutions will be

---

cities. Weeks later, two people chain themselves to machines while 50 more enter the site. A blockade is established, and the Mirrar Gundjehmi people, who are the aboriginal land owners and are working closely with environmental activists, vow to prevent development of the mine until the project is abandoned.

>> April >> The Multilateral Agreement on Investment (MAI), negotiated by the 29 rich nations that form the Organization for Economic Co-operation and Development in a bid to open up the world for "free" trade is postponed after a vigorous international campaign by anti-corporate activists.

>> April 1 >> Hundreds of health care workers, in Tameside, England, defy their union and go on strike against pay cuts, saying, "We realized in the first few weeks of the strike as we traveled round the country that this wasn't just happening to us.... Everywhere you go, it's privatization and slashing wages."

>> April 22 >> Construction begins again illegally on the Maheshwar dam in Madhya Pradesh, India, and over 4,000 people penetrate police barricades to stop it. Despite sweltering heat, police block the protesters' access to clean drinking water and shelter, forcing people to drink oil-contaminated river water. That

derelict and abandoned.

Further up Dowgate Hill, the top entrance to LIFFE was forced open, and people battled up a narrow escalator (crushed glass in the mechanism forced LIFFE staff to use the stairs for the following six months) only to be stopped just yards from the trading floor. Fists flew, flares and smokebombs added to the confusion. I wish I could say I was inside, but by the time I arrived, the riot police had formed a cordon across the entrance, shields held high against a hail of missiles. LIFFE staff were evacuated, but the carnival never reached the trading floor. We'd failed in our under-ambition. Unprepared, we never imagined we could get so close to occupying a trading floor in one of the City's major exchanges. We'd planned the wall, and built it. We'd planned to free the Walbrook, and done it. But we'd stopped short of planning for full-scale occupation.

Then the police rioted. Word must have come down from above that the unexpected rebellion must be put down at any cost. Stepping over piles of burning files and papers, and past a trashed Mercedes show room, we retreated west. Wails of distant sirens merged with cries of distress and anger. A slow motion tidal choreography of rising and falling batons, cracked heads, and dripping red faces, played out around me. The riot police, dumb mutes, high on confiscated amphetamines, hiding behind uniforms, shields and visors, dealt out on-the-spot punishment for anyone who dares to dream or act. Eventually, we were pushed back, and the carnival fractured and fizzled out. A crowd of a few hundred was trapped on Southwark Bridge. Another crowd made their way to Trafalgar Square. Gradually people left the City. It didn't matter. The carnival had happened, and London's financial centre had come to a grinding halt.

By the end of J18, 46 people had been injured by the police. Sixteen had been arrested, and another fifty arrests followed before the end of the year. Three days later in the House of Commons, the Home Secretary, Jack Straw, failed to "...understand the direct connection..." between J18 and the G8 summit. In the House of Lords, Lord Simon of Glaisdale compared J18 in London to "...the storming of the Winter Palace." The Lord Mayor of the City, who'd walked the streets on J18 in disguise, described the area around LIFFE as "...nothing short of a war zone..." and the day itself as "terrorism". A year after, the police were still hunting suspects. Sixty officers trawled through 5,000 hours of CCTV surveillance footage, 138 'offenders' were identified and their photos distributed up and down the country. One man was tracked down by DNA analysis of blood he'd left on the door handle of a riot van. Prison sentences were handed out, as the state sought revenge. The media called us "evil savages", and worse.

Predictably, over the following days, self-styled journalists from so-called newspapers went to town, misrepresenting us all. None of the pictures showed people dancing, peaceful or happy – the only moments deemed sufficiently photogenic for the tabloids and broadsheets are fighting and bleeding and smashed windows. Of course, they'd all missed the real story. It wasn't the practical disruption, the two million pounds of damage. It wasn't the damage suffered by the international reputation of the City. Instead, it was something more subversive. Until J18, the idea that there was a global movement against capitalism remained just that. An idea. I hoped it was true, but I couldn't really feel it. Many of us felt the same way. Now, because of J18, it had become tangible and real. Our movement had passed some invisible threshold. Tearing down the barriers that usually keep us apart. While we shut down the City of London, people were doing the same all around the world. Those that seek to dominate and rule our lives rely on keeping us apart. If you think you're alone in your desires, you're less likely to act. Divide and rule. tolerate single issues but don't let them join up. To spectators it must have seemed that the movement had appeared from nowhere. But nowhere does exist. It's anywhere people dream of leaving capitalism behind. To feel part of this global movement that transcends boundaries of language, culture, distance, and history, is empowering beyond words.

I left the carnival and found myself walking along the river. In the distance, smoke spiralled into the sky over the silhouette of the smouldering financial centre. I stood for a while, looking at the water, following the passage of muddy tides and spinning eddies. Enjoying the silence. Imagining the hidden undertows as the evening light glinted on the water's surface. In nature, small, seemingly insignificant changes can have disproportionately large effects. A trickle can become a flood. Raindrops coalesce, tributaries join. Our movement is like a river. A fractal network of converging and anastomosing channels, defying straightforward analysis, and rising from a thousand distant sources. On J18 a new, stronger current emerged into the light. A flow we need to sustain, keep free, and above the ground.

Wat Tyler is a pseudonym

Resources:

» J18 coverage in *Do or Die* issue 8, See www.eco-action.org/dod/

» Documents and reports of the day: www.infoshop.org/june18.html

---

evening, police arrest 1,200 people. Hundreds more return the next day and are beaten, charged by horses, sexually harassed, and 800 more are arrested. They are replaced by surges of new protesters who, in their determination to prevent the dam's construction, set up seven continuous blockades of the key entry points to the construction site.

>> April 27 >> Half a million Danish workers go on strike (ten per cent of the population) demanding an extra week's holiday and a 35 hour work week. The strike lasts ten days and virtually shuts down heavy industry, transportation, construction, and even newspapers. It ends with a weak compromise between union leaders and the government.

>> May >> For 250 miles, a shipment of high-level radioactive nuclear waste running through Germany meets numerous demonstrations as 10,000 activists along the way blockade train tracks with cars and their own bodies in an attempt to stop what's referred to as "mobile Chernobyl." Many residents living along the route are relocated, and some areas are enclosed by fences. Some people lock themselves to the rail tracks, and eventually police are forced to pull up the entire section of track and lay down a new one. Throughout

Carnival of the Oppressed: resisting the oil occupation of the Niger Delta

by Owens Wiwa

While 10,000 people *held a Carnival Against Capital in the City of London, UK, the indigenous groups of the Niger Delta in Nigeria were waging their own Carnival of the Oppressed against the oil multinationals who have devastated the lives of those in this richly diverse ecological region.*

In 1995, the writer and Ogoni activist Ken Saro Wiwa was hanged with eight others by the military dictatorship. Ken Saro Wiwa was leader of the Movement for Survival of the Ogoni People (MOSOP) who fought for self-determination and against oil companies like Shell who were working with the military dictatorship and drilling for oil on indigenous lands. As a physician in Nigeria, his brother, fellow activist Owens Wiwa treated and documented diseases caused by oil-industry pollution and the injuries of victims of the dictatorship. He was arrested and detained three times and on one occasion tortured. After the execution of his brother he and his wife sought asylum in Canada.

According to a New York Times *investigation, in 1993 Shell not only transported but paid salary bonuses to soldiers taking part in attacks on the Ogoni after claims that they had sabotaged Shell equipment. The officers killed 2,000 Ogoni people and destroyed 30 villages. Shell subsequently pulled out of the oilfields there in the mid-1990s claiming that the local resistance made operations too dangerous.*

In this testimony Owens Wiwa talks about what he found when he returned on a visit to Ogoniland from exile in 1999. The Carnival of the Oppressed was held on the streets of Port Harcourt as a welcome home celebration, and was part of the J18 international day of action against global capitalism. While people around the world took to the streets, Ijaw and Ogoni youth were removing the sign of the main road named after the dictator General Abacha, and renaming it Ken Saro Wiwa Road during their self-described carnival against imperialism and corporate rule.

I left Ogoniland on 21 May 1994. It was after my brother Ken Saro Wiwa was abducted. I remember it was on 22 May that I found out on the radio that I was declared wanted, and so I didn't go back. I went underground in Nigeria for a year and five months, then I went into exile.

I flew into the Nigerian capital of Port Harcourt on 18 June 1999, and 5,000 people came out to receive me. It was a wonderful reception that turned into a mass demonstration against what the corporations have done to the indigenous populations of the Niger Delta.

Twenty-two communities of the Niger Delta took part in the Carnival of the Oppressed, including the Chikoko, Ijaw, Isoko, Ikwerre, the Urhobol National congress, the Itsekiri Youth Vanguard, the Egi Peoples' Forum and Egi Women Movement – many, many different communities came in their truckloads and busloads from all the different corners of the delta. Together they created a convoy that stretched out two miles behind us.

We made a first stop at a major road junction where we laid a wreath in memory of Ken. Then we carried mock coffins to the oil company headquarters of Agip. We went on to Ken's old office and performed a ceremony for his martyrdom and in memory of the others that died with him.

To me the carnival was amazing. There was lots of dancing in the street. I was so honoured. There were so many dancing in the street they blocked the whole city of Port Harcourt! There was carnival dancing, masquerades, music everywhere, everyone in the streets – it was quite a sight to see!

Then we went in the Shell headquarters and repeated the carnivalesque atmosphere, gave rousing speeches, and we blockaded the Shell offices. About 10,000 people took the great risk to come out onto the streets. Luckily we had already taken the precaution of alerting international society so that the government knew they were being watched.

From there we travelled to Ogoniland. From the moment we entered Ogoniland to the point where we reached my own village, there were thousands of people lining the roads the entire way. When we got there, every shop was shut, every market closed, the whole town had shut down and come onto the streets to welcome us home. There were 20,000 people on the roads, routes, and through streets on the way down to my own villages. Masses of people from my village had come, then another 10,000 arrived. Ultimately I would say about 50,000 - 70,000 people in Ogoniland participated in my homecoming. It was very humbling.

"Arise, arise, great Ogoni, arise. We will not allow the world to oppress us any more." – **Ogoni song of struggle**

Shell and the government tried to use force to cower us against our aspiration, but we came out to celebrate anyway.

When I went back to Ogoniland, I saw a group of people who were very visibly proud that they were able to drive one of the biggest transnational corporations in the world off their land. But I also could see that there was a lot of poverty.

Shell had not cleared up any of the spills in Ogoniland, the pipelines were still on the surface, they had not been buried. One thing that had changed, however, was that the gas flares had gone. The Ogoni had put a stop to those. Compared to a few years earlier, when Ken was still alive, the trees were green again. There was a visible change in the vegetation due to the fact that there was no more oil drilling going on.

---

the length of the transport, people resist riot cops with water cannons, dogs, and the military police using up to ten helicopters at a time. Though the shipment eventually reaches its destination, the anti-nuke movement is regalvanized.

>> May 2 >> Hundreds of thousands of peasants, agricultural labourers, tribal people, and industrial workers from all regions of India take to the streets of Hyderabad to reject neoliberal policies and demand the immediate withdrawal of India from the WTO, against the backdrops of a growing wave of peasant suicides.

>> May 5 >> The indigenous Maori in Aotearoa/New Zealand arrive in Auckland after walking 375 miles to increase awareness of and resistance to the MAI.

>> May 15-17 >> GDA Global Street Party

>> May 21 >> The Indonesian government falls after insurrection against the Suharto dictatorship and the country's IMF-dictated austerity policies. Police kill six students.

>> May 27 >> Korean unions hold a general strike against the global rule of capital; denouncing the IMF and MAI.

>> July 6 >> A 48 hour work stoppage entitled the Peoples' Strike Against Privatization takes place across

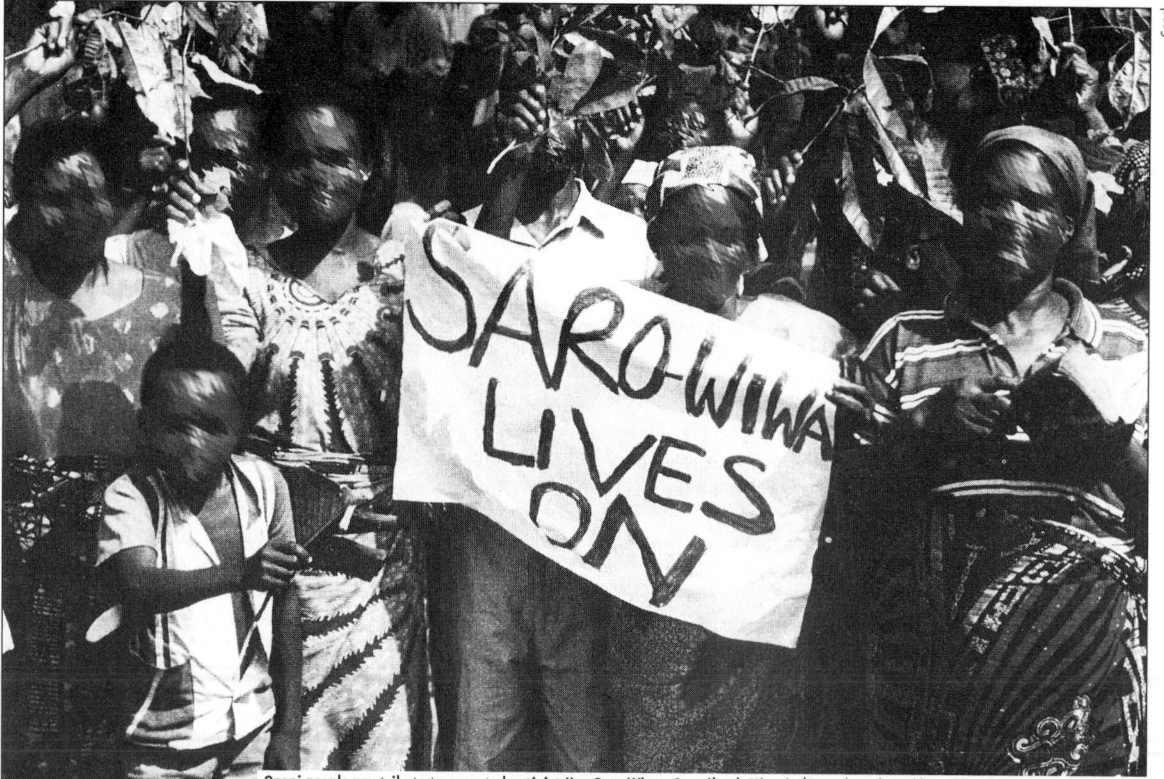

Gopal

Ogoni people pay tribute to executed activist Ken Saro Wiwa. Ogoniland, Nigeria (Faces have been blurred by photographer for security)

But the people were so poor, and the inner anger against Shell was visible in their faces. You could see it in their eyes when the name Shell was mentioned. People in the region had been abused, raped, beaten, tortured. Still there had been no redress, no compensation for the human rights abuse and the destruction of the environment. They've had no redress from Shell. But the people were still very resolute and said that they did not want Shell to ever come back to Ogoniland.

Shell has made a lot of moves to divide people, to get some in the community on their side so that they will help the company back into Ogoni. There is a lot of bribery going on, especially of key people like chiefs, to use their influence to invite Shell back. But the women especially, the women will not be bought over.

Many other groups in the Niger Delta had also become aware of the economic, environmental, and human rights abuses going on and have increased their actions in working against Shell and other oil companies in the area. The oil companies' activities are backed up by the military police. Aside from Shell, the other companies involved in oil drilling in the Niger Delta include Chevron, Agip, Mobil, Elf, and BP. These are the main players in the region.

"For a commercial company trying to make investments, you need a stable environment ... Dictatorships can give you that."

– Naemeka Achebe, Shell's General Manager in Nigeria, a few months before the Nigerian government hanged Ken Saro Wiwa

I also saw more drilling, both on and off-shore, than when Ken was alive – but not in Ogoniland. There was definitely an increased environmental awareness around the whole community, with an increase in civil actions. In relation to government, there was more freedom of speech and association but still incidents of senior military personnel arresting and molesting people, especially those resisting the oil companies.

When I was in Ogoniland, I did not see the community development of which Shell speaks. [Shell's 'Profits and

---

Puerto Rico, protesting against the privatization of the state telephone company. The country is brought to a standstill as the largest demonstration in the island's history shuts everything down, including shopping malls and the airport.

>> July 27-August 25 >> One thousand indigenous people from the Pemon, Karina, Arawaco and Akawaio tribes join together to roll massive logs onto the only highway connecting Venezuela and Brazil. The move reinforces their determined resistance to a proposed 450-mile long electrical transmission line that will rip through their rainforest homeland, particularly damaging the Imataca rainforest, a nine million acre natural reserve. Twice the size of Switzerland, Imataca is home to an extraordinary array of wildlife including jaguars, bearded bluebells, marmosets, and the world's largest eagle, the endangered harpy. After 11 days, the national guard violently disperses the encampment, and bulldozes the crops of nearby villages. Yet the blockades continue for over a month and the government eventually concedes.

>> July 30 >> In Chile, hundreds of indigenous Pehuenche people blockade access to the construction site of the World Bank-funded Ralco dam of the Biobío

principles, does there have to be a choice?' report claims it has built many community development projects in the region.] I saw new roads built by Shell, but these were ringing their own facilities, and served only Shell. The roads I saw were not the priority of the Ogoni people. Ogonis don't have cars, and these roads take up the land and carry loggers to our remaining forests.

The community development priorities of the Ogoni people are to clean up the polluted land, and the polluted rivers, so that they may be used once more for farming and fishing. So that ill health may be tackled, so that the people are no longer drinking polluted water. And so that they will not be malnourished because they can once more get the protein they need from the fish in the rivers. The killing off of the fish in the waters means people are malnourished and especially vulnerable to disease.

So there is a big disconnection between the brand and the reality.

It's very important and strengthening to know that our struggle is not just local. Solidarity is always hopeful in many ways. Linking all our struggles, which we realize are really the same, gives us great encouragement – to see that others are in the struggle. If we connect with people in other places our struggle becomes internationalized, in that way we can look at our programmatic similarities and we don't just remain isolated. And if we stay isolated, we will be wiped out. If the government knows we are part of a wider network they know they have to be more cautious.

Marginalized peoples in all parts of the world need to be

"What Shell and Chevron have done to Ogoni people, land, streams, creeks, and the atmosphere amounts to genocide. The soul of the Ogoni people is dying, and I am witness to the fact." – Ken Saro Wiwa

making connections, coming together to develop conjoined solutions. You can see commonalities between the indigenous peoples in the Amazon, in Australia. The process of globalization has destroyed our wealth, the natural resources we use to sustain ourselves with and that made us prosper.

Still we draw great hope from this globalization from below. It is going well, but it is a very slow process. To do it properly, really from the ground up, is a very slow process. I have grown to understand that good things come slowly to people like us.

And I worry that our collective pace in combating globalization is too slow compared to the rapid rate that economic globalization is occurring. It is creating a space that nothing is filling. Our own slowness of movement cannot catch up with the fast pace of economic globalization – its speed, its momentum is like a train going too fast. Perhaps we do need to speed up our protest and our resistance, roadblock the rails or pursue the train faster. It is very difficult.

I was in Seattle. It was incredibly gratifying to see people from the US on the streets protesting against corporate rule there. But one thing our friends in the North should know: that big corporations, the extractive industries – if you want to stop them, you have got to stop them at the point of production, as well as disrupting the meetings. So it is especially important to disrupt the process at the other end, to support the people who are fighting globalization from the grassroots in Southern countries.

In Ogoniland we use the method of the human shield – a simple, nonviolent human shield. Often it is the women who stand at the forefront. We use the biggest resource we have – humans – to prevent the oil companies from getting access to their weapons of mass destruction – to drill the earth, spoil the earth, drill for oil. Our processes involve making sure everybody is involved through democratic processes, holding a council meeting. We held lots of rallies in every village every week and different groups choose to form together, through self-organization, through self-building. In this way everybody in the community becomes mobilized.

We are working for freedom, for economic and social freedom. The corporations are dictating our lives right now. And I am fighting for my brother's name to be cleared. I want it to be known that he was a man of peace, a man who gave his life so that those struggling against corporate power can do so without being killed, so that people can live in dignity.

Dr Owens Wiwa's book *Politics of Bones: Dr. Owens Wiwa and the Environmental Wars in the Niger Delta* detailing the resistance actions in the Niger Delta is available from November 2003

Resources:

» Movement for the Survival of the Ogoni People, still fighting for life against the oil transnationals in the Niger delta: www.dawodu.net/mosop.htm

---

River, thus enforcing the 1993 Indigenous Law which requires written consent from all 400 Pehuenche that would be displaced by the dam. Nicolasa Quintremán, whose family has owned and lived on the same land for 500 years says, "The only way I'll leave here is dead." Riot police tear gas the blockade, and arrest four people, and the government concedes, demanding that construction be halted until resolution of the dispute is found. A constant vigil is established at the dam site to ensure that the order is obeyed.

>> August >> Fifty children aged between seven and thirteen launch a hunger strike in New Delhi, India to protest at being forced to work as bonded labourers in carpet factories.

>> August 5 >> Ten thousand people take to the streets in Rio de Janeiro, Brazil, protesting against privatization of the nation's largest telecommunications company.

>> October 1 >> The streets of La Paz, Bolivia are quiet except for squads of trade unionists patrolling to enforce a general strike in the city. Public and transport workers form the core of the mass protest against rising telephone, water, and electricity prices. Unions blame the price hikes on large-scale privatization of public

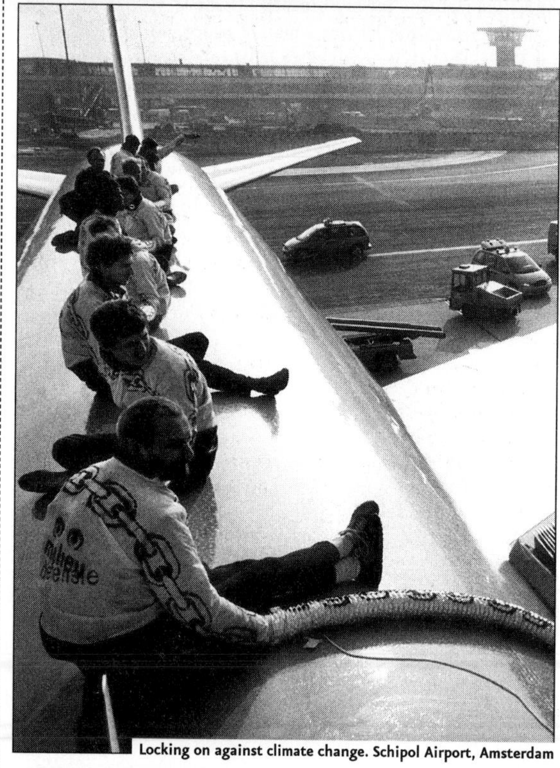
Locking on against climate change. Schipol Airport, Amsterdam

Disobedient Bodies

"With our bodies, with what we are, we came to defend the rights of millions – dignity and justice – even with our lives. In the face of the total control of the world which the owners of money are exercising, we have only our bodies for protesting and rebelling against injustice."
– Italian priest Don Vitaliano, participating in a *Tute Bianche* action.

To engage in direct action means literally embodying our feelings – performing our politics with our whole body. Placing ourselves directly in the cogs of the mega-machine transforms the body into both weapon and statement of resistance – whether it's to delay a bulldozer that's destroying woodland or to enter a corporate HQ. Here are just three techniques, all of which are best done by affinity groups.

Locking on

Locking on is the technique of attaching your body to something so that it's difficult for anyone to remove you. Locking on has been used for delaying evictions, saving ecosystems, preventing delegates from attending summits, and much more. Since time equals money, every minute it takes them to remove you hits them where it hurts – in their pockets. Always remember to go to the toilet – or wear a nappy – before you lock-on to anything!

One of the best tools for locking on are bicycle D-locks or U-locks. They fit neatly around your neck and can attach you to pieces of machinery, gates, etc. Work in pairs when locking on. One person locks themselves down and their buddy keeps the key, and stays nearby to provide food, extra blankets, and other support

Thomas Schlijper

to the person locked down. If locking on to a machine, someone MUST let the driver know that operating it will break someone's neck. You should also be prepared for the lock to be cut off – a pair of safety goggles and ear plugs are essential for this.

Padding up

Developed by the Italian *Tute Bianche* movement as a nonviolent but confrontational tactic, padding up is a method of self defence. Turning the detritus of consumer society – cardboard, old mattresses, inner tubes – into body armour transforms you into a hilarious hybrid of Michelin-man/woman, clown, and gladiator, but most importantly it protects you from police who, you mustn't forget, have been trained to hurt you.

The basic idea is to protect your most exposed and vulnerable parts: your head, neck, and face, lower back, ribs, groin, abdomen, and all of your joints. The best materials are foam (which can be found in old sofas), cardboard, and bubble wrap. Cut the materials to fit parts of your body, and layer them. Ideally cardboard goes on the outside, as it will disperse the pressure from a blow. Use duct/gaffer tape to attach the pieces to yourself. You might want to run, or rapidly remove the armour at some point, so don't wrap yourself up too tightly. Protective head gear is essential, and unfortunately is the only thing you can't really make yourself. There are several options: motorcycle or bicycle helmets, hard hats, or military helmets. And don't forget a gas mask (tear gas) and ear plugs (concussion grenades).

Shields

Watching a phalanx of padded-up *Tute Bianche* attempt to nonviolently push through a police line, using their 'tortoise' formation of shields, evokes Roman army scenes from Hollywood epics – with the addition of jovial singing and coloured balloons. Not only is it great theatre, it also makes for a whole new way of looking at street actions. When a whole group with shields works together, they create the ultimate in mobile barricades. The shield becomes not only a way to defend our bodies, but a way to demand and claim our rights to move freely.

Shields can be made of anything – trash can lids, tarp, foam, plywood, cardboard. The material choice depends on many factors: speed of construction, concealment from police or border guards, type of action, number of users. The most high-tech ones are made of tall sheets of clear Plexiglas on wheels; lower-tech shields can be made from large rubber inner tubes, which are fun and bouncy – and make the police look like they are busting up a beach party.

All of these techniques are incredibly effective, and to do them safely, require further research and planning. Police responses vary from bemusement and befuddlement to attack and outright torture, so having a solid support group is really crucial. Have fun, and remember the proverb, "If you think you are too small to make a difference, try sleeping with a mosquito."

Resources:

» Download BODYHAMMER, a full-colour booklet with tactical info and great tips on making gear for cheap: www.devo.com/sarin/shieldbook.pdf

» Thorough UK site with good links and a broad spectrum of information: www.wombles.org.uk

» Supply lists and where to get gear from New York Ya Basta: www.free.freespeech.org/yabasta/protection.html

Nick Cobbing

The Festival of Resistance heads towards the WTO summit. Seattle, US

Global Day of Action

November 30th 1999

N30 – Shut Down the WTO, Seattle

"I wish every town could be just like Seattle," says World Trade Organization Director-General Michael Moore, just before the police begin rioting. More than 700 organizations and around 75,000 people take part in the protests against the WTO in Seattle, preventing the opening ceremonies from, well, opening, and sending a message to the global elite, many of whom are inside taking notice. "What we hadn't reckoned with", says UK Environment Minister Michael Meacher, "was the Seattle Police Department who single-handedly managed to turn a peaceful protest into a riot."

Days later, the summit collapses in failure due to trade representatives from Africa and the Caribbean refusing to agree to the proposed new round of trade liberalization, in protest against the secret negotiations and bullying of the US and Europe. The *Los Angeles Times* states: "On the tear gas-shrouded

Bette Lee

Protesters lock down to blockade the convention centre. Seattle, US

streets of Seattle, the unruly forces of democracy collided with the elite world of trade policy. And when the meeting ended in failure on Friday, the elitists had lost and the debate had changed forever." While activists in Seattle bring the city to a standstill, internet surfers from around the globe are able to log onto a special website, courtesy of US hacktivists armed with scanners, that broadcasts the sounds of the Seattle police departments' radios, live from the blockaded streets,

Inevitably mainstream media focuses solely on broken windows and the Black Bloc in Seattle, but reports of actions from Hong Kong to Iceland fly across the world, thanks to the newly launched Indymedia website. In France 5,000 farmers gather under the Eiffel Tower with their sheep, ducks, and goats to feast on regional products, while 75,000 people protest in 80 other French cities. Turkish peasants complete a 2,000 mile walk to the capital, having visited 18 towns to discuss the attack on humanity by capitalism. Massive demonstrations take place all over India; in New Delhi hundreds of indigenous people blockade the World Bank building covering it with posters, graffiti, cow dung, and mud; in the

Romeo Ranoco/Reuters

Protest against WTO blocked from reaching US embassy. Manila, Phillipines

Narmada Valley, youth activists hold an anti-WTO bullock cart rally, crying, "The youth of Narmada has awakened – the WTO will flee!"

Banners with slogans that mockingly call for more order, security, and police are paraded in Berlin, while free food is distributed on the streets of Hamburg and Prague. In Amsterdam's airport, over 100 activists demand free tickets to Seattle from the airline companies sponsoring the WTO summit. In Geneva, activists sneak into the WTO headquarters and short circuit the electricity mains, crashing computers and communications for several hours. As 8,000 march in Manila to the US embassy and presidential palace, a virtual sit-in involving 200,000 people floods the WTO website.

Over 8,000 in Muzafer Ghar, Pakistan hit the streets, carrying banners and posters warning about the dangers to agriculture that the WTO poses. In Lisbon, Portugal hundreds stop traffic in the city centre, while others redecorate McDonald's and the city's Christmas tree with graffiti, while in Porto activists hand out fake money in front of a shopping mall. Stock exchanges are targeted in Buenos Aires and Brisbane, where the street is declared a 'beyond the

Panos

The city centre is occupied and the WTO opening ceremonies shut down. Seattle, US

market' zone. In Italy a McDonald's is occupied, a Nestlé factory and Lloyd's Bank get similar treatment in England, while 2,000 people rally in London against the privatization of public transport and are attacked by the police.

Over the following week, actions in solidarity with the 600+ arrested in Seattle take place around the world, notably in Mexico City where 10,000 university students, themselves engaged in a nine month strike against proposed hikes in tuition fees, demonstrate outside the US ambassador's residence, demanding freedom for those arrested and an end to neoliberal policies.

Despite *Fortune* magazine's opinion on Seattle, that "Democracy used to be a good thing, but now it has got into the hands of the wrong people," it seems that the twenty-first century begins early in Seattle, giving hope to people around the world that resistance is alive in the heart of the Empire.

The World Trade Organization *is a corporate coup d'etat in disguise. Through the WTO, the national laws of any country can be challenged if three bureaucrats in a secret dispute settlements committee deem them to be "barriers to trade". Full-time corporate lobbyists are at work to get inconvenient laws challenged at the WTO. Time and time again, laws to protect the environment and workers – from minimum wages, to eco-labelling, from food-safety, to the ban on asbestos – have been construed as barriers to trade, and been overturned. In this way, the WTO promotes the consolidation of power and wealth in the hands of large corporations and financial institutions.*

The WTO is not only about trade – it is about paving the way towards a new form of capitalism, one where the role of government is limited to assuring a stable currency, providing a justice system to arbitrate disputes, enforcing property rights, and maintaining a strong military and police force. Under WTO rules, governments are not allowed to favour local firms and 'discriminate' against foreign-owned corporations; nor subsidize domestic industries. WTO rulings take place in secret, and allow for no appeals. It seemed like an unstoppable force, until 30 November 1999.

N30. The overwhelming unforgettable rejection of the World Trade Organization. 75,000 people on the streets of Seattle, 10,000 taking direct action and preventing the opening ceremonies from taking place. Simultaneous demonstrations in over a hundred other cities around the world. Three days later, headlines screamed from the papers, "Summit Ends In Failure," after delegates from the global South, encouraged by the mass rejection on the outside, withdraw their consent, and prevent a new round of trade deals.

To contrast with well-known events involving tear gas, brutal police, broken corporate windows, and the infamous 'no protest zone,' in which all dissent was banned, here are three of the literally thousands of untold stories of individuals taking action in Seattle, all of which, when combined, add up to much more than we can possibly imagine.

The Anticipated First

by Rowena Kennedy Epstein

I met you somewhere between revolution and my heart. You walked in cold and smooth on the eve of history. Stories whispered by my ear and maps lay on my lap, actions were planned and I signed up to lock down around a cow. You slid in next to me and shook my hand. I said, "Nice to meet you, are you getting arrested?"

You said, "No, not this time." Then you turned on your heels and walked toward the ruckus of the week to come.

I desperately want to say that I thought about you every day, that the revolts on the street were nothing next to the revolts of my heart. But I had been training in a boot camp for combatants against capitalism for the last 19 years, and all I could think of was glory and stories of the movement to come. I hadn't slept in weeks; I couldn't dream of you. I hadn't eaten in days; I was planning our attack. I hadn't loved in months; I was organizing the stories of Salvadoran struggles.

I woke up at 4.00 am on 30 November 1999 from the pre-battle lump in my throat and the 10,000 monarch butterfly skeletons rattling in my belly. I had two hours to get to the park, two hours to meet my affinity group; two hours till I would introduce myself to a hormone injected cow. A cow that would make its way through wet streets and riot police, a cow that moo-ed: "We're cold, we're wet, and we hate Monsanto." I arrived armed with hot tea and a mistrust of the already swarming police. I watched cops confiscate puppets and shopping carts, smirking as they walked away with a 40-foot papier maché carrot that read "UPROOT OPPRESSION."

Bold – that's what we were, all of us, bold and cold. Some with wings and a smile, some with lock-boxes tucked under our Gore-Tex jackets and Bolivian wool sweaters. The ground vibrated beneath our collective fear and anticipation. We sang songs in rhythm with memory, and moved in beat to the stories of those who had fought before. We functioned in narratives. We saw microscopic forms of the present. We longed in future syllables of what may come. We aged.

The smell of wet hair and history sailed into my nostrils as we stepped into those streets. There was a collective sigh of relief as the morning light pierced through the clouds onto the streets that would become our home for the next week. We had fun, the Monsanto hormone-injected cow and I. We ate words of struggle, spitting them out with venom and power, and as day broke night we broke oppression. Empowerment swelled over us; a generation began to understand. Our work was legitimized, our back-alley meetings made sense. And our fates had been sealed by sticky, permanent, revolutionary glue.

I didn't think about you that day. I thought about El Salvador and Chiapas. I thought about Emma Goldman and the Chicago anarchists of 1887. I thought about the fact that I paid for my own tear gas, and wondered if I had got my money's worth. I wondered if my parents were proud, hearing my father say, "They think they can hide, but not this time; people are organizing." I saw them standing in shattered glass; they watched my face and for a moment our lives had reversed – a recognition of their past.

I remember the collective. I remember standing in the intersection of Stewart and Olive and hearing my life change. I remember thinking that I would talk with you about all of this. I remember thinking I would never stop. My body was caving in on me, my eyes were swollen, my feet were bleeding, and I never anticipated stopping. I would like to think a generation never anticipated stopping. I lay down that night and heard drums in my ears, and watched helicopters fly past my high school. I watched riot police stand on the same corners where I used to smoke a

---

services in 1994, and community groups threaten to seize the water and power companies if prices don't drop.

>> October 1 >> In Ecuador cities grind to a halt and schools shut down in a general strike against the IMF austerity package that has triggered currency devaluation, and 400 per cent increases in energy prices. 12,000 police and military troops are deployed in Quito alone, and a bomb explodes outside the US embassy. During clashes, four people are killed and over 90 arrested.

>> October 1 >> In Peru, following demonstrations against president Fujimori's pro-IMF policies, hundreds storm the presidential palace, looting the storage room of the presidential guard and painting the walls with graffiti. Thirty people are arrested and marches the following day demand their release.

>> October 7 >> "Mr. Friedman, it's a good day to pie!" says Special Agent Apple of the Biotic Baking Brigade, as he flops a coconut cream pie in the face of Milton Friedman, neoliberal economist extraordinaire. Friedman is in San Francisco, US, at a conference he organized on privatization of public education. As the agent is dragged away, he is heard shouting, "When it comes to defending the Earth from the scum of the

joint between fourth and fifth periods on Friday afternoons. I watched the beginning and the end of my career as a forgiving activist. I knew that I would soon be a casualty of everyday meetings and the jailhouses of Seattle, Philadelphia, and DC. I don't think I thought much more that week. I had occupied a different mind, trying to organize the events, trying to organize my thoughts, trying to organize the order of the streets I would be running in.

We won that night. A phone call from the jailhouse yielded me my breath. I heard the drums and the chanting and then the words, "We won this battle, there was no new round, we shut down the WTO!" I fell to the floor and cried; I cried an hour before I met you and I cried an hour after I left you. I cried from the acid left in my mouth and numb limbs; I cried for all our defeats. I cried because I never imagined experiencing a victory in my lifetime. And then I ran to my car and came to you, bearing my body and the news of the first victory of this war. I remember you sat down and stopped moving, and looked at me as though the world had just fallen from my tongue. We smiled. We would have kissed if we had known each other; we would have hugged if it hadn't been our first date. And I said, "Should we go downtown?" and you said, "I really want to hang out with you."

That night we sat across from each other sipping tea and singing stories, weaving the past into our present; speaking of yesterday as if it had already been entered and meticulously recorded into the history books. I felt the philosophical knife of my life before and my life after N30 slide deep into my skin. I had broken open; I was seeing new land with views of rebellion and courage, a glimpse that will be with me through the stories of repression and time and survival. That will outlive me. I knew then that I might never have the words to tell this story, our story, a story of re-birth.

I can never forget the history of that week, so I can never forget the history of us. I met you in simple language, at the beginning of a complex battle, somewhere between revolution and my heart.

Rowena Kennedy-Epstein is a poet and activist. She lives in New York City

---

Resources:

» *Whose Trade Organization? Corporate Globalization and the Erosion of Democracy*, Lori Wallach & Michelle Sforza, Public Citizen Foundation, 1999.

» *Voices From the WTO: an anthology of writings from the people who shut down the World Trade Organization*, edited by Stephanie Guillaud and Julia Allen, self-published, available from the Evergreen State College bookstore, by emailing payner@evergreen.edu

Not in Service: the tale of insurgent taxis

by Grey Filastine

One of the lesser known acts of civil disobedience during the days of the Seattle WTO meetings was a strike by the local taxi drivers; a small but effective component in making the city inhospitable to our unwelcome guests. The call was made for all taxi drivers to suspend service within Seattle city limits from 6.00 am to 6.00 pm on Tuesday 30 November 1999.

In some parts of the world, taxi driving is a respectable profession which earns a decent income, by local standards, and which has no negative stigma. The cab drivers I've talked to in Europe, Asia, and North Africa claim to do pretty well and identify with the middle class. This is not the case in the United States, where taxi driving is one of the lowest rungs on the social hierarchy. Taxi drivers in urban areas are overwhelmingly poor immigrants, rural taxi drivers are frequently among the poorest and most marginalized of whites. Seattle's two biggest taxi fleets are primarily owned and operated by East African men from Ethiopia, Somalia, and Eritrea. Another large company is almost entirely Punjabi Sikhs and other North Indians, and another is the last holdout of the working-class Anglo drivers. Drivers lease cars for 12-hour shifts from taxi owners. Most lease the car on a weekly basis, working seven 12-hour shifts per week. We are therefore self-employed, and lacking unions, unemployment insurance, workers' compensation, medical insurance, and any official channel for dealing with exploitation by the companies, which deal with the allocation of cars, collection of lease money, dispatch, and general administration. Cab owners pay dues to the company to support this infrastructure; since there is no oversight, the companies are dens of nepotism and incompetence.

Additional troubles began in the industry when the city government decided to apply a 'zero tolerance' model to the local taxi industry with an ordinance passed in 1997. In one of the many spurious attempts to make Seattle a 'world class' city, perhaps in anticipation of the already scheduled WTO meetings, the taxi industry was targeted for reform. Laws were enacted regulating everything imaginable,

---

corporate universe, the pie's the limit!"

>> October 18 >> Activists in the Earth Liberation Front Network reduce North America's largest ski operation in Vail, Colourado, US to ashes, causing $26 million in damages, in order to halt expansion of the resort. The 12 miles of planned roads and 885 acres of clearcut would decimate the last and best remaining lynx habitat in the state.

>> October 30 >> World Trade Organization Director-General Renato "Rocky" Ruggiero gets lemon pied at a London, UK, conference on trade, investment and the environment. Three members of the People Insurgent Everywhere, or P.I.E. division of the Biotic Baking Brigade catch Rocky by surprise, calling out references to landmark WTO rulings: "That's a present from the dispossessed!" Sploosh! "And that's from the turtles!" Sploosh again. "Are you bananas Mr. Ruggiero?" Splat! The adrenalized trio disappear into the West End crowds, shouting, "We are everywhere!" while Rocky sulks back indoors.

>> November >> A massive internet campaign against the MAI convinces the French government to withdraw, leading to the total collapse of the negotiations and sending a wake-up call to business élites. Lasting results

beginning an era of English language tests, uniforms, enforced cleanliness, consolidation of cab companies, illegalization of independent owner-operators, inspections, and a punitive system for offenders. Curiously absent from these laws was assurance of quality of life, job security, safety, or reliability of income for the taxi drivers – indicating the local government's dominant concern for the superficial experience of tourists and conventioneers over the working conditions of its constituents.

Drivers reacted by forming an organization, called the Cab Drivers' Alliance of King County. This organization has had limited success in challenging the power structure, mostly stymied by the individualist nature of taxi drivers and the implacable nature of politicians. At the very least we have made a career of harassing City Hall, once encircling the building with honking cabs in a four hour wildcat strike, then cruising through downtown as a rolling roadblock.

If this doesn't sound familiar, it should. People from the global South working too hard for too little. Working-class whites pitted against immigrants. Sweatshop hours. A system which caters to the comforts of the wealthy. A popular resistance that gains little ground against a 'business-friendly' government. It is like a script in miniature of capitalism's latest fad, neoliberalism.

For obvious reasons, it wasn't difficult to call for a strike. The difficulty was largely one of information dispersal. Flyers posted at the cab lot were torn down immediately, flyers posted 50 yards from the lot were removed within 24 hours. Management did its best to discredit the strike,

"The WTO is the place where governments collude in private against their domestic pressure groups." – *Financial Times*, 30 April 1998

claiming it to be a fiction to the media. Other management declined comment or made ambiguous statements. At the Anglo company, the management made it clear to me that I was not physically safe to organize or post flyers at their lot. I spent a few nights creeping around all the lots at 3.00 am in the morning, posting flyers under windshield wipers. It is strange that so little has changed in the US – that labour organizing can still get you shot or blacklisted.

Perhaps the most difficult task was to convince the drivers that N30 was the right time for a strike. Most were counting on making heaps of money from the delegates, and were hesitant to give up one of the most lucrative days of the year. A large article was published in our newsletter, detailing the reasons we should act on this day for our own individual interests and for global reasons. Many of the African and Indian drivers were familiar with the WTO, World Bank, and IMF because of the activities of those institutions in their home countries. Eventually most drivers warmed to the idea because of the rare chance to get even with the city government – by denying taxi service when it would hurt the most.

Just four days in advance, the strike was announced to

the media. It was kept secret until the last minute to prevent the companies from coming up with counter-propaganda, or the municipality to avoid the crisis by arranging other transportation. Response from the media was immediate and somewhat overwhelming for our small strike committee. News outlets were desperate for more WTO stories, and I suspect they were also interested because of the dynamic and unpredictable nature of our 'union', lacking careerists and the usual crusty old order of lefties to water down our anger.

The events on N30 are now pretty historic, and there were certainly a lot more exciting things happening then a dearth of cabs. Busy with other actions that day, I felt happy to know that the delegates couldn't use cabs to get through crowds, and were more easy to spot and harass in their limousines, and that no taxis were being shaken or blockaded, which could have shifted some taxi driver's sympathies.

Our strike significantly aided in shutting down the city since bus service was also suspended, and people definitely wouldn't drive into the city after it became clear that the demonstrations had claimed the streets. There was simply no way for people to get to their jobs in the city centre. This, combined with the masses of people who voluntarily chose not to work on N30, suspended any atmosphere of normalcy. The transportation shutdown enabled a situation of de facto general strike.

Grey Filastine drives a taxi as infrequently as possible, but if you are in Seattle try hailing Yellow 509. The rest of his time is spent in various hustles, producing music, or making political trouble.

Resources:

» Information about Grey's other musical and direct action projects: www.postworldindustries.org

---

of the campaign include a global network of connected activists primed for the next battle: that against the launching of a new round of 'free' trade negotiations at the upcoming WTO ministerial in Seattle.

>> **November** >> In an impressive nationally coordinated action, crops in over thirty UK GMO test sites are destroyed in over a dozen cities on the same night.

>> **November 23** >> Following the October pieing of Monsanto's CEO, Robert Shapiro, Operation "Privatize This!" is launched in Berkeley, US in the form of a vegan pumpkin pie to the face of Douglas G. Watson, president and CEO of biotech giant Novartis. According to BBB Special Agent Tarte Classique, the pumpkin pie symbolizes the estimated 60 per cent of food on American tables for Thanksgiving which will contain genetically-engineered products. At the same time, UC-Davis Chancellor Larry Vanderhoof receives a banana cream pie to the face, for the "strategic alliance" he has contracted with the other biotech giant, Monsanto. Agent Cow Pie remarks, "We speak pie to power, and send this epicurean treat to His Honor the Chancellor with love from the BBB."

>> **November 28** >> "Operation Cremate Monsanto"

Affinity group discussion. Andalucia, Spain

Jordi Blanchar

Organizing Chaos

In the days leading up to a mass action, whether in Seattle, London, Washington, Prague, Davos, Québec, Gothenburg, or Genoa, the air is tangibly electric as people arrive in town and prepare themselves and their environment for the demonstrations. Cities are transformed overnight as graffiti and posters mysteriously crowd out corporate advertisements, and billboards are transformed into canvases for radical propaganda. A general framework for the actions at hand has been crafted in advance, in face-to-face meetings, over internet listserves, and on telephone conference calls. Then thousands of people, many of them total strangers, come together in dozens of meetings running late into the night.

The skeletal plan for the direct action to come is made flesh and blood, sometimes outright rejected and turned into something else. These actions will belong to everyone and their success will rely on the level of participation.

To facilitate this vital participation, it's essential that there be a location in which we can gather, and a system through which communication, information sharing, and collective decision-making can happen. Events like the Seattle shut-down owed much of their success to the convergence centre space and the spokescouncil meetings.

Convergence centres

Thousands of people are moving about, clustering in impromptu debates, checking a schedule of workshops on the wall, lining up for a free meal, painting banners, laughing. There is a frantic energy engulfing the massive warehouse space, and ricocheting off the rafters; it is the energy of too many sleepless nights, the energy of anticipation, the energy of a common vision, the energy of history being made.

You've entered a convergence centre, a gathering site for people to come together, learn new skills, meet new allies, hold incredibly long meetings, and together, make plans for the upcoming actions. A convergence centre can be little more than a space in which to gather, or it can be a highly coordinated community centre, offering information to folks from out of town, helping to find accommodation, hosting cultural events, trainings, spokescouncil meetings (see below), health clinics, free meals, art-, puppet- and banner-making, and so on.

The best convergence centres are temporary autonomous zones, outside of the cash economy, miniature and imperfect versions of the world we wish to create, where everyone can participate in feeding and caring for each other, teaching and learning from each other, and developing tactics and strategies together to achieve common goals.

Spokescouncil meetings

The spokescouncil meeting is the coordinating and networking structure that enables very large numbers of people to discuss and decide things, usually by consensus. It is a form that has similarity to decision-making processes of many different cultures over a large span of time, including many indigenous nations around the world, many Bedouin and tribal Arab cultures, and the Spanish anarchists in the years leading up to and during the Spanish Civil War.

Affinity groups, and clusters of affiliated affinity groups choose spokespeople who are empowered to speak for the group. The spokespeople sit in a circle, with their affinity group behind them. In this way, groups can confer during the meeting and participate via their spokesperson, but only spokespeople address everyone, vastly reducing the amount of time required for inclusivity.

Spokespeople are responsible for carrying their group's plans, decisions, and opinions to the spokescouncil, as well as relaying information and decisions back to members of their group who aren't present. Power is decentralized – the group retains its autonomy, and yet is able to closely coordinate with others, all of whom have agreed that this model of communication can best maintain their diversity, while at the same time allowing them to create political space.

As with most things, the spokescouncil model works best when the affinity groups have been together for a while and are skilled both at making quick collective decisions, and at being willing to let go of some of their opinions, trusting in the collective intelligence of the group.

Though the sounds *of breaking glass and concussion grenades were the sounds from Seattle most heavily regurgitated by the corporate media, there was a musical storm brewing in the thickest of tear gas which laughed in the face of the predictable police stand-offs. Wearing Russian-style fuzzy black hats and militaristic green and black uniforms, flanked by a flag corps and rifle twirlers, a radical marching band called the Infernal Noise Brigade (INB) roamed the liberated streets.*

There have been marching bands like these at almost every global day of action since J18: the Committee for Full Enjoyment played at IMF/World Bank meetings in Washington in 2000, the INB turned up again in 2000 in Prague, as did Rhythms of Resistance, a samba band from London which incorporated 50 people playing home-made shakers into a huge festive block. New York's Hungry March Band frequently delights crowds with their dance music and flashy baton twirling; the Front Musicale d'Intervention from France played the Zapatista hymn during the March for Indigenous Dignity in Mexico in 2001; a marching band of internationals played with the Black Bloc in Genoa in 2001; and an anticapitalist marching band in São Paolo came to Porto Alegre for the World Social Forum 2002 – playing a song they learned from a member of the INB!

These marching bands inspire joy, but also help move crowds, bringing reinforcements to high-intensity situations and renewing courage of those engaged in direct action. They also provide music – an essential component of carnival as it crosses barriers of nationality, ideology, and class; like carnival, it embodies self-organization and incites people into "dancing", as US folk singer Casey Neil sings, "on the ruins of multinational corporations." Making music is a way of throwing beauty back into the streets – streets in which people really begin to live again.

Infernal Noise: the soundtrack to insurrection

by Jennifer Whitney

"You know your own music when you hear it one day. You fall into line and dance until you pay the piper." – **Bryon Gysin**

"We have to come up with a new marching pattern," said Grey. Everyone else in the band groaned. Practice was almost over, or so we thought, we'd spent half the time marching around and stepping on each others' heels and not working on improving our tiny repertoire of half-written songs that we were going to have to play in public in two month's time. Besides that, it was freezing – the wind was blowing the rain horizontal, so it battered us under the shelter of a freeway overpass. Over the disgruntled murmuring, Grey continued, "There's never going to be more than about 500 people around us, so we need to figure out a way to look big, and fill up all four lanes."

Five hundred people? I stared at him in disbelief, realizing what different worlds we had been occupying lately. "Look, I know of more than 500 people who are organizing this action." I replied. "There's gonna be thousands of people out there, we'll never have a chance to spread out like that, and we have plenty of other stuff to work on." Everyone murmured in agreement, not because they shared my conviction or believed my slight exaggeration of how many organizers I knew, but because they wanted to either play music or go home.

Cycling home, I was overcome with a sense of excitement, a sense of inevitability, of change. I knew that my band was going to make a huge difference in the action, and that the action would make an even more colossal difference in all of our lives. I marvelled at my own unwavering conviction that thousands of people were going to shut down the WTO meetings in Seattle, and at how rapidly my life had completely transformed in the previous month.

The whole year had been a blur. I learned that February, right before leaving for a long trip to Morocco, that the WTO was coming to Seattle. I didn't know much about the WTO, just enough to know that I would work on organizing protests of some sort when I got back. But then I spent almost six months living in the foothills of the Rif mountains, where there was no electricity or running water, in a tiny, remote village of musicians. I was tour-managing their occasional forays into Europe, and absorbing what I could of their legendary history and trance-inducing music. The global economy was as far from my thoughts as was possible.

Then one evening in August, an acquaintance of mine from Seattle turned up, by massive coincidence, in my village. Dan had come to Morocco from London, and he told me a story of an extraordinary tube ride he had one Friday afternoon in June. He was travelling in central London, when he heard an announcement about some sort of civil unrest causing the closure of the next few stations. He got off and retraced the path of the tube – and found himself, completely by accident, in the middle of the Carnival Against Capital on June 18.

I, of course, knew nothing about J18, having been in the village since March. I listened with awe and slight disbelief as he told me incredible stories of the carnival that disrupted the entire financial district, the samba band that was leading the crowd, the graffiti and the focused property damage targeting transnationals, the plumes of smoke he saw rising from the City as he left. I was completely starved for news of any sort, and hung on to every word. It felt a bit like he was a time traveller, or I was.

Dan and I began speculating about the actions being planned against the WTO meetings, which would take place

---

begins in the village of Maladagudda, India, with the destruction of the first test site of Monsanto's genetically modified cotton. Mr. Basanna, owner of the field where an illegal genetic experiment is being conducted without his knowledge, local peasants, and members of the KRRS, together uproot the genetically modified plants. Afterwards, all the plants in the field are set on fire. "We send today a very clear message to all those who have invested in Monsanto in India and abroad: take your money out now, before we reduce it to ashes," declares the KRRS.

>> December >> Responding to a call by Mon refugee Buddhist monks, Thai activists begin a three month occupation of the proposed route for the Yadana gas pipeline, which, after slicing through Burma's rainforest, is heading for neighbouring Thailand. Oil company's Unocal and Total contracted the Burmese portion of the pipeline with the Burmese military junta, which instituted a scorched-earth campaign along the pipeline route, relocating and destroying entire villages. For three months, construction is stopped, but eventually police move in with construction crews and disperse the crowd with water cannons, arresting 50.

>> December 7 >> A unusual coalition of locked-out

in our city a few months later. Little did we know, but that action would find us together in a marching band, playing rhythms originating from this tiny, off-the-map village in Morocco, rhythms which are close to 1,000 years old, and which are in danger of being lost forever.

When I finally returned to Seattle, I was staying at Grey's house when a friend of his came over with slick anti-WTO agit-prop and a collection of beautiful images of past actions. He told me about the Direct Action Network (DAN), a grassroots coalition of groups and individuals, formed that summer in order to organize a complete shut down of the WTO ministerial. I went to the next meeting. Before I knew it, I was organizing first aid trainings and street medic support for the actions, setting up a clinic for the convergence centre, and working on various other aspects of the action. And then I got a phone call asking me to show up at a meeting to talk about starting a band.

"The Infernal Noise Brigade is a marching drum orchestra and street performance crew activated by massive political and cultural uprisings. We are a tactical mobile rhythmic unit consisting of a majorette, medics, tactical advisors, rifle-twirling contingent, flag corps, and percussionists."

The INB first came together several months before the WTO actions. Some of us had been inspired by hearing of the Barking Bateria, the samba band Dan saw during the J18 actions in London, many of us had worked together before in a political band/performance collective, and all of us wanted something meaningful and fun to do during the actions. Our intent was multi-fold; we wanted to provide entertainment, energy, and support for the hundreds of people who would be locked down in blockades all day; we wanted to be a useful tool that tactical organizers could utilize to move a large crowd to strategic locations to reinforce blockades; we wanted to prevent endless speechifying and break up the sometimes-tiresome chants so people could dance and have a good time rather than just shouting all day long; and we wanted to confuse the police – staving off arrests or police attack if at all possible.

Moving a crowd is a logistical nightmare. No-one listens to anyone with a megaphone anymore, and relying on one person to shout orders to a crowd is risky and disempowering to those being shouted at. So we figured that if we developed good systems of communication, made it clear to organizers what we were there for and how they could interface with us (in other words, don't talk to the musicians while we're playing!) we would be able to dramatically affect the overall strategy of the day.

So we began practice, and I began talking up the band to the other organizers within DAN to ensure that they'd know how to work with us when the time came. We had several meetings to discuss our goals, and how we might best achieve them, talked about the WTO, and tried to live up to the outrageous mission statement Grey crafted, which read: *"Strike fear and incomprehension in the minds of the powerful. Disrupt the dominant trance. Be calculatedly unpredictable and undermine the spectacle by introducing music of a disorienting or ecstatic nature into the sterile political discourse. Disrupt the stale dichotomy of leftist protest and police cliché. Facilitate the self-actualization of the mob. Be the dope propaganda."*

We tried to keep this 'mission' in mind as we practiced, trying to learn to march in step, as summer slipped into fall, and as the cops repeatedly ran us out of public parks. We still needed uniforms, we had no idea how we were going to communicate with each other while playing, and we couldn't come up with anyone who might work as a drum major – someone fearless, performative, fun to work with, good under pressure, who would like our weird niche of an aesthetic (post-industrial, quirky-but-militant), had a strong sense of rhythm, and could devote countless hours over the next two months to practice and meetings. We'd been stuck with the same three songs for at least a month, and we had yet to figure out a name.

We were playing in a park on one of the last sunny days of the year when our fire-spinning acrobat friend Josephina came skipping over on her lunch break. She came right into the centre of the circle we'd formed and leapt into the air, diving, and rolling into a double somersault. She jumped back up, spun around, threw us a wink, and started dancing. I looked at Grey and he looked at me, the same thought running through our minds. I formed the words "drum major" with my lips, and he raised his eyebrows in agreement. Perfect.

Then the rain came, and we moved practice to a run-down industrial part of Seattle. The cops never looked for us there, and as the driving wind blew the rain into our shelter, we reassured each other that it would be good practice for playing all day in the inevitable rain of late November.

Meanwhile, Seattle was slowly becoming an occupied city, as people poured into town to help in the final days of preparing for the actions. Cycling between my house, my work, and my meetings, I made eye contact with innumerable strangers who gave me conspiratorial smiles and winks. Armies of culture jammers armed with spray paint and stencils, or wheatpaste and posters, began their night-time transformation of the city, one neighbourhood at a time. Banners, puppets, and flags were being stockpiled, taken out for test runs in a series of

---

steelworkers, members of the International Workers of the World, the International Longshore and Warehouse Worker's Union, and Earth First! successfully blockade a ship in Tacoma, Washington, US. The ship belongs to MAXXAM Corporation, whose subsidiaries, Kaiser Aluminum and Pacific Lumber, are responsible for locking out 3,000 steelworkers and logging old growth forests, respectively. Some people picket the port, others lock onto a conveyor belt, and a flotilla of small boats blocks the waterway. Most dramatically, braving 75 mph winds, activists hang suspended over the water with a banner, blockading the entry to the dock. Members of the ILWU refuse to cross the picket and when the ship does dock, it remains unloaded for several days as the port's conveyor belt has been mysteriously damaged to the tune of $50,000. "[CEO] Hurwitz Cuts Jobs Like He Cuts Trees," reads the banner above the climber's bodies. **>> December 9 >>** School is definitely out for the kids of Greece: pens and note books are exchanged for petrol bombs and face masks as a wave of mass demonstrations hits 44 cities and 10,000 schools are occupied. Pupils and teachers join forces to oppose legislation which links education directly to fluctuations of the economy with a torrent of actions resulting in imprisonments and a

neighbourhood processions. Designed as outreach tools and serving as morale boosters, the parades grew larger and more colourful each time.

Some folks sussed out vacant buildings, searching for the perfect one to crack open as a mass public squat, an action to bring attention to the housing crisis, brought on by the high-tech industry. DAN meetings grew larger, longer, louder, and more urgent. I finally broke down and got my first cell phone, promising myself I'd only have it for the month of November (yeah, right). Impromptu trainings and practice runs were held across town; I came home from work to find sheepish friends dismantling a tripod they'd erected in my backyard, unbeknownst to my housemates or neighbours.

My life took on a very narrow focus, as I cycled the triangular pattern between my home and workplace, DAN meetings near the university, and band practice on the waterfront. Nothing outside of that triangle mattered anymore. I was operating on the complete conviction that we were going to succeed in shutting down the WTO. I also was convinced, after watching video from the APEC summit in Vancouver, Canada, that the police were going to violently attack us, and so I began doing research about pepper spray and tear gas, trying to figure out what we might do to protect ourselves against it. I spoke with veterans, military dissidents, activists who'd been pepper sprayed, doctors, and chemistry students, reading the scant amounts of documentation about so-called non-lethal weapons, and desperately theorizing and speculating about what might neutralize the painful chemicals. This earned me the scorn of a few organizers, who called me alarmist and fear-mongering; a few were opposed to me talking about these chemical weapons during first aid trainings. Due in part to my minor obsession, and also to what was to become our customary blend of pragmatism and fashion sense, the marching band decided to play it safe and wear respirators with goggles as protection.

"For the World Bank and the WTO, our forests are a marketable commodity. But for us, the forests are a home, our source of livelihood, the dwelling of our gods, the burial ground of our ancestors, the inspiration of our culture. We do not need you to save our forests. We will not let you sell our forests. So go back from our forests and our country." **– letter by Indian adivasi (tribals) handed over as they invaded World Bank offices in New Delhi and plastered its walls with cow dung, 9 November 1999**

"Because humans have too long bleated slogans and carried signs, the aesthetic of the INB is entirely post-textual; we provide tactical psychological support through a 'propaganda of sound'. The street

is the venue for action and symbology, the domain of emotion and intuition; ideology is homework."

According to Hakim Bey, military marching bands were invented by the wine-drinking Bektashi Sufi Order, who made up the Ottoman Empire's Imperial Guard. In an essay entitled 'Utopian Blues', he writes, "Judging by European accounts of [these] bands, which always speak of the sheer terror they induced, these musicians discovered a kind of psychological warfare which certainly bestowed prestige on this very ambiguous group, made up of slaves of the Sultan."

As the weeks slid into months, and we prepared to commit our own style of psychological warfare, band practice started to really come together and we slowly developed more songs. Our rhythms mostly came from members who have studied or travelled in countries not yet steamrolled by the scourge of western popular music. These rhythms are processed into an amalgam of styles, which leads us to mix unexpected elements – for example, a traditional Rajasthani folk rhythm is modified and transposed to snare drums, with a galloping North African Gnaoua line clattering across the top.

It was imperative to us that we not degenerate into meandering 'jam sessions' or let drum circles form up around us – such music is shackled to the lowest common denominator. We wanted not only to provide a soundtrack to the insurrection and tactical support to the organizing strategy, but also to play really tight, well crafted songs. Accusations of elitism have not been uncommon; we maintain that the left is full of mediocrity and we are interested in transcending that. Tight organization plus a high level of skill is the only thing that can constitute a real threat to the powers that be, and like those who invented marching bands, we wanted our music to be threatening.

Meanwhile, we spent hours discussing uniforms (the beginning of an eternal obsession) and trying to come up with a name for the band. After one particularly long and absurd brainstorming session, a small group of us set off for a bar, determined not to leave until we had a name. The brainstorm had yielded a single mandate – our name had to be a three letter acronym, and after a few hours of drinking, we christened ourselves the Infernal Noise Brigade.

Then it came time to add new elements to our mix: a

---

hunger strike. The occupations last for several months, despite massive repression.

\\ 1999 //

>> January >> The twelve year campaign to save Headwaters Forest reaches an important milestone when two ancient groves are transferred into public ownership and five other groves are protected under a 50 year cutting ban. Earth First!ers continue their campaign against the MAXXAM corporation, and strengthen their defence of still-unprotected forest in the area.

>> January >> Years of campaigning pay off for the semi-nomadic Penan tribe of Sarawak, Malaysia. After a decade of vigorous repression against anti-logging activities, with hundreds of Penan people receiving long jail sentences, the police and inform the communities that the Lajung Lumber company has been ordered to leave the area and compensate the Penan for violating its agreement not to log without their permission.

>> January >> Students in Benin City, Nigeria, begin an indefinite strike to protest against conditions at the school. Student stipends, which are paid out sporadically, "have been the same for 21 years," says student council president Alphonse Late Lawson-Helu. "It's really a pittance. The cost of living has gone up

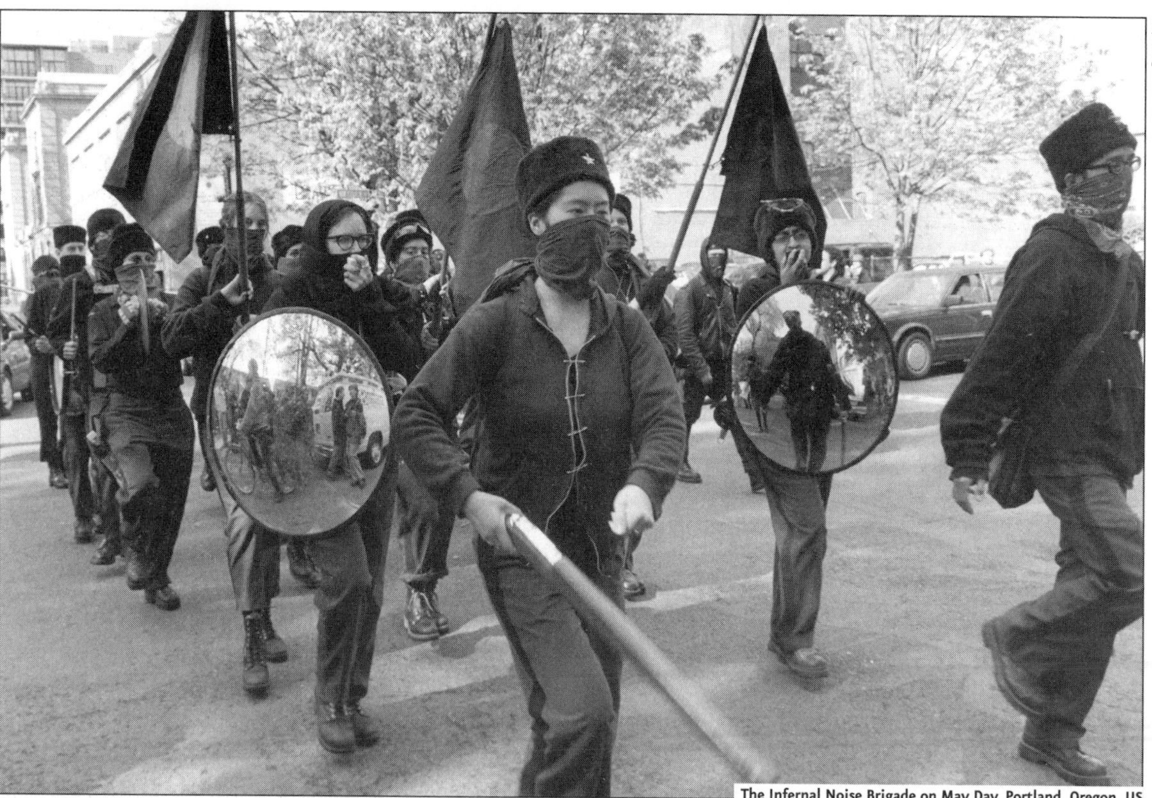

Bette Lee

The Infernal Noise Brigade on May Day. Portland, Oregon, US

team of coordinated rifle twirlers, a flag corps, medics, and scouts. They quickly became indispensable, as not only did they provide a strong visual component, they also acted as eyes and ears for the entire crew, and formed a protective barrier around the musicians in tight crowd situations, enabling us to continue playing without smacking anyone in the face with our drumsticks.

By then we were marching in step most of the time, and working on some formations – things we could do to add more visual interest when the march came to a standstill, or when we wanted to block an intersection, or just wanted to show off. We developed whistle commands and hand signals so the major could indicate for us to go into different formations, stop marching, stop playing, and the like. One night a friend of ours came to practice and gave us a quick-and-dirty workshop on Brazilian samba music, teaching us our first song that anyone could really dance to, and beginning our incessant struggle to learn to play samba right.

I began suffering from sleep deprivation and overstimulation. My worlds were becoming crossed, and I was finding myself tapping out our songs during meetings, and scribbling out tactical ideas and first aid supply needs during band practice. No one really seemed to notice, as everyone else was as overloaded as me.

And then I quit my job, just as the convergence centre opened in an old hip-hop club called Studio 420, about ten blocks from my house. My little triangle of a life became a singular straight line, much narrower and more focused, as I went from home to 420 to practice and back to 420, and home again, with meetings everywhere I turned and a cell phone that wouldn't stop ringing. But although my life became much more hectic with the opening of the convergence centre and the health clinic, which was now providing free care to hundreds of people a day, it also became very simple, very clear. The actions had acquired a momentum of their own, (this probably happened long before I even noticed), and there were now so many people working night and day that I was no longer essential to making things happen. My work was useful and helpful, yes, and I was looked at sternly if I missed a meeting, absolutely, but the thing had grown to proportions so much bigger than me, bigger than most of us had imagined was

---

tremendously, and the university now houses 16,000 students, but was built for 6,000."

>> January 3 >> People without legal papers from Congo, Sierra Leone, Kenya, Algeria, Tunisia and elsewhere occupy a church in Ghent, Belgium, reclaiming their autonomy, declaring their solidarity with the thousands of people without papers occupying churches all across the country, and demanding papers for all.

>> January 4 >> To celebrate Ogoni Day, and in solidarity with Nigerian activists, UK activists occupy the offices of Shell's directors, declaring their intent to send a message to Shell and other corporations that 1999 will be a year of increased globalization of protest. Live footage of the protest is relayed directly from Shell's own offices to an activist website.

>> January 29 >> Thai Greens protest infront of Leonardo DiCaprio's hotel, his new film, *The Beach* is destroying Maya Bay, in a protected National Park. The bay's beach has been planted with 100 non-native coconut trees to give more of a 'tropical' feel!

>> Febuary >> Students continue an indefinite strike at the University of Benin, Togo, to protest conditions at their school. Student stipends, which are only paid out sporadically, "have been the same for 21 years," said

possible, and I was humbled by the vast amount of dedication and conviction in the many strangers who came to my city and quickly became allies. It was an important lesson, and one I've relearned and refined over the years since. I learned how to be useful and hard-working, and yet not to presume myself to be irreplaceable or even essential, because I'm not, none of us are. To act otherwise is to set ourselves up for isolation and targeting by repressive authorities, not to mention denying the capacity of others to adapt to new circumstances, learn new skills, and develop qualities of leadership, including humility.

"We attempt, through our aesthetics and our fierce commitment to the politics of joy and desire, to create a space of carnival, where all rules are broken and anything is possible. We seek to dissolve all barriers between art and politics, participants and spectators, dream and action."

The morning of N30 dawned grey and drizzly, and the INB was late to the march. However, the crowd was so huge that by the time we got there and scrambled into formation, the tail end of the march had yet to leave. I took a deep breath, waiting to fall into line and march towards downtown. We set off. Left, right, left, cursing the light drizzling rain, stomachs knotted up in anticipation of who-knew-what. As we descended the hill and caught our first full view of downtown, I realized something that I had suspected for some time, and was now absolutely sure of – we were making history.

Our first act of mischief was to invade a Starbucks where

"Well they certainly lived up to their name. I don't know if these people have any kind of message other than making noise, but when they have 50,000 of their closest friends downtown with them – well, that's a lot of noise."

– Seattle's KIRO television station, 30 November 1999

people were having their routine morning coffee before work. Marching in, we formed a circle and played for a few minutes to general consternation and astonishment before clattering back out onto the streets again. It was one of my favourite moments of the day, because it was like we were announcing, "Hey, normal life ends here folks, there is a marching band in your Starbucks, you're not going to work today!"

Shortly after, we came to an intersection quite close to one of the entrances to the convention centre, where the WTO's opening ceremonies were to take place. My adrenaline was starting to wear off. I'd almost grown accustomed to the fact that we had completely taken over the city centre, that in every direction I looked were crowds of people dressed as butterflies, waving flags, hoisting the signs of their unions – it's a big myth that all the unions were boycotting our actions in favour of their big rally in a stadium a few miles north. There was a large contingent of Steelworkers and Longshore workers leading one of the marches at 7.00 am, and they were there when we first got gassed.

The whole band seemed a little scattered. We were completely exhilarated, and we weren't prepared for all the cameras, getting in our way, vying for shots of us. I think we were all somewhat in shock about two things – one, that we'd actually managed to pull off this marching band thing, and two, that there was a crowd of 10,000 people we could play for.

We got to the bottom of the hill, marched around a bit, and then took a little break, ate some snacks, said some brilliant things to each other like, "Isn't this cool? Wow, I can't believe it," and the like. Then we started playing a West African rhythm. It wasn't something that we'd actually written and rehearsed, but several of us knew the basic rhythm and it was easy enough for the others to pick up. As we played, the light misty rain stopped, and blue started to take over the sky. Robert pulled out his camera, went and stood in front of the police line, and snapped a photo of himself before climbing on top of a dumpster in the middle of the intersection to check out the crowd. Then, without warning, they started to gas us. Chaos broke loose. Our song trainwrecked to a halt. A tear gas canister hit Robert in the head; another one caught him in the back as he jumped down. We scrambled to find our goggles and respirators – we were prepared for them to gas us, but hadn't expected it at 9.00 am!

Someone started up another song, and those who were able to play dropped into it while we retreated, but Shazz and Dan were walking the wrong way, towards the cops. Disoriented and blinded, they moved into the thick cloud of gas that was now filling the once-blue sky. I grabbed them and we headed out of there; I was breathing slowly, deeply, through my fleece scarf, and walking with my eyes closed, blind leading the blind. I got us around the corner and we caught up to the rest of the band, who seemed giddy, delirious, confused. Everyone around us was shouting and screaming, frightened, angry. It's hard to remember what we did, what I thought, what happened next. I know that several of us were laughing, excited, ready to gear up and jump back into the fray. Someone pointed out that the rhythm we'd been playing before the gas started was a warrior's rhythm, traditionally played while two adversaries fought each other, a ritualized system of settling

---

student council president Alphonse Late Lawson-Helu. "It's really a pittance. The cost of living has gone up tremendously, the univeristy now houses 16,000 students, but was built for only 6,000."

>> February 5 >> Twenty-seven students in Washington DC, US occupy the office of Georgetown University's President, demanding that the administration adopt anti-sweatshop policies.

>> February 6-9 >> At Nairobi University, Kenya, students and others struggle to defend the Karura Forest against development. Riot police attack, and for three days pitched battles fill the streets. Three MPs are arrested and charged with inciting violence, while Wangari Maathai of the Green Belt movement (having been beaten in January when she tried to plant saplings in the forest) barricades herself in her own home to avoid being arrested as well.

>> February 13 >> In Libreville, Gabon, police use force to disperse demonstrations by high school and university students who have been on strike since November 1998, carrying out road blockades to protest shortages of school buses and other facilities.

>> February 22 >> Fifty thousand farmers descend on Brussels to protest at the EU shake up of the Common

disputes. Here we were, 7,000 miles from West Africa, inadvertently inciting a battle. We laughed manicly while adjusting our respirators and getting back into formation. It was the first time that any of us had been tear gassed. And it was the last time we ever ran from it.

"The INB provides subliminal disruption of time, using drums to divide it into disorienting rhythmic patterns which are disturbing to the linear sequence. Songs in different tongues further infect the monoculture. In the path to constructing a better reality, and in deconstructing a system based in the misery of alienation, we choose noise as our tool."

We took a break in the central park, Westlake Center, after trying to meet up with some people who'd planned a Reclaim the Streets action, which seemed a little underambitious at that point, as we'd already successfully reclaimed the entire city centre. So we split up to find food and toilets in the nearby mall and transnational chain stores surrounding us. It was like we were an invading army – we had grown so quickly accustomed to our total occupation of the city that we didn't expect no for an answer. We were in control. We were experiencing a complete shift in the balance of power for the first time in our lives, and it felt amazing. We were manic, ecstatic, every cell vibrating, electric, experiencing freedom in a way we'd only ever dreamt of. History was ours to shape with our own hands.

Regrouping in the park, we formed up, launched into a song, and set off down Fourth Avenue, where we suddenly became the main event. Thunderous applause greeted us, as if we were heroes, and the glaring lights and made-up faces of the mainstream media pressed against us. It was as if we'd stepped into a void, the vacuum which occurs when a performance is running late; perhaps people were waiting (in vain) for the approach of the labour march. Whatever its cause, it jolted us back into the moment and we confidently marched off looking for adventure, feeling like we'd done something truly great. That was part of the magic of Seattle – as one activist put it, everyone who was there came away feeling like they did it.

We marched on, back towards where we'd been gassed, hung a left, and then found ourselves marching parallel to a police line. We went to check it out, and saw a vast expanse of empty pavement stretching away behind the cops and ending at the heels of another police line, two blocks away. In that vast 'demilitarized zone' lay the hotels where US Secretary of State Madeleine Albright and US trade negotiator Charlene Barshefsky were trapped, making frantic, furious phone calls. Just beyond it, where the streets came to life again, was a huge crowd gathered around a burning dumpster. We decided to retrace our steps and head over there; drawn like moths to the flickering flames.

There was a crowd of folks circled up from the Black Bloc, strangely dusted in what looked like ash, or spray from a fire extinguisher. A few people prayed, another few were dancing, most were gazing at the flames, mesmerized. Just beyond the flames stood the riot cops, their monolithic black-clad presence stretching from sidewalk to sidewalk, their visors glinting with reflected light, their image wavering, shimmering behind the waves of heat emanating from the dumpster.

The entire day looked a bit like that, shimmering, not quite real. My memories of it are elusive, more of feelings than of events. A burning dumpster, my first taste of tear gas – these are incidental when held up next to the feeling of power and entitlement shared by everyone in those streets, the feeling that the world belonged to us and that we would not so easily give it back to those who would destroy it to please their shareholders and loan officers.

"Out of the chaos the future emerges in harmony and beauty."

– Emma Goldman

The rest of N30 is history, the future emerged from the chaos, and the world breathed a collective sigh of relief – finally people in the US were waking up to the economic and political reality for the vast majority of the planet. The global movement gained more momentum than it knew what to do with, the WTO hung its head in shame and swore never to meet in a democracy again, and the Infernal Noise Brigade continues playing, trying to write one decent samba rhythm, still having ridiculously long meetings about new uniforms, sending emissaries to far-flung gatherings of musicians, revolutionaries, and those who form bridges between, always trying to jump-start the advent of a better world.

"During times of revolt there is a brilliant flash of direct truth, connecting internal desire with external reality and smashing the barriers between the two. In that instance, that dangerous moment of ultimate presence and clarity, we become alchemists, forging the future from the energy of spontaneous passionate imagining, and fuelling it with infernal noise."

Jennifer Whitney is one of the co-editors of this book

Note: Bold quotes are from INB agit-prop: www.infernalnoise.org

---

Resources:

» Great information on instruments and making your own gear from Rhythms of Resistance in London: www.rhythmsofresistance.co.uk

» Moroccan musicians, the Master Musicians of Jajouka: www.jajouka.com

---

Agricultural Policy. Tear gas is fired and water cannons hose down the farmers. A large part of the city is enclosed behind razor wire barricades. The state closes roads and schools and forbids residents from hanging the EU flag from their windows. Farmer Joseph McNeely from County Donegal said: "I don't know what we'll do if this agriculture reform goes through. It will depopulate our part of Ireland still further. I am the fourth generation of my family to farm our land but I am doubtful if we can carry on."

>> March >> Five thousand civilian Zapatistas conduct a week-long programme of popular education throughout the country, in preparation for a popular referendum, or *consulta*, on indigenous rights and culture. Over three million Mexicans vote at thousands of polling stations, agreeing that the San Andrés Accords should be implemented.

>> March 10 >> The Ecotopia Cell of the Biotic Baking Brigade (BBB) delivers just desserts in the form of three blueberry tofu cream pies to the head of Chevron CEO Kenneth T. Derr, just before he delivers a speech to school kids in San Francisco, US. Special Agent Blueberry says: "From the forests of Colombia to the platforms of Nigeria down to the waters and workers of our own Bay,

Indymedia: don't hate the media, be the media

What follows is a compilation of texts, which explain some of the origins and spirit of Indymedia. First is a log made up of excerpts from the New-IMC network email list that works with new site applications from around the globe. Here they explain their reasons for requesting a new site:

>> GLOBAL IMC LOG >>

IMC PALESTINE

>> Our mission is to help Palestinian activists organize, motivate and inform. We want to help people develop the art of story-telling and debate. We want to be a catalyst for those stories to reach into other media and parts of the planet. We want to break down barriers and encourage the flow of information from people with both good and bad stories to tell, to the people we know are out there who want to hear them. We want to create a physical and virtual space that creates a sense of achievement and reflection but is vibrant and open enough to attract people who are interested in activism; while remaining practical and focused to encourage all people in our audience to contribute.

>> Out of the ten people in our core group, only two are women. Unfortunately this is a trend throughout Palestine that we do not want to follow and we are encouraging more women to attend our meetings and take an active role in the new media centre.

>> New volunteers have asked us who is running this project? Most businesses and organizations in Palestine suffer from over-management and from having too many people in charge. This makes it even more crucial that we strive to create an open and transparent organization whose members report fully to one another and share responsibilities.

From Seattle to South Africa, *Chiapas to Croatia, a radical and democratic peoples' news network for the world has spread like wildfire, recklessly endangering the corporate media's monopoly on information. Known as the Independent Media Centre (IMC, or Indymedia), this network enables hundreds of alternative media organizations and thousands of activists to collaborate through the internet in a joint effort to democratize the media. Since the success of the first IMC in Seattle, Indymedia is the fastest growing alternative media network in the world, with 112 websites spanning six continents as of April 2003 – the most recent addition being IMC Iraq.*

Through Indymedia, people who are directly affected by social and economic policies can directly share their news and views with the world, using innovative 'open publishing' software. This allows anyone with access to the internet to easily and instantaneously publish text, audio, and video files onto the network's newswires. Viewers can comment directly below the original post, creating an open forum for dialogue and debate.

Open publishing is redefining journalism by welcoming people to publish more than just the facts, to tell their tale as they witnessed it. "People all over the world are dipping their story telling toes in the water," says Matthew Arnison, a member of the Indymedia Tech Collective. Without much in the way of rules or style guides, Indymedia is hub for the collection of eclectic and lush story telling, a breeding ground for the exploration of new and creative journalistic styles, and an archive for history as it happens.

Indymedia has evolved into a hopeful vision that a new media landscape is on the horizon, one that gives voice to millions of people. "Those who are looking for a better world, those who are revolting...can no longer rely on corporate [and] mainstream media," says media critic Robert McChesney. "They need their own media. That is precisely the mission of the IMC."

>> IMC NIGERIA

On the issue of the Nigerian government reaction, should they learn that a Nigeria IMC have commenced in the country, we resolved that we are going to operate our IMC though we know that the Nigeria government will never be in support of our new technique in getting real news spread within and outside the country. An activist from Dehura cited the killing of the editor-in-chief and founder of *Newswatch* magazine who was murdered by the federal government because of his unrelenting effort to unfold the ills of the Nigerian government, which is not the usual operation of the corporate press in Nigeria. We all agreed that the field of operation will be rough, but we just have to contribute lots of sacrifice to start and sustain the Nigeria IMC, knowing the positive effect it will have on the Nigeria people as a nation. We agreed that all our discussion-making system shall be non-hierarchical, consensus-based and collective decision process. We also agreed that the Nigerian IMC is not owned by any person or organization.

>> IMC JAKARTA

In a place where internet access is expensive and difficult, an IMC can/must do work primarily off-line to have it be effective. Whether or not an IMC makes media on or off the internet, the general organizing principles are the same – have meetings, have enough people to sustain a group, gather a mission statement and editorial policy, not be dominated by one organization…

>> IMC ECUADOR

In our country the mass media are private monopolized corporations; as a logical consequence they only inform about notices of their interest, not informing about actions of the majority of Ecuadorians. These days, knowing objectives/aims of Indymedia, and after having some meetings of analysis with responsible persons of alternative communication, we found it necessary for Ecuador to join power to create an IMC Ecuador, to inform the world about our struggles, processes, activities, proposals and thoughts.

>> Indymedia is the space of communication, which will help us to inform lots of people about our feelings, thoughts, proposals, actions, and mobilizations like indigenous, campesinos, urban, popular, and other social movements of Ecuador. We will get back the space of communication that the conventional mass media have monopolized, not expressing the reality of people and social movements.

>> IMC ZAMBIA

After covering the Conference of Parties (COP 7) of the United Nations Convention on Climate Change, in Marrakech, Morocco, I feel deeply encouraged to set up an IMC in Lusaka, Zambia. I contributed a series of stories to the IMC-Climate project in Morocco and after reading my stories on the IMC site, I was very much challenged to set up our local IMC. I have familiarized myself and other colleagues and have read the IMC blueprint

---

large petro-chemical corporations display callous disregard for human life and the future of this planet… To their lies, we respond with pies."

>> March 24 >> Thousands of workers denouncing government austerity measures march through Romanian cities and threaten a general strike next month unless their demands are met. Demands include: indexation of wages, new labour legislation, an end to redundancies, lower utility prices for consumers and a grace period for companies unable to pay their debts.

>> March 24 >> In the United States seven Oglala warriors maintain a tipi camp at La Framboise Island in the Missouri River to protest the controversial Mitigation Act, which would turn nearly 200,000 acres of their land over to the state of South Dakota.

>> March 26 – April 5 >> An eight day partial strike against privatization by Spain's Iberia Airlines workers causes the cancellation of about 400 flights, affecting nearly 100,000 passengers.

>> March 31 >> Bahaman telecommunications workers stage a walk-out, accusing the government of deceiving them in negotiations over privatization of the state phone company. Consultants recommend reducing the work force of 2,100 to under 1,000. The walkout leaves

documents. We seek to set up a committed, country-based IMC group that will work consistently and provide up-to-date independent news coverage. We also seek further guidance from already existing and established IMCs. We are neighbours to South Africa and Congo and I hope with effective communication, we can made our dream a reality.

>> IMC GLOBAL

Re: new imc process: We don't want to just have people fill out the form and click off the boxes and say, yeah give us the domain name. To me, personally, that feels like standing in line, filling out a form and getting a drivers license. that is NOT what Indymedia is about. It's not about a site. That would be easy. That would mean we are just a digital network. But we are much more than that and that is why we are a threat. We are a social network combining the best of a decentralized digital network. So think tanks like the RAND Corporation are threatened by us. If we were just a collective of websites linked to a few servers across the globe, with groups of people uploading stories to open publishing sites, that would be cool. But that wouldn't be Indymedia. The work we are doing is not easy. It is not just about filling about a form. It is not just about getting a server going. It's about changing paradigms...and hopefully about listening and learning more from each other so that we really can change the world and communicate without commodification and with more of a vision for how we want to see things.

/Logging off >>

Indymedia: precursors and birth

This is an edited transcript of an October 2000 interview with one of Indymedia's originators in Seattle, Jeff Perlstein, by journalist Miguel Bocanegra. Interspersed between the text of the interview are first-hand accounts of other Indymedia activists which relate to the events Jeff describes.

Miguel Bocanegra: I'm here with Jeff Perlstein of the Independent Media Centre in Seattle. So Jeff, can you talk a little bit about...how you got involved in the issue of the WTO and give a history of the IMC?

Jeff Perlstein: Sure. In January or February [1999], I saw some flyer about a city-wide gathering about the WTO...I went to monthly meetings and started to hear more about the mobilizations that were happening and learn more about the policies of the WTO.

I'd also begun to see how many folks were coming to Seattle, and see these meetings grow and grow. As someone who has done independent media projects, I began to recognize that we couldn't just let CNN and CBS be the ones to tell these stories, that we needed to develop our own alternatives and networks. That's where the idea for the media centre came from – the necessity for communities to control their own message. So we set about to create a community-based peoples' newsroom. That's where the idea came from.

MB: How did the IMC develop, and how did it come out of the WTO process?

JP: Just to back up a bit, I always like to give respect to the media projects that have come before, that have been part and parcel of movements for social justice, because it's a long history and the IMC didn't just come out of nowhere. [Alternative media] is everywhere from Radio Venceremos [clandestine radio station which played a crucial tactical and cultural role in the 1980s liberation struggle in El Salvador] to Liberation News Service in the sixties here in the US, to the Zapatista's use of the internet in 1994 and since then, a project called Counter Media that I was involved with in 1996, [which brought together independent media activists from around the country to document actions during the] Active Resistance anarchist gathering during the Democratic Party's convention in Chicago, and it was kind of the kernel of the idea for the IMC. It was very small-scale – media activists were out shooting video and documenting what was going on in the streets that the networks weren't covering.

And others – Paper Tiger TV, Deep Dish TV, all the activist media over the years lay the groundwork and paved the way for the IMC model, which was really tying all of these people together, nationally and internationally, in a network that would be powerful and vibrant – media for the movement.

>> Logging on >> J18.org

In the UK, the bug for independent media caught at the Carnival Against Capitalism on J18. Australian techies provided a website which allowed easy uploading – the beginnings of the code for open publishing. Experienced media activists from Undercurrents, Squall, and Schnews and others joined in with cameras, notepads, and tape recorders. A strong internet connection was added, and J18.org appeared.

>> "While the carnival was roving in the City of London, I spent most of the day on the other side of the river Thames, in a dark room packed with cables, used teacups and computers. Everybody was busy typing, uploading reports from all over the world to a shared website. Couriers came in with new audio and videotapes to be edited and uploaded. The footage was projected onto the wall. Reports were received on the phone. The room was buzzing with activity, everybody seemed to know what they were doing. When we left at three in the morning, the leftovers from the day were still visible in the quiet streets – graffiti, beer cans, forgotten leaflets. We were worried [about being] caught with our rucksack full of mobile phones, but determined to continue."

BaTelCo with only a skeleton crew as it tries to repair Nassau phone links knocked out by sabotage.

>> April 8 >> State police occupy the autonomous community of San Andrés Sakam'chen, site of the historic San Andrés Accords, and install a PRI mayor. The following day, 3000 unarmed Zapatistas nonviolently force the police to leave the town and re-install their elected representatives.

>> April 17 >> Two members of Argentina's Mothers of the Plaza de Mayo – the vocal mothers of those who disappeared during the right wing dictatorship – travel to Belgrade, Yugoslavia, to deliver a message of peace and dignity to the war-torn capital: "We are not here to support one sector against another, but to say to all of you that the only enemy is imperialism. This Yugoslav land today is fragmented by the interests and the manipulations of the great powers. Beloved Yugoslav mothers, dear women who struggle: we are here together with you to struggle for peace and dignity. We, the Mothers of the Plaza de Mayo, will carry our message to the world, because we don't believe that missiles and bombs are the way to build a peace. We believe in the word, in dialogue, and in the love of life."

>> April 19-21 >> In Jamaica a new tax is

>> The day became a landmark for the emerging global protest movement due to the audacity of the action, but also due to the use of technology that allowed simultaneous, real time reports of events all over the world on a common website. Five months later, the first IMC website successfully reported the anti-WTO protests in Seattle, this time direct from the street, giving Indymedia a dynamic that would keep it moving and developing across the globe. – **UK IMC**
/Logging off >>

JP: In Seattle, we had this notion that we couldn't just wait for the networks to cover this. This was going to be a very important event, and it was right in our own backyard. It was coming to our town, so we had a responsibility to provide some sort of platform, some sort of framework, for people all over the country to plug in and do good media work.

We set about to do that with only about eight weeks before the WTO. We had no organization. We had no space. We had no funding. We had no staff. What we did have was these relationships with media activists who all were very excited about the idea of us coming together, of really amplifying our impact and bringing the resources and passion and skills that each of us could to really be a vibrant network and to provide a true alternative voice out there.

So that's what folks did. People pitched in, on really short notice, locally, nationally… Somebody said, "Well, this is what I can do. I can bring an editing deck, since you guys don't have one. And everybody can use it," or "We'll bring a bunch of camcorders, and we can help rent satellite time."

"In breaking down barriers, sharing ideas with friends and peers, we are creating a new front in the cultural war to decommodify information and our lives. I see this as an online front, working with journalism and activism at its core, the concept of a free and open exchange of ideas is now being built in earnest, thanks to a modestly conceived but paradigm-shattering open community called Indymedia." – Shane Korytko

We were especially concerned with the way the internet has really grown and how access by a certain segment of the population has also grown, and so there's an issue of what's called a 'digital divide,' [wherein the vast majority of the world does not have internet, or even telephone access]. So we set about to do this innovative thing, linking high and low technologies, or old and new technologies. So the internet and the website was the backbone of our distribution.

For example, we posted audio, video, text, and photos, all these different mediums, to the site, and easy to download. Then community radio stations, cable access stations, even community-based organizations internationally could download and distribute them. Here's a good example: Radio Havana pulled down the audio feed, because they had an internet connection in their office, and then they rebroadcast it on the FM dial, and people all over the island could hear it; nine million people could hear it and didn't have to use the internet.

Another example is that we kicked out a daily print publication called The *Blind Spot*, and we only had the money to run off 2,000 hard copies each day. It's expensive to make hard copies, and we gave those away for free, and posted the files on the site. Activists in Brussels then pulled down those files and printed 8,000 copies and handed them out in the streets of Brussels. So, again, that's 8,000 folks that didn't have to check out the internet, right?

MB: So how did the IMC as an organization become formulated? Did the [WTO organizing] process spark it, create a reason to develop this medium?

JP: In the independent and activist media worlds, there was a lot of discussion about networking, the need for us to have a powerful, vibrant network, as a true alternative to the corporation's network – a peoples' network. Subcomandante Marcos, in 1997 made a video communiqué which was screened at the Freeing the Media Conference in New York.

"We have a choice: we can have a cynical attitude in the face of media, to say that nothing can be done about the dollar power that creates itself in images, words, digital communication, and computer systems that invades not just with an invasion of power, but with a way of seeing the world, of how they think the world should look. We could say, well, 'that's the way it is' and do nothing. Or we could simply assume incredulity: we can say that any communication by the media monopolies is a total lie. We can ignore it and go about our lives. But there is a third option that is neither conformity, nor scepticism, nor distrust: that is to construct a different way – to show the world what is really happening – to have a critical worldview and to become interested in the truth of what happens to the people who inhabit every corner of this world …

This truth becomes a knot of resistance against the lie… independent media tries to save history: the present history – saving it and sharing it so it will not disappear, moreover to distribute it to other places, so that this history is not limited to one country, to one region, to one city or social group … The truth that we build … will reach full potential if we join with other truths and realize that what is occurring in other parts of the world is also part of human history."

– Subcomandante Marcos, excerpt from video communiqué

---

implemented to compensate for the $37 million budget shortfall. The tax results in a 30 per cent rise in fuel prices, leading to three days of rioting, which closes down major roads, schools and most businesses throughout the island. Police kill nine people, arrest 152, and eventually the shaken government backs down, cutting the new tax in half.

>> April 20 >> Students at the National Autonomous University of Mexico begin a general strike against a 3,250 per cent tuition increase – from two cents to $65 per semester – and for administrative reform. The strike, which completely shuts down this university of 270,000 students for nine months, catches the attention of people worldwide and inspires many others who are dealing with similar budget cuts, privatization, and the general undermining of public education. Though military police brutally take back the campus the following winter, the Mexican student movement, an inspiration to the world, continues its fight for free education for all.

>> April 20 >> Students occupy Nicaragua's Central Bank in Managua, demanding that the government allocate six per cent of the national budget to the universities as mandated by the constitution. One is

So what we really saw with the WTO was an opportunity to be a spark, to be a catalyst.... And then folks could bring [Indymedia] with them when they went home. The idea was to make it a replicable model they could take with them.

Since Seattle, when people come together for these big manifestations, the resources also come together, we document it, build an alternative, and then some of those resources stay behind, so we're building all these points in this network. Also we're building the personal relationships, not just a virtual world.

Although we are all linked now by this website, Indymedia.org, there's a real emphasis on the physical spaces, because one of the whole points is to reclaim space for ourselves, for people to interact and to come together and dialogue and exchange, and that that can happen in the virtual realm, but most powerfully happens when we're face-to-face, so these physical locations are linked by this virtual connection.

MB: Can you talk a little bit about the process itself. You said that you started organizing about eight weeks prior to the actual protests. Can you go through the timeline of events that occurred with IMC, the first eight weeks to 30 November through 4 December?

JP: We started convening these weekly meetings and became overwhelmed very quickly as to how ambitious this was and what we were trying to do. Like I said, we had no money. Most of us weren't fund-raisers or anything like that. We were grassroots activists.

Very quickly people started getting very involved, and people started, in an amazing way, saying, "This is what I can do. This is what I can contribute here." The first meeting maybe had 15 people. The next week we had maybe 30. The next week we had 40, 50.

So about up to mid-October, we've got about 40, 50 people who are plugging in somehow. That's locally. Also, myself and a few others were keeping in touch with folks nationally and internationally, putting out the call and getting an overwhelming response. People all over the country, saying, "Yes, we're coming, we're coming. This is what we can bring," or "We're going to raise money for this."

A really key moment was that I made a trip to the Public Grassroots Media Conference in mid-October in Austin, Texas, because it was the only face-to-face opportunity that we had to meet up with independent media makers from around the country between the time of the idea and the WTO. Essentially, this project became the talk of the whole weekend. We ended up workshopping how we could make this go with people who had done these things for years. Paper Tiger has been around for 25 years doing activist media in New York, and they've got the experience. People from Free Speech TV from Boulder showed up. They were there with two people, and they basically said, "Well, we'll design the internet, and we'll provide all the resources for the web stuff."

Folks from *Acción Zapatista*, based in Austin, were providing a lot of the ideological framework, a lot of input on the process and the importance of process and how the Zapatistas have put that at the forefront, and also a reclaiming of space and keeping this decentralized network, and this whole idea of "one no and many yeses", that we all can come together in these moments from one unified "no" to globalization, to global capital, to confront power from above, but that the model and the process has to have ways for people to express their different yeses, their different identities, their different ways of expressing themselves.

So the whole project really accelerated then, to the point that when we got back to Seattle, people were really psyched and we located a space downtown owned by a local non-profit Low Income Housing Institute (LIHI). They really liked the idea of the project and they have this storefront that had just been sitting there unused for a few years. They said, "Look, you can use the place for two months. If you clean all the junk out, and you redo the walls and you paint the place, then that will be in exchange for rent." It is a big place, 2,700 square feet, with high ceilings and an ideal location, right in the heart of downtown. We couldn't really ask for much better.

Pieces are starting to come together. Everyone is bringing a different part to it. Still no money, though. This is late October. We're about a month away and we have about $1,500 donated by one group early on. At this point we're starting to see local people subdividing into different groups, different affinity groups almost. There's a video team. There's an audio team. There was a print team that didn't really come together until the week before. People dealing with volunteer coordination. Another team dealing with security. Another with housing for out-of-towners, and stuff like that.

Meetings are happening almost every night of the week to make this thing go on. We're starting to have phone conference calls, people nationally, to really figure out how all these pieces are going to plug in and hopefully make some sense when the week of WTO hits.

Right around the first week of November, we're still pulling all these strands together and trying to get people involved. Because we were a new project and trying to make it go in eight weeks and probably far too ambitious for what we had in place, that the relationship with local organizers, local organizations, wasn't as strong as it could have been, and in my mind should have been.

---

killed by a police officer, 21 others are wounded and 77 are arrested. In response, students take two hostages, burn a vehicle, and attack the building with homemade mortars. That night, they maintain a continuous occupation of the highway passing by the campus' main entrance

>> April 20 >> South Korean docks are idle as shipyard workers walk off the job to protest Daewoo Heavy Industry's threats to auction off its shipbuilding division in order to eliminate half of its $49 billion debt and meet the terms of a $58 billion loan being issued them by the IMF.

>> April 21 >> In Ouro Preto, Minas Gerais, Brazil, 25,000 people protest against rising unemployment and IMF austerity measures. The peaceful No Confidence demonstration calls for President Cardoso's resignation, suggesting that he ought to face criminal charges for his role in the Central Bank scandal.

>> April 26 >> South Korean striking subway workers stand off against 2,000 riot police who are trying to evict them from their protest camp at Seoul's National University. The strike against layoffs is declared illegal with the government threatening to sack any worker who does not return to work immediately.

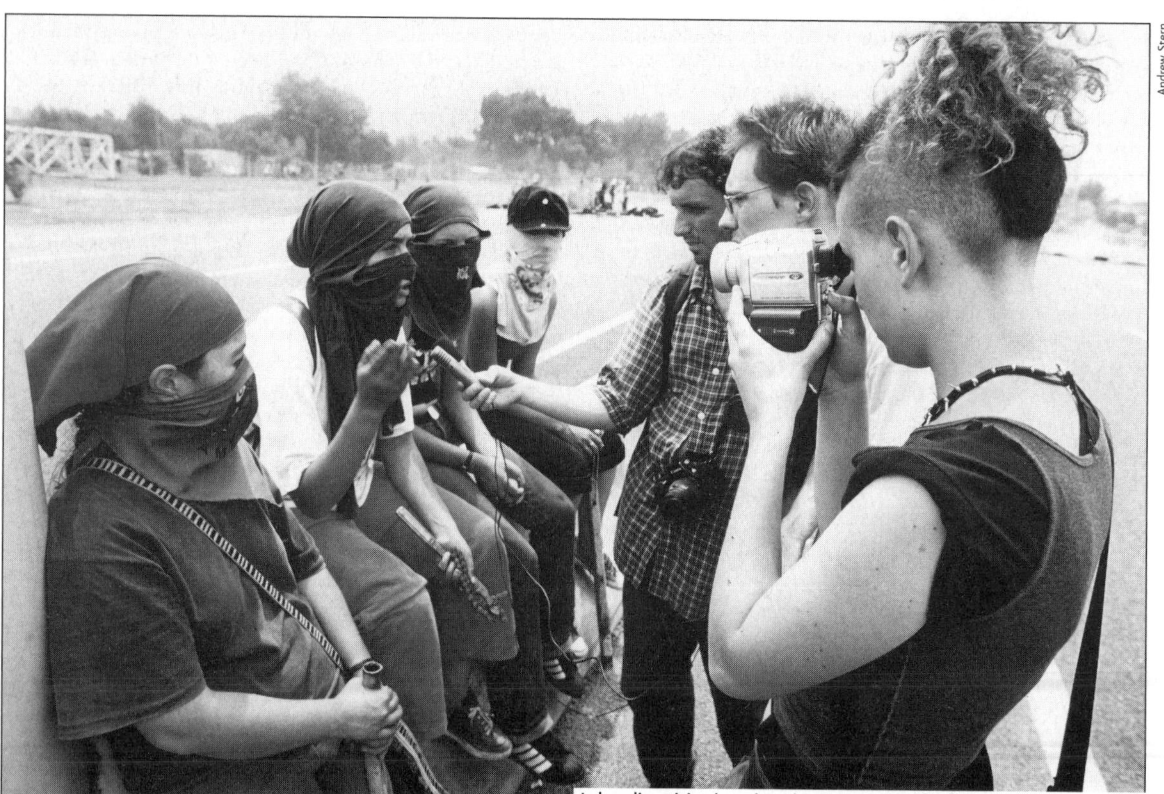

Andrew Stern

Indymedia activists interview *piqueteras* on a road blockade. Buenos Aires, Argentina

So early November, we finally got the space, and not only were we maxxed out just trying to make the media side of things happen, but now all the same people are having to pitch in to sheetrock the walls and paint the floors and put in plumbing and wiring. So many people really put their lives on hold.

Deep Dish TV from New York was on board – they started during the Gulf War, because they recognized the complete media consolidation during the war and how only a narrow thread of information was coming out. Their idea was to break through that blockade by producing video of the critical issues, and then loading it to a cable access station satellite so it would play on community access stations all around the country. For Seattle, they raised money for us to buy [TV] satellite time.

By mid November we have solid core people. We actually got another space donated to use for the video editing, because they had to crunch video all the time, 24 hours a day, in order to produce the nightly satellite broadcast, so footage from the streets had to be logged each day from all the videographers that were going to be out there.

As all this is happening, we're still in crisis mode. For example, we don't have a point person for the print team, and it's two weeks ahead of time. The audio team is just one guy from out of town who basically really wanted to be security and communications and just kind of stepped in to help out. And we're finding out that while lots of people were going to bring camcorders and video gear – the video team was stacked with resources – we couldn't even pull together two mini-disk recorders or even hand-held tape recorders for the audio team.

We didn't know if the phone lines would be installed in time, so there was this huge panic, since so much that we were doing relied on the web. It was our backbone of distribution. If we didn't have phone lines in, and especially high speed internet connection in ... We didn't have a photocopier lined up. Just real basic stuff.

We were having an argument – I should say discussions – about whether we should bother to paint the floor or not, because that meant that we were going to have to pick everything up and move it out, and we were going to lose two days. We were to the point where two days was like two

---

>> May-June >> An intercontinental caravan of 450 activists – the majority of them Indian farmers – from Southern grassroots groups travel around Europe to protest at centres of capital and make links with European social movements.

>> May 4 >> A violent six day national strike by Nicaraguan transport workers ends with the government agreeing to lower fuel prices.

>> May 7-10 >> At least 1,700 delegates attend the second Zapatista encuentro in La Realidad, Mexico. Members of civil society who organized the recent popular referendum discuss the results of their work, and make plans for the future.

>> June 5 >> A street party against economic globalization erupts in Prague, Czech Republic, with between 5,000-8,000 people participating. The US embassy receives a torrent of bottles and cobblestones, seven broken windows, and a barrage of words against NATO's involvement in ex-Yugoslavia.

>> June 18 >> GDA Carnival Against Capital, London.

>> June 18 >> Tens of thousands of people fill the streets from Port Harcourt to Ogoniland, Nigeria, in a festive "Carnival of the Oppressed" to greet Owens Wiwa, brother of Ken Saro-Wiwa, as he returns

weeks in any other point in your life.

Throughout this, there was a real concern about participation and representation. Like I said earlier, lots of local organizers were deeply involved in their own campaign projects. It was short notice. But we were finding that who was coming in the door to participate were mostly white folks – progressive activists, well-intentioned white folks. The intention of the project was to be an opportunity for under-represented groups, groups who not only aren't seen in the media or misrepresented in the media, but may not have access to media production resources. Yet most of the people that were getting involved did have access to this stuff, did have some prior relationship with media making, or had the resources to gain access if they wanted. That was just the way it was playing out, because of who had the 'free time' to get involved and to devote so much time to this project in such a short time frame.

It was a major issue – how questions of privilege play out. Even if we seek to be an alternative, and in some ways we were, there always needs to be an internal critique as well, and that privilege is based on race, class, gender, sexual orientation, age, even. So the question of how to be a really heterogeneous group is a fundamental question that the media centres continue to grapple with, as do many progressive projects.

Another big question we were grappling with was how we were going to get people to check out the material? It is all well and good to come together and make a bunch of media, but if nobody sees it ...? It's like the tree falling in the woods – does it make a sound if no-one can hear it?

One issue with the site is it relies on people coming to the website to find this material and post their own. So people needed to know that it existed, how to find it. Not only didn't we have a budget for advertising, but we didn't have a pre-existing web presence. It wasn't like people had been accessing this web address, Indymedia.org, before. It never existed.

This was a real dilemma, because the site didn't even come online until the day before the WTO week. Yet it still got one and a half million hits that week, which was more than CNN's website, and we know that they have a bunch of advertising money. In some ways, I think what that speaks to is, first of all, the deep, deep desire and need for this sort of information, for this sort of network. People who did find

"Imperfect, insurgent, sleepless, and beautiful, we directly experienced the success of the first IMC in Seattle and saw that the common dream of 'a world in which many worlds fit' is possible – step by step, piece by piece, space by space, pdf by pdf, word by word, over the net, on pirate broadcast, in the streets, streaming live, and most importantly – face to face."

– Greg Ruggiero, media activist and editor with Seven Stories Press

out about it, friends, through the different links of all the partner collaborating organizations, it was resonating so deeply with them that they were letting everybody they knew check it out, and it just rippled outwards, expanding.

So that's one part of its success. Part of it was also that we weren't trying to be in charge. We were very clear that we were trying to facilitate all these pre-existing organizations' and individuals' work, and so it was participatory in that regard and I think people really felt a powerful investment in the project, where they wanted to let everyone that they knew, know about the project. So they put links in their different websites; they were all referring to it.

What was just complete circumstance is that things got pretty crazy and pretty exciting in Seattle that week, and the world was watching. People were speaking their voices powerfully, and that made for really compelling news, compelling coverage. I think that people around the world had some sense that this was an historic moment, that there was a shift happening here.

We had ABC Nightly News showing up at the door of the IMC wanting to do a piece on the media centre, the new model. And CNN and Christian Science Monitor all of a sudden, intrigued by all this.

MB: Can you talk a little bit about the actual week of the WTO, and how the events, like you said, made for a dramatic scene? What was the mainstream media not doing that you guys were able to do so people were going to your site instead of the CNN site?

JP: We opened our doors on Sunday, N28, and signed in over 450 people that week. So that allowed us to put about 100 videographers out in the street with camcorders. That meant that our coverage was in a lot of ways much more comprehensive than any of the networks who had maybe two camera people on staff. A real quick story is that we heard from some network folks later in the week that they actually started looking for intersections where they saw people with the IMC passes. They were bright green, obnoxious bright green. If they saw enough of those people around, they knew something was happening at the intersection.

That's what was so compelling – we were out in the streets talking to people, which mainstream media wasn't doing. They were talking about people; we were talking with

---

from exile.

>> July 1 >> An unofficial "call in sick to work day" keeps one in four Jamaican police officers at home, following a ban on police officers taking industrial action and an ongoing dispute over pay raises. The government brings in the army to help maintain public order.

>> July 5 >> Outraged at IMF-directed social cuts, and massive hikes in food, gas, electricity, diesel and water costs, thousands of Ecuadorians rise up in protest. Taxi drivers block roads, bringing cities to a standstill, demanding a reduction in fuel costs. Indigenous groups also block roads, occupy state electricity offices, and take over communications towers. Teachers, health care, transport, and banana workers all go on strike demanding back payment. Ironically the police also find themselves unpaid. In Latacunga, indigenous groups charge a military vehicle full of troops and the vehicle flees. In all, at least 13 people are shot and 400 are arrested, with the government declaring a state of emergency.

>> July 7 >> Thousands of Iranian university students in Tehran begin demonstrations which rapidly spread throughout the country, and last for six days. In the

people, and handing people the microphone and letting them talk for themselves and be directly engaged.

Monday rolled around and there were all sorts of marches and mobilizing. There was a real palpable sense that Tuesday was going to bring something that we'd never seen before. Nobody knew what that was going to look like, necessarily. Then Tuesday morning, we got reports from way early in the morning. A number of IMC folks were out with the direct action affinity groups. Some had paired up with labour groups. Some had paired up with the [grassroots Filipino-led] People's Assembly march. We got a sense early on that the people in the streets were actually shifting the balance of power, at least in those hours. Even before 10.00 am we could see that the positions of the direct action people were very solid, strategic positions, and that in order for the police to move, there would have to be a whole lot of commotion.

By noon, with the police response we were capturing on film, it was clear that this could not be ignored by mainstream media. So folks went into overdrive to start conveying to and working with them – to make sure that the protesters' methods were really understood, to get the word out as widely as possible.

We were getting in the IMC all sorts of reports. We actually had our own walkie-talkie dispatch system so that the different video teams could report back on what was going on, so people running in and out filing reports could know where to go. As information came in, we began expecting a serious clampdown. So lots of the media team stayed out in the field, to witness whatever might take place. This enabled us to counter a lot of the misinformation that the police department and city officials were putting out.

A really significant example is the denial that they were using plastic bullets. All the networks were carrying this denial from the Police Chief, as if it's law, as if it's the word of God. But yet, we were posting numerous photos of people holding plastic bullets of all sizes, with huge welts all over their bodies.

Just quickly I'll talk about how the curfew played out that night. It was pretty interesting at the Media Centre. We got an announcement of a dusk-to-dawn curfew, that people were going to be cleared out of the downtown area. As I said, we were positioned right in the centre of downtown. It was very unclear whether the Media Centre was going to be cordoned off or raided. A lot of people had to decide quickly if they were going to stay there for the night or if they should take off.

>> Logging on >> Information wars

It was early evening, and beyond the banks of computers, the tangles of radio wires and mikes, the giant map of Seattle's gridded streets pinned to the wall, and dozens of journalists rapidly uploading news reports from the anti-WTO protests onto the website of the Independent Media Centre, thick wisps of tear gas started curling under the front door. We all began coughing, and two men pulled a table across the entrance as the sound of concussion grenades clattered outside, coming nearer and nearer.

Outside the window we could see 'Peacekeepers', the armoured personnel carriers of the National Guard with huge mounted guns driving past in formation. Suddenly the door burst open, and out of the mist stepped a Darth

Vader-like figure, booted, masked, with heavy black cape. Those near the entrance tried to negotiate with the policeman. We were told we were all detained.

Reports were still coming in from video makers, radio journalists, reporters with mobiles dotted around the city. We knew the precise scale of the clampdown against the anti-WTO protesters, who was injured, who was arrested. The tension was rising, and the IMC was stuck right in the middle of the 'no-protest zone' where all constitutional rights had been suspended.

A Dutch woman and I realized that as non-US citizens we would face possible deportation if arrested, and decided we would risk leaving. We climbed out the back window, past a burning dumpster, and looked left down the tiny alleyway. A line of riot police blocked our way. We turned right, only to find another line of police, this time with their backs to us. We found a third alleyway that was clear, and made our escape down it. It was abundantly clear to us as we skulked the 60 blocks back home, often having to turn back on ourselves to avoid more lines of police, that in a globalizing economy, not all information is equal. By the end of the first day of the historic street protests against the World Trade Organization in Seattle almost every single newspaper box in the city had been grafittied with a single word: Lies.

– Report from British Indymedia activist in Seattle

/Logging off >>

JP: After the police left, [without detaining anyone] we were all pretty exhausted and emotionally distressed from the events of the day. We decided to run with just a skeleton crew that night in the centre so everybody else could get some rest and come back into the streets to document stuff the next day. So we basically emptied out the place. There were eight of us who stayed overnight, napping, and keeping stuff running.

That brings us through Tuesday night pretty much, at least the view from inside the Media Centre.

There were lots of memorable events during the rest of the week. One was a public hearing with the City Council on 2 December. People were demanding accountability from the city, in part because of the incidents that happened on Capitol Hill [the most densely populated neighbourhood on the west coast outside of San Francisco] the two nights previous, when police pushed crowds there from downtown with great force, used lots of tear gas and pepper spray, and attacked a lot of people who hadn't been involved in the protests and didn't consider themselves activists – that really politicized folks.

We had people there covering the hearing – it was

---

largest demonstrations since the revolution, people call for a restructuring of the political system and even an overthrow of the religious state. The students' organizing involves many other sectors of society, particularly the unemployed and high school students, and the demonstrations seem to announce a new era in Iran.

>> August 12 >> A McDonald's in Millau, southwest France is dismantled just days before it was due to open. On a sunny afternoon a crowd of farmers, activists, union members, and local families remove doors, roofing, and electrical plates using a tractor, axes, and chain saws and load the rubble onto trucks and tractors, driving it through town and dumping it outside City Hall. The action takes place to protest against the US-imposed 100 per cent import tax on Roquefort cheese (among other European goods) in response to Europe's refusal to allow sale of US hormonally-tainted beef.

>> August 23-26 >> The second conference of Peoples' Global Action is hosted by the KRRS, in Bangalore, India. It is called to plan for global actions against the looming meeting of the World Trade Organization in Seattle in November. A hundred

standing room only, and several hundred people rallied in the rainy streets outside. They actually had to cut off the speakers – each had three minutes, but still it went on for more than six hours and they didn't get to everybody. So they had to schedule another one a few days later. It was just tremendous to see people speaking up. The IMC was getting calls from the hearing, because all the videographers were running out of film and batteries.

The other big moment was the presence of people at the jail, supporting those who had been arrested. Hundreds were camping out and demanding their release, and also making the connection between the arrests and brutality that happened to activists and the arrests and brutality that happens everyday in lots of communities, here and internationally.

So a part of what we've seen since Seattle, I think, is the growth of these international mobilizations and confrontations in Washington, Philadelphia, Los Angeles, Prague. In all these places, people have seen it appropriate to carry the IMC model on, build on it, add to it.

>> Logging on >> Public access point – Prague S26

"Indymedia adds a further aspect to the carnival – a challenge to the boundaries between reporter and activist, documentation and spectacle, expert and amateur, techie and content-producer, cyberspace and real space. Public access points are one way to enforce this challenge. On marches in Belgium and Italy, Indymedia activists used vehicles with sound-systems as reporting hubs and for info distribution. On S26, the direct action day in Prague, the international Indymedia crew tried out the public access point again: "We hooked up to the generator of one of the sound systems in Naměsti Miru, the main square. We didn't have any materials until that morning, but it came all together as the crowds gathered. A door was used as a table for two computers, hastily painted banners pointed to the public access point in Czech, Spanish, and English, and the whole thing was decorated with glitter hanging off the trees. People came and asked lots of questions, others typed or translated reports. It was not so much info-gathering, more a hub to exchange information – and the community that fed and read it extended far beyond Prague." – **IMC UK**

/Logging off >>

Thanks to Jeff Perlstein, Miguel Bocanegra, Ana Nogueira, UK IMC collective, and many anonymous others for contributions to this piece, and to the literally thousands of independent media makers around the world who continue documenting a people's history.

Indymedia: who are we?

>> Statement by IMC Argentina

Permit us to begin by digressing, as we Argentines so enjoy doing. We wish to inform you that from now on, when you speak with Indymedia Argentina, you should know that you are not speaking with Indymedia Argentina.

This sounds strange, but it is so, and it was discovered by DJ Soncho the other day. We believe that we were the 10, 20, 30, 50 or three that met from time to time. We believe that today it was us who wet our hair so we could stand the heat and write these lines. But someone told us we are not these things, and we return to the Zapatista slogan: we are not ourselves – "*Nosotros no somos nosotros.*"

We admit that we are a rock that flew a little over a year ago and got stuck imbedded in the window of a bank. We went for almost a year before discovering it by the old axiom that consciousness runs behind reality and rarely reaches it, but finally DJ spelled it out.

And now we know who we are, or, better said, we know to a scientific certainty that we are not ourselves.

And what are we if we are not?

Are we are a picket line, barricade, burning tyre, masked face, nightstick, bullets that come flying, dining room where all the hands are all one and the mouths are in the thousands? Are we a factory takeover, posted lookout, machine that makes magic, that reproduces love, that returns to us what is ours? Are we a neighbourhood assembly, a woman that changes the life of her family, eyes that yearn, rebelliousness that speaks out? A while ago, shut up in an office (it wasn't as hot as it is right now) we asked permission of everything to be part of everything, and everything gave us permission to be part of itself.

And we disappeared. And we changed into all of the above things, without even realizing it. And our voice got hoarse and spoke in other voices, and later we heard nothing. Then we discovered that others spoke.

That we were not ourselves and we were a protest, a factory, an assembly.

And so it was, simply, that we stopped being ourselves.

So imagine that every time we wanted to have a meeting, and wanted to discuss something, how our voices got mixed with the noises of machines producing, the slogans of *piqueteros*, or the shouts of the woman who prepares the food for everyone. And, once in a while, the police interrupt, or someone flees simply because we're facing an eviction.

And so it is that now with wet hair, to endure the heat of Buenos Aires, it is hard for us to say what we have to say.

English translation by Peter Maiden

Resources:

» Global Indymedia: www.indymedia.org (portal to all local sites)

---

delegates meet from 25 countries agreeing that, as the Indian slogan goes, they must "kill WTO before it kills us."

>> August 25 >> More than 90,000 Brazilians converge on the Congress building in Brasilia, demanding an end to President Fernando Henrique Cardoso's IMF-sponsored austerity drive. "If Cardoso resigns, it would be a gracious gesture, but Cardoso has no grace," says Luis Inacio 'Lula' da Silva, president of the leftist Workers' Party.

>> August 25 >> Rail workers occupy the San Pedro station in Cuzco, Peru, shutting down the line to the ancient Inca city of Machu Picchu. Pickets block freight trains at Cosicha, near the capital. Army helicopters start a replacement service between Cuzco and Machu Picchu. The workers are protesting a deal handing the state-owned railways to a private consortium for 30 years. They are demanding a guarantee of five years' work instead of the one year promised under the deal, and severance payments of $5,000.

>> August 29 >> South Africa sees one of its biggest protest actions in years, as thousands of teachers, with civil servants and nurses strike and take to the streets, against low government wage offers.

Culture Jamming

"If any of you work in advertising or marketing, kill yourself. No, seriously. Kill yourself."
– Bill Hicks, US comedian

Early evening. A crowd of commuters stands on the platform of a San Francisco train station, avoiding eye contact and glancing occasionally at the overhead monitors. Suddenly, a gust of wind indicates an imminent arrival. The crowd looks up to the monitors in unison, checking the train's destination. The stream of adverts switches to the characteristic lettering of a destination message – only it reads, "Capitalism Stops at Nothing." The message blinks twice before giving way to the train's destination. And for a few seconds, hundreds of people scratch their heads and wonder the same thing: "What the hell just happened?"

What just happened was a perfect example of culture jamming. Sometimes known as media hacking, information warfare, or poetic terrorism, it's an assault on advertising and consumer culture involving the deliberate disruption, distortion, or subversion of mainstream media messages to expose their hidden meanings.

Culture jamming ranges from the simple alteration of billboards – with spray paint or pasted up text using similar fonts, the redesign of logos, the printing of spoof newspapers, such as the *The Financial Crimes*, to more complex forms involving hacking websites, or developing intricate press pranks. Although the techniques and media vary, there is one key characteristic: the subversion should feel and look like the real thing. Attention to detail is key and the more closely the jam can mimic the media it is trying to distort, the more successful the action will be.

Here are a few examples of culture jamming to inspire the semiotic guerrillas in all of us:

GI Jane

The voice boxes of hundreds of GI Joes and Barbie dolls are switched, and the dolls placed back into shops. Unsuspecting consumers buy the altered dolls and suddenly have a sparkling Barbie huskily intoning, "Dead men tell no lies", while a combat-ready Joe squeals, "Want to go shopping?" A leaflet hidden in the box tells them to ring their local media, and is signed the Barbie Liberation Front. The media love the story; Mattel, who manufactures the dolls, is outraged.

Rename the streets

As the war on Iraq intensifies, brand new street signs appear in Buenos Aires. The street once called "United States" has been renamed with plaques that look identical to the official municipal ones. The street is now called "People of Iraq".

Billionaires for inequality

"Because inequality is not growing fast enough," reads the byline of "Billionaires for Bush and Gore", a bipartisan coalition of super-rich donors to political parties. Dressed in tuxedos and evening gowns, they have been seen pressing wads of fake money into the cops' pockets and thanking them for repressing dissent, chanting slogans "We don't care who you vote for, we already bought them both" during political party conventions, and holding a press conference after the Enron scandal where they admonished the company, saying "Shame on you Enron for getting caught! You need more creative accountants and better PR!"

Consumer choice
Nike's Express Yourself website gives the customer the chance to have the message of their choice embroidered on a new pair of shoes. Someone logs on and requests shoes embroidered with the word *sweatshop*. Nike refuses the order and the resulting email debate between Nike and the culture jammer is forwarded to millions around the world.

Resources:
» UK artists and subvertisers: www.uhc-collective.org.uk
» Culture Jammer's Encyclopedia: theory, techniques and links everything you need in one place: www.syntac.net/hoax/index.php
» Old masters of the genre: www.billboardliberation.com
» *Adbusters* magazine: the journal of the mental environment. www.adbusters.org
» *Activist Cookbook*, Andrew Boyd, United for a Fair Economy, Boston, 1997.

UHC Collective

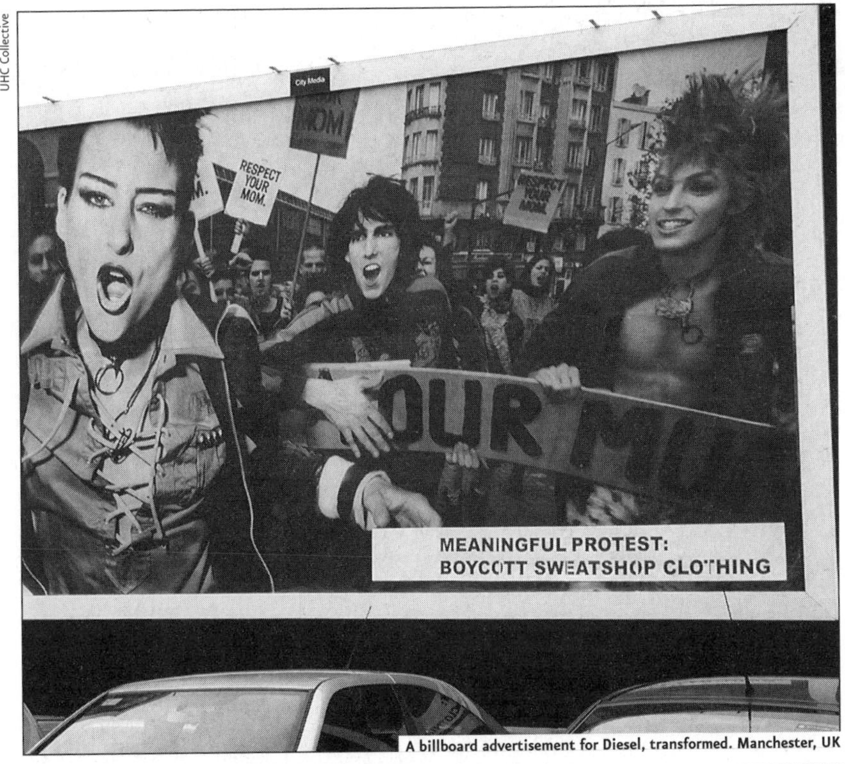
City Media
RESPECT YOUR MOM.
OUR M
MEANINGFUL PROTEST:
BOYCOTT SWEATSHOP CLOTHING

A billboard advertisement for Diesel, transformed. Manchester, UK

Artist-pranksters *The Yes Men expose the ideology of the WTO by actively promoting the most absurd and inhumane ideas, and rationalizing them by the (il)logic of 'free' market fundamentalism.*

With their website www.gatt.org, a clever spoof of that of the WTO's, they tried to provoke outraged anger, yet such reactions almost never materialized. Even mild reactions turned out to be rare, and the bulk of their mail consisted of humdrum requests for this or that bit of data. They began to feel that their work was a failure. Then on 17 May 2000, an entirely new sort of email arrived at gatt.org.

It was addressed directly to WTO Director-General Michael Moore; the e-mail's sender, under the impression he was emailing the real WTO, requested Moore's presence in Salzburg, Austria to speak before a panel of international trade lawyers. After three months of deliberating the risks (prison, ending up much poorer) vs. the benefits (discovering the limits of people's willingness to follow 'free' market theory) The Yes Men accepted.

The mission was a complete success in that the impostors were not detected, and a total failure in that no one batted an eyelid at their enthusiasm for invented 'free' trade initiatives such as the privatization of national elections where US citizens could go to VoteAuction.com and sell their vote to the highest corporate bidder.

They began to fear that consumers of neoliberal economic ideology might indeed believe anything, however insane or inhuman, provided it were presented as a logical part of the workings of the immutable law of the 'free' market. So for a subsequent appearance, they decided to pull out all the stops and deliver something extreme, aided by a PowerPoint presentation and stunningly clear visual effects, something any child could understand …

The Pranksters and the Golden Phallus

by The Yes Men

This lecture by 'Dr Hank Hardy Unruh of the WTO' (aka Andy, from the Yes Men) was the keynote address for the Textiles of the Future conference held at the University of Technology on 18-21 August 2001 in Tampere, Finland. In the audience were 150 international research engineers, businesspeople, officials and academics working in industries ranging from medicine to defence.

Towards the Globalization of Textile Trade

Textilically speaking …

It's an honour to be here in Tampere, addressing the most outstanding textilians in the world today. Looking around at this diverse sea of faces, I see outstanding elements of corporations like Dow, Denkendorf, Lenzing, all at the forefront of consumer satisfaction in textiles. I see members of the European Commission, Euratex, and other important political bodies that aim at easing rules for corporate citizens. I also see professors from great universities walking into a prosperous future hand in hand with industrial partners, using citizen funds to develop great textilic solutions to be sold to consumers for profit and progress.

How do we at the WTO fit in? Well, that's easy: we want to help you achieve dollar results. We want to make sure that protectionism, worry, even violence against physical property doesn't stand in the way of your dollar results.

What do we want? A free and open global economy that will best serve corporate owners and stockholders alike. When do we want it? Now.

How will we do it? We're using a variety of techniques. Lobbying, for example. 'Guerrilla marketing' to cleverly show teenagers the value of liberalization; and so on.

Finally, we have in mind some far more sophisticated solutions for the future. In just 20 minutes, I'm going to unveil the WTO's solution to two of the biggest problems for management: maintaining rapport with a distant workforce, and maintaining healthful amounts of leisure. This solution, appropriately enough, is based in textiles.

I myself am an abolitionist

But how did workers ever get to be a problem? Before unveiling the solution, I'd like to talk a bit about the history of the worker/management problem. The first leg of our journey is back to 1860s America, and the US Civil War. We all know about this war – the bloodiest, least profitable war in the history of the US, a war in which unbelievably huge amounts of money went right down the drain – and all for textiles!

Now believe it or not, even many Americans don't know what caused the Civil War. Why did people fight and die and lose money? The answer is really really simple, but it is surprising. It comes down to one word: freedom.

By the 1860s, the South was utterly flush with cash. It had recently benefited from the cotton gin, an invention that took the seeds out of cotton and the South out of its pre-industrial past. Hundreds of thousands of workers, previously unemployed in their countries of origin, were given useful jobs in textiles.

Into this rosy picture of freedom and boon stepped... you guessed it: the North. The South, of course, wanted to buy industrial equipment where it was cheapest, and to sell raw cotton where it fetched the highest price – in Britain. The North, however, decided the South should not have the freedom to do this, but instead should have to do business with the North, and only with the North.

The North used its majority stake in the country's governance to exploit the Southern landowners and deny them their freedom to choose the cheapest prices; this of course made them very angry. And so the North's abusive

---

>> August 31 >> Twenty million people from Colombia's labour unions, students, and indigenous groups begin the first day of an indefinite national strike in protest at the government's IMF-backed privatization plans and social spending cuts. The demands also include a moratorium on all debt repayment. Small businesses use the strike to begin a campaign of civil disobedience marked by non-payment of taxes, and the Revolutionary Armed Forces of Colombia (FARC) carry out an occupation of the hydro-electric plant, demanding a cut in electricity tariffs and securing an agreement that a regional forum on the issue will be held. An IMF delegation cancels a trip to Bogotá and after three days the government releases all arrested during the strike, and agrees to set up a working group to discuss demands.

>> September 11 >> Several thousand people from diverse groups march to the stock exchange to protest against the dictatorship of the marketplace in Stockholm, Sweden.

>> September 14 >> Despite heavy-handed police tactics, protests and counter-summits shadow the APEC meetings in Auckland, Aotearoa/New Zealand. Meanwhile Chinese Premier Jiang Zemin demands that

tariff practices basically caused what otherwise was a perfectly good market to spiral into a hideously unprofitable war.

Now some Civil-War apologists have stated that the Civil War, for all its faults, at least had the effect of outlawing an Involuntarily Imported Workforce. Now such a labour model is of course a terrible thing; I myself am an abolitionist. But in fact there is no doubt that left to their own devices, markets would have eventually replaced slavery with 'clean' sources of labour. To prove my point, come join me on what Albert Einstein used to call a "thought experiment." Suppose Involuntarily Imported Labour had never been outlawed, that slaves still existed, and that it was easy to own one. What do you think it would cost today to profitably maintain a slave – say, here in Tampere?

Let's see ... A Finnish clothing set costs $50 at the very least. Two meals from McDonald's cost $10 or so. The cheapest small room probably runs for $250/month. To function well, you have to pay for your slave's health care – if its country of origin was polluted, this could get very expensive. And of course what with child labour laws, much of the youth market is simply not available. Now leave the same slave back at home – let's say, Gabon. In Gabon, $10 pays for two weeks of food, not just one day. $250 pays for two years' housing, not a month's. $50 pays for a lifetime of budget clothing! Healthcare is likewise much cheaper. On top of it all, youth can be gainfully employed without restriction.

The biggest benefit of the remote labour system, though, is to the slave. In Gabon, there is no need for the slave not to be free! This is primarily because there are no one-time slave transport costs to recoup, and so the potential losses from fleeing are limited to the slave's rudimentary training. So since the slave can be free, he or she suddenly becomes a worker rather than a slave!

I think it is clear from this little thought experiment that if the North and South had simply let the market sort it out, they would have quickly given up slavery for something more efficient anyway. By forcing the issue, the North not only committed a terrible injustice against the freedom of the South, but also deprived slavery of its natural development into remote labour. Had the leaders of the 1860s understood what our leaders understand today, the Civil War would never have happened.

Now the 'modern' remote labour model, while much better than the imported workforce model – being decentralized – is also much more complicated from a management perspective.

British Empire: its lessons for managers

In a world where the headquarters of a company are in New York, Hong Kong, or Espoo, and the workers are in Gabon, Rangoon, or Estonia, how does a manager maintain proper rapport with the workers, and how does he or she ensure from a distance that workers perform their work in an ethical fashion?

Let's look at a counter example, where managers remained out of touch with remote workers, leading to extreme worker dissatisfaction and the eventual total loss of the worker base. Perhaps we can learn from this case and avoid such catastrophes in the future.

In nineteenth century Britain, just like in the South, things had never looked better. The country was flush with cash, potential, and freedom, thanks to new technology – the spinning jenny. Like the cotton gin in the South, Britain's spinning jenny turned useable cotton into finished textiles, so the British could suddenly mass-produce clothing.

Like in the South, all that was needed was a work force to produce the raw materials that these new tools required. The British took a modern approach: instead of expensively importing workers, they located their employment opportunities where workers already lived – India.

There were problems right from the start. For thousands of years India had made the finest cotton garments in the world, so Indian workers felt humiliated providing raw materials to British industry.

The main rabble-rouser was Mohandas Gandhi, a likeable, well-meaning fellow who wanted to help his fellow workers along, but did not understand the benefits of open markets and free trade. Gandhi thought that through 'self-reliance' – protectionism, really – India could become strong and relearn its own ancient ways of textiles. These rather naive ideas became extremely popular, and a big proportion of the citizenry rose up against the British management system. The British eventually had to leave!

What are the lessons for management here? The big problem in India was clearly a grave lack of management rapport with workers. By making only small adjustments, British management could have kept India on the path to modernity.

For example, one of the things Gandhi and his antiglobalization followers did was make their own clothing at home, to symbolize their independence from the cotton trade. Now as any student can tell you, if management in England had been properly in touch with worker concerns, they could have responded in a timely way – perhaps by making available clothes in the homespun style that the Indians craved. Today you can see clothes like that in many clothing catalogues, like the Whole Earth Catalogue. But of course they didn't have that sort of perspective in Britain and so they couldn't do it.

Now while the British may be excused for losing India because of a want of technology, we have no such excuse. In

---

police disperse the crowd before he will consider attending the banquet, and arrives an hour and half late after they have complied. Protesters are moved out of the Premier's sight; buses are used as visual barricades, and police sirens blare out in an attempt to drown out the sound of opposition.

>> September 24 >> Canadian university students smash up the Montreal stock market and build a bonfire while demanding that budget surpluses be spent on education. "The stock exchange is a symbol of capitalism and the business class who ask the government to make cuts," says one student. Eighteen people are arrested.

>> September 26 >> Fifty people protest outside the annual meeting of the IMF/WB in Washington, US. The IMF's official documents begin to make conciliatory but empty gestures to the growing demands for change by stressing the need to promote both growth and poverty reduction. Little do they know that this will be their last chance to meet with so little opposition!

>> October 6-12 >> Seventy thousand steelworkers stop production of auto parts and 4,333 cars in 15 plants located in the greater São Paulo area, Campinas, and Vale do Paraíba, Brazil, with the objective of receiving a salary raise. Local strikes, referred to as the

these sensitive times when a large percentage of the world's population is nearing the boiling point over problems they imagine with globalization, we need to use all resources at our disposal to help the market help corporations, to assure that things go well, in society just as in nature.

Again, we need to use all the political tools at our disposal, like lobbying. And again, marketing to certain population sectors can change future perceptions. The market, in the form of privatized education, is likely to be our ally in this process of shifting children's awareness from less productive issues and thinkers to more productive ones, but we can help it along as well.

The prototype Employee Visualization Appendage

But even more important than any of this is management's on-the-ground efficiency. To avoid another India, we must ensure that management is constantly in touch with workers. That the manager has direct, visceral access to his or her workers, and can experience their needs in a visceral way.

I'm about to show you an actual prototype of the WTO's solution to two major management problems of today. This solution is intended to get you thinking outside the box on solutions to management problems.

Now we all know that not even the best workplace design can help even the most astute manager keep track of his workers. You need a solution that enables a lot more rapport with workers especially when they're remote.

[Dr Unruh steps out from behind podium.]

Mike, would you please?

"The protesters are simply too focused on reality, and on facts and figures. There's an enormous number of experts at all the greatest universities in the world, who have read all these books, who have read Adam Smith and everything since, to Milton Friedman, and these people have solid theoretical basis for knowing that things will lead to betterment ...

We have to find a way to convince perhaps not the protesters, but the protesters' children, to follow thinkers like Milton Friedman and Darwin and so on rather than what the protesters have been reared on - Trotsky, and Robespierre, and Abbie Hoffman."

– interview with Yes Man 'Granwyth Hulatberi, WTO spokesperson', broadcast live on CNBC's European Marketwrap program, on 19 July 2001, the day before the G8 protests in Genoa

[Mike grabs the front of Dr Unruh's suit at the chest and the crotch, gives a mighty yank, and rips his suit right off. Dr Unruh's gold lamé body suit is revealed. After regaining his equilibrium, Dr Unruh raises his arms to the crowd in a gesture of triumph. Applause.]

Ah! That's better! This is the Management Leisure Suit. This is the WTO's answer to the two central management problems of today: how to maintain rapport with distant workers, and how to maintain one's own mental health as a manager with the proper amount of leisure.

How does the MLS work, besides being very comfortable indeed, as I can assure you it is? Allow me to describe the suit's core features.

[Dr Unruh bends down, grabs a ripcord in his perineal region, and pulls hard. Nothing happens. He tries again. Still nothing. He pulls a second ripcord. This time, there is a hissing sound, and a three-foot long golden phallus inflates forcefully, snapping up and banging Dr Unruh in the face. Dr Unruh, now sporting a meter-long golden phallus, turns to the audience and again raises his arms in triumph. Applause.]

This is the Employee Visualization Appendage – an instantly deployable hip-mounted device with hands-free operation, which allows the manager to see his employees directly, as well as receive all relevant data about them. Signals communicating exact amounts and quality of physical labour are transmitted to the manager not only visually, but directly, through electric channels implanted directly into the manager, in front and behind. The workers, for their part, are fitted with unobtrusive small chips, implanted humanely into the shoulder, that transmit all relevant data directly into the manager.

The MLS truly allows the corporation to be a corpus, by permitting total communication within the corporate body, on a scale never before possible. This is important but the other, equally important, achievement of the MLS has to do with leisure.

In the US, leisure – another word for freedom, really – has been decreasing steadily since the 1970s. Compared with 1973, Americans must now work six weeks more per year to achieve the same standard of living. The MLS permits the manager to reverse this trend by letting him do his work anywhere – all locations are equal.

Strike Festival, take place once a week in different Brazilian states.

>> October 7 >> Over 1,000 men and women from grassroots organizations converge on the capital city of Brasilia, Brazil, having walked 995 miles from 23 states. The Popular March for Brazil meets with more than 200,000 on the way, in schools, churches and associations of all kinds, discussing ways of developing a new politics, holding forums on the economic crisis, and developing proposals for alternative economies.

>> October 21 >> Eighty thousand Filipino farmers protest against feudal exploitation and globalization in nationally coordinated actions. Thousands of farmers caravan for three days to Manila, holding rallies along the way. They denounce the Estrada government's plan to grant 100 per cent foreign ownership of land, demanding genuine land reform instead. Simultaneously, 10,000 farmers and fisherfolk refuse to allow a real estate project that would turn fertile agricultural lands into a tourist paradise for the rich; more than 300 peasant families defend their claims on a portion of the former Clark US Air base in Pampanga which they have tilled for years, and 1,000 peasant families in Bukidnon, Mindanao resist eviction from the government-owned

Now the MLS is good for both managers and workers, but the number of non-corporate solutions, also, is as endless as our imagination. For example, with the MLS I'll be able to not only see protests right here on my screen, but I'll be able to feel them as well. What will the danger level be when the first protester is beheaded? I'm against beheading, but they do that in Qatar, where we're holding our next meeting. The MLS can, in a general sort of way, show us things – it can help us discover new metrics.

This suit – is it a science-fiction scenario? No – everything we've been talking about is possible with technologies we have available today. And even more interesting solutions are being developed. Right here, today and tomorrow, we will be learning about some of the most interesting new solutions from the prime movers themselves.

I am very excited to be here.

Thank you.

Human Resources: behind the scenes

by The Yes Men

'Dr Hank Hardy Unruh', aka Yes Man Andy and his accomplice Mike, explain how they pulled it off ...
Our Finnish adventure began, unfortunately, with the belated realization that the clocks in Finland are set one hour ahead of those in most of the rest of Europe, so when we arrived at the conference centre at what we thought was eight o'clock in the morning, there was only one of the conference organizers left in the lobby. When Andy introduced himself as Hank Hardy Unruh of the WTO, she was relieved. "It is wonderful to see you. They are waiting for you." Waiting for us? An hour before? We looked at the clock on the wall behind her. Then we looked at each other, speechless with horror. "Time zone," Andy finally managed to gasp. "Please follow me," she said. She whooshed towards the door of the conference hall.

Andy followed impulsively, in a panic. Fortunately Mike had managed to conserve some of his wits. "Ah, Dr Unruh," said Mike, "we have that, ah, urgent phone call ..." Andy froze. The Management Leisure Suit!! Andy wasn't wearing it, for it made moving very clumsy, and it had been hard to imagine waddling the half-mile from the hotel to the conference centre. Instead he wore a suit identical to the breakaway suit covering the MLS; we'd planned to change into the real McCoy on arrival. "Ah, ma'am," he called out to the lady just as she opened the door to the conference hall, "we have a very urgent phone call we'll be just a tiny, tiny bit late? I mean later. Two minutes?" Her eyes widened speechlessly for a moment, then she shook her head, pointed to the telephones down the hall, and hurried into the conference hall.

We hoped nobody saw us darting together into the restroom next to the telephones. What would they think? That the WTO representative and the WTO representative's assistant both have urgent bladder problems, simultaneously? And that they lie about it? More frantic than either of us had ever been, Mike pulled the thing out of his bag while Andy stripped down to his underwear. The suit was designed for simplicity, but there's only so simple you can make a three-foot long inflatable phallus. "A fucking hour late," said Andy as he tried to jam his foot into the leg. "Wait, wait, shit, go slow," said Mike, as he bent down to untwist the golden fabric. "Fucking time zone… Okay, push." "One fucking hour," said Andy as he pushed it in and frantically searched for an armhole to fill. After what seemed like an interminable amount of untwisting and zipping and fitting – straps, penis, baboon butt, CO_2 cartridge, second CO_2 cartridge (backup), breakaway pants, breakaway shirt, breakaway jacket – the Management Leisure Suit and its breakaway suit were on.

Fully reassembled, Dr Hank Hardy Unruh emerged from the restroom and waddled into the conference hall as fast as he could without breaking his seams. Three hundred people were waiting. Dr Pertti Nousiainen, the president of the university and primary organizer of the conference, was still explaining to the audience that the keynote speaker encountered a slight adversity of some sort, compounded by a last-minute urgent telephone call, and would arrive soon. When he saw us his eyes lit up – apparently he had gotten to the end of plausible explanations.

Now for our second tightrope act. We had planned to hook up the computer to the projector ahead of time; now we had to do it in front of everyone. Dr Nousiainen used the opportunity to announce the keynote speaker, and to explain again who he was. Andy waved to the audience. The audience did not react. Nor did the computer. For ten minutes, Andy fidgeted with his laptop, under the increasingly icy stares of the audience. Nothing. Fortunately, this had happened before, and we had a CD backup just in case – but it would take at least 15 minutes to copy to another computer, because of the enormous video files.

Mike explained the unfortunate situation to Dr Nousiainen, apologized on behalf of our crappy laptop, and asked to change spots. Our host did everything in his power to accommodate the frantic, absurd, and incompetent team from the WTO. Dr Nousiainen would speak first instead of second; another lecturer would speak second instead of third. We set the files to copying over to Dr Nouisiainen's own computer, which he graciously volunteered, and sat

---

lands of the Central Mindanao University.

>> November 21 >> The Landless Movement (MST) in Brazil occupies land at Igarassu, Pernambuco State, and 620 families set up new homes.

>> November 23 >> More than 300 indigenous people from the Indian state of Madhya Pradesh blockade the World Bank building in Delhi. Covering the building with cow dung, mud, posters, and graffiti, they sing traditional songs, protesting the impact of World Bank forestry projects which threaten their rights to land, forest, and fishing. "We fought against the British and we will fight against the new form of colonialism that you represent with all our might," they declare.

>> November 24 >> Demonstrators in Manila, Philippines break through security lines at the meetings of the Association of South East Asian Nations (ASEAN). A few days earlier, many homeless families who were living near the summit building were brutally evicted so as not to spoil the view of foreign dignitaries on their way from the airport to their hotels. More than 7,000 police and soldiers control the streets, while firefighters turn high-pressure hoses on the crowds.

>> November 25 >> Five thousand French farmers gather with their sheep, goats, and ducks for a picnic

down in the audience. The copying finished with less than one megabyte to spare. (A week later, informed by a reporter that Dr Unruh had been a fake, Dr Nousiainen refused to believe it. "But he was so polite!" he said. "And he had such a very large presentation!") Finally, the incompetent duo was ready. The second lecturer finished, and Dr Nousiainen took the stage to introduce what had been billed as the keynote speaker, and was now the *pièce de résistance*.

Now when a performance is plagued with technical difficulties before it even begins, there are two ways the audience can react. They can sympathize with the performer, proffering increased attentiveness, applause, and big smiles to make her feel better. Alternately, they can manifest petulance – remaining passive, stone-faced, as if to show that their money would have been better spent elsewhere. Our audience was the latter sort; we were relieved when it was time for the climax.

Mike grabbed the front of Andy's suit and ripped it off in two hard yanks. Andy was now wearing only the golden leotard. The audience was suddenly bolt upright at attention. A gold-lamé suit on the WTO representative? Everything changed. Our audience was all smiles, applause, and kindness. As the Employee Visualization Appendage inflated to its three-foot length, the audience was clearly beside itself with excitement. As Dr Unruh enumerated the uses of the EVA – to monitor distant factory workers and administer electric shocks when necessary, to assure leisure time for a grossly encumbered managerial class, to keep tabs on the severity of protests – the audience's attention was riveted. The WTO stood there with its enormous golden phallus, controlling the Third World and parts of the First, and the audience felt nothing but love.

In the heat of a performance, certain things happen. Juices flow, awareness falls away, the entire being is concentrated on a single point of entry or exit. Andy, fully Dr Unruh, was as happy as Dr Unruh would have been to be receiving the adulation of such a respectable audience. But when he saw Mike's face – clearly very depressed – Andy snapped out of his bliss. Something was wrong. And what was wrong was exactly what had seemed right: the triumph of Unruh was the failure of Andy and Mike. As we waddled to lunch, the air slowly leaking out of Andy's EVA, our spirits sagged along with it. We had pulled out all the stops, and we had gotten nothing by way of reaction. We had spent the last three weeks anticipating an extremely dramatic, even dangerous situation, and nothing but applause had resulted. By the time we got to the cafeteria, our cheer picked up slightly. We became certain that someone in the audience must have been violently appalled by the WTO's metre-long member and what it signified. We resolved to find that person.

On the way we spoke to a fellow from Dow ("Interesting lecture!"); a German chemist ("I enjoyed your lecture, but only wondered what was its point"); a fellow from British defence ("Your point was obviously that the market would have replaced slavery, given enough time"); the head of the textiles department at

Ghent University, who insisted we read his position paper on the future of textiles; several assorted others who had enjoyed the lecture in various ways.

Then, right after dinner, we met her, the object of our quest. She had not enjoyed the lecture: so much not, in fact, that it took a great deal of coaxing to get her to speak to us. At last! We managed to convince her that we really wished to hear what she thought. "Well," she finally said, "I think your performance was clear. I think you showed how close the factory owner wants to be to the workers, to control the workers very well. But the way you presented it was not fair." "Fair?" Andy said. "To the factory owners. You present it as, the males are the owners and the females are the workers. But females can be the factory owners too."

Andy and Mike were stunned. Their hearts sank. "It's just the... metaphor?" Andy managed. "Yes," the woman said. "If we varied the... metaphor..." Andy made big circular motions around his chest, as if to show where big golden breasts might be placed. "Yes," she said. "But don't get me wrong," she said, "your performance was brilliant. And you got your point across, that's the main thing." "So the point was clear," Andy said sadly. "Just the shape was unfortunate." "A penis is a nice shape," the woman said. "I'm only speaking of what it meant." "What did it mean?" Mike pushed. "Male perspective," she said. "Too much." Enough was enough. "I'm sorry for interrupting," Mike said, "but it's time to call Mr Bensonhurst-Philidango." "Ah yes! Of course!" Andy exclaimed. "Bensonhurst-Philidango! I am so sorry," he said to his new scientist friend. "Thank you for everything!" he called out to Dr Nouisiainen from across the room, gesturing at Mike as if blaming him for his abduction. Our Waterloo was finally over.

The Yes Men are a genderless, loose-knit association of 300 impostors worldwide. By any means necessary, they enter fortified compounds of commerce, ask questions, and smuggle out stories from the behind-the-scenes world of business. In other words, the Yes Men are team players... but they play for the opposing team.

Resources:

» For the complete works see: www.theyesmen.org

» Quintessential for subversion and pranks: www.rtmark.com

---

under the Eiffel Tower. Feasting on regional products, they denounce the impact of 'free' trade and the WTO.

>> November 30 >> Global Day of Action, WTO actions, Seattle.

>> December >> Over the course of this year, anti-biotech activists have destroyed all the field trials of genetically modified trees in England.

>> December 7 >> Twenty thousand people take to the streets of Seoul, South Korea, demanding a shorter work week and an end to privatization. Organized by the Korean Confederation of Trade Unions, the workers defend themselves with bamboo sticks and metal rods against an attack by riot police, which injures 160 people.

>> December 11 >> In Mexico City, 10,000 striking UNAM students protest outside the American embassy in solidarity with people arrested in the Seattle WTO actions, and also with US political prisoner Mumia Abu Jamal. Police attack and arrest 98 people, charging dozens of them with mutiny.

>> January-February >> Activists break through police lines and invade several immigrant detention centres across Italy, allowing journalists and human rights observers to document inhumane conditions. The

Disobedience Is Happiness: Mujeres Creando

From an interview with Mujeres Creando by Notes from Nowhere

Overnight, in beautiful handwriting, *words appear on the walls of La Paz, the high-altitude capital of Bolivia. They speak truths Bolivian women won't say out loud. Deconstructing machismo, anti-gay prejudice and neoliberalism, Bolivian anarcha-feminist group Mujeres Creando (Women Creating) takes art back to the streets.*

"The face of happiness vanished from art and literature as it began to be reproduced along endless walls and billboards," said the Situationists. Mujeres Creando's graffiti paints happiness back onto the walls. "Coca Cola pays, and paints, so why can't we paint without paying? The problem isn't that the walls are painted, the problem is that it's not paid for," says Julieta Paredes. The street is their canvas, art is political, art is for everyone. Theirs is a politics of creativity, of interventions in everyday life. In exile politically, and sexually, a group of friends started Mujeres Creando in 1992 – a group of "affection and defects, creativity and proposal". Two are the only openly lesbian activists in Bolivia. At the time, they explain, there was little talk of feminism – a militant, radical feminism, a feminism of the streets, of everyday life.

They declare: "The intention to be a transforming movement... a movement of cultural space, art, and social proposals, where we paint, we tell stories, we dance them, we cook them, subverting the patriarchal order." In 2002 they faced arrest for making a TV show in which two women in traditional Bolivian dress and bowler hats were shown passionately kissing.

In another notorious campaign, Mujeres Creando provided pots of paint to the poor women of the barrios, who painted slogans the walls of the bank they owed crippling debts to. A desperate group of debtors strapped themselves with dynamite and held bankers hostage. As soldiers prepared to massacre them, Mujeres Creando formed part of the delegation who negotiated an end to the debt, and safe removal of the protesters.

Crazy people, agitators, rebels, disobedients, subversives, witches, street, *grafiteras*, anarchists, *feministas*, Lesbians and heterosexuals; married and unmarried; students and clerks; Indians, *chotas*, *cholas*, *birlochas*, and *señoritas*; old and young; white and coloured, we are a fabric of solidarities; of identities, of commitments, we are women, WOMEN CREATING.

Mujeres Creando is an anarcha-feminist group which began in the year 1992 in La Paz, with three friends – Maria Galindo, Julieta Paredes and Monica Mendoza. They were very critical of the traditional left. They came out of leftist groups themselves, but were sick of the fact that everything was organized from top down, and that the women only served tea, or their role was a purely sexual one, or they were nothing more than secretaries. And so they said, "No, we cannot carry on doing this. We believe in revolution, we believe in social change, but this organization is not for us."

That's why *Mujeres Creando* is autonomous from political parties, NGOs, the state, hegemonic groups, leaders of unions. We don't want bosses, figureheads or exalted leaders. We organize ourselves horizontally, and nobody represents anybody else – each woman represents herself.

You see, our struggle is not specific – it's not just part of a 'Marxist revolution' or a 'Trotskyite revolution'. It is a struggle with its own character, its own individuality. It is directed at all of society, not only at women, not only at middle class women, or indigenous women, but at everyone – men and women.

We believe that how we relate to people in the street is fundamental. We have a newspaper *Mujer Publica* (Public Woman) which we edit and sell ourselves, and we carry out creative street actions.

We paint graffiti – *las pintadas* – and this is one of the communicative forms that really gets through to people. It started out as a criticism of what the Left is – but also the Right. It was our response to their painting in the streets saying "Vote for so-and-so." They were affirmative or negative phrases, "No to the vote," "Yes to this," "No to that." What we do instead is we appeal to poetry and creativity, to suggest ideas which aren't just "yes" or "no", "Left" or "Right" All the graffiti and paintings we do, wherever they are, are signed *Mujeres Creando* with the anarcha-feminist symbol.

We target all kinds of oppression from a feminist perspective – racism, the dictatorship, debt. Our aims aren't always centred on women's themes like abortion, reproductive rights, motherhood. The government says: "You can dedicate yourselves to those issues, full stop." And we may say "No." Or we may say "Yes, that interests us – we have positions on abortion, birth control, but don't categorize us!" We are involved in everything: we are part of society. And for this reason we paint graffiti about different things. There is graffiti which provokes men, graffiti provoking the government, graffiti which is only directed at women, graffiti about the political situation.

For us, the street is the principal site for our struggle. For us, the street is a space like a common patio, where we

"We're not anarchists by Bakunin or the CNT, but rather by our grandmothers, and that's a beautiful school of anarchism."

– Julieta Paredes, Mujeres Creando

---

invasion is only part of a long campaign against the centers, involving occupations, marches of tens of thousands, and legal pressure. Following a three-day roof occupation, the Via Corelli camp in Milan is closed by the government, but later reopens.

>> January 3 >> The Zapatista Air Force bombards a Federal Army encampment in Chiapas, Mexico with paper aeroplanes.

>> January 11 >> Four thousand peaceful protesters of the Narmada Bachao Andolan (NBA) occupy the site of the Maheshwar dam in Madhya Pradesh, India, bringing work to a halt. Police attack and arrest 1500 people on their way to the dam site action. The past three years have seen strong resistance against the Narmada dam constuction.

>> January 15-22 >> Protesting the dollarization of the Ecuadorian economy, 40,000 members of various indigenous groups converge on Quito to demand the resignation of the president. Thousands more blockade highways throughout the nation. Transportation and oil workers and street vendors declare an indefinite strike to support the indigenous movement. Despite the presence of 30,000 police and troops, protesters occupy the Congress building and the Supreme Court. For a few

can all be, children, everyone. It is very important that what we do in the street interacts with people, that we speak to people, that they see the graffiti, that it provokes something in them, laughter, annoyance, rage....

They have told us that it is quite fucked up in Europe. I have never been, but Maria and Julieta, who have been, tell us that everything is controlled: whether or not you can march, whether or not you can protest, whether or not you can sell things. Here in Bolivia, you go out into the street and you can see it belongs to the people: people doing things, people selling things – the street is ours. It is more fucked up in Europe and in other countries: they control the people – the police, the state, the municipalities, control them.

Creativity is human – it belongs to all women and men.

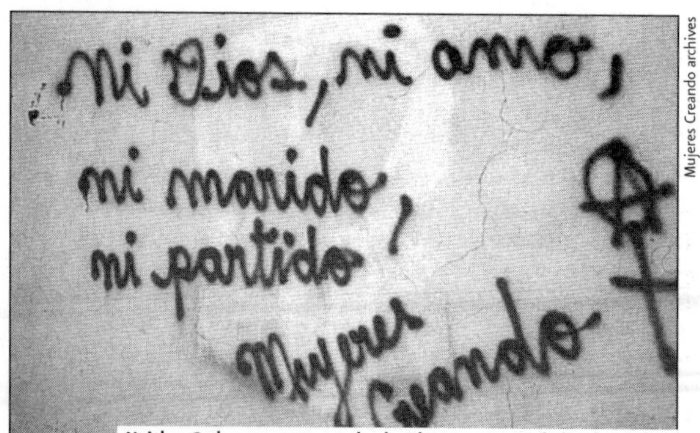

Mujeres Creando archives

Neither God, nor master, nor husband, nor party. Cochabamba, Bolivia

But many want to dispossess us of this creativity, something that is ours. They want to turn creativity into something elitist, saying the artists are the creative ones, the inspired ones, the ones who inspire each other. We do not allow ourselves to be dispossessed of an instrument of struggle and in everything we do, in the books we make, in the street actions, in the graffiti, we include this element which is important and fundamental to us: creativity. Then some people say to us: "You're artists." But we are not artists, we are street activists. All we do is to use something which is totally human: creativity.

We call our actions *Acciónes Callejeras* (street actions), but we don't only carry them out in the street, though we make interventions in different spaces as well. We have intervened, for example at a meeting of the Superintendencia de Bancos, for all those who own the banks. One of us wore a wig, skirt, thick glasses, and, carrying an invitation obtained through a friend, entered the meeting, which would normally be closed to other people. They have a lavish lunch, and wine. So a member of *Mujeres Creando* went in and during lunch distributed leaflets denouncing the banks' interest rates, shouting "You are profiteers!" and she started to distribute some leaflets.

We have resisted neoliberalism in other ways too – we've taken actions against Coca Cola and McDonald's in our newspaper, for example. Before it was published anywhere else in the country, we published information about the Multilateral Agreement on Investment (MAI).

> "Emancipation should make it possible for woman to be human in the truest sense. Everything within her that craves assertion and activity should reach its fullest expression; all artificial barriers should be broken, and the road towards greater freedom cleared of every trace of centuries of submission and slavery."
>
> – **Emma Goldman, *Anarchism and Other Essays*, Dover, 1970**

And we have promoted quite a lot about the protests in Seattle, in Prague.

The last mobilization we carried out against the bankers was very powerful. In our country there are small loans which are given above all to women, but also to men, to peasants. They are called microcredit loans, meant for poor people. Neoliberalism and capitalism asks, "How do we solve the problem of poverty in Latin America? We can't give them social security, we can't give them employment security, we can't give them health, education. So we'll give the poor a little bit of money, so that they can use their initiative and move forward." And then they charge huge interest rates on this money, and use it for their own investments.

In Bolivia, microcredit was introduced in 1992. They said to the women here who sold things, who sold sweets: "Señora, we can lend you some capital: you want money, we'll give it to you," and they would lend them money. The guarantee for this loan was not private property, it was not your house, it was not your car – because these people were poor – it was a group in which each member provides guarantees for each other. So the bank began to lend and after a time there was a microcredit crisis. The people could no longer pay, interest was very high, and the women were fighting amongst themselves, saying, "You're not able to pay the bank," accusing each other. It

---

hours, a three-man junta of indigenous and military leaders takes power, but is soon dissolved by the army, under threat of sanctions by the US. The protest is called off and Vice President Noboa assumes the presidency, continuing with the IMF policies. However, the coup is supported by 71 per cent of the population, and the uprising simmers beneath the surface of everyday life, erupting for years to come.

>> January 27 >> Two thousand industrialists, politicians and other self-proclaimed 'global leaders' meet for the thirtieth World Economic Forum (WEF), in the Swiss ski resort, Davos. Small demonstrations have taken place here since 1994 but this year over a thousand protesters turn up and a counter-conference takes place. The ski-resort's McDonald's loses its windows, and protesters throw snowballs at the police who respond with hard plastic bullets.

>> February 15 >> As Michel Camdessus prepares to give his last major address as head of the International Monetary Fund to the delegates of the United Nations Conference on Trade and Development (UNCTAD) in Bangkok, Thailand, he is greeted unceremoniously with a fruit-and-cream-pie to the face, delivered, according to the pie slinger, "to give a warning to his successor

caused many problems. The interest rates were enormous. If you owed $100, you would end up owing $5,000! You were poor, but after being lent money by the bank for eight or ten years, during which you had been paying them, you were much poorer than before, you were a woman who worked much harder than she worked before microcredit.

In 2001 a group made up mostly of women from the poorest barrios came to La Paz in protest – an organization called *Deudora* (debtor). We joined together with them, started to think and to act together. We spoke to them about pacifism, we carried out some creative actions against these banks and their interest rates, against money... painting murals in the streets. We brought paint, and the *Deudora* group took off their shoes and dipped their feet into the pots, then lifted each other up to leave their footprints on the wall. This was a symbol of their long journey to the capital. We've also marched, we've thrown ourselves onto the floor so the police won't repress us, that sort of thing.

We believe in self-defence, so we appeal to strategies of struggling which are peaceful, but we don't believe in going out to provoke, going out to throw paint around, going out to hit someone. But we do believe in legitimate defence: if somebody hits you, you can react, right? We are careful of our reactions, though, because we know that often to react often means you get harmed by the police.

After three and a half months, we managed to get an agreement. We sat down with the large banking and financial associations, and we negotiated. We made a whole series of complaints to them and we managed to achieve an agreement. The bank recognized this, and said "Yes, we have committed some irregularities with you, so we'll excuse you from your debts." People whose houses were being auctioned off have managed to keep them. So this action has given capitalism a kick, because financial capital here is all-powerful. The state really looks after the interests of investors, people who put money into banks, into mutuals, into NGOs, people who lend money.

For us, to confront this apparatus has been tremendously hard. We are still carrying on – it's still not

"Political activity does not only happen in political parties or in organized groups; it happens as soon as you are conscious of your actions and your decisions – an intuitive kind of feminism.... Through feminism, women come to know themselves and each other, with all our potential, our strengths, our weaknesses, and we discover a freedom that we keep on developing." – **Mujeres Creando**

over. We have the agreements, but we are going to return with an international seminar to denounce microcredit, which has been more just to make money, make money, make money, full stop.

Once an agreement was signed that benefited the debtors, we organized a kind of festival with flowers and bread. The children began to share out the bread with everyone, a symbol of the *olla* (collective cooking pot) of the poor – the poor who share what they have.

Interview by Notes from Nowhere / Katharine Ainger

Resources:

» Carcajada Cultural Café, Almirante Grau, 525 Central, La Paz, Bolivia

» Mujeres Creando: creando@ceibo.entelnet.bo

» *Quiet Rumours: an Anarcha-Feminist Reader*, collected by Dark Star, AK Press, 2002.

---

that we expect different policies." One senior UNCTAD official comments, "Everybody will tell you they disapprove of the act, but I still have to meet somebody who was unhappy that it happened to Camdessus."

>> February 15 >> Hundreds of people gather to defend the Jardín de la Esperanza (the garden of hope) in New York, US. The garden is bulldozed and 31 people are arrested a few hours before legal protection of the garden is issued.

>> February 18 >> One thousand Thai activists march on the UNCTAD conference, burning effigies of IMF director Michel Camdessus, and calling for radical changes to the global financial system, which keeps much of the world locked in poverty. Inside the conference, Algerian President Abdelaziz Bouteflika says in a keynote speech that the African continent is being rubbed off the map by the trade policies of richer nations.

>> March 8 >> Youth activists of colour in San Francisco, US storm the corporate headquarters of Chevron, Hilton, and Pacific Gas and Electric. These corporations are guilty of, among many other crimes, giving tens of thousands of dollars to a campaign to put a proposed juvenile 'justice' measure (Prop 21) on the

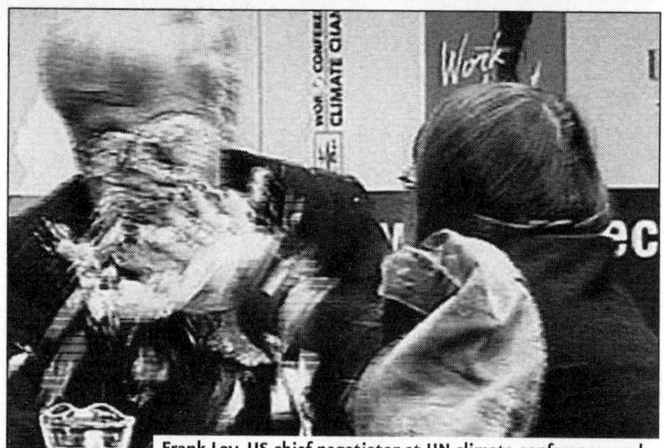
Frank Loy, US chief negotiator at UN climate conference, and...

James Wolfensohn, head of the World Bank, get a taste of pie-rect action

The Pie's the Limit

"It is better to pie on your feet than to live on your knees."
– Emiliano ZaPieta

A phantom flan-flinger appears as if from nowhere and, raises her arm. A pie flies through the air and meets its target – splosh – followed rapidly by indignation, laughter, and a quick getaway that night on the news the world discovers that the man in a suit with his face full of cream has been selling off old-growth forest / rewriting laws that don't concern him / using sweatshop labour and so on, and that some cheeky bunch has pied him for it. The pie may not have changed the world, but the sheer nerve of the act has shed light on some shady corporate (or state) crimes, opened up space for discussion of related issues, and delivered just desserts to an unaccountable and powerful person.

How to deliver just desserts to the powerful:

Step 1: Pick a worthy target
Aim for someone infamous, whose crimes should be revealed, and don't be afraid to think big. You may plot to pie someone for months, or spontaneously decide to do it the next day. Be sure you can clearly articulate the reasons for your choice, and carefully consider the level of security you are prepared to outsmart.

Step 2: Obtain a pie
According to market research, the best full-face coverage comes in the form of a coconut cream pie. Most pie throwers are in agreement that you shouldn't use red filling, as it could be mistaken for blood. Vegan pies are less firm than those with eggs – a problem which results in less theatrical results, but may be worth it to make a political

statement. Give your pie an name – Baked Alaska for a global warming villain, say.

Step 3: Disguise yourself

It doesn't take an economist like Milton Friedman (pied in 1998) to figure out that if you attempt to enter a fancy hotel, you will draw less attention to yourself if you look like everyone else. If you shave, dress up, and keep your hair average, you can go anywhere. You can sneak your pie into the corridors of power concealed in a brown paper bag, or if it's firm enough to go vertical, put a lid on it and carry it in a briefcase.

Step 4: Consider media

A key element of any pie launch is documentation. Because it's difficult to pie while shooting video, it's good to work with a friend or two. Expect not to be the only media present, and be ready to talk intelligibly. This action is essentially one of public theatre – when the media come calling it's good to have pithy soundbytes prepared to highlight your issue.

Step 5: Launch the attack

Some pie slingers work in teams. The splatting of Bill Gates was a masterful coordination of 30 individuals in groups of three, carrying a total of 25 pies. Multiple pies give you more than one chance to score a direct hit. However, some prefer to work solo, finding it more heroic and romantic. Most agree that a quick quip as you hurl the pastry can work wonders, clarifying your intent and message. Be aware that assault charges are not unheard of, so the more gently and lovingly you can cream your target, the better it will look in court.

Step 6: Consider the consequences

Expect shock and chaos. Anything can happen. Everyone may laugh and pretend that they are in on the joke, or security guards may attack violently, and have you arrested or detained. But once you are able to regroup with your allies, it's crucial to celebrate.

Finally, remember that it doesn't take special skills to toss a tart. Anyone with a pie and a vision of a better world can speak pie to power.

"Never doubt that a small and dedicated group of people with pies can change the world. Indeed, it is the only thing that ever has."

– Subcomandante Tofutti, after Margaret Mead

Below: Renato Ruggiero, then Director-General of the WTO, pied. London 1999

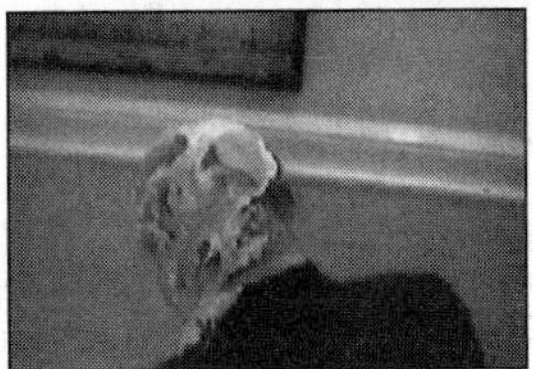

The Water Is Ours, Dammit!

by Jim Shultz

Before April 2000, *few people outside of Bolivia had ever heard of Cochabamba. Four months into the new century that changed. Against all odds – standing down soldiers, resisting a declaration of martial law, and rising up against a wave of worship-the-market economic theology – South America's poorest people evicted one of the world's wealthiest corporations and took back something simple and basic – their water.*

The World Bank laid the foundation for privatization in the mid-1990s, by 'offering' a $14 million loan to expand water service if Cochabamba's water was placed under corporate control. The resulting contract with US corporation Bechtel was a sweet deal. The agreement guaranteed the company an average profit of 16 per cent annually over the 40-year life of the contract. The company was also to be given control over hundreds of rural irrigation systems and community wells, that had been built by local people without government help. Water bills increased by up to 400 per cent. People were even charged for collecting rainwater from their roofs.

The outraged population began organizing, forming a group known as the Coordinadora. *They became convinced that they needed to campaign not just for rolling back water rates to repealing the contract altogether and putting Cochabamba's water under direct public control.*

In March, Coordinadora *leaders took up an organizing strategy pioneered by activists in Mexico, the* consulta popular. *For three days activists set up small tables in plazas and other public gathering places throughout the region, to survey residents with a simple question – should the water contract be cancelled? The answer, by a vote of over 90 per cent, was a resounding yes. Cancellation of Bechtel's contract became the main demand. This was bold, to say the least. Nowhere else on earth had popular protest succeeded in reversing such a major privatization deal. But Cochabamba was about to make history.*

Mountains of silver

Bolivia's experience with the darker forces of globalization began centuries ago, in another Andean city – Potosí. There, in 1545, a modest hill was discovered to be, quite literally, a mountain of silver. For nearly three centuries Spanish colonialists mined the hill, Cero Rico or Rich Hill, of enough silver to virtually bankroll the Spanish empire. They also left behind, in the words of Eduardo Galeano, "eight million Indian corpses". Slave miners were sent into the pitch dark and stale depths for as long as six months at a time. Many of those who survived went blind from re-exposure to sunlight. Bolivia's first lesson about globalization was this one – a people blessed by the Earth with one of the largest single sources of mineral wealth in the history of the planet ended up the poorest nation in South America.

This memory of horrific abuse and the theft of wealth across the sea was not lost on the Bolivian soul when, in the 1980s and 1990s, the World Bank and International Monetary Fund (IMF) decided to make Bolivia a laboratory for their own modern experiments in global economics. World Bank water officials believe in privatization the way other people believe in Jesus, Mohammed, Moses, and Buddha. So they focused their most aggressive campaign for privatization on the public water system of Bolivia's third largest city, Cochabamba.

"The Bolivian government would rather respond to the directives of the World Bank than take into account what the people themselves consider to be their needs. The heart of the problem is this: who decides about the present and the future of the people, resources, work and living conditions. We, with respect to water, want to decide for ourselves: this is what we call democracy."

– communication from the Coordinadora, 28 January 2000

In September 1999, in a closed-door process with just one bidder, Bolivian officials leased off Cochabamba's water until the year 2039, to a mysterious new company named Aguas del Tunari – which was later revealed to be a subsidiary of the California engineering giant, Bechtel. Just weeks after taking over, the company hit local families with rate increases of up to 200 per cent and sometimes higher. Workers living on the local minimum wage of $60 per month were told to pay as much as $15 just to keep the water running out of their tap.

The water war begins

Even before the huge rate hikes were introduced, a citizens' movement began forming to challenge the privatization, a group which came to be known as *La Coordinadora*. Its leadership came from the local factory workers union, irrigators and farmers, environmental groups, local economists, progressive members of Congress, and a broad base at the grassroots. *La Coordinadora* was both urban and rural, both poor and middle class.

In November 1999, the Federation of Irrigators, furious about the planned give away of water systems they had dug with their own hands, staged a 24-hour blockade of the highways leading in and out of Cochabamba. "Our objective was to test what capacity we had to fight," recalls Omar Fernandez, leader of the irrigators' union. "We found out that our base wanted to move faster than even our leadership. In [the small town of] Vinto they blockaded the highway for 48 hours." After the blockades the rural water users formed an alliance with urban users concerned about Bechtel's take-over of the city water system and on 12 November 1999 *La Coordinadora* for the Defence of Water and Life was born.

In January 2000, after the water company announced its huge rate increases, *La Coordinadora* sprang out of nowhere

---

ballot which would give prosecutors the power to decide whether children as young as 14 are tried and jailed as adults. 175 people, mostly high school students and their parents, are arrested at the Hilton in what is referred to as "the first hip-hop generation sit-in".

>> March 12 >> Over a million people in Spain take part in an unofficial referendum on 'Third World' debt. More than 97 per cent vote in favour of Spain's cancellation of external debt with poor countries. The referendum goes ahead despite the Spanish Electoral Committee's ban and despite attempts by the police to shut down voting booths.

>> March 16 >> Pressured by the IMF, the Costa Rican government passes a law allowing the privatization of the state telecommunications company. Widespread protests erupt, resulting in five protesters being shot, one killed, and 60 police officers injured as riot police clash with demonstrators. At least 100 students are arrested. Days later, 40 protests take place all around the country. The following week, 10,000 people descend on the presidential residence demanding the withdrawal of the bill.

>> March 27 >> Three thousand people, including undocumented migrants, occupy trains to take them

with its first public action, a city-wide *paro*, a general strike. For three days Cochabamba was shut down. Blockades closed down the two main highways leading in and out of town, eliminating bus transportation and food shipments. The airport was shut. Roadblocks cut off all traffic in the city. Thousands of Cochabambinos occupied the tree-lined, colonial central plaza. At one corner of the plaza *La Coordinadora* set up its headquarters in the ragged offices of the local factory workers' union and hung a wide banner from the third floor balcony. Bright red with white letters the banner carried the city's new rallying cry, *El Agua es Nuestra Carajo!*, The Water is Ours Dammit!

> *"Men and women of Cochabamba, rights cannot be begged for, they must be fought for. No one is going to fight for ours. We will fight together for what is just or we will tolerate the humiliation of bad government."*
>
> **– declaration to Cochabambinos from the Coordinadora, January 2000**

Just across the plaza sat the offices of Cochabamba's regional governor, an appointee of the President. After a day of refusing to recognize the *Coordinadora* as a legitimate organization, the governor agreed to meet its leaders. During the negotiations the governor could hear the angry chants of thousands of protesters, quite literally at his door. The government finally signed an agreement to review the water company's contract and the new water law, if the protest was suspended. *Coordinadora* leaders gave the government three weeks.

As is political custom in Bolivia, the government broke its word. As January turned to February no change in the rates was forthcoming and the people of Cochabamba were refusing to pay their bills to Bechtel. The company, growing desperate, threatened to shut off people's water. The *Coordinadora* announced that it would stage a take-over of the city's central plaza once again, on 4 February.

What was planned was a simple lunchtime protest to remind the government that the people were still watching. Several hundred protesters would march to the plaza, hear some speeches, prod the government to keep its word, and then go back to work. "We told the minister of government, 'Nothing is going to happen,'" says Oscar Olivera, head of the Cochabamba Factory Workers Union and one of the *Coordinadora*'s most visible leaders. "It is a take-over with white flags, with flowers and bands, like a party."

The government announced that the protest was not going to be allowed and on the morning of the fourth, more than 1,000 heavily armed police and soldiers took control of the city's centre, almost all brought in from other cities (as Cochabamba police could not be counted on to take such a hard line against their own relatives). For the people of Cochabamba, even those who may not have been sympathetic to the water revolt before that, the invasion of police was akin to a declaration of war. Not only was the government refusing to rollback the company's huge price hikes, now it was protecting Bechtel's increases with tear gas and guns.

For two days central Cochabamba turned into a war zone. Every block leading to the plaza was converted into a mini-battle field. At one end police outfitted in full riot gear blocked the streets with tear gas cannons. At the other end protestors – young people, old people, poor and middle class – held their ground with rocks and slingshots. Many wore the impromptu uniform of vinegar-soaked bandanas over the mouth and nose, and baking soda under the eyes as protection against the gas.

> *"The cost of the repression: a six month supply of tear gas was used, 3,840 tear gas grenades, on the first day of the repression. Each grenade costs between $5 and $10.... On Friday $28,000 was spent on tear gas grenades alone. The second day, fewer tear gas grenades were used because their reserves had been depleted... 5,600 grenades were used over the two days of the conflict, at a cost of approximately $42,000. Eighty police officers arrived from La Paz, each having received $7 per day for food and other needs. From this, it can be calculated the government spent $15,480 over five days. It cannot be confirmed but is it supposed that each police officer who participated in the repression received a bonus of $35. The government also incurred costs for a small plane and for the leaflets which were distributed by this means during the first days of the conflict."* – ***Los Tiempos*, 8 February 2000**

As the conflicts continued, the doors of middle class homes would open up and bowls of food and water would appear, an offering of support to those standing up to the government in the streets. In two days more than 175 people were wounded, most all victims of tear gas canisters or police beatings. The government lost whatever public legitimacy it had on the issue. It announced an agreement with the company to invoke a temporary rate rollback for six months. The *Coordinadora* had won its first victory.

The final battle

In April the *Coordinadora* announced what it called *La Ultima Batalla*, the Final Battle. On Tuesday 4 April, Cochabamba was shut down again for the third time in four months by an indefinite general strike and blockade of the highways. The *Coordinadora* issued two key demands – cancellation of the water company's contract and repeal of the national law through which the government planned to give Bechtel control over wells and rural irrigation systems.

On Thursday, after Cochabamba had been shut down for two days, government officials finally agreed to sit down to

---

from Italy to Paris to participate in the Solidarity and Open Borders in Europe demonstration. Everyone travels without identification or travel documents in support of the free movement of citizens regardless of nationality or income. The train drivers union, on strike that day, grant an exception and guarantee their journey to the French border. The train is stopped nine miles from the border and all crossings without documents are banned by the Prime Minister, despite the Schengen Agreement which guarantees EU citizens freedom of movement within the EU. The protesters walk to the border and are trapped in a tunnel by French riot police and Foreign Legion soldiers.

>> April 13 >> A demonstration in Nairobi, Kenya calling for debt relief and an end to IMF's economic conditions is broken up by riot police with 63 protesters arrested, including 13 nuns and two priests. Brother Andre, one of the priests, later writes, "The IMF and World Bank have power over the financial decisions of poor countries. Poor countries have totally lost their autonomy. They are often recolonized, with the powerful countries dictating the terms."

>> April 10 >> After a fierce and bloody struggle, the people of Cochabamba, Bolivia regain control over their

Tom Kruse

Stand-off during the water wars. Cochabamba, Bolivia

talk with *Coordinadora* leaders, in negotiations moderated by Cochabamba's Catholic Archbishop, Tito Solari. Late that night *Coordinadora* leaders began their talks in the state's offices, with the governor, the city mayor, the Archbishop and other officials. Suddenly police under orders from the national government in La Paz burst in and put the *Coordinadora* leaders under arrest. "It was a trap by the government to have us all together, negotiating, so that we could be arrested," says Olivera, who was among those taken into custody. Bishop Solari locked himself in his own office for the night, telling reporters that if the *Coordinadora* was under arrest so was he.

"We aren't going to forget what they have done to us."

– Citizen cited in *Pulso*, 11 February 2000

On Friday, after the Coordinadora leaders were released, Cochabamba residents expected a military take-over of the city at any moment. Bolivia's president, Hugo Banzer, who had ruled as dictator during the 1970s, was well known for his easy use of political repression. The atmosphere in the city was incredibly tense, especially in the central plaza where news of the arrests the night before had drawn a gathering of more than 10,000 people. Many were locals, but thousands of others had marched in long distances from the countryside and had been there for days. Community by community they arrived, to great cheers, each group carrying a banner bearing the name of their *pueblo*. One rural town official, who had marched 44 miles to get to Cochabamba, told me, "This is a struggle for justice, and for the removal of an international business that, even before offering us more water, has begun to charge us prices that are outrageously high."

A meeting was announced for 4.00 pm between the Governor and the *Coordinadora*, to be mediated by Archbishop Solari. After midday it was announced that the Governor would sit down once more with *Coordinadora* leaders, this time in the offices of the Bishop. When word spread that the Governor had failed to show, people in the plaza feared the worst. A half dozen teenage boys climbed to the bell tower of the city's Cathedral, tying ropes to the bells so that they could be rung as a warning when soldiers started to invade the city.

---

water supply and evict US corporation Bechtel, which had imposed rate hikes of 400 per cent.

>> April 15-17 >> Thirty thousand converge in Washington DC, US, to protest the World Bank / IMF annual meeting. Groups from across the world are represented, including affected peoples from South Africa, Guatemala, Haiti, the Philippines, Nigeria, Uganda, and Eastern Europe, as well as labour unions, church groups, NGOs, students and more. During the lock down blockades, a 1,000 strong Black Bloc keeps on the move all day, keeping the cops distracted, and providing welcome solidarity to activists holding intersections. A total of 678 are arrested and report widespread abuses in prison. Though unsuccessful at blockading the meetings entirely, the protests lead to widespread debate in the media. Parallel protests are held in several countries including South Africa, Hungary, Turkey, and Kenya.

>> April 26 >> Scores of protesters in Lusaka, Zambia's capital, demanding an end to IMF austerity measures, picket the hotel where the IMF is meeting with the government. Organized by a leading civil society group, Women for Change (WfC), the protesters blame the IMF and World Bank for continued poverty in their country.

In his plaza office Governor Hugo Galindo could hear the angry crowd outside. Windows had already been broken on the front of the building. A fire was set against the giant wooden main entrance door. At the hour he was supposed to have met with *Coordinadora* leaders, instead he telephoned his superiors in La Paz. He explained that he saw no alternatives except cancellation of the contract or an all out war between the people and government. He recommended that the contract be cancelled. Banzer's people were noncommittal. Galindo then called Bishop Solari, sitting in his office with *Coordinadora* leaders. He told the Bishop that he had urged the President to cancel the contract. When Bishop Solari relayed that message to Olivera and other *Coordinadora* leaders it got transformed into something more dramatic – that the company was leaving.

Minutes later, still wearing a vinegar-soaked red bandana around his neck and with white smudges of baking soda under his eyes, Olivera emerged from a third floor balcony over the plaza. "We have arrived at the moment of an important economic victory over neoliberalism," he yelled with a hoarse voice to the crowd, which erupted in a cheer that rivalled thunder. He thanked the neighbourhoods, the transportation workers, people from the countryside, university students, and others who had made the battle and the victory possible. Cochabambinos celebrated in the streets. Archbishop Solari presided over a packed service of celebration in the Cathedral.

Within hours events took a dark an unexpected turn. Banzer's spokesman refused to confirm the company's departure. Bechtel's local representatives faxed notices to the press declaring that they weren't leaving. At midnight Governor Galindo went on TV live, told city residents that he didn't want to be responsible for a "blood bath", and resigned. Bands of police started to appear at the doors of Coordinadora leaders and their families, arresting all those they could find. Seventeen people were arrested, put on a plane in Cochabamba, and flown off to a mosquito-infested jail in Bolivia's remote eastern jungle. Those that escaped arrest, including Fernandez and Oscar Olivera, went into hiding.

"For many years, governments felt that the supply of fresh water and the safe disposal of wastewater were matters which were too important to be left to business. Now we all know better. International Water has already shown that powerful resources applied skillfully by conscientious private enterprise can lift a huge burden from the shoulders of governments and so transform the lives of citizens. Together, we serve a public which likes what we do."

– website of International Water, a subsidiary of Bechtel

On Saturday morning panicked city residents scrambled to local markets, which had been closed for four days, to stock up on food. At 10.00 am President Hugo Banzer, the former dictator, declared a state of emergency, initiating martial law. Soldiers shut off TV and radio broadcasts. A whole section of the city, the hillside where antennas continued to broadcast news, had its power cut off, taking most of the remaining stations off the air. A curfew was instituted. Public meetings of more than two people were banned. Cochabamba was under a dictatorship.

> *"What can we do when they charge us so much for water that does not even reach our houses? We had to fight in whatever way we could. Of course, what we have seen is that we are fighting between brothers, but they have not left us any other option."*
>
> **- Cochabambino quoted in *Opinión*, 7 April 2000**

The public response was quick and furious. Even with its leaders under arrest and in hiding, the *Coordinadora* called for an immediate reinstitution of the road blockades and work stoppages. In my neighbourhood an old woman with a bent back laid out rocks in our street to block it. Young people, dubbed "the water warriors", headed back downtown to challenge Banzer's troops. Women travelled door to door to collect rice and other food to cook for the people who remained camped in the plaza.

By Saturday afternoon the conflict turned violent. Protesters set fire to a vacant state office building, sending a huge plume of black smoke into Cochabamba's clear blue sky. Soldiers switched from using tear gas to live rounds. A local television station captured footage of an army captain, Robinson Iriarte de La Fuente, a graduate of the US School of the Americas, disguised in plain clothes as he shot live rounds into a crowd of protesters. He was tried later in a Bolivian military court, and was acquitted, then promoted to Major, even though his flying bullets coincided exactly with the time an unarmed seventeen-year-old boy, Victor Hugo Daza, was killed by a bullet through the face. His companions brought his bloody body to the plaza and held an angry, emotional wake.

Cochabamba had reached a bloody stand-off. President Banzer, who now faced spreading protests on other issues in cities all across the nation, made it clear that he was not

---

"The IMF are killing us, especially women and children," says Emily Sikazwe of WfC. The protesters are eventually dispersed by armed riot police.

>> April 26 >> Workers belonging to the Confederation of Turkish Labour Unions begin a walk to Ankara to protest against privatization, to demand their union rights and employment security as well as an end to political labour discrimination. The Confederation's Aegean Region chairman Mustafa Kundakci says; "We are walking for workers' rights and to reject the government's economic policy. This march is the last warning for the Government. If it does not listen to the workers, we will turn Turkey to ashes."

>> May 6 >> The Asian Development Bank (ADB) meeting in a luxury hotel in Chiang Mai, Thailand, is blockaded by farmers and students calling for ADB loans to Thailand to be scrapped. Thai police say they had never seen such a determined crowd, as 5,000 activists break through police lines and crowd control barriers during the opening ceremonies. Later, 100 students manage to scale the wall of the hotel. Weeraporn Sopa, the 33-year-old leader of a farmers' confederation from Thailand's northeast, said the demonstration built on the WTO Seattle protests he

about to cancel a contract with a major multinational corporation. His public relations staff went to work to spin a false story to foreign reporters that the price increases had only been 20 per cent and that the Cochabamba protests were being orchestrated by "narcotraffickers" intent on destabilizing the government. The people of Cochabamba were also not about to back down. The streets were still getting fuller.

Meanwhile, while Bolivians were shedding blood, the water company's foreign owners and managers were escaping accountability altogether. The foreign managers sent in to run the company were laying low in a five star hotel, insistent in their demand to control the water, watching the suffering on television, and hanging up on reporters who got hold of their cell phone numbers. It was then that we decided that the company's vague connection to Bechtel was worth another look.

On Sunday morning, as a funeral service was being held for Victor Hugo Daza downtown, I began looking into the Bechtel-Bolivia connection via the internet. After two hours of examining the webpages of Bechtel and its assortment of international shells and subsidiaries we had the smoking gun. Bechtel was not only a player in the Bolivian water company, it had been its founder and 55 per cent controlling owner. We used The Democracy Center's large email network to send alerts to thousands of activists worldwide, calling on them to pressure Bechtel to leave the country. We also gave them the personal email address of Bechtel's President and CEO, Riley Bechtel.

On Monday the confrontations continued, though more peacefully than on the bloody weekend. That afternoon the government made an announcement. Bechtel officials had left the country and the government declared the contract cancelled. The city celebrated as it would have a World Cup soccer victory, with cars parading along Cochabamba's avenues with horns blaring. The *Coordinadora*'s leaders came out of hiding and were flown back from their jail in the jungle, greeted as heroes.

"There is a sort of rebirth of people's capacity to believe. People want to have faith in themselves again, something that neoliberalism had taken from us. Before, we had to believe in the 'expert', in the sort that barely speaks Spanish, who speaks English instead, in the way they speak at Harvard."

– A. Garcia in *Pulso*, May 2000

In the wake of Bechtel's departure, Cochabamba's water company, SEMAPA, was turned over to a public board appointed by the *Coordinadora* and Cochabamba's city government. Water rates were rolled back to what they had been before Bechtel's price hikes and local water users lined up to pay their bills. *Coordinadora* leaders turned from the high drama of street protest to the headaches of trying to make a water company work more efficiently. Management and system problems remained, but a series of new neighbourhoods were added to the water grid and the company accomplished something else extraordinary. Even at the pre-Bechtel rates, Cochabamba's water company was operating in the black. It also began qualifying for loans, from the Inter American Development Bank and others, to allow for expansion of the water system. Even the powers of international finance had begun to accept that, in Cochabamba, the water was to remain in public hands.

Why they fought and why they won

> *"They want to make us believe that the privatization of water is going to save us, that it is a lifesaver. As if we don't have experience with privatization? Privatization is total chaos, privatization has failed in Bolivia. Now we see that the corporations, the corrupt and the politicians work together against the people."*
>
> **– Cochabambino on the radio, 5 February 2000**

"The privatization of the water was the straw that broke the camel's back," says Tom Kruse, a US researcher who lives in Cochabamba and was an active advisor to the *Coordinadora*. Cochabambinos had endured one privatization after another, always with resistance by those directly affected – the airline workers union, for example – but never with enough force to make a difference. The revolt over water was a revolt over everything, a reaction to official corruption, economic decline, and the clear and broad belief that the government was looking out for everyone but the people. In one neighbourhood a sixteen-year-old boy explained to me how he received his political awakening over a piece of bread. "My mother sent me to the store one morning to buy bread but told me she had no money, not even one Boliviano [about 15 cents at the time] to pay for it. She told me to ask the storeowner if we could pay later. I thought to myself, 'How can it be that my mother works so hard and we don't even have even one Boliviano to buy bread?' It was then that I realized something was really wrong." When the *Coordinadora* came to his neighbourhood to organize resistance to the water privatization, he saw his chance to do something.

"Older people told us stories about the dictatorships but we had never been directly involved in struggles like those," explains Leny Olivera [no relation to Oscar], a 23-year-old university student. She adds, "I think it was a way for our generation to show our courage."

Water is something essential to life, not like an aeroplane or even electricity in a poor country. People know that if they lose control of their water they lose control of their lives. The

---

attended. "I have to warn the ADB and organizations like it – they should listen to us. When you still have a conscience, you can control the streets."

>> May 10 >> Half of South Africa's work force – 200,000 people, since eight out of ten are unemployed – honor a general strike across the country, demanding an end to neoliberal policies which have resulted in mass job losses.

>> May 12 >> Eight thousand Honduran hospital workers go on strike, demanding a pay raise after the IMF mandates cuts, including the privatization of telecommunications, electricity, social security, and the pension system. 28 public hospitals and 500 clinics are affected, and riot police are deployed in and around the hospitals to maintain order.

>> May 15 >> Labour unionists and human-rights activists in Zomba, Malawi try to march to the New State House, where a consultative group of Western donor countries are meeting government officials. The protesters, carrying placards protesting against the effects of structural adjustment, are stopped by police and dispersed by tear gas.

>> May 15 >> In Ecuador the National Educators' Union goes on strike for five weeks over the proposed

Coordinadora gave people a hope that was new. It also unified people from the rural areas and people from the city, which was absolutely key. "Many people say it is impossible to fight against the neoliberal model," says Leny Olivera, the university student. "But we showed that you can, not just in Bolivia but in the world. The humble people are the majority and are more powerful than multinational corporations."

> *"The other great success of this movement is that we have lost our fear. We left our houses and our communities in order to talk among ourselves, in order to get to know one another, in order to learn to trust one another again. We occupied the streets and highways because we are their true owners. We did it counting only upon ourselves. No-one paid us, no-one sent us orders or fined us. For us, urban and rural workers, this is the true meaning of democracy: we decide and do, discuss and carry out. We risked our lives in order to complete what we proposed, that which we consider just. Democracy is the sovereignty of the people and that is what we have achieved."*
>
> **– communication of the Coordinadora, 6 February 2000**

Birth of an international symbol

In the end it was a revolt not just about water but about arrogance, against an attitude by the World Bank, Bechtel, and Banzer that said, 'You are losing control of your water and you are going to pay more for it, take it and shut up.' In its aftermath, Cochabamba's water revolt became an international symbol, a modern day victory of a humble David against a giant corporate Goliath. The water revolt drew broad international media attention. Oscar Olivera was awarded the prestigious international Goldman Prize for environmental activism. Cochabamba became synonymous with the struggle for global economic justice, a source of great inspiration and hope. How the water revolt went from being a local struggle to an international icon is a story in itself, the product of the internet, a great story, and the luck of great timing.

The only international reporting directly from the scene was mine. I was in Cochabamba because that is my home. Each morning as the revolt deepened I would walk down the long hill into the city centre and to the centre of the protests to get the story. Then I would walk back up the hill in the afternoon and send out dispatches to the 2,000 press outlets and activist organizations on The Democracy Centre's email list. How far and fast these spread through the internet was astonishing. My reports were syndicated by Pacific News Service and picked up by publications all across the US and Canada. These stories later sparked other writers, from the *New Yorker*, the *San Francisco Chronicle*, to write their own stories.

More importantly, activists from all over the world picked up Cochabamba's fight and made it their own, sending my alerts far and wide and pummelling Bechtel with messages of "Get out!" Water activists in New Zealand received my alerts and asked what they could to do help. With the revolt still raging across the world in Bolivia, activists in Auckland got hold of a fire truck, covered it with anti-Bechtel and anti-Banzer signs, drove to the Bolivian consulate and before the amazed eyes of local media, hosed it down at high pressure. They sent pictures of the event to us in

Cochabamba which we gave to the local press. One Cochabamba daily, *Gente*, dedicated its first three pages to the story, amazing Cochabambinos with the fact that their local rebellion was drawing the attention of the world.

Also, quite by accident, it turned out that Cochabamba's revolt over water was unfolding just as tens of thousands of young people a hemisphere away were on their way to Washington DC to protest at the joint meeting of the World Bank and IMF, the first major globalization action since Seattle five months earlier. With Oscar Olivera in hiding to avoid government capture, my colleague Tom Kruse came up with the idea that we could buy him some political protection by getting groups in the US to invite Oscar to attend the events in Washington. The idea was never that Oscar would go but that these invitations, which we gave to the Bolivian press, might make the government hesitant to arrest someone who now had an international profile.

On Wednesday, with the water revolt just ended and with the smell of tear gas still hanging thick over the city centre, Oscar told us that he thought he really should go to Washington, to share Cochabamba's story. The Washington protests were just two days away and Oscar had neither a Bolivian passport nor an entry visa from the US (which generally take months to secure if they can be gotten at all). On Thursday morning Oscar went to the local passport office which, by chance, was run by an old schoolmate, and got his passport in less than an hour. Later that day, Oscar and Tom flew to La Paz to attempt the impossible task of convincing the US Embassy that it ought to grant an immediate entry visa to a man wearing a Che Guevara wristwatch who had just led the eviction of a major US corporation. While they were waiting, I received a call from a reporter for a major newspaper chain in the US, begging for help to secure an interview with Oscar. I suggested a bargain. If he would agree to call the US Ambassador and ask if she were going to give Oscar a visa, I would set up the interview. He agreed and a few hours later Oscar strolled out the Embassy doors with the seal of the US stamped in his fresh passport. On Friday Oscar, Tom, and I flew to Washington.

By Sunday, Oscar was at the head of a procession of thousands through the streets of the capital of the most powerful country in the world. Just a week earlier he had

---

IMF cuts in spending and salaries. President Noboa says he will take a tough stance: "I'm willing to go all the way with this. If they want to strike for a year, let them do it. We're not going to back down." Protests by teachers in Quito are dispersed by riot police using tear gas.

>> May 24 >> In Genoa, Italy 10,000 people respond to a call to action against a gathering of pro-GMO scientists and corporate leaders. Among the protesters are members of India's KRRS, and members of Tute Bianche who wear full body padding and carry shields, demanding the right to enter the exhibition hall to debate the issues. Despite a helicopter flying only 33 feet above their heads, and constant attack by police, they manage to push the police line back to the entrance of the hall and block it. The conference is shut down for the rest of the day. The Italian government withdraws its endorsement of the event, and eventually bans GMOs from the country. The media christen the event "Italy's Seattle".

>> May 29 >> Thousands of Bolivians block the nation's most important highway in Alto, the poorest city in the poorest country in Latin America. They issue three separate demands: the creation of an autonomous

Tom Kruse

Citizens resist the clampdown. Cochabamba, Bolivia

been in hiding, and Bolivia was under a state of martial law. Walking next to him I asked Oscar, "So, what do you think of the United States?" He paused a minute and said to me in Spanish, "*Es como Cochabamba. Hay policias y jóvenes en todo lado.*" It is just like Cochabamba. There are young people and police everywhere.

Epilogue – the water war, round two

In November 2001 the Bechtel Corporation launched round two in the Cochabamba water war, filing a lawsuit of $25 million against Bolivia in a secret trade court operated by the World Bank, the same institution that forced the Cochabamba privatization to begin with. "We're not looking for a windfall from Bolivia. We're looking to recover our costs," explains Michael Curtin, the head of Bechtel's Bolivian water company. However, Bechtel didn't invest anything close to $25 million in Bolivia in the few months it operated in Cochabamba. Bechtel officials paid for its rental cars and five star hotel rooms with funds from the public water company it took over and Bechtel left behind an unpaid electric bill of $90,000. Bechtel currently masquerades as a Dutch company, shifting its Bolivian registration to an Amsterdam post office box in hopes of getting covered by a Bolivia-Holland treaty that makes the Bank the arbiter of their investment disputes. With such an obvious sham, it's clear that just as the water revolt became an international symbol in the struggle against privatization, Bechtel vs. Bolivia will become an international symbol for everything wrong with rigged

"After having been passive in the selling off of 60 percent of our economy, we have finally reacted. What we have done means that we have redeemed our honour, in order to construct a common home with our own ideas and our own hands ..." – editorial in *Opinión*, 8 April, 2000

international trade law.

The stakes in the Bechtel vs. Bolivia case are high. $25 million is what Bechtel earns in half a day. In Bolivia that is the annual cost for hiring 3,000 rural doctors, or 12,000 public school teachers, or hooking up 125,000 families who don't have access to the public water system. But the stakes in this case go well beyond Bolivia. The World Bank's secret trade court is the prototype for the proposed Free Trade Area of the Americas (FTAA). The same tool Bechtel is using today against Bolivia could be used by other corporations to repeal environmental laws in California, health regulations in Québec, and worker protections in Venezuela – all in the name of knocking down barriers to trade.

In August 2002 more than 300 citizen groups from 41 different countries launched their own round two in the Bolivian water revolt, filing an International Citizens' Petition with the World Bank, demanding that the doors of its secret trade court be opened up to public scrutiny and participation. "The Bolivian water revolt has had an enormous impact on the global fight for water rights," says Maude Barlow [of the Council of Canadians]. "Many people feel that if some of the planet's poorest and disenfranchised people could stand up to the World Bank and Bechtel, so can all of us. The personal stories of heroism and struggle of the Bolivian people are very powerful and have been recited over and over all around the world."

Jim Shultz is executive director of The Democracy Centre, based in Cochabamba, Bolivia, he also writes extensively on globalization issues and is president of an 80-child orphanage. This piece is copyright Jim Shultz. Contact him if you wish to reprint it. JShultz@democracyctr.org

---

university, repeal of IMF-imposed tax-reforms, and revocation of increases in charges for electricity, fuel, and sewage systems. About 20,000 people converge at City Hall, where they are tear gassed by police. Chanting slogans denouncing the genocidal former dictator and current president Hugo Banzer, they enter the building and smash furniture, computers and windows, setting fire to the building. Police disperse the crowd hours later and arrest six people.

>> May 31 >> Protests against the IMF austerity plan in Argentina which will raise taxes, reduce social spending, and cut salaries, culminate with 100,000 people taking to the streets of Buenos Aires. Protesters liken the IMF to a financial dictatorship and promise "fiscal disobedience" by refusing to pay taxes, which have jumped from 8 to 22 per cent.

>> June 4-6 >> The US-Canada border is shut down on the occasion of the meeting of the Organization of American States, in Windsor, Canada, preventing thousands from demonstrating against the planning session for the FTAA. The Canadian Auto Workers join members of the US and Canadian steelworkers' unions, service employees and Ontario public employees in the streets. The

The Roquefort Rebellion

by Norm Diamond

Since 1999 *the media image of French anticapitalism has been a comic book caricature, an Asterix for the twenty-first century – the Gallic, pipe-smoking figure of José Bové. His interventions from Millau to Seattle and Brazil to Palestine have fascinated journalists – but the story told here is a little different. In August 1999, the destruction of a McDonald's in Millau by farmers from the union* Confédération Paysanne *established Bové as a national hero, but as we learn here, the media icon is merely the tip of a rather large iceberg.*

This act of strategic and symbolic property destruction was not a riot but a community carnival, organized to convey a clear message about WTO sanctions and the cultural imperialism of the United States. Above Millau is the Larzac plateau, where the small farmers that dismantled the McDonald's come from. Famous for producing Roquefort cheese, their livelihoods were threatened by WTO-approved sanctions imposed to punish Europe for refusing the import of US beef injected with growth hormones. Punitive sanctions of this type, which included a prohibitively high import tax on Roquefort entering the US, can devastate local economies, but in picking on Roquefort, the WTO had unwittingly stumbled upon a rather deep seam of resistance.

In the 1970s, newcomers to Larzac arrived to oppose its transition into a military testing range. Traditional ways of living were soon transformed, and in no time large communal plaques with quotations from Mao and Marcuse appeared. The Larzac community launched a newspaper and a satiric journal that continue to this day and the sheep farmers of the Larzac organized themselves under the umbrella of Confédération Paysanne, *which has since become a key node in the growing network of peasant farmers organizations worldwide,* La Via Campesina. *In this piece, the Larzac plateau remains a beacon of resistance and a symbol of continuity and solidarity, a place where Roquefort and rebellion go hand in hand.*

It is early afternoon, 30 June 2000. We are part of a vast chain of people hiking down from the plateau of Larzac to the town of Millau. We walk mostly single file, along what our guides tell us is normally an obscure path for sheep. Much of the time we have fabulous vistas: over the river Tarn and its narrow valley, over the tiled roofs of the ancient town, across to the other plateaus that squeeze Millau. When we are able to look up from the steep path, we see others like ourselves, hundreds, perhaps thousands of us, snaking down the cliff face. We are the impatient ones, the ones who wouldn't wait for organized transport. Eventually we reach a road and have to cross between the steady flow of shuttle buses bringing thousands more. On foot and by bus, we are a guerrilla army taking over the town.

We are in southern France in July 2000, and are here for the trial of ten sheep farmers accused of dismantling a McDonald's and using their tractors to haul away the debris. One of the farmers is José Bové, one of the media stars in the anti-WTO protests in Seattle, who distributed smuggled Roquefort cheese and spoke effectively about the horrors of corporate agriculture. We are in his home territory, and his popularity is immense. National polls show him winning the presidency of France, should he choose to run. Unions, peasant organizations and leftist groups have chartered trains and buses from all across France to show their solidarity.

Along the road we pass the refurbished McDonald's. It has

been open for business, but today it is shuttered. Riot police with three-quarter body length shields surround it, barricaded behind buses and armoured cars. Given our numbers, they hardly appear menacing. Indeed, they are nearly the only police we shall see this day. Even the courthouse relies on marshals from the demonstrators to keep order in the street.

"Seattle on the Tarn," is what organizers name the day, and French media are quick to use the catchy appellation in their headlines. J30 is what we call it for short, identifying it with a continuing list of date-named protests against capitalist globalization worldwide.

So far, each of these protests has gained inspiration, legitimacy, and momentum from the ones that precede it. Each one of these events, however, came out of concrete local conditions, out of the specifically local ways people have been affected by the generalized spread and penetration of the capitalist market. That J30 happened here and now is the product of a particular history and organizing effort. Understanding and building on these events requires recognizing the importance of place.

Spirit of place

I begin with two vignettes: in the first, we are driving along the top of Larzac some days after the demonstration. We are on a modern highway which obliterates the Roman road I knew from past visits. My teenage son is hungry, too much so to wait until we reach the old walled city I want to show him. We pull into a roadside restaurant and are already seated before we notice that the walls are covered with blown-up photos from the Seattle protest. My son walks the perimeter, identifying each of the places where he faced off with WTO delegates or city police.

When I express my surprise to the waitress, she says we're in luck. By coincidence, the photographer is eating with his young son a few tables away. He tells us they are celebrating his return from Colombia, where he had been travelling with Bové to talk strategy with organizations of small farmers like themselves. When the waitress brings us a bottle of the house wine, the label is the same symbol we've seen already on hillside banners, t-shirts, flyers and postcards: a globe with two sites indicated, Seattle and Millau. Half the globe consists of a voracious sesame-seed burger bun. Rising from inside one

---

meeting is surrounded by a ten foot-high fence of mesh steel. A member of the CAW said: "The corporations have their global links with institutions like the WTO, IMF, and OAS in privatizing everything, taking away our self-determination. As their agendas increase globally, so must ours. Workers must fight for each other."

>> June 5 **>>** The Nigerian government imposes IMF-mandated cooking fuel price hikes, and in response the country is crippled by the most serious general strike since the end of military rule. Oil workers are joined by public sector and transport workers in shutting down Lagos' port, highways, airport, and all petrol stations. Sporadic violence is reported across Nigeria's cities, leading to 40 dead, hundreds injured, and more than 1,000 arrested. After a week the government backs down. One observer comments: "In a country where, after several doses of Monetary Fund medicine, the average income is somewhere between one quarter and one tenth of what it was in 1980, SAP is practically a swear word."

>> June 9 >> In continued defiance of the new IMF-prescribed labour laws, Argentina is paralyzed by a 24-hour general strike supported by more than 7.2 million

hemisphere are two hands, handcuffed but raised in triumph, effectively holding off the attacking corporate breadstuff. The day before, when we remarked on one of the postcards in our hole-in-the-wall North African restaurant down in Millau, the counter man told us, "Those guys up on Larzac, they're magnificent. They're all anarchists, you know."

In the second vignette, I have found an injured sheep while wandering outside a small hamlet, also on Larzac, where I spent time in the 1970s. Now my son and I are waiting for two of the farmers to bring her back, to make sure they could follow my directions. In the hamlet, prominent on the rutted trail that winds through it, serving as its main street, we come across a wooden plaque. It is a sort of public penance, a communal expression of regret and atonement.

Here is the story it tells: in the early 1960s, France was engaged in a bitter war to retain Algeria as a colony. Algerian prisoners, small farmers turned independence fighters among them, were brought back to the military camp on Larzac. Though fairly remote, this camp became the target of antiwar and anticolonial protesters, who tried to block its gates and scale its fences. The protesters, nearly all from outside the region, attempted to enlist the small farmers of Larzac. But the latter were "apathetic" (their self-description on the plaque). They saw nothing in common with the prisoners. Instead, they served in the army when they couldn't get out of the obligation and ignored the protesters.

Now they feel ashamed that they let nationality divide them from small farmers like themselves who happened to be from a different country. The plaque is their declaration that they should have joined the protesters 40 years ago against the government. It also says they have done more than offer a remote, carefully carved apology. They have established a program that brings the children of Algerian farmers to live and study on Larzac.

The public nature of the plaque is as remarkable as the vision and practice of class solidarity it expresses. What could account for this extraordinary transformation from the 1960s until now? The key is a series of events in the 1970s that rocked Larzac and, then as now, mobilized France and beyond. J30 shows the continuing significance of this remote plateau to solidarity all across France. It is also an indication of the way that an earlier solidarity has evolved to become anticapitalist.

> **"Faced with a little local image problem, McDonald's [France] … has retired Ronald McDonald as the company's public face and replaced him with Asterix the Gaul …"** – *New Internationalist* magazine, September 2002

The struggle for Larzac

In the early 1970s the French government decided to convert this sparsely settled plateau into a facility for West European militaries to practice tank manoeuvres. France would both take a small step toward independence from NATO and further French-German rapprochement. All this would happen by means of heavy tank treads on a fragile landscape. An advance guard of German tanks rolled in by invitation, less than 30 years after German occupiers were driven out. Speculators began buying properties for resale to the military. The Ministry of Defence issued an edict forbidding any new farm building on the entire expanse of Larzac. Peasant attachment to their own land became a drive for local autonomy which quickly bloomed into anti-militarism and found resonance worldwide.

The struggle over Larzac merged initially with student and other opposition to the US continuation of the Vietnam War. It drew also on the established national network of small farmers. As various leftist groups joined in, the organizers on Larzac made it a priority to reach out to industrial workers. They began to send meat and cheese to workers on strike, and visited rallies at Renault and Peugeot and elsewhere. They developed especially strong ties with workers at the Lip factory, engaged in an extended occupation of their own. Joint posters identifying the two struggles appeared all over France.

Parallel to their own ritual of public oath-taking not to give up their land, the farmers of Larzac organized young men across France to send back their military registration, the equivalent of burning their draft cards. With supporters, they launched a 425-mile march to Paris. Two years later, they camped for a week under the Eiffel Tower. When protesters were arrested at the military camp, they organized demonstrations outside the same tribunal in Millau where we waited for José Bové and friends.

Up on the plateau, in a brilliant organizing move and to defy the Ministry's edict, they began to build an 'illegal' sheep barn. The structure is typical for this region, shaped like a miniature vaulted aeroplane hangar, large enough for hundreds of sheep and made of limestone rocks. The building process and ornamentation, however, were anything but typical. Under its eaves, along both lengths, there are foot-high anti-militarist quotes, on one side from Einstein, on the other from de Gaulle. Each quote is reproduced numerous times, in languages that pair peoples in conflict. Thus the same quote appears in Russian and English, Hebrew and Arabic, Vietnamese and Cambodian, etc. People came from all over France and all over the world to help with the construction, carving the name of their

---

workers. The president, Fernando de la Rua, is reported as saying that the government has no choice but to meet targets set by the IMF.

>> June 14 >> Chanting Zapatista slogans, members of Italy's Tute Bianche, anarchist groups, and communist groups work together and blockade the OECD summit in Bologna, Italy, preventing delegates' access for several hours. Demanding access to the summit so that their voices can be heard alongside those of corporate lobbyists, they advance slowly. The 6,000 police attack with truncheons and tear gas, as the Minister of Industry cries, "Let us meet!"

>> June 15 >> Ecuador's new President faces his first general strike, organized by trade unions and church groups, against continued IMF economic reforms. Among those striking are more than 30,000 doctors, who join with teachers, oil and public sector workers in a 72-hour sit-in. In Quito, protesters who try to march on the government palace are met with tear gas and riot police, who open fire on the crowd, wounding a bystander. In Guayaquíl, a bomb explodes outside Citibank and demonstrators are dispersed with tear gas.

>> June 15 >> Rural villagers from Altiplano, Bolivia

organization or struggle or place of origin into the stones. Especially prominent were young German antiwar and new leftist activists.

The struggle lasted the entire decade before backing the government down. Its persistence and militancy probably contributed to the Socialist Party electoral victory in 1981. Newly elected President Mitterrand then conceded the victory the people of Larzac had already won. Within France, the struggle both reinforced organizational ties among small farmers and provoked splits in pre-existing organizations over tactics. It strengthened mutual support between peasants and industrial workers, and brought an awareness of struggles elsewhere in the world and other ways of thinking about struggle.

John Jordan

McDonald's closes down for the day anticipating May Day protest. London, UK

Why McDonald's?

To the return visitor, rural Larzac looks much the same. The barn stands, as it probably will for centuries, though its soft stones are now weathered, their carved symbols mostly illegible. Roquefort cheese has become more of an international commodity, but it still requires land, sheep, and the distinctive mould found nowhere else. There are now some machines for milking the sheep, but the task is still mainly done by hand – by two fingers, to be exact. One of the pleasures of returning was to see the extraordinary 'illegal' barn in normal, sheep-filled, daily use.

The towns, however, have changed drastically with the new economy. Millau still has about the same number of inhabitants, about 23,000. But 20 years ago, 7,000 people worked in its factories, right in the heart of town, processing animal hides. Now those factories are mostly vacant. They are in transition, shuttered but not yet converted to housing or boutiques. There are still 600 workers, but they live off Millau's reputation, making fancy, one-of-a-kind pairs of gloves on special order. Mass production has gone elsewhere, to cheaper labour in Eastern Europe or the Third World. Instead, Millau has become the hang-gliding capital of Europe, with the northern lip of Larzac being, literally, the jumping off point, and tourism the main industry. This is the economic underpinning of the refurbished and new hotels and fancy shops. It is also the explanation for the, not one but two, new McDonald's.

At every level, international, national and local, McDonald's in Millau is a focal point for the strains and pressures brought by capitalist globalization. As such, it was an evocative and well-chosen target. French cuisine is an integral part of French culture and national identity. This tour guide truism understates the assaults people have felt in the last few years from: mad cow disease, genetically modified organisms, dioxin contaminants, septic residues, listeria, and heavy metals. Each of these has been a significant scare to French consumers. All have been by-products of the new industrial agriculture, with its massive operations integrating fertilizers, feed, pesticides, herbicides, and seeds.

It is that background that stiffened European resolve around bovine growth hormone (BGH), even in the face of a ruling by the court of the World Trade Organization. This court held that Europe could not refuse hormonally-enhanced beef from the United States because such refusal would represent an unfair commercial advantage to its own farmers. (United States, chemicals, and beef: sounds like McDonald's already). Most European farmers don't use the hormone because they would be obligated to label it as such, thus deterring consumers. As a sanction, the US government was granted the right to impose tariffs on selected European products and chose, among others, Roquefort cheese! Add only that McDonald's did not use local labour in its construction. Neither do they sell Roquefort in their cheeseburgers, not even in Millau.

The attack on McDonald's

On 12 August 1999, the McDonald's we hiked by nearly a year later was still under construction. The first reports from the scene were that it had been 'sacked' by rioters. Within a day, damages were reported to be in the millions of francs and the perpetrators in hiding. Overseas accounts emphasized that this was an anti-American action. The impression, hearing about it from abroad, was that it had been some sort of stealthy vanguardist undertaking. Debray's old theories of guerrilla warfare came to mind in trying to make sense of press reports: perhaps the perpetrators thought they were demystifying authority and encouraging the cowed citizens eventually to act on their own. In nearly every respect, the press reports and official accounts were misleading.

What actually happened represents the kind of political organizing developed over the years of the struggle on Larzac. Exactly one week before, on 5 August, a delegation

---

bring their deformed dead sheep to the city of Oruro to prove the seriousness of contamination caused by a massive oil spill from Enron-Shell's pipeline. The spill contaminated 120 miles of rivers and irrigation canals, and affected water used by 127 farming communities. When the police attack the demonstrators, they respond by throwing rocks, sticks, and foetuses of dead sheep. They then march to the corporate offices of Enron-Shell and break windows, hurl stones and Molotov cocktails, and then throw themselves to the ground and refuse to leave when the police attempt to disperse them with tear gas.

>> June 21 >> An unknown group hacks into the official Nike web site and all visitors are automatically redirected to an anticapitalist site prepared for the upcoming actions in Melbourne, Australia against the World Economic Forum. In the six hours it takes Nike technical workers to undo the reroute, the activist site receives almost 900,000 hits.

>> June 22 >> A 48-hour general strike is called in Paraguay in response to the government's plans to privatize its telephone, water, and railroad companies. The privatizations are conditions of an IMF programme that Paraguay must meet in order to access $400 million

representing both the farmers producing sheep's milk and the industrial makers of the cheese met with the Minister of Agriculture, in Paris, to see what could be done to protect the thousands of people hurt by the punitive tariff on Roquefort. The Minister told them there was no way to challenge the WTO court ruling. At best, he could offer modest funds for a stepped-up Roquefort advertising campaign. Emerging from his office, the delegation held a press conference on the steps of the Ministry, linking McDonald's to the attempted importation of the BGH beef and identifying it as a symbol and purveyor of the worst of industrial agriculture.

In the days preceding 12 August, organizers met with the Millau police, agreeing on a time when the construction site would be cleared of all workers and negotiating over the parts of the building that could be dismantled as a symbolic statement. The police offered light switch boxes, the organizers countered with door frames, and bargaining went from there. The rally was publicized, the event billed as a family affair. About 300 people showed up, half from Larzac, half from Millau. Kids frolicked. People pitched in to load the (more or less) agreed-to pieces of the building onto carts. Tractors hauled the carts into town and deposited their contents at the police station. There were speeches, then everyone went home. The damage to the construction was not great. The organizers apparently did not even expect to be arrested.

The unanticipated arrests played into the hands of the experienced organizers, who used the prospect of a trial to hammer at the issues. José Bové focused attention by refusing bail and staying in jail a few extra days. He was already well-known as a spokesperson for international and worker-farmer solidarity and an advocate for small-scale, environmentally sustainable farming. At the time of the McDonald's action, he was on parole for an earlier use of his tractor that destroyed a field of genetically-modified corn. The French press treated him as a media star on his N30 trip to Seattle, and he milked the coverage effectively. Before giving one of the keynote speeches at the anti-WTO protests, he travelled across the US for more than a week, meeting with groups of small farmers and assuring everyone that his target was not the American people but corporate agriculture. Along the way he distributed samples of smuggled Roquefort.

> **"During a counseling session, a corporate executive of Burger King was heard despairing at the fact that yet another McDonald's, and not a Burger King, had been targeted by anticapitalist demonstraters. 'That's global brand recognition for you,' he bemoaned."** – Karen Elliot, *The Burger and the King*

J30 - The trial begins

There were about 100,000 people in Millau for the trial and follow-up festivities. Long after midnight, the highways were still backed up for miles with arriving vehicles. The town undoubtedly was overwhelmed, but everything stayed peaceful. The atmosphere was that of a carnival and concert. The defendants turned the trial into a denunciation of corporate globalization, with witnesses from around the world. The judge tolerated the testimony, but acted uninterested. The real teach-in happened outside the trial, however, with forums and street theatre in the town and the witnesses repeating their testimony to the crowd on the concert grounds. Speeches and music lasted most of the night.

We left not knowing the verdicts. In mid-September, the judge ruled that only Bové would go to prison for three months – a harsher sentence than the prosecutor asked for.

Bové himself walks a fine line. He has become an international star in a movement, both local and global, that thrives on collectivity and professes egalitarianism. "We are all leaders!" has become an international motto. On our last day in Millau, my son and I came across an encouraging sign. There is an age-old working class slogan that radically rejects hierarchy: "Neither God Nor Master." As we wandered one last time in Millau's medieval passageways, we found freshly painted graffiti. Along with support for the defendants, it said: "*Ni Dieu, Ni Maître, Ni José Bové.*" (Neither God, nor master, nor José Bové).

Norm Diamond was president of Pacific Northwest Labour College. He co-authored *The Power In Our Hands* and hosts *The Old Mole Variety Hour* on KBOO-FM in Portland, Oregon.

Note: This is an abridged version of the original, "Seattle on the Tarn, French Solidarity Against Capitalist Globalization", published in *New Politics*, vol. VIII, no. 2 (New Series), Winter 2001

Resources:

» Confédération Paysanne's site: www.confederationpaysanne.fr/

---

in World Bank loans. Police meet the protesters with violence almost immediately, resulting in 20 injuries and at least ten arrests. About 300 protesters are dispersed by police with water cannons.

>> June 26 >> Thousands of Honduran workers take part in a national strike demanding an increase in the minimum wage. Protesters block main roads and the state-run port company, and a number of banana plantations are shut down.

>> June 30 >> In an effort to defend the forests surrounding Bloomington, Indiana, US, activists in the Earth Liberation Front network spike trees in areas designated to be logged this summer. Communiqués are sent and the area containing the spiked trees is clearly marked in order to prevent logger or millworker injury.

>> June 30 >> One Hundred thousand people descend on the tiny town of Millau (population 20,000), France to support José Bové and nine other defendants from the Confédération Paysanne, on trial for causing $114,000 damage to the McDonald's they helped dismantle last August. An enormous festival commemorates the event, with bands, and speakers. "Yes, this action was illegal.... The only regret I have

Meyer / Tendence Floue

Frivolity on the run. Prague, Czech Republic

Global Day of Action September 26th 2000

S26 – Balls to the IMF – Prague, Czech Republic

On S26 European movements pick up the gauntlet that N30 had thrown down for the meetings of the World Bank and IMF in Prague, in September 2000. Activists successfully besiege the conference centre despite the presence of 11,000 police and members of the FBI and UK's special branch who have been sent to Prague to 'advise' the Czech forces. Meanwhile, although the Czech state turns many activists away from its borders, there are no borders to the imagination of those who take actions in 110 cities in solidarity with the demonstrators in Prague. Early morning commuters are greeted with banners hung from motorway bridges in Frankfurt and Seattle. Despite bans on S26 demonstrations in Moscow, activists put out a spoof press release saying they will destroy a McDonald's, and baffle the pursuing media when they pay a noisy visit to the World Bank offices instead. Similar colourful visits

Brazil IMC

S26 solidarity actions in Caracas, Venezuela and...

Brazil IMC

São Paulo, Brazil

Nick Cobbing

Tute Bianche pad up in preparation to push through police lines. Prague

happen in Ankara, New York, Dhaka, Paris, Calcutta, and Kiev. Mirroring the events in Prague, World Bank employees are blockaded into their offices in Delhi, while in Geneva a symbolic sculpture of flesh, bones, and money is built in front of their doors.

Meanwhile in São Paulo, Brazil 1,000 people occupy the streets around the stock exchange, where a banner declares: "Seattle, Prague, São Paulo: We are Everywhere." IMF 'delegates' in pig masks play football with a globe, and a capitalist monster covered in corporate logos eats people in the crowd. When paint and stones are thrown at the building, and a corporate media van is destroyed, the police attack the crowd.

Four other Brazilian cities take action, including Belo Horizonte where a Citibank branch (Citigroup is a major investor in World Bank bonds) is blockaded, while in Berkeley, US one loses its windows, and in San Francisco a 'Shitigroup' float parades through the streets with bankers sitting on planet-shaped toilet bowls. In Wellington, Aotearoa/New Zealand, police attack a carnival against capitalism after people occupy a branch of the Westpac Bank.

Over 150 different actions take place across India,

Nick Cobbing

People get jumpy during the blue march. Prague

including in Mumbai, where people invade a brand new luxury shopping mall, surrounding the McDonald's inside and shouting, "We want food, not burgers, first give us water before you feed us Coca Cola!" In Chennai, Tamil Nadu, 400 women demand the abolition of the World Bank and IMF, and in Pakistan, a caravan made up of 30 organizations visits 31 towns where they are greeted by large crowds.

The joy of resistance is brought to at least five cities in Australia and over 40 in the United States as well as to the streets of Buenos Aires, Bangalore, Capetown, Brussels, Toronto, Warsaw, Belfast, Bergama, Zagreb, Istanbul, Johannesburg, Bawalpur, Izmir, Belfast, Montreal, London, Bristol, Tel Aviv, and beyond ...

On the cobbled streets of Prague itself a new generation of radicals from the Czech Republic, Poland, Hungary, and other Eastern European countries – where visible resistance to capitalism has been snuffed out since 1989 – come together and begin to build new networks.

Despite the efforts of the Bank, the Fund, the corporations, the authorities, and their assembled

Meyer / Tendence Floue

Police defend all routes to the Congress Centre. Prague

press to discredit anticapitalism, to paint the Prague actions as a failure, and the movement as divided, violent, and out-of-control, many within the movements saw S26 as a resounding success: it is the first time a summit is not just blockaded but actually shut down a day early. According to a World Banker, the sound of police firing concussion grenades led to a high state of tension inside the conference centre on the first day of their summit. And on the second day, a great number of delegates were too scared to leave their hotel rooms and attend the meetings. A week later, smoke bombs greet World Bank head James Wolfensohn at a conference in Amsterdam, where he complains, "I'm getting so tired of all the security."

To plan actions *against the IMF and World Bank's meetings in Prague, activists from across Europe and the US came together months earlier and developed a plan to lay siege to the conference centre, blockading the bankers and delegates inside. Because of the diverse nature of the crowd, a 'diversity of tactics' was agreed upon, and 20,000 people divided into four separate marches: blue for those who engaged in more aggressive tactics on the West side, pink for the socialist contingent which carried placards around from the East, yellow for staging a highly visible yet impossible push from the North, and pink and silver, for a carnivalesque approach from the South.*

It was here that a powerful vision emerged, a vision developed by 12 women, who joined forces with a samba band to create Tactical Frivolity. Their idea: to dress up in outrageous costumes – half Bacchanalian ball-gown, half Rio carnival dancer – and confront the police, unmasked, and armed only with feminism and feather dusters.... By exposing their vulnerability, dancing and singing, and generally being silly, they not only subverted the idea of confrontation, but also demanded that the police see them as human beings.

The force of their humour was unstoppable. Hilariously, one tactically frivolous woman was seen alone, advancing on a cluster of cops, who retreated clumsily uphill before the power of her magic wand-like feather duster. Many policemen endured a fierce struggle not to laugh, failing to maintain the grim, deadly serious posture demanded by their position. A few were even caught dancing!

The delegates eventually escaped from their meeting, hours late, and on public transport – probably the first time many of them had seen the inside of a subway. The actions ended in success, with the last day's meetings cancelled after poor attendance the previous day.

It's Got To Be Silver and Pink: on the road with Tactical Frivolity

by Kate Evans

London. Twelve women, two trucks, two men, one ultimately useful journalist. I realize something is different. Usually people tat down to just one small rucksack for a journey. Not this time. Everyone brought everything: tent poles, sewing machines, brewery tubing, tinfoil, space blankets, medical kits, gaffer tape, glue, whatever we thought might be useful, plus personal tat. All in a pile on the floor of my truck. Fuck. Packed it really badly and headed off to Calais with the vehicle leaning five degrees to the left.

Calais. Really fucked already. We park up on the sand dunes to make breakfast for 15 people. Carla performs miracles on the all the tat; ruthlessly subdividing the available space, folding, sorting and beating it into the corners, leaving us with an almost liveable space in the middle. Which is great, but for the rest of the journey we have to ask her where anything is. The rest of us head to the dunes and the sunshine, dragging piles of clothes and fabric. It looks amazing; the hills are strewn with yards of flashing silver and lurid pink. We dig out silver leggings, fluffy waistcoats, frocks, socks, gloves, and hold them up to each other. This is going to be silly. This is going to be good. The journalist wanders around the periphery, sucking a pencil and making notes:

"*First night is the beach outside Calais. By 11.00 am three French botanists studying dune life have stopped in their tracks, dumbfounded. One hundred feet away the women are acting Priscilla of the Desert. Out of the lorry have poured sacks of pink and grey cloth, glitter, bo-peep outfits, sequins, g-strings, bras, fur, crushed velvet, lycra, giant metal costume structures, wings, trimmings and hats.*

"*C'est cool", says Pierre, speechless.*

"*Glam it up, girls. Pink is power. Wearing pink in threatening situations changes everything. It calms the anarchists and the cops," says Kate. "You change minds much faster by celebration and smashing peoples' sense of reality.*" – **the journalist**

The drive was a rush. Up by seven, on the move by ten. Two trucks traveling in convoy, one divining the route, the other following the exhaust. Late at night, parking under a tree, in a field, in a forest, building a fire, some singing, some talking, some crying. Got pulled over by the police just before the Czech border, and they were very amused by our singing, wise cracking, dance routines. They checked our passports and waved us on. Let that be the Czech police's problem, they thought.

At the border everything was different. A lot colder. We suddenly felt stupid in our random silver clothing. And fucking freezing too. Men in black shut me out of my truck and searched it inch by inch for drugs, which freaked me right out, cause they could plant anything. They shook my homeopathy suspiciously, sampled my St John's Wort oil (hope it cheered them up), and stopped just short of searching the drawer with my pink sparkly vibrator in, for which I was extremely grateful. They said we couldn't come into the Czech Republic unless we had money for our stay. Max, quite miraculously, produced £900 from his bum bag which he hadn't wanted to leave behind in his squat. They said our vehicles were not roadworthy. We pointed out that the large black patch under Mel's truck was in fact, not oil, but the overflow from the washing up. They said they did not like campers in the Czech Republic (as another Winnebago sped past) and said they would confiscate our tools and knives. I was hiding my adjustable spanner in my sock when the journalist wandered over to the head of customs, showed him his press card and World Bank

---

now is that I wasn't able to destroy more of it," says Bové, who is sentenced to three months in prison.

>> July 17 >> The Earth Liberation Front destroys two acres of genetically engineered corn and several greenhouses of seedlings in Cold Spring Harbor, New York, US. Graffiti highlighting the hazards of GE adorns the walls.

>> July 21-23 >> The G8 meet in a luxury beach resort on a remote peninsula in Okinawa, Japan, protected by 20,000 heavily armed police, six navy warships and a mile and a half nautical exclusion zone. Debt campaigners send 200,000 protest emails to the G8, protesting that the $750 million cost of the summit would have been enough to cancel the servicing of one year's debt from Guyana, Rwanda, Laos, Zambia, Nicaragua, Benin, Cambodia, and Haiti. Numerous counter-summits and protests take place, including a human chain of 27,000 Okinawans with gags over their mouths surrounding the US's Kadena Air Force Base, demanding the withdrawal of the 26,000 US troops permanently stationed on the island.

>> August 3 >> Over 700,000 Colombian workers go on a 24 hour general strike to protest IMF-imposed austerity measures. The 2001 budget is announced by

The pink and silver posse brightens up the streets. Prague, Czech Republic

"The agenda had been taken over by the protesters. Prague created quite an impression with the World Bank/IMF bureaucracy. I sensed that after Prague, the words of civil society will be taken much more seriously ..."

– World Bank staffer, October 2000

Conference accreditation, and asked if that meant he wasn't allowed in either. The poor man's face crumbled. "But you are not, with ... them?" he whispered incredulously. The journalist replied that he was, actually. And we were allowed in.

That set the tone for our experiences with the Czech authorities. Police arrived at our park-up that night. Plain-clothes police probably followed us into Praha the next afternoon. We were pulled over twice more before we found a camp site and secret police tailed us indiscreetly to the pub. We started a book on how many times we'd been asked to show our passports. "It does make you feel safe", said Kim. "Mm", agreed Ronni, "we're sure not to be raped or mugged". The constant surveillance had taken its toll on fellow activists. We phoned the number on the flyer when we got into Prague, to be told not to leave the vehicles on the street, or in a secure lock-up, they would be impounded,

Katharine Ainger

what were we doing bringing our homes with us anyway? And meet Someone (who was using a code name for this operation) in a Chinese restaurant, opposite a certain metro station, for further instructions which it would be unsafe to issue over the phone. Very fucking cloak and dagger. Some of us went off to meet Agent Paranoia, most of us went to the laundrette, and I napped in the back of the truck.

Where were we going to put the vehicles? I thought bringing my home would be an asset, not a liability. But now we realized we couldn't just expect there to be a traveller site in the middle of Prague. Squatting was illegal; campsites expensive; we couldn't even park on the street for an hour and every time we moved them we got pigged. There was a real possibility I was going to spend September 26 babysitting my truck. Then we got lucky again. Friends told us of Ladronka, a crumbly squatted farmhouse in the middle of a park to the West of the city. With a yard (hee hee). It was inhabited by an indefinable number of people who weren't particularly into being associated with the protest and possibly risking their home, but we met them, and fortunately they all fancied Carla. So we were in.

The convergence centre opened and filled with activists from around the world. So many groovy people! So many sexy groovy people! Unfortunately we wasted all our precious socializing time having interminable, slightly pointless seven-hour meetings in five languages about where we would be on the day. What we didn't discuss was what we would do when we got to where we couldn't agree we would be. And I suppose that was good, because we didn't have interminable, divisive, and slightly pointless discussions about violence versus nonviolence, man, and what is violence anyway when the State is like killing people every day, man. And the people in the World Bank eat Third World babies for breakfast, so if they get bricked then hey, that's their fault, although, of course, symbolically placing a flower on each of their breasts would be great. Yeah, I was quite glad we avoided having a general 'fluffy' versus 'spiky' debate, but afterwards I wished that our affinity group had a chat about what we would do at the police lines.

Back at Ladronka, a riot of pink and silver had erupted from the back of the vans. Vi was going to be a butterfly,

---

the Finance Minister as "the budget of sweat and tears," with 5,000 public sector jobs to go and wage increases to be kept below the rate of inflation. The conditions laid out in the $2.7 billion IMF loan require Colombia to further open its economy, privatize public companies and cut back spending. "This is a protest strike, it's a political strike, to call the Colombian peoples' attention to the need to tell the government that we are not inclined to keep carrying the rich people of this country on our shoulders," says the president of the National Federation of State Service Workers, Wilson Borja.

>> August 16 >> The Biotic Baking Brigade's division on Prince Edward Island successfully carries out Operation "Pie Minister", launching a Roundup-Ready Frankencream pie in the face of Canadian Prime Minister (and first head of state to be pied) Jean Chrétien, in an effort to highlight his failure to take a stand against the introduction of genetically engineered foods into Canada.

>> August 24 >> A 24-hour general strike opposing IMF-backed economic reforms sweeps across Honduras. Organized by the Popular Bloc, and comprising farmers, workers, and students, the protest closes universities, affecting 60,000 students, and blocks services at

Dee a bird; Ronni made a huge spiral dress with polka dot skirts and a feather duster fairy-godmother wand. Caz started constructing nine-foot high samba dancer fantails which filled half the yard. A two foot pink Marie Antoinette wig, a silver flash Superman costume, a floor length tinsel ball gown. Natalie was in pink shin pads and soldier's helmet; Jane was a scaly silver bat-winged thing. The lads in the house would wander through from time to time, shooting us bemused and incredulous glances. One afternoon we were bent over sewing machines in the slanting autumn sunshine, splashes of pink unrolled around us, and crumpled silver foil escaping across the yard. A police helicopter suddenly rose over the rooftop and hovered 80 feet above us with a camera. It must be such a picture. Tuesday came. We all dressed up. We rocked.

What was the action like? I can't really describe it. It was pink. Our whole fucking march was pink. We'd decked out so many people in a totally silly, non-threatening colour, and it had all happened because Caz had been wandering through the scrap store three months earlier, thinking "It's got to be silver and pink." Doing an action in a carnival costume is mental. For women, facing all-male riot police, it is a way of exploiting our vulnerability, making them see that we're people, not just things to be hit. We all got hit anyway, but there were some charmed moments. Caz hung back when others ran, walking in her huge silver costume. With her pink confection of hair and voluminous skirts she was like the figurehead of our march, a woman, alone. She and the line of pigs met, and they didn't hit her, it was as if, for a moment, they couldn't hit her; they pushed her instead. She fell, and the crowd surged back for her, and the police were checked for a moment, seeing us all move. The next instant she was up again, but her wig came off; her head looked naked without it. The crowd surged again for the wig and a copper booted it back to us. Caz was restored to full glory. She kept going, she really had no fear.

"I've become aware that I carry fear, everybody carries fear, you know, but I'll have fear in instances that I don't think I should, like fear of talking to strangers. I've tracked down my fear to see what's at the end of it and it's a man who's faceless who's going to hurt me in some way. That is what I'm ultimately frightened of. I'm not frightened of being on my own or of nature, you know, I'm frightened that some man is going to hurt me. I was aware of this before I went to Prague – that I was actually in some way going there to face this fear because I would end up facing a man in black who had an intention to hurt me at the end of the day.

"So these riot police protecting the World Bank and the IMF had sort of become symbolic for all my fears, all the men out there that might hurt me, and I was actually quite up for it, I wanted to face that, I wanted to go and stand up against the faceless man and just see what happened, you know. But we all got dressed up in our pink and silver and we went on the subway and were whooping and excited, and when we got to the park there was just pink and silver everywhere. And there wasn't time to be fearful." – **Ronni, Tactical Frivolity**

I was dancing alone in a side street while the crowd streamed past me. There was a line of police there and I didn't want them to surge out and attack the crowd from the side. A sweet looking guy in a green camouflage vest tapped me on the elbow. "You come with me, I know a way in. I think it will be a good action, yes?" Fuck yes! He ducked through a door in a side street and gave me a leg up onto the roof of a garage. "I make graffiti often in my home town. And this, I think, makes it easy for me to see a way across the roofs." I scrambled like a spider under a three-foot gap beneath an apple tree (with my fan tail) and through a dark corridor. My companion paused with his hand on the handle of a door. Concussion grenades were going off outside. We emerged slickly into the sunshine and joined a waiting crowd of delegates as inconspicuously as one possibly can in a floor length silver tinsel dress, pink Ascot hat, and a nine-foot fantail of silver streamers. Cop after cop thundered past us to reinforce their lines. The pink march was within 400 yards of the doors of the Congress Centre. The police were moving in with water cannons and [tear] gas. Two women were bundled past with blood flowing down their faces. And there we were, standing with a line of delegates who were waiting for the metro. Very unfortunately, I did not at this point manage to think of single politically incisive statement. High on adrenaline, I made meaningless small talk with a man from the Royal Canadian mint. Then someone asked me what I thought of the World Bank, so I had a little rant at her, but then I realized she was a journalist. The delegates melted away, leaving only newshounds, hungry for pictures of violence, [which I, with my pink feather boa, did not have to offer].

Kate Evans is a cartoonist. Her work includes *Copse, the Cartoon Book of Tree Protesting*, and *Funny Weather We're Having at the Moment*

Resources:

» Kate Evans' cartoons: www.kartoonkate.co.uk

» Since Prague, Pink and Silver has become the colour of creative resistance blocs. For Pink and Silver reports and pics:
www.schnews.org.uk/sotw/rhythms-of-resistance.htm
www.nadir.org/nadir/initiativ/agp/free/genoa/pinksilver.htm

---

hospitals and major highways.

>> September 7 >> Over five million people vote on an independently organized referendum asking if Brazil should discontinue IMF reforms. Organized by the National Council of Bishops, and Jubilee 2000, the 'unofficial' referendum is an overwhelming success, with nearly everyone rejecting the IMF presence. To mark the end of six days of voting and Brazil's Independence Day, a demonstration draws thousands of protesters under the banner of 'Cry of the Excluded'. All of Brazil's major cities see widespread participation, with more than 100,000 people in São Paulo, despite the government's assertion that the referendum was "a stupid, isolated project undertaken by 'minorities'." Solidarity marches take place simultaneously in Ecuador, Colombia, Bolivia, Argentina, Mexico, Honduras, and Paraguay.

>> September 11-13 >> A week-long Carnival for Global Justice takes place in resistance to the World Economic Forum meeting in Melbourne Australia. Activists erect a tent city opposite the casino where the Forum is meeting, and 10,000 activists surround it, preventing one-third of the delegates from entering, and forcing a quick cancellation of the delegates'

The Narmada (the name means "one who endows with bliss") is the longest river in India, sacred to the villagers who live along her banks. They carry on their daily existence under the long shadow of the Sardar Sarovar dam being constructed – synonymous with all that is wrong with big development. In the 1980s, the World Bank funded the Indian government to build 30 big dams, 135 medium and 3,000 small dams along the Narmada Valley, threatening to turn the entire river into a series of lakes which will submerge the villages and displace between 100,000 to 1,000,000 people.

Since 1986, the Narmada Bachao Andolan (NBA Save Narmada Movement) has spread across the villagers in the Valley, against the dam, against submergence, in favour of people's rights to the natural resources they depend upon to survive. The villagers have sworn to stay and drown with their children, preferring death to the inadequate resettlement programme or a life in the slums – for them, another kind of death. They have fasted, sat-in, occupied the dam-site, faced baton charges by police, gone to court and to jail. Time and time again as the monsoon arrives, they have stood up to their necks in the rising, swirling waters.

The dam will not bring the water promised to the drought-prone areas of Gujarat, but to the industrial zones where, already, huge sugar-processing plants are being built in anticipation. Gujarat's minister has declared that the villagers should smile while making the 'small sacrifice' of giving up their homes for the greater common good.

Since then, Medha Patkar has led the fight against the Narmada dams and the NBA, part of the National Association of Peoples' Movements, which unites untold millions of the unrepresented across India. These are Medha's words as she carried a banner through the streets of Prague with the pink and silver group during the September 26 protests against the World Bank and IMF in 2000.

A River Comes to Prague

by Medha Patkar

This day [S26] is not about Northern protest, but about the solidarity all around the world. It's not about the First and Third World, North and South. There is a section of the population that is just as present in the US, and in England – the homeless, unemployed people, on the streets of London – which is also there in the indigenous communities, villages, and farmers of India, Indonesia, the Philippines, Mexico, Brazil. All those who face the backlash of this kind of economics are coming together – to create a newer, people-centred world order.

We're here because our movement is the movement of the people from the Valley of Narmada fighting big dams, which the World Bank was originally involved in. But our movement successfully forced them to withdraw.

We battle for the true kind of development which is equitable and sustainable, and believe very strongly that the World Bank, IMF, the WTO, and the multinational corporations are taking society in exactly the opposite direction. That is, towards an inequitable, non-sustainable, and unjust world. We feel that the corporations and their tentacles have now taken over, not just markets, but the lives of the people. The people have to resist. The people have to say no, not just imports, but to impositions. Imposition of culture, imposition of consumerism, imposition of a new kind of money and market based economics and related politics.

And we know that we cannot fight this alone in our

corner of the world and in an isolated way. It is necessary to build alliances among the women's movement, the fish workers' movement, the farmers' movement, the tribal and indigenous peoples' movement – all those who live on the natural-resource-base and their own labour are being evicted and being impoverished.

And then we have to gather together all the sensitive and sensible people of the world to reject the corporate sector and this kind of lending and the export credit guarantees. And these will be replaced by ordinary people's ways of exchange, of knowledge, ideas, of technology – that will be the real empowerment of the people.

Medha Patkar is at the forefront of the *Narmada Bachao Andolan* (Save Narmada Movement), using Gandhian methods of nonviolent struggle or satyagraha. She is a leading inspiration in challenging capitalist globalization and fascistic nationalism in India.

Resources: » Friends of River Narmada (not *Narmada Bachao Andolan* but a support site) www.narmada.org
» *Drowned Out*, a film on Narmada Bachao Andolan by www.spannerfilms.net

Karen Robinson

Woman prays next to half submerged temple. Narmada River, India

---

banquet at the Hilton. Several delegates' presentations end up being canceled, including Bill Gates', because of the overwhelming protester presence.

>> September 26 >> Global Day of Action, Prague.

>> October 1 >> Thousands march to the US naval base on the island of Vieques, Puerto Rico, and 65 people cut the surrounding fence and trespass onto the base, for which they are arrested. The US navy controls about 70 per cent of the island and uses it to conduct military exercises which have stunted the island's economy, displaced many people, and decimated the environment.

>> October 19 - 20 >> Twenty thousand workers and students erupt onto the streets of Seoul, South Korea against the Asia-Europe Meeting (ASEM) which is sealed off by 30,000 riot and plain clothes police officers and an exclusion zone. "We Oppose Neoliberalization and Globalization!" shouts a banner, as march heads towards the conference centre.

>> November 16-18 >> In Cincinnati, US, thousands protest the meeting of the Trans-Atlantic Business Dialogue (TABD); 500 picket at a supermarket which refuses to support striking farm workers; an "End Corporate Rule" banner is hung during a symphony for

It's a question that is sometimes asked: "I can see why you might target global organizations (G8, WTO, IMF) that are clearly undemocratic, secretive and self-serving, but why target the European Union? Surely protesting against that is the preserve of right wing nationalists and xenophobes...?"

Some answers were to be found on the French Riviera. The EU summit in Nice from 7-11 December 2000 was a crucial meeting, for it continued the expansion of the EU from the Atlantic in the West, to the borders with Russia, and the Ukraine in the East. For corporations who have lobbied for expansion, this signalled new markets, with fewer local controls and lower production costs achieved through a reservoir of cheap yet often highly skilled labour. Of course they also understand that cheaper wages in the East might also be the lever to lower pay in the West!

What activists understand is that the imposition of 'fiscal discipline' and 'liberalization' – as the new entrants try to bring their economies in line with the EU – means that transnational corporations eventually replace domestic production. The export of raw materials will increase with obvious environmental impacts, unemployment will grow, and social provisions will be lowered, leading to greater inequality.

At Nice, the EU also proposed and subsequently implemented the rather grand sounding 'Charter of Fundamental Rights', which despite its name is effectively a retreat from hard won rights gained in struggle. This Charter allows the European Commission to negotiate directly at the WTO in order to deregulate services and erode the conditions of those who work and benefit from them. In the US they call this 'fast track' negotiating power.

As Nice approached, the time had come to begin to tear down the walls of Fortress Europe and to disrupt the creation of yet another extended 'free' trade zone.

Nice – If You Could Only Breathe

by Arnau Facilillo

It's January 2000, at the World Economic Forum in Davos, Switzerland. The ex-communist President of Poland is surrounded by a horde of high-ranking executives asking him about the next privatizations. Without the slightest blush and in full view of the cameras, the director of a transnational demands immediate measures, and licks his moustaches. The president retorts that he has already privatized 75 per cent of the public enterprises, even while admitting that the energy sector is ripe. But the horde wants more, they're hungry, they love to see their prey caught in a trap. Then the prisoner-president pulls back a bit more, and in an excess of Stockholm syndrome [when the kidnapped falls in love with the kidnapper] he quips: "Hey, when everything's private, what's going to be left for you to privatize?" At which point a hyena rises up amidst the laughter, proposing: "The Government!"

The story, which is true, continues with mounting laughter and the president saying yes, he's with the programme, but maybe some of his ministers won't agree. Let's take this as a parable of the European construction as it stands today, amidst the transfer of powers from the parliaments to the boards of directors. All beneath the guiding lights of the Washington Consensus, the theoretical basis for the domineering expansion of the big North

American, Japanese, and European firms, promoted to the rank of owners of the global village, with police support from the single superpower, the United States. Just to sum it all up. So the politicians have nothing left to do but to validate on paper what's already happening in reality. And that's why they all went to Nice. They went to sign for liberalization (with article 133) and the cutback of social rights (with the Charter of Fundamental Rights). And we went to try to stop them.

Unions and social movements from all over Europe marched massively on 6 December, with different agendas but a shared critique – you have to start somewhere. There were 100,000 of us. The next day we weren't quite so many. The big unions went home. The Global Action Express carrying 1,500 Italians was blocked at the border by – 4,500 policemen! Those who tried to go on the free French trains were gassed at their departure cities. But anyway, we hit the streets early Thursday morning, not very organized but full of desire. The confrontations were settled indiscriminately by the cops with volleys of tear gas. A man who went to get information about the prisoners was hit with a tear gas grenade right in the police station, and suffered an epileptic fit. The demonstrators who went to the Central Station to protest against the delay of the Italians were dispersed by apprentice 'robocops', who banged on their shields with truncheons to drive fear into our hearts, and courage into theirs. The ATTAC members – an international network campaigning for a global tax on financial speculation – who tried to 'invade' Monaco to denounce offshore tax-havens also ran up against the forces of disorder when they lay siege with tear gas and water cannons to the gymnasium

"[Enlargement] will bring great economic benefits. These countries will bring ... material resources, including land and energy, and they will bring markets for our products."

– The European Round Table of Industrialists, corporate lobby group

---

the TABD delegates, resulting in a police attack under the chandeliers; and a picket greets the TABD delegates at their banquet. On the final day, the police turn up costumed in brand new riot gear, and busy themselves harassing and issuing tickets to activists. They disrupt the closing march, arresting and tear gassing the group, and the day ends with martial law imposed.

>> November 19-22 >> Fighting the privatization of their water, the Sri Lankan National Alliance for Protection of Water Rights holds four days of action. People from three different parts of the country caravan to Colombo, holding picket lines, distributing handbills exposing and denouncing the WB and WTO policies, and collecting signatures along the way.

>> November 26 >> A caravan of 150 Egyptian people bring donations of food and medicine to Palestine. Intending to set up an art exhibit in tents at the Egyptian border of Palestine in Rafah, the activists are shocked when Egyptian border guards refuse them crossing. They are forced to surrender the donations to representatives from Palestinian NGOs in the city of Aarish, 12 miles before the border. Unexpectedly, demonstrations arise throughout Aarish and on the Palestinian side of the border. Thus is born the Popular

that the municipality had finally conceded to the demonstrators. Tension and bad weather, but no lapse in spirits, with the cry of *"Tous ensemble!"* (we're all together) repeated every moment.

"A great step ahead for the Europe of business": that was the headline of *Le Figaro* the day after the riots in Nice. So not only did we fail to stop the summit, but the great 'decision-makers' went on reinforcing the ultraliberal principles that serve as the guiding spirit and fundamental life-breath for the reconstruction of Europe, while they continued dismantling the social pact that had been put together by the post-war societies. Even with all that,

Meyer / Tendence Floue

Tear gas and water cannons protect the EU summit. Nice, France

"In the West we have mature markets. We are already consuming everything that we are able to consume. You cannot drive two cars at the same time. So we have a slow growth economy ... To the East of us, we have around a hundred million people with sophisticated tastes who lack all the items we are already consuming. They need those items."

– General Zygmunt Tyszkkiewicz, Director of the Union of Industrial and Employers' Confederations of Europe

political infighting and disputes over vested interests kept them from signing things definitively, and for the moment there are only non-binding agreements. In any case the decisions are taken and will continue to be taken, inexorably. Decisions proving that Thatcher and Reagan didn't preach in the desert: the borders close ever more tightly down on people, and open up ever wider to commodities. Genetically modified foods will find their place, with the help of their lobbies. The real decisions drift toward technocratic organs like the European Commission, the European Central Bank. The tax havens and offshore exchanges will go on coughing up speculative bubbles. The employers' organizations will keep on growing, in Brussels, Berlin, or Davos. Not to mention the decisions that won't be made – the decisions that could put an end to this era of transnational feudalism, and give politics back to the citizens.

But it's not all about blocking international summits. In Prague the meetings were put off, but the wealth goes on concentrating around its own navel, the supermarkets are still overflowing with useless junk, the structural adjustment plans are still being applied pretty much everywhere (Europe included: the convergence criteria for the single currency are nothing more than disguised adjustment plans), Banks go on making 20 per cent profits annually, and foreign debt, the arms trade, and open season on immigrants are all doing fine – to give just a few examples.

Still the most important thing about these counter-summits, the dissonant notes of globalization, is not to break the bones of some high-ranking executive but to break out of the ghetto, end the isolation, or in other words, to go on weaving ourselves into a great network, and to nourish a transcontinental cry. Because despite the media circus, these counter-summits are a good opportunity to see each other, and to be seen.

It's about finding spaces where money doesn't measure the value of all things; it's about leaving lies and solitude behind. Next stop: a better world.

Arnau Facilillo currently lives in Can Masdeu, a squatted paradisiacal eco-community in rural Barcelona. He was a freelance participant in the recently dissolved MRG (Global Resistance Movement) – dissolved to avoid the boring politics of representation and branded resistance.

Resources:

» Corporate Observatory Europe, research and campaign group targeting the threats to democracy, equity, social justice and the environment posed by corporations and their lobby groups.Incredible site detailing your worse fears about capital : www.xs4all.nl/~ceo

» State Watch monitors the state and civil liberties in the E.U. Everything you wanted and didnt eant to know about what the state is doing to limit your few remaining freedoms: www.statewatch.org

---

Committee in Solidarity with the Palestinian Intifada.

>> December 6-8 >> At least 90,000 people demonstrate in Nice, France, despite the lifting of the Schengen agreement, which leaves thousands of internationals stranded at the border, and the halting of many domestic Nice-bound trains. The protests are against European Union expansion of 'free' trade negotiating rights, and are the largest Northern protests of their kind to date. Tear gas and pepper spray are used liberally by the 15,000 police, who in their zeal, also manage to gas delegates inside the meeting due to faulty ventilation systems, sending President Chirac into coughing fits during his opening speech.

>> December 9 >> Thirty people from six different countries storm the stage during a closed session of government negotiations over global warming at the UN COP6 climate summit, in Den Haag, Netherlands. The hall is eventually cleared of delegates and sealed off to press while the protesters are assaulted by security. Meanwhile, five activists drop a banner from the roof in protest at emissions trading. Another banner is hung directly outside the Congress Centre, which says "Climate Talks = Money Talks."

>> Continued on page 317 >>

The control society

It's a Friday night in Seattle. A line stretches down the street and around the block, as hundreds queue to get in to see ¡TchKung!, an infamous eco-punk band. Their shows traditionally end with the performers leading the crowd into the streets where anything can happen, from occupying an intersection with a 'construction crew' handing out drum sticks for people to accompany the band on a giant metal sculpture next to a bonfire, to the crowd racing off to trash an under-construction Niketown. Although they haven't played in three years, there are many old fans in the crowd entertaining others with tales of outrageous past shows.

But as people enter the club, they come to what appears to be a registration booth for the newly-created Department of Homeland Security (DHS), a Cabinet-level office of the US Government begun in the aftermath of the September 11 2001 terrorist attacks which unites previously separate agencies: Federal Emergency Management Agency (FEMA), the Coast Guard, the Customs Service, and the Border Patrol, and tasks these agencies with the mission of "defending the homeland". A large American flag is draped over the table, upon which is a patriotic arrangement of flowers and flags and two laptop computers. Camouflage netting surrounds the whole set-up. Two men in suits staff the table, asking people to volunteer to report any suspicious activities, saying, "It's up to people like you to keep this country safe and secure." The laptops feature the website of the Department where one can anonymously submit the name and contact information of any friend, neighbour, or boss who has aroused suspicion. The site also features multiple-choice questions about the 'war on terror' so visitors can test their knowledge. Periodically a woman in military garb comes to consult with the men in suits. She wears the DHS logo and seems to be monitoring activities throughout the club. Occasionally one of the men breaks the rhythm of his patter and starts listening to his earpiece. He then pulls someone aside for more intense questioning, maybe asks to look in their bag. Some people are even given 'cash' rewards for submitting a name.

Meyer / Tendence Floue

This was, of course, a spoof. However Orwellian the DHS seems, as far as anyone knows it has not yet stooped to the level of recruiting snitches at political punk shows. Yet the response to the spoof was astonishing. At each of the six shows on the Pacific Northwest tour, countless people believed that the registration booth was real. Some people entered the club, saw the booth, and angrily stormed out. Many others attempted to sneak past unnoticed, as though getting away with something. Still others expressed their outrage, shouting angrily about their civil rights being violated, and about government intrusion. Plenty of people gave names (which ended up on the bands' mailing lists), and not all of them knew it was a joke.

But what was most disturbing was the group that resentfully complied. Refusing eye contact, they shuffled their feet and reluctantly answered questions, looking for all the world like school kids being called before a strict principal and reprimanded. They submitted to the presumed authority, offered their bags up for search, and even begrudgingly gave a few names. No matter how overtly offensive, terrifying, and over the top you get, certain people will still believe you. These particular people submitted out of fear – fear of government, fear that all of their worst nightmares could become reality, fear of the unknown, fear that they were powerless to stop the deluge of repression.

Fear is powerful. It can be all encompassing, completely debilitating, impossible to ignore. Steve Biko, who was imprisoned in South Africa under apartheid, was referring to the power of fear when he said, "The most powerful weapon of the oppressor is the mind of the oppressed." And it is exactly that fear which the real Department of Homeland Security and its counterparts worldwide rely on to push their agendas further. The more fearful your population the easier it is to get them to accept oppressive measures, whether its censorship, racial and religious profiling, detention of immigrants, or increased powers of surveillance.

"ECONOMIC OPPRESSION AND MILITARY REPRESSION ARE FLIP SIDES OF THE SAME GLOBALIZATION COIN. THE ECONOMIC RAPE OF THE POOR THAT ACCOMPANIES GLOBALIZATION COULD NOT STAND WITHOUT THE REPRESSIVE MILITARY APPARATUS THAT BRUTALIZES PEOPLE WHO RISE UP TO RESIST. THOSE WHO OPPOSE THE GLOBALIZATION OF GREED AND THOSE WHO WORK TO END US TRAINING OF REPRESSIVE FOREIGN ARMIES ARE JOINED IN ONE EFFORT."

- Hendrik Voss, School of the Americas Watch

Wearing masks, we are visible

What was interesting about the iTchKung! theatre piece, and what was so provocative to those who encountered it, was the unmasking of the DHS. All in the audience had heard of this department and yet few had actually encountered a manifestation of it. By bringing into reality a possible scenario of its practices, the performers triggered the imaginations of everyone – what else might the DHS do? Its clandestinity gives it power; as long as it remains unknown it is difficult to resist. But by demystifying it, some of the fear it feeds on is neutralized. Instead it becomes a focal point for anger and defiance.

Clandestinity can be the key to our survival, or it can be our downfall. It can bring us together or deeply divide us. Our clandestinity involves secrecy, marginality, anonymous direct action, breaking the law, hiding, escaping, going underground. It can be a gift to the movement – but it is a dangerous, double-edged gift.

It can render us invisible as secret border-crossers, anonymous web hackers, or workplace saboteurs. It can also neutralize us, if our vast potential support-base only sees us through the lens of spectacularly distorted media as dangerous and frightening. It can render us ineffective if we allow our own fear of repression to create a cult of security that leaves us intolerant, exclusive, suspicious of outsiders and other ways of working, and paranoid. Such groups are among the easiest for the state to break.

We must remember that clandestinity is a tool, one of many that we have available to us. We can learn to use it when appropriate, and set it aside when not.

For our clandestinity is easily misunderstood. When we wear masks or disguises, we are accused of being ashamed of the work we are doing; when we work stealthily or at night, we are assumed to be committing dangerous, violent, or illegal actions.

We have studied history, and we know what happens to those who withdraw their consent and fight back – they sometimes are arrested, tortured, driven mad, isolated. As dissenters, our very survival sometimes hinges on our ability to be clandestine, to be secret, to hide, to stay a few steps ahead of our enemy who would reduce us to thoughtless utopians, raving mad lunatics, rabble-rousers, even terrorists. Yet at the same time, we must refuse to disappear, refuse to retreat to the margins of extreme violence and despair. For these are the places they long for us to inhabit, the places where they can set the terms, where they call the shots, and where we slowly become broken and ineffective.

Clandestinity is about protecting ourselves while opening ourselves up to new possibilities, about creating space and sharing it with people we have never met, people with whom we may disagree. It is about remaining ahead of those in power, but recognizable to each other, to those who share our struggles and are looking for us as we look for them. Our proposals and alternatives must also be recognizable, familiar enough to fit the imaginations of all people, and yet shockingly unfamiliar to those in power, as what we want is above and beyond their wildest dreams.

We have a long legacy of clandestinity behind us, protecting us from those in power, who have interminably criminalized us for being different: for being queer, for being poor, for being women, for being people of colour, for being revolutionary, for refusing marriage, for being landless, for rejecting the expansion of global capital, for wanting to survive, and for wanting more than merely to survive.

Consistently, we have fought back, sometimes overtly, more often by shape shifting, seeming to be what we are not, going in drag, dressing up, dressing down, disguising our faces, changing our names. Eighteenth century pirates Anne Bonny and Mary Read dressed as men and sailed the seas, terrorizing slave traders and looters of the 'New World', trading the drudgery of plantation life and unfortunate marriages for adventure and freedom.

In England the Luddites, faced with what was the largest repressive campaign ever mounted by the English monarchy, disguised themselves as women, clergy, and military officers and disappeared into the shadows after a night of destroying factory machinery which had made their jobs redundant, often walking through crowds prepared to lynch them, if only they could find them! In the US, Harriet Tubman fearlessly conducted over 300 slaves along the Underground Railroad to freedom – often disguised as a man, and relying on an intricate network of safe houses.

Phoolan Devi, the 'Bandit Queen' of India, employed a myriad of disguises after becoming an outlaw at age twenty and spending the next four years living in the desert ravines of northwest India, outwitting the police, leading gangs of bandits in stealing from wealthy higher castes, and distributing the wealth among the poor and lower caste people. In Chiapas, Mexico, an undetermined number of undercover Zapatistas joined the police force, and the military, and then in 1993 volunteered to work on that most difficult shift to fill, New Year's Eve. The rest is history in the making.

The enemy within

"The population immediately [becomes] the internal enemy. Any sign of life, of protest, or even mere doubt, is a dangerous challenge from the standpoint of military doctrine and national security. So complicated mechanisms of prevention and punishment have been developed ... To operate effectively, the repression must appear arbitrary. Apart from breathing, any human activity can constitute a crime ... State terrorism aims to paralyze the population with fear."

– Eduardo Galeano, *Open Veins of Latin America - Five Centuries of the Pillage of a Continent*, Monthly Review Press, 1998

As the wave of resistance to capitalism swells, threatening to overwhelm it with alternative demands for democracy, justice, and freedom, the powerful are developing and refining a familiar strategy. So we have become witness to hasty retreats, brutal repression, mass obfuscation, and serious attempts to completely discredit the movement. Thirty years ago, intelligence agencies used criminalization strategies similar to those used now, in their attempt to thwart vibrant and participatory grassroots movements that had become a serious challenge to the system. Times have not changed much, and we should learn from the history and legacy of our predecessors in order to avoid failure, where many of us end up imprisoned, exiled, dead, or in madhouses.

There is a clearly discernible pattern to criminalization, repeated around the world, and even taught at international policing conferences. The events surrounding the actions in September 2000 against the IMF and World Bank in Prague, Czech Republic described here have direct corollaries in Seattle, London, São Paulo, Cochabamba, Seoul, Melbourne, Cancún, Genoa, Washington – and everywhere people have dared to stand up and say no.

In the months leading up to a mass demonstration the media runs numerous stories in a concerted campaign to terrify local citizens who are not involved in social change and dissuade them from possible participation or support. In Prague, rumours flew between newspapers that international travelling anarchists were descending on the city in order to smash and burn it. Eleven thousand police officers – a quarter of the police in the entire country – patrolled streets during the day, and practiced manoeuvres at night. On 1 August 2000, seven weeks before the actions in Prague, the Czech daily paper *Hospodarske Noviny* quoted President Václav Havel describing the mounting tension in the city, 'as if we were preparing for a civil war'. The following day, the *Prague Post* quoted Prague's mayor, Jan Kasl, saying that some protesters "will kill if possible, if allowed".

The tension generated by these declarations reached such a level of intensity that the Ministry of the Interior published recommendations that the population "stockpile food and medicines". Furthermore, they were instructed to avoid eye contact with demonstrators, refuse their literature, and not engage in conversation with them in order to "avoid suspicious situations that could attract the attention of the police", and they warned citizens against "watching dramatic developments from a close distance because police will not discriminate when suppressing violence and riots." The Ministry of Education closed all public schools in Prague for a week, and many families were actually asked to declare in writing that the students would spend that week outside of Prague to 'protect' them from the protests.

As a result, an estimated one-fifth of the population left town for the week. In the *Prague Post* published just prior to the actions, a lead article erroneously linked anarchists to neo-nazi skinheads. Another detailed the increase in business that the summit's delegates would provide in the city's thriving sex industry, culminating with a list of "erotic entertainment" clubs – convenient and timely advertising targeted at the international money men. Nowhere was there discussion of the key issues, many of which directly affect the Czech Republic, such as the World Bank-funded Temelín nuclear power plant on the Austrian border. Nowhere was space dedicated to an investigation of exactly who these 'murderous' internationals were supposed to be, or quite what they had against Czech plate glass that they would travel from as far away as Colombia, India, Australia, or the United States just to smash windows? The story was written before events had begun to unfold.

This sort of disinformation campaign works on several levels: not only does it undermine any sympathy the local population may have, it sets the stage for the police to move in with the next stage of repression. This generally involves 'evidence' linking the protestors to violent activities. It can take the form of a simple press release, such as unsubstantiated news of a group of people turned away from the border because "they had baseball bats and they were clearly not baseball players," as a spokeswoman for the West Bohemian police force put it. It is unknown if they 'were clearly' protesters, as no one has been observed at protests swinging baseball bats, but the association is implied, and the story is repeated and becomes accepted truth, making it much easier for the police to justify their actions in the days leading up to and during the demonstration. The public has been primed with the message, "Violent protestors will descend on the city causing mayhem and riot," and of course it is always much easier to frighten people than to get them to take the risk of questioning the status quo.

The next stage of repression takes the form of a police action. The Czech Republic was one of the first European nations in recent times to completely shut down its borders to anyone who seemed like they might be a protester. A Dutch collective coming to Prague to set up a kitchen and provide food was refused entry for 24 hours, simply for wanting to feed people! A train from Italy carrying 800 people from various social movements was held at the border for 17 hours. The police had a list drawn from information provided by Interpol and the FBI – of 'known subversives' who were to be denied entry, or possibly deported. Organizers already in Prague were

"ONLY SOMEONE COMPLETELY DISTRUSTFUL OF ALL GOVERNMENT WOULD BE OPPOSED TO WHAT WE ARE DOING WITH SURVEILLANCE CAMERAS."

– NYC Police Commissioner Howard Safir, 27 July 1999

faced with overt surveillance, including being followed and filmed, harassed on the street, and prevented from holding meetings.

Finally, after this long and concerted prelude, came the actions themselves. In Prague, the police chased and beat women in pink carnival gowns who were singing, dancing, and wielding feather dusters; they arrested and brutally beat people on a peaceful blockade, and they menaced people with armoured personnel carriers and water cannons. Overwhelmed by protesters during the day, they made up for it after dark. For at least 36 hours after the main demonstration ended, police patrolled the streets in unmarked vans, indiscriminately beating, gassing, and arresting anyone who looked like a demonstrator, especially people of colour. A black American man was attacked from behind, beaten to the ground with sticks, tied up, and had a hood pulled over his head before being thrown into a car. The situation in the prisons was even worse.

To include more cities in this sort of detailed accounting begins to show a systematized picture of globalized repression. In Washington, Philadelphia,

London, and Gothenburg, police raided the convergence centres, confiscated food, medical supplies, and personal belongings, destroyed giant puppets and banners, and in Washington even claimed to have found a laboratory where protesters were manufacturing pepper spray. This turned out to be a kitchen with bags of dried chili peppers and other spices. In another instance in London, they took DNA samples from cigarette butts and soda cans, before having the squatted building – used to prepare for May Day demonstrations – razed to the ground.

In Port Moresby, Papua New Guinea four students were killed and 24 wounded during a peaceful sit in protesting IMF-mandated cuts to public services. In Barcelona, police infiltrated demonstrations, staged fights, broke windows, and violently dispersed a peaceful crowd gathered in a public plaza, after the demonstration had ended. In Argentina, 34 people were killed in a day while rising up in outrage at IMF-imposed financial and banking restrictions. In Québec City during FTAA protests, police staged a night-time raid on the medical centre, evacuating healthcare workers and patients at gunpoint into the cold dark night. In Cochabamba, young men who took part in protests to defend publicly owned, affordable drinking water were tortured and one young man was killed.

In Genoa, a letter bomb was sent to a police station in Milan and frequent bomb threats occurred at the convergence centre, none of which were thoroughly investigated. This mimicked the 'strategy of tension' tactics used in the state-terror campaign against Italian activists in the 1970s. In the climate of fear they created in Genoa, police shot and killed a young man in the streets, and the next night, planted Molotov cocktails in buildings used by the protesters for media, medical, and legal headquarters. The weapons were then used as pretexts for the infamously brutal midnight raid in which nearly a hundred people were beaten in their sleeping bags, 61 were hospitalized, many of whom continued to be beaten in hospital, and 93 were arrested. This list is never-ending; as long as we resist, they repress.

The costs of this repression are heavy. They include the steady elimination of rights and freedoms obtained through centuries of social struggle, people frightened away from joining protests, diversion from serious discussion of the issues, and a drain on our energy and paltry financial resources as we spend months or years at a time fighting excessive legal charges. They also include long-term physical and psychological damage, and the intensification of internal conflicts as we blame ourselves and each other for the repression, which – apart from technological advancements – has actually changed very little over centuries.

This process of state repression – and the media's collusion through its treatment of our movements as both absurd and threatening – creates a vicious circle which provokes increasingly negative perceptions of activism and struggle, and results in a gradual distancing of the sectors of society that are not directly involved in processes of social change. This enables the state to harden the juridical regime and to redefine as 'extremism' or 'terrorism' activities whose objectives are to increase grassroots participation in new and truly democratic political processes.

But such displays of force paradoxically reveal the state's vulnerability. Its mask begins to slip, and we begin to see that what it is protecting so desperately is not natural, not inevitable, but a carefully constructed system which requires massive force and constant effort to maintain. As the Toronto Globe and Mail wryly observed in the week following the Québec FTAA actions in 2001: "The violent response to protesters does not lend credibility to government reassurances that labour, environmental, and democracy concerns about the proposed FTAA will be addressed."

Engineers of inequity

"Your report of the anarchists that 'most are autonomous, unaccountable, small in numbers, and unwilling to divulge tactics. Prepared to attack people and property.' That just about sums up the global economy."

– John Lodge, *The Guardian* letters page, 23 July 2001

In this time and among a particular few, clandestinity has reached high art. Amidst electronic networks, boardrooms and the banal spaces of a thousand conference centres a tiny band of CEOs, politicians, and the info-tainers of the media are attempting to construct our collective futures. From their remote locations they declare that history has ended, capitalism reigns supreme, and the expansion of

"WE ARE CLANDESTINE BECAUSE WE KNOW THERE IS NO PLACE FOR US IN THE GOVERNMENT, AND IF THE PEOPLE RISE UP IN ARMED STRUGGLE LIKE THIS, THEY KNOW THEY HAVE NO PLACE. THAT'S WHY WE ORGANIZE THIS WAY, SECRETLY."

– Comandante Javier, Clandestine Revolutionary Indigenous Committee, EZLN

the market is inevitable, natural, and correct. These (mostly) men of money are the noble practitioners of the dark arts of the information age, the wizards of Oz, modern day robber barons waging war on humanity.

They are the three trade ministers who preside in secret over the WTO's trade disputes panel, whose decisions result in the overturning of national environmental and labour protections, or in punitive sanctions. They are the authors of the FTAA and MAI texts which were only released to the public after months of intense international campaigning. They are the mayor, the police chief, and all major news networks flatly denying the use of hard plastic bullets in Seattle on N30 – while simultaneously the Indymedia website was flooded with photo evidence to the contrary.

They are Riordan Roett of Chase Manhattan Bank, whose infamous leaked memo of 13 January 1995 read:

"While Chiapas, in our opinion, does not pose a fundamental threat to Mexican political stability, it is perceived to be so by many in the investment community. The government will need to eliminate the Zapatistas to demonstrate their effective control of the national territory and of security policy."

They are influential investors such as Marc Helie, a partner in Wall Street's Gramercy Advisors, who in 2000 refused to agree to a one-month extension on payment of Ecuadorian bonds that he held. Consequently, Ecuador requested a loan from the IMF, who demanded the dollarization of the economy as a loan condition. In January 2000, over a million Ecuadorian indigenous paralyzed the country with protests. And Helie bragged that he was "the man who brought Ecuador to its knees, single handed."

Clandestinity is nothing new to the architects of the global economy. It is the foundation of their entire house of cards, and permeates every structural support.

But their mask is slipping. These wizards behind the curtain are being revealed as lying profiteers playing games with smoke and mirrors, and accounting books. With every corporation forced into bankruptcy, forced into revealing its creative accounting, its complete conflagration of business and government; with every shady deal which comes to light, the mask slips further. Just as with every act of repression – every beating, every murder of a protester, a community leader, a woman or man fighting for a better world – more of their world is revealed, and we deepen our understanding of the true nature of the global economy. It is a nature which institutionalizes poverty, malnutrition, death, and despair, a fact which inspires more and more people to make the leap from believing that there must be something better, to acting on that profound conviction.

As the global justice movement grows, the powerful are forced further into hiding, retreating behind fences, the façades of democracy behind which the decisions are made. These negotiations must remain secretive – after all, they are about the future of continents and the planet, and should not be taken lightly, should not be taken by the people whose lives they will affect. When fences aren't enough, power retreats to the desert, traditionally a place for pilgrimage and cleansing, an appropriate setting for the WTO to attempt to regain legitimacy after their humiliating defeat in Seattle. Less than two months after the World Trade Center attacks, trade ministers set off on a desperate pilgrimage to Qatar for the Fourth Ministerial, armed with gas masks and the anti-anthrax drug Cipro in their briefcases, charged with the task of successfully passing a new round of trade negotiations. Maria Livanos Cattaui, Secretary General of the International Chamber of Commerce, increased the pressure, saying that if a new round were not settled on, the setback "would be acclaimed by all enemies of freer world trade and investment, including those behind the attacks on the World Trade Center and the Pentagon." By linking the anticapitalist movement with terrorism, these people turn tragedy into opportunity, and prepare a global political strategy through which they try to destroy our movements.

It has been the goal of most governments since 11 September to contain and disperse dissenters in order to get on with more serious business – that of 'fighting terrorism', war, closing borders, halting immigration, restructuring federal budgets, and restricting civil liberties in ways that make the McCarthy era seem like a minor inconvenience.

Repression has erupted on a worldwide scale, as governments scramble to pass anti-terrorism laws or strengthen existing ones. The USA PATRIOT Act, which sets a new standard of government control, defines domestic terrorism as "acts dangerous to human life that are a violation of the criminal laws" if they "appear to be intended... to influence the policy of a government by intimidation or coercion," and occur within the US. Because it is written in such vague terms, it can easily be used against peaceful protest, as most protests seek to influence policy, and of course it is the government that determines what constitutes a danger to life. The PATRIOT Act, among other things, also permits indefinite detention of non-citizens based on mere suspicion, expands the Government's ability to conduct secret searches, broadens telephone and internet surveillance by law enforcement agencies, and allows the FBI access to financial, medical, mental health, and educational records without evidence of a crime and without a court order. Similarly over-broad legislation has been enacted all around the world. Countries that have taken radical so-called anti-terrorist measures to crack down on inconvenient internal political dissent include Nepal, Thailand, India, South Korea, the Philippines, Japan, Indonesia, and Britain.

Terms of engagement

"There [has been] much romanticization of frontline action. Some [perceive] frontliners as being "hard-core" activists. The true reality tells us that it is equally demanding to incorporate the struggle into one's everyday life. We aren't trying to criticize those at the frontlines, but we need to take a deeper look at the glorification that we give those frontline actions."

– editorial collective of *Resist!*, Fernwood Publishing, 2001

As we become more effective, we will face increasing repression. For it is not our militancy, not shattered windows or graffiti, and not our moral arguments they are afraid of. It is our popularity. It is the growth of the movement, resonating across borders of nation, class, race, gender, age. The truth is: it is when they are most afraid of us that they order their crackdowns.

Until we can recognize this and develop new forms of communication and outreach, we will continue in the endless Mobius strip of debating violence versus nonviolence, diversity of tactics versus clear action guidelines. So instead, what if we collectively demanded that the Black Bloc, who engage in property damage aimed at symbolic institutions of global capital, among other actions, work at developing solid affinity groups and lines of communication amongst themselves and with the rest of us in order to make infiltration of their ranks more difficult? And what if we demanded that the pacifists, who are more likely to practice nonviolent civil disobedience, work at sharing more of their class and race privileges, along with their access to the media, while making a serious effort to have a dialogue with those who wish to engage in different, and seemingly contradictory tactics?

What if we refuse to repeat familiar mistakes such as these: one group claims ownership of an action and all that it contains, freely condemning any who disagree with them; another group proclaims their greater militancy, joining in the moral clamouring by claiming purity, holding their alienation close to heart where it festers and turns bitter, causing everyone to seem like the enemy. What if we agreed that no-one should break windows next to a nonviolent blockade, as it is vulnerable to police attack, and that no-one should physically or verbally assault people engaged in tactics which endanger no-one, and which are appropriately targeted, regardless of whether or not we agree with them?

The very notion of 'militancy' is problematic. To pretend that it is more militant to mask up and throw cobblestones at police than it is to maintain a peaceful blockade despite beatings, horse charges, and persistent attacks with pepper spray is deluded. It's just as deluded as pretending that leading a march of tens of thousands away from a major international trade summit and ending up in a vacant lot is more legitimate than tearing down a much-despised fence which cuts through the centre of your city, as in Québec City.

Both of these words, militant and legitimate, are infused with a disturbing sense of moral superiority, widening the gap between the groups which claim them as their own. We have seen this trend of romanticized 'militancy' before, and we can see how it threatens to shatter today's movements as it did throughout the seventies in the US and Europe. We have also witnessed the clamouring of certain NGOs for recognition as legitimate dissenters. We should take note of The Economist, which wrote, "The principle reason for the recent boom in NGOs is that Western governments finance them. This is not a matter of charity, but of privatization."

On the flip side, with the vanguardist application of 'militancy', popular movements in the recent past split into legal groupings and clandestine cells, and from there it was a simple campaign for the state to widen that gap, co-opting the former and infiltrating the latter.

Responding to an escalation of state repression with an escalation of violence, (by which we mean actions which intend to kill or maim people) forces entrance into a profound polarization of tactics, a head on engagement with an enemy more violent, more destructive, and more corrupt than we can comprehend. Using weapons of oppression to fight the state not only legitimizes their tactics, but also makes it difficult to discern any great difference between such groups and the state. In such a scenario, the end does not justify the means, because an end achieved through violence is unlikely to contain freedom or justice. To call for and foment such a dichotomy when there is no mass social base demanding such an escalation not only shows no sense of responsibility to the larger community of people in resistance, but also shows a political naiveté and hubris, as if the world needs another small group of elite urban self-defined 'militants' who think that they know what's best for us and will lead us all into the true path of revolution. It seems that there are enough small groups of elites making decisions for us; we don't need those which claim to be on our side any more than we need those who turn up on the other sides of the fences in Québec, Bangkok, Genoa, Cancún, São Paolo, or Davos.

However, responding to tactics with which we don't identify by condemning them and their practitioners, isolating them, in a sense, evicting certain 'elements' from the movement and disowning them, forces a collaboration with the state, however unwittingly. If we truly believe in creating a new world which promotes self-determination, autonomy, direct democracy, and diversity, we must extend that belief to our movements, recognizing that there is a place for rage, for impetuousness, for audacity and fearlessness. We must also recognize that nonviolent civil disobedience is not a universally appropriate tactic. Some Brazilian activists complained bitterly that hundreds of activists who attended a nonviolent direct action training led by US activists were then beaten to a pulp during the anti-FTAA actions in São Paolo in 2001. Sitting down in a blockade in front of the Brazilian police force ended in a blood-bath – predictable, say the more experienced locals, who are still trying to rebuild the trust of those who took such a brutal beating on their very first direct action.

"AFTER TWO YEARS OF INCREASINGLY MILITANT DIRECT ACTION, IT IS STILL IMPOSSIBLE TO PRODUCE A SINGLE EXAMPLE OF ANYONE TO WHOM A US ACTIVIST HAS CAUSED PHYSICAL INJURY.... GOVERNMENTS SIMPLY DO NOT KNOW HOW TO DEAL WITH AN OVERTLY REVOLUTIONARY MOVEMENT THAT REFUSES TO FALL INTO FAMILIAR PATTERNS OF ARMED RESISTANCE."

– David Graeber, "The New Anarchists", ***New Left Review***

Identifying primarily with our tactics (I am a nonviolent activist), or costumes (I'm with the Black Bloc), rather than with our goals, ideas, and dreams makes us rigid and inflexible, completely predictable, unable to evolve. By reducing all of the world's complex problems to a single target with a single solution, we dally with authoritarianism, vanguardism, elitism. As always, we must find the in-between spaces, the exit from the dichotomy. We must examine each tactic in the context of a specific location and circumstance. As Massimo de Angelis puts it, "The only right tactic is one that emerges out of a communal process of engagement with the other." And engage we must, as our very survival depends upon it.

Towards the escape hatch

"The realistic course of action today is to demand what is seemingly impossible, that is, something new."
– Antoni Negri and Michael Hardt

The only way out of the polar terms of engagement laid out by those in power is to recognize that there is no longer anywhere to which we can retreat. There are no safe places in a world which grows critically warmer, a world in which safe drinking water is running out, a world undergoing the greatest mass species extinction since the disappearance of the dinosaurs. We can't keep going back to the land, starting commun(e)ities off the grid, and insulating ourselves with the safety net of subculture. As Naomi Klein said at the 2002 World Social Forum, "The movement is the escape hatch from the war between good and evil. We know that we have more than two choices." The only safety is to act now, with great conviction, with a total commitment to increased resistance, with the broadest possible appeal, and a fierce passion for the development of alternatives.

When we succeed at this, it will be impossible to criminalize us. While it is important that people continue working specifically against repression, we must also maintain and strengthen our vision, unleash our imaginations, broaden our constituencies, and develop communication strategies to make plain what we already know: our ideas are in everyone's minds.

The globalization of repression shows us clearly that our movements around the world have been enormously successful at closing off the spaces into which neoliberalism wishes to expand. It also shows us that no matter how hard they try to beat us, isolate us, imprison us, slander and defame us, infiltrate us, shoot at us, and destroy us, we are winning, we truly are everywhere, and we are not alone.

Notes from Nowhere

Many activists will *tell you that the corporation is taking over from the state, and that the state needs to be strengthened in order to defend against the corporation. However the state and the corporation are separated by a revolving door, with politicians serving on boards of directors, and campaign donations securing legislation. The state is as corrupt as the corporation, in collusion together against the will of the people.*

The US presidential election of 2000, a farcical charade of democracy if ever there was one, provided a perfect example of this. Five months before the election, Florida's Governor Jeb Bush (brother to George W) ordered his Secretary of State, Katherine Harris, to illegally knock 94,000 voters off the registration lists, claiming that they were felons, and therefore, ineligible to vote in Florida. Harris, who was simultaneously running Bush's presidential campaign, complied. Why was this happening in Florida? It's the US' swing state, where the vote is evenly divided. Of the 94,000, 91,000 were innocent of crimes, but half of them were 'guilty' of being African-American or Latino – in other words, Democrats. Since Florida is like South Africa under apartheid in that they list race on voter registration, the purging of black voters was no coincidence.

In addition to that, 179,855 votes were not counted, due to what was referred to as 'irregularity,' or 'spoilage.' As investigative journalist Greg Palast puts it, "People wrote in the name Al Gore because the ballot said, 'Write in candidate's name.' ... If you wrote in Al Gore, because he wasn't a write-in candidate, your ballot was void." The following month, after much hand-wringing, discussion of 'dimples' and 'chads,' and racist insinuations that African-Americans in Florida are perhaps not clever enough to use a ballot properly, George W Bush was declared the winner of the election, by a margin of 537 votes. So it was no great surprise that 20,000 people turned up in Washington to protest the swearing in of such a sore loser. They had seen the future, and the future looked scary.

Anarchists Can Fly

by Sophia Delaney

"If someone had told my dad he'd one day be friends with the President of the United States, he wouldn't have believed it." Fucking moron. I would have smacked her if she had been three-dimensional.

In the library, waiting for the internet terminal, I picked up the latest issue of *TeenPeople*, the glossy-paged teen celebrity magazine. I didn't start reading to "scope some mega-cute skater sweeties!" or dig some lip-gloss likely to get me tongue-kissed after class. Nope – it was lying open where I sat down, and the page facing up was a photo spread of George W Bush's inauguration.

I had been in Washington DC when the President was sworn in. I was curious to see how a magazine that touted shopping and good grades as the answer to every teen-age problem would write up an event like our corrupt system reaching new heights of unscrupulousness, and how their coverage measured up to my memory of it. Not very well. The girl writing the photo captions was the daughter of a friend of Dubya. She got to go celebrate the presidential coup Republican-style, with ball gowns ("I spent about two hours getting ready!"), and Ricky Martin shaking his bon-bon and Bush calling out "T-Bone!" to her daddy, "That's good ol' Bushie's nickname for him!" from the stage right before his speech. Wow, I thought. Ain't no inauguration I went to.

My memories of 20 January are strikingly different, but no less memorable. I was there as a protester, one of the

20,000 who came to deride Bush, not dance at the ball. I was a member of the Revolutionary Anti-Authoritarian Bloc. We were the anarchist Black Bloc, the window-smashing flag-burning mask-wearing 'bad' demonstrators.

There's a photo in my journal – a black and white taken at 14th and K, where police scuffled with protesters – that shows nothing but lights and shadows distorted into a haze of action. Nothing entirely clear, everything moving too fast. I saved the print because that was the way it had felt. This was my first big protest, and there was just too much happening – too many chants, too many conflicting reports on the streets, too many cops, too much rain and hunger and exhaustion. I was new to this and a total wimp, and I ran on autopilot.

There was one moment, though, that seared itself into my memory, seizing a handful of brain cells so tightly it will never escape my mind. It was after hundreds of protesters had bypassed the unconstitutional security checks – goodbye, chain link fences – and got all the way up to the parade route we were supposed to be four blocks away from. The Black Bloc had converged near a small plaza full of flagpoles. We'd met there for protection – the National Organization for Women had staked a claim to some of that space, and while police would charge and beat the anarchists, they might not do that to a crowd of feminist ladies. The crowd was thin and we would be close to the street when the motorcade passed, a good thing.

We anarchists milled about, anxious. The flagpoles – about 30 feet high, set in seven-foot concrete pedestals – were the Navy Memorial. Each of them was strung with three long ropes of ship flags waving in the cold wind. I looked around anxiously, feeling as though my momentary quietude was about to be disrupted.

I was right. A Black Bloc-er, his face covered with sweatshirt hood and black bandana, ran up to the pole and scrambled up the cement base. Three others quickly joined him, and the crowd began to cheer. They struggled to unravel the ropes holding the flags in place, tearing down the monument. As each length of cloth fell the crowd let out a collective yell of joy, happy to see the symbols of the system they wanted so badly to change hit the mud puddles below. I hollered, "Hell yeah!" up to the overcast sky, thrilled with the spectacle.

2001

>> January 1 >> Zimbabwean public workers go on strike to protest against the government's 15 per cent wage increment. With inflation at 70 per cent, the workers argue that the rise is insufficient and leaves them unable to meet the costs of living.

>> January 8 >> Angolan public sector workers go on general strike for four days in most provinces in reaction to government proposals to lower the minimum monthly salary. The state-owned media refuse to report the events.

>> January 20 >> Thousands line the streets of Washington DC, US to protest the inauguration of unelected President George W Bush.

>> January 21 >> Ecuador erupts as indigenous groups are joined by farmers, students, and labour unionists

With the flagpole stripped bare, the anarchists ran up their own symbols: a black flag and a red and black flag. The Republicans standing on bleachers nearby began to yell, "Get down! Get down!" as the four kids clinging to the flagpole began to string an upside-down US flag into place. The anarchist kids yelled, "Stay up! Stay up!" in response. We were louder and more exuberant than the sourpuss Bushites, and the tattered emblem of a state gone wrong rose all the way to the top.

A handful of cops, formerly occupying the curb of Pennsylvania Avenue, were about to disrupt the fun. They moved into the crowd to end the symbolic dissent with a few beatings and arrests. Three of the flagpole liberators saw them coming, leapt down, and ran, hiding themselves in the crowd. The fourth had his back turned, and by the time he saw them it was too late – he was surrounded by angry patriots with pepper spray and batons at the ready. To hop down would be to take a beating and maybe a felony charge, so he did the only thing he could: he breathed deep, lifted his arms, and flung himself straight out over the cops and the crowd, stage-diver style. The crowd let out a collective frightened gasp. It was the shocked response of people watching something so daring it looked, at first glance, suicidal. He was Rocky the Flying Squirrel, Evel Knievel, the antithesis of timidity.

My heart stopped too in that moment. It seemed both lightning-quick and eternal, that one second when the flying anarchist hovered horizontal in the air. When he fell to earth, landing in the arms of his comrades and escaping the police, everything felt different, like we were living in the pages of history, as though in that moment there was a crystal-clear delineation of past and future. Something had just Happened.

But there was no time for the inspired feeling in my gut to move to my left-brain at that moment. The cops were advancing, nightsticks swinging. We panicked a little and retreated, but then the Black Bloc's collective mind seemed to go, "No, fuck these cops." We turned and linked arms, pressing forward and shouting at the police. We yelled at them to back up and, one by one, their confidence suddenly wavering, they did. It was a retreat no one in my affinity group, with hundreds of protest hours logged among us, had ever seen before. Later, when Dubya's motorcade raced by, SWAT team members in full riot gear advanced on us. We did it again, linking arms and screaming, "Cops off the sidewalk!" And they moved back. It was a feeling of incredible strength.

Reading *TeenPeople's* article, I was unamazed to find that there was no mention of protesting. It was as if the day had been nothing but cheerful, waving Republicans and a grinning president, so thrilled to be able to seize power and destroy the country. The history-in-the-making feeling I had gotten at the Navy Memorial was, in the end, only true in the personal sense. It made no headlines, changed no policies, destroyed only a few pieces of cloth – but to me it changed everything. Before Washington I had been to, dig it, two protests. I wasn't an activist and wasn't especially committed to any cause. I was only a voyeur of activism, doubtful of our ability to really change anything. Pre-inauguration, I knew I could walk away from activism altogether. Afterwards, I felt as though I never could.

When the anarchist leapt and the world stopped cold, my heart ceased for one beat and then started up again in a different rhythm. I understood that to turn my back on the world's problems would be to become an accomplice in their perpetuation, and that changing the way things are now is critical to the survival of the world. I understood my right to say "NO", and not consent to living under these rules, and the need to say "YES" to creating something different. My mind had understood human suffering, injustice, destruction and pain; suddenly, my heart did too, and change became vital, a part of my soul.

But the problems in the world had looked impossible before; it was an uphill battle on a hill too steep to climb. In that incredibly bold leap over the heads of the riot police, the option of saving the world from the jaws of destructive, violent capitalism seemed possible somehow. One quick, bold move – it made other acts of amazing audacity seem possible, which made defeat for the powers-that-be seem possible, which meant that our efforts on that cold day and all the other days when people world-wide have marched through the streets, struggling to be heard, were not for show, not a battle fought in vain, not a losing proposition.

It took my hopes of defeating the forces that beat us down and synthesized them into one metaphoric illustration that said, "Yes we fucking can!" A seven-foot leap; a leap of faith. When a handful of kids in black sweatshirts told a SWAT team to back up and they obeyed, that feeling was confirmed. If that flying anarchist taught me nothing else, it was that when shit looks absolutely impossible, don't worry. Don't stop to analyze too much. Be courageous. Do what they don't expect. Take a leap. Anything is possible.

I flipped through the rest of *TeenPeople*, then turned back to the Bush coverage, pulled out a marker, and scrawled "FUCK BUSH" across one page. On the other, I added a new slogan: "ANARCHISTS CAN FLY."

Sophia Delaney was 18 years old when she wrote this piece and has since become an emergency medical technician and visited Palestine

---

Resources:

» Greg Palast, *The Best Democracy Money Can Buy*, Penguin, 2003

---

blocking roads in half the country's provinces. The police and army disperse peaceful demonstrations using tear gas, batons, and rubber bullets. In response, over 10,000 people march on the capital. The protesters, led by a large indigenous coalition, continue to block roads, and establish a camp at the main university, declaring that they will not be moved until the government reverses its plans to impose austerity measures.

>> January 25-30 >> Over 11,000 activists from social movements in 120 countries declare that "another world is possible", as they converge on the Brazilian city of Porto Alegre for the first World Social Forum, an alternative gathering to the WEF meeting in Davos. Taking a break from the thousands of workshops, cultural events, and discussion groups at the Forum, 1,300 farmers destroy five acres of genetically modified Brazilian corn and soybean fields at a nearby farm managed by US biotechnology firm Monsanto. They pull up crops, burn seeds, and destroy documents in the company's offices before returning to the Forum.

>> January 27 >> This year the World Economic Forum in Davos, Switzerland is turned into a fortress and all protests banned once again. However, protest messages from across the world are sent to a website and

It would be easy to label the Zapatistas as terrorists: they are armed, wear ski masks and are still officially at war with the Mexican government. But it isn't that simple. Their primary weapons are their words; they refer to their firearms as "weapons which aspire to be useless". Constantly defying fixed definitions, their war is one fought with words and symbols, while being a matter of life and death.

On 24 February 2001, the Zapatistas did the unthinkable. The most wanted men and women in Mexico emerged from the jungle to begin the March for Indigenous Dignity. Twenty-three commanders of the Zapatista Army for National Liberation, and Subcomandante Marcos, travelled 950 miles across Mexico accompanied by a caravan of 50 buses filled with supporters from across Mexico and the world. They slept in town squares, in gyms, in water-world theme parks. They held masked balls, and no less than 77 public rallies on the way to Mexico City, and each visit became a town fiesta.

As they rode into the capital, two million people lined the streets to greet them as they headed for the central square. "No estan solos!" (You are not alone!) the crowd cried. For the first time in Mexican history, indigenous women addressed Congress, demanding constitutional recognition of the rights and autonomy of Mexico's ten million indigenous inhabitants.

The trip was a huge gamble as death threats against the Zapatistas poured in from state governors and paramilitary groups alike. This story illustrates the enormous difficulty coordinating such an epic event using the Zapatista's guiding principle of "leading by obeying" and shows that history can be made not only by confronting power head-on, but also by defying it creatively and adapting it to the needs of the people.

Civil Emergency: Zapatistas hit the road

by Afra Citlalli

Two days before the Zapatista *comandantes* descended on the cultural capital of Chiapas, San Cristóbal (in the popular imagination) or climbed their way up to the city (in the geographical reality), an atmosphere of madness invaded the spaces and lives of Mexican civil society. Nationals and internationals ran in all directions, from meeting to meeting, from house to house, from NGO to NGO; in the cafés the rumor spread that with the Red Cross' refusal to accompany the Zapatistas to the capital, the Zapatista Information Center still didn't have enough buses or money to cover the trip; in the grassroots organization Melel they were preparing the indigenous communication promoters to cover the journey; in the School of Social Sciences they were fixing up mattresses for the caravaners-to-be; in Café Museo they were holding a press conference; in Junax they were organizing a rag-tag contingent of independent journalists; in the networking hub of the Los Altos Coordination office they referred everyone directly to the feminist bookshop, Luna Creciente; at Luna Creciente the telephone rang every minute asking if there was space in the buses; just outside of San Cristóbal an informal official registered and assigned a number to the vehicles wishing to participate ... In general, only two things were certain: first, there was no official organizer of the caravan, and second, that everything would turn out fine, as usual.

In the afternoon, a long wait for the *comandantes* in the plaza – apparently because all the Zapatista support bases coming to say goodbye had not yet shown up. Then at night, the final details, the final blankets, the final press releases and suitcases. Nobody slept. In the morning, long lines of Zapatistas, ready from the break of dawn to act as a human barricade, escorted the bussed-up *comandantes* all the way to the gates of San Cristóbal. Behind them, almost 50 vehicles, all in disorder, with god knows how many press cars after that. The now-rolling caravaners cried out heartfelt goodbyes from their buses to the rows and rows of indigenous Zapatistas, who answered by waving their hands and calling out their slogans.

The caravan had left, the support bases got back on their sheep trucks to go up/down to their communities, and San Cristóbal was left all alone once again. For those who weren't leaving, the traffic blocked their path and they sat down on the side of the highway. And without the media, with nobody around and no photos being snapped, they slowly let down their ski masks to cease being the support bases of the Zapatista Army of National Liberation, and to once again become just plain indigenous people.

Tuxtla Gutiérrez, La Ventosa, Juchitán, Tehuantepec, Oaxaca, Tahuacán, Orizaba, Puebla, Tlaxcala, Emiliano Zapata, Cd. Sahagún, Pachuca, Actopan, Tepatepec, Ixmiquilpan, el Tephé, Querétaro, Acámbaro, Zinapécuaro, Patzcuaro, Uruapan, Nurio, Morelia, Toluca, Temoaya, La Pila, Cuernavaca, Tepoztlán, Iguala, Cuautla, Emiliano Zapata, Milpa Alta, Xochimilco, Mexico City. On the road, arrival, out onto the street, rally, back into the buses, do it all over again. At night, sometimes on a public square, sometimes on a basketball court, sometimes at a university dorm, sometimes at hot springs, sometimes in a bus, but one thing's for sure: there's always a meeting. Of the San Cristóbal internationals, the independent journalists, the bus coordinators, the security people, the Europeans....

The San Cristóbal internationals named spokespeople who would say nothing except what had been consensually agreed upon. They decided on attitudes and security measures in order not to be caught without a visa and they mistrusted every stranger that came to listen at their round-tables.

The independent journalists told everyone where they

---

projected by laser beam onto the nearby mountain where all can see them. Police use water cannons in the driving snow to drive back 500 protesters who somehow have snuck into the fortress-like ski resort. Meanwhile, inside the conference, some of the richest and most powerful business leaders in the world engage in direct action of their own. Having lost patience with the perpetual security sweeps of the building required by the US security services, the delegates stage a bizarre sit-in which delays President Clinton's speech.

>> February >> Members of the grassroots farmworkers' union, the Coalition of Immokalee Workers, join with students across the state of Florida, US to launch a campaign for fair wages and improved working conditions. The campaign involves a boycott against Taco Bell, the largest purchaser of tomatoes picked by union members. The CIW marks among its long term successes the establishment of a food cooperative providing food to members at nearly wholesale costs, weekly radio programs in Spanish and Haitian Creole, and an education and leadership development program focused on skill acquisition and the integration of culture and politics. "When you look at the difference in power between us as farmworkers

had set up their mobile office – their computers, scanners, mini-discs, video-editing material, all of it on loan. Once inside, some took digital portraits and printed out self-authorized accreditations to go through life and history with a press pass; others typed notes, reports, and chronicles about what had happened that day; others scanned photos; others, with their video cameras, loaded images for editing – and so, from one night to the next, more than a dozen webpages went up to say what's never even mentioned in the mainstream media.

The Europeans, for their part, had discussions about whether it was really worth continuing in their six second-class buses that went too slow and took turns falling apart every day. But from Oaxaca onward they didn't have anything left to discuss, because their buses abandoned them. The drivers told them they should take out their things so they could clean the buses, because they were full of scorpions. Scared, the Europeans took out their stuff, but at five in the morning when it was time to leave, the buses had disappeared. The *comandantes* sent their spokespeople to say that they were sorry, but they couldn't delay the departure because they had too many public meetings that day. So the Europeans were left stranded in Oaxaca, making press releases, refusing the offer of the governor of Oaxaca to bring them six first-class buses for free, and putting together money to rent others and join the caravan again some day. The buses' owner told them that soon after the buses left the group they were fired on, and one of the drivers was wounded. No one ever knew if it was true.

"Listen well: We are the colour of the earth! Without us, money would not exist, and we know well how to live without the colour of money. But do not be concerned. We have not come to exploit anyone, so we shall not engage in competition with you. A house can always remain a house if it lacks the terrace or the upstairs floor, but a house without foundation is nothing but a pile of rubble.

"Lower your voice and listen, because there is now another voice which has not come to steal or to impose, but something more serious: to take your place. This voice is ours. The voice of those who are the colour of the earth." – **EZLN speech upon arriving in Mexico City**

The bus coordinators got together to ask each other, because there was nobody else to ask, why the caravan was sometimes chaotic and sometimes a non-entity. The number that had been assigned with such circumspection in San Cristóbal had been replaced by the speed that each bus could attain. The first night they decided that the two meetings held simultaneously should become one. The second night they agreed that there ought to be a meeting every night. From the third night a series of discussions about civility began. Some argued that the bus numbers ought to be respected, others that it was impossible, given the motor

Tim Russo

An enormous crowd welcomes the Zapatistas to the zócalo. Mexico City, Mexico

and Taco Bell as a billion dollar corporation, you may think we are crazy for taking them on. They have all the money and political power, and we have only one weapon. But that weapon – the truth – is the most powerful thing on earth, so we are certain that we will prevail," says Romeo Ramirez, a member of the Coalition.

>> February 1-7 >> A coalition of indigenous and labour union activists occupy the IMF offices in Quito, Ecuador's capital. The following day the government announces a state of emergency. Undeterred, protesters escalate actions. Hunger strikes begin at the university protest encampment, roadblocks intensify. Protests spread across the country, closely followed by repression, during which four people are killed by troops, 25 others are shot, and hundreds are injured. A week later the government backs down on price hikes and agrees to dialogue with protest groups. An enormous victory march snakes through Quito. The talks last two months and break down because the government refuses to engage seriously.

>> February 8 >> Three hundred angry, naked women confront biologists attempting to conduct a census of the endangered Tana River colobus monkey in Kenya – a

capacities of each vehicle, and the drivers argued that if they didn't take advantage of the downhill slopes they'd never get there. Some said that wanting to be near the *comandantes* was glory-hogging, others said it was just making sense out of their visit, because lagging behind meant never arriving in time for the public meetings, and when they got there it was already time to go. Some argued that no-one should take off before everyone was in their buses, others, that the *comandantes* couldn't wait and that everybody was grown up enough to be ready to go when each meeting was over. Some argued that it was part of the Zapatista spirit to give a ride to those left behind, others, that it was very dangerous to bring strangers into the caravan because they could be only pretending to be part of another bus.

In Querétaro, where the Governor had threatened the Zapatistas with death, one of the buses lost its brakes and collided with two highway patrol cars and the bus carrying the *comandantes*. Fear and silence invaded the caravan; it was stranded for more than two hours. Little by little, without uttering a word, the caravaners surrounded the *comandantes*' bus, linked hands, and formed a thick human shield. They began to hum the national anthem – first quietly like a rumour, then loudly with all their strength. When the buses could finally move on, what had been a four-lane caravan became a thin Indian file that crept away from the scene of the accident. From then on, the assembly decided that the numbers would be transformed into letters giving a new order to the buses, and that the caravan would be divided into a fast and a slow one. But the fast caravan would redistribute the people in the first-class buses so the security section would be with them: the bus carrying the Italian *Tute Bianche* (providing security), and five Mexicans for every other bus.

From then on, the security people also held their assembly every night, but since it was about security, no-one ever knew what was said. What's known is that the *Tute Bianche* gradually came to be hated, first by the media and then by some Mexicans, offended by the rude foreign security. Their defenders argued that there was nothing to complain about: it was not that they were the best organized ones in the caravan, but the only organized ones. But from Nurio onward, the *comandantes* asked them to leave their task in the hands of the National Indigenous Congress, and the *Tute Bianche* sent out a press release to Our Lady of Civil Society explaining only that from then on they would be at the back of the caravan.

And so they continued: the champions of the indigenous, supporting the return to the values of community life, the return to our little bit of a forgotten past. The *Tute Bianche*, the global Indians, who put on their white overalls like ski masks, in order to be seen by a system for which all marginalities are invisible; the counter-globalizers of Seattle, Prague, Nice, Davos, and Cancún, who like the EZLN are for humanity and against this horrid neoliberalism that homogenizes cultures and McDonaldizes the world; the Mexican frontists who stand up without fear as Zapatistas, as their most faithful civilians and their most trusted accomplices in the search for a new politics; the Christians committed to helping the poorest of the poor; the First

Worlders who exchange money for hope; the artists seduced by Marcos, by his irony and poetry, because a movement that laughs and makes poetry is a movement that brings joy; the indignant with their untouchable communications media, soothsaying spokespeople of truth, because it's one thing to dress up the facts and quite another to fall into lying cynicism, and because the struggle to decide which bit of reality will be socialized is also the good fight; the die-hards of the 1970s, because the wall that fell in Berlin went up again in the Lacandón jungle, because behind the word neoliberalism you'll always find capitalism, and because even though it's a pacifist movement, Zapatismo is also an armed rebellion; the South American Guevarists because Marcos looks so much like Che and because the Conquest, the Spanish, and Zapatismo must unite all of Latin America against our enemies in the North; all different, and all advancing for different reasons behind the Zapatistas.

Because theirs is everyone's struggle, because if they win, we all have a hope of winning, because if a masked man enters Congress, pacifism has meaning, because if indigenous autonomy is approved, the struggle for world plurality has a reason to exist.

They advanced, they got themselves indebted up to their ears just to be there, to feel it, they ate the rice and beans that the welcoming committees offered at each stop, they stood out in the blazing sun so as not to miss even one rally, they said goodbye through the window to the thousands of people who rose up in euphoria from the mass feasts. They received applause, greetings, oranges through the windows, flowers from the school kids, teasers from the girls in middle school, benedictions from monks who wished them good fortune drawing crosses in the air... and yes, a few insults as well – all that in order to go in hand in hand, forming a great human barrier – less of security than of solidarity – around the *comandantes*, to finally enter the zócalo together.

Afra Citlalli Mejma Lara is a communicator, and also the author of a documentary film entitled '*En el camino del surco*' (*Along the Furrow's Path*), depicting the introduction of the neoliberal model to the Mexican countryside. She lives in Guadalajara.

English translation by Brian Holmes

---

project funded by the World Bank. The women strip and charge the biologists in a protest against the Bank's plan to turn the area into a nature reserve for the primates, which would result in the displacement of at least 2,000 families.

>> February 16 - March 7 >> The struggle against Daewoo in Pupyong, South Korea reaches a peak, as the union responds to an attempted plant closure with a partial strike. 4,000 riot police seal off the plant and brutally attack the strikers and their families, including children who have come to support the workers. The workers resist the police with their own home-made water cannon, Molotov cocktails, and large sticks. Solidarity demonstrations by students and social movements erupt across the country. Meanwhile the Daewoo Motors Joint Struggle Headquarters Arrest Squad, set up by activists, travels to Europe to locate and bring to justice Kim Woo-Choong, the corrupt CEO responsible for the company's bankruptcy, who has been in hiding since 1999. They find him hidden in his luxury villa in France, where he remains, as the South Korean government refuses to extradite and prosecute him.

>> February 20 >> Protests take place outside development meetings between African leaders and

Jail Solidarity

"Keep your focus on the meaning of what you are doing as your hands are cuffed behind you. Your challenge now and for a long time to come will be to remember, at each stage of what happens to you, that you have a choice: acquiesce or resist. Choose your battles mindfully: there will be many of them and you cannot fight them all. Still every instance of resistance slows the system down, prevents its functioning, lessens its power ... And when you get out of jail you will see where the jail is thinly concealed in the shopping mall, the school, the television program. You will know that at every moment you do truly have a choice: to acquiesce, to resist, to create something new."
– Starhawk, *Making it Real 'initiation instructions'*

Red hand prints cover police station walls. Oaxaca, Mexico

Jails protect those with access to the system from those without, and are used to demoralize and dehumanize us. As a result of our struggle for a better world we are sometimes arrested, either for breaking the law, or often just to intimidate us or get us off the streets. Struggle does not end with arrest. By acting as a strong group, those arrested can have the power to transform jails into places where we continue to look after ourselves and others rather than succumbing to the disempowering system that wants to control us. Jail solidarity is one way of doing this.

Solidarity is protecting each other and ourselves through group decision making, it is a philosophy and an approach, not a set of tactics and it can prove extremely effective in jails and court houses, which are designed to make people feel alone and powerless. In some places jail solidarity has become synonymous with certain non-compliance tactics, such as withholding one's name and identification. While this can be a powerful tactic, it is only one of many – the key is to work together to find out what is the best for everyone in the given situation.

A few of examples of successful jail solidarity are: Nelson Mandela organizing with other prisoners on Robben Island in South Africa to gain better conditions; arrested Suffragettes refusing to eat while in jail, until all women were released together; in Washington DC, during the A16 IMF actions, 150 protesters, through disobeying police and jail guards,

CIPO-RFM

negotiated a plea bargain in which everyone's misdemeanour charges were reduced to a $5 jaywalking ticket, and no one had to give their real name.

So what can jail and court solidarity look like?

» When you are arrested with other activists who you do not know, look around and check in with each other, are their any medical emergencies, is everyone OK? Exchange names or nicknames, and get to know one another.

» Communicate those names or nicknames to someone not arrested. This can mean shouting out of a police vehicle to an activist with a notepad, to then share with a legal collective (see below) group, or your friends.

» As people may be at physical risk while under arrest it is crucial that all tactics are decided collectively, and that all voices are heard. The most effective way to do this is using the consensus process. It is important to have a facilitator and then rotate that person so the police do not single out any one person as a 'leader'.

» Decide collectively how you will respond to certain situations. If the police try to separate one person from the group, which is common, people have used various tactics including piling on top of that person and insisting they are not removed.

» A tactic is something you do (eg: chant incessantly). A demand is something you want (eg some water). You use tactics to get demands met (eg we're going to chant incessantly unless you bring us some water). Matching tactics to demands and appropriate escalation are keys to successfully accomplishing our collective goals. Make sure the cop, guard, judge, etc. one is talking to can meet the demands and is directly affected by the tactics.

» What can we do if our tactics aren't making them meet us our demand? We can stop or escalate. If singing isn't working, try singing off key. Then try screaming; then screaming and pounding on the door; etc. Make sure the tactic is still on the same level as the demand. We may also collectively choose to stop.

» Be ready to use solidarity tactics to protect people who are likely to be separated in jail and prosecuted more harshly in court. Non-citizens, people of colour, people who are seen as leaders, transgender or queer people, people with disabilities, people who dress 'punk' and people with prior arrests are examples of vulnerable people.

» Once out of jail and in the court system, we need to maintain solidarity. This can mean anything: organizing people to attend hearings, demanding collective trials, representing ourselves, creating theatre in the court to show the farce that it is.

» Legal collectives are helpful in any action. A legal collective can be a number of things. A trusted group of activists who work with lawyers to track us through the arrest, jail, and court process is invaluable. Legal collectives are never to tell activists what to do, but help facilitate with communication, advance training, and interfacing with lawyers.

Resources:

» People's Law Collective (US) www.PLC/~tao.ca

» Just Cause Law Collective (US) www.lawcollective.org

» Midnight Special: www.midnightspecial.net

» In the US the National Lawyers Guild, a radical legal association, supports activists in dozens of actions: www.nlg.org

» The Activists' Legal Project, advice on how to run workshops for UK grassroots groups: www.activistslegalproject.org.uk

»Liberty, guide to your rights in the UK: www.yourrights.org.uk/your-rights/index.shtml

In the World Bank's opinion, *there are "too many" African students and their numbers should be cut. Why bother educating those who are destined to be a source of unskilled cheap labour for the West? Where many post-independence governments invested in free education up to university level, the World Bank and IMF structural adjustment programmes (SAPs) imposed drastic cuts to higher education. Most students now pay fees, and no longer receive stipends which once covered meals and supplies.*

According to A Thousand Flowers: Social Struggles Against Structural Adjustment in African Universities: *"On most African campuses, student life today verges on the catastrophic. Overcrowded classrooms, students running on one meal a day, failing water and electricity supplies, collapsing buildings, libraries without journals or books, lack of educational supplies from paper to chalk and even pens are the visible test of what [the IMF], stripped from the ideological smoke, actually provides."*

The higher education student in Africa is an endangered species. Perhaps not coincidentally, African student movements have been the fiercest critics of the World Bank and IMF's new form of colonialism. "The police and/or the army are frequently stationed on or near the campus and classes are filled with informers, to pre-empt or supress students organizing and protesting," A Thousand Flowers *reports.*

African students fighting education cutbacks and economic restructuring over the past 20 years are described as "hoodlums", just like their counterparts in the global North. Hundreds of African students have been killed on protests, paying the ultimate price of resistance. But the following testimony from the Committee for Academic Freedom in Africa speaks not just of death, but of hope, as a new generation of young people – part of the international movement against neoliberal globalization – carry the message of the African student dead to the Washington doorstep of the World Bank and IMF.

An April of Death: African students fight World Bank policies

by the editors of the Committee for Academic Freedom in Africa newsletter

The ten days between 9 April and 18 April 2001 were bloody ones for African students and youth. They epitomized the literal war African states (committed to the structural adjustment ideology of the World Bank and IMF) are waging against African youths who see no future for themselves or their countries in the path these states are following.

On Monday 9 April, a Zimbabwean science student, Batanayi Madzidzi, aged 20, died from injuries suffered during clashes with the police on Sunday. The clashes arose from a demonstration organized to protest the late payments of their stipends. This was one of many demonstrations in the last decade the students of the University of Harare have organized focusing on the rising costs of food, accommodation, and tuition due to the government's structural adjustment policies. The immediate trigger of the students' anger was the apparent suicide on Friday 6 April of a first-year female student who was found dead in a female students' hostel with a note beside her body that referred to a relationship gone sour. Apparently many female students, in the context of the economic crisis, are financing their education through making liaisons with wealthy men. The results are not, however, always under their control.

On Wednesday 11 April, students of the Addis Ababa

University, in Addis Ababa, Ethiopia were demonstrating against the police presence on campus, and demanding elementary academic freedom rights like freedom of assembly and expression on campus. Apparently two plain-clothes policemen were spotted by the students in their midst; this triggered an attack by riot police bent on rescuing their colleagues. The police riot ended in the injury of 50 students that night. In the following days, student demonstrations and strikes were echoed by rioting in the city by youths who state officials called "hoodlums and lumpen." Shops were looted, government buildings burned, and cars were trashed. The state unleashed a deadly response, killing 38 people and wounding 252 others. The deaths were due largely to gunshot wounds caused by police fire. Thousands of students were arrested and sent to a concentration camp in the village of Sendafa, 17 miles north-east of Addis Ababa. Students returned to campus in early May, but continued to demand the release of all their fellows. They eventually left the university campus en masse on 12 June, concluding that the government was not seriously negotiating with them.

On Wednesday 18 April, while the deadly confrontation in Ethiopia between students and police was beginning to quiet, Algerian police killed a student, Germah Massinissa, in the Kabylia region during a demonstration anticipating the huge annual gathering of indigenous Berbers to celebrate "Berber Spring" on 20 April. The killing of the student was followed by demonstrations of protest throughout Kabylia, and by sympathetic demonstrations in Algiers and other parts of Algeria where students chanted, "We are all Berbers!" These demonstrations were met with determined violence by state forces. At least 50 people have been killed in a long series of demonstrations demanding the right to practice Berber culture. But they continue, and they threaten the government's hold on power.

We present these moments of Zimbabwean, Ethiopian, and Algerian state violence as an indication of African states' confirmation of the World Bank's judgment on the students of Africa: there are too many of them; they are expendable. At the same time the political leaders of Zimbabwe, Ethiopia, and Algeria, through their decision to respond with massive mortal force, have lost hold of the future while these

---

heads of the IMF in Bamako, Mali. Banners outside the meetings announce that the World Bank and IMF are assassinating African people, and causing poverty and catastrophe.

>> February 20 >> Direct actionists in the Earth Liberation Front network burn a research cotton gin at Delta and Pine Land Company in Visalia, California, US. Their communiqué announces that the warehouse was chosen "because it contained massive quantities of transgenic cottonseed in storage". No one is injured in the action.

>> February 21 >> Indian farmers disobey police orders, and march towards the port in Mumbai to stage a symbolic protest against import of food grains and the World Trade Organization (WTO). Police arrest over 51,000 of them, release them after several hours, and then disperse the crowd with water cannons.

>> February 24-March 11 >> Following the historic route of Emiliano Zapata into Mexico City, 23 Zapatista commanders and Subcomandante Marcos caravan through 13 Mexican states on the March of Indigenous Dignity. They are joined by thousands of members of national and international civil society. Their demands are constitutional recognition of indigenous rights, the

students, far from defending their ivory tower detachment, are expressing the aspirations of the mass of African youth in the streets.

The main change in this April of Death, however, has not been in the brutality of the African state (for there have already been hundreds of African students killed in anti-SAP demonstrations), but in the attitude of the World Bankers. They used to think that the struggle could not touch them as they were safely ensconced on H Street in Washington. They were happy to have their 'front men' in Africa get their hands dirty dealing with the opposition to their programs. But the antiglobalization movement, which had as one of its sources the persistent anti-SAP student movement in Africa, has finally leaped from the streets of Harare, Addis Ababa, and Algiers into Washington in April, and Prague in September last year. The World Bankers now know that they cannot expect to carry on their planning and comfortable get-together in tranquility. They have been hounded, finally, by a truly international youth movement which has carried the African student dead to their door.

Kenyan Students Resist the World Bank

by Jim Wakhungu Nduruchi

This is an expanded version of the letter addressed to World Bank Bonds Boycott team that was protesting simultaneously with us in Kenya at the World Bank/IMF headquarters in Washington in April 2002, among other cities in the US. It was also addressed to the Movement Members in universities throughout Kenya, Uganda and South Africa.

Comrades,

I don't know what transpired on your side. I only know about what happened in Kenya. We have never had such a fabulous protest. We have never made headlines on TV before. We only came on the scene fighting with the police, as intelligent people who did not know how to use their excessive energy.

Kenyan students have always protested against the IMF/World Bank, although they were not being heard due to government brutality and harassment. For instance, in the year 2001, protests were also staged against them, and two protesters were injured by the police.

We have never gained such acceptance as we did this year! Because there was no money to board a bus, we trekked at 7.00 am to downtown, 11 miles from Kenyatta University. We were over 400 students. Many people joined us and did more than what one can believe in. By the time we were downtown, we were over 1,500. Three professors from the department of history accompanied us. My lawyer, who works with Amnesty International, was with us. In downtown we were joined by comrades from Nairobi University – about 400 students. We straightaway headed for the World Bank offices.

At the World Bank Group headquarters, the chanting went mad. The police were already stationed there to block us, and indeed they did. But they never blocked our mouths from speaking what we know is truth. The officials in the premises could be seen peeping through the window curtains as they swallowed, with pretence, the realities which were coming out of Press For Change members.

The Press For Change Movement is a coalition of University students in Kenya fighting both for justice and accountability in offices of the Government, and to educate people on the ills of the IMF/World Bank's water and electricity privatization, dilution of education, and other bad policies.

The protests were triggered by the World Bank move to privatize water and electricity. Part of the system had already been purchased, but our protests that day salvaged

"Lagos was literally a ghost town last weekend. The streets were empty, except burning tyres and smoking debris and the rhythmic hooting of a few okada (bike) riders. The atmosphere was tense, if not highly charged and palpable. As I moved around observing the mass protests against the IMF-induced fuel price hike, one sight was constant. Youth had turned many of the city's high ways into football pitches. I sat down to watch a match. Suddenly armed police in a station wagon pulled up. Rather than make way, the youth continued to play. The policemen hooted their horns frantically but they were ignored."

– Kwesi Owusu, 'Welcome to Lagos Mr Larry Summers', June 2000

---

release of all Zapatista political prisoners, and the removal of seven of the more than 250 military bases from the state of Chiapas. Comandante Esther makes the first address to Congress by an indigenous woman in Mexican history; however, as yet, none of the Zapatista demands have been met.

>> February 26-27 >> The World Economic Forum meets in a luxury hotel in the resort town of Cancún, México, behind solid metal fencing and lines of riot police. Around 500 activists brave intense surveillance by local, federal, and immigration police – some stage a symbolic face-off, others parade naked between the rows of activists and cops, and other sit down and block the road, while still others attempt to infiltrate the meeting from the beach side. After a few hours, as people begin dispersing, the cops open the barricade and violently batter the stragglers. Media and local support for those imprisoned and hospitalized is enormous - food is delivered to the protesters' encampment, a solidarity demo happens the next day in the capital, local journalists organize their own protest against police brutality, and the WEF scuttles out of town without releasing their customary celebratory communiqué. Popular pressure leads to the release of

Ramadhan Khamis

Opposition to IMF / World Bank privatization policies. Nairobi, Kenya.

the remainder. In addition, the World Bank interference with higher education was looming. They dictated to the Government how many students should be admitted to public universities. The rich were favoured by being allowed to go for "parallel Degrees". This was condoned by the Bank and it diluted education so much, denying such opportunities for the poor who had actually qualified.

The World Bank officials listened to everything we had to say about this, but never came out to comment. But the messages on the placards were enough to make them read our message. One poster read, "We stand in solidarity with those that are protesting in Washington DC today." Another read, "Is it World Bank or Weird Bank?" Another said, "Wolfensohn, you have suffocated us enough, stop now!" Another read, "Where did you hide our education rights?" Another one had a large cartoon showing HIV/AIDS in a limousine called World Bank/IMF. The driver was called Mr SAPs. It was moving on a pot-holed Kenyan highway. The virus, which was too fat, was saying, "Using this vehicle and my competent driver, I shall have conquered 75 per cent of the people by the year 2020. Ahaaa! Lucky me!"

One member of Press for Change, who is an actor, moved the entire crowd into tears after he went before the protesters and faced the headquarters. He personified the IMF/World Bank and sang a self-composed song and a poem revealing how the two are a cruel couple: "We fought for independence in Kenya, we are not going to be colonized by the World Bank and her sister again." It was a very emotional moment. My speech was the concluding remark, everything had been said. The good news is this – they heard everything! We are waiting for their comments.

From there we went to the Ministry of Education headquarters. After chanting and cursing against the corruption in that office, the minister sent a lady to explain that we have to leave, lest the police disperse us. The poor woman was hit with a stone from one protester who was not familiar to us. I was so sorry about it.

Then the dancing and chanting group went to the high court grounds where the noise went mad. Here, the high court judge came out to address us. He gave us time to explain our grievances. Over 20 people came up and ridiculed him and the judicial system so much for letting the mess happen in the judicial system. Francisca, a nice lady who works with Press For Change, blamed the judicial system for turning a blind eye to the plight that fell upon my home last December. She appealed to the Chief Justice to personally get involved to make sure justice is done.

In 1996 my brother was shot dead by the police while protesting against the cancellation of government grants to students. This was forced upon the Government by the World Bank. On 18 December 2001, thugs were sent to invade my home in the upcountry. They killed my dad, brother and had mom raped by six people. She is now HIV+. I was threatened and that's why I had to flee.

At this time my lawyer, who was received with a mad applause, came and told the Chief Justice that he would not rest until justice has been done. I just had tears rolling down and watering the corrupt ground. The Chief Justice promised that some officers in the judicial system were corrupt, and promised that he was going to take action. He asked us to come up with any evidence about corruption against any judge. I answered, "I shall present correct evidence to you. And if you will not do something about it, you shall leave office!" For all that time, three trucks of police officers had been following us at a distance, without opening fire as they have done before.

From here our motorcade took a different tune. We went charitable. We started cleaning dirt from streets. We did it with such efficiency. Dirt has been accumulating for the last two years. The stench was great and we didn't have gloves. But we did it! The media gathered and took pictures of what

---

the prisoners, and even the ruling party condemns the police action, with president Fox apologetically appearing on television days later.

>> March 2-4 >> Thousands of activists gather in Trieste, Italy to protest against a preliminary environmental ministerial meeting of the G8. 3,000 police barricade the streets surrounding the palace where the meeting takes place. Protesters launch fireworks and colored smoke bombs over the barricades and dance to music from a mobile sound system.

>> March 12 >> A four-month-long strike by the San Salvadoran Social Security Union ends favorably, having garnered the support of nearly 12,000 doctors and workers who demand an end to the privatization of the country's health system, the reinstatement of fired workers, and an increase in pay.

>> March 17 >> Twenty thousand protesters take the streets in demonstrations against the Global Forum Conference on e-government, in Naples, Italy. A security cordon rings the conference. The agenda includes discussing introducing an electronic ID card in Italy. Father Vitaliano Della Sala, who took part in the Zapatista march to Mexico City the previous week, says, "It was easier for Subcomandante Marcos

we were doing. We did it without talking. This process took us about two hours. Luckily, I had gotten some money courtesy of the Centre for Economic Justice. So I booked a bus to ferry people back to their respective campuses.

When we came to Kenyatta University where the majority of our members come from, we took donations of old clothes, shoes, foodstuff, blankets, mosquito nets, and utensils and put them in a truck. We headed for the home for the elderly people. We gave them this donation and, I testify, it was such a nice thing. Some of the old guys had no blankets. Some have totally torn clothes. One old woman had nothing to cover her nakedness, but a small rug covering her private parts.

Her chest was all out. Her skinny body was so dirty. Her legs were full of jiggers. She needed a wash. Some were so hungry, and one explained that they had not eaten anything since morning. It was 5.30 in the afternoon. The mentally stable ones explained how they just survive. It was so moving.

One old man was lying outside the men's dormitory and we did not see him when we came. Luckily, I went round the building and saw him. He had no strength to move after being roasted in the hot tropical sun throughout the day. When the attendant who claimed to have gone to buy food came, he told me that the old man had arrived in the home three days earlier. The old inhabitants were not amused at his arrival because it meant more competition over meagre food and resources.

We spent the entire evening washing the dirty bedding, cleaning the home, washing the old nice people, cooking for

"Just between you and me, shouldn't the World Bank be encouraging more migration of the dirty industries to the less developed countries? The economic logic behind dumping a load of toxic waste in the lowest wage country is impeccable, and we should face up to that … Under-populated countries in Africa are vastly under-polluted; their air quality is probably vastly inefficiently low compared to Los Angeles or Mexico City … The concern over an agent that causes a one-in-a-million change in the odds of prostate cancer is obviously going to be much higher in a country where people survive to get prostate cancer than in a country where under-five mortality is 200 per 1000."

– Lawrence Summers, chief economist, World Bank, 1991

them, and just sitting with them to share and hear what they had to say. They are full of wisdom! We told them who we are and they pledged their support to us. Then we sang the old gospel song, He Has Done So Much, and the old guys blessed us. We left the place so rich and full.

This was a national venture. I am yet to receive a full report about what happened in other universities. They did not join us because of financial problems. I only watched on telly the Moi University group talking to their Vice-Chancellor about necessary reforms at the university to make it a better place to live.

Partners, I don't know what I can tell you. You have made all this happen. Without you, we could not have done that, we could not have recognized 20 February. You sent us thoughts of strength.

And to everybody else around the world who participated in yesterday's protests; you are rare guys! You might be living well, without the SAPS. Your country is blessed. You have jobs and refreshments. And yet your love drives you to fight for us, to protest and risk negation and even beatings from the police just for our sake. Thanks brothers and sisters. We are so proud of you, and you are a source of strength for us.

Jim Wakhungu is a founding member of Press for Change, which almost came to a halt following government surveillance and persecutions. He was specifically targeted by the Moi regime, and is now living in exile in South Africa, researching a book, *The African Woman*.

Press for Change is still working hard to keep the wonderful agitation for accountability and transparency on the move, but is in urgent need of international support (jimdaleford@yahoo.com).

Resources:

» *A Thousand Flowers: Social Struggles Against Structural Adjustment in African Universities*, edited by Silvia Federici, George Caffentzis, and Ousseina Alidou, African World Press Inc.

» World Band Boycott campaign: www.worldbankboycott.org

---

to reach Mexico City than for these kids to reach Piazza Plebiscito."

>> March 21 >> Thousands of protesters descend on Johannesburg, South Africa, to demonstrate against the privatization of the city's water supply. The municipal company was sold to the French multinational, Suez Lyonnaise des Eaux. The South African Municipal Workers Union is appalled that the ruling party, which came to power in 1994 with promises of providing free basic public services to those who cannot afford them, is inviting profit-driven multinationals to run the city's water.

>> March 23 >> A 1,000-strong rally in Lagos, capital of Nigeria protests the government's continued persistence to phase in the deregulation of fuel supplies. "We can not pay world prices because we do not earn world incomes," says one speaker. The unions oppose deregulation and liberalization because these reforms inevitably lead to a rise in prices on basic necessities.

>> March 26 >> Ecuadorian transport workers go on strike, bringing cities to a standstill in response to a government increase on Value Added Tax, which will result in many of them going out of business.

>> March 29 >> The Arctic Baking Brigade in Helsinki,

Nick Copper / nickcooper.com

One of many walls of gas throughout the city. Québec City, Canada

Global Day of Action April 20th 2001

A20 – FTAA, No Way! Québec City, Canada

"What you don't understand is that when we negotiate economic agreements with these poorer countries, we are negotiating with people from the same class. That is, people whose interests are like ours – on the side of capital."
– former State Department official at a meeting of the Council on Foreign Relations, *American Prospect*, 12 June 1999

People begin resisting the Sixth Summit of the Americas weeks before the leaders of the 34 countries of the Western Hemisphere (except Cuba) meet behind fences in Québec City to lay the groundwork for the world's largest free trade zone, the Free Trade Area of the Americas (FTAA). Although the FTAA – if implemented – will affect 800 million people, from Alaska to Argentina, the draft documents remained secret for years. In March simultaneous actions demanded the release of the documents to the public. On 7 April in Buenos Aires, Argentina, a city recovering

Meyer / Tendance Floue

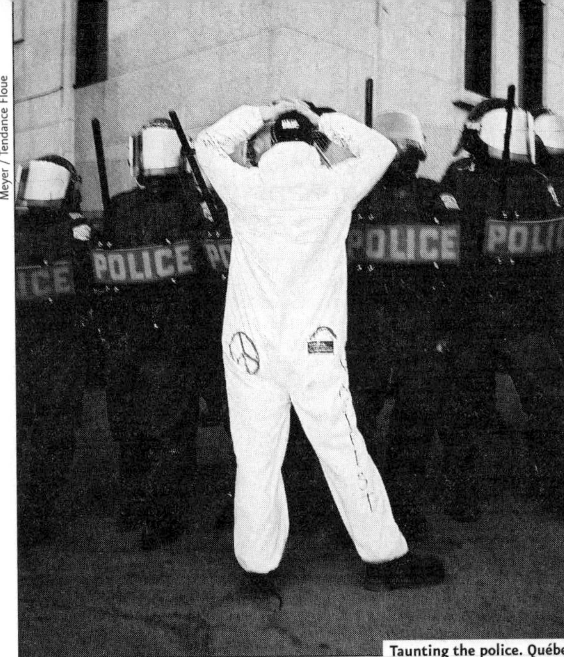

Taunting the police. Québec

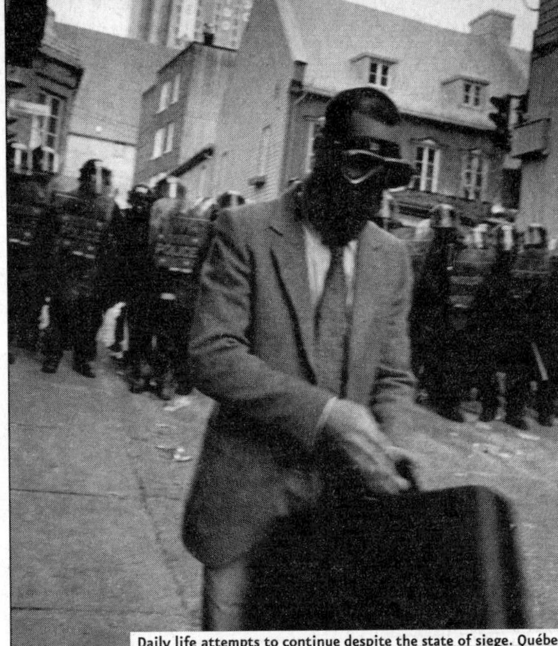

Daily life attempts to continue despite the state of siege. Québec

from two weeks of general strikes against the IMF, trade ministers of the Américas hold pre-FTAA meetings in the Sheraton Hotel and are greeted by 10,000 demonstrators who are fired on by plastic bullets and tear gas. At the end of the meeting the ministers announce to great fanfare that they will make public a rough copy of the agreement before the Québec summit on 20 April. A very partial text with little substance is eventually released at the end of July.

As protesters from across the Américas head to Québec City, which is preparing one the biggest security operations in Canada's history – including a ban on the wearing of all masks and scarves – the community of Las Abejas, in Chiapas, Mexico shows its support for the coming actions by ritually burning coffee crops to protest the starvation prices being forced on small growers.

Many activists are turned back from Canada's borders – one because he has a black hat and is suspected of being a 'member' of the Black Bloc. Others use ingenious tactics to get through: ten US activists pretend they are an Ultimate Frisbee team with custom-made Team Blue Jay jerseys, a van full of Frisbees, and a printed out email-invite to a fictitious

Meyer / Tendance Floue

The labour union march splits and heads towards the fence. Québec

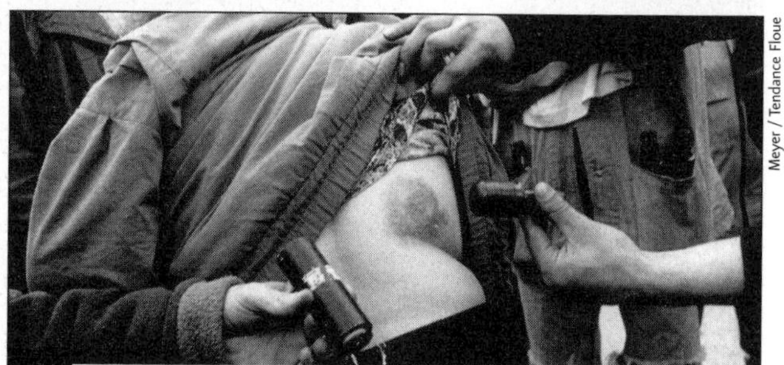
Meyer / Tendance Floue

Local woman shows her injuries from plastic bullets during street assembly. Québec

Frisbee tournament.

The Mohawk Nation plans a solidarity action for the day before the summit, with support from the Ontario Coalition Against Poverty, Anti-Racist Action, the Canadian Union of Public Employees, the Canadian Union of Postal Workers, and high school students, to open the border between Canada and the US which runs through Mohawk territory. Despite weeks of state disinformation telling Mohawk communities that protesters will burn their homes and loot stores in a crazed rampage, the action takes place – but 500 police make sure that few activists actually make it across the border.

A20 dawns and the Carnival Against Capital begins. Before long the fence around the summit is breached. Tear gas fills the entire city and the following day's march organized by unions and NGOs decides to head away from the fence to a distant park to listen to 22 speeches. But tens of thousands disobey stewards and head for the fence instead.

As tear gas rises in Québec, Brazilian police in São Paulo gas and beat anticapitalist demonstrators who carry huge shields of rubber tyres and a three-foot envelope containing a message to the Central Bank of

Meyer / Tendance Floue

Night descends on the city but the tear gas continues to rise. Québec

Brazil: "FTAA – no fucking way". In Uruguay, healthy food is shared with passers by outside a Montevideo McDonald's and in Austin, Texas an 'Anti-Corporate Crawl' visits local transnational companies. All across the US – in Chicago, Boston, Eureka, Jackman, Miami, Seattle, Portland, Vermont, Atlanta, and San Francisco – people take to the streets. Hundreds block the Detroit/Windsor border tunnel; 700 block the Peace Bridge at Blaine/Vancouver, where many dress up as dollar bills and ask the police to let them through because capital is allowed to freely cross borders. Meanwhile on the southern border, several thousand Mexican and US activists join for a festive celebration of transnational resistance whose backdrop is the 14 mile long fence separating San Diego and Tijuana.

As the summit closes, an official press release suggests that "despite protests" an "accord" has been signed. But the reality is that the talks failed – no agreement was reached on an FTAA text, which helps explain why the draft document wasn't released. The accord merely expresses willingness to continue the FTAA process. Meanwhile a pan-Américan alliance of anti-FTAA movements are making ever-stronger links of resistance across borders.

NAFTA, according to *the Zapatistas, was a death warrant. The Free Trade Area of the Americas is sometimes referred to as NAFTA on steroids, a combination of NAFTA and the WTO. It is a trade agreement which would include – if it passes – 34 nations – that is to say, the entire Western Hemisphere except Cuba. It is, unsurprisingly, being heavily promoted by the US, and its goal is to impose the neoliberal model of new corporate investment, patent protections, trade liberalization, deregulation, and privatization hemisphere-wide. It would also include a secret court modeled after the WTO's trade disputes panel, allowing unelected officials with strong corporate ties to determine trade policy.*

The summit organizers made a terrible mistake in choosing Québec City as the site for the Third Summit of the Americas. The people there are friendly, welcoming, and fiercely proud of their unique culture. Those who weren't already against the FTAA became so, as the Government enclosed the heart of the city with a 2.4 mile fence, dubbed the Wall of Shame. Locals queued up to offer housing to visiting protesters, and kept their new-found friends up all night discussing economics and trade. They came in droves to the People's Summit, a conference which focused on alternatives to 'free' trade, and they danced in the streets each night.

During the demonstrations, while police launched tear gas at the rate of more than one canister per minute, local people opened their homes to offer refuge to protesters with children, and ran water hoses out their windows offering relief from the painful tear gas blended with pepper spray. Even the media was on our side, as evidenced by the cover of the main French-language paper. A photograph showing the tear gas blowing away from the demonstrators and engulfing the police sat under the headline, "Un bon vent...." (a good wind)! And indeed, the protest itself was a good wind, which radicalized thousands, and strengthened us in the face of the inevitable repression that followed.

The Bridge at Midnight Trembles

by Starhawk

Under the freeway, they are drumming, picking up sticks and beating on the iron railings, on the metal sculptures that grace this homeless park, on the underpinnings of the overpass that links the lower town to the upper levels of Québec City. They are mostly young and they are angry and jubilant, dancing in the night after two days on the barricades.

From above, the cops fire volleys of tear gas. It billows up in clouds and drifts down like an eerily beautiful, phantom fog, but the dancers keep on dancing. The sound and the rhythm grows and grows, a roar that fills the city, louder than you can imagine, loud enough, it seems, to crack the freeways, bring the old order down. The rumbling of the rapids as you approach the unseen waterfall. A pulsing, throbbing heartbeat of something being born. A carnival, a dance, a battle. No-one has come here expecting a safe or peaceful struggle. Everyone who is here has overcome fear, and must continue to do so moment by moment.

In the chaos, the confusion, the moments of panic, there is also a sweetness, an exuberance. Spring after winter. Freedom. Release. The rough tenderness of a hand holding open an eye to be washed out from tear gas. The kindness of strangers offering their homes to the protesters: come up, use our toilets, eat these muffins we have baked, fill your bottles with water.

We are the Living River: a cluster within the action that sometimes swells to a couple hundred people, sometimes shrinks to 50. Our core is made up of Pagans, who are here because we believe the earth is sacred and that all human beings are part of that living earth. Our goal is to bring attention to issues of water, we say, although our true goal is to embody the element of water under fire.

We carry the Cochabamba Declaration, which was written by a group of people in Bolivia who staged an uprising to retake their water supply after it had been privatized by Bechtel Corporation. They wrote:

"For the right to life, for the respect of nature and the uses and traditions of our ancestors and our peoples, for all time, the following shall be declared as inviolable rights with regard to the uses of water given us by the earth:

1) Water belongs to the earth and all species and is sacred to life, therefore, the world's water must be conserved, reclaimed, and protected for all future generations, and its natural patterns respected.

2) Water is a fundamental human right and a public trust to be guarded by all levels of government, therefore, it should not be commodified, privatized, or traded for commercial purposes. These rights must be enshrined at all levels of government. In particular, an international treaty must ensure these principles are non-controvertible.

3) Water is best protected by local communities and citizens who must be respected as equal partners with governments in the protection and regulation of water. Peoples of the earth are the only vehicle to promote earth democracy and save water."

The Declaration is the alternative. It's what we are fighting for, not against. Our goal is to bring it into the Congress Center, declare the Free Trade Area of the Americas meeting illegitimate because it is not supported by the people, and suggest they begin negotiating to protect the waters. Failing that, we will get as close as we can, and declare the Declaration wherever we are stopped.

As we are mobilizing, our friends in Bolivia stage a March for Life and Sovereignty, which is violently repressed. Oscar Olivera, one of the framers of the Declaration, is arrested, charged with treason, but then released. As we are tear gassed, so their march is tear

---

Finland serves up just desserts to the director of the World Bank, James Wolfensohn, by splooshing two tofu cream pies in his face during a press conference. A surprised Wolfensohn comments, "Mmmm, tastes good, but I'm on a diet." ABB Deputy Commander Marzipan expressed great satisfaction at being the first to throw a pie in Finnish history, saying "We managed to cancel the press conference. It's hard to give an impression of a respected economic leader with your face covered in soya cream." Wolfensohn declines to press charges, although the Finnish prime minister's office later files an official criminal complaint against the two *entarteurs*.

>> March 29 >> South Africans take to the streets of Durban to protest pharmaceutical companies' imposition of patents on essential AIDS medicines. Linking their struggle to that in Brazil, where the drug giant Merck threatens legal action on the same morning as the march, they surrounded Merck's headquarters and hold a rousing rally, complete with traditional *toyi-toyi* dancing and poetry readings.

>> March 31 >> Mass demonstrations by unions and civil society groups clog the streets of Istanbul, Turkey, protesting the financial crisis that began in 2000, and the austere IMF bailout package. "Our problems cannot

gassed, again and again. In Bolivia, two people die, one asphyxiated by the gas. In Quebéc, there are near deaths, a man shot in the trachea by a rubber bullet, asthma attacks from the tear gas, a finger torn off in the assault on the fence. In São Paolo, the youth blockading the Avenida Paulista are brutally attacked and beaten. Broken arms, broken wrists: one of our closest friends is beaten on the head so hard her helmet is split in half, but she refuses to leave because she is a medic. At the private hospital, they refuse to treat the protesters. The police chase them away with live ammunition. Those arrested are tortured, held on their knees for over three hours in tight handcuffs while every fifteen minutes the police come by and beat them on the back. Most are under eighteen.

Friday afternoon. The River has spiralled at the gate at Rene Levésque, where the night before the Women's Action hung our weavings. As we wind up the circle, beginning to raise the power, Evergreen comes up to me with a man in tow who is decked out in the Cuban flag. He is part of a small group of indigenous people who have been holding a vigil at the gate, and our group is so metaphoric, (and we never quite got the signs made that said clearly what we were doing), that somehow he has gotten the impression that we are for the FTAA. We are singing, "The river is flowing," and he is from Honduras and his land is flooded from ecological breakdown and hurricane Mitch, and the only way we can demonstrate our solidarity, he says, is to join him in his chant. "Why not?" I shrug and we begin to chant, "*El pueblo, unido, jamás será vencido!*" (The people, united, will never be defeated).

We dance on down to St Jean Street, where the news comes from our scouts – the CLAC [Anti Capitalist Convergence – one of the groups organizing actions] march has reached the gate we've just left, and the fence is already down. I literally jump for joy. We advance forward and receive cheers – "Hey, it's the River." Closer to the gate, the cops are firing tear gas at the crowd. Young men run out of the crowd, shadows in the fog, and throw them back. The gas billows up and is blown back onto the police lines. We are still able to breathe, and sing, so we start a spiral. The circle grows: other people join hands and dance with us, moving ever closer to the gate, not running away, not giving ground. All along it has been hard to decide what the *action* of this direct action should be. Now we all see that the fence is the action.

We spiral and dance, the drums pounding against the thunder of the projectiles as they shoot tear gas canisters overhead, laughing with the sheer liberation and surrealism of it all. Until at last one shot lands close to us, the gas pours out and engulfs us in a stinging, blinding cloud, and we are forced away.

We decide to flow on, to the blockade on the Côte d'Abraham a few blocks away. We hear that, that gate could also use some energy, and the mission of the River is to flow, so we go on. We could use ten, a hundred Rivers.

The area has been so heavily gassed that many of us can't stay long. The energy peaks, not into a cone of power, but into a wild dance. Our scouts report that riot cops are massing down the street, heading toward us to clear the area. The River flows on. Behind us, we can look back and see the spray of the water cannon, arching high in the air, filled with light like a holy and terrible rain that plays upon the black figures who hold their ground below.

Saturday morning: About 20 of us gather in the house where we're staying. Everyone is braver than before. I am awed. Some of us have been activists for decades, and carry into the actions a slow courage that has grown over many, many years. But some of our people have made that internal journey in one night. And it's one thing to decide, in the safety of your home, to go to a demonstration. It's another thing to face the reality of the chaos, the tear gas, the potential for violence.

I am here, I have done my best to inspire and encourage other people to be here with me, because as scared as I might be of the riot cops and the rubber bullets, I'm a thousand times more scared of what will happen if we aren't here, if we don't challenge that meeting going on behind these walls. Even if the River seems placid, I can hear the roar of the waterfall in my ears. In the beauty of the woods, in the quiet of the morning when I sit outside and listen for the birdsong, in every place that should feel like safety, I know by the feel of the current that we are headed for an irrevocable edge, an ecological/economic/social crash of epic dimensions, for our system is not sustainable and we are running out of room to manuever. In the meeting we are protesting, protected by the fence, wall, riot cops, and the army, they are planning to unleash the plundering forces and remove all controls. Water, land, forests, energy, health, education, all of the human services communities perform for each other will be confirmed as arenas for corporate profit making, with all of our efforts to regulate the damage undermined.

Saturday afternoon: I am standing in the alley with Juniper who has never been in an action before and with Lisa who has been in many. There is an opening in the wall, but the riot cops stand behind, defending it, their shields down, impermeably masked, padded, and gloved, and holding their long sticks ready to strike.

---

be solved unless the IMF and World Bank policies are given up," they declare.

>> April 9 – 12 >> Hundreds of angry black residents of Cincinnati, US storm the local council meeting days after the police murder of Timothy Thomas, an unarmed 19 year old black youth, which was the fifth police killing of a black person in six months. By end of the night an organic and spontaneous rebellion erupts, lasting over three days and fueled by the firing of lead pellet bags at mourners leaving Thomas' funeral. 800 arrests and at least 25 hospitalizations occur, as well as some bridge-building between white antiracist activists and the black communities rising up.

>> April 20-22 >> Global Day of Action, FTAA Québec

>> April 23 >> A two week long March for Life and Sovereignty, which has gathered 30,000 participants from across Bolivia, converges in La Paz. Met with tear gas and repression, the marchers are joined in the struggle by retirees staging a hunger strike to demand raises in their pension.

>> May 8 >> Harvard University students begin a three week occupation of the President of the university's office, demanding that the school pay its employees a minimum hourly wage of $10.25. A year

Willow moves forward, begins to read the Cochabamba Declaration. The cops interrupt, shouting and moving out from behind the fence. Their clubs are ready to strike: one holds the gun that fires tear gas projectiles and points it at us. Lisa and I look at each other, one eye on the cops, the other on the crowd behind us. "What do we want to do here?" she asks me. The cops begin to advance. "Sit down," someone calls behind us, maybe someone we ourselves trained to sit in this very situation. We sit down. The cops tense. We are holding hands. I consider whether we should link up, make a stronger line.

We pass the Cochabamba Declaration back to someone who speaks French and begins to read it out loud. I pass my drum back, hoping one of my friends will pick it up. I see one of the cops slightly lower his baton. Another wavers: their perfect line now shows some variation. They are beginning to relax.

Meyer / Tendance Floue

The entire city is engulfed in tear gas. Québec City, Canada

From behind, someone passes up flowers. Heather brought them in the morning, saying she wanted to do something nonviolent, give them to the police. I remember thinking that hers was an idea so sweet that it belonged in some other universe than the one I anticipated being in that day. She had not looked too happy when I explained that we intended to follow CLAC and the Black Bloc up to the perimeter. "People might think we're supporting them," she said. "Well, we are supporting them," I explained. At least, for some of us that's what we feel called to do – to be right up there with them in the front lines, holding the magic, grounding the energy, not preaching about nonviolence but just trying to embody it. Now Heather and her flowers are here.

Lisa gets up, holding out her hands to the cops in a gesture of peace, and attempts to give them the Declaration. I watch, holding my breath, ready to back her up if they attack. "We can't take it," one of them whispers to her through clenched teeth. She lays it at his feet. A young man comes forward, lays down a flower. A woman follows with another. Somehow, in that moment, it becomes the perfect gesture.

Everyone relaxes. After a time, we decide to make our exit. The River must flow on. Others move forward to take our place. We snake back to the intersection. Behind us, the young men of our cluster are helping to take down the fence along the cemetery. We begin a spiral in the intersection: masses of people join in with us. From a rooftop above, two of the local people shower us with confetti. We dance in a jubilant snow. The power rises, and as it does an absolute scream of rage tears out of my throat. I'm drumming and wailing and sending waves and waves of this energy back at the Congress Centre, and at the same time we are dancing and confetti is swirling down while behind us the tear gas flies and the fence comes down.

In front of the gate on St Jean Street, five young men and one woman stand, their backs to the massed groups of riot cops behind the barrier, their feet apart, one arm up in a peace sign, absolutely still in the midst of of chaos, unmasked, unprotected, in a cloud of tear gas so strong we are choking behind our bandanas. We file behind them, read the Cochabamba statement, and then flow on. They remain, holding the space as their eyes tear, steadfast in their silence, their courage, and their power.

When the Bay Bridge fell in the last San Francisco earthquake, we learned that structures resonate to a frequency. A vibration that matches their internal rhythm can bring them down. Beneath the overpass, they are drumming on the rails. The city is a drum. Massive structures tremble. And a fence is only as strong as its point of attachment to its base.

Starhawk is the author or coauthor of nine books, including *The Spiral Dance*, and *The Fifth Sacred Thing*. She is a veteran of progressive movements and deeply committed to bringing the techniques and creative power of spirituality to political activism.

Note: This is an excerpt; the complete text is available in Starhawk's book, *Webs of Power: notes from the global uprising*, New Society Publishing, 2002

---

later, janitors' and security guards' wages increase and raises for food service workers are negotiated.

>> May 9 >> Five hundred Guatemalan fisherfolk in Retalhuleu begin removing fences installed by privately owned shrimp companies to enclose shrimp breeding grounds. The police open fire on the protesters, killing two young men, 14 and 22 years old, and injuring at least five others.

>> May 9 >> The Asian Development Bank, relocating from its planned meeting place of Seattle for fear of protest, finds itself greeted by activists on the streets of Honolulu, Hawaii despite the largest domestic security operation in US history, which cost an estimated $14,000 per protester present.

>> May 10 >> Panamanians take to the streets against a 66 per cent increase in bus fare and are met with gunfire from the police. It is apparently the most violent demonstration since the US invasion in 1989.

>> May 16 >> Years of organizing against the reroute of Highway 55 outside of Minneapolis, US pays off with the passage of a law protecting the flow of Camp Coldwater Spring, sacred to several Native American tribes. The new law forces the Department of Transportation to halt construction for as long as the

Touching the Violence of the State

by Brian Holmes

The Masks: The world is upside down. Democracy has its face in the mud. Thirty-four of the world's most violent people are enclosed behind their own wall in Québec City. Outside, crowds move freely beneath the cameras of the police. The crimes inside are unbearable, the tension is too great. The Carnival Against Capital is about to begin. Already last night, thousands of bandanas started appearing – orange, red, yellow, the colours of fire. They are hand-printed with a fantastic, grotesque, carnivalesque smile. They are masks. Folded carefully, like a soft weapon. Every gesture, every word of resistance counts. The weapons have these words, on a little photocopied sheet inside:

The Gift of Masks

"A classic crisis of legitimacy has overtaken the key institutions of global economic governance. If legitimacy is not regained, it is only a matter of time before structures collapse ..." – **Walden Bello**

Inevitably as the global movements against neoliberalism and for life have grown and become more vocal, so has the repression. But with each act of repression, the men of money reveal themselves further. No longer can they meet in relative anonymity. Their unmasking has become a carnivalesque ritual, repeated in Seattle, Prague, Seoul, and Buenos Aires...

Now, the fences grow ever higher and the meeting locations ever more remote as the mask of 'tolerance' continues to slip further, revealing an animal that is cornered, knows its time is up, and is fighting for its survival. Besieged by those who desire justice, the men of money are getting scared. They want to name the faces of resistance – name them thugs, terrorists, flat-earthers, delinquents, dreamers. They want to capture, catalogue, and criminalize the faces of those who are saying "enough is enough." They want to wipe the smile of resistance off these faces forever.

"Resistance is the secret of joy." – **Alice Walker**

Carnival and rebellion have identical goals: to invert the social order with joyous abandon and to celebrate our indestructible lust for life. Carnival breaks down the barriers of capital, and releases the creativity of each individual. It throws beauty back into the streets, streets in which people begin to really live again. During Carnival, as in rebellion, we wear masks to free our inhibitions, we wear masks to transform ourselves, we wear masks to show that we are your daughter, your teacher, your bus driver, your boss. Being faceless protects and unites us while they try to divide and persecute. By being faceless we show that who we are is not as important as what we want, and we want everything for everyone.

So we will remain faceless because we refuse the spectacle of celebrity, we will remain faceless because the carnival beckons, we will remain faceless because the world is upside down, we will remain faceless because we are everywhere. By covering our faces we show that our words, dreams, and imaginations are more important than our biographies. By covering our faces we

recover the power of our voices and our deeds. By wearing masks we become visible once again.
– Carnival Against Capital, Québec, 20-22 April 2001.

After the action

How to create new forms of expression, exchange, and debate? How to maintain them over time? How and where – at what scale – to institute new spheres of popular decision-making, and how to link those spheres together in the planetary society?

You think about these kinds of questions, after ... After the "legislative theatre" of the Peoples' Summit and the street theatre of the Peoples' March, orchestrated to transform the city, blending new democratic procedures and old, raising echoes in the press and elsewhere, creating spin-offs and facing parallels in the province, the nation, and across the hemisphere. After the Carnival Against Capital, where so many individuals – from the blackest-clad anarchists to teachers, local residents, intellectuals, artists, children, average folks if there were such a thing – all felt the need to touch the violence of the state, to feel and shake the wall it builds around corporate interests, to taste the tear gas it spits out into the faces of the crowd.

We are not the only ones. Think back on the recent decades: How many anti-IMF riots in Latin America, Africa, Asia? How many local committees, social movements, single-issue and electoral campaigns? How many formal victories for democracy that brought back the police with other explanations?

The ethics, the intelligence, the analysis, the openness, the energy, the creativity, the disruptiveness, and the violence of this dissidence are changing my life, changing the lives of everyone touched by it, from near or far. The stakes are the autonomy and coexistence of all the varieties of human time, against the clock and grid of market exchanges. When we reflect, read, and debate for years, not as experts but as passionate amateurs, it's a very different kind of time. When we dance all night around a huge fire beneath a freeway bridge, drumming with rocks and sticks, it's a different kind of time. When we talk between the bursts of tear gas and the intense work on our own projects, we open up an infinite well of freedom. We are fighting for

---

law remains intact.

>> May 17 >> Greece is brought to a standstill for the second time in three weeks as pensioners, unionists, and young people demonstrate against economic reforms and a general strike closes down most cities. Even state television goes off the air, and radio news stations broadcast only music, interspersed with taped messages from the journalists' union explaining the reasons for the strike.

>> May 17-19 >> More than 1,000 migrants converge on Berlin, Germany and set up a protest camp near the Reichstag, where they conduct workshops and organize small actions. They denounce the illegitimacy of the recently passed Residenzpflicht law (which assigns them to live in a very restricted area). The final day of the camp sees a demonstration of several thousand Berliners in solidarity with the migrants' plight.

>> May 18 >> Thirty-five thousand indigenous and Afro-Colombians march to the city of Cali, Colombia, demanding recognition of their rights to life and autonomy, and expressing their solidarity with the Zapatista caravan.

>> May 22 >> Kenyan state-employed air traffic controllers in Mombasa's main airport go on strike

another time, and for each other's time.

For anyone who went to greet the IMF in Prague, or took part somewhere in a global day of action like June 18th, Québec could come as a kind of revelation. In Prague or London the protesters were like a flying saucer, a message from outer space, with most of the popular support coming from unknown, invisible fringes. Here, the entire city gave us the warmest welcome – because it was mobilized first, many months ago. And support poured in from across the country.

All the complexity and agency of a highly articulated political society was on our side. Tactical debates notwithstanding – 'civil' disobedience, or just plain disobedience – the movement in its different facets showed a coherency that will affect the province of Québec and the nation of Canada in enduring ways, while serving as a model and an inspiration to the world-wide effort that made these revolutionary days possible. The neoliberal project is being torpedoed by those who were to be its 'beneficiaries' – the citizens. Its rhetoric is proving as weak as the absurd fence that fell at the first blows of the crowd.

Counterpowers: on the ground

What was it like for an individual, for someone out in the sea of faces at the FTAA summit protests in Québec City? I don't think many people were alone. Almost everybody was part of some kind of association, from the most organized and abstract civil-society groups – the Hemispheric Social Alliance, the *Réseau Québecois sur l'Integration Continentale*, Common Frontiers, ATTAC, SALAMI, the union federations –

"It's important to draw a distinction between our trade progress and labour and the environment.. We should not link these things together at all costs."

– Canadian trade minister Pierre Pettigrew, June 2000

to your local street-level welcoming committee. Myself, I went as a member of *Ne Pas Plier* (do not bend), which is a small French association that distributes graphic art productions in collaboration with social movements. We deliberately went as a network, inviting artists and graphic designers from the US and England (Cactus), Spain (Las Agéncias), and ex-Yugoslavia (Skart, Emigrative Art), as well as two members of a French social movement (l'APEIS: Association for employment, information and solidarity for jobless and casual workers), and a sociologist working with French radical intellectual Pierre Bourdieu – whose recent statements on the need to encourage a European social movement make a lot of sense to us. We basically wanted to see a translocal social movement in action on a hemispheric scale, and to support it, with the aim of finding out what we could do about that sort of thing at home in Europe.

We held an 'exhibition,' a temporary agit-prop centre in support of the movement, in a Québec City gallery called Le Lieu, which invited us, got housing for us all, and helped us in many ways. The English and American friends brought along the mask project, which four of us developed early on in Montréal with the help of some very generous people – teachers and students at Concordia University. Some 3,500 of these masks – bandanas printed with a laughing face on one side, a gagged face behind chain-link fencing on the other – were silk-screened by hand, at personal expense and with the help of 20 or 30 other people. They were all given away free, a few from the gallery, the majority during the first hours of the protest.

Ne Pas Plier itself brought posters and stickers, distributing a few hundred thousand of them during the 'exhibition'. The stickers included slogans, mostly in French. Another showed the earth as a hamburger, waiting to be consumed. Another said 'free' in various languages. Our idea was to play the political gift against the totalitarianism of the economy, to practice a dispersive art, to spark off conversations through the act of giving signs to strangers – an act which could be performed by anyone, since we gave large quantities to people we didn't know.

The images we distributed were all enigmatic, they asked people to think, to speak, and to play. The city was flooded with them, everyone seemed to love it, it was a fantastic pleasure to do. And all around us, people were doing similar sorts of things.

By the nature of it, the work in the street brought me closest not to the more formal counterpowers of the Peoples' Summit, with its panels of activists and researchers from all over the Américas, but instead to the local activists: OQP2001, who struggled to organize logistics on the ground in Québec City, and the anarchist alliances, CLAC and CASA. With *Ne Pas Plier* we also tried to make contacts with popular education groups and elements of the more traditional cultural and workerist left. In the demonstrations by the fence though, what you saw most was anarchy. So what's the anarchist program? Right-thinking people are always deploring them for being apolitical, spontaneous, violent – not me. I think diversity of tactics is the key.

Mass protest movements, including direct confrontation, are at the heart of any chance we may have to transform society today, and the anarchists seem to know that, maybe better than the others. In these actions, where art has a central role to play and everyone can act artistically, at least

---

demanding better terms of employment and salary increases.

>> May 23 >> Four hundred children reach Buenos Aires at the end of a mammoth 1,242 mile trek aimed at bringing attention to child poverty. It is estimated that 43 per cent of children in Argentina are living below the poverty line.

>> May 25 >> Airline workers set up blockades by parking planes across the runways of the Ezeiza airport in Buenos Aires, Argentina to protest cut-backs and lay offs on Aerolineas Argentinas. Riot police are brought in to disperse workers' actions inside the airport.

>> May 26 >> A coalition of Pakistan's NGOs protest outside the World Bank building in Islamabad. Protesters carry banners saying: "IMF: International Monetary Fraud," and, "World Bank policies: poverty elevation or alleviation?" In a press statement the coalition states that the IMF and World Bank have violated Pakistan's national sovereignty by trying to influence the country's budget.

>> June 3 >> Haitian Cointreau orange workers and local farmers occupy a plantation protesting discrimination against their union's organizers. Every year during off-season the plantation owners

three things happen, which can change your life. The first is that you touch the concrete limits of your rights: you face the police, the gas, the fence, you feel the worst of the system in your own body, and you need that. Touch the state and be radicalized. It's a way to get beyond the cool media screen, to verify what oppression is, to better imagine how it works far away. It was clear that people needed it, and particularly clear in the stories of everyone who left the union march to climb the stairways up to the fence and find out where the real protest was.

The second thing is solidarity, mutual support: we're all here to help each other, with almost nothing on our backs, no armour, no hierarchies, and when someone has the courage to throw the tear gas canister back at the police, you love that someone. Love on the barricades. You can talk to anyone in the crowd, say things you never said for years to your colleagues or even your friends, you can act collectively in simple but essential ways. And the third thing is freedom, the freedom of the city. Walk on a freeway, dress in an outlandish costume, give away your art, build a bonfire on the street at night. Dance in the streets. The power of the drumming, hundreds, maybe thousands of sticks and stones on the roadside barriers, beating out a wild, threatening, supportive, joyful, Dionysian rhythm that came together at times into an incredibly sophisticated beat: that's something you can never forget, you carry it within you. The carnival is a counterpower too.

Québec City looked a lot like the beginning of what I'd seen the end of back in the early 1970s: a countercultural movement with a powerful, articulated politics. We know how that older movement was dismantled, not only through its own internal contradictions, not only through the secret police picking off key people (as they're already doing now), but also by channelling rock music and other spaces of freedom into commodity zones.

What I see today, in the wake of that, is a situation where the only party in town, the only one that can really get you high, is 100 per cent political. Québec City, my friends, was the biggest party you've ever seen, maybe the beginnings of a new political party. It was collective Dionysian political theater. And everyone knows it. There was no real violence: almost no gratuitous smashing of private property (some would say not enough broken banks), no deaths as there might easily have been, not even many broken bones. That level of sublimation was deliberate, and Canadians can be proud of forcing compliance from their cops, who simply were not given the right to break bones and kill. Because the idea is not for us to become the terrorists they want us to be – the idea is to go somewhere we've never been before, to change politics, to change life. To express the violence of contemporary capitalism, to make it real here and now where the power is, and to go beyond it in the same movement. We don't know what 'the revolution' will look like. But we know so many other things: about the nature and structure of exploitation and domination in the present, about the way it is ideologically supported and engineered to bypass any democratic political process, about its key points of weakness, about the new possibilities for organization, and the sharing of both information and decisions. We also know about the course of radical democratic and socialist movements in the past, about the traces and resources they've left in our societies and our hearts, about the political and social rights we've gained collectively over centuries, rights that the state can't take away without losing all its legitimacy and increasing the force of the movement, as it is doing right now.

We know all that, and that's why no one is allowed to dominate, why no-one's in control. But more and more people are starting to play the great revolution game – carefully, with love and intelligence, urgency and foresight, and with the sense that if you make the right moves now, someone else may surprise you tomorrow. As 60,000 people surprised us, beyond all hopes, and in ways we still have yet to thoroughly understand, last week in Québec City.

Brain Holmes is a writer, translator and activist, living in Paris and working with various artist-activist groups in Europe

Note: These texts are from three emails sent at the time

Resources:

» Hemispheric Campaign Against the FTAA: www.movimientos.org/noalca
» Dinero Gratis: www.sindominio.net/eldinerogratis/
» Yomango: www.yomango.net/
» Cactus Network: www.cactusnetwork.org.uk
» Ne Pas Plier: www.nepasplier.fr
» Tendance Floue: www.tendancefloue.net/
» Universite Tangente: www.universite-tangente.fr.st

---

distribute land parcels, allowing the workers to grow millet and corn, and requiring that they give half of the harvest back to the owners. Union organizers are frequently assigned to the smallest portions of the least fertile land.

>> June 7 >> Demanding that the government revive the industry, 12,000 miners converge on La Paz, Bolivia, and vow to stage daily marches and blockades until their demands for better housing, working conditions, nationally negotiated contracts, and debt forgiveness are met.

>> June 7 >> Massive demonstrations shut down much of Colombia's urban centres as a month of strikes and work slow-downs by teachers, state workers, and students culminate in actions targeting an IMF meeting with the government. Major riots take place across Bogota, and the police respond with water cannons, tear gas, and truncheons, while the city bans liquor sales indefinitely. Highways are blocked nationwide.

>> June 15 >> The All-Indonesian Trade Union organizes a massive strike against the government decree proposing to dilute labour laws and cut severance pay for retiring and resigning workers. Under the threat of the strike, the Government backs down.

Meyer/Tendance Floue

Helicopters drop tear gas canisters from above. Genoa, Italy

Global Day of Action

July 20th 2001

J20 – You Are G8, We Are 6 Billion, Genoa, Italy

In the final weeks leading up to the G8 meeting, a wave of industrial action sweeps Italy in anticipation of social unrest to come. Hundreds of thousands of metalworkers around the country take to the streets while a strike by pilots, flight attendants, and air traffic controllers causes the cancellation of more than 200 flights. The protests' coordinator, the Genoa Social Forum, sends speakers to the rallies, asking the strikers to come to Genoa. The strikers spontaneously respond, "We're going to Genoa!" As the demonstrations commence and the tear gas flies, thousands of pairs of underpants flutter in the breeze above the violent clashes. In protest against the G8, Genovese citizens defy a mayoral request to refrain from hanging "unsightly" laundry out to dry. The protests are the biggest to date, with 300,000 taking to the streets; they also are perhaps the most violent, ending with hundreds of people injured, and 23 year old Carlo Giuliani shot dead by conscripted police.

Meyer/Tendance Floue

Hundreds of thousands converge on the G8 from the four corners of the world. Genoa

For over a month, and all around the world, Italian embassies and consulates are targeted in a variety of ways as the most tangible symbol of the murderous Italian state, and the focus of much rage and mourning. Memorials to Giuliani are constructed, red paint is splashed and red wine dumped, slogans are spray painted in Italian and local languages, paint bombs, rocks, and underpants are thrown at the windows, and silent candlelight vigils are held.

In Athens, about 2,500 people march to the Italian embassy, smashing windows of a Benetton and the Ministry of Trade, and burning ten banks along the way. That night, many Italian cars are torched at Fiat and Alpha Romeo dealerships. Several more marches, arsons, and occupations follow.

In Vienna, as hundreds demonstrate at the consulate, a group of people dressed as the Black Bloc run onto the lawn and strip off their clothes. Their naked bodies are painted with the numbers of people still imprisoned or missing in Genoa. Bodies are painted on the ground in Geneva in front of the consulate, McDonald's, and other corporations, while 900 protesters march in Bern, Switzerland, and several attack a police station with paint 'bombs'.

Meyer/Tendance Floue

Police clear the streets with tanks and gas. Genoa

Recent Deaths in
Anti-Capitalist Struggle
GENOA – 1 demonstrator
Papua New Guinea – 3 anti-IMF demonstrators
Argentina – 2 workers at a road block demo
Ecuador – 13 farmers/demonstrators
"Canada", Ipperwash indigenous Nation – 1 demonstrator
Columbia – continuous massacres & assassinations
Acteal, Mexico – 48 Indigenous Zapatistas
Nigeria – 9 Ogoni demonstrators
Don't forget where you stand in the struggle.

George Danez

Sign posted outside the convergence centre. Genoa

In Warsaw, the square opposite the Italian embassy is renamed Carlo Giuliani square, and a grave and altar are established. In London, the Canadian embassy (located around the corner from the Italian embassy) is spray-painted with the words, "You are next!" in reference to the G8 meeting in 2002.

In Kiev, Ukraine, an altar is built and a silent street theatre re-enactment of Carlo's death takes place in front of the embassy. Letters of solidarity pour into Italy from India's Narmada dam movement, the Zapatistas in Chiapas, indigenous movements in Bolivia, and many other people and places where the struggle for survival often precludes solidarity marches.

While 600 march in Helsinki, Finland, Stockholm sees 800 people march, and the Italian tourist information centre is smashed up and spray-painted.

In Manchester, Britain, activists sneak into the Italian consulate, graffiti walls, and spray fire extinguishers into the computers. Then they set off the fire alarm, causing an evacuation of the entire building. Upon leaving the consulate, activists hear consulate staff members muttering, "This would not have happened if Mussolini was still in power."

In Berkeley, US, hundreds join in a demonstration

Meyer/Tendance Floue

Anger erupts after the carabinieri kill Carlo Giuliani. Genoa

blocking rush hour traffic. Dressed in black as a sign of mourning, they link the brutality in Genoa to local issues of police violence. In Buenos Aires, hundreds march to an Italian bank and demand that those imprisoned in Genoa be released.

Representatives from the landless peasants' movement (MST) in Recife, Brazil speak about repression, and a samba band plays and people dance in front of the Italian consulate. In São Paulo, hundreds blockade the entrance to the consulate trapping those inside for over three hours.

On the US West coast, members of the dockworkers' union successfully prevent an Italian ship from unloading its cargo in Portland, and in Oakland, the unloading is delayed by a day. The ship is operated by Italy's main shipping company, which is run by a major financial backer of the Berlusconi government.

Canada's Prime Minister announces that the G8 meeting scheduled in Ottawa the following year will instead convene in Kananaskis, a small and largely inaccessible resort town in the Canadian Rocky Mountains. This leaves one protester to wonder, "Where will they meet next, outer space?"

__In Genoa__, the Group of Eight (the leaders of the seven most advanced industrial nations plus Russia) brought their war of terror to the people. Finally, with no holds barred, this was to be a pre-emptive murderous assault against every political and organizational hue, every colour of action and allegiance. All were to be beaten, laid low before the might of the 'gang of eight,' the Mafiosi of neoliberalism. As the days of action accumulated, it became increasingly obvious that the state might soon resort to its monopoly on deadly force. By the end of 20 July 2001, after thousands had participated in direct action, often in the face of police ambush and unprovoked attacks, Carlo Giuliani lay dead, shot in the head and repeatedly run over by the Carabinieri.

The next day a 300,000 strong demonstration sustained hours of police attack, culminating in chaotic retreats, street fighting, and many injuries and arrests. That night, sleeping activists were beaten in their sleeping bags in the Diaz school, donated by the City of Genoa and opposite the Indymedia Centre, injuring over 60 of the 92 people arrested there and hospitalizing nearly two dozen. Gianfranco Fini, the Deputy Prime Minister of Italy and leader of the National Alliance, a 'post-Fascist' party, had been at police headquarters for two days. Encouraged by Berlusconi, Blair, and Bush and their public support of the police despite the death of Carlo Giuliani, Fini pushed just a little further, and the results were all too bloodily predictable.

Genoa was a key moment; for many in the North it was the moment when the war came home, not the silent, everyday war of repression, poverty, and exclusion, but the visible war waged by an empire that will tolerate no breach in its façade. It was also a moment to mourn our loss, to pause and consider tactics, and to re-group, plan, and think. What follows is a collage of descriptions, experiences, and reflections that came from this process, a mosaic within which the Genoa protests might be glimpsed.

Genoa:
the new beginnings of an old war

Extract from email 'Death and Terror in Genoa' by Ramor Ryan

The walls went up around the old quarter of Genoa, enclosing the G8 and their cohorts: huge heavy walls of concrete and metal, like medieval fortifications or prison fences, walls to keep the people out, the world leaders penned in.

Genoa is a beautiful renaissance city carved out of a treacherous mountain slope that seems to slide irrevocably into the sea. Its pulsating streets, the mystery of its dense labyrinth, and the expansive calm of the seafront created a surreal theatre for the battle that would consume it. Leading up to the summit, the authorities closed down the airport, the main railway stations, and severely restricted access by road. Aside from the centre of town (the red zone), which was completely forbidden to citizens, the area surrounding the red zone was also restricted (the yellow zone) with people enduring random stop-and-searches. Local people fled the town in droves, and most businesses closed for the duration of the summit. The G8 had transformed Genoa from a thriving commercial and tourist metropolis to a war zone under a form of martial law.

As if to justify the extraordinary security measures, the media reported various bomb scares and explosive finds, all of which protesters viewed sceptically. No groups claimed responsibility, and these are not tactics used by the alternative globalization movement. The Italian military brought in an array of defensive missiles, and war ships were stationed in the bay. A state of paranoid terror was created to dissuade protesters from coming, and to criminalize the protesters who did.

Friday 20 July. The aim was to shut down the G8. The strategy was to attempt to breach the fortifications from a variety of positions. The tactics were direct action. The first task was to break through the myriad fortified police lines. The strongest contingent was the *Ya Basta/Tute Bianche* grouping, numbering more than 10,000 militants. They used a previously successful tactic of wearing layers of protective padding and helmets while using plastic shields to push through the police lines. Some wore gas masks. The preparations began with talks and then training sessions. Resembling an army preparing for war, men and women, predominantly young and Italian, spent all morning taping up their fragile bodies with foam and padding. The atmosphere was tense, the mood defiant. It really seemed anything was possible. There was an ecstatic mood of celebration when we finally set off on the two and a half mile march to the city centre, an endless sea of bobbing helmets, a vast array of flags of every hue and colour, led at the front by a long line of *Tute Bianche* militants behind a wall of plastic shields.

Despite all the ominous reports, we swept down the wide boulevard confidently – we were so many! Like an unstoppable river! So many people prepared to use their bodies to break through, to defend themselves, to struggle.

"*El Pueblo Unido, Jamas Sera Vencido*," we chanted. "*Genova Libera!*" "E-Z-L-N!". Rage Against The Machine blasted from the mobile PA – "Fuck You, I Won't Do What You Tell Me!" screamed along by thousands. It was momentarily powerful and wonderful. Then about a mile from the red zone, the police attacked us. First a frantic barrage of tear gas, lobbing over the front lines, deep into the heart of the demonstration; nobody here had gas masks. The poisonous gas first blinds you, then hurts, and then disorients you. It is immediate and devastating. The people, packed in tightly, panicked and surged backwards. The chaos was manic. Five hundred heavily armed riot police stormed the front lines. In brutal scenes and despite brave resistance, the *Tute Bianche* militants' defence crumbled and they were battered.

>> June 15 >> Over 50,000 workers from 126 South Korean unions stop work, despite the strike being declared illegal by the government. All Korean Airlines flights are canceled and efforts by the police to arrest 14 union leaders of the airline are blocked by workers. Nearly 9,000 hospital workers later join the strike, taking action against government plans to restructure. **>> June 15-17 >>** Thousands converge on Gothenberg, Sweden to participate in the For Another Europe conference and the Reclaim the City street party, counter points to the summit meeting of EU heads of state. Despite protest groups' prior negotiations with authorities, a campaign of criminalization, including scare stories in the media about "armed terrorists" creates a climate of fear and tension. Police SWAT teams armed with laser-guided machine guns besiege the convergence centre, using freight containers to barricade streets, while police with dogs and horses attack, arresting 200 people inside . This pattern of containment and provocative policing continues throughout the summit, culminating in police firing live rounds into the crowd at the street party, hitting three people, and sending thousands into panic. Months later, despite conclusive evidence that Swedish police

People screamed, turned, fled, falling over each other. We retreated up the road. The sky was heavy with gas and helicopters hovered overhead. A water cannon blasted away, throwing bodies around like paper bags.

What now? People looked to the *Tute Bianche* leadership in all this horrible disarray but there was no Plan B. Silence from the microphone that had being commanding us to follow their directions the whole march. People retreated further and further, eventually sitting down. The *Tute Bianche* leaders told people to hold this space, this nowhere space over a mile outside the city centre, signifying nothing. Meanwhile the frontlines struggled to hold on, and the fighting was intense, the tear gas volleys raining down, the police hitting out viciously, as the plastic shields shattered, the helmets cracked. Injured people were rushed to the back, injuries to the head, people who had been shot in the face with tear gas canisters. We were defeated before having even begun the nonviolent direct action tactics, active defence crushed in the face of decisively brutal police tactics. As the majority of the march sat down further up the road, thousands of others streamed off into the side streets. The right side was blocked by the railway track, but the left side was a labyrinth of tight chaotic enclosed streets.

Open new fronts! Break through police lines at two, three, four different points! A couple thousand people stormed into the side streets. The *Tute Bianche* loudspeaker requested people to stay put on the road, far from the red zone. In a beautiful old *barrio*, the battle raged. Protesters charged up tight streets flinging stones at the police lines. The police, protected head to toe, amassed behind shields and flanked by armoured vehicles, responded with tear gas and by flinging back the rocks. The ferocious spirit of the protesters rather than the paltry stones pushed back the police lines. Then barricades were built, with dumpsters, cars, anything at hand. The front lines retreated, nursing wounds and poisoned eyes. The more seriously injured were carried to ambulances. One man was carried by with blood spurting from his eye where a canister had hit him. New people rushed to the front, others tore up the pavement for ammunition. A tall Irish man fell back, saying, "We almost got through, we just need a few more people ...!"

Another surge, everybody rushed forward on two or three different streets. Some riot cops got stranded in their retreat and hand-to-hand fighting ensued. The people fighting are not necessarily in black, although some are masked. Some have helmets. It is not the Black Bloc, and there are no agent provocateurs. This is a militant energy driven by people who have said – "*Ya basta!* (enough), fuck the police", with rage, energy, resolve. They move forward; tear gas everywhere, the police retreating. An armoured vehicle is captured and the occupants flee. It is smashed up and set ablaze. This armoured *Carabinieri* truck, symbol of what they hate, is ablaze and everyone is cheering and filled with rebel joy. Someone sprays "We Are Winning!" on the side of the carcass of the armoured beast. Now they are almost in Piazza Alimondo. They are pushing the police back, two, three blocks, the protesters are euphoric, storming forward, overwhelming the despised *Carabinieri*.

Getting closer to the detested wall of the G8; "Here we are," they chant, "We resist!" Hundreds strong, they pour into the expansive Piazza Alimondo. Two police vehicles drive recklessly into the crowd, one drives away, the other stalls; people rush towards the vehicle. Then shots ring out. Plastic bullets? No, the ominous thud of live ammunition.
The air heaves. The protesters stop, reel around, and flee. Carlo Guiliani was 23 years old. A rebel. The papers belittled him, called him a ne'er do well, a bum, a hobo. But we know him as a comrade and a revolutionary. He fought the paramilitary police bravely, fearlessly. He was involved in the Zapata Social Centre of Genoa. Zapata lives. Carlo's death was not heroic, nor tragic. It was the consequence of his life, how he lived, how he resisted. Moments before he was shot in the face, Carlo probably felt the extraordinary rebel joy of this spontaneous uprising against power in the little side streets of Genoa. He died instantly, or when the police drove over him, not once but twice, as if to make sure he was dead, really dead. For the police, Carlo had to die. Now they must kill us, because we are beginning to really threaten their power. Carlo was murdered. We are all Carlo.

"Genoa is Bupyeong where the Daewoo Motors workers were bloodied, is Ulsan where Hyosung workers protesting against restructuring were threatened with knives, and is also Yeoido where striking cement-mixer drivers were attacked by police armed with axes and hammers. What is definite at this time is that there can be no compromise between neoliberal globalization and lives of the workers and people. They have already started to aim their guns and proclaim war against the peoples around the world."

– Mi-Kyeong Ryu, Secretary of KoPA (Korean union association) in Genoa, comparing it to repression experienced by Korean workers

---

creatively edited video footage used as evidence, heavy jail sentences are passed on many of the 600 arrestees. UK prime minister Tony Blair declares that "...there is no place in democracy for an anarchists' traveling circus that goes from summit to summit with the sole purpose of causing as much mayhem as possible."
>> June 18 >> Students and ordinary citizens join striking bus drivers in the streets of Jakarta, Indonesia, jointly declaring that the proposed removal of fuel subsidies will make it impossible for bus drivers to earn their living without raising fares. Police respond with plastic bullets and tear gas, and 42,000 Indonesian military personnel are put on high alert after running battles in the streets. Local authorities decide that rather than maintaining subsidies, they will increase bus fares by 30 per cent, vastly compromising the ability of poor people to get to work.
>> June 18 >> In Zimbabwe, protesters block roads in response to a 70 per cent rise in fuel prices. The Congress of Trade Unions renews its threat to call a general strike if the Government does not revoke the price rise.
>> June 21 >> Special Agent Chocolate Supreme generously delivers a blueberry tofu cream pie to the

Assassini: the day after

extract from email report by Uri Gordon

Saturday arrives, and until noon it seems like the march will go through peacefully. I don't join, not seeing the point of walking four hours in the sun, and stay instead at the media centre with a girl who is too afraid to leave there. The march begins, and I go to a high place to see it from above. I can't believe my eyes. The police massively attack part of the demonstration for absolutely no reason, tear gassing the whole area, including the parking lot that serves as the Genoa Social Forum convergence centre, and a nearby beach. Some people are forced to jump into the sea just to escape. The march breaks up; more than 150,000 people fill the beach promenade for miles, some dispersing to side streets. The riots go on, spread again all over town. People at the back of the march manage to retreat, others choke and get beaten up. Some Black Bloc-ers advance to defend them, and again the sights of burned cars, defended retreat lines, smashed windows, and wounded protesters.

Then, on Saturday night, on the pretext of looking for the people who had caused the violence, the police come outside the media centre where I am. This is the headquarters of the mainstream, nonviolent NGOs in the Genoa Social Forum. Certain that they're about to raid the building, I run up to help barricade the top floor, trying to buy time to get rid of sensitive material. I get cut off; the barricade has already closed. I climb to the roof, and see them entering the school opposite the centre. They start smashing people up, screams and shouts all over the place. And then they're in our building. I try to get back down and almost run straight into the hands of the police. I turn around and escape back up – I still don't know how they didn't see me. The roof is empty now, and I find a niche to hide in, some kind of a store-room that has a window off the roof. The police are now all over the building, and I later hear that all the people had to stand with hands against the walls of the halls. Police gathered all journalists, and then searched the rooms. They confiscated mini discs, digital cameras, and 'weapons' such as Swiss army and kitchen knives.

I spent the longest 30 minutes of my life in that enclave, certain that if I were found I'd be killed. I just breathed, avoided the helicopter searchlights and waited for it to pass. At the end, activists came onto the roof and I knew the police had gone. I stepped out, and saw hundreds of police down the street, and ambulances coming in to clear the carnage at the opposite school. People were screaming "Assassini!" and "We won't forget." They had beaten up everyone to the extent that most of the people could not walk out and had to be carried in stretchers out of the school. I don't know how many people were badly injured because we lost count of the amount of stretchers carried out of the school, but they brought about 30 ambulances for the injured people. The police also brought at least one body bag outside, maybe two, and at the time we thought there might be more people dead. [It was later revealed that the body bags were used to transport the injured, as paramedics had run out of stretchers.]

Testimony of Terror

statement of Morgan Katherine Hager

State of Oregon. ss. County of Multnomah

I, Morgan Katherine Hager, being first duly sworn, do depose and say as follows:

The following is a summary of what I recall about the incidents of the morning of Sunday 22 July and the events that followed. Even though I was injured and afraid at the time, my memories are clear (although some minor details may be inaccurate). This statement focuses on what I directly experienced or saw. When I refer to events I didn't directly experience or see, I have so indicated.

Sherman Sparks and I, together with our friend Angeline, traveled to Genoa and participated in the peaceful protest marches there. We at no time engaged in any violence against persons or property. The G8 ended on Saturday 21 July and about 9.00 or 10.00 pm on Saturday night, Sherman and I went back to the school where we had slept the night before. We were looking for Angeline. Angeline wasn't there, so I checked my email and sent an email to my parents, telling them that everything was fine, the protests had ended, we were safe, and we were going to leave Genoa first thing the next morning. We considered joining Angeline, who was sleeping at another location (one of many camps in and around Genoa), but by this time we were too tired to find another place to sleep. Anyway, we thought the school would be the safest place to sleep. The camps didn't seem to be safe because we had been told the police had visited them on a number of occasions and the encounters were not pleasant, although not violent. Also, the school was across the street from the Indymedia Centre and the clinic, so we perceived that the closeness gave the school some protection.

Sherman and I lay down in our sleeping bags on the first floor at about 11.00 pm. We fell asleep. I can't remember if Sherman woke me, or if I woke because of all the noise. Regardless, I woke to crashing and yelling outside. There was chaos everywhere. People were running around trying to collect their belongings. There was a great deal of noise. The police were breaking down the doors and smashing the windows. I later heard that someone had barricaded the

---

face of Enron Corporation CEO Jeffrey Skilling in San Francisco, US, where he is scheduled to speak on "The Roles and Responsibilities of the Energy Industry". Agent Chocolate Supreme pies Skilling, saying: "This is for the millions you've stolen from California's real working people." The accomplished *entarteur* continued, "Mr. Skilling, who personally made $132 million this year, creamed us – so I, Agent Chocolate Supreme, felt obligated to cream him back."

>> June 22 >> Municipal workers go on strike in Kakamega, Nigeria, to demand payment of their salary arrears. Workers say that without payment of salaries they cannot continue to meet family obligations and buy basic necessities.

>> June 24 >> Unions and activists stage a celebratory march, having prevented the World Bank from holding their annual meeting in Barcelona, Spain. World Bankers around the world regret the loss of the opportunity to snack on *tapas* together ostentatiously as they are forced to conduct their meeting online. A major scandal erupts in the following week as it is disclosed by the mainstream media that police broke windows, started fights, and instigated riots at the end of the march.

>> June 26 >> Students stage a five-day blockade of

doors after the trouble started out in the street and at the media centre. I quickly began collecting my belongings, but I didn't manage to get my shoes on or collect my belongings before the police entered the room.

Sherman and I were sleeping behind a wall so we did not have a view of the main entrance to the school. People across the room had a direct view of the entry. The first thing I noticed was that they were getting down on their knees and putting their hands up in signs of peace or non-resistance, surrender. All of those across the room, about 15 in total, were doing that. Sherman and I immediately did the same thing.

The police rushed into the room. They were dressed in dark clothing, and may have had protective vests under their clothing because they looked exceedingly bulky. They wore helmets with plastic face covers, heavy boots, gloves, and carried batons. I am certain no skin was showing on any of them. I later learned that these police were part of an anti-terrorist force called the DIGOS. I know the Italian press has reported that 20 policemen were hospitalized after the raid on the school, but that is difficult to believe based on what I saw and experienced.

The first thing I recall the police doing was kicking a chair into the group of people kneeling on the floor. I could hear things smashing this whole time. A few police (between five and seven) ran into the room. One came over to our corner and, as I was kneeling with my hands extended, he kicked me in the side of the head, knocking me to the floor. Sherman and another man who had been sleeping near us helped me back up to my knees. Another policeman came to where I was kneeling and started beating me with his club. I was up against the wall, and I curled over with my right side against the wall and my hands and arms covering my head for protection. I tried not to move because I thought he would stop beating me sooner if I lay still. I am not sure how many policemen were beating me. I looked up and saw Sherman being beaten. After they stopped beating us, Sherman and I lay curled up by the wall for about five minutes or so. I think at this point the police were bringing people down from the upper two floors.

I noticed that there was a lot of blood around us, and that blood was smeared on the wall. I think it was our blood because we were both bleeding from the head, and I was bleeding from my hands and wrists. About five minutes later, the police ordered everyone in the room to go over against the opposite wall. As I was walking across the room to do so, the policeman who told us to move struck me in the butt with his club. We all curled up against the opposite wall. At this point I noticed that my bleeding right hand was swollen, and my little finger was sticking out at a strange angle. Sherman's eyes looked glazed and he wasn't responding to questions normally.

We sat against the wall as more people were herded into the room and basically piled up with us against the wall. All had been beaten, and some had to be carried down the stairs by others who had also been beaten. I was shaking and couldn't stop. We stayed against the wall for five or ten minutes more until paramedics in orange suits started arriving. By this time the original policemen who had done the beatings were gone and the room was full of different riot police wearing the *Carabinieri* uniforms.

Every once in a while, the police would take a few people out of the room, making them walk with their hands above their heads and shouting at them and pushing them out. The paramedics began laying the most severely injured out on sleeping rolls and covering them with sleeping bags. Eventually, they got stretchers into the room. All the paramedics did was pass around some rags with disinfectant because they were not equipped to deal with the number and severity of the injuries.

I smelled human excrement and blood in the room as I lay against the wall. The man to our left had a severely broken arm and I could see the bone ends pushing up on his skin. It was enormously swollen and he was in extreme pain. The people to our right – one man was bleeding from the head and wavering in and out of consciousness. A girl curled onto the floor and was shaking.

The paramedics told us that everyone who didn't need to go to the hospital was to move to one side. Initially I didn't want to go to the hospital, so Sherman and I moved to that side of the room. The paramedic stopped us and told us we needed to go to the hospital.

People were being carried out on stretchers and, about 30 minutes later, we walked out behind the stretcher of the man with the broken arm. Outside the courtyard of the school, there were very large numbers of police, and they were lining up as if to create barriers. I saw some media people and saw flashes from cameras. I covered my face. People were in the windows of the media centre and behind the lined up police, and they were yelling *assassini* (assassins).

I had about seven X-rays: both hands, head, chest, ribs, legs, and back (as best I recall). The person who did the X-rays spoke no English; he would just grab me and push me to get into position. It hurt a great deal. When he was X-raying my hands, he wanted them flat on a screen and he tried to force them flat. I cried out in pain. Neither hand would go flat because of the injuries. Finally, his assistant stopped him and said *roto* (broken). After the X-rays, they pushed me back into the hallway.

---

university and government buildings in Port Moresby, Papua New Guinea in protests against World Bank plans to privatize national assets like the PNG Banking Corporation and Air Niugini. As they exit the university with their hands up, the police fire shotguns and M-16s at close range, killing four people and injuring twenty. The students' demands are the expulsion of the IMF and World Bank, the cessation of Government borrowing from the Bank, and the resignation of the government if this does not happen. After the refusal of local police to disperse them, Prime Minister Mekere Morauta transfers riot police from their usual job of protecting pipelines and gold mines owned by the US and Canada. A month later the Government's privatization plans falter and the students claim a partial victory.

>> July 1-3 >> Thousands manage to slip across the militarized border and join Austrians in protest against the WEF meeting in Salzburg. Despite 5,000 police who threaten to shoot at protesters, and a ban on most protests, the main demonstration is quite lively until it is surrounded by police, penning people in for six hours.

>> July 18-19 >> Argentina's main union calls a two-day strike following President De la Rua's public admission that the country is forced to implement IMF-

They told me one bone in my hand had two fractures and that my ribs were also fractured. After my parents arrived in Italy, I saw another doctor, had new X-rays, and was referred to an orthopedist: three different bones in my right hand are fractured. Both hands and my left forearm were terribly swollen. I was in pain during this time.

At this point, I really started noticing the police (they were the *Carabinieri*, which are paramilitary riot police). I went to sleep and woke up to see three police officers standing there staring at me from across the hall. I was told that police in the hallways were slapping their clubs into the palms of their hands as threats to those in the beds as they roamed up and down the halls, and also that they were tapping the beds with their clubs. After another long while, I was taken to have a cast put on my hand and was then returned to the hallway. I was semi-delirious at this point and drifting in and out of sleep.

I woke up being pushed on a stretcher down a hallway into emptier parts of the hospital. It frightened me because I didn't know where I was going. I asked the orderly in Italian several times where we were going and he ignored me. I remember being afraid that I was being taken somewhere to be beaten again. They put me into a room at about 6.00 am I slept, but kept waking up and realizing that I was in different places. I remember that they took blood. When I woke up everything was gone from my pockets except my wallet, which had been emptied of everything except the money and my identification. They also took the card the American consul had given me. At all times, our room was guarded by *Carabinieri*, who prevented us from moving around or looking out of the window, and eventually ordered us to sit on our beds. Basically, the hospital had been turned into a prison.

A Canadian girl and I were taken to get a CT scan. We were then fed. I was not offered pain medication. We were told to dress, and then escorted from the hospital room and handcuffed together. In the hallway, we were turned over to detention centre officers. When I shifted around in the handcuffs to try to get them off the cuts on my wrist that was not in a cast, the detention officers tightened the handcuffs. They grabbed us by the handcuffs and pulled us to the transport van. When we arrived at the detention centre, they pulled us out of the van by the handcuffs. As we were being led through the lobby of the detention centre, an officer came up and grabbed me by the back of the head. He pushed and held my head downward and yelled something in Italian. We were never told we were under arrest and never told that we had any rights.

We were put into a detention cell (a square room with a stone floor and no furnishings at all) with about seven or eight others from the school, both male and female. We were all very afraid that we were going to be beaten again. Eventually they came and took the males away and brought in about 20-25 females, all of whom had come from the school.

During this time, they came and took people out one by one for fingerprinting and processing. They told me to sign some papers when I was being fingerprinted, but I refused.

The papers were in Italian.

Some girls who had been in there since the night before had not yet been given water or food. About four hours later, we were each given a ham sandwich and water. At about midnight, they gave us four or five blankets for all of us (we numbered about 31 by then). The windows of the cell were covered by bars and screens only, and the wind was blowing. It was very cold in the cell, and we were trying to sleep on stone floors with our various injuries.

During the whole time, we were repeatedly told differing stories about what was going to happen to us. Sometimes they said we'd be free the next day; sometimes they said we'd be in jail for at least a week; sometimes they said they were going to start taking each of us out individually for "interviews" to see if we would go free; sometimes they said they were going to take us to a different jail that night to sleep and shower.

In the middle of the night, they started taking people out of the cell one by one again. I don't believe anyone was brought back. My turn came around daylight. I was taken into a room where they took my belt by cutting my belt loops. (They had returned my clothes at some point before this). They told me to take out my earrings, so I took out the ones that I could given the fact that my hands were too injured to do much. They made me take my clothes off and stand in front of a man who then asked me if I did drugs or had any health problems. I was taken to another room where they again demanded I take out the rest of my earrings (the ones that remained were thick metal that I could not bend to take out), and all I could tell them was that I could not and gesture at my cast. A guy came in with a knife and gestured that he would just cut them out. Eventually, the two guards bent the earrings enough to take them off and threw them in the garbage. Then they used scissors to cut my hair off (they left a ragged inch or so all over my head).

At this point, differentiating the days is very difficult. Basically, I spent one night in the detention centre, two full nights in Voghera Prison, and was transported from Voghera to Pavia Prison at about midnight on the third night. The first night at Voghera, the Italian prisoners were released.

During one of the recesses in the yard, a priest came to us

---

imposed austerity measures because the country's "sovereignty is limited" due to difficulties in repaying its $128 billion debt. Outraged at proposals to cut public salaries by 13 per cent and cut pensions benefits, tens of thousands of workers take to the streets, blocking roads, shutting banks and government offices and marching on Congress.

>> July 19-21 >> Global Day of Action, Genoa G8.

>> July 25 >> Ten million Indian state employees go on general strike against privatization plans and call for a halt to IMF, World Bank, and WTO policies. A union spokesperson said that the government policy of backing globalization is selling the country to the transnational companies and foreign interests, adding that: "This will serve as a warning to the government against their anti-worker polices."

>> July 31 >> More than 500 Nepalese protesters denounce a 40 per cent electricity price hike by the Nepal Electricity Authority, which succumbed to pressure from the Asian Development- and World Banks to raise prices as a precondition for fresh loans on water resource development.

>> August 6 >> In Maputo, Mozambique a strike by the railway services and dockworkers at the port brings

with information about charges being made against us, and a list of weapons the Italian police claimed were found in the school. The weapons listed that I remember were things like Swiss army knives, wallet chains, helmets, sticks (I know there were sticks there that had been taken from banners), and metal poles (the Canadian girl I was with said she saw police cutting open backpacks and taking poles out of the frames). They also said they found two Molotov cocktails. [Later revealed to have been planted by the police]

On the third day, I had a preliminary hearing at the prison. This is the first time I saw my lawyer, and was allowed a two minute session alone with him only after I asked for it. I answered questions from the judge and made a statement to the judge about what had happened to me at the school, the detention centre, and in prison. I was formally told the charges against me, which the judge said were resisting arrest, being part of a criminal organization, causing bodily harm to the police, and possession of weapons. I understood that according to Italian law, after the first appearance before a judge, I was entitled to a phone call, which I didn't get. I was taken back to my cell.

Later, we were brought down one by one to hear the verdicts in our cases. I was told that I was free to go and would be released in one to two hours. There was no mention of deportation. We waited for many hours in our cell for the anticipated release. Finally, they took us downstairs where they gave us bags with what was left of what was on our persons when we were taken to the hospital. They had us sign a paper saying everything was

"[The G8] are in a position of all ruling elites, who must preside over the flow of wealth from poor to rich, without appearing to do so." – **Jeremy Seabrook, *The No-Nonsense Guide to Class, Caste and Hierarchy*, New Internationalist/Verso, 2002**

there. My Italian money that had been in my wallet was gone, and they explained that it had been taken to pay for anything I wanted to purchase in the prison. (I purchased nothing). My friend Angeline recovered my backpack, boots, sketchbook, and coat from the school after the police had finished searching; however, all of my other belongings, including $200 in American money, $300 in travelers checks, and my return airline ticket, were missing.

We were put into another holding cell and then taken one by one to a police van and driven to Pavia Prison. On this ride, the police talked loudly in praising terms of Mussolini and Pinochet. They took us into Pavia Prison and put us into a small room where eventually the German consul came and informed the German citizens of their deportation. Nobody ever told me I was deported. I didn't know what was going on at this point, but we stayed in Pavia for five to seven hours. One by one, we were again photographed and fingerprinted and told to sign a deportation order. We were taken to a small airport in Milan (no US flights) and left there by the police. I heard a rumour that we had 24 hours to leave the country, but was never told that directly. The deportation papers actually said (as translated by the American consul) that we had been taken to the border and were to leave the country immediately from there. This was not true, but we would not have been able to prove to the police, if we had been stopped, that we were left at an airport in Milan with no money, not at the border. None of us had any money, and some had no passports. Two volunteers from a human rights group offered to take us to a safe house to sleep and to try to make arrangements to leave the country. We went to the safe house for the night. Sherman and I were reunited with our parents at the American Consulate the following day, and I flew home with my parents on 28 July.

Although I am grateful for the large amount of media attention the beatings have received in Italy and the rest of Europe, because I am sure the attention hastened our release, I also realize that the focus has been drawn away from the overarching issues and reasons for our presence in Genoa in the first place. I sincerely regret this.

Will A Death in the Family Breathe Life Into the Movement?

by Richard K. Moore

Seattle may have been some sort of watershed, but Carlo's killing in Genoa is a turning point for the anticapitalist movement (if we can call it that). How we play it from here will have repercussions far beyond the blood-stained streets of Northern Italy. It was no freak cub-cop overreaction that left one mother mourning and several others preparing to, as the sun hit the sea on Friday night, but a deliberate act of terror, in the most basic sense of the word.

The snowball that's been gaining weight and speed as it rolled through Geneva, Prague, and Gothenburg has become far too jagged a spike in the side of those steering the planetary carve-up. So bullets meet brains, and young people are shot dead for daring to think there can be another way.

The message from the world's authorities is clear: go back to your homes, do not meddle in what doesn't concern

---

the south of the country to a standstill. The workers protest plans to cut the work force, one of the largest in the country, by half under a World Bank restructuring program. In the third week, strikers fire their union leaders and set up an independent negotiating team. The few trains that continue operating do so under armed guard.

>> August 7 >> Frustrated by failed attempts to persuade the government to give subsidies and to end food imports, Colombian farmers join rural communities in setting up roadblocks across the country. Two protesters are killed by police. Meanwhile, labour unions in Bogota go on solidarity strike in support of bus and taxi drivers, who are protesting increased taxes. Hector Fajardo, Secretary-General of the United Workers Federation says: "We [are out in] the streets to support Bogota's drivers and protest against the neoliberal program emerging in Colombia." Meanwhile, in Sydney, Australia, a group of 25 Colombians take over the Colombian consulate, demanding an end to US influence over Bogota.

>> August 13 >> Strikes and protests gather momentum in Argentina with a nationwide mobilization of *piqueteros*, the militant unemployed movement, which

you, return to your televisions, to smoking dope and stealing traffic cones, and leave the intricacies of global economics alone – because if you don't we will kill you. The same way we killed Carlo Giuliani.

For decades, the poorest of the planet's families from Asia, Africa, and Latin America have been burying the fathers, the sisters, and the first born sons who have dared to confront the forces of global capitalism. But Carlo's death spells something different. For the first time the global elite has begun to kill the children of its own people. Dissent will no longer be tolerated. The whip of economic dictatorship is finally cracking at home.

But where we go from here is still up for grabs. The globalizers would dearly love to see us run scared, or split our ranks with paranoid accusations of "whose side are you on?" Tactical difference should not be confused with police-collusion and counter-revolutionary activity ... or vice-versa.

True enough, there were cops in ski-masks leading the more excitable and naive among Genoa's young bloods on attacks on corner shops, bus stops, and post offices. But the agitators can be addressed. If everyone who takes any action knows why they are taking it, and knows what sort of action they think is necessary to achieve their goal, then the police will not be able to steer the crowds, the meetings, the discussion groups, or the movement as a whole. The problem is less one of infiltration, more one of focus.

The more liberal elements of groups (such as the Genoa Social Forum – GSF – or Prague's INPEG) need to understand that just because they have the ear of the newspapers doesn't mean they speak with the voice of the people. The reformist agenda of these groups – who call for more legislation, more institutions, and stronger government control over the runaway capitalist train – is an entire philosophy away from the genuine participatory democracy sought by many.

Instead of calling for the deployment of "nonviolent methods of restraining and defusing violent behaviour" for those who fail to adhere to "the political and ethical parameters of our mass actions" (Walden Bello, I expected so much more from you), perhaps the up-in-arms brigade should be questioning their own attempted coup of the global resistance movement. Both INPEG and the GSF produced documents laying down "rules" for "participation" in what were illegal blockades of international meetings. The GSF tactical manifesto was insulting to the resistance history of many of its signatory groups. The anarchists were perhaps the only people (police included) who took to the streets with honest intentions, both about their goals and what they were prepared to do to achieve them. The anarchists have long been aware that power (be it economic or governmental) is the problem – not who holds it – and needs, therefore, to be removed altogether. The Black Bloc do not detract from 'the message' – they have a different message. And unlike the liberals and the hierarchical groups of the organized left who would, at best, replace those in power with their own institutions manned by their own people, and at worst, settle for a seat at the G8 table, the anarchist's message is not a lunge for the throne shrouded in the smoke screen language of 'justice' and 'liberty'. The anarchists recognize that a power-wielding state is no better than a power-wielding corporation, and they are well aware that the police are the front-line defence for both.

This is not to dispel organization. Organization is imperative. Co-operation and communication between the disparate groups involved in the resistance is key. But an insurrectionary pseudo-government (complete with pseudo-police if Walden gets his way)? Hmmm ... it's two legs good, four legs bad time already.

The strength of this movement/loose-amalgamation-of-people-who-ain't-taking-any-more-shit has always been its leaderless fluidity, its constantly changing strategy, its unpredictable tactics and targets. This is why the authorities (until now) have found it so hard to get a handle on what we were up to – we weren't following patterns or playing by any discernible rules. Now, as we witnessed in Genoa, the Man has caught up. Infiltration is the price of protesting-by-numbers. Though Italy was an ideal venue for us to mobilize an unprecedented number of insurrectionaries, it was also a touch for the global authorities who could mobilize one of the West's most corrupt, right wing, and violent state security forces. Recent history has shown the Italian security services are prepared to stoop to anything in order to undermine subversive movements. Genoa proved they haven't lost their touch.

The point has been made that if the nonviolent protesters came up with something that worked, maybe more people would adopt their tactics. However, nonviolence should not be confused with not rocking the boat – as often appears to be the case. Those who feel the 'violent anarchists' are curbing their successes should maybe look at how successful their own tactics are. It is no coincidence that Tony Blair 'welcomes' peaceful calls for debt reform – the communiqués are duly issued, the lip service paid, and then ... nothing changes, and the global carve-up getting mapped in the Oval Office doesn't miss a step.

Maybe the movement's time would be better spent skipping the anarchist witch-hunt and focusing on our common enemies. One of the more eye opening moments in Genoa came when the nonviolent protesters and the Black Bloc crossed paths. At around three o'clock on 20 July, a

---

shuts down over 300 highways across the country. Over 100,000 unemployed workers participate and the economy is effectively paralyzed. Thousands are arrested and five killed, but the movement continues building momentum and support.

>> August 15 >> Activists in Mauvezin, France tear up three plots of land where genetically engineered corn trials are growing. It is the third action since June when the Agriculture Ministry was forced to publish the list of GMO test sites.

>> August 16-20 >> The Dignity in Resistance Congress in Toez, Columbia sees 20,000 indigenous people gather to approve by consensus their position and plan of action for peace.

>> August 16 >> The Yes Men send their WTO 'representative' to deliver the keynote address at the 'Textiles of the Future' conference in Tampere, Finland, where he models the Management Leisure Suit, with its gilded Employee Visualization Appendage.

>> August 28 >> Angolan teachers defy a ban on their three day strike and take to the streets demanding that the Education Ministry adhere to the agreed wage package negotiated by their union.

>> August 28 >> Teachers in Blantyre, Malawi

Black Bloc tried to cross the Piazza Manin en route to the red zone. The nonviolent white-handed pacifists in the square refused to let them pass. Discussions between the two groups were interrupted by a vicious police attack during which the white hand protesters sat down, hands aloft, and took a severe beating without fighting back (as is their prerogative). However, an hour later when three masked youth walked back through the square, the (understandably upset) pacifists threw first a stick, then a bottle, then a rock at them. They saw the Black Bloc as the cause for their pain. No violence had been directed at the police wielding the boots, the clubs, and the tear gas, but strict pacifist adherence could be suspended in order to attack anyone without authority who had not stuck to 'their' tactical code. Perhaps this pacifist submission to authority says more about the the authoritarian nature of the society they seek, than about their abhorrence of the Black Bloc's tactics.

The more reasoned voices of Italy's *Ya Basta* collective are already admitting the error of attacking the brick throwers (there is something twisted about an elite *Tute Bianche* hit squad in Subcomandante Marcos t-shirts beating people with crash helmets for wearing bandanas over their faces). However, the security services will no doubt be fuelling the fire of division and will embrace the 'peace-policers' (as they did during the anti-war protests of the 1960s) who, they hope in turn, will return the anticapitalist front-line to the letters pages of the *Washington Post*.

The rats inside the global red zone want us to crawl back to our workplaces, to the fear of unemployment, and to the gratitude for an irregular playtime. But we can say no. We can say: we do not care how well protected you are with your armies, your police, your banks, or your brands, because we have had enough and we will not run from your guns.

These would-be leaders can scuttle off to Qatar, or cruise ships, or Rocky Mountain retreats, but we know their meetings have little impact on the real decisions made elsewhere. Perhaps we in the West should follow the example of India's farmers who removed Monsanto's headquarters brick by brick and took it away. If we don't like Bush's missile defence plans, we could go to Flyingdales and take it away... brick by brick, bullet by bullet. We have the ability to take capitalism out piece by piece, pound by pound. We could pick a company, say Balfour Beatty [construction conglomerate which builds dams, among other things] and put them out of business. A thousand actions at a thousand sites, dismantling every facet of their insidious business – would their shareholders bail them out? Unlikely. Then we could move on and up. When we can coordinate our actions as millions of people, then maybe we can dismantle the oil industry, the arms industry, the jail industry, the government industry ...

The mass street actions we have been able to mount, and the dedication, planning, and application of those on the streets has shown us that we have the wherewithal to make decisions and carry them out regardless of what the state may think or threaten. If we put this dynamic to work away from the mega-summits we can become a threat again. But we need to be imaginative and we need to stay ahead of the beast. Where we choose to go from here is crucial to whether we are in the process of sparking serious global change or whether we are merely in the death throes of another cycle of resistance.

If we don't want corporate activity in our neighbourhoods, let's chuck the corporations out. If we don't want the police or the government flexing their muscle in our neighbourhoods, let's stop recognizing their bogus authority and encourage others to do the same. Let's link our communities together – not through state or business initiatives – but through people who share a common struggle. If we believe in making changes and creating something better, and if we are prepared to take the risks and put in the time, then let's do it. Let's not let Carlo's death be in vain. Because when one of us catches a bullet, a club, or a jail sentence, a little bit of all of us dies. But together we are alive and together we can, and we will, win.

Protecting the Movement and its Unity: a realistic approach

by El Viejo (excerpt from an email)

Genoa showed that antiglobalization has become a vast social movement: 300,000 people demonstrated, despite the intense criminalization campaign conducted since Prague and Gothenberg. And opinion polls in countries as different as Greece, Switzerland, France, and Italy indicate that a large majority is in favour of the movement.

To this massive popular pressure, our rulers (right and 'left') have not made even the slightest, the most reformist concession over the past three years. They have only one answer: police violence. Their plan is simple: frighten as many as possible so that they stay home and condemn the radical part of the movement; radicalize and criminalize the rest.

We must all abandon (at least in the short run) our self-important illusions that we can persuade or impose a single perspective on the whole movement. Debate must continue of course, but whatever our particular position within the

---

demonstrate, demanding payment of back salaries, and the reinstatement of benefits, cut as part of austerity measures. Police respond with tear gas.

>> August 29 >> Farmers in South Cotabato, Philippines join with local Earth First! activists to destroy genetically engineered corn. Tearing down fences and tearing up fields, the activists destroy the test site in five minutes. Police leave the scene when confronted by the media, while Monsanto employees photograph the protesters, all of whom escape successfully.

>> August 30-31 >> All major South African towns and cities are nearly shut down as nearly four million people participate in a two day strike against privatization and lay-offs. A union spokesperson says: "We want to broaden the public sphere and limit the space in our society that is dominated by unelected, undemocratic, profit-driven forces."

>> August 31 >> Over 20,000 people march against the UN World Conference Against Racism in Durban, South Africa, saying that racial apartheid has been replaced by economic apartheid.

>> September 2-7 >> A massive grassroots campaign, the Cry of the Excluded, organizes a

movement, the really subversive approach is to think how to protect the whole movement and make it grow. This is true of movements in general, and even more of this one in particular, for whom diversity is a central value and goal. Any attempt to hegemonize the movement is a blow against it.

Over and above our very real differences, paradoxically we actually need each other. Without the 'radicals' this whole movement wouldn't have existed and would now be quickly recuperated, co-opted. Without the 'reformists,' we would be isolated and wiped out. We are at once opposed and allied. And the sooner the regime can drive a wedge between us, the more difficult it will be for us.

So we would like to say to the 'nonviolent' side: If you try to impose nonviolence without discussion as though it was obviously the only legitimate means, you will lose all credit with the young radicals, for you will appear to align yourselves on the position of the police and to implicitly accept the idea that the changes needed are possible without challenging the rules of the game set by the regime, and its legitimacy. Should we really scrupulously respect the property of multinationals amassed through murder and exploitation? Rightly or wrongly, violence of different kinds has been inseparable from practically every movement for radical change in our culture, and has often been considered necessary to provoke real change.

The 'Black Bloc,' as such, doesn't really exist. There are just different persons and groups – often dressed in black – who share the opinion that destruction of property, and in some cases violence against police, can be an effective and legitimate political tool. Implicitly, they invoke the legitimacy of self-defence against a regime whose own illegitimacy and incredible violence is every day more obvious.

So repeating the enemy's revolting propaganda about these people (that they are purely destructive, nihilists, etc.) will not moderate or dissuade them. On the contrary, it can only confirm their desperate suspicion that they are alone in a sea of corruption and political naivety. On the other hand, it is urgent to start a serious debate on the pros and cons of violence with them. Because we have been through all this already. We have seen the most generous and determined of a generation abandoned in isolation cells, suicided or killed. And the world is in too bad a state to let history go on stuttering.

To the 'Black Bloc,' we could say: We refuse to renounce the right to violence as a legitimate right of self-defence against an inherently violent system. And that is an important idea. But at the same time we recognize that perhaps our principle demand is a less violent society and that the movement that builds that society must resemble the society we want. So our violence must always be as minimal as possible. We won't win by force, we will win because people like our practices and the ideas behind them. And the right to self-defence is just one of our ideas. Let's not get hung up on it or identified politically only with that.

Another of our ideas is precisely that we want a less macho society, in which force isn't the only recognized way of deciding things. And that idea is much better expressed by nonviolent direct action, by the sober and determined refusal to accept injustice. Yet, another idea is that we are for a diverse and non-hierarchical society in which all can be heard, without being silenced by the behaviour of others.

It is also important that our movement should not always be expressing rage, but also the joy, the life and laughter of a real movement of liberation. We want to leave this grey and violent world behind, reproducing it as little as possible in our forms of struggle. All these ideas, and more, are as important as the legitimacy of our violence, and can all be eclipsed by the excessive imposition of violent methods.

Victorious movements are ones that can adapt to circumstances, use violence when really necessary, but also humour, music, reason, patience; being stubborn in one case and negotiating in another. Flexibility is the secret of survival for any living thing.

Anyhow, no one part or tendency of the movement can seriously expect to convince the others in the short term. And if they seek to destroy the others, they will assure the victory of the enemy. For me, consciously trying to spoil other groups' game or to impose their opinions on others is the only thing that can de facto put a group outside the movement. Whether those who do this kind of thing consider themselves anarchists or autonomous or pacifists, they are acting like Stalinists. The movement must be like the society it is building: a place of autonomy, diversity, and respect.

Objectively speaking, this movement would not exist without the 'radicals.' It was nonviolent but illegal action and the Black Bloc that reawoke the world's political imagination. But without the mass of 'moderates,' the radicals would all be in jail already. Is it not possible for us to see, beyond our narrow views, how to preserve the whole movement, keep ALL of it as safe and wise as possible, make it grow?

The debate will continue. But there are also other urgent things to discuss. In particular, how to profit from the truly historic opportunity, that the human tide of Genoa is a small part of. The regime has not appeared so totally illegitimate for decades. In three years, the antiglobalization movement has practically become a subject of consensus.

Anticapitalism is following close behind.

---

national popular referendum throughout Brazil on the internal and external debt. Over six million Brazilians vote that the government should cease payments on the external debt.

>> September 4 >> Environmental groups protest outside the Brazilian Congress in response to a controversial bill which would allow farmers to clear larger areas of the Amazon for agriculture. The new bill stands to increase the proportion of forest that can be cleared for export farming, from 20 per cent to 50-80 per cent.

>> September 10 >> Two thousand people defy security forces and flood Midan al-Tahrir in central Cairo, Egypt, in solidarity with the Palestinian intifada. Demanding an end to US aid to Israel, the protest is the first public demonstration in the square since 1977, and launches a revitalization of Egyptian activism, particularly among women and students.

>> September 13 >> Mexico City is brought to a standstill as thousands protest in response to plans to impose taxes on certain foods and medicines.

>> September 13 >> Villagers from the Kajarg community of South Sulawesi, Indonesia carry out a traditional ritual as part of a demonstration against

Street medic during S26. Prague, Czech Republic

Action Medical

It may seem strange to think about first aid as a form of direct action, but the reality is that our needs as radicals are different, and groups such as the Red Cross/Crescent don't meet them. Emergency medical services tend to coordinate with the police; during demonstrations this frequently means they can't or won't cross police lines in order to treat the injured. And they certainly don't have much experience removing the contact lenses and scrubbing the bodies of hundreds of people after they've been pepper sprayed by the police. This is where street medics come in.

It doesn't take an expert with lots of certifications to help keep people safe and secure during an action. A neurosurgeon who can't work collectively is less useful than someone who has no technical skills, is really nice, and has lots of water to share. Some of the most important stuff can be done by anyone. It's always useful to try and spread calm. You can try and negotiate with police to allow an ambulance to come, or to delay a police charge until a patient has been evacuated. You can even help by handing out information about healthcare post-action, or lists of free / activist-friendly clinics and practitioners.

How to fight the power and do no harm:

Step 1: Prepare yourself
Because you'll sometimes be working in extreme conditions, it can be good to mentally prepare. Talk with other healthcare workers (activist or not, some of the issues are universal) about the stress and the gratification; watch videos of mass actions to get a sense of crowd dynamics and tactics used, and envision yourself working in similarly chaotic situations; go on actions and see if you can

Meyer/Tendance Floue

find medics in the crowd. It's good to be aware that medics may be arrested, as the police generally won't treat you differently than other protesters. Prepare yourself also for boredom – long marches where nothing happens, no one gets hurt, and you're stuck carrying loads of water.

Step 2: Get first-aid training
Start with a basic course, and if you like what you learn, get more training. There are several radical healthcare collectives in the US and in Europe that teach first aid courses addressing our special needs as activists. But if there isn't one near you, the next best thing would be to find something like a wilderness first responder course. This may seem strange if you're an urbanite planning a street party, but if you imagine the city filled with riot police, road blockades, public transport strikes, or other disruptions associated with large actions, you can see that the trip to the hospital which normally takes ten minutes might take three hours during an action. You might as well be in the wilderness in terms of your access to high tech healthcare. The Red Cross/Crescent offers trainings as well, designed more for family care than crisis, but they'll teach you basic skills applicable in the streets.

Step 3: Assemble your gear
Street medics are often 'gear-heads', and so there are innumerable variations on what to carry and how. In terms of first aid materials, carry only what you're confident with and trained to use. Over time you'll figure out what is essential. Most everyone agrees that packs that are worn on the hips are most easily accessible and backpacks are the least. Some people wear helmets and gas masks and others wouldn't dream of it. Protection from the elements, a sun hat or rain gear, is really nice. Comfortable shoes are crucial. Multiple pockets. Lots of water and latex or nitrile gloves are essential. A good attitude, even more so. And don't forget a bandana or two.

Step 4: Coordinate with others
Working with a partner is highly recommended, in fact, you'd be completely crazy not to. This is for safety reasons as well as practical reasons – it's nice to have someone to watch your back, call for help, and shoo away the media while you're focused on helping someone. You could be a medic for your affinity group, or you could form a group in which all members are medics. Whatever you do, it's good to figure out your limitations, not only in terms of medical skills, but also regarding your level of comfort. Do you want to be in the front lines all the time, or do you want to wait around the corner and catch people as they run from police charges? Don't be afraid to say, "I don't know how to deal with this injury," and seek someone who does; don't shy away from saying "I don't feel comfortable staying here." Respecting your limits is one of the most important things you can do on the streets.

Step 5: Take care of yourself
Witnessing lots of injuries can be hard. Debriefing with others after actions, even if only for ten minutes, can really help prevent trauma, burn out, and feelings of isolation. Be sure and drink lots of water, and be good to your body and mind. It's crucial to work sustainably.

Hopefully this information helps you to be safer and stronger in your activism. Remember that we do this because it's important and fun, and that at least some danger is essential to life.

Resources:
» Info on protest safety, trainings, and pepper spray/tear gas: www.blackcrosscollective.org
» US network of street medics: www.action-medical.net

When the state of Israel was initially founded, it provided a much-needed sanctuary for Jews around the world whose communities have been oppressed for thousands of years, particularly crucial for the tens of thousands of refugees who narrowly escaped extermination during the Jewish Holocaust. Having sought asylum in numerous countries and been rejected, they came with relief to Israel to find refuge and repose.

Tragically, the state of Israel was formed at the expense of the Palestinian people. In 1947, a UN resolution partitioned the land, giving the Israelis about 56 per cent of the land despite numbering only one-third of the population. In the war that followed, over 700,000 Palestinians were driven off the land, 400 villages were depopulated, and innumerable Palestinians were massacred. It is therefore no coincidence that Israel's independence day is the same day that Palestinians observe al Nakba, the day of catastrophe.

As the global balance of power shifted from Britain to the US, and as Israel proved itself to be a strong and capable player in the region, the US found it strategically advantageous having Israel as a junior partner to its empire. Despite what many perceive as strong US support for Israel, the current situation is not beneficial for the people of Israel, except perhaps in the very short term.

The September 2000, with the beginning of the second intifada (literally, uprising), extraordinary violence has come from both sides of the conflict. It is clear that the waves of suicide bombings commited by fundamentalist Islamists and/or underground guerrilla organizations are both morally reprehensible and politically counter-productive. However, Israel's army has killed more civilians than have the Palestinians, and has implemented: severe restrictions on movement between towns, internal closures which function as seiges (preventing the entry and exit of people, food, or goods), and curfews, which effectively imprison entire populations in their homes – violations frequently result in arrests, indefinite incarceration and torture, or death.

The suicide bombings are directly tied to this occupation and the violation of international law, and so it is unrealistic to imagine the Palestinians unilaterally halting all aspects of their uprising – attacks on the occupying military as well as suicide bombings – without any concrete change in Israeli policy. As Stephen Zunes writes, in Tinderbox, "International law sees terrorism as a war crime, but recognizes the right of people under foreign military occupation to armed resistance against the occupying forces. Unfortunately, both sides have muddied the issue. Some Palestinians claim that suicide bombings against Israelis civilians … constitutes legitimate resistance. On the other side, the American and Israeli governments condemn Palestinian attacks against uniformed Israeli occupation forces as 'terrorism'."

All civilians of the region effectively have their hands tied. A large majority of Israelis in a 2002 public opinion poll supported peace talks, and said that the problem of terrorism couldn't be resolved without them. The Palestinians, for their part, suffer under what Zunes says "may be the worst leadership of virtually any national liberation movement in recent decades", with large segments of the population alienated by Yasser Arafat and the Palestinian Authority.

Although it is clear that there is nothing grassroots about the structure or funding of the Palestinian Authority, or some other players in the intifada, many individuals and families are coming together to create new forms of resistance, and to provide much needed services and infrastructure to their communities. They are being joined by international activists working with the International Solidarity Movement (ISM), which was formed shortly after the beginning of the second intifada. ISM has a mandate of nonviolent direct action against the occupation, and has facilitated participation and solidarity work for hundreds of internationals who join Palestinians in putting their lives on the line in an effort to stop the violence and open a space where peace can take root and flourish.

International Solidarity: accompanying ambulances in Palestine

By Ewa Jasiewicz

> *"If you have come here to help me, you are wasting your time ... But if you have come because your liberation is bound up with mine, then let us work together."*
>
> **- Lilla Watson, aboriginal educator and activist**

People have often viewed the Palestinian/Israeli struggle as somehow outside of the anticapitalist movement. Palestinians want their own state. Anti-capitalists, by and large, want to see the dissolution of the state, since the state reproduces and reifies capital, perpetuates capitalism. The Palestinian resistance, in mainstream media representation, is often reduced to one for an Islamic state, waged by masked fundamentalists. What can activists do in the face of so many competing armed factions? Do you really want to be complicit in the creation of an Islamic state? Where does the struggle fit in our imagining of a world without borders when so much of it is about securing borders? On the surface, the struggle does not fit neatly into the trajectory of anticapitalist international struggles which we can identify with in the West, those which mirror our aims and desires, such as that of Argentineans rejecting politicians and government; the West Papuan Freedom Movement which resists the state and technocracy, or the direct democracy-generating Zapatistas.

Yet ultimately, the Palestinian struggle is a fight against colonialism, state fascism, and endemic racism. The final outcome of what it is for and what shape this will take is undecided. It may be an Islamic state, a Marxist-Leninist state; a liberal parliamentary democratic state; a US-overseen free market-driven state; a police state; or an autonomous zone recognized as an independent state. The land that Palestinian people live upon is a resource exploited by Israel and the US, and requires the eviction of the Palestinian populace numbering just 3.5 million – approximately half the population of London. The struggle

---

Monsanto's genetically engineered Bollgard cotton. The protesters wear black headbands and brandish swords while burning scarecrows along with two tons of GMO cotton. They demand that all transgenic crops be banned from South Sulawesi.

>> September 17 >> One hundred-thousand farmers gather in New Delhi, India in a last ditch battle against plans by the World Trade Organization to liberalize agriculture. Farmers are worried about highly subsidized imports of agricultural goods from rich countries flooding their country. Mahendra Singh Tikait from the Bharatiya Kisan Union says, "Unless you organize and come into the streets, nobody will listen to you."

>> September 17 >> In Cochabamba, Bolivia, the third conference of Peoples' Global Action begins, despite having been described as a meeting of "potential terrorists" by the governor. Post-September 11 panic among security forces results in the stranding of thousands at the Bolivian border, threatened deportation of delegates, and immigration authorities stating, "Visas for PGA people are no longer valid." In this chaotic environment, 300 delegates meet from 35 countries, and reaffirm their commitment to the struggle against capitalism and for life.

is against that exploitation and expropriation, and its dynamic is mirrored throughout the world.

As internationals, we come as spanners in the corpse machine. We come as a small chance to free up new possibilities, for resistance and imaginings of a new reality – whatever that will finally be. It means walking with people, listening to them, absorbing their stories and pain, then speaking it out to death-numbed Western audiences. It means accompaniment, riding with ambulances, witnessing atrocity – often with no powers to stop it – staying with the kids in the street when they're fighting back and dying. All the camera-grabbing stuff – the placing of your body between soldiers, guns, and tank-fire – that's minor compared to the living-with, daily, non-spectacular emotional support solidarity is about. An international grassroots presence can also help break down barriers of suspicion and myths of Western populations' acceptance and support of what their nation-states are perpetrating with the help of their taxes and silence. As my Irish friend says, "We go also to show that the West has more to export than just bombs and bloodshed." We go to show that their oppression is linked to ours, that we are fighting our own states as much as they are; and that ultimately, their liberation will be ours too.

I came to the Occupied Palestinian Territories by myself and immediately hooked up with the main coordinating body for international volunteers in Palestine – the International Solidarity Movement. ISM was created to bring internationals into the territories to witness, document, demonstrate, and protect people living under the occupation. This is to be done by exploiting the enduring pathology of white supremacy, wherein a Western life is worth more than that of a Palestinian. Spilt Western blood is a global news story; spilt Palestinian blood is *aade*, usual, as regular as breathing.

I've been riding with the ambulances of the Jenin *Helal Ahmar Falastini* (Palestine Red Crescent Society—PRCS) for three weeks now. For all intents and purposes, the *Helal* is the equivalent of ambulance service in the UK, but smaller, more decentralized, and aims to minimize hospital admissions by carrying out emergency procedures in mobile clinics and Red Crescent Centres. Many of the ambulance drivers and doctors are also highly qualified surgeons and physicians with ample experience and verve in dealing with all types of emergency and chronic cases.

Started up in 1968 when the Palestine National Council issued a mandate to provide social health and welfare services for the Palestinian people, the PRCS relies heavily on medical volunteers – local and international – plus donations for its survival. It represents the largest Arab Red Crescent Society, constituting a network of over 70 hospitals, 300 clinics, and dozens of health and social welfare centres. Since this *intifada* and the escalation of the occupation, it also occasionally doubles up as a taxi service, fire-engine fleet – when water trucks or fire engines are blocked – and, since the Palestinian Authority cops scattered during the first invasion in March, the local police service.

The *Helal* centre is basic. The walls are adorned with

glossy shaheed (martyr) posters of Dr Khalil Suliman. Dr Suliman was incinerated in March when a tank fired a shell at the ambulance he was in. The IDF said the ambulance was booby-trapped, stacked with bombs, but everybody in Jenin knows that it was attempting to reach the dying in the refugee camp.

Cream and white marble steps lead through iron doors into a simple reception area, consisting of a grey marble floor, plastic white lattice stools, a cream marble and wood coffee table, an overused payphone, and a simple, bashed up and bandaged phone — the emergency line, which also receives hundreds of hoax calls each day. Volunteers sleep on mattresses on the floor of the office and beds in a dormitory. Mice skip-scuttle across the floor at intervals, and people sit around, tired, trying to keep alert by drinking tiny cups of amber mint tea or thick sweet Arabic coffee. A comfy old ambulance seat rests on the porch. Everyone takes turns answering the emergency phone, and ambulance shifts rotate according to exhaustion levels. The operation runs smoothly and loosely. There are about four ambulances, mostly old 1960s vans with creaky steel door handles, a driver and passenger seat in front, and a wobbly plastic stool in the middle. The newer model sports sliding doors, three seats in the front and a swifter, smoother ride due to the sophisticated suspension, steering, and gears. The fleet of four serves 200,000 people every night, according to the Red Crescent. Usually though, there's just two in use.

I wandered into the centre one afternoon at 3.30 pm and didn't leave until 8.00 am the next morning. There I met Ashraff, head of the ambulance service volunteers, a wide-eyed, animated, irreverent 26-year-old who speaks fluent Ukrainian. Then I was sussed out by a paramedic named Jalaa, a tough, elegant Muslim woman who improved my Palestinian vocabulary in exchange for Polish obscenities.

Our first patient of the night is a pregnant woman. All the pregnant women attended to are either a month or more overdue, or need a caesarean. Our ambulance crew (me, Jalaa, and Ghassan – a nervy ambulance driver and former US resident) has to go to a newly-imposed army checkpoint on the outskirts of Jenin and meet another ambulance carrying the woman. I have to request permission for her to pass the checkpoint and walk with me

---

>> September 17 >> Activists in Ayvalik-Sarimsakli, Turkey storm the conference hall where the twelfth Biotechnology Congress is taking place. Wearing Frankenstein masks, they hang banners and distribute leaflets until security forces attack and evict them.
>> September 29 >> Kenyan teachers strike in opposition to a government housing allowance initiative, which subsidizes the rent of some teachers but not others. The strike, which lasts for over a week, ends up with running battles with the police. Meanwhile Mombasa Council workers start dumping municipal rubbish in the streets to protest against continued non-payment of three month's salaries. The littering protest continues until the Council promises to pay.
>> October >> Hospital workers in Blantyre, Malawi stage a three week strike over nonpayment of promised wage increases. The central hospital is looted during its shut down, and a large supply of drugs stolen. The strike is resolved when the government agreed to pay interim monthly awards until the wage increases are implemented.
>> October 4-13 >> Massive protests rock the region of occupied Western Sahara and southern Morocco, as

to the other ambulance.

At night the drivers guide the ambulances fluently, slowing just in time to avoid or breach concrete speed bumps, tank-shot trenches, shell-smashed holes, bare end-of-the-tarmac drops and any other Occupation-created hazards. The nights are the hardest. Six military checkpoints ring Jenin. New roadblocks – mini mountains or unexpected valleys – slam up randomly. You never know what might turn up, abort your route and maybe cost a life. And when darkness falls, there's an increase of fear, soldier agitation, and friction between the few Palestinians still moving and the young, edgy troops.

It's dark and balmy on the way there as we wind, with windows down and elbows out, through clear streets lit warm by the lights of garden *shisha* cafes and grocery stores which double as drop-in centres. The revolving lights splash red over rock-and-rubble side-roads, hillsides, and the wasted outskirts – grey pulverized asphalt, ankle deep, like a moonscape in the dry night. Ghassan tells me. "You know we never used to have this problem with the checkpoints. We used to pass through, they would know us, we would know them. They didn't treat us like they do now."

We approach the checkpoint – a tank and an armoured personnel carrier (APC) – stationed just in front of a broken-through road block. High piles of heavy limestone rubble and dust have been manipulated into a narrow weave-through passage. The air is spiced with the smell of pines, craning from the scrub banks flanking the road.

I walk up to the tank. It and the APC are virtually invisible, blending into the arid landscape in khaki, encrusted with dust. The smell of the pines makes me feel good, it's like cool caves and frankincense smoke. The tank shines its searchlight squarely onto me. "*Shalom*," I say, peace, shielding my eyes. I am ordered to go to the APC and am followed by its mounted gun. I have to explain to the APC and unit commander, an olive-skinned, steely-eyed man that the woman in the ambulance 30 feet away from him really is going to have a baby, and yes, it really is an emergency, and could she please pass? He asks me where I'm from, what I'm doing here. I answer and throw the questions back at him. When reminded about the emergency case of the pregnant woman needing to give birth, he flicks his hand as if to say, "Bring her forth." She steps out of the ambulance heavily, supported by her mother, walking gingerly and looking increasingly distraught, as the tank and APC loom closer. The APC gun tracks her. The soldier doesn't take his eyes off her. "*Ma-ye, ma-ye*," she gasps, water, water. I think she must be thirsty and assure her there's water in the ambulance. She looks feverish and on the verge of collapse, stumbling along, gripping one side of her maroon velvet dress. I take it in my hand and realize it's soaking wet - her waters have broken. The soldier lets us through eventually, after a five minute lecture letting me know that ambulances are regularly used by terrorists to transport weapons and suicide bombers.

Ten minutes later we're back at the same checkpoint. This time it's to bring across a young boy with a metal spike lodged in his throat. Everything has to come out of the ambulance. Ghassan lifts out crutches, plastic blankets, luminous foam neck braces, cotton gauze packets. We're eventually allowed through to bring him further down the road to us. Coming back with him we have to stop and all pile out while they search the ambulance again.

Next it's a boy suffering from a scorpion bite to his knee. Same checkpoint. The soldiers are getting angry now; it's the third time in 40 minutes that they've seen us. Two search the ambulance. The kid looks petrified. This time they say they're holding back his uncle. It's taking them ages to check his ID. My passport is subjected to extra long scrutiny too. Initially I refuse to let go of it. Me and the commander get into a bit of a mini tug-of-war with it, which ends with him finally gripping it, rock-still, and glaring at me darkly. I let go.

Ghassan says he's going to the hospital with the kid and asks the soldier to let the uncle start walking towards Jenin; he'll be back to pick him up. "If the ID is clear then yes," says the soldier. I say I'm staying with the uncle. "OK," says Ghassan and the ambulance doors slam shut, top lights revolve into life; it speeds off. We watch the tail-lights melt from red to black. The pine trees emit their heady, sweet, musky scent. The soldiers talk to us until Ghassan returns, then they pass down the uncle's ID card from the APC and we walk rapidly to the ambulance.

Back at the *Helal*, Ashraff is sitting on an old wicker chair, feet on the edge of the coffee table, tapping his knee and singing a popular Arabic chart-topper. We all sit down, chill out for a bit. He answers a few calls – most of them hoaxes. He's getting restless. "Hey, let me show you a picture," he says, brightly, and bounds off to get it. I doodle new Arabic words in my notebook and listen to the sound of the walkie-talkies crackling out commands. He returns as the phone rings, slaps the photos on the table, and answers it. "'Ello?" They say hello instead of *marhaba*. I take a look. At first glance I think it's a female patient, badly injured, with a doll by her side. A grown woman lying with a doll, a broken and rather creepy looking, dirt-covered doll. On closer inspection I see that it's a little girl with the top of her head blown off. She must be about six or seven years old. The top of her skull is gone, replaced by just a craggy, diagonal, jagged line sloping down to her right ear. Her

---

demonstrators converge on town halls in Asrir, Assa, El Layoun, and Smara demanding self-determination and independence of the indigenous people, a release of political prisoners, and an end to repression of the Saharawi people. Meanwhile, in order to expedite the plunder of resources, the Moroccan government illegally grants concessions for off-shore oil exploration on the entire Saharan coast to oil companies from the US, UK, South Africa, and France (Kerr-McGee, Enterprise Oil, Energy Africa, and TotalFinaElf).

>> October 26 >> In São Paolo, Brazil, police captain Francisco Roher is pied while attempting to present his master's dissertation thesis on human rights, while 150 protesters block the room in which he is meant to present. Captain Roher was commander of the force that violently repressed demonstrations against the FTAA six months previously. As a result of his command, 100 people were injured, 69 were arrested, ten were tortured in prison, and one was shot. His dissertation, apparently without intended irony, is on community policing, and explores the difficulty police officers trained during the military dictatorship face under civilian rule.

>> October 30 >> In solidarity with their striking teachers, Nigerian students invade the main highway

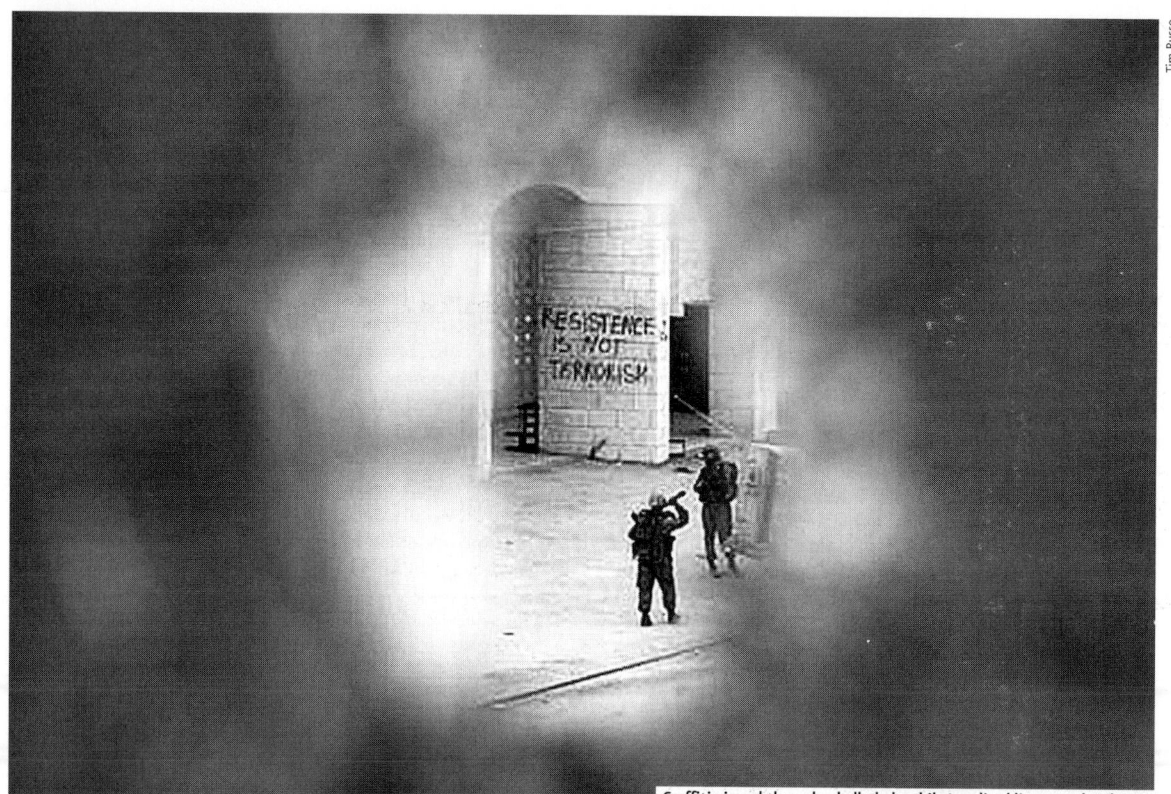

Tim Russo

Graffiti viewed through a bullethole while Israeli soldiers patrol. Palestine

mouth is slightly open, a long caked streak of blood stretching out across her cheek, and her eyes are looking slightly down, not bulged in shock, just normal, but slightly forlorn. Her and her mother's clothing are drenched and charred dark black-red with blood. "They were shot by a tank," says Ashraff, slamming the phone down, tapping his thigh, looking about. "They were out picking olives."

Abdel Rahim walks through the door. He's tall and skinny with bright black eyes and a small moustache furring his upper lip. He's the shyest but one of the hardest working volunteers at the centre. He got involved after the April invasion, giving up his days and nights, four days in a row sometimes, to drive the endangered. The Israeli Occupation Force (IOF) demolished his house a couple of days ago. I was on shift when we got the call. Abdel's brother was the military head of *Jihad Islami* in the West Bank. He was a huge, combat-wearing, out-and-out fighter, who walked around the camp armed to the teeth and ready, as many wanted people have to be. He was also incredibly gentle, always stopping to ruffle kids' hair, muck about, make jokes, responding all the way to the greetings and questions shouted to him. He was eventually captured during the April invasion. Now he's locked up in an Israeli jail, sentenced to hundreds of years.

We had gotten in an ambulance and driven up as close as possible, and then walked, hands up, yards apart, towards the operation. Two white Mohabarat (Israeli M15) jeeps, three ordinary jeeps, a couple of trucks, and about 20 soldiers were at the scene, relaxed, idly watching a military bulldozer claw into Abdel's home. There was no one inside. Most of his stuff was gone. We knew we couldn't stop the demolition itself, but we were concerned about the neighbours, wondering if evacuation procedures had been carried out properly. A few months ago during a home demolition, a woman in a neighbouring house was severely disabled and two children killed.

We all watched as the bulldozer gnashed its way through painted walls. On a wall still standing, a picture of al-Aqsa Mosque still hung, while the floors collapsed from above. We spoke to the commanders about the safety of other residents. Captain Hosney, the "good-cop" counterfoil to the area's insane "bad-cop," Captain Jamal, assured us

---

into Lagos, blockading the road and bringing rush-hour traffic to a standstill. The professors, who are not being paid and have been on strike for several weeks, reiterate their opposition to the government's position on salary payments and conditions of work.

>> November 6 >> 500,000 people rally in New Delhi, India to protest the World Trade Organization. The Indian Peoples' Campaign Against the WTO call for a sustained movement to stop the Government from surrendering India's economic sovereignty and destroying the Indian economy and peoples' livelihoods.

>> November 6-14 >> Global Day of Action, WTO, Doha.

>> November 8 >> Local government officials and thousands of people stage a mass rally, organized by labour unions, in Ankara, Turkey, protesting the government's subservience to IMF policies.

>> November 15 >> Students in Ghana siege government buildings and about 300 more blockade the University of Ghana campus in protest against non-existence of loans promised to them for their studies.

>> November 19 >> More than 2,000 demonstrators converge on three major dams in the southern African nation of Lesotho. Protesting the lack of compensation for property lost to the dams, the people demand a ten

procedures had been followed. The soldiers just eyed us.

The next few nights we were woken up by the sound of building-shaking explosions. I learned to strain my ears for the rushing sound of streaming dust, debris, broken furniture, burst water pipes – the physical after-sigh of a house falling down. And then we'd jump into action, driving to smoking slabs of floor criss-crossed over broken walls, where children sat in saucer-eyed silence, wrapped in blankets, or talking energetically, breathlessly. The *Helal* guys would check them out, treat them for shock, sometimes take them to the hospital. Sometimes we'd get a call instead. Woman having a breakdown. House demolition about to begin. She'd have to be gently dragged. She'd have to be listened to. Everything she was telling you, how she'd lost her sons, one to a targeted Apache helicopter assassination, the other in jail, and now her home.... You'd have to take it in, over and over and over, how ever many times she repeated it, however many times it got harder and harder to make out.

Back at the *Helal*, Abdel is sitting on the ambulance seat outside, smoking, staring down. I ask him about his brother. What happened to him? He tells me the story. The April invasion was drawing to an end. After the ambush and killing of 13 soldiers by the resistance, the soldiers went nuts. That's when the demolitions, the bulldozers, and escalation of killing really intensified. His brother and two others were cornered in a wrecked house and had been fighting from within. They had used up all their ammunition. He had nothing left, trapped inside with nothing but a knife. He and the others had been told by the Israelis that if they didn't surrender, they'd carpetbomb the entire camp. At that point, 350 homes had been levelled and 52 people from the camp had been killed. No relief agency, no ambulances, nothing had been allowed in the camp for ten days. People had bled to death from easily-treatable shrapnel wounds, yards from the local hospital. Tanks had deliberately flattened a wheelchair-bound man into a sheath. They didn't think the Israelis were bluffing, they really thought they would do it. So he gave himself up.

Everyone has a story. I discovered my friend Mahmoud, a driver and medic from Tulkarem was the driver of a famous as-seen-on-TV ambulance, plowed into by a tank. The footage is repeated almost every night on the *intifada* montage of attack and resistance, all set to a militant fighter hymn background. It follows the Syrian-broadcast Palestinian news. "My wife was so worried about me," he hoots when I ask him what the hell it was like. "It was crazy. She saw it on the TV and she was frantic. I was injured in the head, chest and right shoulder, from shrapnel." The second PCRS ambulance crew were not so lucky. The driver, Ibrahim Mohammad As'ad, was shot in the shoulder. As he tried to escape his ambulance, which was riddled by flying bullets, he was chased by soldiers and fell to the ground. As he attempted to crawl to safety, they ended him, shot him at point-blank range in the head.

The following days would see *Helal* medics Ashraff, Ghassan, and two other medics arrested during a second invasion. Arbitrarily. They were returned to us before the day was out, giving us a grim re-enactment of the incident, mock-stumbling out of the back of the ambulance, blindfolded, with their wrists bound with plastic cord. They didn't get beaten. But the blood keeps flowing. They shot an Irish woman in the leg, deliberately; they shot and killed Ian Hook, the head of the UN in the area; they demolished my family's house in Nablus with dynamite, taking out half the neighbour's home too; they killed some more kids, assassinated some wanted men. The daily gulps of fresh horror sink undigested. Only the winding rides from Jenin to Shuhada at three am, fighter music on the stereo, swapped for Fairouz or Lionel Ritchie when a roadblock looms ahead, wild dogs gnashing and barking up our ambulance, bounding behind us on the bullet torn roads. The checkpoints keep breeding. The pines keep releasing their cool, heady scent. The *Helal Ahmar* keeps moving....

Ewa Jasiewicz is a 25-year-old Polish Londoner living in Jenin, who has been active in the anticapitalist movement since 1999. Recently she has worked as a freelance interpreter, mainly with Polish Roma refugees, and did the odd bit of radio presenting on Resonance FM with the SlowSmallPeasants.

Resources:

» International Solidarity Movement website: www.palsolidarity.org

» News, commentary, and analysis from a Palestinian perspective: www.electronicintifada.net

---

per cent share of royalties generated from the dams and an inquiry into the dams' impact on local people. The Lesotho Highlands Water Project is the World Bank's largest infrastructure project in sub-Saharan Africa, and is designed to divert water from Lesotho to the urban and industrial Gauteng region of South Africa (including Johannesburg). The first three dams in the plan of six have displaced 27,000 people, only 2,000 of whom have been resettled.

>> November 21 >> About 30 Okinawa citizens begin a hunger strike to protest the dispatch of Japan's Self-Defense Forces (SDF) to lend noncombat support to the US military operations in Afghanistan. The hunger strikers hold their protest at an open space in front of the Okinawa prefectural government office in Naha.

>> November 21 >> Angry protesters storm the Buenos Aires stock exchange after MerVal, the leading stock index, falls more than six per cent, leading to the resignation of a top economic aid to Finance Minister Domingo Cavallo. Trading is halted for 20 minutes as chanting and drumming protesters take control of the exchange.

>> Continued on page 399 >>

Power building it without taking it

"I want a revolution that changes the very nature of how power is structured and perceived, that challenges all systems of domination and control, that nurtures the empowerment of individuals and the collective power we can wield when we act together in solidarity" – **Starhawk, US activist and writer**

"Meet me by the giant fist!" I can hardly hear my friend's voice above the roar of the crowd. "Giant fist?" I shout into the cell phone. "Yes", she laughs, "it's huge, pink, and made of paper maché. You can't miss it." And sure enough, above the sea of heads, I see it: an eight-foot high fist, defiantly erect and utterly ugly, rising above the tens of thousands of people who are here in the main square of Buenos Aires, the Plaza de Mayo. We are celebrating the first anniversary of the day in December 2001 when Argentina's economic collapse caused a popular uprising in the streets, ousting the Government and kick-starting a countrywide rebellion that became a crucible for popular politics.

The fist had been placed there by one of the traditional leftist political parties – political dinosaurs who had attempted to take over the Plaza with a huge stage and long line-up of ranting speakers, calling for a revolutionary workers' government. It was a desperate attempt to co-opt this genuinely popular movement which was born of disgust with party politics and politicians. Somehow the giant raised fist, so crude and aggressive, said it all. It was so clearly an icon of the politics of the past, something that one might find among the dusty items in the antique shop of failed revolutions, a monolithic symbol of a time when revolution had a simple formula: you built a huge party, waited for the right historical moment, stormed the government buildings, replaced the government, and took power.

The raised, clenched fist is a symbol of people-power worldwide, and yet it is made by a body that is tense, angry, and threatening. It's a hard, closed, hostile gesture, something that seems alien to what the contemporary spirit of global anticapitalism is about. With a clenched fist you can't reach out to a stranger, you can't give or receive gifts, you can't shake hands. You accept nothing, learn nothing, you can only fight – and the thing for which you fight is power acquired through force. In contrast, perhaps the greatest advantage of our movement of movements is that it struggles to avoid taking power, seeking instead to shatter it into little pieces, to share it amongst ourselves, to open up spaces where everyone can develop the power to create, and to destroy the power that dominates.

Andrew Stern

"Power poisons the blood and clouds the mind," said Subcomandante Marcos during the Zapatista caravan that travelled 950 miles from the jungle to the heart of Mexican political power, the central square or Zócalo in Mexico City in the spring of 2001. Though seven years previously they had declared war on the Mexican state, they were trying neither to secede from nor overthrow it. Instead, they were demanding dignity and autonomy, and developing new ways of seeing revolution. By the time they entered the enormous Zócalo, which echoed with the voices of 200,000 supporters chanting "*No están solos!*" (You are not alone!) the Zapatistas had grown into a vast movement with supporters nationally and internationally sharing a contagious idea: that power is about claiming dignity, about taking back control of our communities, and not about holding a seat in government.

Revolutionaries of the past would tell us that a guerrilla force entering a capital city with 200,000 supporters would be in a prime position to spark off an insurrection, occupy parliament, and take power. But the Zapatistas sought none of this. Unarmed, standing on a ramshackle wooden stage with their backs towards the Congress building, they spoke to the crowd in calm, poetic voices:

"*We are not those who aspire to make themselves powerful and then impose the way and the word. We will never be them …*
We are not those who wait, naively, for justice to come from above, when it only comes from below…liberty which can only be achieved with everyone…democracy which supports all of us and is fought for all the time … "

The desire to conquer the state maintains the illusion that the state is the foundation of sovereignty and autonomy. But in the networked world of global capital, the state is merely a node in a web of power, woven between the banks, stock exchanges, corporate headquarters and multilateral institutions. Any government that steps out of line encounters punishment in the form of trade sanctions, capital flight, or military intervention.

Yet the world must be changed. This we know and desire more and more urgently as we witness the destruction and despair brought by capitalism engulfing every corner of our lives. We are in desperate need of another politics. But it is no longer the politics of the clenched fist, the punch of power. Ours is the politics of interlaced fingers, a politics that develops when the 'I' and the 'you' come together as 'we', when people clasp their hands, warm palms touching, fingers woven together, and build a rebellion that deeply interconnects us, a rebellion of relationships which embraces differences, a rebellion that desires to share rather than to take power.

Fragmenting power

"*The state is not something that can be destroyed by a revolution but is a condition, a certain relationship between human beings, a mode of human behaviour. We destroy it by behaving differently, by contracting other relationships.*"

– Gustav Landauer, early-twentieth-century revolutionary theorist

What is power? The dictionary tells us that power is 'the ability to do or act'. In French and Spanish the word power is the same as the verb 'to be able' – *pouvoir, poder*. It shares its etymological root with the words potent and potential. Put simply, power is our ability to do things, to change things. It is the creative force behind all our experience. It is what makes something possible.

It's easy to imagine power as something that is outside of us, that is safely guarded and exercised by 'the powerful', a tool wielded by the other, the patriarchs, the capitalists, the oppressors. But power does not just reside in one place. It's not just found in the seat of government, on the screens of the stock exchanges, at the end of the swinging club of the police officer. These are simply places and moments where power has accumulated and become fixed.

All of us use power everyday. We use it when we speak, we use it when we relate to our loved ones, when we play with our children, when we cook a meal, when we write. Power is not a tool. It's not a thing that one person or a group can wield in isolation: it's a process that is deeply embedded in a complex set of social relationships.

We cannot exercise power without affecting others. It's something that flows between us and all of us are embedded in its diffuse and complex web. We cannot escape it, but we can learn to recognize different forms of power, where they come from, and how they can be transformed and allowed to flow unheeded, without accumulating, without becoming fixed in one place.

We live in a society where one type of power is dominant. This is 'power-over' – coercive power, the opposite of 'power-to', which is creative power. 'Power over' is someone controlling something outside of themselves: the power of the police officer who prevents you from squatting a building to set up a shelter for the homeless, the power of the corporate executive who slashes their workforce to increase profits for shareholders. It's the power of the abusive husband who strikes his wife, the power of the international bankers whose actions destabilize national economies disrupting the lives of millions; it's the power of the revolutionary central committee that leads the revolution. 'Power-over' tends to be wielded from a distance, physical as well as emotional: it relies on separation, on objectifying, devaluing, dehumanizing. It is the power at the core of capital, the power that takes away our ability to do, separates us from our own land, our own time, our own creativity. It is the power that attempts to disrupt our ability to self-organize, to determine what we wish to do; it is the power that demands that we be indebted to a distant owner, dependent on remote experts, no longer in control of our own lives.

'Power-to', however, is power that affects something in our own lives, close to us, within reach. It is not power that demands others do things for us, but power which enables our own doing. It is empowerment, power that flows without restriction, builds relationships, opens up spaces for possibility, enables others to develop their own 'power-to'. It is the power to create that radiates from direct democracy and direct action, the productive power that flows between the groups and individuals that make up the network of movements of movements.

Bring power closer to home; reduce the distance of decision-making and those the decisions affect – this is the demand that resonates from the valleys of Narmada to the plains of Ecuador, from the squatted European social centres to the spokescouncils of Seattle, from the township meetings in Durban to the neighbourhood assemblies of Buenos Aires. The movement of movements demands power that is not on paper, that is not abstract nor far way, but exercised in our streets, our land, and our lives.

Perhaps the best way to imagine power, in all its forms, is to think of it like water: when it is allowed to flow between us it is 'power-to', the power that nurtures, the fertile flow that makes possible. When it freezes or stagnates in one place – in leaders, governments, distant institutions, vanguards, and committees – it becomes 'power-over': the power that prevents our ability to refuse what is and decays our ability to create what could be.

From a mountaintop to the streets

"Ultimately it is in the streets that power must be dissolved – for the streets, where daily life is endured, suffered and eroded, and where power is confronted and fought, must be turned into the domain where daily life is enjoyed, created, and nourished." – **London Reclaim the Streets agitprop, 1997**

Billionaire Klaus Schwab, founder and president of World Economic Forum (WEF) disagrees: "The hard work of improving the state of the world will not be done in the streets," he declared in 2001 in response to the anticapitalist protesters outside. For Schwab, the correct place for such work to be done is in a luxury retreat from that world, on a mountaintop in Switzerland in the five-star ski resort of Davos, where every year 2,000 'global leaders' gather for the WEF. Described by one observer as: "A spectacle of fur coats tottering on high heels, watched over by marksmen on the roof," the WEF's self-proclaimed role is to "mould solutions" and "shape the global agenda". Billed as the "leading interface for global business and government interaction", this extraordinary mingling of the elite aims to create "opportunities for the formation of global partnerships and alliances". Everyone attending must be personally invited by Schwab, who first started to assemble people in 1971, "in a unique club atmosphere" to discuss how to renovate a commercial world he saw slipping into a socialist mire. Ever since then, this exclusive self-appointed think tank has met annually and has been at the forefront of developing the neoliberal agenda.

Mountains have always been the abode of the gods, the place from which the Ten Commandments descended, a place of aloof power and immutability. And so it is at Davos: the masters of the universe are all here. Rubbing shoulders in the restaurant during the 2003 meeting were

Microsoft's Bill Gates, the Secretary General of NATO, the head of the Organization for Economic Co-operation and Development, the head of Interpol, and US Secretary of State Colin Powell. The chief executives of Nestlé, British Petroleum, Sony, Novartis, and Goldman Sachs frolicked on the ski slope with the Prime Ministers of Malaysia and Peru. All were being slapped on the back by the editors in chief of Reuters, CNBC, and the *Wall Street Journal*.

This exclusive mountaintop club for the architects of global capitalism, is protected from uninvited protestors by razor wire, riot police, and soldiers in a security operation that now costs the Swiss state more money than any operation since the Second World War. It embodies the ultimate form of detached power – an unelected elite governing from afar, accountable to no-one but themselves. They also represent a globalized form of power that is difficult to resist – an imperial, flexible, nomadic, and diffuse power, much like the supple transnational capitalism that they seek to promote. Most of the select few who attend the WEF are not bound to particular places or nation-states, and the membership changes when necessary: the CEOs of Enron and WorldCom, for example, were conspicuously absent from the list of invitees in 2003. In its own words the WEF is "tied to no political, partisan, or national interest". It is the savvy mutable capitalism of the off-shore bank account, the speedy money markets, the flexible production systems, and the lean-and-mean corporation. It is capitalism without a centre. Power without a palace. Empire without a Rome.

But all gods have a secret vulnerability: they cease to exist when people no longer believe in them. Trust is the fuel of power. As corporate collapses and financial scandals rock the markets, and the democratic deficit expands as people desert the charade of participation by voting, trust is in short supply. And failure of belief in a system spreads fast. A contagious whisper, it ripples through the multitude, rising to a roar.

The roar was responded to by the World Economic Forum in 2003, when it chose 'Rebuilding Trust' as the theme for the gathering. As preparation for the meeting it commissioned a massive public opinion survey representing the views of 1.4 billion people spanning every continent. The results, according to the WEF, revealed "that trust in many key institutions has fallen to critical proportions". The least-trusted of the 17 institutions in the survey were national governments and corporations. Two-thirds of those surveyed worldwide disagreed that their country is "governed by the will of the people" and half distrusted the WTO and the IMF to operate in the best interest of society. The crisis of legitimacy has hit uncontainable proportions. According to a leaked email from a writer invited to Davos in that year the fear amongst the guests was palpable. "These people are freaked out", she wrote, describing her dinner conversations with the elite. Despite their privilege and wealth, they know that their legitimacy is waning, that we have seen through them, that when trust has been eroded it becomes increasingly difficult to wield power.

Refusing to co-operate

"The tap root of power lies below the surface. It is obedience, co-operation, collusion: the social glue that ensures that each day proceeds much like the last. Every single one of us has the power to give or withhold our willing participation. To 'reproduce' or reshape society." **– Alex Begg, *Empowering the Earth: strategies for social change*, Green Books**

We are led to believe that the system of power is like a pyramid, similar to a food chain with the dominant species at the top maintaining its control over those at the bottom through superior strength and violence. But if an avalanche swept away all at Davos tomorrow, not much would really change because the power the Davos class accrues, through their ownership of capital, extends everywhere.

There is a secret, however, that those on the mountaintop rarely reveal, which is that their power exists to some extent because we allow it to. They want us to believe that they wield power over us with their weapons and armies and police forces, and although their violence is highly effective in disrupting our movements, hurting our bodies and making us afraid, violence alone can't guarantee their continued existence. Ultimately, it depends upon us believing in their power, in their immutability, and failing to recognize our own. This was the substance of Shelley's furious ballad of 1819 when he wrote the famous lines to Manchester's working poor after troops fired on them in the Peterloo massacre:

"Rise, like lions after slumber, In unvanquishable number, Shake your chains to earth like dew, Which in sleep had fall'n on you! Ye are many, and they are few."

In reality, the system is more like a huge wedding cake than a pyramid: multiple layers of dominance held up by many pillars – pillars which are institutions and individuals, values and belief systems. Successful movement strategies, therefore, are those that identify the key pillars in society, and work to weaken their compliance until they break. As we take away one pillar, others begin to wobble and the system trembles.

When people in South African townships fight the privatization of services by illegally reconnecting their water and electricity; when Scottish conductors refuse to operate trains transporting weapons; when the Italian *Disobbedienti* take apart a detention centre for asylum-seekers; when hacktivists break into the CIA web site and rename it Central Stupidity Agency, they are knocking away pillars. With their disobedience they remove the false aura of legitimacy around the powerful, regain their own dignity, and discover the sheer potency of their 'power to'.

"We renounce power", says activist Raul Gatica, from the Mexican Indigenous People's Council of Oaxaca, "and build in the immediate now a different way of being." Keeping the balance between resistance and reconstruction, between saying no to 'power-over' and building our collective 'power-to' at the same time, is key to the success of our movements. In other words, we say no by constructing our yeses.

We need to construct alternative institutions, cultural and economic projects based on cooperative and collective models while simultaneously confronting the oppression of the system. This idea, sometimes referred to as *dual power*, is key to our success. We must confront and create together.

When those resisting on the streets are also involved in the creative acts of building new ways of living, we reduce the danger that our radical political analysis might become disconnected from the everyday needs of ordinary people. When those working to develop alternatives participate in moments of confrontation and conflict, they are reminded of the system of oppression, they reaffirm their identity as different and they remember what it is they don't want to build.

Confrontation and construction – Argentina's *piqueteros*

"We think that counterpower is something that the state can't control. It is a power that comes up from below, from the neighbourhoods, the assemblies and within each person, each subject, it is very difficult to control." **– Nekka, piquetera from Solano unemployed workers movement, Argentina**

But how do these ideas of power work out in the 'real world' context of a serious social crisis? An inspiring example of resisting power from above while constructing alternatives through building power from below, is emerging from Argentina.

The recent economic catastrophe there has become one of the most gaping wounds in capitalism's global crisis, while simultaneously becoming a laboratory for new forms of popular power. Once the star pupil of the 'Washington Consensus', several decades of neoliberal onslaught have hollowed out the Argentinean economy. Foreign capital flowed in during the mid 1990s, seeking quick profits. Everything was privatized, from the post office to the zoo. When the crisis in the Asian markets hit in 1998, foreign capital turned on its heels and fled South America, fearing a contagion there too. Investment dried up, jobs disappeared, poverty mushroomed, and the growing external debt became unpayable. Argentina's wealthy citizens moved $140 billion – more than the country's Gross Domestic Product and foreign debt combined – into foreign bank accounts and the IMF clamoured for debt payment.

In December 2001, fearing a further run on the banks which would sink the economy, the Government announced limits on the money Argentineans could withdraw from their accounts. The middle class was furious. The IMF refused to lend any more money and within weeks Argentina defaulted on its loans, the first time this had happened to a country in years. From this moment, the economy was in free fall. On 13 December a general strike brought the country to a grinding halt. Then six days later, when the poor began to loot supermarkets for food, the Government imposed a state of emergency, constitutional rights were disbanded and meetings of more than three people banned. Before the President's televised announcement of the state of emergency was even over, people were in the streets disobeying it. Over a million people took part, all demanding an end to neoliberal policies and the corrupt Government. On 20 December the President resigned, and Argentina was set on a major high-speed collision-course with the needs and desires of its people on one side and the demands of the IMF, the inept Government, and global capitalism on the other.

This collision manifested itself in the most remarkable of ways. For the crippling tragedy befalling Argentina was being transformed by its suffering population into an extraordinary laboratory for creating alternative economic models and for reinventing political power from below. Thousands of workers occupying and running their factories, neighbourhood assemblies practicing street-level direct-democracy, and the radical unemployed movements setting up road blockades and pickets – hence their name *piqueteros* – all began experimenting with new ways of exercising power.

The *piqueteros*, for exampla, are the living embodiment of the idea of building power from below. They were an early manifestation of the rebellion, active from the mid-1990s onwards with their road blockades during which families demand unemployment subsidies, food, and jobs. The Argentinean media's image of the *piqueteros* has been one of masked youths blocking roads with burning tyres. But concentrating on the confrontational tactics, the media has ignored the constructive aspects of the movement, such as bakeries, communal kitchens, and popular education schemes - for the smell of teargas makes better headlines than that of baking bread.

Carlos, an unemployed telephone technician in his 50s, is part of one of the most radical branches of the *piqueteros*, the MTD (Movement of Unemployed Workers). His group is transforming a huge, abandoned electronics factory into a self-managed organic farm, clinic, and media centre. He said that his most profound political moment since the December 2001 uprising was seeing three young *piqueteros* faint from hunger. "Our main aim now is to have enough bread for each other," he said. "After that, we can concentrate on other things."

The *piqueteros'* daily work is creating what they call the 'solidarity economy', an autonomous, non-profit economic system based on need. During the blockades, they demand a specific number of unemployment subsidies, and usually squeeze them out of the local government, despite the pressure of the IMF to cut social spending. The subsidies are then shared and used to fund community projects. Most *piquetero* groups don't delegate leaders to meet officials, but instead demand that the officials come to the blockades so that everyone can collectively decide whether to accept any offers – they have too often seen leaders and delegates bought off, corrupted, killed, or otherwise tainted by power.

Maxi, one of the founders of the Almiralte Brown MTD, took me on a tour around his neighbourhood. He listed the range of activities they had organized. "We have a group building sewage systems, and another that helps people who only have tin roofs put proper roofs on their houses. There is a press group that produces our newsletter and makes links with the outside media. We have the *Copa de Leche*, which provides a glass of milk to children and a free meal every day. We have a store that distributes second-hand clothes, two new bakeries, vegetable plots, and a library."

That afternoon, we visited one of the two weekly assemblies that were happening simultaneously in Almiralte Brown. A group of 70 people stood in a circle. They discussed plans for demonstrations, the problems of the past week, how to get children's shoes, and how to resolve conflicts between group members. It was mostly women who spoke. One of them named Yolanda told me later how women are hit hardest by unemployment: when there is no food on the table, no clothes for the children, it is women who are at the sharp end of poverty. Often the men feel rejected and paralyzed by the loss of identity that followed unemployment, and it is the women who are first to take part in roadblocks. "Women's struggle is the pillar of the movement," Yolanda explained.

The story of Ariel, whose mother had joined the movement before him, seemed typical. He had a job selling loans for new cars and every time he saw his elderly mother on TV, masked up and blocking the highways, he would cringe with embarrassment. But no one buys cars now. His job disappeared and feeding his three children was becoming difficult. So one day he went to the *piquetero* assembly out of curiosity, and he saw how women, many of them elderly, many of whom had never had the chance to make decisions or express important things about their lives, were able to put up their hands and talk freely and people listened to them. They proposed good ideas and then went and blocked the roads. Ariel soon realized that he too had to join the movement.

When I asked what had changed in their lives since they became involved in the *piquetero* movement, they told me that the loneliness and isolation of unemployment and poverty had disappeared. Marta, a punky 21-year-old in charge of the *piqueteros*' security, said: "The biggest change was the relationship with other people in the neighbourhood, the development of friendships, and the possibility of sharing... When you're on a roadblock and you have nothing to eat, the people next to you share their food. Now I feel I'm living in a large family – my neighbours are my family."

After the assembly, Maxi showed me the *Copa de Leche* housed in an abandoned municipal building next to a plot of land. The *piqueteros* had taken down the fences and used them to build the base of a huge, roaring outdoor oven on the edge of a football pitch surrounded by newly-dug vegetable plots. Fences torn down and turned into something practical struck me as a beautiful metaphor for the transformation of the private spaces of profit into shared tools of social change – a transformation that involves people building the life they want and defending it, rather than simply protesting against what they don't want. The *piqueteros* know you can gain little or nothing by winning power. They don't want to take over the crumbling centre; they want to reclaim the edges, bring back into their community a life that's worth living. "We are building power, not taking it," is how Maxi described it.

The power of the neighbourhoods

"*People reject the political parties. To get out of this crisis requires real politics. These meetings of common people on the street are the fundamental form of doing politics.*" – **Roli, an accountant and participant in the Almagro neighbourhood assembly**

Pablo, an unemployed sociologist in his 60s, and an active member of his local assembly describes the night of the uprising of 19 December 2001, saying that there were no political party banners, no placards or flags, just a multitude banging pots and pans – the *cacerolazo*. "Finally the noise became words and those words were '*que se vayan todos*'," (out with them all) sung to a catchy tune by a chorus of hundreds of thousands. Now it has become the defining slogan uniting all the movements in Argentina. To many, it was a demand that the entire political class should go, every politician from every party, the Supreme Court, the IMF, the transnational corporations, the banks – everyone – so that the people could decide the fate of this economically crippled country themselves. To others it was simply a demand to bring in a new set of politicians, without corruption and free from the leashes of the IMF. And although it is clearly not a proposal for a new way of running society, the impossibility of the demand cleared the decks of old words and old ways of thinking about politics. Like the many bare, unrented billboards in this city, somewhat beautiful in their enormous emptiness, freed from the images of commerce and consumption, *que se vayan todos* opened up space. Like a blank page waiting to be filled, it seemed to make anything possible. And in that space, people began talking to each other in the streets, in the silences between the crashing pots and pans, and a new political form emerged: the local neighbourhood assembly.

The local assemblies meet weekly, and are open to anyone, so long as they don't represent a political party. The first one we attended involved some 40 people: a breastfeeding mother, a lawyer, a hippy in batik flares, a taxi driver, a nursing student ... a slice of Argentinean society standing on a street corner, passing around a megaphone and discussing how to take back control of their lives. It seemed so normal, yet this was perhaps the most extraordinary radical political event we'd ever witnessed: neighbours discussing self-management, understanding direct democracy and putting it into practice.

Despite the rising poverty, destitution, and despair, self-managed neighbourhood assembly projects have popped up across the city. In one of several occupied banks *asamblistas* cook meals for 150 people every weekend, and on the top floor independent media activists update their website. Assemblies plant organic vegetable gardens in vacant lots, while a self-managed clinic for workers in the occupied factories is being set up. The assemblies have also become a on-call citizens' force against police repression. Every time an occupied factory is threatened with eviction, the assambleas mobilize and in several cases have managed to resist the attempts by police to reclaim the factories for the owners.

Hope is a verb

"I don't feel hope abstractly, only when I'm doing something do I feel it," Pablo tells me. In this economically devastated country, hope has become a verb – not an abstract noun, but a process. Politics has been freed from the icy grip of intangible ideologies, liberated from abstract fantasies of a pending revolution. The futile dream of taking power and running governments has been abandoned, and politics has returned to the physical processes of everyday life, to the necessities of the immediate moment. In Argentina, politics thinks by doing.

And whether you talk to a middle-class member of an assembly or an unemployed *piquetero*, there is a common understanding that you can't change society overnight. They understand that change is a step-by-step process of talking and listening, of dreaming and constructing alternatives that are rooted in relationships and neighbourhoods, and that each neighbourhood, each participant, each place must be profoundly interconnected and mutually supported.

"We can't do it on our own, and we shouldn't do it on our own," says Fabian, a member of an autonomous peasants' movement. "No one can construct a new world by themselves." When I met Fabian, he was attending a meeting to develop the national 'solidarity economy', where goats from the provinces can be swapped for bread from *piquetero* bakeries, seeds can be traded for popular education, and so on.

"The resistance can't stand still," he says. "It has to keep moving to stay healthy. We have always made mistakes. It's important to make mistakes." He frowns deeply. "At first we were like this," – his huge brown hand jerks up and down like a roller coaster – "but now we realize that sustainable change is slow." His hand pauses in mid-air and begins to trace a gently undulating wave, gradually rising higher and higher. And it's that gently undulating wave, like a steady tide, that best describes the reinvention of popular politics that is taking place in Argentina.

If Chiapas was the place from which the seeds of the first round of this movement blew, then Argentina is one of the many places where some of those seeds landed, began to sprout, and are putting down roots – roots which have penetrated deeply into the lives of individuals and communities, and have empowered them to radically change their world without taking power. And whatever happens at the top in Argentina, it is the lessons from below – the lessons of what is possible when the powerless realize that they are nothing of the kind – that will continue to spread and take root everywhere.

Notes from Nowhere

When the revolutionary African National Congress (ANC) overthrew apartheid and brought democracy to South Africa, activists around the world celebrated the victory. Since then, through bitter experience, South African activists and social movements have come to understand that the ANC made a Faustian pact with international finance: you can take power, the bankers said, but leave the economy to us. By 1996 the promises of redistributing wealth were forgotten. In the new South Africa, half of all rural black children go hungry every day, and it now has the greatest divide between rich and poor of any nation on earth. Once again, power betrayed the people it had promised to free.

While unemployment grows and public services and housing projects are privatized, more and more people are being pushed to the margins. Since 1994, when the ANC came into power, ten million South Africans have had their water and electricity cut off as they cannot pay the new rates, while two million have been evicted from their homes. Resistance to these policies are met with tear gas, mass arrests, and live bullets.

Feeling utterly betrayed by the ANC's assault on the poor, people are challenging state power, developing new strategies, rejecting neoliberalism, merging subsistence struggle with the language and tactics of the global movement, and championing locally-based direct action. A new coalition of landless, anti-AIDS, anti-eviction, and anti-privatization activists launched a common struggle against what they call 'global apartheid' through the Durban Social Forum. The DSF was created to highlight issues not on the agenda as South Africa hosted the United Nations' World Conference Against Racism. The following declaration was adopted at a mass meeting, held in the township of Mpumalanga, and is a message of solidarity with oppressed people around the world.

Durban Social Forum Declaration

28 August 2001

It has been seven years since apartheid ended in the country where we live. It has been seven years since the open wound of colonialism was finally stitched closed on the continent of Africa. The defeat of political systems, which for over 350 years created so much human degradation and racial violence against Africans, brought a moment of hope and a moment of rest for many of us who live below the Limpopo River. By 1994 the tireless exertions of the workers, the militance of the people in the townships, as well as the sacrifices of the gallant youth during the 1980s, finally had brought down the white-minority Government. In the process, we had built strong, democratic organizations, and elected individuals to lead us whom we trusted as honest and principled people. Of course, we still had to start building a new society ourselves. But we looked to our leaders for policies that would make this possible by redistributing the wealth held by a tiny group of families and corporations in South Africa. Who could blame us for wanting to beat our swords into ploughshares?

For a while we really hoped things would get better, even though we kept being told of delays and compromises and new economic plans to satisfy the West. We thought, "If not for us, then for our children." But things started to go wrong. The important people – increasingly just appointed to lead us – we knew them not. Before elections they spoke many fine words, but by their deeds we saw that they no longer cared about us. When we looked around, we saw that many of our leaders had not struggled for freedom with us or suffered like we had. And even those who had been with us started keeping their distance. We read the soft words they spoke to the rich men in our country, and soon we heard the harsh words they began speaking to us.

We were told to pay money or be thrown out of our homes, to pay school-fees or have our children prevented from learning. We were told that without money we would be given no water or lights, and minimal medical care. They gave this an indigenous name, Masakhane, to pretend that they acted for our own good. But all the while, jobs were being cut by the hundred-thousands and there was no money coming into our communities anymore. One day we woke up to learn that it was now the Government's actual policy to lose jobs, to cut off the water of the indigent, to reduce child-care grants by half, and to evict with violence those who could not pay for a piece of land or a roof over their heads. Most shocking, as hospitals and clinics were closed down all over the countryside, we were told that 'our' Government would refuse us medicine for HIV/AIDS, even when it could prevent babies being infected by this terrible plague.

The leaders became unrecognizable to us. Even physically. They became bloated with gravy and their faces distorted behind the dark glass of their luxury cars. They seemed to be much happier overseas grovelling in front of world leaders when, not long ago, we had all shared an understanding that it was the powerful in the West and the North that had an interest in our exploitation.

We are sad to report that since 1999 things have become very bad in this country for Black people and the poor. The policies this regime is pursuing have caused outbreaks of serious diseases like cholera. Half of all Black children in rural areas go hungry every day and, although a few Black people in the upper echelons of the ANC have become fantastically wealthy, South Africa now has the greatest divide between rich and poor of any country in the world. Our president's arrogance and cowardice has caused

>> November 26 >> Thousands of workers rally in Seoul, South Korea, demanding shorter working hours and the release of Dan Byong-Ho, leader of the Korean Confederation of Trade Unions, who was arrested for organizing 'illegal' protests in October.

>> December 2 >> Activists in various capital cities sabotage what newspapers describe as "the most idiotic protest ever," the Walk for Capitalism, or D2, as the organizers call it. No protest draws more than around 25 attendees and in many places protesting capitalists are outnumbered by global justice activists, who dress in thrift store suits and carry signs saying, "Child labor=huge profits," "The more efficiently you work, the more of you we can lay off," and "Our stock is more important than your family."

>> December 10 >> The Revolutionary Association of the Women of Afghanistan holds a demonstration in honour of thousands of preventable AIDS deaths. The police shoot students dead again who protest against unaffordable fees and the closing down of unprofitable departments. Instead of a solution to the land hunger of our people, we have evictions of families living on land stolen from their forefathers, carried out with a brutality we never thought we would live to see again.

And so, reluctantly at first but now with a deepening fury, communities have started to resist. In Chatsworth and Mpumalanga in KwaZulu Natal, bloody battles have been fought against evictions and water cutoffs. The same has happened in Tafelsig on the Cape Flats. And in Bredell

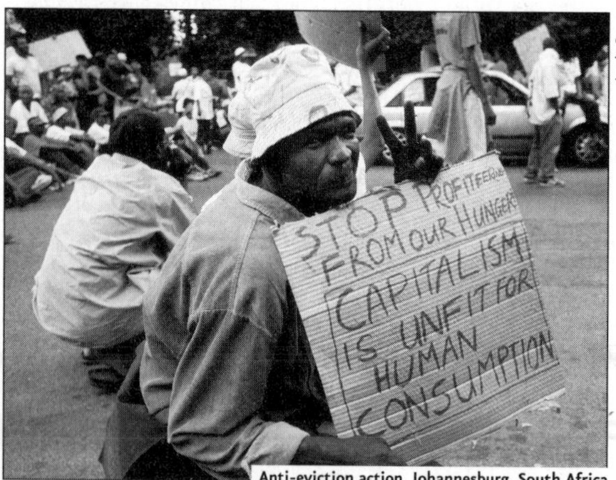

Justin Rowe

Anti-eviction action. Johannesburg, South Africa

"South Africa is in the hands of global capital. That's why it can't meet the legitimate demands of its people."

– George Soros, financial speculator

in Gauteng, landless people seized their birthright. They were defeated, but will always be remembered as the beginning of a movement for radical redistribution of land, away from those who do not need it and towards those who are desperate for any piece they can get. In Isipingo, the community has voted out of office all political parties, and elected instead a local council member directly accountable to them. In Soweto, people are trained to reconnect electricity and water and occupy the smart offices of the companies that urge service cut-offs. In Johannesburg, an anti-privatization group, which unites comrades from many different traditions of activism, is growing from strength to strength.

These local community struggles have shone a light not only by their courage in the face of the enemy, but also courage in the face of our own prejudices. It is supremely ironic, and tragic, that this Government's policies continue to barricade the poor into racial ghettoes to fight over neoliberalism's crumbs while a few of the rulers share out the loot. The result, increasingly, is the creation of race hate. Nonetheless, our courage can free us. For example, in this city of Durban where colonial rulers encouraged divisions between Indian, coloured, and African people, a sense of non-racialism is defiantly entrenched in the community organizations as we confront our common lot, not as separate races, but as *the poors*.

Recently, we have come to understand more about the 'global village', and are ashamed about the role our Government has chosen to play as an *induna* of the West. We wish to apologize to the people of Palestine, Harlem, East Timor, Congo, Chiapas, Algeria, Burma, Sudan, Iraq, the Dalits of India, the workers in Asian sweatshops, the women downtrodden in Afghanistan, the street-children in São Paulo, the political prisoners in the United States, the villagers in the Maluti Mountain Valley, the Aborigines in Australia, the immigrants of Europe and North America, and every other place in our world where injustice is perpetuated while the leaders of our country keep conveniently quiet, or even support your oppressors. We are learning about economic globalization too. We realize that while some wounds from the past have been sewn shut, many others have been torn open – on the body of the earth and on the bodies of human beings. Colonialism is dead but new overlords impose themselves: the World Bank, WEF, G8, IMF, and WTO. They are supported, not only by lackey governments like our own, but also by a legion of other forked-tongue abbreviations: NGOs, UNOs, USAIDs, and WCARs, of which we are all deeply suspicious, despite their pretence at caring for us.

But we don't despair. We are encouraged by what we have read, heard on the radio, or seen on TV, about how our brothers and sisters in the North are bravely struggling to determine the character of the new world economy. Their ways of struggling are at once so different and so similar to ours. As our struggles merge, we are going to learn better and stronger ways of fighting against those who hurt us. We will not make the mistakes of the past, when all too often we trusted leaders or parties or nations or races to save us. We know now that only the freedom and justice we the people build together has the strength to resist oppression.

International Human Rights Day in Peshawar, Afghanistan. Two hundred people gather and condemn the Northern Alliance for their continued patriarchy and lack of democracy, while calling for the participation of women in the political process of building a secular democratic state.

>> December 11-13 >> Moroccan teachers' unions stage a three day strike with nearly 100 per cent participation by the 215,500 teachers in the public school system. Teachers stage sit-ins in front of the Ministry of Education and the university president's offices, demanding adherence to commitments to raise wages and improve conditions.

>> December 12 >> In Zambia, over 2,000 Lusaka City Council workers go on strike against the nonpayment of over three months' salary.

>> December 14 >> In the Democratic Republic of the Congo, 3,000 students of the University of Kinshasa take to the streets demanding a reduction in tuition fees. Earlier in the week, tuition fees in Lubumbashi were reduced following demonstrations in which two students were killed by police.

>> December 18 >> Workers at the Brukman textile factory in Argentina take control of their workplace when its owners abandon it. The action serves as an inspiration to workers across the country, and countless other

We Mekin Histri

by Pravasan Pillay and Richard Pithouse

"it's no mistri – we mekin histri" – **Linton Kwesi Johnson**

The streets of Durban widened and softened a little to make space for a new humanity. Under unusually dark and restless skies the will to self-determination triumphed over the pull of authority. Barricades were torn down. Old ideologies and demagogues crashed and burned like forgotten satellites falling from the sky. New and forbidden ideas that were once whispered in the backstreets and on anonymous emails were shouted through loud-speakers and printed boldly on t-shirts and banners.

"Thabo Mbeki – You are a Liar!"
"ANC – Agent of Global Apartheid!"
"Mbeki, Don't Sell Our Future!"
"Mbeki, AIDS is as real as cANCer!"
"Mbeki, Give Us Our Land Now!"

The United Nations World Conference Against Racism (WCAR) came to Durban to do its business in the new democratic South Africa. That sounds like a magnificent moment: the people of the world gathering to denounce racism in a country where ordinary people have recently triumphed over organized racism. Mr Motsepe, from Pimville, Soweto, thought so too. Along with 250 others, mostly pensioners, many of whom were infirm and unwell, he went to the Johannesburg Central Station to catch a train to Durban. They wanted to tell the WCAR that in the new South Africa they couldn't pay their electricity bills and that men with guns and sunglasses were invading their homes and disconnecting their electricity. Mr Motsepe and his friends waited well into the dangerous Jo'burg night before a train arrived. When they got to Durban, on Thursday 30 August, they were hungry and exhausted. They needed food, a place to sit, and decent toilets. So they walked to the NGO forum, held in tents erected on a sports field outside the main conference. They knew that they could never afford the $100 that it cost to get into the NGO Forum but they hoped to be able to sit down on the grass for a while and perhaps use the toilets. When they arrived the delegates panicked and the organizers of the NGO Forum called the army and the police. Perhaps you might like to read that sentence again: when they arrived the delegates panicked and the organizers of the NGO Forum called the army and the police. Mr Motsepe and his friends were scattered into the city's hard streets. There they stumbled across a Congress of South African Trade Unions (COSATU) march against the ANC's plans to privatize the provision of electricity and telephone services. The COSATU marchers welcomed them into their river of humanity. Later, ordinary Durban people, people with no pretensions to being progressive and no time or money for NGO conferences, found food and shelter for the exhausted Jo'burg contingent. They spent the night in a hall, under a sparkling dome of stories.

Walking through the same streets that raised fighters like Steve Biko and Ashwin Desai can give your walk

"Apartheid based on race has been replaced with apartheid based on class." - **Trevor Ngwane, former ANC councillor, now Anti-Privatization Forum activist**

something of an arrogant swagger. You may find that you lift your eyes up off the ground and say to your master: "Who are you? Why are you here?" You may begin to believe that you own the streets – to greet your friends warmly and to spit at your enemies. You may feel that oppression makes for righteous impoliteness. Sometimes Durban sweats revolution. Everybody knows that something has to give. Something will give. And why not here? Why not now?

The next morning more than 20,000 people gathered to join the Durban Social Forum's (DSF) march on the WCAR. The DSF had been set up specifically to facilitate networking for the march. In South Africa, protest actions have historically been tightly controlled by small groups of people in single or formally aligned organizations. The multitude has been organized into clear channels.

But following the model developed in actions against the Durban offices of pharmaceutical company Merck and the World Economic Forum's Durban meeting earlier in the year it was decided that DSF would be a loose networking point for a variety of autonomous rebel organizations and individuals. Only the ANC were excluded. All the plans were laid with personal time and personal money.

The organizations that affiliated to the DSF included the Soweto Electricity Crisis Committee, the South African Landless Peoples' Movement, the South African National NGO Commission, Jubilee South Africa, the Taflesig Anti-Eviction Committee, the Palestinian National Forum, AIDS Action, and a range of Durban community organizations from places like Chatsworth, Wentworth, Isipingo, and Mpumalanga. Organizations representing Palestinians, Dalits, Tibetans, Sri Lankan Tamils, Zambian, and Zimbabwean communities and others were given observer status at the planning of the march and invited to join the march.

Prior to the march, the DSF had drawn up a memorandum which stated that: "We march in solidarity with those who have struggled internationally against

---

factories are occupied and run under worker control.

>> **December 18** >> In Zomba, Malawi, the university is closed because of protests by students and other citizens against unemployment and the increasing cost of living, including soaring maize prices. Police, who use live ammunition, rubber bullets, and tear gas, kill one student while breaking up the demonstrations.

>> **December 19-21** >> Argentina's largest and most widespread protests in over ten years erupt across the country. The protests last for two days, despite (or in response to) the imposition of a state of emergency which bans all demonstrations. Over a million people banging pots and pans take to the streets of the capital, and hundreds of thousands more occupy the streets of other cities, leading to the Financial Minister's resignation, followed by the resignation of the President, who escapes his residence in a helicopter. Riot police attack, killing at least 30 people and wounding countless others.

>> **December 21** >> An international coalition of Women in Black in occupied Palestine remove one of the Israeli roadblocks which prevent Palestinian villagers going to work. They lie in front of Israeli tanks rolling down the streets of Ramallah in the West Bank, to draw attention to the 800 Palestinians killed by Israeli troops during the last

neoliberalism and global apartheid. At the same time we are marching against the South African government and its conservative economic policy, GEAR [Growth, Employment and Redistribution, the South African's Government's self-imposed structural adjustment programme which replaced the ANC's initial moderate social democratic programme in 1996] that is making the poor poorer. Under the leadership of Thabo Mbeki our government has not used the liberated state to confront global apartheid. On the contrary the government has acted as an agent of global apartheid." The memorandum went on to demand the scrapping of a massively corrupt arms deal, the institution of a social wage, the development of a principled foreign policy, an end to privatization, and the provision of affordable medicine to HIV-positive people.

Most of the marchers had funded their trip to the march themselves. Some had shrugged off threatening telephone calls from the National Intelligence Agency (South Africa's CIA). All had braved newspaper reports warning that the NIA had infiltrated the organizations planning the march and had 'information' that a group of 20 people were on their way from the Genoa protests to cause violence. Many marchers carried homemade banners and posters with slogans like "Mbeki is a Liar", "Stop the Assault on the Poor – Reverse GEAR" and "AIDS Treatment Now." Thousands of marchers wore headbands reading "Durban Social Forum Says Phansi GEAR".

The Dalits brought drums. The anarchists brought juggling, stilts, and unicycles. The landless farm workers brought ancient battle songs. Students brought photocopied pamphlets. Anti-Zionist Rabbis linked arms with Palestinians. The mood was festive, restless, militant, excited. There were no leaders. Just a fractious multitude who had forgotten their place, didn't care about the NIA cameras, and sought only to become something and to make something. Here and now.

Five hundred people who had travelled all night on the train from Cape Town arrived, to welcoming cheers, in time

"August 2001 ... was a time of deep frustration and even despair [on the West Bank] ... But then, at the very end of the month, something happened to provide a spark of hope. It was the Durban Social Forum at the World Conference Against Racism. I have never in my life seen so much hope and so much strength in the Palestinian people as I saw during those few days in Durban. The march captured everyone's imagination."

– Andy Clarno, *From Durban to the West Bank*

to join the march in Leopold Street. No-one bothered to wonder if the brutal Belgian king was turning in his grave. It was their street and their day. The future was wide open.

Later Lorenzo Komboa Ervin, writing for the Black Radical Congress in the US, declared: "I have never been in a protest march like this one, though I had been to a lifetime of protests all over the world. Elders and the youth alike sprang into action, literally jumping and running many parts of the route, while screaming slogans. The march itself lasted almost three and a half hours, over a course of about five miles. Thousands of ordinary working class and poor people came out of their houses, churches, stores, and other places to join in, and thousands of others stood on the sidewalks to spur us on. It literally stopped all action in Durban, a city of 3.2 million people. I know I will never forget this march, and felt that I was part of a great historical happening." Most felt that this was the start of a new movement, a poor peoples' movement which would not be denied or ignored, and that the poor population would begin to speak with a loud voice. They were insistent that neither ANC government bureaucrats, heads of state, nor anybody else would speak for them anymore. They would not be victims in a country they had fought to create in the battle to overturn apartheid, and they forcefully said that they would take control of their own destiny.

All those grinding years of no land, no water, no electricity, no country, no dignity, and no hope. All the lies from above. All the little compromises from below in lives lived under the long shadow of the Party, the Leader, and the Market. Suddenly something was in the air. People cast off their respect and ran, carelessly and joyously, into the future. The gospel was the gossip: the only loyalty is to humanity, here and now. Saying it out loud, even to the wind, can get you in trouble. Almost everybody was ready to get in trouble. It was a very, very beautiful thing to see. And hear. And feel. No one will forget how it tastes. How it sings in the nostrils.

When the marchers reach the police blockade at the International Convention Centre (ICC), where the conference is being held, the mood is militant. The Dalits drum harder and quicker. The police roll out more rusty razor wire. There are leaders now, standing on a pick-up

---

year and the occupation of Palestinian land. The tanks stop at the last minute, after firing shots in the air.

>> December 21 >> The regional farmers' organization Bharatiya Kisan Union (BKU) of Haryana, India launches its campaign against the privatization of electricity and water in the region under World Bank auspices with a 20,000 strong rally. Police open fire and farmers respond with stones and traditional weapons, forcing the police into retreat. The agitation continues for four months, and warrants for the arrest of 63 peasant leaders are issued under new terrorist legislation.

>> December 25 >> Protesting against imminent privatization, 800 workers occupy the 17 story headquarters of Bogota's water, electricity, and telecom company EMCALI. The occupation is the culmination of ten months of community organizing, which included the donation of utility usage to the poor on weekends. Thousands of people provide constant support outside the building, including a community kitchen and concerts. Solidarity marches, strikes, and road blocks also take place. After a month of occupation, the union wins its demands to keep the company in public hands and maintain low utility prices for the poor.

>> December 30 >> Argentina erupts again, this time

truck with a microphone. But people are cool with that because the leaders are the kind of people who are always outside and always brave, and the banners hanging on the truck shout "Mbeki is a liar" and "The ANC is an Agent of Global Apartheid". The police are just standing there, but that makes the leaders acutely aware of their responsibility. It is, after all, just over a year since a student was gunned down by the police at a Durban university during a peaceful protest against the exclusion of poor students. The leaders call Thabo Mbeki and Kofi Anan to receive the memorandum. A low-level UN official is sent out. People shout and whistle their disgust. An old woman, unimpressed with the President's reluctance to meet the people, says "*Hei*, that man is cheeky!" There is laughter and the mood mellows.

A nearby grass embankment became the peoples' Geneva, the peoples' ICC. Everybody is a Dalit. Muslims face Mecca for Friday *namaaz*. Everybody agrees that the Market is not God. A woman with shining eyes, long dreads, car tyre sandals, an "I am Red Judas" t-shirt, and dirty jeans walks past the police with a sign that reads, in red: "Mbeki's Lies are the Real Disease". A boy with a Palestinian *keffalah* around his shoulders and a Rage Against the Machine t-Shirt squeezes forward and nervously give her his worn copy of Pablo Neruda's *Odes*. She takes it with grace and a warm smile. It's that kind of moment.

Then the leaders tell the multitude that its time to move on to Hoy Park for a rally. There is a spontaneous chant of "ICC! ICC! ICC!" and a rush to the barricades. A DSF marshal flings her arms out and hysterically shouts "Go back! Go back!" She is ignored but people take care to run around her. Up against the riot shields the chant gets louder. The visors on the police helmets come down. The *toyi toyi* dance starts. War dances work. The protesters feel stronger and stronger. A marshal in a "Landlessness is Racism" t-shirt is taken through the barricades and the police lines and up on to a truck where he is given a loud-hailer. He tells people to move on to Hoy Park for the speeches. They tell him: "Fuck off!" and a chant goes up: "Whose Side Are You On?" He tries some anti-apartheid slogans but is drowned out and gives up. DSF marshals link arms and form a barricade between the protesters and the police. Someone takes up Shona Malanga (The Sun Will Shine) and everyone points to the ICC when the chorus, with its lyric about ambushing the enemy with a bazooka, comes around. Suddenly the first barricade is down and then the second. The police move forward. A marshal, standing in front of the police, screams at the protesters to get back. A protester shouts back "*Voetsak!*" (fuck off). The marshal lunges forward in violent anger. He's attacked and brought down before he can get near his target. The police watch. The spell is broken. The singing and dancing start again but it's not the same. Big drops of cold rain start to fall. A critical mass moves on to Hoy Park for speeches and biryani. The people who have been up against the barricades disappear into the city.

That night one of the DSF leaders, Ashwin Desai, was on the television telling the nation that the social movements that marched on the ICC are a major new force in South

African politics. And that, for the first time, there is now a nationally organized and mass-based force that is directly opposed to the ANC, the President, and their Thatcherite economic policies.

History had been made. On the streets and on television.

Some of the marchers were disappointed that the march was steered away from the barricades and towards the Hoy Park rally. There may be some splintering to the left. But the organizations that made the DSF march such a success have more confidence than ever before and are already planning even larger actions in other parts of the country. Civil society has re-gathered and reasserted itself after being co-opted by the ANC in the years following the victory over legal apartheid.

The people are now the official opposition.

The next day the ANC have their march. Large full-colour posters have been up all over town for weeks and there's free transport into the city. They get around 7,000 people on the streets. Angela Davis chooses to walk with the ANC. Maybe you should read that sentence again: Angela Davis chooses to walk with the ANC. With a Minister who refused to pay any rent for his mansion, while the poor, many of whom lost their jobs as a direct result of the ANC's Thatcherite economic policies, are brutally evicted from their homes because they can't make the rent.

What do we tell the children? We all make our choices. We are all, only, who we are right here and right now.

Pravasan Pillay and Richard Pithouse have a graft teaching philosophy in Durban. They scheme that if you're ever parking off in Durban and you're lus for serious chow you should waai to Johnny's, in Sparks Road, and tune the oe to score you a chip'n'cheese roti. It's not as kiff as the prawn roti but it'll fill you up for two days, ja. And it gives the munchies a moerse klap, one-time, ja, full-on.

Resources:

» Movement news and views with a Southern African focus at the Centre for Civil Society site: www.nu.ac.za/ccs

» For up-to-the-minute news: southafrica.indymedia.org

---

against the newly formed Government coalition. The Parliament building is stormed by protesters and set on fire. One demonstrator says: "The Government has changed but the economic policy is just as bad", as another Government falls.

\\ 2002 //

>> January 4 >> India's banking sector completely grinds to a halt because of the decision by Standard Chartered Bank to forcibly relocate about 30 administrative staff. About 70 per cent of all bank workers – more than 600,000 staff – refuse to work in response.

>> January 9 >> A nationwide general strike shuts down Bangladesh as people protest against price hikes on fuel, gas, water, and electricity, which despite remaining at the minimum levels on the international commodities market, are being priced at maximum levels, according to organizers The Awami League.

>> January 15 >> Over 7,000 people in Santa Fe, Argentina, take to the streets and attack banks with eggs, rocks and hammers, in protest against devaluation of the national currency, when everyone's savings accounts were reduced by two-thirds overnight. Police attack with tear gas and plastic bullets. Similar scenes occur throughout the Jujuy province, where government employees, who had

Ten days after *the streets of South Africa were filled with inspiration, terror seemed to chase away hope. The crisis that enveloped the US in the wake of 11 September 2001 seemed to blast away dreams of a better, saner world. Some Northern activists had identified recent actions in Genoa as being the end of a phase, or the beginning of a new one. The altered political terrain which emerged after the fall of the Twin Towers confirmed that idea.*

In the North, activists retreated, pulling out of protests and hunkering down for as long as it took, whatever it turned out to be. Many predicted the subsequent wave of repression: the surgical excising of civil rights, the violence against anyone perceived to be Muslim or Arab, the consolidation of power, the secret detentions and deportations – they came one after the other, a steadily building crescendo, and we couldn't fight back fast enough, couldn't maintain and defend all the spaces we'd opened up in previous years. Many of us despaired. Meanwhile, voices from the South emerged, saying that this 'new' war was nothing new. Telling a Colombian labour organizer, a Guatemalan truth-commission worker, a South African with AIDS who cannot afford the patented drugs, a Palestinian in a refugee camp, a Mexican human rights lawyer that a war was just beginning, (a war which for them has never ended), made as much sense as Bush pretending that his sudden interest in war against Iraq had nothing to do with oil.

Though our movements' work was harder than before, and hate and fear were stalking the planet, curiously, a new space began to open. Suddenly, people in the US were talking about foreign policy and considering the connections between the venerated 'American way of life' and the poverty, violence, and blood spilled across the planet. An unprecedented, pre-emptive world-wide anti-war movement emerged from the ashes of the Twin Towers. Closing the door on an unsustainable paradigm, we began to walk forwards, and in walking, began creating new pathways into another possible world. This piece is not a first-hand testimony, but a reflection on that moment.

The Altered Landscape

by Jordi Pigem

1973. It's the year when Picasso and Neruda pass away. The year when the last US combat troops leave Vietnam, and Watergate begins to engulf Nixon. The year of the oil crisis: the exporting countries turn the tap off – in protest at the 'First World's' backing of Israel's expansionism – and the breathless modern economy, so reliant on oil, starts to gasp. It's the year of the Wounded Knee uprising: at the site of a callous massacre of their ancestors, a group of Native Americans resist US forces for ten weeks. It's the year when, precisely on 11 September, night falls over Chile, the heartless night of the coup orchestrated by Kissinger and the CIA. In that same year, the jury of an upside-down world condemns Kissinger to the Nobel Peace Prize.

In 1973, EF Schumacher publishes *Small is Beautiful*, the first great manifesto for ecological economics, "economics as if people mattered". The architect Minoru Yamasaki proclaims the opposite. He is the father of the Twin Towers, which were baptized on 4 April that same year. Supported by 192,000 tonnes of steel, they were born to be the sturdiest and most impressive buildings in the world. From their sky-high windows, "people looked very small". That is: they did not matter. Those Towers (not the victims who perished with them) symbolized our contemporary economy: awesome concentration of power, striking efficacy, global reach – and as a corollary of that, lofty indifference, the cherished illusion of being above the land and the breathing beings that walk upon it.

Some of his colleagues called Yamasaki "the architect of terror", given his taste for bewildering structures that defied common sense. In the 1950s he designed in St Louis the Pruitt-Igoe housing development, which also resembled the contemporary economy: so rational, homogeneous, and decontextualized that it fostered anomie and crime, to the point that it was dynamited as uninhabitable. The moment of its demolition, 3.32 pm, 15 July 1972, is referred to as the birth of post-modernity.

Almost three decades later, Saturn returns to the celestial point it occupied as the Towers were baptized, and now it is exactly opposed by Pluto (symbol of the underworld, of primordial destruction and regeneration). It is 2001, the year of the Human Genome Project, of the Zapatista march to Mexico City, of the brutal repression in Genoa. In September, in Manhattan, the streets of finance and glamour get covered with the ashes of the innocent.

Rediscovering America

As far as one can tell, no Muslim has any problem with America. Or does America mean the US? America stretches from Ellesmere Island to Tierra del Fuego. Brazilians, Patagonians and Canadians are as American as any Californian. Its pretension to monopolize the word America was the momentous first colonial act of the nascent United States: you start by colonizing a word and you end up trying to control earth and heavens (Star Wars) and even life's fertility (Monsanto).

The bishop of San Cristóbal de las Casas – a North American tropical city in the Zapatista heartland – condemns the ghastly deaths in the Towers but acknowledges that the policies of the neighbouring country "reap what they had sown". Many voices, mostly quietly, say the same in the US: "Does anybody think that we can send the USS New Jersey to lob Volkswagen-sized shells into Lebanese villages – Reagan, 1983 – or set loose 'smart bombs' on civilians seeking shelter in a Baghdad bunker – Bush, 1991 – or fire cruise missiles on a Sudanese pharmaceutical factory – Clinton, 1998 – and not receive, some day, our share in kind?" asks author Micah Sifry. Back in 1967, Dr Martin Luther King Jr said: "My government is the world's

---

not been paid in six weeks, attack five banks, throwing computers, bookshelves, and office furniture into the streets. Others destroy the façade of the provincial energy company, which had repeatedly raised its rates until they were unpayable.

>> January 16 >> Despite being declared illegal by the government, a 24 hour general strike in Nigeria paralyzes most of the country's main cities and brings commercial life to a standstill as workers protest against an 18 per cent rise in fuel prices.

>> January 25 >> In Bologna, Italy, an immigrant detention camp under construction is invaded and completely dismantled. Hundreds of activists from the Italian movement of *Disobbedienti* (which replaced the White Overalls), including members of parliament, take part in the action, which is attacked by riot police who beat up many, including MP's and one of the negotiating police officers.

>> February 1-4 >> Defying 10,000 militarized police as well as those who said that protest couldn't happen post-September 11, 20,000 people hit the streets of New York City, US to protest the World Economic Forum's meeting. The action is organized entirely without the support of unions or NGOs, still under the misconception that protest is over. Declaring their solidarity with the people of

leading purveyor of violence." Noam Chomsky has long been remarking that the industrial-banking-political-military conglomerate that rules the US is the most powerful terrorist organization in world history. But, needless to say, one kind of terrorism doesn't justify another.

In 1996, US Secretary of State Madeleine Albright, when asked on television how she felt about the 500,000 children that had died in Iraq, replied that "all things considered, we think the price is worth it". If you could add and subtract human lives, half a million children would weigh more than 3,000 adults, although those reckonings would be as heartless as the acts of 11 September or the embargo on Iraq. The point is that those children were not US citizens – and in the Secretary of State's parlance *justice* sounds like *just us*.

The problem, though, is not the US, nor even its government: the problem is a system of which we all partake. Only fanatics can rage at whole countries or peoples. To mistake US citizens for their government (most of them didn't vote for Bush, and the great majority know very little about foreign policy) is as senseless as mistaking poor Afghani people for the Taliban.

Dreams and reality

Before 11 September, the foreign world as seen from the US didn't seem to be fully real – it looked rather blurry and intangible, like a dreamland that one could visit but was lacking real substance. No wonder its elite refused to sign (let alone fulfill) international treaties on climate change, arms control, and chemical or biological weapons. No wonder they spurned the UN Conference on Racism in early September and, in spite of their wealth, ran up the biggest debt with the UN. They were aloof, asleep in the 'American dream', with little or no awareness that this daydream was a nightmare for people and ecosystems outside (and inside) their borders. The American dream: a somnambulating giant fantasizing it was God in the plastic promised land of technology and consumerism. A reverie as beautiful as it was unsustainable.

Loaded with fuel and fanaticism, the planes crash into the Towers and create hell (temperatures that would melt steel, one hundred floors pulverizing the fire-fighters), and that hell bursts the bubble in which the great somnambulist was floating. Reality, buried for so long, emerges among the rubble and the tears. For the first time, many US citizens start to wake up and realize that they are as much citizens of the world as anyone else, and that their opulence is built with the blood of others – many of whom are aware of it, some of whom won't forgive it.

But the American dream was also the European and Australian and Japanese dream; it was the dream of the World Bank and the World Trade Organization, the dream of a mentality that longs to be above the earth and life and death. These latest dreams of immortality (biotechnology, artificial intelligence, and nanotechnology) can self-replicate and evict the dreamer from the earth – not to mention from the dream.

Pacifying the economy

According to Buddhist philosophy, three poisons undermine our lives: greed, ill-will, and delusion. These poisons today reach unprecedented levels while colonizing the very fabric of our world: structural greed in our economic system; structural ill-will in the policies of many states and in the arms trade (thriving as the world sinks into suffering); and structural delusions propagated by the 'infotainment' industry.

Year after year, economic globalization helps to enrich the rich (mainly corporations and people from the North) while impoverishing the poor (mostly countries and people from the South): the richest 20 per cent of humanity is already 80 times richer than the poorest 20 per cent. Mind the gap. Meanwhile the structural greed of the system results, per day, in 24,000 deaths from malnutrition and the extinction of 140 species.

The violence of our economic system is the source of many other forms of violence. The pacification of our world calls for the pacification of our economy and the abolition of the obscene inequalities it creates. It calls for the economy to be brought down to earth by prioritizing ecological and social concerns over the 'freedom' of corporations. Cancelling 'Third World' debt, taxing capital flows, creating an ecotax for transport: these are steps towards a world of true democracy, with justice and freedom available for all people – rather than for economic abstractions.

Awakening

The unsustainability of our world is becoming more and more blatant, and the system would do anything rather than acknowledge that, starting by criminalizing dissent and writing off liberties. But crisis also means opportunity. The further we are into the night, the closer is the dawn. Our current predicament is a call to wake up from our personal and collective delusions and to realize who we are, where we are going, and how we are living.

If we look deeply, we know that a lot of what we dislike in others is a projection of what we fail to acknowledge in ourselves, that an eye for an eye makes the whole world blind, and that violence, even if victorious, never leads to peace. We know that only fanatics can believe that whoever is

---

Argentina, demonstrators chant "They are Enron! We are Argentina!" outside the offices of Andersen Consulting, Enron's disgraced accountants, and hold a *milonga* (tango dance party) in the streets, then move on to the Argentinian consulate. "This is a provocation. While thousands of New Yorkers are still burying their dead… the richest and most powerful men on earth have decided to come and party on the wreckage – to celebrate, no doubt, the billions of dollars of taxpayer money they've just been handed by their respective governments and explore new opportunities to profiteer from permanent global warfare," said the Anti-Capitalist Convergence in its statement for the weekend protests. Referring to recent actions of fire-fighters shut out of the clean up of the Twin Towers wreckage, the statement continues, "As our heroic fire-fighters have shown us, the moratorium on direct action in New York is over. We are the future and the future is of resistance!"

>> February 1-5 >> The World Social Forum gathers again in Porto Alegre, Brasil, with 60,000 global activists converging. Even the *Financial Times* is forced to admit, "The strong turnout showed that the movement had regained some of the momentum it had lost after the terrorist attacks in September." Meanwhile, regional social

not with them is against them, that only fanatics demonize their antagonists and instigate crusades to rid the world of evil. Bush and bin Laden share more than they suspect.

We know that a world which is bewitched by symptoms and ignores the context, seeing life in terms of genes and freedom in terms of money, is a sick and ill-fated world. We know that a world that worships Progress, with its trinity of Science (inscrutable and omniscient Father), Technology (Son bringing us closer to deliverance), and the Market (Holy Ghost that blows where it wills) is a world as deluded as it is unsustainable.

Albert Schweitzer, a deserving Nobel Peace Prize recipient, emphasized that we must rediscover a sense of awe in the presence of life, and gratefully revel in its mystery. We need a new vision enabling us to overcome dualisms and to see in every person and every culture a valid source of self-understanding, without renouncing our convictions nor the actions that are born from them. We know we must provide for others what we wish for ourselves, and that integrity is our best protection. As Gandhi taught, the practice of *satyagraha* – clinging to the truths that are born in each of us – will open the paths we must travel. All this we know. Is it not enough?

Jordi Pigem is a Catalan philosopher based in England, who is combining writing with research into the roots of our alienation from ourselves, from each other, and from the Earth

---

Resources: » *Another World is Possible: conversations in a time of terror*, ed. Jee Kim, Jeremy Glick. New Mouth From Dirty South Press, 2001

The third conference *of Peoples' Global Action (Against 'Free' Trade and the WTO), held in Cochabamba Bolivia, began on 14 September 2001 – a dangerous time to be fighting the 'free' trade agenda with one of its most potent symbols – the World Trade Center – in ruins. George W Bush made it clear: you are with him, or with the terrorists. The Governor of Cochabamba District absorbed these instructions rapidly and announced to the press that the PGA conference was a meeting of "international terrorists". On arrival in La Paz, many activists heading for the conference were interrogated and detained by intelligence officials. Dozens were threatened with deportation.*

Stanis, an unflappable Papua New Guinean, had the longest, strangest journey of all. It began, in a sense, when he started using the internet, which required walking to a friend's house two hours from his village in New Guinea. In this way he discovered, to his delight and astonishment, that many others around the world are, like him, opposing the policies of the World Bank. After a long trek to the capital, Port Moresby, he took a plane to Sydney. Flight disruption after the 11 September attacks delayed him there for three days, and then he caught a plane to Los Angeles. Despite being in transit, he was held in a hotel under armed guard for two nights by US immigration officials who didn't believe that a large, affable rural Papuan with radical literature in his luggage could be anything other than a terrorist.

Stanis was finally sent on to La Paz, where he was detained for two more days, sitting in a small office in the customs lounge with no bed, no food, and $10 in his pocket. Having been jailed in the past for organizing protests against the World Bank in Papua New Guinea, he merely sat there and implacably refused their hamburgers. Eventually he was released, and he came to Cochabamba to share his story. This is an edited transcript of an interview.

We Discovered We Weren't Alone: surfing the net in Papua New Guinea

an interview with Stanis Kaka by Notes from Nowhere

Economic independence struggle

In Papua New Guinea we got our independence from Australia in 1975. It was given, as a gift. We never struggled for independence. They just gave it to us, and we accepted. But it wasn't an economic independence, it was only political independence. But without economic independence we can't run our country. And what is actually happening now is they are trying to take over our lives.

The World Bank and the IMF came in [in 1991] and offered 'assistance', and the Papua New Guinean Government accepted. Since then we have been told that we are millions of dollar in debt to them, but we can't afford to repay. In 1995 the World Bank and the IMF declared our debt unpayable, and came up with 27 policy conditions that the government had to implement by 1996, or Papua New Guinea would not be able to access any more loans.

[Those policies] include the Customary Land Registration Act – 97 per cent of our land is customary [tribal or collective] land. Most of the people cannot afford to register land, and so are losing it to the state.

We were against those policies and we led a strike in 1996, in which two people were killed. There followed a general strike against the World Bank then, and the government gave orders that the people who were leading should be arrested – including myself. We thought that we were the only ones who were controlled by the World Bank and the IMF. And I, too, thought that when I was leading the strike.

We were waiting to see if our government would continue pursuing these policies. And what happened was in 2001 the World Bank and IMF pushed for the same conditions for the next loan. As a result, all of the university students went on a peaceful sitting protest, and four of them were killed on 25 June 2001. They were sitting all day in front of the parliament building, and that

---

forums begin to spring up on every contintent.

>> February 8 >> Ukrainians in Kharkov say *"Nyet!"* to McDonald's, as 6,000 turn out to stop the construction of a new franchise in the city centre. Dressed in bloody aprons and wielding dripping knives, the people decry the company as the leading serial killer (of animals) in the world. Local authorities concede to demands, and prohibit the construction from taking place!

>> February 9 >> Following days of protests and blockades by coca workers, resulting in several deaths, Bolivian officials agree to suspend coca eradication efforts and guarantee the normal functioning of the coca leaf market at Sacaba, Cochabamba, for 90 days while a commission of government representatives and *campesino* leaders reviews laws which criminalize the transport and sale of coca leaves. Many of the protesters' deaths are attributed to the Special Security Group, a police unit popularly known as *Dálmatas* (dalmatians), which was trained by the US military. One *Dálmata* officer claims that the unit has "a certain specialty and an affinity for dealing with confrontational civilian groups."

>> February 18 >> Thirty Korean students from *Hanchongryon* (Federation of Korean University Student's Association) barricade themselves in the American

evening the police asked them to leave, but they refused. The police came and used firearms to disperse them, and killed four of them, and 17 were hospitalized.

And since then I've opened my eyes, collected information. Concerned people were getting in touch with me, writing letters and saying, "That's what the World Bank is doing to Malaysia, to Africa, and to other parts of the world." And I thought, wow, other people in all these different countries are struggling – well that is not a bad thing.

And so I'm interested in making international links. Earlier this year when I was using my friend's internet I began to realize the internet is access to everything. I find it very easy, instead of waiting two to three months to get a letter. So when I was invited to come [to the PGA conference], it was a great opportunity for me to see what people from other countries are experiencing and get experiences from them.

"Since 1993/1994 when we began the campaign against the corporate take-over of Papua New Guinea by the World Bank/IMF, the struggle has been long and bitter ... And it has also been bloody, with our students paying with their lives ... We know too, that our struggle and campaign is the same being waged all over the world by those of you who, like us, are opposed to the take-over and domination of our world by multinational and transnational corporations."

- Powes Parkop, Anti-Privatization Alliance, Papua New Guinea

Burgers from Interpol

When I arrived in La Paz the immigration officer asked me where I was going and I said to travel 'round. They started saying to me, "You're not going there, you don't have a place to stay." I said that someone was picking me up at the airport, and they rang Cochabamba to check. Then I said I was going to a hotel and they could get in touch with me there and they said, "No you're not, you're going back to Papua New Guinea." And I said, "Why am I going back?!" And they said, "You don't have any legitimate reason to be here. And you are going to that PGA conference so we are sending you back." The man who interrogated me was working with Interpol [the international police force] and I gave him my telephone number and told him everything, and said, "If you want to ring my family, ring them and they will tell you the truth." They were trying to see if there was space on the plane to deport me but there were no seats. Finally, a lawyer rang and came and bailed me out.

I stayed in that airport office for two nights – sitting and sleeping. They sometimes came with burgers but I didn't take them. I just ate one piece and left it on the shelf, saying, "I didn't come all this way to sit here and eat this kind of food." The man who came to bail me out shook my hand and said "Good luck."

I will tell my people

I work with Kasalapalou, a community organization which raises awareness campaigns about our land, and fights the appropriation of our land through the Land Registration Act. We have a lot of mineral resources in our province. The experience of many provinces in my country is that corporations come in and log and mine – but they don't care about the environment, they just do what they like. That's why we formed our group. It wasn't made with outside influence or help, it just consists of village people.

Despite the fact that the university strikes came out against the World Bank, many village people think these policies are only to do with the educated people, like the students, and that it won't affect them. They say, "That's nothing to do with us, we enjoy our life here, we have food and shelter." But they don't know that the government is making laws that will affect them, everyone, not just the few people struggling.

Most village people are not educated but we communicate well with them. There are no telephones or other forms of communication; we use word of mouth and we have a local radio program. There are six districts in the Inga province in which we go around talking to people.

Eighty-five per cent of our population live in the villages. We live in extended families and most of us are pretty happy. Like me, I had a job, but left it and for the last 15 years I've been in the village. But I can survive. I have land there. I can grow my own food. I have three houses in the village, whereas in the city I would have to rent a place! But in the village I have three houses and I own them. I don't have to pay for anything! I don't have electricity bills and I don't have water bills and I don't pay rent. Actually I find it very easy! And that's what I judge things by. Because I see people are struggling under the rules of the World Bank and the IMF, and I find out that the world's people in other countries are struggling also and seeing them as enemies, and then I know there must be something wrong with these institutions.

When I go back home I will tell my people, "Listen, we

Chamber of Commerce in downtown Seoul to protest against a range of military and economic issues associated with President Bush's visit. Occupying the office in the World Trade tower for four hours before being arrested, they knock out windows and replace them with a large sign which reads, "No War! No Bush!"

>> February 18 >> In Buenos Aires, Argentina, a group of hundreds of depositors, whose savings accounts have been 'structurally adjusted' by the government, tour the financial district. Banging pots and pans, they demand the return of their money, and smash up 17 banks in broad daylight and in full view of the police, who follow them sheepishly from bank to bank.

>> February 19 >> Dutch activists from the group *Amsterdamse Radicale Klimaatactivisten* cause a stink at a carbon trading conference in Amsterdam. Wearing blue wigs and armed with water pistols and farting-gas to emphasize that "carbon trading stinks", they occupy the conference room, holding up the conference for two hours, and forcing delegates to be relocated. Outside the conference, in hail and icy gusts of wind, a group distributes flyers, plays samba music, and does street theatre for the passersby.

>> February 20 >> Public employees, teachers, doctors,

think we are helpless, but we're not." My people normally come and they say, "You're nobody. You're not a politician. You're nobody special. You're just a village person and you are struggling out here and these people are coming with money. These people have all the power. And they can kill you." And what I'm telling the people now is that what I am doing will have a big impact in the future. That's what I tell them. So when I was invited to come here, they realized that something was happening across the world.

We can outnumber them

Awareness and distribution of the message in Papua New Guinea is slim. A Malaysian logging company runs our second newspaper, so when we put anything about mining or logging in the newspaper they will never publish it. I have tried to write about this ten or twenty times and when I ring them to find out what has happened to my article they say the Chief Editor has refused to publish it. So when I go back I am going to put my program on a provincial radio station. Now they are banning our form of awareness-raising through the radio station. The radio station manager is my friend, so he lets me speak. But gradually they will stop it. That is why I am looking at ways to set up my own community radio station, so awareness will carry on being built there. We have no other means of communicating so we put our programs out to let people know what the mining and logging people are doing – every fortnight.

We have lots of mineral resources in our ground and thick rainforest, and the big companies are coming in and taking out our resources in raw form without them even being processed in Papua New Guinea. [These 'rip and ship' policies prevent the development of manufacturing in resource-rich countries, while avoiding higher *tariffs* or import taxes for Northern corporations]. So it's going out raw, not even as timber. Some big companies – especially Japanese and Malaysian ones – are logging. And our government can't pay back the money to the World Bank.

And yet our government is inviting them in. I don't why. I don't know what's wrong with the governments of this world. We normally vote our representative into the parliament, and before they get elected we educate them, question them, and all that. We ask them, "Are you going to fight for us?" But they promise us everything, and once they get into the parliament they are 100 per cent different. They just dance to the tune of the IMF and World Bank and the government. So when they come back we say, "When we elected you, you told us different things, but since you got into the parliament you haven't raised your voice and you haven't done anything."

They say, "I am only one person myself and I can't do

"We are like rats fighting the elephants. People struggling for the land are being killed for it, but the word is more important than violence ... We the people are going to make a big hole for the elephant to fall in."

– Stanis Kaka at an international climate change gathering, 2002

anything. We have got a democratic system, but this is what happens." But the population of Papua New Guinea is four million. And if four million of us stand up for what is right – there are, I think, only 109 members of parliament – we can outnumber them. That's what I say to them when I go to the villages. I say, "There are four million of us, four million people of Papua New Guinea; we can speak for our own rights better than those people. Our elected members in parliament don't have any authority – we do." That's our message. We have got a right. That's what I believe in.

So I would say that this is the real independence struggle of Papua New Guinea. Political independence was gained, but we are struggling for economic independence now. And so far two people died in 1996, four died in June – and probably we are looking at 1,000 people dying before we get economic independence. With the blood of those people, we will get economic independence.

It's not that I am going to end it. When I become old and die, that's not the end. I have children. And I have told them, "Fight to the end of your life." So I am training them. I am educating them so they will say, "What my father fought for, I am fighting for too."

I used to work for an Australian company doing mining in my own province, but I pulled out. I was working in a laboratory analyzing everything for them and I saw the amount of the waste going in the water system. I didn't agree with this and so I pulled out. And that is the reason for me being really active. People said to me: "You had a job there! You had a good wage! Why don't you just close your mouth and just go along with them?" I replied that this is my province, and I know what is actually happening. And if I close my mouth and enjoy what is given to me, when I am dead my children will just take out my bones and throw them away. That's why I resigned my job and am now telling my people what is actually happening.

Stanis Kaka can be contacted at kakastanley@hotmail.com
Interview by Notes from Nowhere / Katharine Ainger

Resources: » Interviews from the Cochabamba conference make up the book: *Desire for Change – women on the front line of global restistance* from: LARC, 62 Fieldgate Street, London E1 1ES, UK or pgabolivia@yahoo.co.uk

---

the unemployed, account-holders, pensioners, and students flood the streets in Buenos Aires and at least ten provinces of Argentina. Unemployed workers protest at the central offices of Repsol-YPF, a transnational oil company, demanding "50,000 real jobs and urgent food aid". The head of the teachers' union says, "Every day, another 1,700 workers are left without a job and enter the circuit of poverty. And those of us who do not lose our jobs have to put up with salary cuts, unpaid wages, and restructuring in the midst of an inflationary process."

>> February 20-25 >> Indigenous people, farmers, and municipal workers occupy the oil industry infrastructure in the northeastern provinces of Sucumbios and Orellana, Ecuador. Local residents erect roadblocks, blockade the airport, and occupy oil wells, demanding compensation for ecological damage wrought by a crude oil pipeline. The President declares a state of emergency; one person is killed and nine seriously injured by the police. The following month, a tree village established in an attempt to protect the Mindo-Nambillo forest, is brutally evicted. The Government eventually concedes and declares that ten per cent of revenues generated by the pipeline will return to local communities affected by it. So the IMF withdraws a loan, as they oppose the ten per cent allocation.

Cho Yong-soo/Reuters

International workers from 16 countries join South Korean unionists against the WTO. Seoul, South Korea

Global Day of Action

November 9th 2001

WTO Retreats to the Desert, Doha, Qatar. Decentralized actions against the Ministerial meeting:

Armed with anthrax antidote and gas masks, delegates flock to the WTO's fourth ministerial in Doha, Qatar, a desert dictatorship where all protest is banned. Meanwhile, across the Persian Gulf, US cluster bombs fall on Afghanistan during the first stage of the 'war on terror'. The summit nearly collapses again, but heavy pressure by the US and EU on poor countries force into place a new round of trade liberalization. "We are made to feel that we are holding up the rescue of the global economy if we don't agree to a new trade round here," says the Jamaican delegate. Weeks before, US Trade Representative Robert Zoellick warned the developing world that no serious opposition to the American trade agenda would be tolerated. "Our new coalition [against terrorism] depends on economic growth," he said. He ends the summit saying, "Today the members of the World

Nayef Hashlamoun/Reuters

Guarding the delegates at the WTO conference centre. Doha, Qatar

Trade Organization have sent a powerful signal… we have removed the stain of Seattle."

A decentralized global day of action is called by Peoples' Global Action under the slogan, "They can run, but they can't hide: we are everywhere." Numerous NGOs and labour unions also call for actions. An unprecedented number of events take place, many of them linking war and neoliberalism. At least 71 countries participate – from the Congo to Cameroon, Burkina Faso to Bosnia-Herzegovina, Sweden to South Africa, Mauritius to Mongolia, Taiwan to Tunisia, Bulgaria to Bangladesh.

In Thailand alone, 100 cities take action against the WTO. In one village, protesters express outrage about US patents on indigenous jasmine rice by cursing the summit with the traditional ritual burning of chili and salt to bring bad luck. In Geneva, Switzerland, (home of WTO headquarters) 10,000 people march and plaster huge hand-made posters over the façades of banks and corporate headquarters. "Governments have taken refuge in Doha because they are afraid of the people who elected them," says Swiss peasant leader Fernand Cuche.

Italian Prime Minister and media tycoon Silvio

Kamal Kishore/Reuters

Huge crowds take to the streets of the capital rejecting the WTO. New Delhi, India

Berlusconi, declares a 'USA Day' and busses thousands of people into Rome in an attempt to outdo the protests. Despite blanket media coverage by his own TV stations, only 30,000 turn up, while 150,000 march under the slogan, "No to this military, social, and economic war", and actions take place in 100 other cities across Italy. Meanwhile, in Washington DC, a 70 foot tall dragon spews smoke at the offices of US trade representatives.

Public institutions are given mock privatization ceremonies in Barcelona, Spain, as WTO 'delegates' jump out of a special show bus which tours the city with its sound system blasting anti-WTO messages, ending up in a large street party. At the same time, thousands from the National Alliance of Peoples' Movements, a grassroots coalition of farmers and other groups, force their way into grain warehouses across India to distribute the surplus grain to the poor, and 500,000 take to the streets of Delhi.

The (self-described) first ever antiglobalization gathering in the Middle East takes place in Beirut, with hundreds of activists from across the region attending and planning future actions, while 500 workers and students rally in Iran, and a ferry is

Romeo Ranoco/Reuters

Protesters head towards the US embassy. Manila, Philippines

occupied in Copenhagen by activists demanding that the Danish government provide transport to Qatar for WTO protesters. In Aotearoa/New Zealand, the hometown of WTO Director-General Michael Moore, several hundred people go on a "tour of capitalist greed"; Niketown, Starbucks, several banks, and a telecom office are visited. Despite heavy snow in Slovenia, 2,000 people have a street party in downtown Ljubljana, while a caravan of 400 workers and the unemployed crosses Turkey. In Seoul, South Korea, 20,000 workers march and two days later 10,000 rice farmers armed with bamboo sticks clash with police. "[The WTO] is trying to kill us," says the farmers' spokesperson Lee Ho-joong. "We don't have any more ground to lose."

In the early months of 2002, while the mainstream media declared the movements dead and issues of economic globalization irrelevant in the face of the 'war on terror', something happened that no one expected. Through the movements' emails, websites and face-to-face gatherings, stories emerged from Argentina of politicians so universally hated they couldn't walk the streets safely, of angry middle class women smashing up banks, workers occupying factories and running them, seven million people using cash-free barter networks, ordinary people holding meetings to decide how to run their own neighbourhoods, and thousands of unemployed people blocking highways and demanded food and jobs.

Recession had struck Argentina in 1998. The only way the Argentinean government could pay the $132 billion debt – some of which dated from the military dictatorship (1976-1983) was more cuts in social spending. Pensions, unemployment benefits, healthcare, and education all got slashed, yet jobs were disappearing and poverty growing exponentially.

In the mid-nineties, protests began to simmer across the country, but on 19-20 December 2002, they erupted onto the streets of urban centres with unprecedented ferocity. Following the declaration of a state of emergency in Buenos Aires, a million people from every class disobeyed the curfew and took to the streets, banging pots and pans and converging on the Presidential Palace. A cry rose up from the crowd, directed at the politicians, the bankers, the IMF: "Que se vayan todos," (out with them all) so that the people can decide the fate of their economically crippled country themselves. The despised government was ousted, three more were toppled within two weeks, and Argentina's popular rebellion spread to every corner of society.

Pots, Pans and Popular Power: the neighbourhood assemblies of Buenos Aires

by Ezequiel Adamovsky

Coming together

On 19 and 20 December, 2001, my life changed forever. Just as unexpected as any other milestone in history, rebellion caught us all in the middle of the banalities of everyday life – I was painting my flat. Late in the evening, my brother Pablo phoned and we chatted away about nothing in particular when he suddenly interrupted me, and asked, "I hear a funny noise – I don't what it is, but it sounds like pots banging. Can you hear it?" "No. That's strange," was my only answer, not paying much attention.

A moment later, I heard a similar banging near my home. The sound of the first *cacerolazo* [named after the saucepans] had scattered all across Buenos Aires, from downtown where Pablo lives all the way to my neighbourhood. I abruptly put the phone down and ran outside to find out what was going on. That was when I met those strangers for the first time: my own neighbours.

Then came the rebellion of 20 December, long hours of fighting with the police. The President was toppled from the government. Repression snatched the lives of seven protesters near the Plaza de Mayo, and 35 across the country. Fate determined this time that I would not be one of them.

During the following days, at the beginning of January 2002, a rumour – almost a legend – spread throughout the city, setting fire to our imagination. Groups of neighbours had begun meeting spontaneously in 'neighbourhood assemblies' on the street corners, in order to discuss their problems. "They are soviets!" screamed the panicked headlines of some conservative newspapers.

I looked for one near my house, and soon I joined the Cid Campeador Popular Assembly. Romina, aged 26 and with no previous political experience, had spent an entire week giving out leaflets to call for its first meeting. I arrived on time, but could hardly speak with anyone due to shyness. The images I remember from the first meetings are of chaos, disorder, people shouting at each other, arguing over the megaphone, interminable speeches of pure catharsis...

Gathered under a monument at a crossroads of the noisiest streets in the city, 80 neighbours were trying to come to an agreement to do something in the midst of our shipwrecked country. When I recall that scene today, I find it sweet and powerful at the same time.

Negotiating identities

There were people of all ages, sexes, and professions, with and without previous political experience. Many thought we would not last a single month together. What did we have in common? We were on our own, in a country devastated by capitalism. We yearned to decide for ourselves how to live, and no longer trusted any representative. It's the only thing that we shared. Almost nothing. Almost everything. Since then, we have been negotiating our differences, searching for our own path, our own identities, recognizing ourselves and 'contaminating' each other reciprocally.

Who are we? Where to trace the line between what we want and don't want? The questions hide, and travel with each step that we take. Like in one of the debates we had at the very beginning, "We have to be united; we're all Argentineans, that's what matters", said Claudia, who had no political past. "That's not what matters", snapped back a group of Trotskyists, "We should first focus on whether we are with the workers or not." As the debate heated up, Claudio said, "Our neighbour Francisco, who has just given a great speech, is from Uruguay. Does that

---

>> **February 26** >> The Korean Confederation of Trade Unions leads massive strikes of more than 50,000 workers in 94 workplaces in the railway, power, and gas sectors against privatization. The President of the railway union is arrested. Lee Sang-youn, Head of the Confederation, states, "Public services are the property of the nation. It is not acceptable to sell people's property without their permission or agreement".

>> **March** >> The month sees mass demonstrations of workers and farmers across China, protesting against cuts in benefits and subsidies. For two weeks, 50,000 people gather daily at the Daqing oil field in Heilongjiang province. In industrial Liaoyang, 600 workers block the highway to the provincial capital, and are dispersed violently by police at midnight. Another 1,000 lay siege to city hall, demanding unpaid wages and the release of four detained labour leaders. Smaller demonstrations take place in Beijing, and across the province of Sichuan, as the country moves towards neoliberalism.

>> **March 7-13** >> In Fortaleza, Brazil, over 40 finance ministers and presidents from three Latin American countries meet with businessmen and diplomats to discuss the policies of the InterAmerican Development Bank (IDB). Large parts of the city are cordoned off to prevent

make him a foreigner to our assembly?" That day we learned that what unites us is much more than nationality.

I can recall another story of reciprocal 'contamination', when we co-ordinated a joint meeting with gay and lesbian collectives. After two hours of discussion, Raúl stood and acknowledged with great emotion, "I am 75 years old and my education is old-fashioned. But today I've realized that those kids are human beings and do not deserve to be discriminated against". As it turned out, a 19 year old member of one of the gay groups, Rodrigo, happened to live in our neighbourhood, and he joined our assembly that very day.

Andrew Stern

People gather in an assembly of assemblies. Buenos Aires, Argentina

Empowering ourselves

Many complain that assemblies lack clear "political content" or a "revolutionary programme" to "take power". I am all the time more convinced that our content is present in our form, and that our 'programme' is to build a world in the image and likeness of the assembly, where everybody can make their own decisions. Nothing more, nothing less. Our assembly is a laboratory where a new world is being built every day, where we learn to decide and participate, rather than delegating and obeying. Isn't that a revolution, after all?

Stella Maris and Jackie are for me two of the most inspiring examples of empowerment. Neither of them had any previous political experience to draw upon. Stella Maris, age 41, was suspicious at first of "those who spoke of politics in the assembly". For her, *politics* (especially left wing politics) was a dirty word. Now, a year later, she identifies herself as anticapitalist, and defends the 'horizontality' of the assembly with tooth and claw. She never misses a chance to tell her story to whoever will listen: "I was born into politics in this assembly," she says with pride.

Jackie is 19 and for five months she silently observed every meeting. One day, she timidly began to speak, and she spoke well. One year later, nobody could stop her.

Stella Maris and Jackie today are fundamental parts of our assembly.

A new world in our neighbourhood

In July, our assembly took a risky move. After some weeks of careful planning, we decided to occupy an abandoned three-story building, an old branch of a now bankrupted bank.

It had become the thing to do for assemblies to occupy places illegally, and we didn't want to be left behind. So one Sunday morning, in front of some astonished onlookers, we broke into the building. Did we really need to have that building? In retrospect, probably not. Mostly, what we wanted was to disobey, the sensation of being beyond the law, an action that would mark us as brothers and sisters in rebellion.

Today in that 'reclaimed' building is a café, a community kitchen, classes in theatre, tango, and popular education, tutoring for the students, and cultural activities. Indymedia has an office there too. The only condition we put on using the space is that it be used for participatory and non-profit activities. In a few months, the 'home' of our assembly has transformed into a truly social centre, open to the neighbourhood. For assembly-goers, this means new challenges, for example, providing security 24 hours a day to protect the building, but it also means the opportunity to grow as an assembly and deepen our work.

With the opening of this autonomous space in the heart of the city, organized by rules which differ from those of capitalism, we faced one of the first direct conflicts with the state and the corporations. Two months after our occupation, police raided the building and charged nine assembly-goers with 'trespassing'. The plaintiff is Banco Comafi, a bank long connected with money laundering (called "the gold Mafia"), and government corruption. It is said that the real owner is Emilio Massera, one of the main leaders of the last military dictatorship.

The struggle of the assembly against the monolith of corruption is to me a powerful symbol of resistance of the oppressed in this country against the aggression of capitalism. Banco Comafi epitomizes economic exploitation, financial speculation, corruption, and state terrorism – the major calamities of recent decades. Will David defeat Goliath this time?

Facing contradictions

However, antagonism is not only external. It is not all a bed of roses in the life of the assembly. For example, an unresolved conflict exists between independent assembly-goers and those who belong to political parties. The former

---

protests, and many buses carrying protesters are turned back. Nevertheless, various actions take place including a public assembly in a poor community which will be evicted due to an IDB project which will widen their street and replace their homes with fancy hotels.

>> March 15 >> Despite the closing of borders and a simultaneous football match across town between Madrid and Barcelona, 400,000-500,000 people take to the streets of Barcelona, Spain to protest the EU summit. Promoting over 25 decentralized actions, organizers explain, "We didn't want the terrain they were preparing for us, the direct confrontation where we had to lose". Three activists leap onto the football pitch and chain themselves to the goalposts, halting the game until they are removed and arrested. Speaking of the need to remain flexible, one protester says, "We are not afraid. The entire police strategy is based on creating a state of exception, where people stay inside their houses, and an activist elite confronts 10,000 police. Given this reality, the movement should go back to using its creativity and decentralization. Achieving, through that, a more complete visualization of the resistances, of their diversity, beyond the framework of a medieval joust, which is what the police are proposing."

>> March 19 >> The construction site of a new

reproach the latter for using the assembly to benefit their parties; the latter respond with accusations of McCarthyism. Mutual hostility sometimes seriously compromises our ability to function, and so far we haven't found a way to resolve this problem.

Other kinds of contradictions have become apparent, for example, generation gaps. We are also struggling with deep-rooted class prejudices. Cohabitation in the reclaimed building with unemployed and homeless assembly-goers has generated conflict and friction. The distribution of 'political' and 'domestic' tasks always leads to problems.

Such conflicts are reflected on the nick-names people give each other. Some independents call party-members "the central committee", while some unemployed folks call middle-class people "the managers". In humour, as everyone knows, there always is a bit of truth.

Building coalitions

There is a permanent concern in the assembly movement: how to go beyond our neighbourhood and take part in a more general political life? How can we coordinate with other assemblies and social movements without recreating hierarchies? Between October and December 2002, our assembly helped to organize a political action that may offer some clues to solve this dilemma. After an internal debate, we launched a call to action addressed to all assemblies and popular movements. The idea was to organize a direct action against the places and symbols of economic power on the anniversary of rebellion.

Over 45 different groups responded to the call and in a completely horizontal way we organized a blockade of the Central Bank, the stock exchange, and other financial institutions. Our objective was to warn that the owners of banks, businesses, and large corporations were also included in our call, "*que se vayan todos,*" (out with them all) as they are responsible for the devastation of our country. Moreover, we wanted to show that assemblies can take their own political initiatives and that coordinated actions can be organized in a horizontal way.

Taking part in the blockades – called urban *piquete*, in honour of the *piqueteros'* struggles – were several assemblies, *piquetero* organizations, radical trade unions, political parties, artists' collectives, gay and lesbian groups, associations of *ahorristas* [savers – the middle class whose savings was decimated with the collapse of the economy], global resistance collectives, students, environmentalists, and human rights associations. It was the first time that such a multiplicity of social movements converged as one coalition in Argentina.

But I think the greatest achievement of the urban *piquete* can be summed up in the words of 19 year old Marian, a member of our assembly: "In the urban *piquete* I felt that I was the real protagonist." And that is what it is all about.

My neighbourhood assembly is one year old

One year after that first time I participated in my assembly, I feel, as Jaime said one day, that "I can no longer think of my life without the assembly". The geography of my neighbourhood has completely changed for me, as has my sense of what is important and what isn't, and how I use my free time. Even my mood fluctuates with the assembly: if the meeting is full of conflict one week, my distress lasts until the next; if it is marvelous, I feel euphoric.

I have not the slightest idea of our future. I like to think that, without knowing it, we are participating in the birth of a new global era of emancipatory struggles. I like to imagine that one day the whole world will be like our assembly's building: a place to meet as equals, a place to live in freedom, to listen and to be heard, to be the protagonists of our own lives.

The future, without exception, always bears a question mark. Maybe assemblies will disappear, or maybe they will grow in number and in quality. Maybe we will end up sick of them, or maybe we will end up with the world which makes us sick. What I am certain of is that, even if we disappear, the legend of the assemblies will remain in the collective memory. The mark of this intense experience of participation, horizontality, and autonomy cannot be deleted.

Ezequiel Adamovsky is an anticapitalist activist and writer. He takes part in the movement of the assemblies in Buenos Aires, and in Intergalactika – Laboratory of Global Resistance. He is the author of the forthcoming book *Anticapitalism for Beginners*.

English translation by Romina Propato

Resources: Updated information about Argentina's popular rebellion: www.nadir.org/nadir/initiativ/agp/free/imf/argentina/index.htm

---

McDonald's in Voronezh, Romania is blockaded. For six days, activists prevent work from taking place in the former public park by sitting on diggers and pulling down fences, until the police break up the blockade and construction resumes.

>> March 21 >> In South Africa, the Soweto Electricity Crisis Committee (who illegally reconnect peoples' electricity if they are cut off due to non-payment) and the Anti-Privatization Forum stage a protest to demand that cut-offs of service for those too poor to pay are stopped. According to the Government's Human Sciences Research Council, nearly ten million South Africans have had their power disconnected, and over two million have been evicted from their homes because they cannot afford their water or electric bills.

>> March 24 >> Egypt's Palestinian solidarity movement organizes 450 people to join a second caravan to the border town of Aarish, carrying over 90 tonnes of food and medicine. When the Egyptian security prevent them from entering the town, they occupy the streets. Three months later, a third caravan brings 150 tonnes of food and 600,000 Egyptian pounds worth of medicine, and organizes a public conference about Palestine in Aarish.

>> March 28-30 >> Backed by a Korean drum group, and

No Borders, No Nations

No-one is illegal

The barbarism of migration regimes cause thousands of deaths along the borders between East and West, North and South. As it gets easier for the flow of money, goods, and capital to roam around the globe, for most people, crossing a border to escape poverty, war, catastrophe, or political repression becomes more and more difficult. Inspired by the autonomous direct actions and self-organization of the *sans-papiers* refugees in France in the early 1990s, activists in many countries have begun developing new tactics to disrupt these migration regimes.

Flying deportation class

Many airlines are committed to enforcing inhumane asylum policies by flying refuges back to the places from which they fled.

Most of the refugees, who are transported against their will, try to resist their deportations. Law enforcement agencies have used extreme force, including sedatives and handcuffs, against those who are forced to fly 'deportation class'. This has led to several fatalities. Legally out of any national jurisdiction, the captain of a plane has ultimate responsibility for the lives of all passengers, and the guards accompanying the deportee have no more legal status than that of any other passenger. Thus passengers who intervene in incidents which pose a direct danger for life or physical safety of their fellow passengers, including such deportations, are acting lawfully and do not have to fear being prosecuted on grounds of resisting enforcement officers.

Ways of obstructing the policies of airlines deporting refugees and asylum seekers are many, ranging from participating in email campaigns to object to the deportation, to visiting refugees inside detention centers – all the way up to

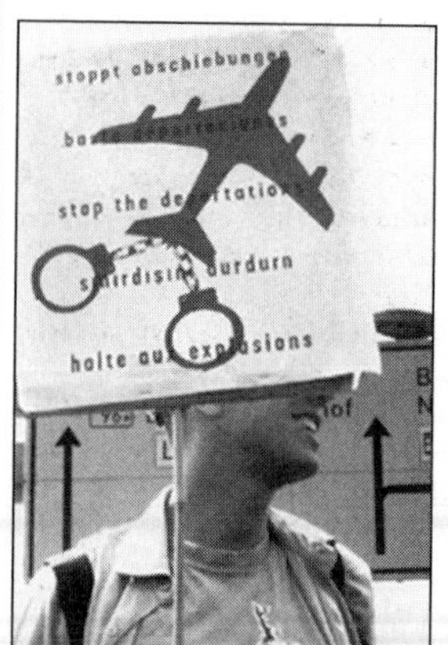

Outrageous
return flight.
Your deportation agent. KLM

deportation class

Sandy K / Deportation Alliance / Brian Holmes

using direct action to prevent the deportations. This is one particularly inspiring example:

An man who had befriended a refugee on the other side of the fence at a UK detention centre discovered that his friend was about to be deported without an appeal. The man bought a ticket for the flight the refugee was to be deported on. After the doors were closed, but before the plane was able to take off, he removed his seat belt, folded his arms so no-one would be frightened of his intentions, and declared that the plane was being used to deport an asylum seeker and that he would not sit down until the refugee was taken off the plane. Eventually he was removed by security, but as he left, he yelled that there were 20 others on the plane who were prepared do the same thing unless the refugee was released (more a statement of optimism than fact). The pilot refused to take off until the refugee was removed from the plane. The refugee's lawyer waiting at the airport used the extra hours to successfully get a new hearing in the refugee's claim for asylum.

No Border camps

No Border camps have been mushrooming across Europe, Australia, and the US. A temporary camp is set up as close to a border as possible. The camps become sites for the exchange of political experiences, as well as cultural and media activities. They create a space, often in remote areas, to gather, discuss, and make connections, as well as to take direct actions to disrupt the border posts or help refugees cross safely. No Border camps have appeared on the shores of the Straits of Gibraltar, the beach of Tijuana, in the desert at Woomera, Australia, and on the borders of Ukraine and Slovakia, Poland and Belorus to name a few.

Even Frankfurt's international airport became a site for a 1000-strong border camp in July 2001, forcing police to cordon off the entire airport to anyone without tickets for a week. Actions included an illegal classical music concert inside one of the terminals.

Targeting detention centres

Writing to refugees inside detention centres and sending them international phone cards (their lifeline to their families) is one of the easiest actions one can take.

Disrupting the building of new centres is one way to highlight the issues locally. A new detention centre in Italy was demolished by a group, which included priests and members of parliament, and two more were closed down due to protest.

In Baxter, Australia, actions were accompanied by an independent radio broadcast in the immediate area of the detention centre. It took in-coming phone calls from the refugees inside, and thus established a two-way line of communication with the people imprisoned.

Some have gone as far as to tear down fences and free refugees. This requires, among many things, solid support networks and living spaces for escaped refugees.

Resources:

»No Border network, fighting for freedom of movement for all: www.noborder.org

»Annual US/Mexican borderhack event: www.borderhack.org

»UK National Coalition of Anti-Deportation Campaigns: www.ncadc.org.uk

»Australian support for escaped refugees: www.spareroomsforrefugees.com

In Australia, concentration camps have been built to intern migrants from poor countries. The largest on-shore refugee detention centre in Australia was built in the desert at Woomera in October 1999. In the first year of its operation there were riots, fires, a mass escape, many suicide attempts, and allegations of sexual abuse. During February 2001, a mass hunger strike of over 300 people went on for up to 30 days; some participants sewed their lips shut.

All of the migrants held there are asylum seekers, most of whose claims have been rejected. Many have been held for over three years – even the blind and the pregnant are detained behind razor wire. The transnational corporation (Group 4) that runs the detention centre also runs private prisons in the US and detention centres in the UK, and earns US$65 a day for each refugee detainee held in Australia.

Protests inside Australia's refugee camps have been ongoing for a decade, and it is only since they escalated in 2000 that people on the outside have protested against the existence of the camps. On 30 March 2002, 1,000 people broke into the Woomera asylum seekers' prison and more than 50 detainees escaped. This was part of the Woomera 2002 Festival Of Freedom – a tour of actions held around the desert town organized jointly by urban activists and local Kokatha and Arabunna peoples, who had received messages from the prisoners requesting help and support.

Though many escapees were recaptured, a few former prisoners remain free. Detainees inside Woomera refused to let guards conduct a headcount in order to ascertain who had escaped. Guards responded with tear gas and beatings. Woomera detention centre, the centre of so much controversy, has since been closed down, but Baxter– a detention centre with an even fiercer regime – has opened and resistance continues: in January 2003, simultaneous fires occurred in every refugee detention centre in Australia.

We Are Human Beings: the Woomera breakout

by Jess Whyte

From inside the Woomera refugee internment camp in the South Australian desert, people screamed out at us. "We are human," they yelled over and over again, "we are not animals". One man called out: "We are people. There are no animals here." These were the calls of desperate people caught in a system so dehumanizing that when they were faced with other people – people who came in solidarity – their first instinct was to convince us they were human.

The call to action for this protest talked of our humanity being obliterated in Woomera. Here, in the desert, we felt the full extent of what that really meant. We realized that it applied not only to those inside the fence but to all of us who are 'free' on the outside. And so we fought for the freedom we had been told we already had. We fought alongside people and knew them as such, and we discovered, amidst the horror, a common humanity.

Arriving in Woomera, the first thing I was struck by was the incredible isolation. I imagined being a newly arrived migrant, driven through the desert to this place. I imagined feeling the dry heat for the first time, being whipped by the dust and then being left here, behind the fence. It would be easy to believe that no one knew this place existed. It would be so easy to feel utterly alone. "The future of people is anonymous," an escapee told me later that night. "They don't know how long [it will be until they are] released. Some have been here years. Their family can't contact them. They don't know if they are alive or have disappeared."

On Friday night 1,000 of us marched towards the camp to show those inside that they were not alone – that we knew, that we cared, and that we would fight alongside them. As we walked through the thistles towards the camp, orange flares were released, spewing clouds of orange smoke into the sunset. The flares were a signal of distress, a signal of the desperate emergency that lay before us. This time the call was answered – not by some distant boat on the horizon, like the unfortunate Tampa, whose captain had followed the law of the sea and his own conscience [by picking up a boat of stranded migrants], and found himself a pawn in a political game [when Australia refused to let him dock] – but by thousands of people fighting together on either side of the razor wire.

Outside the fence we rushed forward. We waited for the riot police. We waited for the tear gas and the water cannons many of us had seen used on those inside to be turned on us. The police didn't arrive.

Suddenly we were face to face with the razor wire. We had talked about ripping down the fences, tearing down the cages, destroying the barriers that divided us. Few of us had believed our own rhetoric. But now we were faced with a fence. In the distance, on the other side, people were locked up. This fence symbolized everything we had come here to oppose. For a moment we were daunted by it. We pulled at it in anger, watching it sway, but hardly believing it when it came down. The coils of razor wire that ran along its top, designed to rip and tear at the flesh of those who attempted to scale it, were soon powerless, pinned to the desert floor by sandbags, which seemed to have been provided for the purpose.

We learned later we could have walked around that fence. Perhaps if we had, everything would have been different. Seeing that razor wire come down changed everything. It changed us. Suddenly everything seemed possible. We helped each other over, mocking the once-foreboding coils now lying limp before us. And still the police didn't arrive. With the fence down, there seemed no other choice but to continue on. Even those who would not

---

shouting "The working class has no borders", close to 1,000 people occupy the Los Angeles International Airport in protest against a week of raids by the Immigration and Naturalization Service, and against a state supreme court ruling which denies back-pay to undocumented workers fired for union organizing. The people are part of a coalition of immigrant rights groups, unions, and community and religious organizations. Southwest Airlines participated closely with the INS in Operation Tarmac, launched in the wake of 11 September. The airline is profiling passengers with one-way tickets, cash purchases, and Latino-sounding surnames, and is allowing undercover agents to demand identification, often chasing fleeing workers into oncoming traffic.

>> March 29 >> Over 1,000 people assist refugees to escape from Australia's Woomera Detention Centre.

>> April 1 >> After a 30 year campaign involving direct action, popular education, and constant legal challenges, forest activists in Aotearoa/New Zealand achieve massive victory when the government bans all logging of publicly owned temperate rain forests. National parks are extended, and two new conservation parks are created, resulting in the West Coast region having over 85 per cent of its land protected as public preserve. Padlocks are removed, fences

Desert Indymedia

Preparing to tear down the fence surrounding the detention centre. Woomera, Australia

have joined the civil disobedience action scheduled for the following day were here now. They too had seen the fence come down. They too had been changed, and they moved with us to the next fence.

If the last fence was symbolic, this one was chillingly real. Behind its bars were people like us, people who were crying or screaming for freedom. Many of them were injured. Topless men stood before us, their chests slashed and bloody. People raised mangled hands, ripped by the razor wire. They too had already pulled down a fence. Now they screamed out at us, desperate to convince us they were human. While Immigration Minister, Philip Ruddock, talks of the "illegals" or the "queue-jumpers", we talk of the "refugees", the "asylum seekers", the "detainees". Too rarely do we go beyond our mythical categories and think about the people. But now we were faced with these people, and we realized how severely the fences they stood behind imprison us all.

A small boy stood at the bars, pulling at them while tears poured down his face. Around him people held hands through the fence. Above them, people from the inside and outside met and wrestled with the razor wire that stretched around the perimeter. This was the razor wire news crews had filmed a man throwing himself onto in desperation months earlier. At one point a man climbed to the top of the first fence and stood contemplating the wire below. For a horrific moment we expected to see a replay of the scene we had all seen played out on our television screens. People on both sides screamed out to him, "NO!" He looked out at the people in front of him, people in tears, people who seemed to care if he lived or died, and slowly he climbed back down.

Around him other refugees used towels and gloves to protect themselves as they tore at the fence. They didn't want to harm themselves and now there was another option. That option was to fight, to escape, to tear down the fences as we on the outside had talked about. When the steel bars finally buckled it wasn't those on the outside who tore them down. It was the people inside who had been constrained by them for so long. And suddenly they were jumping out. The first to escape scrambled out to be hugged by people outside. Moments later, as the police finally moved in, more flew threw the air and stage dived into our arms. A man ran through the crowd grabbing people and

---

come down, and public access is restored to the spectacular region. Using words unfamiliar to most capitalist policy-makers, the forestry minister tells Parliament, "These lowland forests are considered by many New Zealanders to be a unique and significant part of our natural heritage, too valuable for logging of any sort to continue."

>> April 3-5 >> Continent-wide demonstrations in solidarity with the Palestinian struggle take place across Latin America. More than 1,000 Brazilians, including members of the MST, march to the US consulate in Sao Paulo. In Brasilia, *Via Campesina* members hold an overnight vigil and encampment in front of the Israeli embassy, while 500 people in Rio de Janeiro protest at the Israeli consulate. 1,000 people, most of them of Palestinian descent, march in Santana do Livramento, and across the border in Rivera, Uruguay; in Chile 1,000 people gather in Santiago to condemn the Israeli assault. In Quito, Ecuador, a protest takes place at the Israeli embassy and in Lima, Peru, about 100 Palestinians demonstrate outside the Israeli embassy. In Nicaragua, 2,000 people march to the UN office in Managua to present written demands calling for the withdrawal of the Israeli army; participants included many Nicaraguans of Palestinian and Arab origin and members of the leftist Sandinista National Liberation

telling them: "I am refugee. I've been inside two years." I held his hand and began to walk, to walk away from the fence, away from where the police had moved in, blocking the escape of those who had been too slow to get out.

As we walked we tore off his prison clothes and pulled a "Free the Refugees" t-shirt over his head. He looked like any of us. Except that unlike us he was a hunted man, an escapee. As we crossed back through the dust towards our campsite, he asked me again and again, "Now what is your plan? How do we get away?" I wished I had a better answer than, "We'll do everything we can." We kept walking faster now as just in front of us, six police dragged a man back to the other side of the razor wire. We tried to look the other way as we kept walking.

That night we spent many hours with this man. We asked him to choose a name in case the police raided our campsite. He said he'd use an Australian name and chose Chang. We offered him cigarettes, which he took, and we sat in a tent smoking rollies and talking. He was intelligent and articulate and incredibly calm. We offered him food, but he refused. He was on hunger strike. "We had a demonstration in the afternoon saying 'welcome' to protesters," he told us. Australasian Correctional Management (ACM – a subsidiary of Wackenhut Corrections, now owned by global private prison operators Group 4) guards had disrupted the protest and told the detainees that three protesters (who had been injured in a car accident) had been killed. They told the protesting refugees it was their fault. "Today all on hunger strike in solidarity with demonstrators in car accident," Chang told me. "No one inside is eating. In morning we raised black flag in sorrow."

"When there is damage to a detention centre, the TV cameras are invited in to show the ruined buildings to the world, but no journalist has ever been allowed inside to document the destruction of our souls."

– appeal from the asylum seekers of Australia, January 2003

This story was the flip side of the arguments we had heard on the outside before the protest. Some lawyers representing Woomera detainees had expressed concern over our protests, arguing that if refugees were attacked by ACM, or self-harmed, we would be responsible. This argument was taken up by the media and the government who attempted to paint protesters as irresponsible and unconcerned for the welfare of refugees, and foster a split between radical and conservative wings of the movement. At the time, many people involved in the Woomera 2002 network in Melbourne had argued against painting people inside Woomera as lacking in agency. We had pointed out that this movement we were part of was started by people within the camps – the first Woomera breakout was the event that had spurred on protests outside the camps. We had pointed to the fact that inside Woomera people were organized, that many were serious activists before they arrived here and that they, like us, were capable of making decisions about how and when they were to protest, and of evaluating the possible ramifications.

Now before us sat two of these men; men who had escaped from Afghanistan. "The Taliban used to take our people, the Hazaras, for the front lines, then professional soldiers go after," Chang told us. "We were compelled to escape." They were men who had reached Australia against incredible odds and who now were fighting for their freedom. They asked us for one thing: solidarity.

That solidarity came in many forms, and crucially it served to give hope to people who were beginning to believe there was none. "They say no hope, disappointment," Chang said of the people inside the camp. "But when they hear all people of Australia coming they found a glimmer of hope." Throughout the night, he repeated these words again and again. "Before we had no hope. You have given us hope."

Chang will need that hope. Like many others who escaped, he was later recaptured. Chang will not get refugee status. He is what Philip Ruddock referred to during the protest as a "rejectee". The persecution he outlined to us is not enough for him to qualify for refugee status. It seems the continuing 'war on terror' has made Afghanistan safe for people like Chang in the eyes of our Government. Afghanistan has been bombed to pieces, our Government claims it has been bombed to peace. "This [refugee application] process is so complex, even you native Australians would not be successful," Chang told us that night. For people like him, success is even more elusive. "Tajik and Pashtun interpreters inside ACM hate us Hazaras," he explains. "We say something, they something different." There are always technicalities to lock people out, to slam up more barriers to real freedom.

For the people who marched towards the fences that Friday night, chanting "No borders. No nations. No deportations," the technicalities are irrelevant. We did not come to ask for minor amendments to the refugee convention, for faster processing, or more 'humane' incarceration. We came to fight for the free movement of people, for a real globalization, based not on the freedom of

---

Front, among others.

>> April 6 >> More than 100 members of the Soweto Electricity Crisis Committee, in South Africa, a group which reconnects power lines when service to poor communities gets cut, gather outside the home of Johannesburg's mayor's home, and attempt to deliver a memorandum, when they are fired upon with live ammunition. Chanting slogans, flinging garbage around the garden, and otherwise trashing the house ensues in the outraged aftermath before 87 are arrested

>> April 9 >> After six years of bitter struggle, the Cascadia Forest Alliance celebrates the cancellation of Eagle Creek timber sales in the Mt. Hood National Forest, Oregon, US. While not technically old growth, many stands of trees are 150 years old and naturally regenerated after wildfires in the late 1880s. The forest has been defended by road blockades, sit-ins, and three years of continuous occupation of threatened trees. Tragically, 22-year-old Beth 'Horehound' O'Brian falls 150 feet to her death in the days between the announcement of the cancellation and the receipt of documentation, as activists continue their constant vigil, having learned from experience that the word of the Forest Service is virtually worthless.

>> April 10 >> Farmers in Nairobi, Kenya take to the

capital to exploit the world's people with ease, but on global solidarity and justice. We came to assert that the people locked in cages were just like us, and had as much right to be here as we did. On Friday night Chang told me, "We come to be refuged by the people of Australia, not by Philip Ruddock or John Howard." At Woomera, 1,000 of us attempted to provide that refuge; to break down the barriers that existed between us, be they in the form of fences, lies, or institutionalized racism.

After Woomera there are people who remain uncaptured. Others continue to be locked up indefinitely. Those of us who are told we're 'free' Australians learned a lot about freedom, and gained a new determination to fight for it, both for ourselves, and for all of our friends whose cages are more tangible than ours. This time we will not fight on their behalf, but for our own liberation. We left Woomera with the realization that the people inside the camps struggle as much for our freedom as we struggle for theirs. Seeing these people – people who had sat with us, talking, smoking, and even laughing – being dragged back into the camps was heartbreaking. Seeing them with their fists still raised in the air was exhilarating. On Friday night Chang told me quietly, "We are happy that we got out. Even if we are arrested, we are happy we saw outside the fence." So now we continue to struggle, to destroy the fences so that people like Chang can join us in a fenceless, borderless world.

"We came here looking for freedom, safety, and justice. Instead we found nothing but traps, built of steel bars, bad laws, and dishonest politics. Inside these cages, children have grown into adults. Young men's hair has turned white. Babies have been born, taken their first steps, spoken their first words. Most of us, separated from our families, have become like ghosts to our mothers, our wives, our children."

– appeal from the asylum seekers of Australia, sent to refugee advocate Betty Dixon, January 2003

Escape From Woomera

by Sadiq Ali

My name is Sadiq Ali. I am 19 years old. I am from Afghanistan. My province is Ghazni and my village is Sang-e Masha. I came to Australia in February last year. I was in Woomera detention centre till March. On Easter Good Friday I escaped from Woomera, and now I am free. Life in Woomera is like a hell. We have a difficult life in the camp.

I was rejected from the immigration department. When they rejected me first, they said, "The language analysis said that you are not from Afghanistan, we believe you are Hazara". But second time they rejected me they said, "We do not have doubts about your language. Your language is right. You speak Hazargi (Dari), your mother tongue. But you are not from Afghanistan, only your language is from Afghanistan."

In Woomera everyone goes insane. Every day men, women and children cut themselves with razor blades, drink shampoo, and hang themselves. They commit suicide. The ACM who run the camp are very bad with us. They abuse us and say, "Australia is not your father's country. This is your punishment for coming Australia."

Last year on 7 June, the ACM guard beat one of the Afghani detainees. When the other detainees tried to protest about their cruelty they brought more than 200 guards into the camp with large sticks, and wearing full riot protection, and they beat us very badly. They hit the faces and heads of detainees with sticks so that nearly everyone was bleeding. They broke the hand of a detainee and he fell down on the ground. They took him to the medical centre and they pressed his broken finger with pliers because they said he was faking. His entire finger became blue, and they had to take him to Adelaide hospital by emergency flight. The ACM guard told the nurses and the doctor that this detainee is a criminal, and if you aren't careful he will kill you. They also captured more than other 40 detainees, I along with them. They used handcuffs and they beat us very badly. After that they searched our rooms two or three times every month until I escaped.

Last year in our holy month of Ramadan they separated us from the other Afghanis, but when we try to protest and

---

streets in protest against a new policy instituted by the National Cereals and Produce Board where they will receive payment in seeds, fuel, and fertilizer instead of cash. In the past, the Board offered a guaranteed minimum payment for the crops of all small farmers. The farmers demand cash, as they need it to pay IMF-imposed school fees.

>> April 12 >> *Taoiseach* Bertie Ahern (Prime Minister) had an unfortunate run-in with Secret Agent Whatever of the Irish division of the Biotic Baking Brigade, which resulted in the second pieing of a head of state in eight months. When pressed for comment, Agent Whatever said, "We have no idea who our next target will be. There is no shortage of corrupt politicians in Ireland. A pie thrown randomly near any government building would have a hard time not hitting some corrupt old git. That's the main reason we have been inactive so far; it isn't really much of a challenge."

>> April 16 >> Ten million state-employed workers in India strike to protest recently approved liberalization of labour laws, which allow for easier firing. Trade unions are also concerned about the government's plans to speed up the privatization of nationalized industries. In West Bengal, planes and trains in Calcutta are halted by workers, who block access to the airport and railway stations. Most coal miners and dock workers also honor the strike nationwide.

we said to them this is our holy month of Ramadan and we want to stay together because we have a special prayers in this night they dismissed our protest. They used force against us, with four ACM guards for one person. There were 11 unaccompanied minors (under 18 years without parents), and I was also with them. The ACM guard beat us all very badly. They beat me with their knees, with their big shoes they kicked me, they punched me and they smashed me in the ground and after, smashed me against the wall. Not just me, my other friend too, and they used handcuffs and separated us. After that they were doing many bad things

Pip Starr/Rockhopper Productions

An asylum seeker leaps to freedom. Woomera, Australia

against me until the hunger strike.

In hunger strike all Afghanis sat under the sun and were on hunger strike for 15 days. It was very hot and the people were very thin and feeling dizzy. At first the ACM guards laughed at us and we were in very bad condition. The government sent advisory group. They came. They promised us many things and at last we finished our hunger strike, but the advisory group forget their promises and they failed to do anything for us.

During these hunger strikes, the young man named Mazhi Ali [in an act of self-harm] jumped on the razor wire. At first, the immigration department said that he wanted to escape, but afterwards they change their comments. After the hunger strike, our people, who were working in the camps for one dollar an hour, the ACM finished their works as a punishment. Some days after our strike, they removed us from one compound to another compound, the ACM again began searching our rooms, giving us date-expired food, and their abuse until Easter.

One day the ACM centre manager called our delegate and said to him that at Easter there are people coming to Woomera, and that he must tell the detainees, "Don't do anything." They said, "The Government is sending us more force and if you try anything we'll use force and beat your people. And the protesters are going back after two days but we are always here. If you people try anything it won't be good for you."

But on Good Friday when the people came to Woomera we broke the fence and we came out. We were very scared and it was very cold night and we were waiting until 2.00 am, but we were happy. At last after so much struggle we escaped. We were finished listening to the abuse and enduring the beatings of ACM and their guards with their black sticks. And we came to city. Now I and my friend are happy, but we are also sad about our other brothers and sisters that are still there in Woomera and I hope that they will be free soon, and that everything will get better for us too.

But finally we got our freedom, and we are free.

Previously published in *Desert Storm* at:
www.antimedia.net/desertstorm/escapee.shtml

Resources:

» Archived and updated reports from Woomera:
www.melbourne.indymedia.org

» More reflection and analysis on the woomera actions:
antimedia.net/desertstorm

» Website of the Woomera 2002 actions woomera2002.antimedia.net

"We left our homes because we had no choice but to flee from brutal, dictatorial regimes. Many of us faced imprisonment, torture, or murder, and have already seen our relatives suffer those fates. We have been persecuted for our religious beliefs, our ethnic group, our political opinions, or even the family we belonged to. We would gladly have stayed in our homelands and lived ordinary lives, but that is exactly what it has been made impossible for us to do."

– appeal from the asylum seekers of Australia, January 2003

>> April 16 >> Italian industry grinds to a halt in the first general strike in 20 years. An estimated 11-12 million workers put down their tools of trade and took to the streets to protest against government labour reform plans, which reduce the national jobless fund and makes it much easier to fire workers. Temporary employment agencies are occupied, or find their entrances sealed shut with glue. The strike virtually shuts down air, rail and local transport, hospitals provide emergency services only, and no newspapers appear on the streets, as printers and journalists participate en masse.

>> April 17 >> A rally of 200,000 coconut farmers in Dharwar, India is organized by the KRRS and the Green Brigade on the occasion of World Farmer's Day. A spokesperson for the KRRS uses the opportunity to issue a demand to Chief Minister S M Krishna: that he spend some time studying science before introducing genetically modified cotton seed into the state. The spokesperson points out that leading scientists representing 36 nations have submitted a report to the UN recommending the ban of such seeds, and that until Minister Krishna has their level of education, he should refrain from tampering with biodiversity.

>> April 20 >> In a mass global coincidence, the

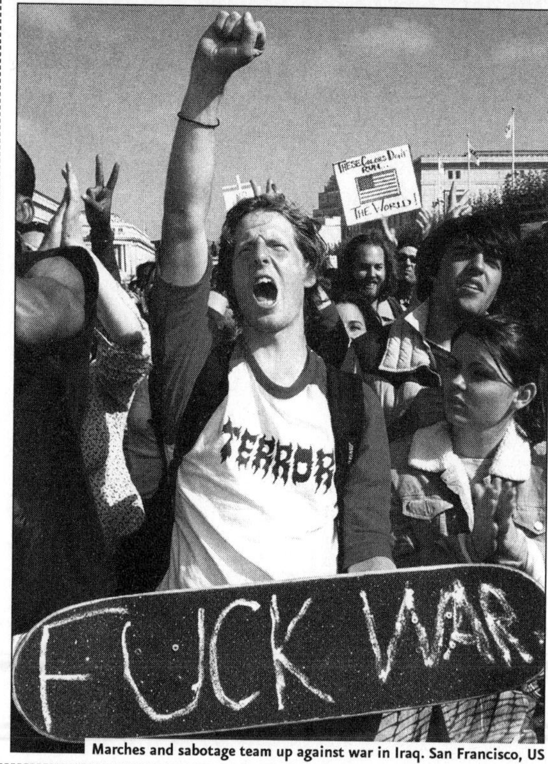

Marches and sabotage team up against war in Iraq. San Francisco, US

Dismantling War

How do you resist the war-mongers, when they have the guns, the bombs, the soldiers, the bankers and the money on their side? Find tactical pressure points. Make it cost more to continue waging war rather than ending it – and cost can be public opinion, political credibility, as well as spiralling budgets. Giant rallies certainly have their place, but there are other strategic and creative ways to resist too. Here are just a few examples.

Spanner in the works

Military bases are built where local resistance is expected to be minimal. So get busy. In the 1980s, women camped outside the US military base at Greenham Common in the UK and set rows of rubber ducks into the concrete on the runways so the planes couldn't take off. In Viéques, Puerto Rico, site of a vast US military base, locals resisting the testing of bombs camped out for over a year on the bombing range in 2000. After they were cleared off by force, local fishermen remained hiding there, risking their lives to stop the bombing.

During the Gulf War of 2003, numerous acts of sabotage occurred. At a US spy base in Yorkshire, UK, people came with miles of tin foil in an attempt to disrupt satellite communications. Others flew helium balloons in an attempt to prevent aircraft taking off. Access roads into the base were blocked. Some locked themselves to dragnets across runways. One woman destroyed a fleet of military vehicles used to service the bombers by pouring sand and treacle into the engines. In Ireland, military aircraft on their way to bomb Iraq had to stop refuelling at Shannon airport, such was the level of protest.

Peter Maiden/SF Indymedia

In Scotland, workers refused to load trains with munitions. In Italy, activists got on passenger trains in front of freight trains carrying arms and pulled the emergency cord, blocking the line. One woman broke into a military base in Scotland and smashed up a Hawk Jet.

In 1996 the same woman with three others had smashed the control panels of a $22 million Hawk Jet, putting it out of action. It had been due to be exported to Indonesia. In court they claimed they had acted lawfully to prevent a greater crime – genocide by the Indonesian military occupying East Timor. The evidence was so powerful the stunned jury found the women not guilty.

Cannon fodder

Thousands of British Conscientious Objectors were imprisoned for over two years – 73 of whom died there during the first world war. During the Vietnam War, dodging the draft became a major preoccupation of young men in the US. Today enforced conscription does not occur in the US or the UK, but is still an issue in many countries, and people around the world are in jail for refusing to serve.

In Israel, every citizen is drafted into the army. Many refusniks are in prison for refusing to serve in the military, in protest at the Occupation.

But even where there is no draft, military recruiters come to schools and colleges, where they can also be met with resistance. In the US poor, black, and Latino communities are targets for military recruitment. Half of frontline US soldiers in the 1992 Gulf War were people of colour. This is 'economic conscription' – when kids with few options join up for the tuition, scholarships and training. Activists are setting up alternative stalls next to army recruitment drives. In Oxford, school children left class, occupied the town centre, and blockaded an army recruitment stall for several hours .

Target the profiteers

One of the most powerful long-term strategies is to unmask and obstruct those who have a direct interest in the pursuit of war. Go for the moneymen.

A week before the 2003 Iraq war started, 20 activists disrupted trading at London's International Petroleum Exchange, Europe's major centre for trading in futures contracts for crude oil, highlighting the links between war in Iraq and the West's compulsive oil habit. Despite being set upon by traders, the protesters unplugged telephones and computers and brought trading to a standstill for two hours. In other places petrol stations were shut down.

Others have concentrated on the battle for resources that helps to fuel wars. Coltan in mobile phones fuels war in the Congo; oil and access to oil fuels wars from Colombia to Chechnya to Iraq; diamond money fuelled conflict in Sierra Leone. Boycotts (eg of coltan) and alternatives (eg converting vehicles to biodiesel) can be innovative ways of highlighting the issue and stopping the root causes of war.

There are increasing numbers of private corporations and mercenaries directly involved in war. British firm Sandline International sent mercenaries to crush the 1996 Bougainville rebellion in Papua New Guinea and is implicated in the Sierra Leone conflict. US firm Dyncorp is contracted by the US military to undertake operations in Colombia. Pipeline builders like Halliburton and Bechtel, arms dealers like Lockheed Martin have all been ripe targets for office protests and anti-war direct action.

Resources:

» Guide to military dismantling: www.tridentploughshares.org

» UK direct action against war: www.disobedience.org.uk

Former Yugoslavia is *where Western and Eastern Europe meets the Middle East. Dominating the crossroads of Europe's most important trade routes, it is key to US plans to extend its sphere of influence within the Balkans, thereby diminishing Russia's control over the Central Asian republics and gaining control of Caspian Sea oil reserves.*

But Yugoslavia is no more. On 4 February 2003 it was replaced by the new state of Serbia and Montenegro, literally a 'state of emergency' since the assassination of neoliberal Prime Minister Zoran Djindjic on 12 March 2003. As Walter Benjamin said, "The tradition of the oppressed teaches us that the 'state of emergency' in which we live is not the exception but the rule."

Certainly, this has been the case for Yugoslavia over the last 25 years. Until 1980, Yugoslavia was seen by some as a socialist utopia under the 'benign dictatorship' of Marshall Tito, the war-time leader of the partisans and subsequent ruler of Communist Yugoslavia. The country was a regional industrial power and economic success, with a multi-ethnic population boasting a high literacy rate and free education and healthcare.

However, as leader of a communist state not aligned to the Soviet Union, Tito sought to integrate Yugoslavia with the capitalist system, and borrowed heavily from Western banks. By the 1980s, Yugoslavia had the highest debt-to-income ratio in Europe, and in 1983 when the European Community and Western banks refused to allow it to re-schedule its debts, it placed itself in the hands of the IMF. What followed was catastrophic social meltdown and economic collapse. Essential social services were cut, regional inequalities increased, and unemployment rose. By 1989, Kosovo's unemployment rate was 50 per cent; in Serbia, Bosnia, Montenegro, and Macedonia, it ranged between 20-30 per cent. In 1991, Yugoslavia began to break-up as Slovenia, Croatia and Macedonia declared independence; Bosnia-Herzegovina did too in 1992. Nearly a decade of civil war followed.

The West has largely ignored these economic and political fault-lines, preferring instead to see the violence as the result of purely ethnic and religious hatred – Serbian aggression, Croat fascism, clashes between orthodox Christianity, Catholicism or Islam – the past decade is presented as the continuation of the barbarous history of Yugoslavia as the 'other', different, better left alone, too difficult to understand. Easier to send the troops and F16s to sort them out.

NATO's intervention in Kosovo in 1999 under the guise of protecting the Kosovar Albanians demonstrates the axiom of military strategist Carl Von Clausewitz: "War is the continuation of politics by other means." As Massimo de Angelis and Silvia Federici wrote at the height of the bombings, "First the economic and financial élites imposed impoverishing neoliberal policies in the region, policies that shattered the social fabric and created the context in which brutal and murderous nationalisms have flourished. Then they seized the opportunity for military action resulting in further death and environmental devastation. Soon again they will wear the banker's hat to 'help' in the reconstruction, cashing in new interest payments and especially, prospecting a more 'stable' environment for business, thanks to NATO's heavy military presence in the region." By intervening, NATO, led by the UK and US, demonstrated the extent of their ambition. This was less a humanitarian gesture than a sign of things to come, the iron fist in a velvet glove used to subjugate all before the military and economic hegemony of the US and its privileged position within the Imperial constitution of the new Empire.

But as the exceptional state of emergency recedes in post-Yugoslavia and the so-called Europeanization of Serbia continues apace, new movements are starting to emerge. In Belgrade, the movement Drugaciji Svet je Moguc (Another World Is Possible) is now convenor of Peoples' Global Action in Europe and is calling anticapitalist activists to look east.

It's Great We Are Everywhere, We Thought We Were Quite Alone: a letter from post-Yugoslavia

by Ivana Momcilovic

Dark objects of desire

In 1968, the Socialist Federal Republic of Yugoslavia turned 24 and I turned 4. We were living in the skyscraper suburb of new promises, New Belgrade, when my father brought me a present – my first 'Texas trousers' from Trieste (Italy, Western Europe, capitalism). Giving it a second thought, I realize today that this was my first step into the mainstream: of the 20 million ex-Yugoslavs, almost half must have had fantasies at some point about the 'original' blue jeans, the uniform of the West. Jeans used to be smuggled in from Italy like gold, since German, English, and Italian tourists did not exchange cheap jeans and nylon stockings in their hotels for local currency (like they did in the countries of the 'real' Eastern bloc). What gave us real pleasure (and also nurtured our sense of 'freedom') was actually the night trip by train to the Italian border (touching with one's own hands as many 'dark objects of desire' as possible) and then catching the train back with a brightly coloured plastic bag in hand.

Jeans were more than just jeans; they signified freedom, wealth, better living, happiness. A lust for a flirtation outside one's rather dull marriage to the socialist dream. Exactly what home was not.

You used to buy Levi's but what you were actually doing was buying fantasies about a new community. Democracy, in a colourful bag.

Even when textile producers in the south of Serbia (Novi Pazar) started producing counterfeit jeans, it was no use. This was false happiness, for there was no male model promising the Levi's style of living. Our economy consisted of powerless 'local raw materials', unbranded and insufficient for conjuring up the Levi's phantasm, that myth of the denim that brings better and eternal life, emancipation, and democracy, had to be savoured directly from the source.

International Monetary Fund responds to a call for an international day of action by having their annual meeting. A call for an international *cacerolazo* in solidarity with Argentina, put out by Argentinean anticapitalist activists, and the day is to commemorate the five month anniversary of the uprising. Cities respond worldwide, some banging on pots and pans, others on bells and drums, some unaware that their actions are linked to Argentina, others unaware of the links to the IMF. Actions take place in Washington DC, New York, Seattle, London and São Paolo, among others.

>> April 20 >> Students take to the streets in Nairobi, Kenya in protest against World Bank-imposed privatizations and restrictions on university admissions.

>> April 22 >> Rejecting the notion that Coca Cola is an acceptable substitute for water, 2,000 indigenous people and *dalits* (oppressed castes) gather at the gates of the Hindustan Coca Cola factory in Plachimada, Kerala, India. The company has been mining groundwater, drying up many wells, and contaminating the rest. The villages demand restoration of the damaged groundwater aquifers and long term water supply to all those affected. The picket is sustained for 49 days, with the company continuing its excavation under police guard. On 9 June,

This is what we thought back in 1968. We were thirsty and we craved adventures.

The first sparks

And while the Western 1968 revolutionaries on the barricades fantasized about our perceived 'socialist utopia', we fantasized as well – not about more socialism but about the things we were missing in our own marriage to it. In other words, by rejecting our own revolution, we rushed to throw the baby out with the bathwater.

The point is that we had something, and yet we were craving something else – the dream of capitalism. But its reality was smaller, and that is exactly where the problem lay. But some things you can't know before you try them. After all, love is a neurosis.

Seduced by capitalism

You see, the reality in Yugoslavia was free education, free health care, and free housing. And we enjoyed this, of course. Only, we yearned for something more than this freedom, won by our anti-fascist grandfathers, and paid for with their lives.

Throughout the cold war, Western capitalism perfected the tricks of an experienced seducer, proffering warm, instant delight. No seducer has ever been as skilful, smiling, smart, perfumed, young, immortal, and seductive as the advertising campaigns of Coca Cola, Winston, Adidas, Dior, all of which lured us into crossing 'the border'. Capitalism should rightfully be known as the Lover of the Century.

Its only shortcoming was that flirting is so ephemeral! The moment you kiss your desire, cross the border, get the sports shoes, a crush-proof pack of Marlboros, or a mobile phone, you realize that true love doesn't lie in these objects, after all, but in something else – in the zone of half-light, of infatuation, the borderless zone, which fills the existential void lurking in every one of us, and which only the miracle of life can fill with meaning.

Capitalism is hysterical, hyperbolic; its perpetual exaggerations are reminiscent of an obsessive desire that can never be satisfied. Producing more than any other socio-economic system, supposedly in order to satisfy human needs (as Marx pointed out), capitalism actually exists in order to create the need that creates the need. No quantity is ever sufficient, no worker is productive enough, no profit is big enough. To say enough is enough would mean to say that more would not be better.

"I can't get no, satisfaction ..." But, the hardest thing of all is that when you finally realize this, you will already have been alone for a long time ....

Alone

Now it is 2003, and Yugoslavia is no more. It has ended up on the dump of history, along with the ardent love life of the Yugoslavs, the impossible flirting between the East and the West. All that remains is the steel embrace of the West.

Hanging above the seductive promises of Marxist self-management there is the promise of Darwinist capitalism where chance alone – the caprice of the stock exchange (as

Westerners are discovering when they check their pension funds) – determines the destiny of humankind. And so the world turns its attention back to Yugoslavia, now that its price has dropped due to the market fluctuation produced by horror and war; now it is a saleable commodity. Paradoxically, the anticapitalist movement feels like it turned its []eyes away from us, as it searched for joyful, colourful victories in Seattle and elsewhere – victories that are simply impossible in our country under total defeat and with this phantom 'transition' to neoliberalism.

Today, Yugoslavia is a country with 250,000 killed in the war which began in 1991 and has not completely ended. One and a half million people were internally displaced, did not return to their homes, large numbers have emigrated, while an unknown number of people are crossing, illegally or not, the border of the Schengen agreement [the border control agreement within the EU which non-EU citizens cannot cross without visas and passports], which is the new Berlin wall, separating the new Roman empire from the threatening hordes of 'Barbarians'. The number of disappeared increases daily, as mass graves are exhumed, and the remains of unidentified people wait in white bags, eventually moved from one administrative status to another, their 'cases' closed.

Because of all of this, the most important news of our society is not on the covers of newspapers, but buried in the back pages, somewhere between sports and culture, in the supermarket of classified ads. Read these ads and there you'll find the appeals of laid-off people selling their labour, legal or illegal Schengen visas, and human organs on offer, as clandestinely people offer their kidneys for sale on the black market in order to provide an education for their children.

This brings the paradox to a peak, since capitalism brought us 'peace', if you believe the Western media and the international community. By bombing the country, they helped to overthrow the 'last communist of the century', Slobodan Milosevic, creating conditions for the importation of democracy, and capitalism. What they don't say is that their 'peace' initiated the greatest theft of public property (through privatization and fortune making) of our time.

But people have started to realize this.

---

the police attack, violently arresting 130, including children and infants, and harassing and tearing clothing off several women.

>> April 27 >> Five hundred Roma people set up a protest camp in Essen, Germany to protest their imminent deportation to ex-Yugoslavia. Then they set off on a caravan to bring attention to their plight. Passing through Müenster, Koln and Berlin, arriving in Dusseldorf on 20 June, where they establish another camp. Conditions in the camp are hard, as the Roma endure racist attacks and constant police harassment. But they insist that Germany has an obligation, after its Holocaust policies against the Roma, to allow them to stay.

>> May >> Police in the district of Rohtak, India try to arrest the Regional President of the farmers' organization, Bharatiya Kisan Union, and are taken hostage by the villagers. Similarly at Kandela, five state officials are held hostage. Thousands swarm into Kandela district to fortify it against state retaliation. Three or four rings of men and women, armed with stones and traditional weapons, stand guard until 2,000 armed police arrive to release the hostages. Road blocks multiply, shutting down the entire region. 11 peasants are killed by police; hundreds are injured and hundreds more arrested. The involvement of women in

'Farewell to political parties', posters cover election lies. Belgrade, ex-Yugoslavia

Never alone again!

For all these reasons, confusion is at its peak in post-Yugoslavia today. The civil war, military aggression (by our own military), NATO aggression and occupation, privatization, restoration, parliamentarianism, negationism, rampaging capitalism, ethno-fascism, modern atavism, atavistic modernism, mass destitution, to sum it up – the black dream of importing a European reality, are only a few of the reasons for the Yugoslavs' feeling of complete isolation from the rest of the 'normal' world, a world that has not experienced a civil war and the political nonsenses listed above in the past decade.

Also, the absurd feeling of returning into something that already existed, the bloody breaking up of the 'United Yugoslav States' in order to enter the 'United States of Market Europe' is but another element of the average Yugoslav's feeling of hopelessness, driven into the 'joyful expectation of the civilized Europe'.

But in such a climate and despite these days of fog, a constellation has recently emerged – the size of which we still do not know because it is being born before our very eyes. The global movement of movements has reached us. The resin of hopelessness is finally turning into the amber of a new existence.

Loneliness and isolation are transforming into the joy of togetherness. Instead of the brotherhood of market unity, through the stories of these movements we are discovering a new counter-solidarity of gratuity and new values. We are together, not in order to be stronger, but to

Ivana

expand the circle for all.

Refugees, workers made redundant, war invalids, Roma people, the unemployed, the missing persons committee, the apathetic silent majority – the list of those in our country to whom the movement can and should give real solidarity (unlike those false NGOs and their hollow discourse of human rights) is huge.

The movement's platform is expanding, meetings are flourishing, the form of organization is changing and moving moment by moment. People of various ages and professions are gathering regularly, when a few years ago, some of them would have given a kingdom for just one such gathering. They come in order to attend an evening of solidarity with the rebelling people of Argentina, and then stay afterwards in order to discuss local issues from radically different, non-parliamentary, and non-party positions. The impossible becomes possible, the prohibited becomes allowed. In the beautiful mist of the unsaid, a place finally appears for the suppressed rapture of long ago, for the true freedom to flourish.

The ideological horror of the 1980s, and the more tangible horror of the 1990s whose black hole swallowed our former and future country, is finally behind us. The prohibited memory and the direct continuity with the non-aligned movement which our country helped initiate in the 1950s is once again becoming the reality of the day.

The (old) new beginning

We are attending a birth, the creation of a new form of the old non-acceptance and resistance, and witnessing the first explosion of grassroots movements and direct democracies. A few months ago, even the most cheerful of optimists would have bet their life on their non-existence. But attending a birth is certainly one of the most powerful events in human life.

Our position is not to fight at any cost for the new: a new brand, new trend, new advertisement, new doctrine of victory, all of which are doctrines of capital. Therefore, we do not start from the absolute beginning; we give old questions new answers, a new non-authoritarian colour, and a horizontal form of old rebellions and emancipatory decisions, which began through the lust for life we

---

the struggle inspires them to start a women's organization. In opposition to World Bank diktats, the state government agrees a 75 per cent reduction in electricity charges, plus compensation to the families of the dead.

>> May 2 >> Workers begin an occupation of the Ozarów Cable Factory in Ozarów, Poland, in response to the factory's closure by new owner Telefonica. The brutal six day eviction of the occupation begins on 26 November, with police and a drunken private security force paying threatening visits to the kindergarten where worker's children are in school. When they attack, they target women and supportive community members, arresting 50 and sending four to the hospital. The workers maintain that they will continue the struggle.

>> May 3 >> Victory not only for the U'wa people of Colombia and for all communities fighting against the devastation of resource extraction around the world comes as Occidental Petroleum announces that it is returning oil concessions on the U'wa land to the Colombian Government, and abandoning its plans to drill in the region. OXY has decided there is no oil under U'wa land despite eight years of assuring investors of a major oil strike. The announcement comes nearly a year after OXY retreated from a site which thousands of U'wa, local

inherited from our rebel forefathers and mothers.

An increasing number of people are becoming aware that the world in which we are living is not a world for everyone. It is a world where, as French philosopher Alain Badiou says, "if you are born in Europe, you will be well nourished, taken good care of, educated, and you will live to be eighty. On the other hand, if you are born in Africa or Asia, like hundreds of thousands of women and men, you will be hungry, ill, illiterate, and you will die at the age of two or thirty. The fundaments of our World are disparate, non-uniform, inconstant."

But Yugoslavia is still not Europe – from which it is still separated by the Schengen wall. Yugoslavia is finally in the non-partisan, global movement, and the movement in turn needs our local content.

We are everywhere – especially here

Over the past ten years, dilemmas have been as dead as victims of war all over the globe, ideological marriages have been broken, and everything seems like an enormous ruin upon which the Empire is being rebuilt most successfully. To grasp this rebuilding, one only has to see the army of glaziers doing their work the day after 'violent' anticapitalist demonstrations have taken place, or the transnationals as they invade to 'reconstruct' countries that have been ravaged by wars, just days after 'peace' has been declared. The big question that remains is how long can capitalism be a synonym for peace?

They say that over the past years capitalism has brought stability and peace. It is rumoured that everybody wants to have parliamentary democracy. And so the idea that 'We Are Everywhere' is one of those important ideas that makes the heart beat stronger again. 'We Are Everywhere' is, actually, a much better name than 'antiglobalization'. I shun anything that is anti. In socialism we had to deal with professional dissidents, anti-communists. It is dangerous when your whole identity is built upon a negation. Solzhenytzin, one of such professionals of the anti-Soviet revolution, revealed to us ultimately that he was actually a monarchist, a national-chauvinist and a radical-conservative. When people define themselves anti something, you never know what jester is going to leap out of the box! I have the same premonition in relation to anticapitalists.

This is why it is important to deal with politics on the side of the people – to engage in a new politics of the people and for the people. I am deeply convinced that there are indefatigable issues, epicentres from which new policies for emancipation can come. These issues relate to people and their destinies – to people and their dreams. Starting always from the marginalized, those who are said not to have a right to having any rights, and continuing from there, everyone in their own struggle and coming together, since we know all rivers consist of tributaries. It remains up to us to adjust the imported contagious optimism of the movement of the movements of the whole world, so that it fits in the context of our problems and entanglements, our inventions and imagination. What is important is not only to see, but also to know.

PS: And let us be ready ... the seducer is never at rest! We must make allies with those who do not yet know the emptiness of his promises and are ready to throw themselves into his arms (especially those who remain under his spell after so many years, like our friends from the West). Levi's have finally arrived in our country too. There is a chance for us to definitively protect ourselves, and reject the toxic embrace before it poisons us and then evaporates. However, detoxification takes time and confidence, both of which must be encouraged. We can begin by making small steps (the local, the everyday, the work on a national level) with occasional dashes towards the goal (mass actions, the awareness of an international network), which give breathing space to our little factory of oxygen-dependent optimism. We need it all, no matter where we are. And as we will know from now on, we are everywhere ...

Ivana Momcilovic is a dramaturge of post-Yugoslav origin who has lived in Belgium since 1991 when the civil war began. She has not written fiction since. She has worked for ten years with the collective Eimigrative Art

---

Resources:

» Peoples' Global Action info point in ex-Yugoslavia: Drugaciji Svet je Moguc collective, drugacijisvet@mail.com

AZIN-DSM, 11 000 Belgrade, Post-Yugoslavia Majke Jevrosime 39

» Temporary Yugoslavia IMC site: www.belgrade.indymedia.it

---

campesinos, trade unionists and students had occupied to prevent oil drilling. After using the Colombian military to brutally evict the protesters and militarize the region, OXY was unable to find oil at the site. This came as no surprise to the U'wa whose *Werjayas* (wise elders) had spent months praying to move the oil away from OXY's drills.

>> May 6 >> Over a thousand Ecuadorian banana workers go on strike at the plantation complex Los Alamos. Ten days later, armed men break through the picket line of nonviolent, unarmed workers and take 25 of them as hostages. Eventually, they are freed by their fellow strikers, though two workers are wounded by shotgun fire. The gun-toting thugs are employed by Presidential candidate Alvaro Noboa, whose fiercely anti-union company exports bananas.

>> May 12 >> About 80,000 people demonstrate in Tel Aviv, Israel in the largest peace rally since the beginning of the second *intifada* 19 months ago, demanding that Israel withdraw from the occupied Palestinian territories. Also 150 members of the Arab-Jewish group *Taayush* (co-existence in Arabic) visit the Kissufim crossing point between Israel and the Gaza Strip and call on soldiers stationed there to abandon their posts and return home.

>> May 15 >> Hundreds of families in Caloocan City,

***Just as the capitalist** dream hasn't spread effectively to most people in the global South, it is benefiting few in Central Europe. The end of the Cold War brought the glittering trappings of capitalism – fancy shops, imported foods, and luxury cars – for some but it also brought unemployment, depressed wages, inflation, and cut-throat business practices. The betrayal of capitalism here looks much like it does in Argentina, South Africa, and other countries where neoliberal policies have been rapidly implemented – the results are utterly devastating, and there is deep fear of what the future will bring.*

Poland is the geographical gateway between East and West, and is a sort of testing ground for the regional transition economies. Rapid privatization has resulted in crisis, and many people are realizing that capitalism has even less to offer than did the state-controlled economy. They know that to guarantee a decent job and a good life, they will have to overcome their instincts to compete for scarce resources, and struggle together.

In 2001 the threat of liquidation of the shipyard in Szczecin forced workers to strike. Wildcat miners' strikes continue as their union negotiates with the government to close mines. In Wroclaw, a struggle for the survival of a hospital has resulted in creative actions including a mass funeral march for the death of health care, a group of hospital workers giving away their passports and revoking their citizenship, and the hospital applying for asylum in Holland and Germany – which resulted in the German consul offering the workers jobs in Germany! The neighbourhood surrounding the hospital, as in El Salvador and Argentina, is offering the strongest support in the struggle.

All across the country are tiny pockets where people are learning to work together at a very local level. Squatters and anarchists are joining forces with workers and neighbours and on a small scale, are beginning to visualize and create a world in which principled action takes priority over ideology, a world which has space enough for everyone.

Forging Links in Ozarów

an interview with Zbyszek, by V. of Abolishing Borders from Below

Ozarów is a small town near Warsaw, with an economy entirely centred around a cable manufacturing factory. This factory fell victim to a hostile takeover in the spring of 2002 by the Polish monopoly, Telefonika, whose owner liquidated the plant and attempted to relocate the machinery to his two other production facilities, where workers' wages are lower. The workers in Ozarów responded immediately by barricading the exits of their factory and refusing to allow trucks to remove the machinery. Keeping the plant running is a matter of survival for them, since no other work is available in town, and so their primary demand is that the factory remain open, preferably under worker control. They are well aware that their struggle is connected to others in Poland, which has seen entire cities virtually dismantled over the last twelve years of economic restructuring and privatization.

As winter set in, locals developed a new strategy to prevent the removal of machinery; they continually poured water on the roads, which then froze in the –4Fh temperatures, and prevented the removal trucks from entering or leaving the premises! The winter also saw the development of an unusual coalition, as anarchists from across the country came to Ozarów in solidarity with the workers. They provided support by doing basic legal trainings, assisting with organizing press conferences, relieving workers on the picket line, joining in defence against the attacks by police and security guards, donating fuel, food, and money, and publicizing the struggle through international activist networks.

Abolishing Borders from Below: What was the first reaction of workers and the local community after the decision to close the factory? What form of protest did they choose at first, and how was it developed over the next months?
Zbyszek: Telefonika didn't even try to communicate with the workers, they just closed the factory and announced that the equipment would be taken out. So people decided to blockade the main entrance. Most of the protesters are Ozarów residents; the local police even promised not to intervene against them, though eventually, of course, they did. The non-stop occupation started with people living in two tents, believing that they would save their workplace. The next months came and went without a resolution, so the workers organized a march into the capital. They counted heavily on the support of Solidarnosc (Solidarity), one of the two biggest Polish trade unions. Unfortunately their help was insufficient, so the workers decided to create their own organization. With the crew from other factories in similar situations, they initiated the Polish Protest Committee (OKP); a new and important branch in the nation's trade union movement. The chair of OKP became the leader of the protesters from Ozarów.

ABB: How have events in Ozarów been covered by the media? What is the view among Polish society? From where did the workers get the most support?
Z: Initially the media reported on the occupation in a reliable and factual way. It couldn't be ignored, as Ozarów is one of many places where Polish industry faces such problems, and it's a big story. However, as the workers became more radicalized and the coalition began to strengthen, reporters started to present events as hooligan-led riots, and the protesters as dreamers out of touch with reality.

Much support comes from the local community, which has brought food and other essentials. We anarchists started coming to Ozarów in the first weeks of the protest, and early on we proposed a broad offer of support, which was turned down after a few hours of discussion. We are not

---

Philippines stage a noise protest against new charges to their electric bills. Bills are sent in, unpaid, and marked "Under protest." In Sawata, thousands protest the charges by refusing to use electricity at all. The protests spread across the country throughout the year.
>> May 17 >> Activists in Québec City, Canada march to demand social housing, concluding the march by occupying a house, which is then used by the local community as a gathering place, and children are participating in painting and decorating it. They have three main demands: that the house be transformed into a self-managed housing cooperative, that a moratorium on any new condominium projects be implemented until the vacancy rate goes up 3 per cent, and that the provincial government start a program to build 8,000 social housing units a year.
>> May 23 >> Several hundred Russians burn American flags to denounce President Bush during his summit talks in Moscow. Braving identity checks, detention, and intimidation by snipers on the rooftops, protesters speak out against the indefinite war on terrorism and the neoliberal policies which have sent their country into extreme economic turmoil.
>> May 23 >> The Korean Health and Medical Workers' Union launches strikes in 16 hospitals; two engage in full-

sure if this was because at that time they saw our movement as too radical, or if they were forced to refuse contact with us by the Solidarnosc Union, which was still involved at that time. It is possible that someone from Solidarnosc gave them the choice between dealing with their union or with us anarchists. So, as we feel that there is no sense in supporting someone who has rejected our support, we stayed on the sidelines for a while. But not for long ...

ABB: How did it come about that you finally joined the protests and began playing such an important role? What was the reaction of the locals in Ozarów when they saw anarchists coming from all around the country to join them?

Z: Well, the situation changed a lot when anarchists from Poznan and Szczecin started to work closely within OKP structures. But the first solid contact came after the brutal attacks of IMPEL, a private security firm, in late November, after 219 days of occupation. At about 4.30 in the morning, this firm violently attacked people who were blockading the factory's entrance. The security guards were drunk and extremely brutal, spraying tear gas on old women and beating up everyone around. Two local fire trucks arrived to help the workers, drenching the security guards with their hoses. Police then joined the security guards, and took over the factory, even though the protest was legal! When word spread about this attack, workers from Ozarów called for anyone to come and support them, and immediately many more anarchists from Poznan, Szczecin, Bialystok, Lodz, and Warsaw came to Ozarów.

Everyone was fighting to prevent the trucks from taking cables and equipment out of the factory, throwing stones, firecrackers, Molotov cocktails, etc. But we were outnumbered by police – there were 600-700 riot cops with water cannons – and the workers' enthusiasm was falling from day to day. So by the third day of almost non-stop confrontation, most of the people still fighting were anarchists.

Resisting factory closure. Ozarów, Poland

ABB: What have the results been of mixing the workers' anger and world views, with those of the anarchists?
Z: It's hard to say, because many anarchists decided to focus more on helping people through direct actions and didn't talk so much about their politics. They were talking with the workers, of course, but there was a broad spectrum there – the Catholic National Front with their rhetoric, the Trotskyists with their newspapers, etc. I would venture to say that among all these groups, the anarchists were the least pushy with their views on the workers. When we first went to Ozarów, one of our people wanted us not to tell the locals that we are anarchists 'cause he thought people would have a bad reaction to us. But I saw a scene where one of our lot gave the workers a few packages of tea and coffee, and someone asked: "Who does this come from?" We replied, "It's from an anarchist." The woman's response was, "Oh God, I wish all people would be like these anarchists!"

ABB: How do you see what is happening in Ozarów in the context of overall changes in Poland?
Z: In Poland there is a big crisis now – the current system is completely incapable – many people are living in really bad situations and people are starting to do something about it. Maybe one day we will see the riot acts like in 1980 when the Solidarnosc movement was born. I see in every sector more disappointment with capitalism, current political structures, and official propaganda of the media. The question is whether we can turn this disappointment into rebellion against the political and economic authority, or if the right wing will be allowed to use the frustration for their aims – for example, there is a popular movement behind Andrzej Lepper, who is a charismatic leader of a farmers' movement and who is known for his radical critique of the EU from an extreme right position.

ABB: What kind of repression are the authorities using to suppress these protests?
Z: Usually they just use truncheons, but the fact is that when there are 10,000 workers on the street, the police are afraid of using violence, 'cause they know that we are not playing a game, that it is not just about another 200 *zloty* ($53) per month. People are taking to the streets with more

---

scale walkouts, while the others initiate partial strikes. Demands include abolishing the distinction between full- and part-time workers. On the same day, 5,000 members of other unions hold a sit-in at Jongmyo Park inSeoul in opposition to privatization plans.
>> June 4 >> Peasants march 87 miles from Coronel Oviedo to Asuncion, Paraguay to demand the revocation of a law allowing for privatization, and to prevent the sale of the public telephone company, a sale which has been suspended six times due to corruption investigations. The 7,000 peasants attempt to break through a police cordon in order to continue the march, and are attacked. A farmer is killed by a bullet to the head, another is critically wounded by a shot to the stomach, and several others are injured. A general strike takes place two days later, with the nation's main trade union demanding that the government, "reject the prescription of the IMF and WB and defend our sovereignty".
>> June 4 >> The Dutch network *GroenFront!*, a branch of Earth First!, occupies a construction crane set to build a new docking pier in the expansion of Schiphol Amsterdam Airport. Work is stopped. Banners hang from the crane, saying "Stop Jet Expansion" and "Nature Will Strike Back". This action adds to *GroenFront!*'s ongoing campaign, which

determination, they know why they're in the streets, and even when they fight the police, they understand why they are doing it. It's not a blind aggression, as the media portrays it. Another form of repression is economic pressure – many people have harsh living conditions in Poland. Many people could not meet their comrades in Ozarów because they don't have a job and are too poor to travel, others who have jobs are not allowed to take two or three days off work. The [state welfare] subsidy in Poland is minimal, and fear of losing a job is incredibly strong. It's a very stressful situation typical for many Polish communities. It seems that it cannot continue much longer and something must change.

ABB: What is the current situation in Ozarów, and what are the plans of the workers? How do you and other anarchists envision your participation in the future?

Z: It is still unclear what will happen with the workers – whether they will succeed in creating their own company, which would require certain negotiations with local authorities, or if the company will take back the whole factory and its contents. The problem is that Telefonika's owner prefers to keep the machines shut down and going to ruin rather than give them to the workers. He announced that he will sell the factory back to the government, but there is no way to create a brand new cable factory. But the workers don't want any other job. They are very highly qualified in their profession and if the factory is sold, it could become, let's say, a potato chip factory and what then – they have to peel potatoes for the rest of their lives?!

At the moment our role, as anarchists from Warsaw and other cities, is to do what we can with financial help, and to remain in contact with people from Ozarów. We are planning some collaborative projects – for example, we are working on making a video about the history of this struggle, and we will have it translated into different languages. We gave them fuel to keep their tents warm, and we are trying to get some more. We're trying to give very practical support. We've got some far-reaching plans as well, but it's too early to speak about it yet.

ABB: Do you believe that the events in Ozarów have changed anything in the overall Polish reality?

Z: Ozarów for sure has become a symbol of resistance across the country. Maybe there are now just a few people left at the factory gates but they are still there – in harsh freezing weather. They are transforming themselves through struggling, and are very effective in what they are doing. Their story has become legend, and has travelled so widely that when any of them are applying for a job and the interviewer learns that they come from the cable factory in Ozarów, they don't continue the interview, because they are afraid of people who can fight for their employment and who are so conscious about their rights. That's what some of them have personally told me. And what is amazing is that they don't say it with regret or despair at not getting the job, they say it with a kind of pride in their voices ...

Update: After almost one year of striking, workers in Ozarów have attained a partial victory. In cooperation with the Industrial Development Agency, and local authorities, the workers succeeded in gaining control over two production facilities and their own company. Unfortunately, it seems that they will not be producing cables; however all former cable factory workers are guaranteed jobs. The organizers would like to thank all who have supported them in any way during their year-long struggle, and invite them to visit occasionally for celebrations.

Zbyszek has been a member of the Warsaw Anarchist Federation for ten years. Before that he organized against the communist regime, as most people in Poland did at that time. He currently works with the antiglobalization movement, and is a journalist.

V. is a co-founder of Abolishing the Borders from Below, an international anarchist collective focused on Eastern European activism, which publishes a paper by the same name. Born in Warsaw, Poland, V. left in 1993 and is now an unemployed squatter, occasional underground musician, writer, anarcho-punk vegetarian living in Berlin.

ABB also organizes a prisoner support group, a libertarian library, various solidarity actions, and cultural events in order to support local and global struggle against all kinds of oppression and with support for development of an anarchist movement across the borders.

Resources:

» *Abolishing the Borders from Below – an anarchist courier from Eastern Europe* Available from Active Distribution. www.activedistribution.org
» Information about the protest in Ozarów (some in English): www.fko.prv.pl
» Website of Anarchist Workers' Initiative: republika.pl/paspartooo/wi

---

has included digging up a new landing strip in the Transport Minister's garden.
>> June 7 >> One hundred people protested against the WEF in Durban, South Africa, bringing attention to the New Plan for African Development (NEPAD). "NEPAD will deliver in Africa, but only to the elite. The poor will just get poorer. President Mbeki is looking after the interests of the emerging élite in Africa", says Ashwin Desai of the Concerned Citizens Group. "We regard NEPAD as a new form of colonization with the consent of African leaders", adds Professor Dennis Brutus of Jubilee South Africa. Protesters are confined to Speaker's Corner, about 110 yards away from the WEF meeting, but about 30 manage to slip away engage WEF delegates in discussion about NEPAD until police remove them.
>> June 13 >> Massive demonstrations in Arequipa, Peru's second largest city, and in Tacna on the Chilean border turn into riots after 90,000 police mobilize and attack. Protests nationwide are underway due to the government having auctioned two state-owned electricity companies to Tractebel, a Belgian company, for $167 million. One demonstrator is killed after being struck by a tear gas canister. Protesters vandalize the airport, smashing landing lights and stealing equipment, and

Solidarity and Sabotage

"Sabotage is aimed directly at 'the boss' and at his profits, in the belief that that is the solar plexus of the employer, that is his heart, his religion, his sentiment, his patriotism."
– Elizabeth Gurley Flynn, *The Conscious Withdrawal of the Workers' Industrial Efficiency*, 1916

The term sabotage often brings to mind media images of people hurling bricks through the windows of transnational companies, or of small covert groups committing acts of property damage under cover of darkness. These actions can put economic pressure on large corporations and draw attention to their shady business practices, however, they can also have negative repercussions – such as brutal repression – as they are largely high risk, unsustainable, and are often inarticulate, as their very nature requires anonymity.

John Jordan

Sabotage is not just about property destruction. Barcelona, Spain

However, sabotage takes many other forms. In France, the Confédération Paysanne dismantled a McDonald's in broad daylight, and the KRRS has burned acres of GM crops in India. And of course, sabotage also takes place regularly in workplaces everywhere.

The word *sabotage* actually emerges from the labour movement. There are many unverifiable anecdotes about this, and all connect it to workers, and agree that it comes from the French, *sabot*, which was the wooden shoe worn by the French peasantry, the wearing of which made one clumsy and slow-moving – less efficient.

Sabotage in the workplace frequently involves individualistic one-off actions, or pranks, which may be expensive or damaging to the business' reputation, but which, alone, are limited in their effectiveness. This sort of action, while often entertaining, serving to blow off steam, and clearly measurable in broad economic terms – just ask any business owner about the costs of absenteeism, worker theft, and vandalism – generally doesn't lead to an improvement in working conditions, as the individual often disappears shortly after the prank, leaving no sustained pressure on the employer.

What's important for sustainable and effective workplace solidarity is building the power and community of the workers, using a spectrum of tactics which can be escalated as necessary, and achieving short term goals while working towards long-term visions.

Of course, the most commonly used tactic of workplace solidarity is the strike. Strikes can be incredibly effective, however, striking workers don't getpaid, and are often locked out of the workplace. This doesn't mean strikes aren't useful, but it's important to be creative. This is about reclaiming what unionism really is – workers acting together in their common interests, plain and simple. There are plenty of possibilities for action with or without the support of a union; many don't even require you to miss a single paycheck. Wobblies (members of the Industrial Workers of the World) call it "striking on the job". Here are just a few tactics:

Open mouth: Most effective in the service industry, the key to this is coordinating throughout the business. Workers are open and honest with customers and state their true feelings about working under grueling conditions for low pay when asked: "How are you?" Complete honesty is also subversive – stating that goods are overpriced, of low quality, and can be found cheaper elsewhere makes an interesting sales pitch! With trust and advance preparation, workers can avoid obvious manipulation such as singling out "ringleaders", and can use this as leverage to force their boss to negotiate. If this doesn't work, an escalation of tactics can follow.

Good work strike: Doing essential work competently may not seem like sabotage, but in France, hospital workers who were afraid that a strike would compromise the health of their patients came up with an excellent strategy. They refused to file billing slips for drugs, lab work, or any other procedures, and spent more of their time with patients. The hospital's income dropped by half, and after three days, the hospital conceded to all of the worker's demands.

Work-to-rule: In most workplaces, the boss imposes a set of rules and structures to run the business. The workers then determine more efficient, and often safer ways of working. Think of all the silly rules at the various jobs you have had, which, if you followed them, would have resulted in, reduced productivity, or even a complete collapse of the business. The notion of the work-to-rule is brilliantly simple — workers follow every rule, no matter how foolish, inefficient, or ill-advised. They break no laws, cause as much disruption as a strike, yet everyone still gets paid! In Austria, where national law requires that postal workers weigh each piece of mail to determine the required postage, workers ceased the common practice of estimating weights, and began weighing every single piece. By the second day, post offices were completely congested with unweighed mail, and the government swiftly entered into negotiations. Dockworkers on the US West coastrecently instituted a work-to-rule, in which they followed all health and safety regulations. Since working on the docks is incredibly dangerous, there are innumerable safety rules. By following them, workers reduced efficiency coast-wide by 50 per cent. The employer was forced to complain that the workers were obeying the rules, and the workers were empowered in the knowledge that they know the best way to run the business.

Resources:

» *The Troublemaker's Handbook: how to fight back where you work, and win!* by Dan LaBotz, Labor Notes, 1991

» Wobblies' website: www.iww.org

The ultimate power *of global capital is its threat to leave, to move somewhere else, saying: "If you don't accept lower wages, if you force environmental legislation on us, we will go somewhere else, you will be left without jobs or money". As the economy collapsed in Argentina, capital acted on that threat, and fled. Businesses closed down, unemployment soared from 6.5 per cent in 1990 to over 40 per cent in 2002 and half the country's population, once comfortably well off in Latin America's largest middle class, fell below the poverty line. Many Argentinean workers, in the face of such statistics and the threat of capital flight, have simply replied, "Fine, leave us alone and we will run the factories ourselves, just don't take the machinery!"*

Over 150 businesses, bankrupt and abandoned by their owners, have been taken over by their workers and turned into co-operatives or collectives. At tractor plants, supermarkets, ceramics factories, textile manufacturers, bakeries, and pizza parlours, decisions about company policy are now voted on in open assemblies, and profits are split equally among the workers. Owners' attempts to evict the workers are often unsuccessful because members of local neighbourhood assemblies show up en masse to support the workers and prevent the evictions.

The idea is contagious and is spreading to schools, soda plants, public transport companies, and even a hotel. A 'solidarity economy' is developing – for example, an occupied health clinic set up to treat workers from the occupied factories is having its sheets sewn by garment workers from an occupied textile plant. A supermarket turned into a workers' cooperative sells pasta from an occupied pasta factory; occupied bakeries are building ovens with tiles from an occupied ceramic plant. On their own, these occupations are not necessarily a threat to capital, however, as they link up, they begin to create the possibility of an autonomous network working on an unprecedented national scale.

We're Nothing; We Want To Be Everything

by Pamela Colombo and Tomás Bril Mascarenhas

Argentina in the 1990s was a land which worshiped individualism, where the success of neoliberal 'culture' was esteemed so highly it made you want to retch. In this ocean of egos, this frenetic society with its alienated people, there began to arise, catalyzed by the events of 19 and 20 December, a counter-culture of solidarity – not charity, but solidarity. Now everyone smells the stench of a rotting Argentina, but we know how to let some fresh air in.

"Our bosses didn't take into account the way we might react if we were fired. Our response was to turn the tables. Take what was theirs and become the owners!"

Eight workers have been holding out in the Chilavert printing press, which for more than a month has been occupied to prevent its assets from being auctioned off. Outside, the number of police is much larger. Eight armoured cars stand by as assembly members, workers from other occupied factories, and neighbours gather at the entrance of the printing press. They've come to resist. They block the entry with trucks and put up barricades.

Meanwhile, inside the factory walls, a new book is being printed, born out of the ongoing struggle, entitled *What are the Neighbourhood Assemblies?* The printers work with the looming threat of the police breaking in, evicting them, and closing down the factory. *You know the police are going to come and beat you*. The judge issued a ruling that forbade starting production, but orders in a corrupt country are not binding: and the workers aren't going to stop. The presses were set in motion; there was a book to be finished in time for delivery the next morning, even if it had to be done in clandestinity.

The atmosphere is tense, the factory doors could be broken down at any minute, they could be evicted and the book confiscated. A few bricks are removed from the factory wall. A hole is opened up. Through it pass the books as they're finished. And a neighbour piles them up in his patio. They've defied the prohibition.

The workers in the Chilavert printing press have demolished more than just a wall. When you begin to make holes in the walls that mark the limits of the system, you have to rethink everything. Outside there's no longer a fatherly guide, beyond the hole there's freedom but there's also a void – a void which fills with actions, enabling creativity. Today the hole at Chilavert has been covered with bricks again. But inside a new reality is being created. *"The reaction was and is spontaneous. Anger unites and moves us."* Strangers, neighbours in the *barrio*, people who only learned about the eight workers because of their struggle defended them and prevented the press from being shut down. Without the support of those new radical participants, the struggle would have been so unevenly matched that it would have quickly ended.

"We share what we earn. We take over, we hold out, and now we produce. And to think the boss said to me: "Do you lazy slobs really think you can run a company?""

Today voices have broken the silence, echoing through the empty factory, and they are joined by over ten thousand mouths shouting, "An injury to one is an injury to all." Liberated voices, with the right to speak. They've decided to defend their space, they have succeeded in ending their suffering, they have decided to begin living.

"I was crying inside, but outside I didn't cry. I never thought I'd want to enter this factory again."

Centralized power hates horizontal organizing; it knows it's contagious. Horizontality wins the struggle against the system, and once it spreads, can only be stopped by force, if at all. One Sunday in November, at six-thirty in the morning (Buenos Aires sleeps) a group of policemen break

---

blocking runways with burning tyres. Days later, as protests continue to spread and tanks roll in Lima, the President cancels the sale, promising that the companies will remain in state hands after all.

>> June 20 >> Coinciding with the EU summit, undocumented North African immigrants occupy several buildings at the Pablo Olavide University in Seville, Spain, demanding regularization papers and job security. The 400 immigrants represent 5,000-6,000 strawberry pickers who have worked for years in the region's fields, have made significant organizing efforts, and have garnered local support for their struggle. This year anti-Arab discrimination has combined with corporate profit-seeking and led to the contract going to Polish workers, who have virtually no knowledge of local conditions, nor likelihood to attract local support. The North Africans are allowed only to work during breaks, and not provided with food, housing, or health care. Half of the occupying workers are given papers, the other half is evicted after two months, and 128 immigrants are locked in a detention in Ceuta, Spain, on the North African coast.

>> June 25 >> The head of the IMF's delegation to Argentina is cornered outside his Buenos Aires hotel room by television reporters. They hand him a set of large,

Nicolas Pousthomis

Andrew Stern

Marina Sitrin

Nicolas Pousthomis

Self-management and direct democracy in Argentina's occupied factories

into one of the bastions of the democracy built with our own hands, democracy that abhors representation. The operation attempts to destroy the eleven month occupation of the Brukman clothes factory, run by its fifty workers.

"The management thought that if they gave each of us two suits we'd accept being sacked."

Sewing machines and seamstresses are attacked; a little girl is arrested. The web pages of Indymedia Argentina fills with messages calling for support and resistance, "All assemblies, go at once to Brukman."

The police follow their orders and try to break up Argentina's icons of collectivity. They destroy Brukman, smash everything. Politics should go on appearing to be out of reach to ordinary people (the great achievement of neoliberalism). Politics is made by a few and it's done in a palace, not in a factory, or a square, or a blockade. That's what they say as yet another truncheon strikes, and they arrest six workers on that unprepared Sunday morning. Politics should be, for the ordinary person, a dirty word, something distant, done by others; something reduced to the ballot box alone.

The police can act each time with less impunity, as they're surrounded by people who are joining forces. The leisurely weekend, sipping *mate* and watching Sunday morning television can wait. People gather under the shadow of the traditional left parties flags, new politics and old politics merge on the crowded Jujuy Street. Together, from the street and inside the factory, Brukman is taken by the workers once again. Following hours of panic and tension, check to the factory owner, though he has yet to be checkmated.

"Now, we all know how it all works."

"Struggle, Work and Culture" can be read on a piece of pottery surrounded by many other works of art in the culture centre, in the attic of the labyrinthine IMPA building. It's no ordinary factory. Inside, there's the smell of melting plastic and the sound of machines repeating their blows again and again; it's a confusing experience, as if two eras have been fused together in the heart of Buenos Aires. One carries the memory of the old industry from the days of import substitution; the other is unlike anything ever experienced. The unknown factor is the mixture of

---

plastic Halloween vampire teeth. "We found these lodged in President Duhalde's neck," they tell him, "and wanted to return them to you."

>> June 26-27 >> The G8 retreat to the remote mountainous resort of Kananaskis, Alberta, Canada, protected by $300-400 million worth of security measures. Meanwhile, in the nearby city of Calgary, activists challenge the police to a soccer match. The police forfeit, but refuse to fulfill conditions of forfeiture which includes handing over their expensive bicycles and arresting the eight heads of state at their meeting.

>> June 28 >> The largest strike by city workers in Canada begins, with a walkout by 23,500 municipal workers, paralyzing Toronto. After nine days, piles of rotting rubbish line the streets and the strike is joined by Toronto's indoor municipal workers. Fearful of losing jobs if the city privatizes public services, the workers are striking over job security, not money. After 16 days, the strikers are forced to return to their jobs, due to newly passed national back-to-work legislation. The city's Mayor predictably asks, "Where are we going to get the money to meet their demands?" Maybe he's unaware of the expenses of the G8 summit in Kananaskis....

>> July 8-18 >> Women in Ugborodo, Escravos, Nigeria

three words, never found together, yet now so close together: struggle, work, and culture.

Struggle. Over a hundred workers try to avoid joining the ranks of the newly unemployed, and regressing to the years of top-down Mafia authority. *Work*. They recycle aluminium, something almost revolutionary in a country where aluminium, like so much else, is a monopoly. *Culture*. Surrounded by the sound of machines in the workshop, is created by artists making new images that transform the workplace. The untidy workshop inspires creativity, almost begs for it. Ceramics, paintings, drawings and nearby, a photo lab, and a portrait that takes you by surprise, inviting you to vote for Perón in 1952. You can inhale the sense of pride that emanates from the workers and artists here, different, but not really. Both fighting, both working.

Before, the factory had places which were out of bounds, restricted, these no-go zones led to rivalry, servility, blackmail – no-go zones, like the executive offices reclaimed by the workers who divide their time between producing doorknobs and making decisions concerning over a hundred of their compañeros who work in the factory.

In IMPA, production continues being alienating, the assembly lines haven't disappeared. Yet the workers have disappeared fear, idleness, and individualism; this gives the assembly line new meaning, as they know that beneath this job lies their latent struggle to work. This is clearly not part of some superficial struggle; they're not fighting out of selfless devotion to a political party. The movement is born of something much deeper, it sets out to defend what

Those who are still alive should never
say never.
The inevitable is not inevitable,
The way things are won't last.
When those who govern have spoken,
The governed will speak out.

Who dares to say never?
On whom does continued
oppression depend?
On us.
On whom does breaking it depend?
Once more, on us.

If you are knocked down, get up,
If you are lost, fight.
How can those who understand their own
situation ever be stopped?

The defeated of today
Will be the defeaters of tomorrow
And 'never' will be 'now'.

– poetry found on the walls of Brukman factory

belongs to us: work and its product. A factory is occupied because of the explicit need to survive. *The only way to maintain the struggle was by getting back to production. If not, hunger would go on killing us.*

The workers intend for this movement to grow; they can't conceieve of the changes they've wrought disappearing. That would require keeping quiet about what they already know – that they can do it themselves and they are many. *Now, we're dangerous workers.*

The struggle never slackens; if it did everything would collapse quite easily. That's why they put their bodies on the line. The end is always uncertain, and the fear is tangible. They know that the old structures are corroded. In an Argentina where one-fourth of the population is unemployed, struggling to work is revolutionary; it's asking the powers-that-be for something everyone knows they can't give. The workers won't wait for a response. The struggle continues, day after day, tearing down hierarchies, evading repression.

"Look after yourself, Daddy, my children in Bolivia beg me. And I, in my letters, tell them I'm struggling for my compañeros."

Update: *In April 2003 the Bruckman workers were evicted from their factory. Thousands came to the factory to support the workers returning to their jobs and reclaiming their work place. An attempt to take back the factory was violently repressed. Depsite this set back, the occupied factory movement continues to grow across Argentina.*

Pamela Colombo studies sociology, plays the sax and writes. Tomás Bril Mascarenhas studies political science and, from time to time, writes and breathes. Both live in Buenos Aires.

English translation by Julian Cooper

All quotes are statements by workers interviewed

Resources:

» Reports direct from the streets: www.argentina.indymedia.org

» *Que Se Vayan Todos: an eyewitness report of the rebellion:* www.nadir.org/nadir/initiativ/agp/free/imf/argentina/txt/ 2002/0918que_se_vayan.htm

---

take control of the Chevron/Texaco oil terminal and threaten to remove their clothes – a traditional shaming gesture aimed at humiliating the company. The 600 women from villages around the terminal block access to the helipad, airstrip, and docks. They are demanding that the transnational invest some of its riches in development of water supply, schools, electricity hookups, and clinics, as well as reparation of mass erosion damage from dredging. Seven hundred company employees – Nigerians, Americans, Britons, and Canadians – are trapped in the terminal while negotiations are held between a representative of the village chief and an oil executive. Meanwhile, in the air-field, two dozen women dance in the rain alongside four helicopters and a plane, singing "This is our land!" After 11 days, the company concedes to their demands, and the occupation ends.

>> July 11-16 >> Peasant farmers of San Salvador Atenco, Mexico demonstrate against government plans to build a new international airport on top of their farmland on the outskirts of Mexico City. Rejecting an insulting offer to buy the farmland for about .60¢ per square yard, the community blockades highways and use machetes and Molotovs to fend off more than 10,000 riot police, who kill one protester and injure countless others. The

In the year *2000 approximately 60,000 families were evicted from their homes in Ontario, Canada. This figure has grown by ten per cent per year since the provincial government's abolition of rental controls in 1998, just one in a number of neoliberal measures that have become familiar worldwide and one instance where the willingness of anticapitalists to fight back has outraged the powerful and emboldened the poor. The Ontario Coalition Against Poverty has been compared to the piqueteros of Argentina. They have a broad and diverse membership, they are well organized, committed to direct action and – most alarming for the state – they are often successful.*

Whether it's actively supporting asylum seekers through direct action and legal casework, coordinating with Mohawk hunters to distribute meat to low income families, converting empty buildings into housing and community facilities, or laying siege to the Ontario Provincial Legislature in an attempt to have the voices of the poor recognized, OCAP is on the frontline.

OCAP's continued growth and broad appeal illuminates one of the many ways forward for Northern movements caught between the local and global, working with communities of activists, or communities in struggle. By understanding and respecting their radical history, and by organizing alongside unions and people of First Nations, they have managed to combine the tradition and culture of community organizing with its emphasis on education and the defence of hard-won gains, with a preference for direct action that is no-nonsense and effective.

Fighting To Win: the Ontario Coalition Against Poverty

by Jeff Shantz

The preamble to the Constitution of the Industrial Workers of the World begins magnificently: "The working class and the employing class have nothing in common." Gathering steam, it continues: "There can be no peace so long as hunger and want are found among millions of the working people and the few who make up the employing class have all the good things in life." In the Ontario Coalition Against Poverty (OCAP) we have taken this message to heart.

From the beginning, OCAP has been dedicated to militant direct action rather than consultation and compromise. Our actions are determined by the real needs of our members, and we take a course of action in which we do whatever it takes to meet those needs. OCAP is a poor people's movement and we organize among the diverse members of the working class rather than trying to reach out to small business people or middle-class liberals. We do not organize as a broad but meaningless coalition

There's a line that goes: "the barricades run through the neighbourhoods." That's where you'll find the Ontario Coalition Against Poverty (OCAP). Our members are the people in our neighbourhoods, the working class in all its diversity: young, old, students, First Nations, disabled, unemployed, psychiatric survivors, immigrants, refugees, low-wage workers, rank-and-file unionists, artists and playwrights, sex workers, homeless, and assorted ne'er-do-wells and even some older Greek Communists.

We fight together and we win. We know what class we're in and we take our lead from our own needs, interests, and desires rather than what the various bosses and bureaucrats tell us we should be happy with. OCAP is about dignity and self-respect in a system that refuses us both.

Direct actions get the goods

OCAP is a 'do-it-ourself' organization and so we don't rely on representatives, vanguards, or experts to do things for us. Our collective power of disruption is applied both to defend individuals and families and to challenge broader political practices. This allows us to win real victories in the here and now while also building the struggles necessary to bring the system down. Right now, direct action at the point of oppression is the most effective means we have to oppose hostile conditions and make gains on our own terms.

As a tactic of self-defence OCAP has developed 'direct action casework'. This involves bringing large numbers of members and allies directly to an offending agency, landlord, or workplace and staying until we get what we came for. If people are facing an eviction, we go directly to their home to make the eviction impossible for the landlord and sheriff. If someone is being denied back pay, we take a picket right to the boss and disrupt business until the money is forthcoming. If an acceptable settlement is not forthcoming, we raise the costs of offending agencies to the point where it is no longer worthwhile for them to act in an oppressive way.

Often this means directly targeting businesses. When a Hollywood movie production drove sex workers from a downtown street without compensation (which had been given to small businesses for lost earnings during the shoot), we disrupted filming with a contingent of people. The next day an envelope full of bills arrived at our office for the workers. When a restaurant owner successfully lobbied to close a downtown shelter, we ran an ongoing picket at his business until he asked the City to allow the shelter to be reopened.

For people who are excluded from channels of power and don't want to deal with such rotten channels anyway, direct action – taking responsibility for the decisions that affect

---

repression backfires and support for the farmers' cause increases exponentially – police cars are burnt, Coca-Cola trucks are seized and used to blockade the national highway, and 13 government and police officials are taken hostage in a successful bid to free their own prisoners. Days later, victory is celebrated as the government announces the cancellation of its airport plans. The peasants vow to continue struggling, declaring their opposition to Plan Puebla Panama and the FTAA.

>> July 15 >> Activists from the KRRS and the Green Army in Davangere, India invade a shop selling genetically engineered Bt cotton seeds and set fire to the seeds. The KRRS notes that they are merely fulfilling a commitment they made to the government, that if Bt cotton seeds were sold, they would destroy them immediately.

>> July 17 >> As the Escravos protest ends, over 3,000 women in Abiteye, Makaraba, Dibi, and Olero Creek, Nigeria occupy four more Chevron/Texaco flow stations, and have their demands quickly agreed upon.

>> July 18-28 >> A No Borders camp, organized in large part by immigrant organizations from France and Germany, sees 3,000 people gather from across Europe, North Africa and Latin America in Strasbourg, France for discussion and action. Strasbourg was chosen because of the Schengen

Jeff Shantz

An empty building becomes a home. Pope Squat, Toronto, Canada

our lives and acting on our own needs and interests – is the most effective means of building collective power.

These methods of collective direct action are also applied to broader struggles. In 2001, OCAP organized in cities, workplaces, towns, and reserves throughout Ontario, working towards a series of acts of political and economic disruption throughout Ontario and beyond. The Ontario Common Front (OCF) tried to build a network among allied organizations (unions, First Nations, other OCAP-style direct action groups) which would target significant corporate backers of the conservative Tories, especially the major banks and real estate developers, in different parts of Ontario.

Among the notable actions around the province was a blockade of a major trucking route by Mohawks, and a march through Bay Street in Toronto (Canada's equivalent of Wall Street). The OCF still exists as a network of action groups in a number of Ontario cities and continues building OCAP-style work in cities such as Sudbury, Ottawa, Kingston, and Belleville.

It has often been said that the first casualty of war is the truth. If that's the case then the second casualty is dissent (connected as they so often are). After the events of 11 September, many activists in Toronto and beyond argued that we should call off the economic disruption planned for 16 October in Toronto's financial district. "The symbolism is too sharp; tensions are too high," they said. The altered context after 9/11 suggested to some that direct action was no longer a viable tactic. Some union leaders said that protest was no longer possible.

Indeed, in the days and weeks after the attacks in the US, we gave much thought and discussion to the possibilities for action on O16. In the end, however, we came to almost unanimous agreement that the economic disruption must go ahead and must not be merely symbolic in nature. The reason for this conclusion was simple: the Tory government in Ontario has in no way backed off from its vicious neoliberal agenda of attacks on poor people in the province. In fact, only days after 11 September, the Tories announced that new corporate tax cuts scheduled for January would be instituted immediately (something which proved unworkable). Even more ominously, they established a new provincial security detail to carry out surveillance and harassment of immigrants and refugees.

As an internationalist organization having only contempt for the borders that divide working class and poor people and shelter capital, defence of immigrants and refugees is an important aspect of our work. Along with our allies in the Canadian Union of Public Employees Local 3903 flying squad, we have gone directly to Pearson International Airport to stop deportations. We've handed out leaflets to passengers alerting them to the situation and gone directly to the Immigration Canada deportation office in the basement of Terminal One. During one airport visit, we successfully stopped three deportations, a testament to the powers of direct action, especially when backed by labour.

We have also fought against borders by building active alliances with anti-poverty and workers' organizations in other countries. During the World Summit on Sustainable Development in Johannesburg, OCAP responded to a call by our allies in the West Cape Tenants' Group by taking a picket to the offices of the South African Trade Consulate. A couple of weeks later, at the request of the Equality Trade Union of South Korea, OCAP held a picket against Korean Air in solidarity with migrant workers in Korea who were being attacked by the South Korean government. In this case, we targeted the capitalists who support, direct, and benefit from government policies rather than the government itself.

Direct actions are also about education, especially self-education. When we do an action we learn that despite this system's best efforts to beat us down, we can actually enjoy some victories. We also learn that the authorities are not

---

Information System computer which is located there, and contains information on all the known immigrants and asylum seekers in Europe. Despite police attacks with tear gas and rubber bullets on numerous occasions, resulting in a broken leg, countless other injuries, and at least 30 arrests, the camp perseveres.

>> July 22-23 >> Healthcare workers across Niger go on strike, providing minimum health services for emergency cases only. They demand a housing allowance, and more training, as well as more secure jobs for auxiliary staff.

>> July 25 >> During the Pope's visit to Toronto, members of the Ontario Coalition Against Poverty occupy a building in Toronto, Canada and name it the Pope Squat. It serves as a thriving community centre for over three months until its eviction.

>> August 4 >> Farmers of the KRRS destroy two acres of Bt cotton in Rudranakatte, India, after convincing the farmers cultivating the crop that it poses a grave threat to the environment. Police are therefore unable to intervene, as the farmers participate in destroying their own crops.

>> August 4 >> Montevideo, Uruguay sees the largest demonstrations in a decade as thousands respond to a general strike called by 62 unions. The strike, accompanied by looting, is in response to the closure of banks and the

all-powerful or beyond our grasp, and we are not as alone as we might sometimes feel. Actions teach us how bureaucracies work, that decisions are often arbitrary and based on nothing more than expediency or the hope that we'll accept no for an answer. Institutions that appear mysterious or impenetrable often come undone when confronted by a delegation of 10-20 people who are sure of their purpose. Direct action lets us see the fear in the eyes of bosses, cops, bureaucrats and landlords when they have to face our unleashed collective anger borne by the strength of our solidarity. It teaches us that we can shake those in power and build a movement that fundamentally challenges the existing arrangement.

Reform *and* revolution?

Although we do press governments and bosses for resources that we need to sustain us and help us build our capacity to fight, OCAP is not a reformist group. OCAP is an explicitly anticapitalist organization, so our long-term goal is the end of capitalism and the development of a society based upon mutual support and self-determination. Along the way we have a responsibility to take care of each other, defend ourselves against bosses, landlords, cops and courts. Since, the state's and the bosses' resources are all stolen from the working class anyway, why shouldn't we take back all that we can get?

OCAP tends to agree with Lorenzo Komboa Ervin's [of the Black Radical Congress] position that reforms are part of our survival pending revolution. When people are losing their home or can't feed their children, it's tough to fight for the revolution. Even small victories give people a sense that they can actually win. This breaks the demoralization and apathy, and also gives us a taste for bigger victories.

"I'd be lying if I said we weren't inspired by OCAP ... We need to have direct action to understand who we are fighting against. Direct action and direct confrontation are very important"

– Ivan Drury, a community worker at the Downtown Eastside homeless shelter, Vancouver, Canada

Having said this, it is important to understand the place of reforms in longer-term strategies and not limit our focus to reforms. OCAP does not pursue reform for reform's sake and we do not organize primarily to win more or better reforms. As stated above, we take whatever we can get to make our lives a little better and to give us the strength and momentum to keep fighting, but we never lose sight of the fact that things are only really going to get better if we get rid of capitalism and build something new. At the same time we have to realize that there is a tension between the reformist and anticapitalist aspects of OCAP's work, and must always work to ensure that the day-to-day 'reformist' work does not come to dominate our activities or obscure the bigger picture.

Some European social movements push wide-ranging and

diverse demands on the state to make reforms that they know it cannot make. Revealing the state's limitations and playing on its inherent contradictions can press the state to potential crisis. There is still much debate about this perspective and, while it makes some sense, it can only be a part of broader organizing work.

The failure to recognize the limits of reforms and to situate demands for reforms within a broader strategy is a problem that still afflicts much of the labour movement in Canada. Many union leaders still give all of their hopes to an idea that the welfare state will be rebuilt. They continue to offer compromises long after the other party has walked away from the table. For many union 'leaders' there was nothing before the welfare state and workers only faced desperation. They forget that at one time in the history of the labour movement, unions offered the basis for such dual power, providing medical clinics, elderly care, hostels, underground railroads and schools for workers. Today unions neglect this work, leaving the state to provide these things for workers. This has done a great deal to undermine working class autonomy.

Building dual power

At the same time we recognize that one of the areas where we've needed to do more work is in building dual power institutions [which confront the state while developing alternatives to it] that can meet our needs in the here and now without having to rely on claims against the state. These dual power institutions would offer real alternatives and a self-determined base for developing our strength.

Our recent squatting efforts are part of a turn towards building more permanent dual power institutions where we provide for our necessities – in this case, shelter – whether the state acts or not. When we took over the abandoned building that became known as the Pope Squat during the Pope's visit to Toronto in the summer of 2002, our intention was not to turn the squat over to any level of government to manage but rather to self-manage the space as social housing and a community resource centre.

For four months, the Pope Squat offered a beautiful community space. Guerrilla gardeners came by the squat to plant seeds of hope in a lovely garden where there had been only an overgrown mass of weeds on the building's front

---

devaluation of the peso, as Uruguay shares the economic catastrophe of Argentina.

>> August 7 >> Several thousand dockworkers in Szczecin, Poland invade the Odra clothes factory where women workers have not received pay for several months. The textile workers are on partial strike; they stop working for six hours a day. The intruders throw eggs on the boss, and perform the age-old firing-your-boss ritual of driving him out of the factory in a wheelbarrow. The police refuse to intervene, due to "fear of enraging the demonstrators."

>> August 14 >> Perseverance pays off for farmers of Karnataka, India where the state government decides to ban the cultivation of genetically engineered Bt cotton as a commercial crop until experts produce a report on potential adverse effects. Sown in other Indian states, the Bt cotton crop fails dismally come harvest time.

>> August 20 >> In New York, US, the city sells 11 apartments buildings for $1 a piece to a nonprofit agency who passes ownership on to the squatting inhabitants, many of whom have lived there openly for over ten years. Acquisition of the 167 apartments is an immense victory – the buildings were nearly lost in a 1995 eviction, which was overturned in court.

>> August 30 >> About 500 protesters gather in

lawn. Similarly, the first days of the squat also saw artists and non-artists alike take part in a mural painting on the front of the building in an act of shared public creativity which broke down the divisions between artist and audience. The mural also made the connection between housing as privatized space and the privatization of creativity in the restricted spaces of galleries and museums. Additionally the mural, as part of the living space, took art away from the commodified form of *objets d'art*.

Other events included a day-long street festival, filling the squat's yard with a variety of sound ranging from protest folk to experimental rock. Community-oriented events throughout the week included movie showings on the side of the building. A yard sale raised over $400 and brought several neighbours over to take at look.

One summer evening, Naomi Klein and her partner Avi Lewis gave the Canadian premier of their documentary on political and economic repression in Argentina. The short but intense video which commemorated the life of Gustavo Benedetto, a young unemployed man killed by security guards, was well received by the 300 or so people who watched it in the backyard. Lewis and Klein properly drew connections between groups like OCAP in Ontario and the *piqueteros*, unemployed and poor people in Argentina, fighting against the machinations of global capital which would obliterate them.

As is usually the case in such participatory forms of community-building, decision-making developed through trial and error and experiment. Community assemblies were held in the yard every evening around 8.00 pm and involved upwards of 60 people. Squatters gave reports and updates of the day's activities inside the building before the assembly took up discussions of strategies for dealing with issues involved in keeping the project open.

The Pope Squat signalled a partial shift in strategy towards a focus on constructing alternatives, and do-it-ourselves institution-building, rather than protest-style demands made upon government institutions. In this regard the squat was an aspect of constituting dual power structures in which participants build the capacity to meet their own needs. The Pope Squat was an integral part of preparing the facilities to house a self-managed social housing and community centre.

In November, the provincial government finally moved to evict the squatters and take control of the building. As of January 2003, armed guards still occupy 1510 King Street. The government has decided it has hundreds of thousands of dollars to guard an empty building rather than spend nothing just to let people build a home for themselves. Such is the true character of the state.

OCAP and our allies refuse to let the Province's actions stop their work of building squatting movements in a country where all squatting is illegal. This year, people are organizing for a cross-country squatting campaign.

This emergent squatting movement is partly the result of widespread frustrations among anticapitalist activists, whether focused on fighting global capitalist institutions or on local manifestations, with the reactive or oppositional character of most recent actions. Squats represent positive and constructive acts of building community-based alternatives to capital in the here and now of everyday life. Making a real contribution to meeting peoples' human needs rather than condemning capital for failing to meet those needs offers a glimpse into how things might be done differently while materially beginning the process of providing real social change (as opposed to social critique).

Doing what's effective

We don't do protests anymore. OCAP learned a long time ago that marches and rallies to protest, register our dissent, or to shame governments that have no shame are almost completely useless. Protest rituals and reliance on moral arguments confine struggles to the terrain of what the state and bosses find permissible and thus are ineffective for making real gains on our terms and in ways that meet our needs. Our members just don't have the time and means to come out for purely symbolic actions.

Recognizing that we have no interests or values in common with the economic and political elite, we don't try to reach them on any level. Instead we attack them directly where it hurts: in their bank accounts. Part of that strategy means acting in ways that raise their costs of doing business. It also means refusing to accept any right they might claim to make the decisions that fundamentally affect us. We neither recognize nor respect government or corporate authority and see it plainly for what it is: an impediment to our self-determination and an attempt to monopolize social power in their own hands. We do whatever we can to make it impossible for the exploiters to implement and carry out their agenda.

Jeff Shantz has been active with the Ontario Coalition Against Poverty for several years. He is co-host of the Anti-Poverty Report on community radio station CHRY in Toronto and a founding member of his union's Anti-Poverty Working Group.

Resources:

» OCAP website: www.ocap.ca

» No Logo website: www.nologo.org

Helsingborg, Sweden for a street party and a friendly game of dart-throwing at artfully displayed election propaganda. While a sound system rages outside, a summit entitled 'Partners in Prevention' is held by a coalition of representatives from NATO, EU, UN, and OSSE. The demonstration focuses on the use of terror by these organizations to criminalize dissent, and highlights the cancellation of the planned educational forum due to police pressure on the property owner.

>> September 1 >> Following up from the Seed *Satyagraha* begun in 1993, Indian farmers in Jyothigowdanapura, Karnataka, India inaugurate an international centre for sustainable development called Amrita Bhoomi, or The Eternal Planet. The facilities are comprised of over a hundred acres of land, have a national seed bank to collect and conserve seeds from all available indigenous varieties of plants, trees, and medicinal herbs, and contain a Green School which offers classes on environmental issues and civil disobedience techniques and philosophies. Run by national and international advisory bodies and held as a public trust, the centre promises to provide support to international movements in designing a way of life to live with nature without damaging it.

>> September 6 >> Tens of thousands of workers in

One of the most *powerful catalysts for Argentina's uprising of 19-20 December 2001 was the* piquetero *movement – a radical mobilization of unemployed workers which erupted across the country in the mid 1990s and grew to become the world's largest movement of the unemployed. The* piqueteros' *tactic of blockading major highways – sometimes for days – has proved extraordinarily successful. Whole families take part in the roadblocks, setting up collective kitchens and tents in the middle of the street barricaded with burning tyres. Many of the participants are young, and over 60 per cent are women. Over the years this loosely federated autonomous movement based in local neighbourhoods has forced concessions from local and state governments, in the form of welfare payments, food packages, and part-time job allocations.*

With a practice founded on direct democracy and the desire to create social change in the present, the piqueteros *use their welfare payments to develop alternative structures in their neighbourhoods, building community kitchens, bakeries, popular education workshops, libraries, vegetable gardens, and more – all part of what they call "the solidarity economy". Beyond building solutions to material problems, the* piquetero *movement also works towards the creation of a new kind of dignity, as they believe that people who are actors in their own lives are key to building power in the neighbourhoods.*

There are hundreds of different piquetero *groups and networks across the country, some with affiliations to unions and left wing parties, and others which follow more independent tendencies. The following interviews were with members of the MTD (movement of unemployed workers) based in three different neighbourhoods in the southern part of greater Buenos Aires: Solano, Almiralte Brown, and Lanus. The MTDs are part of the Aníbal Veron network, which is explicitly anticapitalist and autonomous, and is developing new forms of struggle with links to movements such as the MST and the Zapatistas.*

The Power of the *Piqueteros*

an interview with members of Argentina's movement of unemployed workers, by Notes from Nowhere with Marina Sitrin

MTD Lanus

Notes from Nowhere: Can you explain the *piquetero* movement?

Pablo: Unemployment skyrocketed following the devastating neoliberal reforms in Argentina in the mid 1990s. Across the country the newly privatized factories cut jobs and civil servants were fired. In the interior of the country, some towns, especially those that depended on the state oil company (now privatized), were gutted, the population was completely marginalized and excluded by mass unemployment and that's when the first *piquetes*, or roadblocks occured.

So, these were the first roadblocks, the first *piquetes*, in the interior towns that were left practically abandoned by the withdrawal of the state-run companies. The *piquete* was an old tactic for the workers to protest at the gates of the factories, to bring attention to a strike or consolidate a struggle. Now these tactics were brought to the highways where that oil was transported or the merchandise from those companies was transported. So the unemployed workers, the abandoned townspeople, began to find a way on the highways to bring attention to their cause and protest against the government.

There was strong state repression, but despite this the struggle continued and in 1997 the government was forced to agree to a small welfare subsidy to unemployed workers. So in the places where there were large numbers of unemployed people, those that struggled continued to be recipients of this state subsidy. And the *piquetero* movement grew by using that method of roadblocks. We analyzed this and we said well, even if capitalism has changed and you need less people in the factories, you still need the goods to be transported. Since we were left without work in the factories, we sought a way to block the transportation of those goods. That's how the class struggle began and that's how the different *piquetero* movements began.

Now the *piquetero* groups are growing tremendously and becoming much more established, and this has been our vision. At first the struggles were much more spontaneous and self-organized. For example, we would decide that the negotiations with the government [for the subsidy] hadn't advanced in the meetings or petitions. So in the neighbourhoods we would take 15 days to quietly plan an action, without anyone knowing what highway we would block or when. And then we would go organized, we would get there before the police and then we would have to stand

"When women no longer have the resources to feed their children, the government is coming down, no matter what type of government it is." – **Rosa, MTD**

firm despite the police pressure. This meant burning tyres, making some sort of barricade, and keeping our families safe in the middle of the *piquete* and protected by the *compañeros* that would stand in the front in case of police repression. That's where the image of young people with bandanas masking their faces and holding sticks as tools of self-defence, came from. This became a symbol of the *piquetero* struggle against the police.

MTD Solano

Notes from Nowhere: The *piqueteros* talk about another way of thinking about work, can you tell us about that?

Magda: For us in the MTD it's about staying on the sidelines

Colombia stage a national strike against the new President's adherence to IMF economic policies, and against the violent intimidation campaign against trade unions.

>> September 10 >> Months after forcing the government to abandon airport construction plans, the radical farmers of San Salvador Atenco, Mexico declare the town to be autonomous. It is one of the first autonomous municipalities outside of the southern state of Chiapas, where Zapatistas run some towns. "We are aware that the Government will not recognize this action by the people, but they have no choice but to respect our decision," a new, 14-member People's Council said in a statement read at their swearing-in ceremony. Council members said Tuesday's declaration, developed through neighbourhood assembly meetings, meant that police and government officials would no longer be allowed to enter the town so that villagers could decide for themselves how to meet their community's needs.

>> September 16 >> Dawn breaks on Mexico City, 192 years after Mexicans declared their independence from Spain, and reveals a redecoration campaign throughout the capital. Over 30 statues of the heroes of the independence struggle have flowers at their bases and are dressed in black balaclavas, red bandanas, and are draped with the

of the consumption system, the capitalist system, it started to generate this feeling that, well, we're not interested in going back, really, to a capitalist system, we want to generate something different. We don't want them to open the factories and incorporate us just to be exploited again, we want other things.

Notes from Nowhere: Can you explain what other things you are creating?
Magda: The slogans we're organized under are Work, Dignity, and Social Change. In respect to work, dignified work is not going back to a factory to work 16 hours and be exploited. We want to generate different projects, projects without bosses, where the workers themselves, the same *compañeros* decide what to do with the production. We think that dignity as well as social change has to be built by us. It's not something we demand from the government. We think that we have to build that up and they have to allow us to do so.
Orlando: We are regaining dignity from having organized ourselves, from fighting capitalism. But what do we want to be? I mean, we don't want to make their mistakes but put together a new society, to build a more fair society where there would be neither oppressors nor oppressed, a society where there wouldn't be exploiters and exploited. It's hard for us because we live inside this system they call 'democracy', supposedly we live in a democratic country, and if democracy means to starve, if democracy means that they beat you down every time you go out to protest, or that children are dying every day at Solano's hospital because there are no sterile bandages, that democracy makes me think that, actually we have a stronger dictatorship today than before.

MTD Lanus

Notes from Nowhere: How did the emergence of the *piquetero* movement change the communities, change people's sense of themselves and their future?
Pablo: It happened to us in the neighbourhoods. So many years of a politics with state control over the people, over modest people, generated a lack of self-esteem in us. Our neighbours, our *compañeros* – we didn't feel it was possible for us to fight the politicians. The *piquete* kind of broke that passivity and people are able to recover their self-esteem. It demonstrated through those struggles that it is possible to face the whole government machine, the repressive machine, with our organized forces, and without depending on the old structures – such as unions – that didn't have an answer to this problem. Or the traditional parties, including the left, that for many years didn't understand this phenomenon. And all these movements began growing by themselves from the neighbourhoods and always with some people that had some previous experience with unions or militancy. But we wanted to create something new that is based primarily on our strength as neighbours. And the first subjective change is that change of mood, recovering that confidence in ourselves that we can change things – at least the small things – that we couldn't resolve in an office but we can resolve in a *piquete*.

Notes from Nowhere: Being a *piquetero* implies more than just blocking a road. What does it mean for you to be a *piquetero*?
Pablo: For us, the identity that we began forming as *piqueteros* has primarily to do with dignity. And dignity is built in the neighbourhoods, not just during a roadblock fighting for the work subsidies, but also by trying to solve community problems.

It's the idea of strength, of dignity, and a capacity for transformation of the small things that today are in our reach. We are a grassroots movement organized in the neighbourhoods and there are things that perhaps we can't change today, but the immediate challenge is this: fighting for dignity, conquering some spaces of justice in this fucked up social situation that we are living in.

Notes from Nowhere: How do you understand horizontality and autonomy? What do they mean to you in practice?
Pablo: We started to shape the unemployed movement in such a way that it didn't reproduce certain things from other social organizations. I mentioned before that some *compañeros* or militants had union or political experience. But the structure was always hierarchical. It was years and years of frustration, of deception and experiences that didn't end well. So beginning with the idea that we wanted to avoid that entirely, we started looking for a neighbourhood organization that had very basic principles. We hadn't read about autonomous experiences, but we did want our grassroots organization, our neighbourhood force not be subordinated by partisans or unions or be subordinated by the logic proposed by the state. And that's how we started organizing, with the idea of that the assembly should be the place where decisions are made. This logic was carried out to the *piquetes* as well. And that's how we started to learn. And soon after, we started seeing different experiences and seeing that other sectors valued us because of the way we were organized. And today we can say that with regards to horizontality and autonomy there is a conceptual framework that maintains our criteria of organization.

It sort of marks our path, because although we don't have a clear path of how we are going to advance, we are sure of the way we do not want to advance. We are not going to advance by generating centralized organizations or forms

flag of the Zapatista Army. Several streets bearing the names of the independence fighters are also bedecked with Zapatista flags and stickers. Several other municipalities also report particularly well-dressed statues and a surge in pro-EZLN graffiti.
>> October >> Over 240,000 teachers in Kenya go on strike for four weeks, demanding that the Government pay a salary increase agreed upon in 1997.
>> October 2 >> University professors at the only public university in Angola go on strike demanding an increase in wages and payment of salary arrears. Four days later, students take to the streets in an attempt to pressure the Ministry of Education into meeting their teachers' demands.
>> October 12 >> Global Day of Action, Américas
>> October 24 >> A massive crowd of over 15,000 protest in Colombo, Sri Lanka against the passage of 36 bills passed by Parliament which will expedite privatization of state institutions and natural resources, believed to be directly legislating IMF-recommended structural adjustment programmes. It is the first time that a large protest against capitalist globalization has happened in the nation.
>> October 26 >> About one million people around the planet demonstrate against the US plans to attack Iraq. With nearly 100,000 in San Francisco, US, tens of

of interaction that exclude the people from making decisions. We prefer to continue to support our assemblies and to continue generating organizations that don't depend on other structures that create subordination.

Notes from Nowhere: Continuing with that idea, how do you make decisions, how do the assemblies work?
Pablo: It's pretty simple: a group of neighbours has a weekly assembly; the discussion that needs to happen, the information that needs to be shared, and the decisions that need to be made are all done at the assembly. It's that simple and direct, it's the way that democracy works in the neighbourhood. When we have to co-ordinate various neighbourhoods and when the organization grows, it becomes a bit more complex and debates are held on how to co-ordinate in a way that doesn't create an atmosphere of centralized decision making. Within that debate we discuss the election of delegates and the way that they rotate, it's a way we found so that it's not always the same people playing the same role.

Often passivity, and all those years of a culture where others make the decisions for you generates a feeling where you don't care that other groups are making the decisions for you. So when we develop autonomy and the capacity to make decisions in our assemblies, we have to make damn sure that we keep the decision-making there and not have it expand to other places, because that's when centralized forces – even if we don't want them to – start to make the decisions for us.

"The biggest change was the relationship with other people in the neighbourhood, the development of friendship and the possibility of sharing ... When you're on a roadblock and you have nothing to eat, the people next to you share their food. Now I feel I'm living in a large family, my neighbours are my family." – **Marta, MTD Darío Santillán**

MTD Darío Santillán
Notes from Nowhere: Why a horizontal movement, using direct democracy? This is something new here in Argentina. It is very inspiring. How did it get to be that way?
Daniela: It seems to me that history and experience have shown us many different organizations that function in a vertical [top-down] way, which is also the way this system and government work, and we are breaking with that and we're basically starting from scratch. That's how we came about, from concrete necessities – that's our reality. To me it seems like we are tired of people coming around and telling us what needs to be done and then leaving and then us doing things ourselves. So, it's breaking away from that and beginning to create new things, the collective decision, the

participation of everyone, direct democracy. Here everyone has a voice and a vote, everyone can express their opinion, it's not like no-one knows anything but that we all know something. And it's not easy, I tell you, it's very hard, because in the assemblies it's hard for the *compañeros* to speak, for everyone to express themselves. Many participants don't realize what it is they are creating, how new this way of working is for us, this is a completely new chapter in the history of Argentina.

Notes from Nowhere: How has your life changed since you started participating in an MTD?

Daniela: Before I got involved I was really shy, much too shy, and it was hard for me to interact with people. That has changed a lot. I've changed 'cause in the day-to-day you have to talk to people, all kinds of different people, you're never really quiet at anytime. Now I'm chatting all the time.

I've grown in every aspect. I'm 19 years old now, and I was 16 when I entered the MTD. At first you change what you talk about, the concept of values and the relationships with the people around you and you just grow in every way – on an activist level and on a personal level because you learn to deal with things and you get to know new things. You start to see life in a different way, you see the reality, you become more realistic, more conscious of everything. And on top of that I met a lot of people, a lot of really amazing people. Eventually I brought my dad and my sister to the MTD. I believe it changed my life, it changed a lot. I believe that from here on out the things that I do will always be put in perspective; I will never abandon the struggle, I'm always going to be doing this.

Notes from Nowhere: Its seems that many women are at the forefront of the *piquetero* movement?

Daniela: Yes, it seems to me that within society, in this system the woman is subjected to all kinds of things, but in our organizations, the woman is the protagonist, because when the movements begin they are made up of *compañeras* more than anyone. Because it's the women who go out and put everything on the line to get food for their children. The husband stays home because he's getting depressed due to lack of work. All their lives the men have gone out and

---

thousands in Zaragoza, Spain, Berlin, Germany, Washington, US, and thousands more from Seattle to São Paulo, people around the globe make it clear that they are organized and strongly opposed to war.

>> October 31 >> Thirty badgers armed with water pistols storm a Starbucks in London, UK, claiming it as their ancestral home. Using the logic of Israeli settlers the badgers evict some of the customers and erect the first badger settlement in London. With placards proclaiming "If it works in Palestine why not here" and "It's ours because we say so" the self-styled Badger Defence Force set up checkpoints to inspect shoppers and tourists for concealed weapons. "If they're not a badger, they could be a terrorist" a spokesbadger said. The badgers have selected the store for their settlement because of the role of its CEO as a major supporter of the Israeli state.

>> October 31-November >> Ten thousand mostly indigenous activists converge on Quito, Ecuador to protest the FTAA meetings. A delegation of about 40 people manage to get in and directly address the hemisphere's trade delegates, who stared uncomfortably at their shoes while listening to the words of Leonidas Iza, the President of CONAIE (the Ecuadorian indigenous federation): "We are in desperate shape. You couldn't possibly understand,

MTD Aníbal Veron

Early morning at an MTD bakery. Buenos Aires, Argentina

MTD Aníbal Veron

Piqueteros transform their neighbourhood. Buenos Aires, Argentina

fought for work, to bring home the food, and suddenly when they are without work they fall into a depressive cycle and it's the women who then go out to fight. In Ariel's case his mother brought him to the MTD for the first time, then she got her husband involved. I believe that the women here have a fundamental role. The men also, of course, but the women are completely devoted, it's intense. Even more so with the girls. I don't say this 'cause I'm a woman but I believe that those that have ovaries tend to put themselves in front and say what has to be done. We all do it and there is so much energy, tonnes. They know that it's not just their life and future which is at risk, but also that of their children, their entire family, and that is very important.

The system tells you that women will submit to anything. You have to be home and take charge of the kitchen and the kids and don't leave there, your role is that of housewife, you can't think, you don't have an opinion ... As things change in these movements it comes out that the woman begins to have a voice that can express what she feels. I believe that it radically changes her whole quality of life, because a woman, a *compañera* from the MTD, is not the same as a woman who is not within the movement, and those outside are going to notice the differences.

I believe this is really new, brand new. You go to the movement and you see that it's filled with women. And the MTD woman feels good because it's like she found her place where she can be herself, where she can say what she feels and that is incredible, to find one's place.

Ariel: Yeah, I recently told Dani that in my house, when I had a job, I would get home from work and I'd find all these things done... there was the food, my clothes, I went to the bathroom and my shirt was hanging and now I get home and I don't have any of that [he laughs].

Sometimes it happens that I get home and my partner says, "You're here, good because I have to go out." My wife is active in another *barrio* called Don Orione. I come here more than anywhere; I was born here in this neighbourhood, in Cerrito. I lived here 26 years, I have been in Don Orione for five years and my wife is active in the MTD in Don Orione. Sometimes I get home and she says- "I'm going to work at the *Copa de Leche* [children's milk distribution] afternoon shift."

I'm here in the morning and I'd like to go out but I have to stay with the kids and now that I'm here I have to see if there are clothes to be washed, I have to lend a hand, then maybe I'm told that she left the *Copa de Leche* and she's going to the MTD bakery to make some sweet bread because tomorrow there is an event and they are going to try raise funds for the community kitchen. She has other activities; on Tuesday there is the assembly, since that's today I had to go to pick up the kids at school.

Notes from Nowhere: A little personal question – has involvement in the MTD therefore made your relationship better?
Ariel: Yes, of course, because my partner now feels really good about herself.

Notes from Nowhere: One of the things I want to ask is about the dreams for the future, for the *barrio*, for your children.
Daniela: More than anything I think that I want to have children and I want my children to have a future with dignity. That is why I have taken on this struggle and believe that dignity has to be fought for – to be able to live in dignity, with work. And with a more just society, one that is equal for everyone.
Ariel: Yes, I agree with Dani. I hope that in the future my children don't have to go to the hospital with a stick in their hands and a mask on their face and say to them: "Attend to my children." That they don't have to go to some health ministry and make them understand that it is our right, and that this thing about being masked and grabbing a stick has to continue to implement these necessities. I hope that in the future those that are on top use their

---

you who were born in golden cradles and have never suffered. But we don't have food to feed our children... We have no way to live, and the FTAA will only make it worse. When we complain, the US government calls us terrorists. We are not threatening anything, but we are hungry and tired and things have to change."
>> November 4-5 >> Over 30,000 members of the Korean Government Employees Union hold a public rally, opposing proposed legislation which would deny all civil service workers the name and status of a trade union as well as the right to organize. Twenty-seven leaders of the union were pre-emptively arrested days prior to the rally, which is violently attacked by the police, injuring many unionists, and resulting in the arrest of thousands. The police then surround the union headquarters, block the entrances, and raid the place, confiscating documents.
>> November 6-10 >> A European Social Forum takes place in Florence, Italy with hundreds of activists gathering for in-depth reflection, democratic debate, free exchange of experiences, and planning of actions leading towards building a better world. The Forum culminates in a march against the looming US war on Iraq, with half a million people participating.
>> November 7 >> In Minsk, Belarus a peaceful

conscience, stop stealing, and stop screwing us over. And if they don't gain consciousness and keep doing it, they are always going to find resistance everywhere. I am going to stay in this for however old I become, for my grandchildren and for everyone.

Daniela: And it's a long road.

Ariel: The road is long.

Daniela: And there are lots of hold-ups along the way.

Notes from Nowhere: How is building a community kitchen, a bakery, organic gardens, and popular libraries and so on a threat to the state?

Daniela: In some ways it seems so insignificant, but for them it's a lot, because they see that the people are suddenly organizing and acquiring new skills, other ways of thinking and are saying "Enough of this!" Very young people begin to gain consciousness from the neighbourhood; they stand up to the state and say, "We don't want any more of this! We have come to demand what belongs to us by right," and we confront them, we stop being dominated and break out. I believe that is what they are afraid of, of people with a conscience, of people that think, of people that get together and fight. The state is very afraid. And that's why they first dominate you on an ideological level and then they repress you and beat you down in the street. On 26 June last year, we lost two *compañeros*, and the 19 and 20 of December 2001 were terrible, and not long ago they repressed those of us that went to support the occupied Brukman factory. That's the way it is, the government clubs you but at the same time it sees more resistance on our side, and it's afraid of that. And here in the neighbourhood it's very hard because the concept of repression is obviously very deep and it's something the people are scared of.

On 26 June it was proven. We lost a *compañero* that was very close to us, Darío Santillán, and he is very alive within us now. That's why we also try to work on a neighbourhood level, more than anything, because it's harder for the people to mobilize in the streets, but we try to work on the neighbourhood level and make sure that this work is not in vain, not lost.

Ariel: Yeah, we are a zit on the state's ass, and it really bothers them. So they portray us in the media as violent, saying that all we do is block traffic. We know that we are a minority, but at the same time we get them to listen to us and it worries them. The presidential candidates in the last elections emphasized that they were going to impose order, that they weren't going let any more road blockades take place, but I don't know how they will ever stop this. Nothing changes, they don't provide anything for people, no education – nothing. And here we are at the base, in the neighbourhoods, guaranteeing at least the basic needs, such as food and education. The movements have libraries, popular education workshops, everything. It's the bare minimum, but we are doing it ourselves. It bothers them that the local political party bosses who used to say: "I'll give you a bag of groceries if you go to this support rally," or: "I'll give you this welfare payment but you have to go around wearing this political shirt all day," no longer control us.

Since we threw the political bosses out of the neighbourhoods, we know that they send people to spy on us during our open assemblies but when they talk we all realize who they are, especially when they try to lay down a party line. We don't accept any politicians. And now even during the electoral campaigns, they are respecting our space and are not coming too close to us because they know we're not going to cut a deal with them. We don't cut deals. Not even if they win, not for subsidies, not for anything.

There is a song about a rebel Argentina, the song begins: "Argentina is rebellious, it has guts. We are all rebels because hunger is violence, and if today's hunger is the law, then rebellion is justice."

Pablo Solana is an unemployed electrician and works with MTD Lanus.
Daniela works in the community kitchen and does security in MTD Darío Santillán, Almirante Brown.
Ariel works in the bakery and as a group facilitator with MTD Darío Santillán, Almirante Brown.
Magda and Orlando work in MTD Solano.

Interview by Notes from Nowhere / John Jordan
Marina Sitrin has been an anticapitalist activist for the last fifteen years, most recently working with the Direct Action Network and People's Law Collective in New York. She is currently in Argentina working on a book of interviews with autonomous social movements.

These interviews were transcribed and translated by Roberto Litzenberger, Irina Brunetti, and Paula Talesnik

---

Resources:
»MTD: www24.brinkster.com/movtd/escritos/pariendo.htm
»Excellent and constantly updated site on radical struggles in Latin America: www.rebelion.org

---

demonstration against the war takes place, organized by the Belarussian Anarchist Federation.
>> November 11 >> Three hundred people march through the streets of downtown Montreal, Canada demanding an immediate regularization of the status of the more than 1,000 non-status Algerians living in Canada. Stressing that the situation for Algerians is one of asylum and protection, not immigration, the march is comprised of First Nations activists, members of the Ontario Coalition Against Poverty, and students, and points out the contradiction of deporting asylum seekers to a nation under a Canadian travel advisory warning due to the ongoing civil war.
>> November 12 >> Hundreds of nurses and hospital workers go on strike in Wroclaw, Poland, occupying a hospital and demanding payment of the nurses' back wages. A broad coalition of supporters come out in support, Food Not Bombs serves food at the hospital, neighbours help blockade a major street, and local anarchists help defend nurses' homes under threat of eviction. Police attack the street action and send 11 people to the hospital, two of whom are arrested for throwing potatoes and eggs at the police. Meanwhile, the Polish government knows where its priorities lie as it hems and haws over which war planes to

Jorge Silva/Reuters

Guatemalan farmers block the highway from Huehuetenango to the Mexican border. La Mesilla, Guatemala

Global Day of Action
October 12th 2002

We Will Not be Recolonized, Las Américas

The month of October sees massive resistance throughout the Américas, from Canada to Chile, as outraged people rise up against the new colonialism, focusing particularly on Plan Puebla-Panama (PPP, a $20 billion project of industrial and transportation infrastructure encompassing all of Central America and half of Mexico, which will greatly affect the region's 64 million inhabitants, displacing rural communities, and leaving ecological destruction in its wake), and the Free Trade Area of the Americas, and demanding an end to the militarization that accompanies 'free' trade, especially Plan Colombia.

The 510th anniversary of the first invasion of the Américas by Christopher Columbus is called as a hemispheric day of action by the Latin American Cry of the Excluded network. In El Salvador over 20,000 people initiate 11 simultaneous blockades, paralyzing the country, bringing commerce to a halt, and shutting down the four largest border crossings. Bus drivers and

Ken Lambert / AP

WANTED
CHRISTOPHER COLUMB
GRAND THEFT, GENOCIDE, R
INITIATING THE DESTRUCTION OF A CULTURE,
RAPE, TORTURE, AND MAIMING OF INDIGENOUS
PEOPLE, AND INSTIGATOR OF THE BIG LIE.
500 YEARS OF TOURISM
A NATIVE AMERICAN PERSPECTIVE
go ahead, steal this poster... you've stolen everything else

Sioux activist is arrested while protesting at Columbus Day parade. Washington, US

money-changers at the border join in spontaneously as traffic backs up into Guatemala; police close the border in response. In Comalapa, residents join the airport workers' union and shut down the airport (home to a US military base). The largest blockade is at the Puente de Oro, where over 5,000 *campesinos* block the coastal highway for six hours. Local bands play on a stage in the middle of the highway, while clowns on stilts entertain the children. In Sonsonate, several women's groups block the highway to the port, targeted for development by private industry. When the blockades are lifted, thousands march to state-run hospitals and clinics around the country to support striking health care workers. A peasant organizer declares, "We think that this sent an important message to our government, to the other Central American governments, and to the US that we are not going to stand back and let our countries, our *pueblos* be annexed to the US. This is just the first of many actions yet to come."

Meanwhile, in Mexico, thousands of indigenous people march through the streets of Mexico City, while Zapatista base communities blockade 20 highways, ports, and airports in Chiapas; the Pan American Highway is also blocked in Oaxaca. In Guatemala, 1,000

Claudia Daut/Reuters

Pehuenche women perform a traditional dance during Columbus Day demonstrations. Santiago, Chile

indigenous people block the Pan American Highway, and 6,000 block airports and border crossings in Petén. In Honduras, marches draw thousands of people protesting against the privatization of health care, water, and education, while unionized teachers support the blockade at the Salvadoran border, and a network of over 30 organizations and 4,000 people block the borders to Nicaragua and Guatemala. In Nicaragua, thousands protest in front of the Inter-American Development Bank headquarters in Managua, and the Pan American Highway is blocked in Esteli, while in San José, Costa Rica, protests rage against the PPP-driven construction of the Terraba Dam, which will evict thousands of small farmers. Indigenous activists from Panama march 200 miles from Costa Rica to Panama City, to protest the ecological destruction caused by mining on their lands.

Further south, in Santiago, Chile, thousands of indigenous protesters are joined by hundreds of gay and lesbian rights activists in their protest against the FTAA, while over 1,000 people march in Buenos Aires, singing, dancing, and demanding that land be returned to the indigenous. In Quito, Ecuador, the Hemispheric Social Forum concludes with a festival; 1,000 people fill the

Victor Ruiz Caballero/AP

Salvadorian protesters paralyze the country with simultaneous roadblocks. Los Chorros, El Salvador

Plaza del Teatro. In Barcelona, 500 people denounce the new massacre of people and culture heralded by the FTAA; in Paris, hundreds listen to indigenous speakers from the Américas.

In the US, two dozen cities respond to calls made by the Latin American Solidarity Coalition and the American Indian Movement (AIM). Defying harsh restrictions around the US-Mexico border, people from all over Arizona, US and Sonora, Mexico organize a joint action; Mexican activists, restricted from setting foot on 'US soil' block traffic while US marchers easily cross into Mexico for a cultural exchange and fiesta. The US/Canada border is also a target as hundreds gather in Washington State and British Colombia. A member of AIM in Washington DC breaks a vial of his blood on a Columbus statue, demanding the release of AIM's Leonard Peltier, wrongfully imprisoned for decades. Just two weeks later, actions against the FTAA summit in Ecuador spring up across the hemisphere, as people cry out, "Another integration is possible!"

While 'economic apartheid' *is waging an all out war on the poor of new South Africa it has also galvanized some unique new movements. Reclaiming their dignity in the face of rising destitution, the poors, as they are called, use imaginative forms of direct action to oppose housing evictions and water and electricity cut-offs. Rejecting pure protest in favour of pragmatic locally-based action, neighbours in townships across the country are working together to find radical solutions to their immediate needs. Thousands have illegally reconnected their electricity and water, evicted residents have been put back into their houses, and evictions have consistently and often successfully been resisted.*

Other forms of action have piled pressure on those involved in the neoliberal onslaught on their communities. The mayor of Johannesburg had his water disconnected, bank offices in Cape Town were occupied, and community groups laid siege to the debt collection building in Durban. As the movements grow, so does repression, with numerous arrests, police attacks, trumped up charges, and the murder of community activists. "[T]he black ruling elite," says academic Ebrahim Harvey, "has not hesitated to act against protesters with the jackboot that we are so familiar with under apartheid."

These community movements have challenged the boundaries of what was seen as politics in South Africa. Working outside of formal parties, unions, and NGOs, they have brought radical political action back home to the everyday lives of ordinary people. Without grand ideologies or illusions about state power, and by directly addressing their local situation, they challenge global capitalism and the distribution of power through building community and neighbourliness. They also are beginning to make contacts with other movements which echo their practices, such as the piqueteros of Argentina, the water warriors of Bolivia, and the Ontario Coalition Against Poverty. Here Ahswin Desai, writer and community activist, talks to Holly Wren Spaulding about the significance of the rise of this new form of liberation struggle for South Africa.

Between The Broken And The Built: power to the neighbourhoods

an interview with Ashwin Desai by Holly Wren Spaulding

Holly Wren Spaulding: It seems we are all, as you have written, "between the broken and the built." What are the new tools of liberation?

Ashwin Desai: What are the new repertoires of struggle? Simply rebuilding, in many senses, community structures. But they are not to have the familiar leftist designs imprinted upon them. We need to struggle less for the Revolution and more for a humble and decent life. Of course this brings one up against the capitalist system. What some used to call, somewhat dismissively, "bread and butter struggles" have now mutated, assuming real constitutive force, and generating meaningful and sustained moments of counter power.

Many of these communities have 80 per cent unemployment: eight out of ten people don't work, and probably will never work. That's their life. While the poors do not have the sophisticated organizational structures of the unions, they have the need to fight to hang onto their shelters and there is no reluctance to engage in illegality and there is a great deal of innovation. This will to a dignified life involves very basic things: love, respect, consideration; freedom to move around your neighbourhood.

These are seemingly very minor events – manifesting over a communal cooking pot for example, but they are infused with a lot of politics, a lot of feeling. The new politics is driven by families participating as households, including the lumpen, the rabble, the single mother, the proto-gangster, the young children and the aunties – the unorganizable – and nobody is out of the loop.

There's a sense that these collectives should also be about rebuilding shattered lives, assuming some role in secular and religious celebrations, even pronouncing on who should be in the national cricket team. They settle some fairly serious community disputes and solicit charity and outside resources in a most sophisticated manner. They do seem woven into the everyday fabric of life in the townships to the extent that even after a lull in activity of three or four months, when a new crisis arises, their ranks are swelled.

Having said all this, however, because of the nature of the ANC's trajectory, which is a very brutal form of Reaganomics, community movements do find themselves, most often, confronting the state, which has become a fellow traveller with neoliberalism.

HWS: The history of liberation movements in South Africa leading up to 1994 is vivid, and somewhat familiar to international observers. What is the landscape of resistance in this new climate of supposed liberation?

AD: National liberation is infused with a lot of contradictory impulses, and sometimes it is so hard for people to grasp that. It's not about romance; it's not just about slaying the great monster. Inside that great struggle, the terrain is trespassed and criss-crossed with so much chauvinism and narrow nationalism that could easily turn into one-party fascism and xenophobia. At times there was a lack of democracy completely unjustified by any operational necessities: orders were given and orders were carried out, almost like a factory. Sometimes national liberation movements work in the very manner of company executives and underlings.

These days, part of building community movements is unlearning old ways of doing things. The fact that community movements engender more horizontal linkages and don't deify leaders is a very valuable part of the new repertoire of struggle.

---

purchase for several billion *zloty*.

>> November 13 >> Activists in Prague shut down a seminar on NATO and EU cooperation without even leaving the pub! Police arrive at the scheduled location of the seminar about half an hour before it is to start and tell the delegates that a huge anarchist action is planned against them. The terrified delegates panic, and send for their chartered buses to whisk them away to the EU embassy on the other side of Prague, where the meeting commences under great tension. Activists are delighted to hear the news, as they never knew the meeting's location, and had no intention of protesting it.

>> November 14 >> Thousands take the streets in Homebush, Sydney, Australia, to protest the WTO meeting and the US war, and to highlight the connections between military adventurism and corporate rule. A sound system pumps beats from a rubbish bin on wheels, and the route of the march is determined by games of Spin the Bottle with a six-foot paper maché bottle, which is confiscated by police. "It's bad enough the police stopped us getting to the hotel, but when they stop us snogging each other, it's just un-Australian," says a member of the Bottle Bloc. The next day, a pirate radio broadcast by the Institute for Applied Piracy jams commercial radio signals for ten

HWS: You talk about casting off political labels and walking naked ...

AD: For me personally, and for many people, it's been one of the more harrowing things, but one of the most liberating things. In South Africa, the way you shook somebody's hand or clenched your fist, said which family you were in – whether you were PAC (Pan Africanist Congress) or ANC (African National Congress), or part of the Black Consciousness movement. Movements literally became your family. This is probably best epitomized by Govan Mbeki's response when asked what he thought when his son became president. He said, "I never had a son. All the cadres were my children, were my family." That's all people knew, that was their social and emotional circle.

Many of us have had to cast off old political affiliations, become strangers for a while, alone, and then rebuild something and redress ourselves in completely new clothing, and march against the very people we had previously marched alongside, and shared prison cells with.

Leaving political ideologies behind is a big deal; excising that part of your identity that depended on membership to a particular clique or creed was even bigger. In this new movement there is a need to break away from that, and from electoral politics. It's like marching against your parents: stoning them, forsaking them, and decrying them.

Many people's biographies are written with all kinds of contradictions, often displayed as schizophrenia. If Thabo Mbeki comes around, or Mandela, to remember the 16 June Soweto Uprising, people still see the need to go to the meeting and chant the slogans of the party of liberation: the ANC, slayer of apartheid. But the next day they are fighting evictions, and denouncing the ANC as a party of neoliberalism. A militant opposition has happened in other places in the world, but in South Africa it has happened very quickly. The miracle here is how quickly the ANC has donned the cape of the IMF and World Bank, unsheathed the sword of structural adjustment. Because of this, the pace of opposition has had to move pretty quickly.

"Women of Chatsworth unite
Women lead the fight
Pick up the stones
Break Council's bones
Fatima Meer is in the house ..."

– Psyche, Chatsworth hip-hop artist

HWS: Who is involved in these movements?

AD: In the beginning, almost all over the country, community movements were infused with almost 80 per cent older women, simply because they were the first ones affected by the ravages of neoliberalism. Child maintenance grants were slashed, for example, and they were the first ones expelled from jobs as the enforcement of the reduction of tariffs sank in.

Women are the ones all over this city of Durban who are

working in sweatshops, working Monday to Sunday, earning $65-75. Basic upkeep for a single woman with one child is about $230, which is just really basic poverty. So they became part of the movement to boycott paying for services. They would be very docile in the workplace toward the boss – they wanted that $65 – but they would be militant in the community by not paying for water and electric. They are topping up their salary, insinuating a social wage through their actions, saying, "This fucking state wants to allow people to pay us $65, but they want us to pay $105 in rent, so we are going to take that $40 from the state by not paying." At the level of lived experience translating into activism, women were, and are the real power.

HWS: Are youth involved as well, or are they creating their own movements at this time?
AD: When younger people come out, they bring their own style of taking action, and a different attitude – they want music, and to dance, and they get pissed off and do more militant things. They care very little about the CVs of former MKs [Umkhonto we Sizwe guerrilla army, now disbanded] and those with long struggle histories. They care about what is happening right now and have a wonderfully cynical nose when it comes to the platitudes of politicians and other authority figures.

Of course young people are still fascinated by the local drug lord, the gangster, the rap artist and so on, and they find a sense of meaning through these things rather than through boring old struggle again. The youth still organize separately and youth movements have sprung up in some places, for example, the *Vulumanzi*, or water boys are a youth group that teaches others how to reconnect the water.

HWS: Are communities consciously organizing to be 'non-racial communities'?
AD: In Wentworth and Merebank – Indian and Coloured communities here in Durban – people are organizing against some of the worst kinds of pollution. The city manager, Mike Sutcliffe, an ANC guy, says that African workers want the jobs there, and by fighting Shell and Engen, they will be denied work. The state apparatus can use race as a battering ram to divide people, and racial

---

minutes to transmit across all stations a report on the WTO and its abuses against human and worker rights, public health, and the environment.
>> November 15 >> After a two month long national strike by health care workers, the people of El Salvador win an historic victory. The legislature passes a law outlawing privatization of health care, and defining the state's obligation to provide accessible quality health care to every Salvadoran near their home, regardless of ability to pay. Strike leaders urge striking workers and supporters to throw their weight and experience into the struggle against privatization of electricity and against the Central American Free Trade Agreement, which would supersede the new law and mandate privatization of all services.
>> November 16 >> An estimated 10,000 people marched in Auckland, Aotearoa / New Zealand today for a GMO-free nation. The colorful, diverse crowd take their carnival to a park where they dance to live music and eat GMO-free food.
>> November 20-21 >> Banging pots, pans, and drums while declaring their solidarity with the Argentinean people in their struggle to build a new society, activists from Eastern Europe gather in Prague, Czech Republic to protest against the NATO summit. While official delegates

Justin Rowe

Electrical worker illegally reconnects the power for the *poors*. Wentworth, South Africa

division in this country is 300 years in the making – it won't be unmade by some single individual or through natural processes.

We are building, but we have been sober about what we can achieve in the immediate. South Africa is understood as a black and white society. People are called "so-called Indian", "so-called coloured", "so-called Zulu", as if we could wipe out 300 years of history by putting "so-called" in front of those words. As the rubric of Black has been rendered asunder, and there has been a flowering of all kinds of weird ethnicities and so on, yes, we have tried to build a sort of non-racialism as a culture.

Recently the Concerned Citizens' Forum, (a loose grouping of community movements in Durban), and the Landless People's Movement have engaged in joint marches in an attempt to bridge the urban and rural divide. Young and old, rural and urban, families, and migrant workers who have lost their lands after decades of labouring on the mines recently stormed the Durban City Hall. For a while at least, the shapeless mass was a multitude, chanting "Down with the ANC."

HWS: What are some of the tactics used to build a militant culture? On the ground, how does it look?

AD: We take traditional important events, the Bambata Rebellion of 1906 and Diwali, for example, and the neighbourhoods participate completely, because there are deliberate attempts to rethink that in this South Africa. Bambata is celebrated not as some minor Zulu chief, but as somebody who was a brazen and brave fighter against colonialism, and therefore even in Indian communities, gets embraced before Gandhi because he was carrying a stretcher for the British Imperial Army, while Bambata was attempting to chase the imperial army out. It's hard, but people are embracing those kinds of traditions as their own; histories infused with a fight against imperialism – not the accommodation of it.

HWS: What kind of tradition, if any, explains the willingness of say, Indian flat-dwellers in Chatsworth to stand in an act of passive resistance to defend a black man who is being evicted from his flat down the row?

AD: I think that's a crucial question. A lot of people on what

---

enjoy a posh banquet, hundreds of people give out free food under anti-war banners. Under the oppressive gaze of the heaviest surveillance ever seen in the country, with some organizers being detained as many as 15 times daily, 4,000 people take the streets under the close watch of 12,000 police, unknown numbers of soldiers, and US Air Force jets. The action leaves people exhilarated; many come from communities with very small resistance movements, and most feel empowered after having built and strengthened networks of resistance across the region.

>> November 21 >> In Timisoara, Romania, a massive postering campaign takes place before dawn, resulting in the entire city proclaiming anti-NATO and anti-war slogans from its walls. Additionally, two banners are dropped over major highways, sending the police into a confused flurry, fearing that major demonstrations might follow. The propaganda campaign gets enormous media coverage, even more than did the announcement of NATO's invitation to Romania to join, and many interviewed on the streets are in agreement with the campaign.

>> November 27 >> In Tbilisi, Georgia, activists protest outside the office of the Georgian International Oil Company, who has partnered with British Petroleum to construct the Baku-Ceyhan pipeline. The pipeline would

they call the Left, decry and are very cynical about community movements because their militancy is not palpable – they're not storming the barricades, they're not building the Paris Commune; they do not know the exact difference between the IMF and World Bank and don't particularly care to know either. But I think what we are doing is building our neighbourhoods, which is as effectively anti-World Bank as any demonstration or resolution coming out of an NGO workshop.

In one case where this happened in Chatsworth, Mr Mhlongo was what they call a bush mechanic in the area. He looked after people's cars and they looked after him, through bartering. When Council security guards and the police turned up to evict his family, over 150 people, mainly women, drove them away. They blockaded the stairs that led to his flat. There were gunshots and tear gas, and at least six casualties, but the residents had vowed to prevent the evictions. It was not just a battle for Mhlongo, but for their collective dignity as human beings. That's the beauty of neighbourhoods: this idea of sharing with, and defending each other, and something beautiful and precious is being born.

Where does one struggle and how does one struggle? It would appear to me that marches in Seattle and Genoa get directed toward that more macro financial level and at systems. They take in Starbucks along the way as well, but it's almost like when you go shopping at the supermarket and you buy something you didn't have on your list, and that's great. But the struggle in South Africa wouldn't be smashing McDonald's. It's a more guttural, barricadey kind of struggle of just trying to defend what you have. But in doing that you are linking almost everything; by not allowing the state to 'cost-recover' and privatize and so on, you are forcing it to even greater forms of oppression, and thus the divide becomes more stark; to begin to say to the IMF and World Bank, "We can't abide by these policies, because in certain of our townships neoliberalism just is not possible." It's not like you're building something new in one community in isolation. People have a resonance of what happens elsewhere, but the targets for their anger are local.

HWS: Can you explain the significance of "living spaces that are not bound to the dollar sign"?

AD: The Housing Act in the constitution says that that rental housing must be provided through local municipalities and the state. While that's an Act, they're selling off or forcing upon the poorest people individual title deeds, and then you get Body Corporates emerging and so on. These Body Corporates, consisting of community members, are the ones who enforce payment of levies and evict those who cannot pay. It is a dividing of the poor and the poorest because the poorest can't pay, so they get put in other houses far out of town where they will be policed and won't be a problem. Some of them have lived in the same flat for 35 years (forcibly brought to these places by apartheid), are old, and this is their community and they are not going to leave.

Meanwhile, as the state is slimming down their provision of maintenance and social welfare for the poorest of the poor, you need more and more money in order to survive as everything becomes privatized. This visits the most horrendous deprivation upon people; water and lights get cut off; parks get cordoned off with razor wire, and kids in one neighbourhood can't play in the park that was once a public space. The people who have access to the park are poor themselves, but they put up fences and they guard that zealously. By becoming owners, a process of separation from the community takes place, and the struggle becomes individualized as living spaces are privatized.

HWS: As social movements continue to grow, what are some of the most hopeful tactics and signs of change you have experienced as one who is active in community movements?
AD: A deep sense of what people in South Africa call *gatvol* – we're fucking fed up, would be the loose translation. The hopeful thing is actually a sense amongst people that this government will never deliver and that we're going to have to start building our own lives.

There was a sense that a developmental state would produce a largesse: houses would spring up when you got up in the morning, water taps would be installed, and so on. It's disempowering because the government can't allow people to do it themselves by giving them the rudiments to build houses, tar roads, construct parks, because in loosening people's energies to take over their own lives, people get mobilized. These kinds of governments operate on a kind of "demobilization" you vote once every four years and you wait, and you wait and you wait, and the father figure – yesterday Mandela, today Mbeki – will deliver. Well, we are tired of father figures.

There's a sense that the state won't deliver, and people are making connections at the local level. Incredible bonds are being built between people as they imagine a new world. These are small things, but they're very big things.

What is happening right now is very jarring to old style Leftists – this almost imperceptible growth and flowering of social agents that don't have any manifesto containing their precise position on say, nationalization. There is even some hostility towards the very organic leadership that ensues in community movements. But the flowering I spoke of doesn't want leaders to represent its bloom.

The leadership in communities is people who may never

---

run 1,090 miles from Azerbaijan, through Georgia and into Turkey, creating a two and a half mile wide militarized corridor, destablizing the region, increasing human rights abuses, and degrading the environment.

>> December 1 >> About 1,500 people converge at Wat Don Chai in Song district, Thailand for the largest protest in 13 years against the proposed construction of the Kaeng Sua Ten dam. After erecting a 20 foot teak pole to invoke the spirits in Hor Daeng village, they set afloat a banana leaf container, to carry away bad omens, and later burn a straw effigy of Somporn Chuenkam, the Phrae senator who supports the dam.

>> December 6 >> More than 200 *sans-papiers* (people without papers) and support groups occupy the International Employment Office (IOM) in Paris, France. Many foreigners working under IOM contracts receive no social benefits, are not entitled to welfare funds, are required to pay 170 euros for an annual medical exam, and never get residency visas, no matter how long they work in the country. The occupiers demands are that the IOM comply with France's social legislation, and that all *sans-papiers* be legalized, receiving permanent work permit and equal access to social benefits. The occupation ends when it becomes clear that the police are about to intervene and

have had any education, formally, but are powerful figures because they are so rooted. It's not a haughty leadership, and people have very few illusions about the inherent value of the leader as individual. Those who may be called leaders have a particular sense of themselves, which has something to do with the progressive erosion and confrontation of internal violence.

Fanon has a wonderful line about this, something like "A native who has a knife will turn on another native who has a knife rather than on the European." That happens. But you will find that in communities with social movements there are much lower figures of rape and child abuse, for example.

This rootedness, flatness, and suspicion of leadership is only one half of the equation. I have seen the beauty, and much of this, of course, is anathema to those who desire to use their anger to build up the political machine. You know, the working class party and so on. It has been nine years and people don't care about the ballot box. They might even vote but they know it is all a joke. A guy comes, a local Councillor, there are firecrackers and food, and then little flags and balloons for the kids; people probably give a vote, but they know that it is resignation at that level.

So if a house goes empty it's not the local Councillor who decides who goes in there, it's the community. They take someone off the street and give them a roof. We really are creating liberated zones in a way. People say, "Councillors earn a lot of money but they've got no work." Councillors are being rendered redundant because they don't worry about utilities, jobs, and putting people in houses. People confront their own misery by taking over local fields and doing market gardening. It's not as widespread as water and electricity "theft," but it exists. Land invasions are happening in South Africa, not just in Zimbabwe. People here are taking the state's land – Mugabe is taking land for the state – and so we are learning from other struggles and their pitfalls, but that's why South Africa is such a vital part of this "we are everywhere" movement.

"We don't ask why or when people are cut off, we just switch them back on. Everyone should have electricity." – **Virginia Setshedi, Soweto Electricity Crisis Committee, November 2001**

HWS: Finally, what are the struggles on the international scene that provide inspiration here in communities? Are they paying attention to what's happening outside South Africa, does that matter, is international solidarity important to people in communities?

AD: I think it's a complex kind of unfolding of things. The ANC government still likes to trade on its legitimacy; it's trying something new and what can it do, you know, they are victims. This posturing and rhetoric hides the inhumanity and greed of this new elite.

There are simple things that matter very much to us: the

international figures who criticize the ANC hurt them more than we do – we're always moaning and groaning. When the Maude Barlows, John Sauls, and Naomi Kleins, and other individuals come and ask the critical questions, the ANC acts as if they expect something different. This needs to be understood in the context that those in power want to take advantage of the privileges that were accumulated by the whites when they were in power. When they are criticized, the rest of the world is forced to be cognizant.

We are still fighting a national liberation struggle: this is our government, they have betrayed us, and therefore we must crush them. Immediately people will say "But how can you think you have been betrayed? You should have known beforehand, this is the ANC, they were a bourgeois party, bla bla bla," and the wise-aleck mantra comes out. Of course it is a betrayal because the teeming mass of humanity that got into the streets to be both part of the struggle, and to celebrate it, would have had expectations. Because of this, people are building, in much deeper ways, more deeply embedded structures than a flimsy NGO in a house.

The international event that probably has had the most resonance is the Argentina situation. Some people from here have gone there and met the *piqueteros* and we were all surprised to hear of some of their direct action tactics. In our own discussions we were slowly drifting there as well, and discovering the physical and discursive efficacy of these types of actions.

The very nature of the Argentinean struggle appeals to us; it eschews trade union bureaucrats and NGO-types almost as much as it does Left parliamentarians. It is based not on a struggle captured and defined by tired Left dogma but seems centred on the experiences and desires of people who have a much greater say in the direction of the struggle than we are used to. Now we have the benefit of a rich and ready history.

I myself was completely taken by the fact that when the Municipal Services Project held a big conference, a lot of communities went up because they allowed a side show to happen. A lot of us were saying "Right, we're gonna show videos of Chatsworth, Khayelitsha, Soweto," and the Indymedia people were like, "Let's show something international," and there were videos from Seattle,

---

another action is planned later this month.

>> December 9 >> The government of Zambia makes a surprise announcement that the planned privatization of 51 per cent of the national bank would be halted, due to public and union pressure. In immediate retaliation, the IMF declares that Zambia will not receive debt relief, saying "If they don't sell, they don't get the money. Over one billion US dollars could be delayed." Days later, thousands march in Lusaka in support of the decision. The President of the Federation of Free Trade Unions speaks at the rally saying, "Now let somebody out there tell us, having privatized 80 per cent of our economy, why is it that we have become one of the poorest countries in Africa and in the whole world?"

>> December 10 >> "The farmers are walking towards death", says Alberto Gómez, executive director of UNORCA, a national union of 30 regional peasant groups protesting today against agricultural provisions of NAFTA in Mexico City, Mexico. More than 2,000 peasant farmers gather outside the Congress building, denouncing new trade liberalization – part of NAFTA's time-released formula – that is scheduled for implementation in January, eliminating tariffs on 21 farm products. If the implementation were to be

France, other American videos, and we thought people would be very bored. But that wasn't the case. *This is What Democracy Looks Like*, about Seattle, was the most seen and appreciated video.

To know that from the beast of the apocalypse people are revolting and inventive is very powerful. There was one video where someone was talking and activists abseiled [rapelled] onto the stage and so on. Of course it's an inspiration. We're very conservative actually, we respect persons in authority generally, and this encouraged people to be disrespectful of authority in new and unpredictable ways. There are increasing amounts of disrespect.

We've breached this idea of legal and illegal – to be illegal is something romantic. People now carry banners that say: "Stop squeezing the poor, you bastards," and there is no longer a sense that we must be dignified.

About two months ago in Mandela Park in Khayelitsha, Cape Town, the City Manager who has been evicting and cutting people's water went to address a mass meeting. He wanted to go to the toilet in the middle of it, but there is no water, so they brought him a bucket. Of course, try as he might, he couldn't pee in front of a thousand peering faces. But that would never have happened in the past, people would have actually stopped the meeting to allow the person to go to the loo. That has changed.

People are not showing solidarity with South Africa like during the anti-apartheid struggle. They are fighting where they are, and it makes a hell of a difference. They too are building under very difficult circumstances, and they are being locked up, hurt, beaten. In many ways, at that level, it's a meeting of equals. This kind of solidarity is much different than the anti-Apartheid solidarity; the relationship isn't so much about funds – boycott South Africa products in Chicago, or whatever. People are saying "Boycott products made in America." People are taking their own situation and saying, "We're not going to live off of, and be parasitic on other people's struggles; we come with struggle and we go back to struggle."

Different figures arrive here, and are able to tell us their stories; ACT UP, [and other] AIDS activists who have taken on pharmaceutical companies. Greenpeace came and people immediately said "Don't touch this, these guys are this and that." We went down to meet the ship and they said they wanted us to organize certain things, and we said: "Well this is what we desire," and there was actually quite a gelling. I don't know much about this organization, but there was something very sobering about that experience because a lot of community members were at the meeting when Greenpeace said, "Look, we know you guys have to be in this town and already have criminal cases. We're prepared to go and be charged, so don't do it. Give us this cover, or organize placards, or whatever, but we are going to enter Shell. We don't expect you to come."

It was a hell of a thing for people because actually, it's often the opposite. People give us the money and say, "Go do your struggle now, and we'll just park off in the back." That kind of solidarity work was quite powerful. The media went gaga and put it on the front pages with these guys abseiling in saying, "We're prepared to be charged, but also charge Shell. We accept our fine." When people are prepared to give of their lives like that, those connections can be quite sobering.

I think people's stories are being told for the first time. Not Mandela's story, but the real lives of ordinary South African people are being taken seriously, and the stories are about how they have received the transition, and what has happened to them now.

The poors of South Africa are ready to struggle one more time. They will make history. Again.

Ashwin Desai is a public intellectual, sometime newspaper columnist, teacher, and uncompromising community activist. He is the author of *Blacks in Whites*, University of Natal Publishers, 2002, *We Are the Poors*, Monthly Review Press, 2002, *South Africa: Still Revolting*, Madiba Publishers, 1999, and *Arise Ye Coolies*, Impact Africa Publishing, 1996.

Holly Wren Spaulding is a poet, teacher, Indymedia reporter, and community activist. She works toward the insurrection of water and stones from her home above a fertile swamp in northern Michigan.

Resources:

» Totally comprehensive site with views and analysis of South African movements: www.nu.ac.za/ccs/

---

suspended, it would mean the revocation of Mexico's recognition of the treaty. This seems like a small price to pay – in only nine years of existence, NAFTA has resulted in the loss of over 24.7 million acres of cultivated land, pushing at least 15 million peasants off the land and into urban centres or into clandestinity in the US, according to a study by UNAM. Protests continue into the next year.

\\ 2003 //

>> January 1 >> Thirty-thousand Zapatistas from across Chiapas converge on San Cristóbal de las Casas, for the anniversary of the 1994 uprising. Each carries a machete, a bag of fire wood, and a festive but determined sense of dignity. The evening is marked by fire-lit speeches from the Zapatista commanders. They are punctuated by the clanking of machetes and impassioned chants of: "The three powers of the Mexican government are racist", "Long live the rebellion in Argentina", and "PAN is the same as the PRI". Then the cold of the mountain night dissipates as each adds their wood to the blazing bonfires. As flames leap 30 feet in the air, a sea of machetes held aloft in thousands of small hands reflects and magnifies the message and the warning of the Zapatistas.

>> To be continued everywhere ... >>

Walking we ask questions

"Utopia is on the horizon: when I walk two steps, it takes two steps back … I walk ten steps, and it is ten steps further away. What is utopia for? It is for this, for walking."
– Eduardo Galeano

The anticapitalist movement has played the role of the child in the crowd as the parade of the powerful wheels by. While the pundits applauded and marketeers cheered, we yelled that the Empire had no clothes. Its cloaks of finery were woven from financial fictions. Its promise of universal salvation through neoliberalism was a global imperial project of resource-grabbing and domination. Its 'humanitarian interventions' left a trail of dead human beings in its wake. We always knew the cheerleading of their brutal global project would eventually stop.

Today, capitalism is being unmasked to the global crowd. The last decade has seen the increasing delegitimization of the neoliberal model as a movement of movements has sprung up on every continent, from Chiapas to Genoa, Seattle to Porto Alegre, Bangalore to Soweto.

Like this book, the movement is a web of interconnected strands, of recurring themes and discernable patterns. Autonomy. Participation. Democracy. Diversity. The reinvention of power. The importance of creativity and subjectivity. Real and basic needs rather than ideology as the basis of political action. Access to the 'commons' – whether water, public space, software, seeds, or the manufacture of medicines. And constant questioning and innovation, especially when the movement is most self-satisfied or most despairing.

For movement implies motion, journeying, change. The first stage of the movement that this book documents, from the Zapatista uprising in 1994 to 2001, has been extraordinarily successful in delegitimizing the institutions of global capitalism. But as we move forward in a changing world, we are evolving, transforming once more, innovating tactics. The question now on our lips in the second stage of this movement is: "How do we build on our success and take the movements to another level?" There are many answers. In the words of the Spanish poet Antonio Machado:

"Wanderer, your footsteps are the road, and nothing more;
wanderer, there is no road, the road is made by walking."

When a movement stops asking questions, of itself, of the world, it becomes orthodoxy – an idea that has run out of ideas. It becomes fixed, static, brittle, rather than fluid. Water can resist the most savage of blows, ice shatters. It is only armed with our questions that we can change history.

Nicolas Pousthomis/Argentina IMC

Charting the journey

"This is how the true men and women learned that questions are for walking, not just for sitting around and doing nothing. And since then, when true men and women want to walk, they ask questions. When they want to arrive they take leave. And when they want to leave, they say hello. They are never still."

– Old Antonio in 'Story of Questions', by Subcomandante Marcos

In making this journey into tomorrow, it is important to understand yesterday, to try and trace possible futures in the contours of the present. Mahatma Gandhi offers us some signposts for our journey in his summary of the Indian independence struggle: "First they ignore you. Then they laugh at you. Then they fight you. Then you win." We can follow the path of the anticapitalist movement using these signposts from 1994 to the present.

First they ignore you: Between 1994 and 1999 we were largely invisible. As far as the powerful were concerned, there was no opposition to capitalism, no alternative to the 'free' market. As Thomas Friedman, the ultimate proselytizer of globalization, wrote in his book *The Lexus and the Olive Tree: Understanding Globalization*, "There is no more chocolate chip, there is no more strawberry swirl, no more lemon-lime, there is only plain vanilla and North Korea." Vanilla, you understand, being corporate capitalism, the pinnacle of human evolution. Moreover, he argued, "Not only is all we've got plain vanilla, but everyone is basically happy about it." Something had to give.

Then they laugh at you: 1999 was the summer of corporate love, when the dot-com bubble was at its height and business forecasters, with stunning hubris, were predicting that from here on the stock market would simply continue to go up – forever. Not coincidentally, this was the summer the anticapitalist movement emerged as a global event, when an earthy, rambunctious carnival against capital interrupted trading in the City of London. The contagion spread with the Seattle WTO shutdown later that year. We were raucous, outrageous, riotous, wearing silly costumes, and impossible to ignore. So they laughed at us. "A Noah's ark of flat-earth advocates, protectionist trade unions, and yuppies looking for their 1960s fix," jibed Thomas Friedman, furious that his vanilla ice cream theory of history had been disproved. *The Wall Street Journal* jeered at the, "Global village idiots ... bringing their bibs and bottles."

By the time of the World Bank protests in Prague in September 2000, the laughing was sounding forced. *The Economist*'s editorial was shrill, making its "case for globalization" with the picture of a poor African child – purportedly a future beneficiary of globalization – on its front cover. They were sounding less sure of themselves as they insisted that economic globalization is the "best of many possible futures for the world economy".

Then they fight you: The confrontations got worse. In Gothenberg in the summer of 2001 police shot live ammunition at two protesters, who survived. It was clear that escalating summit protests would end in death. Months later, Genoa saw the most brutal suppression of the movement in the global North to date, when they shot Carlo Giuliani dead and beat 97 sleeping activists in their sleeping bags. At least 18 other live rounds were fired at activists that day.

At every summit the stakes got higher – they were learning about us and working out how to contain us, while we had ceased to evolve our tactics of spectacular summit blockades. Carnivals against capital are wonderful at delegitimizing global capital – but in Genoa they declared war against us. They would shoot us rather than ever let us get into the 'red zone'. In any case, we had to stop and ask what would we do if we ever did get there? Preventing the G8 from meeting would never, alone, create the world we wanted. After Genoa, our direct action summit blockade tactics, which just two years before had shut down Seattle, could never happen again in the same way. The next step if we followed that path – really a cul de sac – which they want us to take was to declare all out war in a military battle we could never win. But as the blood dried on the cobblestones and white walls of the raided Diaz school, we realized that the struggle needed, once again, to be on our terms, not theirs. We needed to reflect, study the lessons of the movements so far, and evolve.

Genoa was the largest protest of its kind thus far. By this time, the movement was being taken enormously seriously, from corporate boardrooms to international police conferences to the columns of the business press.

Six weeks after the Genoa protests, the first of a five-part series of full page articles appeared in the UK edition of the *Financial Times* under the title 'Capitalism Under Siege: Globalization's children strike back'. It claimed: "Just over a decade after the fall of the Berlin Wall ... there is a growing sense that global capitalism is once again fighting to win the argument." Hours after the paper hit the newsstands, Islamist terrorists attacked New York and Washington. Suddenly, hope was replaced by despair and fear. The politics of transformation we had been revelling in were suddenly forced to become defensive rear guard actions – defence of human and civil rights, against war, against nationalism. Italian Prime Minister Berlusconi was not alone in his opportunism when he noted the "strange unanimity" between the movement and Islamic terrorists, who were both "enemies of Western civilization". US Trade Representative Robert Zoellick, gunning for a new trade round at the WTO that November, was utterly cynical in his use of the dead from the Twin Towers, saying, "On 11 September, America, its open society, and its ideas came under attack by a malevolence that craves our panic, retreat, and abdication of global leadership... This President and this administration will fight for open markets. We will not be intimidated by those who have taken to the streets to blame trade – and America – for the world's ills." We were not just described as terrorists. Pundits who were five years late in noticing our emergence were now eager to be the first to proclaim us dead. The editor of *The Guardian* wrote, "Since September 11, there is no appetite for anticapitalism, no interest, and the issues that were all-consuming a few months ago seem irrelevant now." The *FT* series was pulled.

Bush's declaration of a 'war on terror', a crackdown on domestic dissent, a new era of pre-emptive strikes, and a war without end forced a reappraisal among many activists. It has challenged us all to take a deep breath, put our rhetoric into practice, and think strategically, and fast. Not only have these been dangerous times for dissidents, but the nature of the power we face has been transforming rapidly.

For movements in the global South, however, there was far less disjunction. For them – for the MST, for the Zapatistas, for the Colombian *campesinos* – this has always been a war. Spectacular street protests and global days of action were nothing but an opportunity to link their daily struggles – to be fed, to survive, to be paid, to grow food, to be healthy – to a growing global movement. "For us, every day is a day of action," a Bolivian trade unionist said.

And so rumours of the movement's death were greatly exaggerated. Even in New York City itself, a few months after 11 September, 20,000 protested against the World Economic Forum in the most difficult political landscape. Believing no-one would dare to protest their "act of solidarity", the WEF met in New York City in

"IF YOU HAVE BUILT CASTLES IN THE AIR, YOUR WORK NEED NOT BE LOST; THAT IS WHERE THEY SHOULD BE. NOW PUT THE FOUNDATION UNDER THEM." – **Henry David Thoreau**

January 2002 - the first time it had left its mountaintop resort in Davos, Switzerland for 30 years. Simultaneously in Porto Alegre, Brazil, over 60,000 – six times more than the previous year – met for the World Social Forum under the optimistic slogan, "Another world is possible". The protests were still growing exponentially. That March in Barcelona, half a million people taking part in protests against the European Union summit showed they understood the new reality they faced after Genoa: "It wasn't about laying siege to the summit", organizers said of this action, "but about breaking the siege of our city," (referring to the siege created by the summiteers and their police). The protesters in Barcelona also refused the declaration of war, as the anarchist trade union CGT explained: "We have to regain the furiously festive and subversive nature of our activities, breaking military frameworks (the summit-blockade-clash with police) the powers want to confine us to." By November, with the threat of war on Iraq looming, two million took to the streets of Florence to join the closing march of the European Social Forum.

What Genoa and 11 September marked, in fact, was the

end of the first, emergent stage of the movement that had erupted in 1994. It showed up some of the limitations of a momentum – and event-based politics that concentrated primarily on interrupting and delegitmizing economic institutions. And so, against the spectacle, we turned our attention to the politics of necessity. We switched our main focus away from the rapid explosions of the days of action for slow-burning, gradually built, but enormous fires. From the ground up, we were building something new – and on our own terms. The movement had grown up. It was digging in for the long haul, the next stage of struggle – the fight, and as Gandhi predicted, the winning.

"The protesters are winning. They are winning on the streets. Before too long they will be winning the arguments. Globalization is fast becoming a cause without credible arguments." – ***Financial Times*, 17 August 2001**

Then you win: Perhaps the biggest challenge the global movements face now is to realize that the first round is over, and that the slogan first sprayed on a building in Seattle and last seen on a burning police van in Genoa, "We Are Winning", is coming true. What we need to do now is decide what winning actually means for us – disintegrating capitalism, or creating the world we want? They are not the same thing. Meanwhile, Western capitalism's "crisis of legitimacy" in the various ways it wields power – from economic policy to military might – expands exponentially every day.

There has been a "nearly complete collapse of the prevailing economic theory", according to economist James K Galbraith. Corporations and even whole countries that had been capitalism's poster boys throughout the 1990s have gone bankrupt. Chaos reigned – not just in Argentina but in capitalism's heartlands, the corridors of Enron, WorldCom, and many other powerful corporations. We are now in the most severe corporate crisis since the 1930s. "System Failure!" screams the front cover of capitalism's in-house magazine *Fortune* – a sentiment that, during the late 1990s, you would find only in hip counter-cultural periodicals like *Adbusters*. Nowhere is that failure more clear than in Latin America, which contains the largest of the ever-spreading cracks in the edifice of neoliberalism, and the continent burns with an en masse rejection of globalization, as from Argentina to Uruguay schoolchildren eat grass to stave off hunger pangs. After Seattle, *Fortune* wrote the prophetic words: "If we are not careful, the 'Washington Consensus' [the economic ideology of globalization] will be a consensus of one." The fire is building elsewhere, too, and almost entirely unreported. Asian labour activist Trini Leung reports that as China embraces a market economy: "Unrest has been growing among the retrenched workers and displaced farmers in the past decade. At least hundreds of protest actions such as sit-ins, street demonstrations, and road-blocks take place daily across the country. At times violent protests such as physical assaults and bomb attacks have also been assumed by angry and desperate protesters. This looks set to worsen as long as their livelihood and displacement do not get better but worse."

More and more, as the corporate consensus unravels, what you might call 'soft power' targets of the movement, such as corporate gatherings and trade rules, are overshadowed by 'hard power' – war, fascism, militarism. Of course, the velvet glove of 'soft power' has always had the iron fist of 'hard power' behind it. To quote Thomas Friedman again: "The hidden hand of the market will never work without a hidden fist. McDonald's cannot flourish without McDonnell Douglas ... And the hidden fist that keeps the world safe for Silicon Valley's technologies to flourish is called the US Army, Air Force, Navy, and Marine Corps." It is important not to simply move on from soft power institutions as the focus for dissent, nor to forget that it is global capitalism and not just the US military that we are opposing. However, our strategies must reflect the new reality.

The largest global day of action that the world has ever seen happened on 15 February 2003, a month before the US and UK led a renewed invasion of Iraq. Twenty million people took part. Effective resistance to the new imperialism is only possible through global networks of resistance, and it is the forms, links, and networks of the anticapitalist movement as a global political project that have made this level of mobilization and popular education possible. As the *New York Times* noted: "The huge anti-war demonstrations around the world this weekend are reminders that there may still be two superpowers on the planet: the United States and international public opinion."

Back in 1994 the Zapatistas told us they were fighting the Fourth World War (the Third was the Cold War). Ten years later, the people of the world have realized that we are all in that battle together.

Centres and margins

"Life will not be a pyramid with the apex sustained by the bottom. But it will be an oceanic circle whose centre will be the individual always ready to perish for the village, the latter ready to perish for the circle of villages, until at last the whole becomes one life composed of individuals... the outermost circumference will not wield power to crush the inner circle but will give strength to all within and derive its strength from it."
– *The Essential Writings of Mahatma Gandhi*, ed Raghavan Iyer, Oxford University Press, 1990

The second stage of the movement will be harder than the first. It's a stage of working closer to home, a stage where mass action on the streets is balanced (but not entirely replaced) with creating alternatives to capitalism in our neighbourhoods, our towns and cities. A politics which moves between construction and conflict, based on longer-term visions, where we seek to construct alternatives that will sustain us into the future – and yet remembers that any true alternatives to capital will throw us into conflict with the system and that we need to strategize continually to defend ourselves against it.

Yet returning to our neighbourhoods, we must not fetishize the local, retreat into subcultural ghettos, nor forget that we are the world's first grassroots-led global political project. We must not undo the global ties that bind us together in a world-wide network. These powers cannot be fought alone, or by single factions. They will pick us off one by one if we attempt to do so. And our resistance still needs to be as transnational as capital, as financial speculation, as climate change, as debt, as corporate power.

Maintaining the movement as a global phenomenon is also crucial for another reason. The nationalism inherent in a purely localized response to globalization has a dangerous appeal for the world's population. In a recent survey of university students in India, Hitler came third after Gandhi and their current Hindu nationalist Prime Minister Vajpayee as the greatest leader in history. Many in the Middle East, Africa, and Asia are turning to authoritarian Islamism as the only hope for a true opposition. In this context, the newly formed Anti-Globalization Egyptian Group, a rare example of this kind of movement in the Middle East, offers a hopeful alternative. Egyptian Marxist development economist Samir Amin points out that their sophisticated analysis of the real nature of domination in the region is a cause for hope, and internationalist networks that include these kinds of groups must be part of the movement's future.

But being global does not necessarily mean being centralized: the international Indymedia network should teach us that. And though many groups and political parties at the World Social Forum (WSF), for example, believe that it is they who are at the 'centre' of things, directing the movement, they are mistaken. It is in the WSF's corridors, the gym halls, the plastic-sheeted MST encampment under the overpass, where social movements and the marginalized from five continents meet, where the real revolution is being forged.

As one statement to come out of the WSF workshop, 'The Labour of the Multitude' put it: "It was not in the centre of Porto Alegre that we and others were mostly interested ... Social movements always just use – joyfully or cynically, in a healthy or genial way – the paraphernalia created by the 'centres' and their self-satisfied navels." We desperately need a space to strategize as a global movement. Not a world parliament, but a world network. When the marginalized combine, the world shifts a little on its axis. And, as the Multitude text points out: "Sooner or later our course will have to be towards the 'centre'; we will have to cross it as the Argentinean demonstrators do by banging on their pots or forming pickets while marching from their neighbourhoods to their meeting points. The work of the multitude – our work – is to bridge the gaps between peripheries so that they can make the 'centre' explode ... It is better, anyway, that the 'centre' does not realize any of this. It might become afraid. We won't tell it till the last moment."

Of movement and stillness

How can we discover the paths we should take? How will we know they are the right ones? For is there any revolution in history that has not taken a wrong turn eventually, ending in bloodshed and betrayal – ultimately, in failure?

The anticapitalist movement is the most sustained recent attempt to reinvent the notion of revolution into a constantly evolving process rather than the triumph of an ideology. One thing we have tried to learn from history is that the means we choose determine the ends. Too many times we have seen power-seekers gradually compromise every principle they hold until by the time they succeed in gaining power, they must be resisted because they have betrayed everything they stood for. We are not creating a new ideology to impose from above, to 'replace' capitalism, but evolving a new, radically participatory methodology from below. Rather than seeking a map to tomorrow, we are developing our own journeys, individually and collectively, as we travel.

As the activist Starhawk asks, "Can we think like no other social movement has ever thought?" Can we act as no other rebellion has ever acted? Can we create a politics that isn't left up to specialists, a politics that is not just relevant to but part of everyday life, a politics that doesn't look or feel like politics?

To that paradox, let us add a few more to describe this movement that is many movements. This ancient struggle that is new. This movement that is left-wing but has rejected the traces of the leftist state-authoritarianism of the twentieth-century. This movement that masks itself in order to be seen. This movement that dreams of other possible worlds here on earth, but has only hunches, not certainties about the way to get to them. This movement with no name. This movement, the most globalized in history, which was labelled "antiglobalization". This movement which has no leaders, but whose leaders lead by obeying. This movement in which farmers from competing economies, North and South, stand together. This movement that shows the limits of an economic accounting – not with recalculated sums but with carnival – in order to reveal those things that do not show up as losses on the balance sheet: nature, people, culture, and lost souls.

Ancient Greek philosophers used paradoxical, indeterminate, and self-contradictory statements to which there was no resolution, known as *aporia*, in order to evoke a questioning spirit, awe, and speculation in their students, rather than put them to sleep with ready-made answers. It forces the thinker to take responsibility for themselves. Aporia creates wonder and amazement before the confusing puzzles and paradoxes of our lives and of the universe. The origin of the word means to lack a *poros* – a path, a passage, a way.

Is this what the Zapatistas mean when they say, "Walking, we ask questions"? Do we have the courage to move – sometimes stumbling, sometimes running – towards an unknowable destination? Would you be willing to suspend your disbelief if we told you we had all the answers? And if we did and you followed them, how would that help you, in the long run?

The idea of a revolutionary movement that genuinely listens is itself a paradox. Revolutionaries normally shout, they chant, they try to make their screams heard above the roar of a system that bulldozes their means of living, their desires. Yet the idea of listening is central to many in these movements. When a vanguardist Maoist urban guerilla-intellectual first went to Chiapas and spoke to the indigenous in an attempt to revolutionize them, they didn't understand him. Eventually he overcame the arrogance of the revolutionary and he learned to listen. People now call him Subcomandante Marcos. Out of this experience was born *Zapatismo*, a form of rebellion that leads by obeying. This idea of a listening rebellion turns preconceived notions of struggle on their head. *Zapatismo* throws political certainty to the wind, and out of the shape shifting, flowing mist, it grasps change; change not as banal revolutionary slogan, but as actual process. Change as the ability of revolutionaries to admit wrong, to stop and question everything. Change as the desire to dissolve the vertical structures of power and replace them with radical horizontality: real popular participation. Change as the willingness to listen, the wisdom to grow, the commitment to transform.

Getting lost 'without a path' might even be an important part of that process. Making mistakes, having profound doubt, perhaps for sustained periods – this is part of learning to walk. Learning also means understanding why we fail. This isn't a personal crime or flaw – often it is a legacy of history. Learning true democracy is not something you arrive at, and then sit still, clutching it tightly. It falters, starts up again, requires constant rejuvenation and experimentation. It is a series of skills that require practice, self-knowledge, self-confidence, self-awareness. Walking, and asking questions.

A movement that stops asking questions will become more ruthless, possibly more 'effective' in the short term, but ultimately, repressive, doctrinaire, unable to respond to new threats or opportunities. We begin, in short, to resemble what we oppose. We ossify, and are toppled by those who innovate while we stagnate and pontificate. We refuse this fate which has befallen so many radical movements. We commit ourselves to move on and reconstitute rather than let that happen.

Rebels or revolutionaries

"Each generation must, out of relative obscurity, discover its mission, fulfil it, or betray it."
– Frantz Fanon, *The Wretched of the Earth*, 1966

"I cannot give you the answer you are clamouring for. Go home and think! I cannot decree your pet, text-book revolution. I want instead to excite general enlightenment by forcing all the people to examine the condition of their lives … I don't want to foreclose it with a catchy, half-baked orthodoxy. My critics say: There is no time for your beautiful educational

programme; the masses are ready and will be enlightened in the course of the struggle. And they quote Fanon on the sin of betraying the revolution. They do not realize that revolutions are betrayed just as much by stupidity, incompetence, impatience, and precipitate action as by doing nothing at all."
– Chinua Achebe, *Anthills of the Savannah*, 1987

Why do revolutions fail? Let us ask history. The uprisings of the 1960s and 1970s – huge in scale and international in scope – are a reference point for many radicals today. Yet while those movements transformed the world – the social progress on race, gender, imperialism for example was extraordinary – eventually they were broken, co-opted and conquered. How did this happen? How can we avoid making the same mistakes again?

Mike Albert of Z-Net says: "The fact that my generation hasn't shared with yours the lessons we learned out of the failures and successes of the 1960s and 1970s is a sin of humanity." He observed that activists in the US in the 1960s were like "front runners in a marathon where the mass of people were following along some way behind. In fact, those people would have been better off running in amidst that crowd, not way out in front."

PR Watch, a radical investigative group in the US, uncovered the advice of Ronald Duchin, of US public relations intelligence gathering firm Mongoven, Biscoe and Duchin, on how to break anti-corporate groups: isolate the extremists, and through dialogue, co-opt the idealists so that they become 'realists'. In other words, divide and conquer. In the 1970s, some of those radicals who were "running way out in front" of the crowd turned to guerrilla tactics. This allowed the authorities to use incredible force to crack down on the movements, whilst persuading many who were only spectators that they would never join the running crowd.

"FUZZY BORDERS FAVOUR THE DISENFRANCHIZED. IF THE ZAPATISTAS HAD TRIED TO HOLD THEIR LINES AND FIGHT, THEY WOULD HAVE BEEN DEFEATED LONG AGO. THEIR ADVANTAGE LIES IN FLUIDITY AND LACK OF DEFINITION. THE ZAPATISTA WOMEN I SPOKE WITH ALSO DEMONSTRATED A LACK OF BORDERS WITHIN THEIR INDIVIDUAL LIVES... FOR THEM, THE PERSONAL IS POLITICAL, THOUGH IT WOULD NEVER OCCUR TO THEM TO SAY SO. THEIR CONVERSATION REVEALS A PERSPECTIVE THAT DOES NOT DIVIDE AND NEVER HAS DIVIDED THEIR LIVES INTO DISTINCT SPHERES." **– Ellen Calmus, "We Are All Ramona: Artists, Revolutionaries, and Zapatistas with Petticoat"**

Quite apart from the moral arguments, why hand the authorities just what they need to destroy us? This would be a suicidal tactic for a movement that has so far managed to base itself on breaking down dualisms. It would push us towards the "with us or against us" dualisms of Bush's 'war on terror'. In any case, how can you use weapons to defeat powers with the mightiest weapons in the world? We require a far more strategic, jujitsu style to prevail.

George Lakey, a direct action peace trainer working with Indonesian students in 2001 who were fighting an oppressive government and powerful military, explains how reasons for them to use violence were everywhere. He says: "One young man's eyes filled with tears as he described to me what it was like to watch comrades die on the street where they'd been shot by soldiers during a demonstration. 'I want payback,' he admitted softly." Without denying the legitimate feelings of anger, the trainers asked the group: how will violence affect the array of political actors in Indonesia and bring some of them to your support?

Lakey says: "The participants plunged into vigorous dialogue, fingers poking at the graphic display of potential allies. A sudden silence came to the group when one person, forefinger stabbing the air, exclaimed, 'And that's why the government pays provocateurs to come among us to get the violence going!'"

The point of this story is to show how important strategic thinking is, rather than to try and say that violence is never justified as a tactic. We need to analyze the enemies we face, what would benefit them and what would undermine them. We should never underestimate the power of a broad social base of popular support. We need to be able to use self-defence when required, but not descend into pitched battles we can't win, that alienate others, and help to break us. We need constant cross-generational and cross-cultural strategic learning.

Like the Indonesian students, we need to redefine what we need to do, not just to fight, but to prevail. Are we content to remain rebels, outside of society – or are we revolutionaries who wish to transform it? Are there nurses in the movement? Are there schoolkids? Are there grandmothers? What does it mean if our movement doesn't look like our society? What kind of a world are we building if we don't involve everyone in its construction?

Everywhere and nowhere

"Keep walking, though there's no place to get to.
Don't try to see through the distances.
That's not for human beings. Move within,
But don't move the way fear makes you move."
– Rumi, thirteenth-century Sufi poet

"When we lose our fear, we lose our feelings," says Gaby, a young Argentinean activist when asked how it feels to be a radical in a country in which 30,000 left-wing activists were 'disappeared' by the military dictatorship in the late 1970s. Often in the process of struggling for the things we want, we sacrifice our humanity. Struggle can require us to become soldiers. Eventually, like soldiers, we become unable to feel. Facing oppression, beatings, torture, seeing our friends imprisoned or even killed, our hearts harden. We become better fighters, but worse human beings. We may become more determined, angry revolutionaries, but we also make it more likely that our revolution will be imposed upon, and in turn oppress, others.

Seeking to understand how the oppressed become oppressors – the most common dynamic in all revolutionary history – is vital. We need to explore not just what we say in public, but the intimate spaces of revolution, to work out not just how we stay alive, but stay human. It is extraordinarily difficult to withstand that fear, and their violence, while continuing to innovate as a movement. Asking questions of received movement wisdom at these moments of fear and insecurity requires enormous courage, can get you labelled a traitor, a reformist, or a sell-out – and yet is vital.

Those who have experienced conflict and war, including the economic war of extreme poverty, can carry a depth of rage, resistance and humiliation inside them that can fuel the strength of revolutionary movement but fatally weaken it by actually preventing the activist from being able to listen, being able to communicate to those outside the movement, subverting its democracy and efficacy.

'Give up Activism' was the title of an influential article written after J18 in London. It asked some important questions: "The role of the activist is threatened by change ... If everyone is becoming revolutionary then you're not so special anymore, are you?" And: "It is not enough merely to seek to link together all the activists in the world, neither is it enough to seek to transform more people into activists." What is needed is not for more people to become activists, but for the everyday fabric of society to become engaged. That involves risking our own identity as a movement, and our own sense of our place in the world. It's only through letting go of our precious identities, letting go of our egos and our subcultures, that we can remove the limits we place upon own achievements and move into the kind of pluralist politics that we need now more than ever.

"WE CAN CONTINUE ON THE RIGHT PATH, IF WE, THE YOU, WHO ARE US, WALK TOGETHER"

– opening remarks by the EZLN to first International Encuentro for Humanity and against Neoliberalism, Chiapas, July 1996

As Jeremy Gilbert, a British academic and activist, wrote in an email to us during the production of this book: "We are everywhere? We're not, you know – but we could be. And if we're going to be, then we have to acknowledge what a scary thought that really is: for once 'we' are everywhere then there will be nothing to define ourselves against, and so 'we' will be nowhere. If we really want to make the world a better place then that's what we have to want. But learning to want it will take courage, the courage to accept the risk to our identities which real change always poses."

So let's have the courage, let's have the heart that lies in the root of the word courage, *le coeur* – the heart to build a rebellion that embraces, the heart to insist on an insurrection that listens, the heart to create a revolution that when it looks in the mirror understands that its not just about rage, but that it begins with the word 'lover'. Let's have the courage to demand nothing for us, but everything for everyone, the courage to keep the spaces that this movement of movements has created, radically open, rebelliously inviting, and profoundly popular....

For when 'we' are truly everywhere, we will be nowhere – for we will be everyone.

Notes from Nowhere

"Another world is not only possible, she is on her way. On a quiet day, I can hear her breathing."

– Arundhati Roy, World Social Forum, 2003

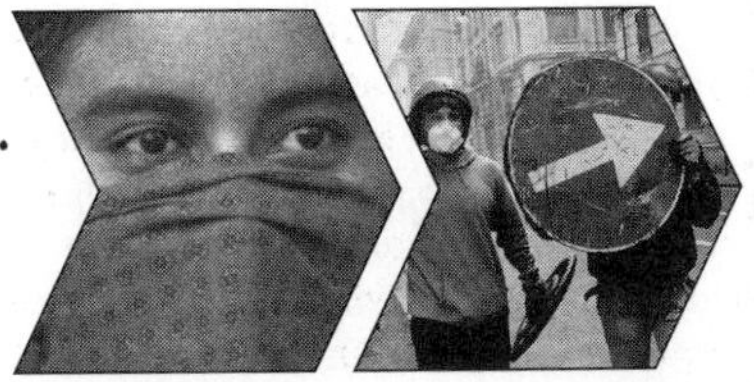

About Notes from Nowhere

"*But nowhere does exist. It's everywhere people dream of leaving capitalism behind.*" – **from *Dancing on the Edge of Chaos***

"*Men fight and lose the battle, and the thing that they fought for comes about in spite of their defeat, and then it turns out not to be what they meant, and other men have to fight for what they meant under another name.*"
– **William Morris, *News from Nowhere*, 1890**

The word *utopia* means nowhere, but also a happy or fortunate place. Our editorial collective, Notes from Nowhere, converged over a period of two and a half years to work on this project; now that it is over we will disappear once again like an affinity group melting into a crowd. We are activists, editors, writers, teachers, and artists. All of us have deep connections to the movement for freedom, autonomy, life, dignity, and democracy. Some of us were involved in the shut-down of the WTO in Seattle, others have worked in movements of the global South, or were involved in London Reclaim the Streets; some are deeply rooted in their local struggles, others are nomadic organizers; some spend time teaching, others writing; some work with Indymedia, several are raising children, and somehow we manage to juggle all of these things. Living in different countries, on different continents, we remain connected by our irresistible optimism and our insatiable desire to turn the world upside down.

Notes From Nowhere is:

Katharine Ainger, a writer, activist and co-editor of the *New Internationalist* magazine. She believes that releasing all the untold stories in the world might transform it. Half British and half Indian, she grew up between Asia and Europe, and over the years has periodically returned to work with and learn from Asian social movements. She has written for all sorts of outlets from serious broadsheets, to disreputable radical publications. She currently lives on an island in the middle of the Thames.

Graeme Chesters, a writer and educator based at Edge Hill College in the northwest of England. He is a co-founder of the Shifting Ground co-operative and is involved in a number of activist and academic networks, some of which curiously and sometimes fruitfully overlap. Presently researching and writing on issues as diverse as global complexity, civil society, and participatory democracy, his biggest challenge is figuring out how to juggle parenthood with paid employment and still remain on the streets. He continues to derive inspiration from the everyday acts of solidarity and defiance that sometimes go unnoticed amidst the more spectacular moments of contention, although he enjoys participating in either. He lives on the edge of the Lake District with Gwyneth and their two children Dylan and Joel.

Tony Credland, a London-based activist and designer involved with Reclaim the Streets, Indymedia, and the Cactus Network.

John Jordan, who spends his time trying to find a space where the imagination of art and the social engagement of politics can be brought together. For 10 years he was a co-director of Platform, an art and social science group, and also worked on a social art project about men and pornography. Since 1994 he has worked in the direct action movements, principally with Reclaim the Streets (1995-2001). He has written and lectured extensively about the anticapitalist movement and was a senior lecturer in fine art at Sheffield Hallam University (1994-2003). He lives in London and mixes his time between trying to creatively overthrow capitalism and looking after his son Jack. He has recently fallen in love with the popular rebellion in Argentina and is involved in numerous projects to spread news and inspiration of the events unfolding there.

Andrew Stern, an activist and documentary photographer who has been involved in the anticapitalist movement in various capacities since a friend dragged him off to his first anarchist gathering some years ago. He can be found working on various photography projects in different parts of the world, including helping to organize a caravan of Indymedia activists to travel throughout South America soon after the economic collapse and popular uprising in Argentina. He is equally comfortable on the front lines of actions with camera in hand or not, and many times will leave his camera at home to play with creative forms of direct action in the streets. Like other members of the collective, the fusion of art and politics is a primary goal in anything he does, along with collecting and sharing stories that are not normally told. His work has been shown in galleries throughout the world and can be found on various Indymedia web sites as well as in the many different publications he works with.

Jennifer Whitney, who is currently engaged in several balancing acts – reconciling her desire to bring thousands of people together in the streets for inspiring mass actions with her commitment to longer-term struggles of the local and everyday variety; merging her creativity and imagination through writing, dance, and music with her more technical and less sexy skills; and fulfilling her passion for travel, languages, cross-cultural skill-sharing and adventure, as well as her love of gardening, community-building, and other things requiring deep roots. She is a health care worker, and organizes clinics and street medic teams for direct actions. When she's at home in the Pacific Northwest, she can be found working with the Black Cross Health Collective in Portland, or drumming with the Infernal Noise Brigade. She derives much inspiration from Latin America, where rebellion has penetrated many corners of society and erupts into the streets with increasing frequency, and she hopes to continue disseminating those stories of people shaping history.

Bibliography

This is not a complete bibliography but simply a selection of well-thumbed favourites that litter our bookshelves and have fuelled our lives and actions. See resources at the end of each section for web links and other books.

Emergence

- **Rebels Against the Future: the Luddites and their war on the industrial revolution-lessons for the computer age** by Kirkpatrick Sale (1996) Quartet Books.
- **No Logo: taking aim at the brand bullies** by Naomi Klein (2000) Flamingo.
- **The Battle of Seattle: the new challenge to capitalist globalization** ed. George Katsiaficas, Eddie Yuen, and Daniel Burton-Rose (2002) Soft Skull Press.
- **First World, Ha, Ha, Ha! the Zapatista challenge** ed. Elaine Katzenberger (1995) City Lights.
- **The Case Against the Global Economy: and for a turn toward the local** ed. by Jerry Mander & Edward Goldsmith (1996) Sierra Club.
- **Globalization from Below: the power of solidarity** by Jeremy Brecher, Tim Costello, and Brendan Smith (2002) South End Press.
- **Year 501: the conquest continues** by Noam Chomsky (1993) South End Press. (Available online at: www.zmag.org/chomsky/year/year-contents.html)
- **Blue Gold: the battle against corporate theft of the world's water** by Maude Barlow and Tony Clarke (2002) Earthscan.
- **Biopiracy: the plunder of nature and knowledge** by Vandana Shiva (1998) Green Books.

Networks

- **Linked: the new science of networks** by Alberto-László Barabási (2002) Perseus.
- **Small World: uncovering nature's hidden networks** by Mark Buchanan (2002) Weidenfeld and Nicolson.
- **The Hidden Connections: a science for sustainable living** by Fritjof Capra (2002) Harper Collins.
- **'The Rise of the Network Society'**, Volume 1 of **The Information Age: economy, society and culture** by Manuel Castells (1996) Blackwell.
- **Steps to an Ecology of Mind** by Gregory Bateson (1973) Paladin Press.
- **Emergence: the connected lives of ants, brains, cities, and software** by Steven Johnson (2002) Penguin Books.
- **The Murray Bookchin Reader** ed. Janet Biehl (1997) Cassell.
- **Networks and Netwars: the future of terror, crime, and militancy** by John Arquilla and David Ronfeldt (2001) RAND. (Available online at www.rand.org)
- **Anarchism and Ecology** by Graham Purchase (1997) Black Rose Books.
- **Schnews Annual: stories that shook the world** (2002). Justice Contact: www.schnews.org.uk
- **Squall Annual: the best of independent media.** Contact: www.squall.org.uk

Autonomy

- **European Autonomous Social Movements and the Decolonization of Everyday Life** by George Katsiaficas (1997) Humanities Press International.
- **The Algebra of Infinite Justice** by Arundhati Roy (2002) Flamingo.
- **Stolen Harvest: the hijacking of the global food supply** by Vandana Shiva (1999) South End Press.
- **Basta! Land and the Zapatista Rebellion in Chiapas** by George Collier, with Elizabeth Lowery Quaratiello (1999) Food First Books.
- **The Temporary Autonomous Zone: ontological anarchy, poetic terrorism** by Hakim Bey (1991) Semiotext(e). (Available online www.hermetic.com/bey/index.html)
- **One Market Under God: extreme capitalism, market populism, and the end of economic democracy** by Thomas Frank (2002) Vintage.

Carnival

- **Rabelais and His World** by Mikhail Bakhtin (1984) Indiana University Press.

A Carnival of Revolution: Central Europe 1989 by Padraic Kenney (2002) Princeton University Press.

- **Upside Down: a primer for the looking-glass world** by Eduardo Galeano (2001) Picador.
- **Lipstick Traces: a brief history of the twentieth century** by Greil Marcus (1989) Picador.
- **The Revolution of Everyday Life** by Raoul Vaneigem (1994) Rebel Press/Left Bank Books. (Available online: http://library.nothingness.org/articles/SI/

- **Drunken Boat: art, rebellion, anarchy** ed. Max Blechman (1994) Autonomedia/Left Bank Books.
- **The Cultural Resistance Reader** ed. Stephen Duncombe (2002) Verso.
- **The Best of Abbie Hoffman** ed. Daniel Simon and Norman Mailer (1989) Four Walls Eight Windows.
- **The Most Radical Gesture: the Situationist International in a postmodern age** by Sadie Plant (1992) Routledge.
- **Pranks!** edited Andrea Juno and V. spaceVale (1987) Re/Search Publications.
- **Commodify your Dissent: the business of culture in the new gilded age** ed. Thomas Frank and Matt Weiland (1997) Norton and Co.
- **The Action-Image of Society: on cultural politicization** by Alfred Willener (1970) Tavistock.

Clandestinity

- **The Silencing of Political Dissent: how post-September 11 anti-terrorism measures threaten our civil liberties** by Nancy Chang (2002) Seven Stories Press.
- **Power and Terror: post 9-11 talks and interviews** by Noam Chomsky (2003) Seven Stories Press.
- **Open Veins of Latin America: five centuries of the pillage of a continent** by Eduardo Galeano, (2000) Monthly Review Press.
- **Bitter Fruit: the untold story of the American coup in Guatemala** by Stephen C. Schlesinger and Stephen Kinzer (1990) Random House.
- **On Fire: the battle of Genoa and the anticapitalist movement** ed. One Off Press (2001) One Off Press.
- **Resist: A grassroots collection of stories, poetry, photos and analyses from Québec City FTAA protests and beyond** ed. Jen Chang et al. (2001) Fernwood Publishing.
- **Desire for Change: women on the front line of global restistance** by PGA Women (2002) LARC press. Email pgabolivia@yahoo.co.uk
- **War At Home: covert action against US activists and what we can do about it** by Brian Glick (1989) South End Press.

Power

- **Society of the Spectacle** by Guy Debord (1970) Black and Red.
- **Discipline and Punish** by Michel Foucault (1977) Penguin.
- **Empire** by Michael Hardt and Antonio Negri (2000) Harvard University Press.
- **Change the World: without taking power** by John Holloway (2002) Pluto Press.
- **The Prince** by Niccolo Machiavelli (1961) Penguin.
- **Demanding the Impossible: a history of anarchism** by Peter Marshall (1993) Fontana.
- **Empowering the Earth: strategies for social change** by Alex Begg (2000) Green Books.
- **Post-Scarcity Anarchism** by Murray Bookchin (1986) Black Rose Books.
- **Restructuring and resistance: diverse voices of struggle in Western Europe** edited by Kolya Abramsky (2000). For copies AK Press distribution UK, www.akuk.org email resresrev@yahoo.com
- **Storming Heaven: Class composition and struggle in Italian Autonomist Marxism** by Steve Wright (2002) Pluto Press.

Walking

- **Naming the Enemy: anti-corporate movements confront globalization** by Amory Starr (2001) Zed Books.
- **Ecology of Everyday Life: rethinking the desire for nature** by Chaia Heller (1999) Black Rose Books.
- **Message of a Wise Kabouter** by Roel Van Duyn (1969) Duckworth.
- **Pedagogy of Hope: reliving 'pedagogy of the oppressed'** by Paulo Freire (1994) Continuum.
- **Activism!: direct action, hacktivism and the future of society** by Tim Jordan (2002) Reaktion.
- **Utopistics: or, historical choices of the twenty-first century** by Immanuel Wallerstein (1998) New Press.
- **Wanderlust: a history of walking** by Rebecca Solnit (2001) Verso.
- **The Dispossessed: an ambiguous utopia** by Ursula K. Le Guin (1974) Panther Press.

> **"I would like my books to be Molotov cocktails or minefields; I would like them to self-destruct after use, like fireworks."** – Michel Foucault

Acknowledgements

Thousands of thanks are due; these are just a few of the special ones. Firstly, thank you to all our neglected friends and family; Zoe, Liz, and Wayland Young for sanctuary; Gavin Everall and Sebastien Budgen at Verso for faith; Brian Holmes for translations and keeping us smiling, and Peoples' Global Action folks everywhere.

Paul for love and endless patience, Heidi for intelligent proofreading, Jacquie and Caroline for translation help. NI allies, all those amazing people who helped along the way including Sanjay, Wiphaphan, Pongtip, Jim, Nico, and the mad anticapitalist bastards at Escanda.

Jack for being the most inspiring eight year old on the streets. Mum for everlasting love; Caro, the kids and Bill for grounding; James for always. All of London's street reclaimers; Naomi for belief; everyone in the fine art department at Sheffield-Hallam University, for years of supporting the unconventional; Steve "the pro" for web wonders; Christine Michael for tireless fact checking.

Gwyneth, Dylan, and Joel for love and patience, laughter and inspiration; Norman and Jennifer Chesters for wanting to understand and understanding; Heather Chesters, the eponymous 16 year old in Dixons, a sister and a rebel; Tom Cahill, Dave Horton, Ian Welsh, Alan Johnson, and all associated with Shifting Ground.

Shan, Erica, Mom, and Dad for turning out to be the best family I could ever ask for and for support at every turn of the road; Nuka and Maija for having the courage to believe in true love and for putting up with hours of my absence; Sherry for friendship and common vision, and for always believing in me; Anikka for giving me the inspiration to follow my path; Ed for saving my life and showing me that there is another way to live; Jason for spiritual brotherhood; Dave for everything we have been through together and for never giving up; Ana just for being her amazing self.

Josephine, whose support means so much, and whose curiosity as well as the willingness to ask hard questions gives me hope; the Black Cross Health Collective for teaching me about community; Kim, whose friendship and understanding is invaluable; Grey for past and future adventures; Clayton for always having my back; the INB for making the streets come alive and for constant challenge and inspiration.

Love and respect to Scéhérazade and Leila, Glenn Orton, the Indymedia UK posse and all at London Action Resource Centre.

Last but not least, we particularly want to thank all the talented and dedicated photographers and writers out there who have so generously given us their hard work and made it possible for this book to be beautiful. We owe this to you.

The project was financially supported in part by *Akademie Solitude* and *Sheffield-Hallam University*.

Index

This index can also serve as a glossary.
Page references set in brackets indicate definition or thorough treatment of a topic.
Please note that the timeline is not indexed.

Credits for front cover: Left to right – Tim Russo, South Africa IMC, KRRS Archive, Meyer/Tendance Floue (www.tendancefloue.net), Karen Robinson, Nick Cobbing (www.cobb-web.org), Meyer/Tendance Floue, Meyer/Tendance Floue, CIPO-RFM, Tom Kruse, Andrew Stern.
Back cover: Credit unknown, Credit unknown, South Africa IMC, Meyer/Tendance Floue.

Captions and credits for the opening photo essay: *Text by Subcomandante Insurgente Marcos* **1)** Zapatista women surround military base, Chiapas, Mexico (Tim Russo) **2)** Civilian 'weapons inspectors' invade US air force base, UK (Andrew Stern) **3)** Pushing down the wall of shame, FTAA summit protest, Québec City, Canada (Meyer/Tendance Floue) **4)** Breaching the red zone, G8 summit, Genoa, Italy (Jess Hurd www.reportdigital.co.uk) **5)** Former playground fenced off by privatized housing, Durban, South Africa (Justin Rowe) **6)** Detention centre fence torn down, Woomera, Australia (Desert Indymedia) **7)** Police barriers surround Asian Development Bank meeting, Chiang Mai, Thailand (Sukree Sukplang/Reuters) **8)** Mexican children illegally cross into the US, US/Mexico border (Todd Bigelow/Aurora Photos)

Captions for chapters: Emergence - Welcoming visitors to a Zapatista Autonomous Municipality, Chiapas, Mexico. **Networks** - Indymedia UK Public Access Point in Parliament Square, London, May Day 2000, UK. **Autonomy** - Brazil's landless peasants celebrate occupying new land. **Carnival** - The Carnival Against Capital begins, J18, City of London, UK. **Clandestinity** - The *Disobbedienti* protect themselves from repression, J20, Genoa, Italy. **Power** - *Piqueteros* blockade a highway on the outskirts of Buenos Aires, Argentina. **Walking** - Love and uprising on the streets of Buenos Aires, 19-20 December 2002, Argentina.

Captions and credits for the final photo essay: *Text by Subcomandante Insurgente Marcos* **1)** Children play during a May Day celebration. Olympia, US (Andrew Stern) **2)** Under the hooped-skirt Reclaim the Streets plant trees in the fast lane, M41 motorway, London, UK (Julia Guest) **3)** Anti-dam protesters on what was the bank of the Narmada river, India (Karen Robinson) **4)** Running battles with police, 19 December 2001, Buenos Aires, Argentina (Nicolas Pousthomis/Argentina IMC) **5)** Revellers liberate the streets during FTAA summit, Québec City, Canada (Meyer/Tendance Floue) **6)** Movimento Sem Terra occupies unused farmland, Brazil (Sebastião Salgado/Amazonas Images) **7)** *Piquetero* road blockade, Buenos Aires, Argentina (Andrew Stern) **8)** Neighbourhood assembly meeting, Buenos Aires, Argentina (Nicolas Pousthomis/Argentina IMC).

Every effort has been made to correctly credit photographs used. Please contact us with any additional information.

We are the end, the
continuation, and the beginning.

We are the mirror that is a
lens that is a mirror
that is a lens.

We are rebelliousness

We are the stubborn history that repeats itself in order to no longer repeat itself, the looking back to be able to walk forward.

We are neoliberalism's
maximum defiance,

the most beautiful absurdity, the most
irreverent delirium, the most human madness.

We are human beings doing
what must be done in reality:
we are dreaming...